12 $\frac{50}{-22}$
US
59267

TAKING SIDES

Clashing Views on Controversial

Issues in American History
Since 1945

SECOND EDITION

D0064498

TAKING SIDES

Clashing Views on Controversial

Issues in American History
Since 1945

SECOND EDITION

Selected, Edited, and with Introductions by

Larry Madaras
Howard Community College

McGraw-Hill/Dushkin
A Division of The McGraw-Hill Companies

*Dedicated to Maggie Cullen, a very
special person in my life.*

Photo Acknowledgment
Cover image: © 2003 by PhotoDisc, Inc.

Cover Art Acknowledgment
Charles Vitelli

Copyright © 2003 by McGraw-Hill/Dushkin,
A Division of The McGraw-Hill Companies, Inc., Guilford, Connecticut 06437

Copyright law prohibits the reproduction, storage, or transmission in any form by any means of any
portion of this publication without the express written permission of McGraw-Hill/Dushkin and of
the copyright holder (if different) of the part of the publication to be reproduced. The Guidelines for
Classroom Copying endorsed by Congress explicitly state that unauthorized copying may not be
used to create, to replace, or to substitute for anthologies, compilations, or collective works.

Taking Sides ® is a registered trademark of McGraw-Hill/Dushkin

Manufactured in the United States of America

Second Edition

123456789BAHBAH6543

Library of Congress Cataloging-in-Publication Data
Main entry under title:
Taking sides: clashing views on controversial issues in American history since 1945/selected,
edited, and with introductions by Larry Madaras.—2nd ed.
Includes bibliographical references and index.
1. United States—History—1945–. I. Madaras, Larry, *comp.*
973.92
0-07-282821-8
ISSN: 1530-0765

Printed on Recycled Paper

Preface

The success of the first eight editions of *Taking Sides: Clashing Views on Controversial Issues in American History* encouraged me to develop a volume that specializes in controversial issues in American history since 1945. I remain faithful to the series' original objectives, methods, and format. My aim has been to create an effective instrument to enhance classroom learning and to foster critical thinking. Historical facts presented in a vacuum are of little value to the educational process. For students, whose search for historical truth often concentrates on *when* something happened rather than *why* and on specific events rather than on the *significance* of those events, *Taking Sides* is designed to offer an interesting and valuable departure. The understanding that the reader arrives at based on the evidence that emerges from the clash of views encourages the reader to view history as an *interpretive* discipline, not one of rote memorization.

The issues in this book are arranged in chronological order and can be easily incorporated into any American history survey course. Each issue has an issue *introduction,* which sets the stage for the debate that follows in the pro and con selections and provides historical and methodological background to the problem that the issue examines. Each issue concludes with a *postscript,* which ties the readings together, briefly mentions alternative interpretations, and supplies detailed *suggestions for further reading* for the student who wishes to pursue the topics raised in the issue. Also, Internet site addresses (URLs) have been provided on the *On the Internet* page that accompanies each part opener, which should prove useful as starting points for further research. At the back of the book is a listing of all the *contributors to this volume* with a brief biographical sketch of each of the prominent figures whose views are debated here.

Changes to this edition In this edition I have continued my efforts to maintain a balance between the traditional political, diplomatic, and cultural issues and the new social history, which depicts a society that benefited from the presence of African Americans, women, and workers of various racial and ethnic backgrounds. With this is mind, I present four entirely new issues: *Did Lee Harvey Oswald Kill President Kennedy by Himself?* (Issue 5); *Did President George Bush Achieve His Objectives in the Gulf War?* (Issue 12); *Did the Supreme Court Hijack the 2000 Presidential Election From Al Gore?* (Issue 15); and *Environmentalism: Is the Earth Out of Balance?* (Issue 16). In addition, for Issue 13 (*Should America Remain a Nation of Immigrants?*) and Issue 14 (*Will History Consider William Jefferson Clinton a Reasonably Good Chief Executive?*) one or both sides have been replaced to bring a fresh perspective to the debates. In all, there are 11 new selections.

i

A word to the instructor   An *Instructor's Manual With Test Questions* (multiple-choice and essay) is available through the publisher for the instructor using *Taking Sides* in the classroom. A general guidebook, *Using Taking Sides in the Classroom,* which discusses methods and techniques for integrating the pro-con approach into any classroom setting, is also available. An online version of *Using Taking Sides in the Classroom* and a correspondence service for *Taking Sides* adopters can be found at http://www.dushkin.com/usingts/.

　　Taking Sides: Clashing Views on Controversial Issues in American History Since 1945 is only one title in the Taking Sides series. If you are interested in seeing the table of contents for any of the other titles, please visit the Taking Sides Web site at http://www.dushkin.com/takingsides/.

Acknowledgments   Many individuals have contributed to the successful completion of this text. I am particularly indebted to Maggie Cullen, the late Barry A. Crouch, Virginia Kirk, Joseph and Helen Mitchell, Jean Soto, and David Stebenne, who shared their ideas and pointed me toward potentially useful historical works. A special note of gratitude goes to a former student, Christopher Higgins. Though we find ourselves on opposite sides of the political spectrum, I gained numerous ideas from our conversations and from his suggested lists of books and articles, which have found their way into this reader. My thanks also are extended to Megan Arnold, who performed indispensable typing duties connected with this project. Ela Ciborowski, James Johnson, and Sharen Gover in the library at Howard Community College provided essential help in acquiring books and articles on the computer and on interlibrary loan. Finally, I am sincerely grateful for the commitment, encouragement, and patience provided over the years by David Brackley, senior developmental editor for the Taking Sides series, and the entire staff of McGraw-Hill/Dushkin.

Larry Madaras
Howard Community College

Contents In Brief

Contents

Professor of history Thomas G. Paterson argues that the Truman administration exaggerated the Soviet threat after World War II because the United
States had expansionist political and economic global needs. Professor
of history John Lewis Gaddis argues that the power vacuum that existed
in Europe at the end of World War II exaggerated and made almost inevitable a clash between the democratic, capitalist United States and the
totalitarian, communist USSR.

History professors John Earl Haynes and Harvey Klehr argue that army
code-breakers during World War II's "Venona Project" uncovered a disturbing number of high-ranking U.S. government officials who seriously
damaged American interests by passing sensitive information to the Soviet
Union. Professor of history Richard M. Fried argues that the early 1950s
were a "nightmare in red" during which American citizens had their First
and Fifth Amendment rights suspended when a host of national and state
investigating committees searched for Communists in government agencies, Hollywood, labor unions, foundations, universities, public schools,
and even public libraries.

Professor of political science John S. Spanier argues that General Douglas MacArthur was fired because he publicly disagreed with the Truman administration's "Europe first" policy and its limited war strategy of containing communism in Korea. Biographer D. Clayton James and assistant editor Anne Sharp Wells argue that General MacArthur was relieved of duty because there was a lack of communication between the Joint Chiefs of Staff and the headstrong general, which led to a misperception over the appropriate strategy in fighting the Korean War.

Professor of history and sociology Melvyn Dubofsky and professor of history Athan Theoharis argue that throughout the 1950s, the U.S. economy dominated much of the globe and created a period of unprecedented growth and prosperity for the percentage of the American population that made it into the middle class. Professor of history Douglas T. Miller and journalist Marion Nowak argue that the nostalgia craze, which re-creates the 1950s as a sweet, simple, golden age of harmony, masks the fact that the decade was an era of conformity in which Americans feared the bomb, Communists, crime, and the loss of a national purpose.

The President's Commission on the Assassination of President John F. Kennedy argues that Lee Harvey Oswald was the sole assassin of President Kennedy and that he was not part of any organized conspiracy, domestic or foreign. Professor of history Michael L. Kurtz argues that the Warren commission ignores evidence of Oswald's connections with organized criminals and with pro-Castro and anti-Castro supporters, as well as forensic evidence that points to multiple assassins

Professor of history Adam Fairclough argues that Martin Luther King, Jr., was a pragmatic reformer who organized nonviolent direct action protests in strategically targeted local communities, which provoked violence from his opponents, gaining publicity and sympathy for the civil rights movement. Professor of history Clayborne Carson concludes that the civil rights struggle would have followed a similar course of development even if King had never lived because its successes depended upon mass activism, not the actions of a single leader.

Issue 7.   Did the Great Society Fail?   150

Conservative social critic Charles Murray argues that not only did the Great Society's retraining, anticrime, and welfare programs not work, but they actually contributed to the worsening plight of U.S. inner cities. Joseph A. Califano, Jr., a former aide to President Lyndon Johnson, maintains that the Great Society programs brought about positive revolutionary changes in the areas of civil rights, education, health care, the environment, and consumer protection.

Issue 8.   Was the Americanization of the War in Vietnam Inevitable?   168

Professor of history Brian VanDeMark argues that President Lyndon Johnson failed to question the viability of increasing U.S. involvement in the Vietnam War because he was a prisoner of America's global containment policy and because he did not want his opponents to accuse him of being soft on communism or endanger support for his Great Society reforms. H. R. McMaster, an active-duty army tanker, maintains that the Vietnam disaster was not inevitable but a uniquely human failure whose responsibility was shared by President Johnson and his principal military and civilian advisers.

Issue 9.   Has the Women's Liberation Movement Been Harmful to American Women?   190

Writer and lecturer F. Carolyn Graglia argues that women should stay at home and practice the values of "true motherhood" because contemporary feminists have discredited marriage, devalued traditional homemaking, and encouraged sexual promiscuity. Feminist Jo Freeman argues that in the late 1960s activists challenged the notion of women's inferior status in society through lawsuits and through "consciousness-raising" sessions to develop egalitarian and liberation values.

Issue 10.   Will History Forgive Richard Nixon?   214

According to professor of history Joan Hoff-Wilson, the Nixon presidency reorganized the executive branch and portions of the federal bureaucracy and implemented domestic reforms in civil rights, welfare, and economic planning, despite its limited foreign policy successes and the Watergate scandal. Professor and political commentator Stanley I. Kutler argues that President Nixon was a crass, cynical, narrow-minded politician who unnecessarily prolonged the Vietnam War to ensure his reelection and implemented domestic reforms only when he could outflank his liberal opponents.

PART 3   POSTINDUSTRIAL AMERICA AND THE END OF THE COLD WAR: 1974–2001   237

Issue 11.   Did President Reagan Win the Cold War?   238

Professor of history John Lewis Gaddis argues that President Reagan combined a policy of militancy and operational pragmatism to bring about the most significant improvement in Soviet-American relations since the end of World War II. Professors of political science Daniel Deudney and G. John Ikenberry contend that the cold war ended only when Soviet president Gorbachev accepted Western liberal values and the need for global cooperation.

Issue 12.   Did President George Bush Achieve His Objectives in the Gulf War?   262

Secretary of State Colin L. Powell argues that the American armed forces successfully achieved their limited and specific objective in the Gulf War, which was to liberate Kuwait from the occupation army of Iraq. Journalist Michael R. Gordon and Bernard E. Trainor, a retired lieutenant general of the U.S. Marine Corps, argue that the Bush administration's lack of a clear political strategy for postwar Iraq allowed Saddam Hussein to remain in power with half of his important Republican Guard military tank units intact.

Issue 13.   Should America Remain a Nation of Immigrants?   292

Social scientist Tamar Jacoby maintains that the newest immigrants keep America's economy strong because they work harder and take jobs that native-born Americans reject. Syndicated columnist Patrick J. Buchanan argues that America is no longer a nation because immigrants from Mexico and other Third World Latin American and Asian countries have turned America into a series of fragmented multicultural ethnic enclaves that lack a common culture.

Issue 14.   Will History Consider William Jefferson Clinton a Reasonably Good Chief Executive?   318

Journalist Nicholas Thompson argues that President Bill Clinton's governing style of simultaneously pushing and pulling in hundreds of directions led Americans to be better off in 2000 than they were when Clinton first took office eight years earlier. Political scientists James MacGregor Burns and Georgia J. Sorenson et al. argue that Clinton will not rank among the near-great presidents because he was a transactional broker who lacked the ideological commitment to tackle the big issues facing American society.

Issue 15.   Did the Supreme Court Hijack the 2000 Presidential Election From Al Gore?   344

Professor of law Stephen Holmes maintains that the U.S. Supreme Court acted in a highly partisan and hypocritical fashion in the case of *Bush v. Gore* when it utilized the equal protection clause of the Fourteenth Amendment to prevent the Florida Supreme Court from ordering a recount of the election returns in certain disputed counties. Professor of law John C. Yoo argues that "rather than acting hypocritically and lawlessly, the Court's decision to bring the Florida election dispute to a timely, and final, end not only restored stability to the political system but was also consistent with the institutional role the Court has shaped for itself over the last decade."

Issue 16. Environmentalism: Is the Earth Out of Balance? 372

Otis L. Graham, Jr., a professor emeritus of history, maintains that the status of the biophysical basis of our economies, such as "atmospheric pollution affecting global climate, habitat destruction, [and] species extinction," is negative and in some cases irreversible in the long run. Associate professor of statistics Bjorn Lomborg argues that the doomsday scenario for earth has been exaggerated and that, according to almost every measurable indicator, mankind's lot has improved.

Introduction

The Study of History

Larry Madaras

In a pluralistic society such as ours, the study of history is bound to be a complex process. How an event is interpreted depends not only on the existing evidence but also on the perspective of the interpreter. Consequently, understanding history presupposes the evaluation of information, a task that often leads to conflicting conclusions. An understanding of history, then, requires the acceptance of the idea of historical relativism. Relativism means that redefinition of our past is always possible and desirable. History shifts, changes, and grows with new and different evidence and interpretations. As with the law and even with medicine, beliefs that were unquestioned 100 or 200 years ago have been discredited or discarded since.

Relativism, then, encourages revisionism. There is a maxim that "the past must remain useful to the present." Historian Carl Becker argued that every generation should examine history for itself, thus ensuring constant scrutiny of our collective experience through new perspectives. History, consequently, does not remain static, in part because historians cannot avoid being influenced by the times in which they live. Almost all historians commit themselves to revising the views of other historians, synthesizing theories into macrointerpretations, or revising the revisionists.

Schools of Thought

Three predominant schools of thought have emerged in American history since the first graduate seminars in history were given at the Johns Hopkins University in Baltimore, Maryland, in the 1870s. The progressive school dominated the professional field in the first half of the twentieth century. Influenced by the reform currents of Populism, progressivism, and the New Deal, these historians explored the social and economic forces that energized America. The progressive scholars tended to view the past in terms of conflicts between groups, and they sympathized with the underdog.

The post–World War II period witnessed the emergence of a new group of historians who viewed the conflict thesis as overly simplistic. Writing against the backdrop of the cold war, these neoconservative, or consensus, historians argued that Americans possess a shared set of values and that the areas of agreement within the nation's basic democratic and capitalistic framework were more important than the areas of disagreement.

In the 1960s, however, the civil rights movement, women's liberation, and the student rebellion (with its condemnation of the war in Vietnam) fragmented the consensus of values upon which historians and social scientists of the 1950s centered their interpretations. This turmoil set the stage for the emergence of another group of scholars. New Left historians began to reinterpret the past once again. They emphasized the significance of conflict in American history, and they resurrected interest in those groups ignored by the consensus school. In addition, New Left historians critiqued the expansionist policies of the United States and emphasized the difficulties confronted by Native Americans, African Americans, women, and urban workers in gaining full citizenship status.

Consensus and New Left history is still being written. The most recent generation of scholars, however, focuses upon social history. Their primary concern is to discover what the lives of "ordinary Americans" were really like. These new social historians employ previously overlooked court and church documents, house deeds and tax records, letters and diaries, photographs, and census data to reconstruct the everyday lives of average Americans. Some employ new methodologies, such as quantification (enhanced by advancing computer applications) and oral history, while others borrow from the disciplines of political science, economics, sociology, anthropology, and psychology for their historical investigations.

Contemporary history divides less easily into discernable schools of thought and is often difficult to interpret because of the short time span— at most 55 years—that has elapsed. Consensus and New Left history is still being written, but a new conservative historiography that is often aligned with the modern conservative political movement has also begun to emerge and is reflected in several issues in this reader.

Writers of the recent past have been less affected by social history—the framework used by most professional historians to interpret America. Most history written about America since 1945 centers on the traditional political, military, and diplomatic perspectives. There are several reasons for this. In the twentieth century—and especially since the passage of the New Deal—the role of the national government as a social service and regulatory institution has become a dominant force in people's individual lives. The traditional roles of the president as commander in chief and chief diplomat were transformed by World War II and the subsequent cold war. Because of the development of the atomic bomb and subsequent nuclear weapons, which accompany the world's strongest armed forces, the United States has abandoned its traditional policy of political isolationism. The controversies surrounding America's role in world affairs is reflected in several issues in this reader.

Interpretations of recent American history are driven in part by the availability of primary sources. Many traditional sources are missing, while modern technology has created new types of material. Social historians are hampered by the fact that detailed information about individuals from the U.S. census is closed to researchers for 100 years. Furthermore, historians have to compete with psychologists, economists, sociologists, and journalists in evaluating the modern social and cultural atmosphere. A time perspective about significant or insignificant changes or continuities in American life is also missing.

There is, however, an abundance of official records available with which to interpret the recent past. In addition to congressional investigations and documents published in the Foreign Relations of the United States series, the Freedom of Information Act has enabled researchers to access—often with many bureaucratic snags—FBI and other intelligence and cabinet agencies' files. These records have altered historians' interpretations of foreign policy, as reflected in several of the issues in this reader. The traditional historian misses the old-fashioned correspondence, however. The eloquent letters of Presidents Theodore Roosevelt and Woodrow Wilson are absent among our modern presidents. There is not enough material to fill a 46-volume edition of the personal papers of George Bush or Bill Clinton, unlike earlier presidents. New sources, such as oral histories, phone logs, and diaries (an old source), cannot make up for the missing letters. Tape recordings of phone conversations and official meetings—especially during the Kennedy, Johnson, and Nixon administrations—are quite revealing. Unfortunately, because the "Watergate tapes" forced Richard Nixon's resignation, subsequent presidents have been reluctant to tape their daily meetings. Airplane diplomacy with only officially issued communiqués, fax memos, and e-mail have also altered the sources that future historians will use. The long-term effect of "Monicagate" may not be the impeachment of President Clinton, but it may make any public official reluctant to put into writing the (public) affairs of the moment.

The proliferation of historical approaches, which are reflected in the issues debated in this book, has had mixed results. On the one hand, historians have become so specialized in their respective time periods and methodological styles that it is difficult to synthesize the recent scholarship into a comprehensive text for the general reader. On the other hand, historians now know more about the American past than at any other time in our history. They dare to ask new questions or ones that were previously considered to be germane only to scholars in other social sciences. Although there is little agreement about the answers to these questions, the methods employed and issues explored make the "new history" a very exciting field to study.

The topics that follow represent a variety of perspectives and approaches. Each of these controversial issues can be studied for its individual importance to American history. Taken as a group, they interact with one another to illustrate larger historical themes. When grouped thematically, the issues reveal continuing motifs in the development of American history.

War, Diplomacy, and Internal Security

World War II brought the end of Nazi Germany and imperial Japan. But a new rivalry soon began between the United States and the Soviet Union. Who started the cold war? Was it inevitable, or should one side take more of the blame? Issue 1 tackles the question of responsibility. Thomas G. Paterson blames the United States for exaggerating the Soviet threat to world peace. He argues that the United States, untouched physically by the war and having emerged as the world's greatest military and economic power, tried to reshape the world's political and economic structures to meet the needs of American capitalism. John Lewis Gaddis, taking a different position, argues that the power vacuum that existed in Europe at the end of World War II exaggerated the countries' differences and made a clash between the democratic, capitalist United States and the totalitarian, communist Soviet Union almost inevitable.

After World War II, many Americans believed that the Russians not only threatened world peace but also could subvert America's own democratic form of government. How legitimate was the second great red scare? Did communist subversion threaten America's internal security? In Issue 2, John Earl Haynes and Harvey Klehr contend that recently released World War II intelligence intercepts prove that a sizable number of high-level governmental officials passed sensitive information to Russian intelligence. But Richard M. Fried argues that the 1950s became a "red nightmare" when state and national government agencies overreacted in their search for Communists in government agencies, schools, labor unions, and even Hollywood, violating citizens' rights of free speech and defense against self-incrimination under the First and Fifth Amendments.

No discussion of American foreign policy is complete without some consideration of the Vietnam War. Was America's escalation of the war inevitable in 1965? In Issue 8, Brian VanDeMark argues that President Lyndon Johnson was a prisoner of America's global "containment" policy and was afraid to pull out of Vietnam because he feared that his opponents would accuse him of being soft on communism and that they would also destroy his Great Society reforms. H. R. McMaster blames Johnson and his civilian and military advisers for failing to develop a coherent policy in Vietnam.

Now that the cold war is over, historians must assess why it ended so suddenly and unexpectedly. Did President Ronald Reagan's military buildup in the 1980s force the Soviet Union into economic bankruptcy? In Issue 11, John Lewis Gaddis gives Reagan high marks for ending the cold war. By combining a policy of militancy and operational pragmatism, he argues, Reagan brought about the most significant improvement in Soviet-American relations since the end of World War II. According to Daniel Deudney and G. John Ikenberry, however, the cold war ended only when the Soviets saw the need for international cooperation to end the arms race, prevent a nuclear holocaust, and liberalize their economy. They contend that Western global ideas, not the hard-line containment policy of the early Reagan administration, caused Soviet president Mikhail Gorbachev to abandon traditional Russian communism.

In the summer of 1990 Iraq took over the small but rich oil-producing nation of Kuwait. The United States felt that this situation threatened its national interests and prepared to attack. Issue 12 discusses the Gulf War, which was fought in the winter of 1990–1991. Did President Bush achieve his goals in this war? In the first selection, Colin L. Powell argues that the American armed forces successfully achieved their limited and specific objective in the Gulf War, which was to liberate Kuwait from the occupation army of Iraq. In the second selection, Michael R. Gordon and Bernard E. Trainor maintain that the Bush administration's lack of a clear political strategy for postwar

Iraq allowed Iraqi leader Saddam Hussein to remain in power with half of his important Republican Guard military tank units intact.

American Presidents Since World War II

The Korean War provided the first military test case of America's cold war policy of "containing" the expansion of communism. The conflict explored in Issue 3 also provided a classic case of civilian control over military officials. Should President Truman have fired General Douglas MacArthur? John S. Spanier argues that MacArthur was fired because he publicly disagreed with the Truman administration's Europe-first policy and its limited war strategy of containing communism in Korea. D. Clayton James, writing with Anne Sharp Wells, maintains that General MacArthur was relieved of duty because there was a lack of communication between the Joint Chiefs of Staff and the headstrong general as well as a misperception over the appropriate strategy for fighting the Korean War.

The perspective gained by the passage of time often allows us to reevaluate the achievements and failures of a given individual. Such is the case with Richard Nixon, president of the United States from 1969 to 1974. Because he was forced to resign the presidency to avoid impeachment proceedings resulting from his role in the Watergate scandal, Nixon remains a controversial political figure. How will Nixon, who died in 1994, be remembered? In Issue 10, Joan Hoff-Wilson downplays the significance of the Watergate scandal in assessing Nixon's legacy. Instead, she argues, Nixon should be applauded for reorganizing the executive branch of the federal government and implementing important civil rights, welfare, and economic planning programs. Stanley I. Kutler, in opposition, asserts that Nixon was a crass, cynical, narrow-minded politician who unnecessarily prolonged the Vietnam War to ensure his reelection and who implemented domestic reforms only to outflank his liberal opponents.

The last president of the twentieth century, William Jefferson Clinton, was the first president to be impeached since President Andrew Johnson (1865–1869). Both presidents, however, were tried by the Senate but not convicted of their impeachment charges. Most historians consider Johnson a below-average president. Will history rank Bill Clinton as a near-great, average, or below-average president? In the first selection of Issue 14, Nicholas Thompson contends that by simultaneously pushing and pulling in hundreds of directions, Clinton was responsible for Americans' being better off in 2000 than they were when he first took office eight years earlier. In the second selection, James MacGregor Burns and Georgia J. Sorenson et al. argue that Clinton will not rank among the near-great presidents because he was a transactional broker who lacked the ideological commitment and overall vision to tackle the big issues facing American society.

The presidential election of 2000 ranks among the most controversial elections in U.S. history. Not since the 1888 election has a candidate who received fewer popular votes than his opponent taken office (although President George W. Bush did win the electoral college). Issue 15 asks, did the Supreme Court hijack the 2000 presidential election from candidate Al Gore? In the first selection, Stephen Holmes maintains that the U.S. Supreme Court acted in a highly partisan and hypocritical fashion in the case of *Bush v. Gore* when it utilized the equal protection clause of the Fourteenth Amendment to prevent the Florida Supreme Court from ordering a recount of the election returns in certain disputed counties. In the second selection, John C. Yoo defends the Supreme Court's decision. He argues that "rather than acting hypocritically and lawlessly, the Court's decision to bring the Florida election dispute to a timely, and final, end not only restored stability to the political system but was also consistent with the institutional role the Court has shaped for itself over the last decade."

Social, Cultural, and Economic Changes Since 1945

Carl N. Degler, a professor emeritus of American history, has labeled the years from 1945 to 1960 the age of "anxiety and affluence." Issue 4 deals with this unique period in U.S. history. Were the 1950s America's "Happy Days"? Melvyn Dubofsky and Athan Theoharis stress the global superpower role of the United States and the prosperity of the middle class, which they feel made those years an era of happiness and optimism. Douglas T. Miller and Marion Nowak detect an underlying anxiety in the decade, with shadows of the cold war, communism, and the atomic bomb looming.

The 1960s was an era of great turmoil. President Johnson hoped to be remembered as the president who extended the New Deal reforms of the 1930s to the bottom third of the population. So controversial were Johnson's domestic reforms that some members of the Bush administration blamed the Los Angeles riots in the spring of 1992 on the Great Society. In Issue 7, Charles Murray argues along this line. Not only did the retraining, anticrime, and welfare programs of the Great Society not work, says Murray, but they also contributed to the worsening plight of U.S. inner cities today. In contrast, Joseph A. Califano, Jr., maintains that the 1960s reforms brought about positive revolutionary changes in the area of civil rights, education, health care, the environment, and consumer protection.

Americans' anxiety peaked on November 22, 1963, when President John F. Kennedy was assassinated while riding in a motorcade through downtown Dallas, Texas. The identity of the president's killer or killers has been a matter of great controversy and speculation ever since. In Issue 5, the President's Commission on the Assassination of President John F. Kennedy concludes that Lee Harvey Oswald was the sole assassin of President Kennedy and that he was not part of any organized conspiracy. Michael L. Kurtz disagrees with the conclusions of the commission, which he maintains ignored evidence of Oswald's connections with organized criminals and pro-Castro and anti-Castro supporters as well as forensic evidence that pointed to multiple assassins.

Two ongoing controversies that have continued into the twenty-first century are analyzed in this reader. Issue 13 debates whether or not the United States should remain a nation of immigrants. Tamar Jacoby, who supports allowing immigration to continue, maintains that the newest immigrants keep

America's economy strong because they work harder and take jobs that native-born Americans reject. Patrick J. Buchanan, however, argues that America is no longer a nation because immigrants from Mexico and other Third World Latin American and Asian countries have turned it into a series of fragmented multicultural ethnic enclaves that lack a common culture. Therefore, he contends, immigration should be drastically curbed.

The final issue in this book (Issue 16) is of great concern to most Americans: Is the earth out of balance? In other words, is there really an environmental crisis? Otis L. Graham, Jr., concedes that severe increases in population and declines in forests, water, and air quality did not occur as some futurists had projected. However, he holds that the status of the biophysical basis of our economies—"atmospheric pollution affecting global climate, habitat destruction, [and] species extinction"—is negative and, in some cases, irreversible in the long run. Bjorn Lomborg, in reply, argues that the doomsday scenario for earth has been exaggerated and that, by about every measurable indicator, mankind's lot has improved.

The Outsiders: African Americans, Women, and Immigrants

Groups outside the mainstream made great strides in the 1960s. This was particularly true of African Americans, who regained civil and political rights denied them since the end of the 1890s. Issue 6 focuses on the second revolution and, in particular, the role of Martin Luther King, Jr. In the first selection, Adam Fairclough demonstrates the importance of King's leadership to the civil rights movement in 1960. In the second selection, Clayborne Carson plays down the mythical image of King and asserts that bestowing praise solely upon King for the civil rights movement takes credit away from many of the local leaders who desegregated their communities through the creation of grassroots organizations. Carson argues that King is a product of a movement that would have occurred even if King had never lived.

Issue 9 debates whether the women's liberation movement that began in the turbulent 1960s has hurt or helped today's women. F. Carolyn Graglia defends the traditional role of women in contemporary America and argues that women should stay at home and practice the values of "true motherhood." Contemporary feminists, she contends, have devalued traditional homemaking, encouraged sexual promiscuity, and discredited marriage as a career for women. In contrast, Jo Freeman applauds the efforts of the two branches of the women's liberation of the late 1960s and early 1970s: the first group challenged women's inferior status in society through lawsuits; the second wing engaged in "consciousness raising" sessions to develop egalitarian and liberation values in an attempt to create a "feminist humanistic" society.

Conclusion

The process of historical study should rely more on thinking than on memorizing data. Once the basics of who, what, when, and where are determined, historical thinking shifts to a higher gear. Analysis, comparison and contrast, evaluation, and explanation take command. These skills not only increase our knowledge of the past but they also provide general tools for the comprehension of all the topics about which human beings think.

The diversity of a pluralistic society, however, creates some obstacles to comprehending the past. The spectrum of differing opinions on any particular subject eliminates the possibility of quick and easy answers. In the final analysis, conclusions are often built through a synthesis of several different interpretations, but even then they may be partial and tentative.

The study of history in a pluralistic society allows each citizen the opportunity to reach independent conclusions about the past. Since most, if not all, historical issues affect the present and future, understanding the past becomes necessary if society is to progress. Many of today's problems have a direct connection with the past. Additionally, other contemporary issues may lack obvious direct antecedents, but historical investigation can provide illuminating analogies. At first, it may appear confusing to read and to think about opposing historical views, but the survival of our democratic society depends on such critical thinking by acute and discerning minds.

Cold War Policies 1945–1991

This site presents U.S. government policies during the cold war, listed year by year from 1945 through 1991, as well as links to related sites.

`http://ac.acusd.edu/history/20th/coldwar0.html`

Oingo: History of the Korean War

This Oingo site provides dozens of links on the Korean War covering the history of the war, specific missions, political and social issues, and General Douglas MacArthur.

`http://www.oingo.com/topic/53/53130.html`

CNN Interactive: Cold War

Experience CNN's landmark documentary series in this award-winning Web site covering the cold war years. Navigate interactive maps, see rare archival footage online, and read recently declassified documents, among other activities.

`http://www.cnn.com/SPECIALS/cold.war/`

The Cold War Museum

Click on a decade on this site's timeline for information about important events that took place during those years, including the Korean War, the Cuban Missile Crisis, and the assassination of President John F. Kennedy.

`http://www.coldwar.org`

The Lee Harvey Oswald Research Page

The purpose of this site, maintained by independent researcher W. Tracy Parnell, is to provide information to researchers and students about Lee Harvey Oswald, accused assassin of President John F. Kennedy, as well as general assassination-related material.

`http://www.madbbs.com/~tracy/lho/`

PART 1

American High: 1945–1963

*T*he post-war years were a period of both affluence and anxiety. America emerged from World War II as one of the strongest nations in the world, both militarily and economically. Both the reconstruction and revitalization of world trade were dependent upon American loans and its industrial production. Presidents Truman, Eisenhower, and Kennedy managed an economy whose major problem was to keep inflation under control for a prosperous blue-collar labor force and an emerging baby boomer, white-collar class. The rich got richer, and the middle class did likewise. African Americans, working women, and rural America were not only left behind but invisible.

World War II ended in 1945. But the peace that everyone had hoped for never came. An "iron curtain" was hung over Eastern Europe, and by 1947 a "cold war" between the Western powers and the Russians was in full swing. In 1949 China came under communist control, the Russians developed an atomic bomb, and communist subversion of high-level officials in the State and Treasury Departments of the U.S. government was uncovered. A year later American soldiers were fighting a hot war of "containment" against communist expansion in Korea.

For the most part, Americans were wealthy beyond their fondest dreams. But they were also scared of losing it all in a third world war. It almost came in October 1962, when the Americans and the Russians faced off in the Cuban Missile Crisis. Both sides backed off, but it appeared to be a victory for the United States when the Russians pulled their missiles out of Cuba. The Kennedy promise came to an abrupt halt 13 months later, when the president was assassinated. The "American high" was over.

- Was the United States Responsible for the Cold War?

- Did Communism Threaten America's Internal Security After World War II?

- Should President Truman Have Fired General MacArthur?

- Were the 1950s America's "Happy Days"?

- Did Lee Harvey Oswald Kill President Kennedy by Himself?

ISSUE 1

Was the United States Responsible for the Cold War?

YES: Thomas G. Paterson, from *Meeting the Communist Threat: Truman to Reagan* (Oxford University Press, 1988)

NO: John Lewis Gaddis, from *Russia, the Soviet Union, and the United States: An Interpretive History,* 2d ed. (McGraw-Hill, 1990)

ISSUE SUMMARY

YES: Professor of history Thomas G. Paterson argues that the Truman administration exaggerated the Soviet threat after World War II because the United States had expansionist political and economic global needs.

NO: Professor of history John Lewis Gaddis argues that the power vacuum that existed in Europe at the end of World War II exaggerated and made almost inevitable a clash between the democratic, capitalist United States and the totalitarian, communist USSR.

Historians are unable to agree on exactly when the cold war began. This is because of the rocky relationship that existed between the United States and the Soviet Union since World War I. The Wilson administration became upset when the communist government declared its neutrality in the war and pulled Russia out of the allied coalition. The Russian leader V. I. Lenin resented the allied intervention in Siberia from 1918 to 1920 because he believed that the pretext for rescuing Czech troops was an excuse to undermine Russia's communist government. The relationship between the two countries improved in 1933 after President Franklin D. Roosevelt accorded diplomatic recognition to the communist government. In the late 1930s the relationship soured once again. Russia, unable to negotiate a security treaty with France, signed a nonaggression pact with Germany on August 23, 1939. This allowed Adolf Hitler to attack Poland in early September and Soviet leader Joseph Stalin to attack Finland and take over the Baltic states Latvia, Lithuania, and Estonia. In September 1939, as World War II was breaking out in Europe, the United States—like the USSR —was officially neutral. But the Roosevelt administration pushed modifications of the neutrality laws through Congress, which enabled significant amounts of economic and military assistance to be extended to England and France. In one of history's great ironies, Stalin, who distrusted everyone, ignored British prime minister Winston Churchill's warnings and was caught completely off guard when Hitler occupied the Balkans and then launched his surprise attack against the Russians in June 1941. By November, lend-lease was extended to the Russians, who would receive a total of $11 billion by the end of the war.

The wartime coalition of the United States, Great Britain, and the USSR was an odd combination. Their common goal—defeat Hitler—temporarily submerged political differences. During the war the United States actually sided with Russia against Great Britain over the appropriate military strategy. Russia and the United States wanted a second front established in France.

As the military victory in Europe became clear, political differences began to crack open the alliance. A number of wartime conferences were held to coordinate military strategy; to establish political and economic international agencies, such as the United Nations and the International Monetary Fund; and to plan the reestablishment of governments in Eastern and Western Europe. Differences developed over the structure of the United Nations; the composition of the Polish and other Eastern European governments; and the boundaries, reparations, and occupational questions surrounding postwar Germany.

The military situation dominated the Yalta Conference in February 1945. Since the atomic bomb had not yet been tested, the United States thought that a landed invasion of the Japanese mainland would be necessary to win the war. At this time Russia and Japan were neutral toward each other. Stalin promised that three months after the war in Europe ended he would invade Japan. In return Roosevelt promised Stalin the territories and sphere of influence Russia held in Asia prior to 1905, which she had lost in a war with Japan.

Sole possession of the atomic bomb by the United States loomed in the background as the two powers failed to settle their differences after the war. Secretary of State James Byrnes hoped that the bomb would make the Russians more "manageable" in Europe, but atomic diplomacy was never really practiced. Nor were attempts at economic coercion successful.

By 1946 the cold war had begun. In February Stalin gave a speech declaring that communism and capitalism were incompatible and that future wars were inevitable. The next month, at a commencement address with President Harry S. Truman at his side, Churchill declared that an "iron curtain" had descended over Eastern Europe. In May 1946 the allies refused to send any more industrial equipment to the Russian zone in Germany.

Who started the cold war? Was it inevitable, or should one side take more of the blame? In the following selection, Thomas G. Paterson argues that the Truman administration exaggerated the Soviet threat to world peace after World War II because the United States had its own expansionist, political, and economic global needs. In the second selection, John Lewis Gaddis asserts that the power vacuum that existed in Europe at the end of World War II exaggerated ideological, political, and economic differences and made a clash between the United States and the USSR almost inevitable.

3

Thomas G. Paterson

 **YES**

Harry S Truman, American Power, and the Soviet Threat

President Harry S Truman and his Secretary of State Dean Acheson, Henry A. Kissinger once remarked, "ushered in the most creative period in the history of American foreign policy." Presidents from Eisenhower to Reagan have exalted Truman for his decisiveness and success in launching the Truman Doctrine, the Marshall Plan, and NATO [North Atlantic Treaty Organization], and for staring the Soviets down in Berlin during those hair-trigger days of the blockade and airlift. John F. Kennedy and Lyndon B. Johnson invoked memories of Truman and the containment doctrine again and again to explain American intervention in Vietnam. Jimmy Carter has written in his memoirs that Truman had served as his model—that he studied Truman's career more than that of any other president and came to admire greatly his courage, honesty, and willingness "to be unpopular if he believed his actions were the best for the country." Some historians have gone so far as to claim that Truman saved humankind from World War III. On the other hand, he has drawn a diverse set of critics. The diplomat and analyst George F. Kennan, the journalist Walter Lippmann, the political scientist Hans Morgenthau, politicians of the left and right, like Henry A. Wallace and Robert A. Taft, and many historians have questioned Truman's penchant for his quick, simple answer, blunt, careless rhetoric, and facile analogies, his moralism that obscured the complexity of causation, his militarization of American foreign policy, his impatience with diplomacy itself, and his exaggeration of the Soviet threat....

Because of America's unusual postwar power, the Truman Administration could expand the United States sphere of influence beyond the Western Hemisphere and also intervene to protect American interests. But this begs a key question: Why did President Truman think it necessary to project American power abroad, to pursue an activist, global foreign policy unprecedented in United States history? The answer has several parts. First, Americans drew lessons from their experience in the 1930s. While indulging in their so-called "isolationism," they had watched economic depression spawn political extremism, which in turn, produced aggression and war. Never again, they vowed. No more appeasement with totalitarians, no more Munichs. "Red Fascism" became a popular phrase to express this American idea. The message seemed evident: To

From Thomas G. Paterson, *Meeting the Communist Threat: Truman to Reagan* (Oxford University Press, 1988). Copyright © 1988 by Thomas G. Paterson. Reprinted by permission of Oxford University Press, Inc. Notes omitted.

prevent a reincarnation of the 1930s, the United Sates would have to use its vast power to fight economic instability abroad. Americans felt compelled to project their power, second, because they feared, in the peace-and-prosperity thinking of the time, economic doom stemming from an economic sickness abroad that might spread to the United States, and from American dependency on overseas supplies of raw materials. To aid Europeans and other people would not only help them, but also sustain a high American standard of living and gain political friends, as in the case of Italy, where American foreign aid and advice influenced national elections and brought defeat to the left. The American fear of postwar shortages of petroleum also encouraged the Truman Administration to penetrate Middle Eastern oil in a major way. In Saudi Arabia, for example, Americans built and operated the strategically important Dhahran Airport and dominated that nation's oil resources.

Another reason why Truman projected American power so boldly derived from new strategic thinking. Because of the advent of the air age, travel across the world was shortened in time. Strategists spoke of the shrinkage of the globe. Places once deemed beyond American curiosity or interest now loomed important. Airplanes could travel great distances to deliver bombs. Powerful as it was, then, the United States also appeared vulnerable, especially to air attack. As General Carl A. Spaatz emphasized: "As top dog, America becomes target No. 1." He went on to argue that fast aircraft left no warning time for the United States. "The Pearl Harbor of a future war might well be Chicago, or Detroit, or even Washington." To prevent such an occurrence, American leaders worked to acquire overseas bases in both the Pacific and Atlantic, thereby denying a potential enemy an attack route to the Western Hemisphere. Forward bases would also permit the United States to conduct offensive operations more effectively. The American strategic frontier had to be pushed outward. Thus the United States took the former Japanese-controlled Pacific islands of the Carolines, Marshalls, and Marianas, maintained garrisons in Germany and Japan, and sent military missions to Iran, Turkey, Greece, Saudi Arabia, China, and to fourteen Latin American states. The joint Chiefs of Staff and Department of State lists of desired foreign bases, and of sites where air transit rights were sought, included such far-flung spots as Algeria, India, French Indochina, New Zealand, Iceland, and the Azores. When asked where the American Navy would float, Navy Secretary James Forrestal replied: "Wherever there is a sea." Today we may take the presumption of a global American presence for granted, but in Truman's day it was new, even radical thinking, especially after the "isolationist" 1930s.

These several explanations for American globalism suggest that the United States would have been an expansionist power whether or not the obstructionist Soviets were lurking about. That is, America's own needs—ideological, political, economic, strategic—encouraged such a projection of power. As the influential National Security Council Paper No. 68 (NSC-68) noted in April 1950, the "overall policy" of the United States was "designed to foster a world environment in which the American system can survive and flourish." This policy "we would probably pursue even if there were no Soviet threat."

Americans, of course, did perceive a Soviet threat. Thus we turn to yet another explanation for the United States' dramatic extension of power early in the Cold War: to contain the Soviets. The Soviets unsettled Americans in so many ways. Their harsh Communist dogma and propagandistic slogans were not only monotonous; they also seemed threatening because of their call for world revolution and for the demise of capitalism. In the United Nations the Soviets cast vetoes and even on occasion walked out of the organization. At international conferences their *"nyets"* stung American ears. When they negotiated, the Soviets annoyed their interlocuters by repeating the same point over and over again, delaying meetings, or abruptly shifting positions. Truman labeled them "pigheaded," and Dean Acheson thought them so coarse and insulting that he once allowed that they were not "housebroken."

The Soviet Union, moreover, had territorial ambitions, grabbing parts of Poland, Rumania, and Finland, and demanding parts of Turkey. In Eastern Europe, with their Red Army positioned to intimidate, the Soviets quickly manhandled the Poles and Rumanians. Communists in 1947 and 1948 seized power in Hungary and Czechoslovakia. Some Americans predicted that the Soviet military would roll across Western Europe. In general, Truman officials pictured the Soviet Union as an implaccable foe to an open world, an opportunistic nation that would probe for weak spots, exploit economic misery, snuff out individual freedom, and thwart self-determination. Americans thought the worst, some claiming that a Soviet-inspired international conspiracy insured perennial hostility and a creeping aggression aimed at American interests. To Truman and his advisers, the Soviets stood as the world's bully, and the very existence of this menacing bear necessitated an activist American foreign policy and an exertion of American power as a "counterforce."

But Truman officials exaggerated the Soviet threat, imagining an adversary that never measured up to the galloping monster so often depicted by alarmist Americans. Even if the Soviets intended to dominate the world, or just Western Europe, they lacked the capabilities to do so. The Soviets had no foreign aid to dispense; outside Russia Communist parties were minorities; the Soviet economy was seriously crippled by the war; and the Soviet military suffered significant weaknesses. The Soviets lacked a modern navy, a strategic air force, the atomic bomb, and air defenses. Their wrecked economy could not support or supply an army in the field for very long, and their technology was antiquated. Their ground forces lacked motorized transportation, adequate equipment, and troop morale. A Soviet *blitzkrieg* invasion of Western Europe had little chance of success and would have proven suicidal for the Soviets, for even if they managed to gain temporary control of Western Europe by a military thrust, they could not strike the United States. So they would have to assume defensive positions and await crushing American attacks, probably including atomic bombings of Soviet Russia itself—plans for which existed.

Other evidence also suggests that a Soviet military threat to Western Europe was more myth than reality. The Soviet Union demobilized its forces after the war, dropping to about 2.9 million personnel in 1948. Many of its 175 divisions were under-strength, and large numbers of them were engaged in occupation duties, resisting challenges to Soviet authority in Eastern Europe. American intelligence sources reported as well that the Soviets could not count on troops of the occupied countries, which were quite unreliable, if not rebellious. At most, the Soviets had 700,000 to 800,000 troops available for an attack against the West. To resist such an attack, the West had about 800,000 troops, or approximate parity. For these reasons, top American leaders did not expect a Soviet onslaught against Western Europe. They and their intelligence sources emphasized Soviet military and economic weaknesses, not strengths, Soviet hesitancy, not boldness.

Why then did Americans so fear the Soviets? Why did the Central Intelligence Agency, the Joint Chiefs of Staff, and the President exaggerate the Soviet threat? The first explanation is that their intelligence estimates were just that—estimates. The American intelligence community was still in a state of infancy, hardly the well-developed system it would become in the 1950s and 1960s. So Americans lacked complete assurance that their figures on Soviet force deployment or armaments were accurate or close to the mark. When leaders do not know, they tend to assume the worst of an adversary's intentions and capabilities, or to think that the Soviets might miscalculate, sparking a war they did not want. In a chaotic world, the conception of a single, inexorably aggressive adversary also brought a comforting sense of knowing and consistency.

Truman officials also exaggerated the Soviet threat in order "to extricate the United States from commitments and restraints that were no longer considered desirable." For example, they loudly chastised the Soviets for violating the Yalta agreements; yet Truman and his advisers knew the Yalta provisions were at best vague and open to differing interpretations. But, more, they purposefully misrepresented the Yalta agreement on the vital question of the composition of the Polish government. In so doing, they hoped to decrease the high degree of Communist participation that the Yalta conferees had insured when they stated that the new Polish regime would be formed by reorganizing the provisional Lublin (Communist) government. Through charges of Soviet malfeasance Washington sought to justify its own retreat from Yalta, such as its abandonment of the $20 billion reparations figure for Germany (half of which was supposed to go to the Soviet Union).

Another reason for the exaggeration: Truman liked things in black and white, as his aide Clark Clifford noted. Nuances, ambiguities, and counterevidence were often discounted to satisfy the President's preference for the simpler answer or his pre-conceived notions of Soviet aggressiveness. In mid-1946, for example, the Joint Chiefs of Staff deleted from a report to Truman a section that stressed Soviet weaknesses. American leaders also exaggerated the Soviet threat because it was useful in galvanizing and unifying American public opinion for an abandonment of recent and still lingering "isolationism" and support for an expansive foreign policy. Kennan quoted a colleague as saying that "if it [Soviet threat] had never existed, we would have had to invent it, to create a sense of urgency we need to bring us to the point of decisive action." The military particularly overplayed the Soviet threat in order to persuade Congress to endorse larger defense budgets. This happened in 1948–49 with the creation of the North Atlantic Treaty Organization. NATO was established not to halt a Soviet military attack, because none was anticipated, but to give Europeans a psychological boost—a "will to resist." American officials believed that the European Recovery Program would falter unless there was a "sense of security" to buttress it. They nurtured apprehension, too, that some European nations might lean toward neutralism unless they were brought together under a security umbrella. NATO also seemed essential to help members resist internal subversion. The exaggerated, popular view that NATO was formed to deter a Soviet invasion of Western Europe by conventional forces stems, in part, from Truman's faulty recollection in his published memoirs.

Still another explanation for why Americans exaggerated the Soviet threat is found in their attention since the Bolshevik Revolution of 1917 to the utopian Communist goal of world revolution, confusing goals with actual behavior. Thus Americans believed that the sinister Soviets and their Communist allies would exploit postwar economic, social, and political disorder, not through a direct military thrust, but rather through covert subversion. The recovery of Germany and Japan became necessary, then, to deny the Communists political opportunities to thwart American plans for the integration of these former enemies into an American system of trade and defense. And because economic instability troubled so much of Eurasia, Communist gains through subversion might deny the United States strategic raw materials.

Why dwell on this question of the American exaggeration of the Soviet threat? Because it over-simplified international realities by under-estimating local conditions that might thwart Soviet/Communist successes and by over-estimating the Soviet ability to act. Because it encouraged the Soviets to fear encirclement and to enlarge their military establishment, thereby contributing to a dangerous weapons race. Because it led to indiscriminate globalism. Because it put a damper on diplomacy; American officials were hesitant to negotiate with an opponent variously described as malevolent, deceitful, and inhuman. They especially did not warm to negotiations when some critics were ready to cry that diplomacy, which could produce compromises, was evidence in itself of softness toward Communism.

Exaggeration of the threat also led Americans to misinterpret events and in so doing to prompt the Soviets to make decisions contrary to American wishes. For example, the Soviet presence in Eastern Europe, once considered a simple question of the Soviets' building an iron curtain or bloc after the war, is now seen by historians in more complex terms. The Soviets did not seem to have a master plan for the region and followed different policies in different countries. Poland and Rumania were subjugated right away; Yugoslavia, on the other hand, was an independent Communist state led by Josip Tito, who broke dramatically with Stalin in 1948; Hungary conducted elections in the fall of 1945 (the Communists got only 17 percent of the vote) and did not suffer a Communist coup until 1947; in Czechoslovakia, free elections in May 1946 produced a non-Communist government that functioned until 1948; Finland, although under Soviet scrutiny, affirmed its independence. The Soviets did not have a firm grip on Eastern Europe before 1948—a prime reason why many American leaders believed the Soviets harbored weaknesses.

American policies were designed to roll the Soviets back. The United States reconstruction loan policy, encouragement of dissident groups, and appeal for free elections alarmed Moscow, contributing to a Soviet push to secure the area. The issue of free elections illustrates the point. Such a call was consistent with cherished American principle. But in the context of Eastern Europe and the Cold War, problems arose. First, Americans conspicuously followed a double standard which foreigners noted time and again; that is, if the principle of free elections really mattered, why not hold such elections in the United States' sphere of influence in Latin America, where an unsavory lot of dictators ruled? Second, free elections would have produced victories for anti-Soviet groups. Such results could only unsettle the Soviets and invite them to intervene to protect their interests in neighboring states—just as the United States had intervened in Cuba and Mexico in the twentieth century when hostile groups assumed power. In Hungary, for example, it was the non-Communist leader Ferenc Nagy who delayed elections in late 1946 because he knew the Communist Party would lose badly, thereby possibly triggering a repressive Soviet response. And, third, the United States had so little influence in Eastern Europe that it had no way of insuring free elections—no way of backing up its demands with power.

Walter Lippmann, among others, thought that the United States should tame its meddling in the region and make the best out of a bad arrangement of power. "I do believe," he said in 1947, "we shall have to recognize the principle of boundaries of spheres of influence which either side will not cross and have to proceed on the old principle that a good fence makes good neighbors." Kennan shared this view, as did one State Department official who argued that the United States was incapable of becoming a successful watchdog in Eastern Europe. American "barkings, growlings, snappings, and occasional bitings," Cloyce K. Huston prophesized, would only irritate the Soviets without reducing their power. Better still, argued some analysts, if the United States tempered its ventures into European affairs, then the Soviets, surely less alarmed, might tolerate more openness. But the United States did not stay out. Americans tried to project their power into a region where they had little chance of succeeding, but had substantial opportunity to irritate and alarm the always suspicious Soviets. In this way, it has been suggested, the United States itself helped pull down the iron curtain.

Another example of the exaggeration of the Soviet threat at work is found in the Truman Doctrine of 1947. Greece was beset by civil war, and the British could no longer fund a war against Communist-led insurgents who had a considerable non-Communist following. On March 12, Truman enunciated a universal doctrine: It "must be the policy of the United States to support free peoples who are resisting attempted subjugation by armed minorities or by outside pressures." Although he never mentioned the Soviet Union by name, his juxtaposition of words like "democratic" and "totalitarian" and his references to Eastern Europe made the menace to Greece appear to be the Soviets. But there was and is no evidence of Soviet involvement in the Greek civil war. In fact, the Soviets had urged both the Greek Communists and their allies the Yugoslavs to stop the fighting for fear that the conflict would draw the United States into the Mediterranean. And the Greek Communists were strong nationalists. The United States nonetheless intervened in a major way in Greek affairs, becoming responsible for right-wing repression and a military establishment that plagued Greek politics through much of its postwar history. As for Turkey, official Washington did not expect the Soviet Union to strike militarily against that bordering nation. The Soviets were too weak in 1947 to undertake such a major operation, and they were asking for joint control of the Dardanelles largely for defense, for security. Then why did the President, in the Truman Doctrine speech, suggest that Turkey was imminently threatened? American strategists worried that Russia's long-term objective was the subjugation of its neighbor. But they also wished to exploit an opportunity to enhance the American military position in the Mediterranean region and in a state bordering the Soviet Union. The Greek crisis and the Truman Doctrine speech provided an appropriate environment to build up an American military presence in the Eastern Mediterranean for use against the Soviets should the unwanted war ever come.

Truman's alarmist language further fixed the mistaken idea in the American mind that the Soviets were unrelenting aggressors intent upon undermining peace, and that the United States, almost alone, had to meet them everywhere. Truman's exaggerations and his commitment to the containment doctrine did not go unchallenged. Secretary Marshall himself was startled by the President's muscular anti-communist rhetoric, and he questioned the wisdom of overstating the case. The Soviet specialist Llewellyn Thompson urged "caution" in swinging too far toward "outright opposition to Russia...." Walter Lippmann, in reacting to both Truman's speech and George F. Kennan's now famous "Mr. 'X'" article in the July 1947 issue of the journal *Foreign Affairs*, labeled containment a "strategic monstrosity," because it made no distinctions between important or vital and not-so-important or peripheral areas. Because American power was not omnipresent, Lippmann further argued, the "policy can be implemented only by recruiting, subsidizing and supporting a heterogeneous array of satellites, clients, dependents and puppets." He also criticized the containment doctrine for placing more emphasis on confrontation than on diplomacy.

Truman himself came to see that there were dangers in stating imprecise, universal doctrines. He became boxed by his own rhetoric. When Mao Zedong's forces claimed victory in 1949 over Jiang's regime, conservative Republicans, angry Democrats, and various McCarthyites pilloried the President for letting China "fall." China lost itself, he retorted. But his critics pressed the point: if containment was to be applied everywhere, as the President had said in the Truman Doctrine, why not China? Truman appeared inconsistent, when, in fact, in the case of China, he was ultimately prudent in cutting American losses where the United States proved incapable of reaching its goals. Unable to disarm his detractors on this issue, Truman stood vulnerable in the early 1950s to political demagogues who fueled McCarthyism. The long-term consequences in this example have been grave. Democrats believed they could never lose "another China"—never permit Communists or Marxists, whether or not linked to Moscow, to assume power abroad. President John F. Kennedy later said, for example, that he could not withdraw from Vietnam because that might be perceived as "another China" and spark charges that he was soft on Communism. America, in fact, could not bring itself to open diplomatic relations with the People's Republic of China until 1979.

Jiang's collapse joined the Soviet explosion of an atomic bomb, the formation of the German Democratic Republic (East Germany), and the Sino-Soviet Friendship Treaty to arouse American feeling in late 1949 and early 1950 that the Soviet threat had dramatically escalated. Although Kennan told his State Department colleagues that such feeling was "largely of our own making" rather than an accurate accounting of Soviet actions, the composers of NSC-68 preferred to dwell on a more dangerous Soviet menace in extreme rhetoric not usually found in a secret report. But because the April 1950 document was aimed at President Truman, we can certainly understand why its language was hyperbolic. The fanatical and militant Soviets, concluded NSC-68, were seeking to impose "absolute authority over the rest of the world." America had to frustrate the global "design" of the "evil men" of the Kremlin, who were unrelentingly bent on "piecemeal aggression" against the "free world" through military force, infiltration, and intimidation. The report called for a huge American and allied military build-up and nuclear arms development.

NSC-68, most scholars agree, was a flawed, even amateurish document. It assumed a Communist monolith that did not exist, drew alarmist conclusions based upon vague and inaccurate information about Soviet capabilities, made grand, unsubstantiated claims about Soviet intentions, glossed over the presence of many non-democratic countries in the "free world," and recommended against negotiations with Moscow at the very time the Soviets were advancing toward a policy of "peaceful co-existence." One State Department expert on the Soviet Union, Charles E. Bohlen, although generally happy with the report's conclusions, faulted NSC-68 for assuming a Soviet plot for world conquest—for "oversimplifying the problem." No, he advised, the Soviets sought foremostly to maintain their regime and to extend it abroad "to the degree that is possible without serious risk to the internal regime." In short, there were limits to Soviet behavior. But few were listening to such cautionary voices. NSC-68 became American dogma, especially when the outbreak of the Korean War in June of 1950 sanctified it as a prophetic "we told you so."

The story of Truman's foreign policy is basically an accounting of how the United States, because of its own expansionism and exaggeration of the Soviet threat, became a global power. Truman projected American power after the Second World War to rehabilitate Western Europe, secure new allies, guarantee strategic and economic links, and block Communist or Soviet influence. He firmly implanted the image of the Soviets as relentless, worldwide transgressors with whom it is futile to negotiate. Through his exaggeration of the Soviet threat, Truman made it very likely that the United States would continue to practice global interventionism years after he left the White House.

The Origins of the Cold War: 1945–1953

It is, of course, a truism that coalitions tend not to survive their enemies' defeat. Certainly during World War II most observers of the international scene had expected differences eventually to arise among the victors. The hope had been, though, that a sufficiently strong framework of common interests— whether the United Nations or some mutually acceptable agreement on spheres of influence—would develop that could keep these differences within reasonable limits. This did not happen. Although both sides sought security, although neither side wanted a new war, disagreements over how to achieve those goals proved too great to overcome. With a rapidity that dismayed policymakers in both Washington and Moscow, allies shortly before united against the Axis found themselves in a confrontation with each other that would determine the shape of the postwar era. Russian-American relations, once a problem of rarely more than peripheral concern for the two countries involved, now became an object of rapt attention and anxiety for the entire world.

It is no simple matter to explain how national leaders in the United States and the Soviet Union came to hold such dissimilar concepts of postwar security. There did exist, in the history of the two countries' encounters with one another, an ample basis for mutual distrust. But there were also strong motives for cooperation, not the least of which was that, had they been able to act in concert, Russians and Americans might have achieved something close to absolute security in an insecure world. Their failure to do so may be attributed, ultimately, to irreconcilable differences in four critical areas: perceptions of history, ideology, technology, and personality.

Clearly the divergent historical experiences of the two countries conditioned their respective views of how best to attain security. The Russians tended to think of security in terms of space—not a surprising attitude, considering the frequency with which their country had been invaded, or the way in which they had used distance to defeat their adversaries. That such a concept might be outmoded in an age of atomic weapons and long-range bombers appears not to

From John Lewis Gaddis, *Russia, the Soviet Union, and the United States: An Interpretive History,* 2d ed. (McGraw-Hill, 1990). Copyright © 1990 by The McGraw-Hill Companies. Reprinted by permission. Notes omitted.

have occurred to Stalin; Hitler's defeat brought no alteration in his determination to control as much territory along the periphery of the Soviet Union as possible. "He regarded as sure only whatever he held in his fist," the Yugoslav Communist Milovan Djilas has written. "Everything beyond the control of his police was a potential enemy."

Americans, on the other hand, tended to see security in institutional terms: conditioned by their own atypical historical experience, they assumed that if representative governments could be established as widely as possible, together with a collective security organization capable of resolving differences between them, peace would be assured. That such governments might not always harbor peaceful intentions toward their neighbors, that the United Nations, in the absence of great power agreement, might lack the means of settling disputes, occurred to only a few informed observers. The general public, upon whose support foreign policy ultimately depended, tended to accept Cordell Hull's vision of a postwar world in which "there will no longer be need for spheres of influence, for alliances, for balance of power, or any of the special arrangements through which, in the unhappy past, the nations sought to safeguard their security or to promote their interests."

There was, of course, room for compromising these conflicting viewpoints. Neither the United States nor its British ally had been prepared wholly to abandon spheres of influence as a means of achieving their own postwar security; both accepted the premise that the USSR was entitled to have friendly countries along its borders. The great difficulty was that, unlike the expansion of American and British influence into Western Europe and the Mediterranean, the Soviet Union's gains took place without the approval of most of the governments and most of the people in the areas involved. The Anglo-Americans simply did not find it necessary, in the same measure as did the Russians, to ensure their own security by depriving people within their sphere of influence of the right to self-determination. Given Western convictions that only the diffusion of democratic institutions could guarantee peace, given Hitler's all-too-vivid precedent, Moscow's imposition of influence in Eastern Europe seemed ominous, whatever its motives. Stalin found himself able to implement his vision of security only by appearing to violate that of the West. The result was to create for the Soviet Union new sources of hostility and, ultimately, insecurity in the world.

Ideological differences constituted a second source of antagonism. Stalin had deliberately downplayed the Soviet commitment to communism during the war, even to the point of abolishing the Comintern in 1943. Some Americans concluded that the Russians had abandoned that ideology altogether, if on no other grounds than that a nation that fought Germans so effectively could not be all bad. The European communist movement remained very much the instrument of Soviet policy, however, and the Russians used it to facilitate their projection of influence into Eastern Europe. This development raised fears in the West that Soviet collaboration against the Axis had been nothing but a marriage of convenience and that, victory having been achieved, the Kremlin was now embarking upon a renewed crusade for world revolution.

This was, it now appears, a mistaken view. Stalin had always placed the security of the Soviet state above the interests of international communism; it had been the former, not the latter, that had motivated his expansion into Eastern Europe. Far from encouraging communists outside the Soviet Union to seize power, Stalin initially advised restraint, especially in his dealings with such movements in France, Italy, Greece, and China. But the Soviet leader's caution was not all that clear in the West. Faced with the sudden intrusion of Russian power into Europe, faced with a revival of anticapitalist rhetoric among communists throughout the world, faced with painful evidence from the recent past of what happened when dictators' rhetoric was not taken seriously, observers in both Western Europe and the United States jumped to the conclusion that Stalin, like Hitler, had insatiable ambitions, and would not stop until contained.

Technological differences created a third source of tension. The United States alone emerged from World War II with an industrial plant superior to what it had possessed before that conflict started; the Soviet Union, in turn, had come out of the war with its land ravaged, much of its industry destroyed, and some twenty million of its citizens dead. The resulting disparity of power caused some Americans to exaggerate their ability to influence events in the rest of the world; it simultaneously produced in the Russians deep feelings of inferiority and vulnerability.

This problem manifested itself most obviously with regard to reconstruction. Stalin had hoped to repair war damage with the help of Lend-Lease and a postwar loan from the United States; his conviction that Americans would soon be facing a postwar depression led him to believe—drawing on clear Leninist principles—that Washington would have no choice but to provide such aid as a means of generating foreign markets for surplus products. His surprise was great when the United States passed up the economic benefits it would have derived from granting a loan in favor of the political concessions it hoped to obtain by withholding it. Nor would Washington allow the use of Lend-Lease for reconstruction; to compound the offense, the Truman administration also cut off, in 1946, the flow of reparations from the American zone in Germany. Whether more generous policies on these matters would have produced better relations with the Soviet Union is impossible to prove—certainly the Russians were never in such need of aid as to be willing to make major political concessions in order to get it. There is no doubt, though, that they bitterly resented their exclusion from these "fruits" of Western technology.

Another "fruit" of Western technology that impressed the Russians was, of course, the atomic bomb. Although Soviet leaders carefully avoided signs of concern about this new weapon, they did secretly accelerate their own bomb development project while simultaneously calling for the abolition of all such weapons of mass destruction. After much debate within the government, the United States, in the summer of 1946, proposed the Baruch Plan, which would have transferred control of all fissionable materials to the United Nations. In fact, however, neither the Russians nor the Americans had sufficient faith in the world organization to entrust their security completely to it. Washington at no point was willing to surrender its bombs until the control system had gone into effect, while Moscow was unwilling to accept the inspection provisions which would allow the plan to operate. Both sides had concluded by 1947 that they would find greater security in an arms race than in an unproven system of international control.

Finally, accidents of personality made it more difficult than it might otherwise have been to achieve a mutually agreeable settlement. The Russians perceived in the transition from Roosevelt to Truman an abrupt shift from an attitude of cooperation to one of confrontation. "The policy pursued by the US ruling circles after the death of Franklin D. Roosevelt," the official history of Soviet foreign policy asserts, "amounted to renunciation of dependable and mutually beneficial cooperation with the Soviet Union, a cooperation that was so effective... in the period of joint struggle against the nazi aggressors." In fact, though, Roosevelt's policy had been firmer than Stalin realized; Truman's was not as uncompromising as his rhetoric suggested. What was different was style: where Roosevelt had sought to woo the Soviet leader by meeting his demands wherever possible, the new chief executive, like a good poker player, tried to deal from positions of rhetorical, if not actual, strength. His tough talk was designed to facilitate, not impede, negotiations—any appearance of weakness, he thought, would only encourage the Russians to ask for more.

What Truman failed to take into account was the possibility that Stalin might also be bluffing. Given the history of Western intervention to crush Bolshevism, given the Soviet Union's ruined economy and weakened population, and given the atomic bomb's unexpected confirmation of American technological superiority, it seems likely that the aging Soviet dictator was as frightened of the West as the West was of him. Truman's tough rhetoric, together with Hiroshima's example, may well have reinforced Stalin's conviction that if *he* showed any signs of weakness, all would be lost. Both leaders had learned too well the lesson of the 1930s: that appeasement never pays. Prospects for an amicable resolution of differences suffered accordingly.

There was nothing in this set of circumstances that made the Cold War inevitable—few things ever are inevitable in history. But a situation such as existed in Europe in 1945, with two great powers separated only by a power vacuum, seemed almost predestined to produce hostility, whether either side willed it or not. As a result, the United States, the Soviet Union, and much of the rest of the world as well would have to suffer through that prolonged period of insecurity that observers at the time, and historians since, have called the "Cold War."

~◎~

The evolution of United States policy toward the Soviet Union between 1945 and 1947 can be seen as a three-stage process of relating national interests to national capabilities. From V-J Day through early 1946, there existed genuine confusion in Washington as to both Soviet intentions and appropriate methods for dealing with them. Coordination between power and policy was, as a result, minimal. By the spring of 1946, a consensus had developed favoring resistance to further Soviet expansion, but little had been done to determine what resources would be necessary to accomplish that goal or to differentiate between areas of primary and secondary concern. It was not until 1947 that there began to emerge an approach to the Soviet Union that bore some reasonable relationship to American capabilities for projecting influence in the world.

There appeared to be no lack of power available to the United States for the purpose of ordering the postwar environment as it saw fit, but the task of transforming technological superiority into political influence proved frustratingly difficult. Secretary of State James F. Byrnes had hoped to trade reconstruction assistance and a commitment to the international control of atomic energy for Soviet concessions on such outstanding issues as implementation of the Yalta Declaration on Liberated Europe, peace treaties with former German satellites, and, ultimately, a final resolution of the German question itself. But the Russians maintained a posture of ostentatious unconcern about the atomic bomb, nor would they yield on significant issues to obtain reconstruction assistance. Congressional skepticism about Moscow's intentions ensured that any loan would carry a political price far beyond what the Russians would willingly pay, while public opinion pushed Truman into a decision to seek United Nations control of atomic energy before Byrnes had made any attempt to extract Soviet concessions in return. Economic and technological superiority thus won the United States surprisingly few practical benefits in its early postwar dealings with the USSR.

In Washington, moreover, there still existed a substantial number of officials who viewed Soviet hostility as the product of misunderstandings and who expected that, with restraint on both sides, a mutually satisfactory resolution of differences might still occur. It is significant that as late as November, 1945, a State Department representative could rebuke the Joint Chiefs of Staff for confidentially suggesting that the wartime alliance might not survive victory. "We must always bear in mind," a Department memorandum noted the following month, "that because of the differences between the economic and political systems [of the United States and the Soviet Union], the conduct of our relations requires more patience and diligence than with other countries." Despite his tough rhetoric, President Truman shared this view. Disagreements with the Russians were to be expected once the common bond of military necessity had been removed, he told his advisers; in time, they would disappear because "Stalin was a fine man who wanted to do the right thing."

But events made this position increasingly difficult to sustain. The Russians remained adamant in their determination to exclude Western influence from Eastern Europe and the Balkans, while a continued Soviet presence in Iran and Manchuria raised fears that Moscow might try to impose control over those territories as well. Russian interest in the eastern Mediterranean seemed to be growing, with demands for trusteeships over former Italian colonies, boundary rectifications at Turkey's expense, and a revision of the Montreux Convention governing passage through the Dardanelles. And in February, 1946, news of Soviet atomic espionage became public for the first time with the revelation that the Canadian government had arrested a group of Russian agents for trying to steal information about the bomb. That same month, Stalin in his first major postwar foreign policy speech stressed the incompatibility between communism and capitalism, implying that future wars were inevitable until the world economic system was restructured along Soviet lines.

It was at this point that there arrived at the State Department a dispatch from George F. Kennan, now *chargé d'affaires* at the American embassy in Moscow, which did much to clarify official thinking regarding Soviet behavior. Russian hostility toward the West, Kennan argued, stemmed chiefly from the internal necessities of the Stalinist regime: the Soviet dictator required a hostile outside world in order to justify his own autocratic rule. Marxism provided Soviet leaders with

> justification for their instinctive fear of the outside world, for the dictatorship without which they did not know how to rule, for cruelties they did not dare not to inflict, for sacrifices they felt bound to demand.... Today they cannot dispense with it. It is the fig leaf of their moral and intellectual respectability.

It followed that Stalin was, by nature, incapable of being reassured. "Nothing short of complete disarmament, delivery of our air and naval forces to Russia and resigning of the powers of government to American Communists would even dent this problem," Kennan noted in a subsequent dispatch, "and even then Moscow would smell a trap and would continue to harbor the most baleful misgivings." The solution, Kennan suggested, was to strengthen Western institutions in order to render them invulnerable to the Soviet challenge while simultaneously awaiting the eventual mellowing of the Soviet regime.

There was little in Kennan's analysis that he and other career Soviet experts had not been saying for some time. What was new was Washington's receptivity to the message, a condition brought about both by frustration over Soviet behavior and by growing public and Congressional resistance to further concessions. In contrast to its earlier optimism about relations with Moscow, the State Department now endorsed Kennan's analysis as "the most probable explanation of present Soviet policies and attitudes." The United States, it concluded, should demonstrate to the Kremlin, "in the first instance by diplomatic means and in the last analysis by military force if necessary that the present course of its foreign policy can only lead to disaster for the Soviet Union."

The spring and summer of 1946 did see a noticeable toughening of United States policy toward the Soviet Union. In early March, Truman lent public sanction to Winston Churchill's strongly anti-Soviet "iron curtain" speech by appearing on the platform with him at Fulton, Missouri. That same month, Secretary of State Byrnes insisted on placing the issue of Iran before the United Nations, even after the Russians had agreed to withdraw their troops from that country. The termination of German reparations shipments came in May; three months later, Byrnes publicly committed the United States to support German rehabilitation, with or without the Russians. In July, Truman endorsed the continued presence of American troops in southern Korea on the grounds that that country constituted "an ideological battleground upon which our whole success in Asia may depend." Soviet pressure on Turkey for bases produced a decision in August to maintain an American naval force indefinitely in the eastern Mediterranean. In September, White House aide Clark Clifford submitted a report to the president, prepared after consultation with top military and diplomatic advisers, arguing that "this government should be prepared... to resist vigorously and successfully any efforts of the U.S.S.R. to expand into areas vital to American security."

But these policies were decided upon without precise assessments as to whether the means existed to carry them out. The atomic bomb was of little use for such purposes, given the strong inhibitions American officials felt about brandishing their new weapon in peacetime and given the limited number of bombs and properly equipped bombers available, if war came. Nor could the administration hold out the prospect of economic aid as a means of inducing more cooperative Soviet behavior, in the face of continued Congressional reluctance to appropriate funds for such purposes. Such conventional military power as the United States possessed was rapidly melting away under the pressures of demobilization, and although most Americans supported firmer policies toward the Soviet Union, the election of an economy-minded, Republican-controlled Congress in November suggested that few were prepared to assume the burdens, in the form of high taxes and military manpower levels, such policies would require.

Shortly thereafter a severe economic crisis, the product of remaining wartime dislocations and an unusually harsh winter, hit Western Europe. This development caused the British to announce their intention, in February, 1947, of terminating economic and military aid to Greece and Turkey, countries that had, up to that point, been regarded as within London's sphere of responsibility. It also raised the longer-range but even more frightening prospect that economic conditions in Western Europe generally might deteriorate to the point that communist parties there could seize power through coups or even free elections. Suddenly the whole European balance of power, which the United States had gone to war to restore, seemed once again in peril.

This situation, which appeared so to threaten European stability, was one the Russians had done little if anything to instigate; it was rather the product primarily of internal conditions within the countries involved. But there was little doubt of Moscow's ability to exploit the European economic crisis if nothing was done to alleviate it. And action was taken, with such energy and dispatch that the fifteen weeks between late February and early June, 1947, have come to be regarded as a great moment in the history of American diplomacy, a rare instance in which "the government of the United States operat[ed] at its very finest, efficiently and effectively."

Such plaudits may be too generous. Certainly the language Truman used to justify aid to Greece and Turkey ("at the present moment in world history nearly every nation must choose between alternative ways of life.... I believe that it must be the policy of the United States to support free peoples who are resisting attempted subjugation by armed minorities or by outside pressures") represented a projection of rhetoric far beyond either the administration's intentions or capabilities. Whatever its usefulness in prying funds out of a parsimonious Congress, the sweeping language of the "Truman Doctrine" would cause problems later on as the president and his foreign policy advisers sought to clarify distinctions between vital and peripheral interests in the world. That such distinctions were important became apparent with the announcement in June, 1947, of the Marshall Plan, an ambitious initiative that reflected, far more than did the Truman Doctrine, the careful calibration of ends to means characteristic of the administration's policy during this period.

The European Recovery Program, to use its official title, proposed spending some $17 billion for economic assistance to the non-communist nations of Europe over the next four years. (Aid was offered to the Soviet Union and its East European satellites as well, but with the expectation, which proved to be correct, that Moscow would turn it down.) It was a plan directed, not against Soviet military attack, a contingency United States officials considered remote, but against the economic malaise that had sapped self-confidence among European allies, rendering them vulnerable to internal communist takeovers. It involved no direct military commitments; rather, its architects assumed, much as had advocates of the "arsenal of democracy" concept before World War II, that the United States could most efficiently help restore the balance of power in Europe by contributing its technology and raw materials, but not its manpower. It represented a deliberate decision to focus American energies on the recovery of Europe at the expense of commitments elsewhere: it is significant that the spring of 1947 also saw the Truman administration move toward liquidating its remaining responsibilities in China and Korea. What took place in Washington during the famous "fifteen weeks," then, was not so much a proliferation of commitments as a reordering of priorities, executed with a sharp awareness of what the United States would have to accept in the world and what, given limited resources, it could realistically expect to change.

Unfortunately, rhetoric again obscured the point, this time by way of a mysterious article, entitled "The Sources of Soviet Conduct," which appeared in the July, 1947, issue of *Foreign Affairs*. Attributed only to a "Mr. X," it advanced the notion that

> the main element of any United States policy toward the Soviet Union must be that of a long-term, patient but firm and vigilant containment of Russian expansive tendencies.... Soviet pressure against the free institutions of the Western world is something that can be contained by the adroit and vigilant application of counter-force at a series of constantly shifting geographical and political points, corresponding to the shifts and maneuvers of Soviet policy.

Then, as now, nothing remained secret for very long, and word soon leaked out that "Mr. X" had been none other than Kennan, who had recently become head of the State Department's new Policy Planning Staff. This information gave the "X" article something of the character of an official document, and it quickly came to be seen as the definitive expression of administration policy toward the Soviet Union.

In fact, Kennan had not intended his article as a comprehensive prescription for future action; it was, rather, an elaboration of the analysis of Soviet behavior he had submitted in his February, 1946, telegram to the State Department. Such policy recommendations as Kennan did include reflected only in the most approximate and incomplete way the range of his thinking on Soviet-American relations. The article implied an automatic commitment to resist Russian expansionism wherever it occurred; there was in it little sense of the administration's preoccupation with limited means and of the consequent need to distinguish between primary and secondary interests. Nor did the piece make it clear that economic rather than military methods were to be employed as the chief instrument of containment. The safest generalization that can be made about the "X" article is that, like the Truman Doctrine, it was an outstanding demonstration of the obfuscatory potential of imprecise prose. It was not an accurate description of the policies the United States was, at that moment, in the process of implementing.

Kennan provided a much clearer explanation of what he meant by "containment" in a secret review of the world situation prepared for Secretary of State George C. Marshall in November, 1947. Soviet efforts to fill power vacuums left by German and Japanese defeats had largely been halted, Kennan argued, but this accomplishment had dangerously strained American resources: "The program of aid to Europe which we are now proposing to undertake will probably be the last major effort of this nature which our people could, or should, make.... It is clearly unwise for us to continue the attempt to carry alone, or largely singlehanded, the opposition to Soviet expansion." Further dispersal of resources could be avoided only by identifying clearly those parts of the world upon whose defense American security depended. Aside from the Western Hemisphere, Kennan's list included only non-communist Europe, the Middle East, and Japan. In China there was little the West could do, although there were as well "definite limitations on both the military and economic capabilities of the Russians in that area." Since Korea was "not of decisive strategic importance to us, our main task is to extricate ourselves without too great a loss of prestige." All in all, Kennan concluded, "our best answer is to strengthen in every way local forces of resistance, and persuade others to bear a greater part of the burden of opposing communism."

"Containment," then, involved no indiscriminate projection of commitments around the world: it was, instead, a policy precise in its identification of American interests, specific in its assessment of threats to those interests, frugal in its calculation of means required to ward off those threats, vague only in its public presentation. But this very vagueness would, in time, corrupt the concept, for where gaps between policy and rhetoric exist, it is often easier to bring the former into line with the latter than the other way around. The eventual consequence would be the promulgation of policies under the rubric of "containment" far removed from what that doctrine had been originally intended to mean.

◦◦◦

Despite its limited character, the vigor of the American response to Soviet postwar probes apparently caught Stalin by surprise. His response was to try to strengthen further the security of his own regime; first by increasing safeguards against Western influences inside the Soviet Union; second, by tightening control over Russia's East European satellites; and finally by working to ensure central direction of the international communist movement. By a perverse kind of logic, each of these moves backfired, as did a much earlier Soviet initiative whose existence only came to light at this point—the establishment, in the United States during the 1930s, of a major espionage network directed from Moscow. The result, in each of these cases, was to produce consequences that only made it more difficult for Stalin to obtain the kind of security he sought.

Soviet leaders had always faced a dilemma regarding contacts with the West. Such associations might carry substantial benefits—certainly this had been true of collaboration with Great Britain and the United States during World War II. But there were also costs, not the least of which was the possibility that prolonged exposure to Western ideas and institutions might erode the still vulnerable base of the Soviet regime. It is an indication of the seriousness with which Stalin viewed this problem that he shipped hundreds of thousands of returning prisoners-of-war off to labor camps in 1945, much to the horror of Americans who had forcibly repatriated many of them at the Russians' request. By 1947, Moscow's campaign against Western influence had extended to literature, music, history, economics, and even genetics. As a result, Soviet prestige suffered throughout the world; the effect of these policies on science, and, in turn, on the advancement of Russian military capabilities, can only be guessed at.

Even more striking in its impact on the West, though, was Stalin's harsh effort to consolidate his control over Eastern Europe. Subservience to Moscow, not ideological uniformity, had been the chief Soviet priority in that area until 1947, but in June of that year the Russians imposed a communist-dominated government in Hungary, a country in which relatively free elections had been held in the fall of 1945. "I think it's an outrage," President Truman told a press conference on June 5. "The Hungarian situation is a terrible one." In February, 1948, the Communist Party of Czechoslovakia overthrew the duly-constituted government of that country—an event that produced the death, by either murder or suicide, of the popular Czech foreign minister, Jan Masaryk. It would be difficult to exaggerate the impact of this development in the West, where guilty consciences still existed over what had been done to the Czechs at Munich ten years before. One immediate effect was to ensure Congressional passage of the Marshall Plan; another was to provoke Britain, France, and the Benelux countries into forming the Western Union, the first step toward a joint defensive alliance among the non-communist nations of Europe. There also followed the stimulation of something approaching a war scare in the United States, an administration request for Universal Military Training and the reinstitution of the draft, and a public condemnation by Truman of the Soviet Union as the "one nation [that] has not only refused to cooperate in the establishment of a just and honorable peace, but—even worse—has actively sought to prevent it."

Meanwhile, attempts to resolve the question of divided Germany had produced no results, despite protracted and tedious negotiations. In February, 1948, the three Western occupying powers, plus the Benelux countries, met in London and decided to move toward formation of an independent West German state. Stalin's response, after initial hesitation, was to impose a blockade on land access to Berlin, which the World War II settlement had left a hundred miles inside the Soviet zone. The Berlin crisis brought the United States and the Soviet Union as close to war as they would come during the early postwar years. Truman was determined that Western forces would stay in the beleaguered city, however untenable their military position there, and to reinforce this policy he ostentatiously transferred to British bases three squadrons of B-29 bombers. No atomic bombs accompanied these planes, nor were they even equipped to carry them. But this visible reminder of American nuclear superiority may well have deterred the Russians from interfering with air access to Berlin, and through this means the United States and its allies were able to keep their sectors of the city supplied for almost a year. Stalin finally agreed to lift the blockade in May, 1949, but not before repeating the dubious distinction he had achieved in the Russo-Finnish War a decade earlier: of appearing to be brutal and incompetent at the same time.

The Berlin blockade had two important consequences, both of which were detrimental from the Soviet point of view. It provided the impetus necessary to transform the Western Union into the North Atlantic Treaty Organization, a defensive alliance linking the United States, Canada, and ten Western European nations, established in April, 1949. Simultaneously, the blockade lessened prospects for a settlement of the German problem in collaboration with the Russians; the result was to accelerate implementation of the London program, a goal accomplished with the formation, in September, 1949, of the Federal Republic of Germany.

POSTSCRIPT

Was the United States Responsible
for the Cold War?

Paterson's selection contains most of the arguments advanced by the revisionist critics of America's cold war policies: Truman's diplomatic style was blunt and impetuous, and he tended to oversimplify complex issues into black and white alternatives. Paterson believes that the Truman administration exaggerated the Russian threat to the balance of power in Europe. It is not clear whether this was a deliberate miscalculation or whether the Truman administration misperceived the motive behind the "iron curtain" that Russia drew around Eastern Europe. The author maintains that Stalin was more concerned with Russia's security needs than with world conquest.

Gaddis is much less critical than Paterson of America's postwar policy. He believes that the United States and Russia would inevitably clash once the common enemy—Hitler—was defeated because the two countries had fundamentally different political and economic systems. Gaddis maintains that for nearly two years there was confusion and uncertainty in the United States' foreign policy in Europe. Truman, he says, did not reverse Roosevelt's policy. His manner was more blunt and, consequently, he showed less patience in dealing with Stalin.

Gaddis acknowledges revisionist criticisms that the Americans misperceived Stalin's attempts to control Eastern Europe. The Soviet premier used expansionist rhetoric when he was primarily concerned about protecting Russia from another invasion. By early 1946 both sides were pursuing policies that would lead to an impasse.

In his book *We Now Know: Rethinking Cold War History* (Oxford University Press, 1997), Gaddis argues more strongly than he has in his previous works that Stalin was primarily responsible for the cold war. Based upon newly discovered, partially opened Soviet archival materials, Gaddis describes Stalin, Khrushchev, and even Chairman Mao as prisoners of a peculiar world view: "Aging Ponce de Leons in search of an ideological fountain of youth."

Students who wish to study the cold war in greater detail should consult *Containment: Documents on American Policy and Strategy, 1945-1950* edited by Thomas H. Etzold and John Lewis Gaddis (Columbia University Press, 1978). Another comprehensive work is Melvyn P. Leffler, *A Preponderance of Power: National Security, the Truman Administration, and the Cold War* (Stanford University Press, 1992). The two best readers to excerpt the various viewpoints on the cold war are Thomas G. Paterson and Robert J. McMahon, eds., *The Origins of the Cold War*, 3rd ed. (D. C. Heath, 1991) and Melvyn P. Leffler and David S. Painter, eds., *Origins of the Cold War: An International History* (Routledge, 1994). Finally, David Reynolds has edited a series of essays in *The Origins of the Cold War: International Perspectives* (Yale University Press, 1994).

ISSUE 2

Did Communism Threaten America's Internal Security After World War II?

YES: John Earl Haynes and Harvey Klehr, from *Venona: Decoding Soviet Espionage in America* (Yale University Press, 1999)

NO: Richard M. Fried, from *Nightmare in Red: The McCarthy Era in Perspective* (Oxford University Press, 1990)

ISSUE SUMMARY

YES: History professors John Earl Haynes and Harvey Klehr argue that army code-breakers during World War II's "Venona Project" uncovered a disturbing number of high-ranking U.S. government officials who seriously damaged American interests by passing sensitive information to the Soviet Union.

NO: Professor of history Richard M. Fried argues that the early 1950s were a "nightmare in red" during which American citizens had their First and Fifth Amendment rights suspended when a host of national and state investigating committees searched for Communists in government agencies, Hollywood, labor unions, foundations, universities, public schools, and even public libraries.

The 1917 triumph of the Bolshevik revolution in Russia and the ensuing spread of revolution to other parts of Eastern Europe and Germany inspired American radicals that the revolution was near. It also led to a wave of anti-Bolshevik hysteria. In the fall of 1919 two groups of radicals—one native-born, the other foreign-born—formed the Communist and Communist Labor Parties. Ultimately they would merge, yet between them they contained only 25,000 to 40,000 members.

The popular "front" policy, which lasted from 1935 to 1939, was the most successful venture undertaken by American Communists. The chief aim of the American Communists became not to increase party membership but to infiltrate progressive organizations. They achieved their greatest successes in the labor movement, which badly needed union organizers. As a consequence Communists controlled several major unions, such as the West Coast longshoremen and the electrical workers, and attained key offices in the powerful United

Autoworkers. Many American novelists, screenwriters, and actors also joined communist front organizations, such as the League of American Writers, and the Theatre Collective produced "proletarian" plays.

In the 1930s and 1940s the American Communist Party's major success was its ability to establish a conspiratorial underground in Washington. The release of the Venona intercepts of American intelligence during World War II indicates that some 349 American citizens and residents had a covert relationship with Soviet intelligence agencies.

During the war the Federal Bureau of Investigation (FBI) and Office of Strategic Services (OSS) conducted security clearances that permitted Communist supporters to work at high-level jobs if they met the qualifications. This changed in February 1947. In order to impress the Republicans that he wished to attack communism at home, President Harry S. Truman issued an executive order that inaugurated a comprehensive investigation of the loyalty of all government employees by the FBI and the Civil Service Commission.

Truman's loyalty program temporarily protected him from charges that he was "soft" on communism. His ability to ward off attacks on his soft containment policy against communism ran out in his second term. Alger Hiss, a high-level state department official, was convicted in 1949 of lying about his membership in the Ware Communist cell group. In September Truman announced to the American public that the Russians had successfully tested an atomic bomb. Shortly thereafter the Chinese Communists secured control over all of China when their nationalist opponents retreated to the island of Taiwan. Then on June 24, 1950, North Korea crossed the "containment" line at the 38th parallel and attacked South Korea.

The Republican response to these events was swift, critical, and partisan. Before his conviction, Hiss had been thoroughly investigated by the House Un-American Activities Committee. Had he led President Franklin D. Roosevelt and others to a sell-out of the Eastern European countries at the Yalta Conference in February 1945? Who lost China? Did liberal and leftist state department officials stationed in China give a pro-Communist slant to U.S. foreign policies in Asia?

Within this atmosphere Truman's attempt to forge a bipartisan policy to counter internal subversion of government agencies by Communists received a mortal blow when Senator Joseph A. McCarthy of Wisconsin publicly identified 205 cases of individuals who appeared to be either card-carrying members or loyal to the Communist Party.

How legitimate was the second great red scare? Did communism threaten America's internal security in the cold war era? In the following selections, John Earl Haynes and Harvey Klehr contend that a sizeable number of high-level government officials had passed sensitive information to Russian intelligence, while Richard M. Fried argues that the 1950s became a "red nightmare" when state and national government agencies overreacted in their search for Communists, violating citizens' rights of free speech and a defense against self-incrimination under the First and Fifth Amendments.

John Earl Haynes and Harvey Klehr  **YES**

Venona and the Cold War

The Venona Project began because Carter Clarke did not trust Joseph Stalin. Colonel Clarke was chief of the U.S. Army's Special Branch, part of the War Department's Military Intelligence Division, and in 1943 its officers heard vague rumors of secret German-Soviet peace negotiations. With the vivid example of the August 1939 Nazi-Soviet Pact in mind, Clarke feared that a separate peace between Moscow and Berlin would allow Nazi Germany to concentrate its formidable war machine against the United States and Great Britain. Clarke thought he had a way to find out whether such negotiations were under way.

Clarke's Special Branch supervised the Signal Intelligence Service, the Army's elite group of code-breakers and the predecessor of the National Security Agency. In February 1943 Clarke ordered the service to establish a small program to examine ciphered Soviet diplomatic cablegrams. Since the beginning of World War II in 1939, the federal government had collected copies of international cables leaving and entering the United States. If the cipher used in the Soviet cables could be broken, Clarke believed, the private exchanges between Soviet diplomats in the United States and their superiors in Moscow would show whether Stalin was seriously pursuing a separate peace.

The coded Soviet cables, however, proved to be far more difficult to read than Clarke had expected. American code-breakers discovered that the Soviet Union was using a complex two-part ciphering system involving a "one-time pad" code that in theory was unbreakable. The Venona code-breakers, however, combined acute intellectual analysis with painstaking examination of thousands of coded telegraphic cables to spot a Soviet procedural error that opened the cipher to attack. But by the time they had rendered the first messages into readable text in 1946, the war was over and Clarke's initial goal was moot. Nor did the messages show evidence of a Soviet quest for a separate peace. What they did demonstrate, however, stunned American officials. Messages thought to be between Soviet diplomats at the Soviet consulate in New York and the People's Commissariat of Foreign Affairs in Moscow turned out to be cables between professional intelligence field officers and Gen. Pavel Fitin, head of the foreign intelligence directorate of the KGB in Moscow. Espionage, not diplomacy, was the subject of these cables. One of the first cables rendered into coherent

From John Earl Haynes and Harvey Klehr, *Venona: Decoding Soviet Espionage in America* (Yale University Press, 1999). Copyright © 1999 by Yale University. Reprinted by permission of Yale University Press. Notes omitted.

text was a 1944 message from KGB officers in New York showing that the Soviet Union had infiltrated America's most secret enterprise, the atomic bomb project.

By 1948 the accumulating evidence from other decoded Venona cables showed that the Soviets had recruited spies in virtually every major American government agency of military or diplomatic importance. American authorities learned that since 1942 the United States had been the target of a Soviet espionage onslaught involving dozens of professional Soviet intelligence officers and hundreds of Americans, many of whom were members of the American Communist party (CPUSA). The deciphered cables of the Venona Project identify 349 citizens, immigrants, and permanent residents of the United States who had had a covert relationship with Soviet intelligence agencies. Further, American cryptanalysts in the Venona Project deciphered only a fraction of the Soviet intelligence traffic, so it was only logical to conclude that many additional agents were discussed in the thousands of unread messages. Some were identified from other sources, such as defectors' testimony and the confessions of Soviet spies.

The deciphered Venona messages also showed that a disturbing number of high-ranking U.S. government officials consciously maintained a clandestine relationship with Soviet intelligence agencies and had passed extraordinarily sensitive information to the Soviet Union that had seriously damaged American interests. Harry White—the second most powerful official in the U.S. Treasury Department, one of the most influential officials in the government, and part of the American delegation at the founding of the United Nations—had advised the KGB about how American diplomatic strategy could be frustrated. A trusted personal assistant to President Franklin Roosevelt, Lauchlin Currie, warned the KGB that the FBI had started an investigation of one of the Soviets' key American agents, Gregory Silvermaster. This warning allowed Silvermaster, who headed a highly productive espionage ring, to escape detection and continue spying. Maurice Halperin, the head of a research section of the Office of Strategic Services (OSS), then America's chief intelligence arm, turned over hundreds of pages of secret American diplomatic cables to the KGB. William Perl, a brilliant young government aeronautical scientist, provided the Soviets with the results of the highly secret tests and design experiments for American jet engines and jet aircraft. His betrayal assisted the Soviet Union in quickly overcoming the American technological lead in the development of jets. In the Korean War, U.S. military leaders expected the Air Force to dominate the skies, on the assumption that the Soviet aircraft used by North Korea and Communist China would be no match for American aircraft. They were shocked when Soviet MiG-15 jet fighters not only flew rings around U.S. propeller-driven aircraft but were conspicuously superior to the first generation of American jets as well. Only the hurried deployment of America's newest jet fighter, the F-86 Saber, allowed the United States to match the technological capabilities of the MiG-15. The Air Force prevailed, owing more to the skill of American pilots than to the design of American aircraft.

And then there were the atomic spies. From within the Manhattan Project two physicists, Klaus Fuchs and Theodore Hall, and one technician, David

Greenglass, transmitted the complex formula for extracting bomb-grade uranium from ordinary uranium, the technical plans for production facilities, and the engineering principles for the "implosion" technique. The latter process made possible an atomic bomb using plutonium, a substance much easier to manufacture than bomb-grade uranium.

The betrayal of American atomic secrets to the Soviets allowed the Soviet Union to develop atomic weapons several years sooner and at a substantially lower cost than it otherwise would have. Joseph Stalin's knowledge that espionage assured the Soviet Union of quickly breaking the American atomic monopoly emboldened his diplomatic strategy in his early Cold War clashes with the United States. It is doubtful that Stalin, rarely a risk-taker, would have supplied the military wherewithal and authorized North Korea to invade South Korea in 1950 had the Soviet Union not exploded an atomic bomb in 1949. Otherwise Stalin might have feared that President Harry Truman would stanch any North Korean invasion by threatening to use atomic weapons. After all, as soon as the atomic bomb had been developed, Truman had not hesitated to use it twice to end the war with Japan. But in 1950, with Stalin in possession of the atomic bomb, Truman was deterred from using atomic weapons in Korea, even in the late summer when initially unprepared American forces were driven back into the tip of Korea and in danger of being pushed into the sea, and then again in the winter when Communist Chinese forces entered the war in massive numbers. The killing and maiming of hundreds of thousands of soldiers and civilians on both sides of the war in Korea might have been averted had the Soviets not been able to parry the American atomic threat.

Early Soviet possession of the atomic bomb had an important psychological consequence. When the Soviet Union exploded a nuclear device in 1949, ordinary Americans as well as the nation's leaders realized that a cruel despot, Joseph Stalin, had just gained the power to destroy cities at will. This perception colored the early Cold War with the hues of apocalypse. Though the Cold War never lost the potential of becoming a civilization-destroying conflict, Stalin's death in March 1953 noticeably relaxed Soviet-American tensions. With less successful espionage, the Soviet Union might not have developed the bomb until after Stalin's death, and the early Cold War might have proceeded on a far less frightening path.

Venona decryptions identified most of the Soviet spies uncovered by American counterintelligence between 1948 and the mid-1950s. The skill and perseverance of the Venona code-breakers led the U.S. Federal Bureau of Investigation (FBI) and British counterintelligence (MI5) to the atomic spy Klaus Fuchs. Venona documents unmistakably identified Julius Rosenberg as the head of a Soviet spy ring and David Greenglass, his brother-in-law, as a Soviet source at the secret atomic bomb facility at Los Alamos, New Mexico. Leads from decrypted telegrams exposed the senior British diplomat Donald Maclean as a major spy in the British embassy in Washington and precipitated his flight to the Soviet Union, along with his fellow diplomat and spy Guy Burgess. The arrest and prosecution of such spies as Judith Coplon, Robert Soblen, and Jack Soble was possible because American intelligence was able to read Soviet reports about their activities. The charges by the former Soviet spy Elizabeth Bentley that several dozen mid-level government officials, mostly secret Communists, had assisted Soviet intelligence were corroborated in Venona documents and assured American authorities of her veracity.

With the advent of the Cold War, however, the spies clearly identified in the Venona decryptions were the least of the problem. Coplon, Rosenberg, Greenglass, Fuchs, Soble, and Soblen were prosecuted, and the rest were eased out of the government or otherwise neutralized as threats to national security. But that still left a security nightmare. Of the 349 Americans the deciphered Venona cables revealed as having covert ties to Soviet intelligence agencies, less than half could be identified by their real names and nearly two hundred remained hidden behind cover names. American officials assumed that some of the latter surely were still working in sensitive positions. Had they been promoted and moved into policy-making jobs? Had Muse, the unidentified female agent in the OSS, succeeded in transferring to the State Department or the Central Intelligence Agency (CIA), the successor to the OSS? What of Source No. 19, who had been senior enough to meet privately with Churchill and Roosevelt at the Trident Conference? Was the unidentified KGB source Bibi working for one of America's foreign assistance agencies? Was Donald, the unidentified Navy captain who was a GRU (Soviet military intelligence) source, still in uniform, perhaps by this time holding the rank of admiral? And what of the two unidentified atomic spies Quantum and Pers? They had given Stalin the secrets of the uranium and plutonium bomb: were they now passing on the secrets of the even more destructive hydrogen bomb? And how about Dodger, Godmother, and Fakir? Deciphered Venona messages showed that all three had provided the KGB with information on American diplomats who specialized in Soviet matters. Fakir was himself being considered for an assignment representing the United States in Moscow. Which of the American foreign service officers who were also Soviet specialists were traitors? How could Americans successfully negotiate with the Soviet Union when the American negotiating team included someone working for the other side? Western Europe, clearly, would be the chief battleground of the Cold War. To lose there was to lose all: the task of rebuilding stable democracies in postwar Europe and forging the NATO military alliance was America's chief diplomatic challenge. Yet Venona showed that the KGB had Mole, the appropriate cover name of a Soviet source inside the Washington establishment who had passed on to Moscow high-level American diplomatic policy guidance on Europe. When American officials met to discuss sensitive matters dealing with France, Britain, Italy, or Germany, was Mole present and working to frustrate American goals? Stalin's espionage offensive had not only uncovered American secrets, it had also undermined the mutual trust that American officials had for each other.

The Truman administration had expected the end of World War II to allow the dismantling of the massive military machine created to defeat Nazi Germany and Imperial Japan. The government slashed military budgets, turned weapons factories over to civilian production, ended conscription, and returned millions of soldiers to civilian life. So, too, the wartime intelligence and security apparatus was demobilized. Anticipating only limited need for foreign intelligence and stating that he wanted no American Gestapo, President Truman abolished America's chief intelligence agency, the Office of Strategic Services. With the coming of peace, emergency wartime rules for security vetting of many government employees lapsed or were ignored.

In late 1945 and in 1946, the White House had reacted with a mixture of indifference and skepticism to FBI reports indicating significant Soviet espionage activity in the United States. Truman administration officials even whitewashed evidence pointing to the theft of American classified documents in the 1945 *Amerasia* case because they did not wish to put at risk the continuation of the wartime Soviet-American alliance and wanted to avoid the political embarrassment of a security scandal. By early 1947, however, this indifference ended. The accumulation of information from defectors such as Elizabeth Bentley and Igor Gouzenko, along with the Venona decryptions, made senior Truman administration officials realize that reports of Soviet spying constituted more than FBI paranoia. No government could operate successfully if it ignored the challenge to its integrity that Stalin's espionage offensive represented. In addition, the White House sensed that there was sufficient substance to the emerging picture of a massive Soviet espionage campaign, one assisted by American Communists, that the Truman administration was vulnerable to Republican charges of having ignored a serious threat to American security. President Truman reversed course and in March 1947 issued a sweeping executive order establishing a comprehensive security vetting program for U.S. government employees. He also created the Central Intelligence Agency, a stronger and larger version of the OSS, which he had abolished just two years earlier. In 1948 the Truman administration followed up these acts by indicting the leaders of the CPUSA under the sedition sections of the 1940 Smith Act. While the Venona Project and the decrypted messages themselves remained secret, the substance of the messages with the names of scores of Americans who had assisted Soviet espionage circulated among American military and civilian security officials. From the security officials the information went to senior executive-branch political appointees and members of Congress. They, in turn, passed it on to journalists and commentators, who conveyed the alarming news to the general public.

Americans' Understanding of Soviet and Communist Espionage

During the early Cold War, in the late 1940s and early 1950s, every few months newspaper headlines trumpeted the exposure of yet another network of Communists who had infiltrated an American laboratory, labor union, or government agency. Americans worried that a Communist fifth column, more loyal to the Soviet Union than to the United States, had moved into their institutions. By the mid-1950s, following the trials and convictions for espionage-related crimes of Alger Hiss, a senior diplomat, and Julius and Ethel Rosenberg for atomic spying, there was a widespread public consensus on three points: that Soviet espionage was serious, that American Communists assisted the Soviets, and that several senior government officials had betrayed the United States.

The deciphered Venona messages provide a solid factual basis for this consensus. But the government did not release the Venona decryptions to the public, and it successfully disguised the source of its information about Soviet espionage. This decision denied the public the incontestable evidence afforded by the messages of the Soviet Union's own spies. Since the information about Soviet espionage and American Communist participation derived largely from the testimony of defectors and a mass of circumstantial evidence, the public's belief in those reports rested on faith in the integrity of government security officials. These sources are inherently more ambiguous than the hard evidence of the Venona messages, and this ambiguity had unfortunate consequences for American politics and Americans' understanding of their own history.

The decision to keep Venona secret from the public, and to restrict knowledge of it even within the government, was made essentially by senior Army officers in consultation with the FBI and the CIA. Aside from the Venona codebreakers, only a limited number of military intelligence officers, FBI agents, and CIA officials knew of the project. The CIA in fact was not made an active partner in Venona until 1952 and did not receive copies of the deciphered messages until 1953. The evidence is not entirely clear, but it appears that Army Chief of Staff Omar Bradley, mindful of the White House's tendency to leak politically sensitive information, decided to deny President Truman direct knowledge of the Venona Project. The president was informed about the substance of the Venona messages as it came to him through FBI and Justice Department memorandums on espionage investigations and CIA reports on intelligence matters. He was not told that much of this information derived from reading Soviet cable traffic. This omission is important because Truman was mistrustful of J. Edgar Hoover, the head of the FBI, and suspected that the reports of Soviet espionage were exaggerated for political purposes. Had he been aware of Venona, and known that Soviet cables confirmed the testimony of Elizabeth Bentley and Whittaker Chambers, it is unlikely that his aides would have considered undertaking a campaign to discredit Bentley and indict Chambers for perjury, or would have allowed themselves to be taken in by the disinformation being spread by the American Communist party and Alger Hiss's partisans that Chambers had at one time been committed to an insane asylum.

There were sensible reasons ... for the decision to keep Venona a highly compartmentalized secret within the government. In retrospect, however, the negative consequences of this policy are glaring. Had Venona been made public, it is unlikely there would have been a forty-year campaign to prove that the Rosenbergs were innocent. The Venona messages clearly display Julius Rosenberg's role as the leader of a productive ring of Soviet spies. Nor would there have been any basis for doubting his involvement in atomic espionage, because the deciphered messages document his recruitment of his brother-in-law, David Greenglass, as a spy. It is also unlikely, had the messages been made public or even circulated more widely within the government than they did, that Ethel Rosenberg would have been executed. The Venona messages do not throw her guilt in doubt; indeed, they confirm that she was a participant in her husband's espionage and in the recruitment of her brother for atomic espionage. But they suggest that she was essentially an accessory to her husband's activity, having knowledge of it and assisting him but not acting as a principal. Had they been introduced at the Rosenberg trial, the Venona messages would have confirmed Ethel's guilt but also reduced the importance of her role.

Further, the Venona messages, if made public, would have made Julius Rosenberg's execution less likely. When Julius Rosenberg faced trial, only two Soviet atomic spies were known: David Greenglass, whom Rosenberg had recruited and run as a source, and Klaus Fuchs. Fuchs, however, was in England, so Greenglass was the only Soviet atomic spy in the media spotlight in the United States. Greenglass's confession left Julius Rosenberg as the target of public outrage at atomic espionage. That prosecutors would ask for and get the death penalty under those circumstances is not surprising.

In addition to Fuchs and Greenglass, however, the Venona messages identify three other Soviet sources within the Manhattan Project. The messages show that Theodore Hall, a young physicist at Los Alamos, was a far more valuable source than Greenglass, a machinist. Hall withstood FBI interrogation, and the government had no direct evidence of his crimes except the Venona messages, which because of their secrecy could not be used in court; he therefore escaped prosecution. The real identities of the sources Fogel and Quantum are not known, but the information they turned over to the Soviets suggests that Quantum was a scientist of some standing and that Fogel was either a scientist or an engineer. Both were probably more valuable sources than David Greenglass. Had Venona been made public, Greenglass would have shared the stage with three other atomic spies and not just with Fuchs, and all three would have appeared to have done more damage to American security than he. With Greenglass's role diminished, that of his recruiter, Julius Rosenberg, would have been reduced as well. Rosenberg would assuredly have been convicted, but his penalty might well have been life in prison rather than execution.

There were broader consequences, as well, of the decision to keep Venona secret. The overlapping issues of Communists in government, Soviet espionage, and the loyalty of American Communists quickly became a partisan battleground. Led by Republican senator Joseph McCarthy of Wisconsin, some conservatives and partisan Republicans launched a comprehensive attack on the loyalties of the Roosevelt and Truman administrations. Some painted the entire New Deal as a disguised Communist plot and depicted Dean Acheson, Truman's secretary of state, and George C. Marshall, the Army chief of staff under Roosevelt and secretary of state and secretary of defense under Truman, as participants, in Senator McCarthy's words, in "a conspiracy on a scale so immense as to dwarf any previous such venture in the history of man. A conspiracy of infamy so black that, when it is finally exposed, its principals shall be forever deserving of the maledictions of all honest men." There is no basis in Venona for implicating Acheson or Marshall in a Communist conspiracy, but because the deciphered Venona messages were classified and unknown to the public, demagogues such as McCarthy had the opportunity to mix together accurate information about betrayal by men such as Harry White and Alger Hiss with falsehoods about Acheson and Marshall that served partisan political goals.

A number of liberals and radicals pointed to the excesses of McCarthy's charges as justification for rejecting the allegations altogether. Anticommunism further lost credibility in the late 1960s when critics of U.S. involvement in the Vietnam War blamed it for America's ill-fated participation. By the 1980s many commentators, and perhaps most academic historians, had concluded that Soviet espionage had been minor, that few American Communists had assisted the Soviets, and that no high officials had betrayed the United States. Many history texts depicted America in the late 1940s and 1950s as a "nightmare in red" during which Americans were "sweat-drenched in fear" of a figment of their own paranoid imaginations. As for American Communists, they were widely portrayed as having no connection with espionage. One influential book asserted emphatically, "There is no documentation in the public record of a direct connection between the American Communist Party and espionage during the entire postwar period."

Consequently, Communists were depicted as innocent victims of an irrational and oppressive American government. In this sinister but widely accepted portrait of America in the 1940s and 1950s, an idealistic New Dealer (Alger Hiss) was thrown into prison on the perjured testimony of a mentally sick anti-Communist fanatic (Whittaker Chambers), innocent progressives (the Rosenbergs) were sent to the electric chair on trumped-up charges of espionage laced with anti-Semitism, and dozens of blameless civil servants had their careers ruined by the smears of a professional anti-Communist (Elizabeth Bentley). According to this version of events, one government official (Harry White) was killed by a heart attack brought on by Bentley's lies, and another (Laurence Duggan, a senior diplomat) was driven to suicide by more of Chambers's malignant falsehoods. Similarly, in many textbooks President Truman's executive order denying government employment to those who posed security risks, and other laws aimed at espionage and Communist subversion, were and still are described not as having been motivated by a real concern for American security (since the existence of any serious espionage or subversion was denied) but instead as consciously antidemocratic attacks on basic freedoms. As one commentator wrote, "The statute books groaned under several seasons of legislation designed to outlaw dissent."

Despite its central role in the history of American counterintelligence, the Venona Project remained among the most tightly held government secrets. By the time the project shut down, it had decrypted nearly three thousand messages sent between the Soviet Union and its embassies and consulates around the world. Remarkably, although rumors and a few snippets of information about the project had become public in the 1980s, the actual texts and the enormous import of the messages remained secret until 1995. The U.S. government often has been successful in keeping secrets in the short term, but over a longer period secrets, particularly newsworthy ones, have proven to be very difficult for the government to keep. It is all the more amazing, then, how little got out about the Venona Project in the fifty-three years before it was made public.

Unfortunately, the success of government secrecy in this case has seriously distorted our understanding of post–World War II history. Hundreds of books and thousands of essays on McCarthyism, the federal loyalty security program, Soviet espionage, American communism, and the early Cold War have perpetuated many myths that have given Americans a warped view of the nation's history in the 1930s, 1940s, and 1950s. The information that these messages reveal substantially revises the basis for understanding the early history of the Cold War and of America's concern with Soviet espionage and Communist subversion.

In the late 1970s the FBI began releasing material from its hitherto secret files as a consequence of the passage of the Freedom of Information Act (FOIA). Although this act opened some files to public scrutiny, it has not as yet provided access to the full range of FBI investigative records. The enormous backlog of FOIA requests has led to lengthy delays in releasing documents; it is not uncommon to wait more than five years to receive material. Capricious and zealous enforcement of regulations exempting some material from release frequently has elicited useless documents consisting of occasional phrases interspersed with long sections of redacted (blacked-out) text. And, of course, even the unexpurgated FBI files show only what the FBI learned about Soviet espionage and are only part of the story. Even given these hindrances, however, each year more files are opened, and the growing body of FBI documentation has significantly enhanced the opportunity for a reconstruction of what actually happened.

The collapse of the Union of Soviet Socialist Republics in 1991 led to the opening of Soviet archives that had never been examined by independent scholars. The historically rich documentation first made available in Moscow's archives in 1992 has resulted in an outpouring of new historical writing, as these records allow a far more complete and accurate understanding of central events of the twentieth century. But many archives in Russia are open only in part, and some are still closed. In particular, the archives of the foreign intelligence operations of Soviet military intelligence and those of the foreign intelligence arm of the KGB are not open to researchers. Given the institutional continuity between the former Soviet intelligence agencies and their current Russian successors, the opening of these archives is not anticipated anytime soon. However, Soviet intelligence agencies had cooperated with other Soviet institutions, whose newly opened archives therefore hold some intelligence-related material and provide a back door into the still-closed intelligence archives.

But the most significant source of fresh insight into Soviet espionage in the United States comes from the decoded messages produced by the Venona Project. These documents, after all, constitute a portion of the materials that are still locked up in Russian intelligence archives. Not only do the Venona files supply information in their own right, but because of their inherent reliability they also provide a touchstone for judging the credibility of other sources, such as defectors' testimony and FBI investigative files.

Stalin's Espionage Assault on the United States

Through most of the twentieth century, governments of powerful nations have conducted intelligence operations of some sort during both peace and war. None, however, used espionage as an instrument of state policy as extensively as did the Soviet Union under Joseph Stalin. In the late 1920s and 1930s, Stalin directed most of the resources of Soviet intelligence at nearby targets in Europe and Asia. America was still distant from Stalin's immediate concerns, the threat to Soviet goals posed by Nazi Germany and Imperial Japan. This perception changed, however, after the United States entered the world war in December 1941. Stalin realized that once Germany and Japan were defeated, the world would be left with only three powers able to project their influence across the globe: the Soviet Union, Great Britain, and the United States. And of these, the strongest would be the United States. With that in mind, Stalin's intelligence agencies shifted their focus toward America.

The Soviet Union, Great Britain, and the United States formed a military alliance in early 1942 to defeat Nazi Germany and its allies. The Soviet Union quickly became a major recipient of American military (Lend-Lease) aid, second only to Great Britain; it eventually received more than nine billion dollars. As part of the aid arrangements, the United States invited the Soviets to greatly expand their diplomatic staffs and to establish special offices to facilitate aid arrangements. Thousands of Soviet military officers, engineers, and technicians entered the United States to review what aid was available and choose which machinery, weapons, vehicles (nearly 400,000 American trucks went to the Soviet Union), aircraft, and other matériel would most assist the Soviet war effort. Soviet personnel had to be trained to maintain the American equipment, manuals had to be translated into Russian, shipments to the Soviet Union had to be inspected to ensure that what was ordered had been delivered, properly loaded, and dispatched on the right ships. Entire Soviet naval crews arrived for training to take over American combat and cargo ships to be handed over to the Soviet Union.

Scores of Soviet intelligence officers of the KGB (the chief Soviet foreign intelligence and security agency), the GRU (the Soviet military intelligence agency), and the Naval GRU (the Soviet naval intelligence agency) were among the Soviet personnel arriving in America. These intelligence officers pursued two missions. One, security, was only indirectly connected with the United States. The internal security arm of the KGB employed several hundred thousand full-time personnel, assisted by several million part-time informants, to ensure the political loyalty of Soviet citizens. When the Soviets sent thousands of their citizens to the United States to assist with the Lend-Lease arrangement, they sent this internal security apparatus as well. A significant portion of the Venona messages deciphered by American code-breakers reported on this task. The messages show that every Soviet cargo ship that arrived at an American port to pick up Lend-Lease supplies had in its crew at least one, often two, and sometimes three informants who reported either to the KGB or to the Naval GRU. Their task was not to spy on Americans but to watch the Soviet merchant seamen for signs of political dissidence and potential defection. Some of the messages show Soviet security officers tracking down merchant seamen who had jumped ship, kidnapping them, and spiriting them back aboard Soviet ships in disregard of American law. Similarly, other messages discuss informants, recruited or planted by the KGB in every Soviet office in the United States, whose task was to report signs of ideological deviation or potential defection among Soviet personnel.

A second mission of these Soviet intelligence officers, however, was espionage against the United States.... The deciphered Venona cables do more than reveal the remarkable success that the Soviet Union had in recruiting spies and gaining access to many important U.S. government agencies and laboratories dealing with secret information. They expose beyond cavil the American Communist party as an auxiliary of the intelligence agencies of the Soviet Union. While not every Soviet spy was a Communist, most were. And while not every American Communist was a spy, hundreds were. The CPUSA itself worked closely with Soviet intelligence agencies to facilitate their espionage. Party leaders were not only aware of the liaison; they actively worked to assist the relationship.

Information from the Venona decryptions underlay the policies of U.S. government officials in their approach to the issue of domestic communism. The investigations and prosecutions of American Communists undertaken by the federal government in the late 1940s and early 1950s were premised on an assumption that the CPUSA had assisted Soviet espionage. This view contributed to the Truman administration's executive order in 1947, reinforced in the early 1950s under the Eisenhower administration, that U.S. government employees be subjected to loyalty and security investigations. The understanding also lay behind the 1948 decision by Truman's attorney general to prosecute the leaders of the CPUSA under the sedition sections of the Smith Act. It was an explicit assumption behind congressional investigations of domestic communism in the late 1940s and 1950s, and it permeated public attitudes toward domestic communism.

The Soviet Union's unrestrained espionage against the United States from 1942 to 1945 was of the type that a nation directs at an enemy state. By the late 1940s the evidence provided by Venona of the massive size and intense hostility of Soviet intelligence operations caused both American counterintelligence professionals and high-level policy-makers to conclude that Stalin had already launched a covert attack on the United States. In their minds, the Soviet espionage offensive indicated that the Cold War had begun not after World War II but many years earlier.

NO

Richard M. Fried

"Bitter Days": The Heyday of Anti-Communism

Even independent of [Joseph] McCarthy, the years 1950–1954 marked the climax of anti-communism in American life. The Korean stalemate generated both a bruising debate over containment and a sourness in national politics. Korea's sapping effect and a series of minor scandals heightened the Democratic Party's anemia. In addition, the 1950 congressional campaign, revealing McCarthyism's apparent sway over the voters and encouraging the GOP's right wing, signaled that anti-communism occupied the core of American political culture. "These," said liberal commentator Elmer Davis in January 1951, "are bitter days—full of envy, hatred, malice, and all uncharitableness."

Critics of these trends in American politics had scant power or spirit. Outside government, foes of anti-Communist excesses moved cautiously lest they be redbaited and rarely took effective countermeasures. Liberals seldom strayed from the safety of the anti-Communist consensus. Radicals met the hostility of the dominant political forces in Cold War America and fared poorly. In government, anti-communism ruled. Senate resistance to McCarthy was scattered and weak. In the House, HUAC [House Un-American Activities Committee] did much as it pleased. [President Harry S.] Truman upheld civil liberties with occasional eloquence, but he remained on the defensive, and his Justice Department often seemed locked in near-alliance with the Right in Congress. [Dwight D.] Eisenhower, when not appeasing the McCarthyites, appeared at times no more able to curb them than had Truman.

Even at his peak, McCarthy was not the sole anti-Communist paladin, though he cultivated that impression. As McCarthyism in its broader sense outlived the personal defeat of McCarthy himself, so, in its prime, it exceeded his reach. Its strength owed much to the wide acceptance, even by McCarthy's critics, of the era's anti-Communist premises. Along with McCarthy, they made the first half of the 1950s the acme of noisy anti-communism and of the ills to which it gave birth.

Soon after the 1950 campaign, skirmishing over the Communist issue renewed in earnest. In December Senator Pat McCarran joined the hunt for subversives by creating the Senate Internal Security Subcommittee (SISS). As chairman of that panel (and the parent Judiciary Committee), the crusty Nevada

From Richard M. Fried, *Nightmare in Red: The McCarthy Era in Perspective* (Oxford University Press, 1990). Copyright © 1990 by Oxford University Press, Inc. Reprinted by permission. Notes omitted.

Democrat packed it with such like-minded colleagues as Democrats James Eastland and Willis Smith and Republicans Homer Ferguson and William Jenner. While McCarthy darted about unpredictably, McCarran moved glacially but steadily to his objective, crushing opposition.

McCarran's panel spotlighted themes that McCarthy had raised giving them a more sympathetic hearing than had the Tydings Committee. In February 1951, federal agents swooped down on a barn in Lee, Massachusetts, seized the dead files of the Institute of Pacific Relations (IPR) and trucked them under guard to Washington. After sifting this haul, a SISS subcommittee opened an extended probe of the IPR, which led to a new inquest on "who lost China" and resulted in renewed loyalty and security proceedings, dismissals from the State Department and prosecution—all to McCarthy's greater, reflected glory.

The subcommittee acquired a reputation—more cultivated than deserved —for honoring due process. SISS was punctilious on some points: evidence was formally introduced (when an excerpt was read, the full text was put in the record); hearings were exhaustive (over 5,000 pages); witnesses were heard in executive session before they named names in public; their credentials and the relevance of their testimony were set forth; and some outward courtesies were extended.

The fairness was only skin-deep, however. Witnesses were badgered about obscure events from years back and about nuances of aging reports. Diplomat John Carter Vincent was even asked if he had plans to move to Sarasota, Florida. When he termed it a most "curious" question, counsel could only suggest that perhaps the Florida Chamber of Commerce had taken an interest. The subcommittee strove to ensnare witnesses in perjury. One China Hand called the sessions "generally Dostoyevskian attacks not only on a man's mind but also his memory." To have predicted Jiang's decline or Mao's rise was interpreted as both premeditating and helping to cause that outcome.

A product of the internationalist do-goodery of YMCA leaders in the 1920s, the IPR sought to promote peace and understanding in the Pacific. It had both national branches in countries interested in the Pacific and an international secretariat. Well funded by corporations and foundations in its palmier days, the IPR had more pedigree than power. McCarran's subcommittee insisted that IPR's publications pushed the Communist line on China. Louis Budenz testified that the Kremlin had assigned Owen Lattimore the job of giving the IPR journal, *Pacific Affairs,* a Party-line tilt. Budenz claimed that when he was in the Party, he received "official communications" describing Lattimore (and several China Hands) as Communists.

McCarran's panel spent a year grilling Lattimore, other IPR officials, and various China experts and diplomats as it tried to knit a fabric of conspiracy out of its evidence and presuppositions. McCarran claimed that, but for the machinations of the coterie that ran IPR, "China today would be free and a bulwark against the further advance of the Red hordes into the Far East." He charged that the IPR-USSR connection had led to infiltration of the government by persons aligned with the Soviets, of faculties by Red professors, and of textbooks by pro-Communist ideas. He called Lattimore "a conscious and articulate instrument of the Soviet conspiracy."

The hearings revealed naiveté about communism, showed that IPR principals had access to important officials during the war, and turned up levels of maneuvering that sullied IPR's reputation for scholarly detachment. Proven or accused Reds did associate with the IPR and may well have sought leverage through it. There were tendentious claims in IPR publications, as in one author's simplistic dichotomy of Mao's "democratic China" and Jiang's "feudal China." Lattimore was a more partisan editor of *Pacific Affairs* than he conceded. However, in political scientist Earl Latham's measured assessment, the hearings "show something less than subversive conspiracy in the making of foreign policy, and something more than quiet routine." Nor was it proven that IPR had much influence over policy. Perhaps the China Hands had been naive to think that a reoriented policy might prevent China's Communists from falling "by default" under Soviet control and thus might maintain American leverage. Yet those who argued that unblinking support of Jiang could have prevented China's "loss" were more naive still.

Unable to prove, in scholarly terms, its thesis of a successful pro-Communist conspiracy against China, SISS could still carry it politically. The loyalty-security program helped enforce it. New charges, however stale, motivated the State Department Loyalty-Security Board to reexamine old cases of suspected employees, even if they had been previously cleared. Moreover, nudged by the Right, Truman toughened the loyalty standard in April 1951, putting a heavier burden of proof on the accused. Thus under Hiram Bingham, a Republican conservative, the Loyalty Review Board ordered new inquiries in cases decided under the old standard....

The purge of the China Hands had long-term impact. American attitudes toward China remained frozen for two decades. Battered by McCarthyite attacks, the State Department's Far Eastern Division assumed a conservative bunkerlike mentality. Selected by President John F. Kennedy to shake the division up, Assistant Secretary of State Averell Harriman found it "a disaster area filled with human wreckage." Personnel who did not bear wounds from previous battles were chosen to handle Asian problems. Vincent's successor on the China desk was an impeccably conservative diplomat whose experience lay in Europe. JFK named an ambassador to South Vietnam whose prior work had been with NATO. In the 1950s, the field of Asian studies felt the blindfold of conformity as the momentum of U.S. foreign policy carried the country toward the vortex of Vietnam.

The IPR Investigation was but one of many inquiries during the early 1950s that delved into Communist activities. The Eighty-first Congress spawned 24 probes of communism; the Eighty-second, 34; and the Eighty-third, 51. HUAC busily sought new triumphs. In 1953, 185 of the 221 Republican Congressmen asked to serve on it. But HUAC faced the problem all monopolies meet when competitors pour into the market. Besides McCarran and McCarthy, a Senate labor subcommittee probed Red influences in labor unions, two committees combed the U.N. Secretariat for Communists, and others dipped an oar in when the occasion arose.

In part HUAC met the competition with strenuous travel. Hearings often bore titles like "Communist Activities in the Chicago Area"—or Los Angeles, Detroit, or Hawaii. The Detroit hearings got a musician fired, a college student expelled, and UAW Local 600 taken over by the national union. In 1956 two Fisher Body employees were called before a HUAC hearing in St. Louis. When angry fellow workers chalked such slogans as "Russia has no Fifth amendment" on auto bodies and staged a work stoppage, the two men were suspended. The impact of junketing congressional probers was often felt in such local fallout rather than in federal punishments (though many witnesses were cited for contempt of Congress). That indeed was the point. A witness might use the Fifth Amendment to avoid perjury charges, but appearing before a committee of Congress left him open to local sanctions.

Lawmakers fretted over communism in the labor movement. The presence of left-wing unionists in a defense plant offered a frequent pretext for congressional excursions. HUAC addressed the issue often; McCarthy, occasionally; House and Senate labor subcommittees paid close heed. The liberal anti-Communist Hubert Humphrey held an inquiry designed both to meet the problem and to protect clean unions from scattershot redbaiting. Lest unions be handled too softly, in 1952 Pat McCarran, Herman Welker, and John Marshall Butler conceived the formidably labeled "Task Force Investigating Communist Domination of Certain Labor Organizations."

Attacks on radical union leadership from both within and without the labor movement proliferated in the early 1950s. During 1952 hearings in Chicago, HUAC jousted with negotiators for the Communist-led United Electrical Workers just as they mounted a strike against International Harvester. In 1953 McCarthy's subcommittee also bedeviled UE locals in New York and Massachusetts. Such hearings often led to firings and encouraged or counterpointed raids by rival unions. They hastened the decline of the left wing of the labor movement.

The UE was beset on all sides. When the anti-communist International United Electrical Workers Union (IUE), led by James Carey, was founded, Truman Administration officials intoned blessings. The Atomic Energy Commission pressured employers like General Electric to freeze out the UE; IUE literature warned that plants represented by the UE would lose defense contracts. The CIO lavishly funded Carey's war with the UE. Three days before a 1950 election to decide control of a Pittsburgh area local, the vocal anti-Communist Judge Michael Musmanno arrived at a plant gate to campaign for the IUE. Bedecked in naval uniform, he was convoyed by a detachment of National Guardsmen, bayonets fixed and flags unfurled. Many local Catholic clergy urged their flocks to vote for the IUE on the basis of anti-communism. Carey's union won a narrow victory.

These labor wars sometimes produced odd bedfellows. Carey criticized McCarthy, but the latter's 1953 Boston hearings helped the IUE keep control of key GE plants in the area. GE management declared before the hearings that it would fire workers who admitted they were Reds; it would suspend those who declined to testify and, if they did not subsequently answer the charges, would dismiss them. Thus besieged, the UE often settled labor disputes on a take-what-it-could basis.

Where left-wing unions maintained reputations for effective bargaining, anti-communism had limited effect. The UE's tactical surrender of its youthful militancy probably eroded its rank-and-file support more than did any redbaiting. Yet the Longshoremen's Union, despite Smith Act prosecutions against its leaders in Hawaii and the effort to deport Harry Bridges, kept control of West Coast docks. (Indeed, having come to tolerate Bridges by the 1950s, business leaders had lost enthusiasm for persecuting him.) Similarly, the Mine, Mill and Smelter Workers Union held onto some strongholds despite recurrent redbaiting. Weaker leftist unions like the United Public Workers or the Fur and Leather Workers succumbed to raiding and harassment.

In an era when mainline labor was cautious, organizing initiatives often did originate with more radical unions and so fell prey to anti-Communist attack. In 1953 a CIO retail workers' union, some of whose organizers were Communists, struck stores in Port Arthur, Texas. A commission of inquiry named by Governor Allen Shivers (then seeking reelection) found "clear and present danger" of Communist sway over Texas labor. Shivers claimed he had foiled a Communist-led union's "well-laid plans to spread its tentacles all along the Gulf Coast and eventually into *your* community." Other Southern organizing drives succumbed to redbaiting too.

By the 1950s, labor's assertiveness had waned; where it persisted, it met defeat; and new organizing drives were few. Internal dissent—indeed, debate —was virtually stilled. Its momentum sapped and its membership reduced by over a third, the CIO merged with the AFL in a 1955 "shotgun wedding." Having won a place within the American consensus, labor paid a dear price to keep it.

Conservatives feared Communist influence in the nation's schools as well as in its factories. The influence of the "Reducators" and of subversive ideas that ranged, in various investigators' minds, from outright communism to "progressive education" perennially intrigued legislators at the state and national levels.

The Communists' long-running control of the New York Teachers Union alarmed the Senate Internal Security Subcommittee. Previously, the 1940–41 Rapp-Coudert inquiry had led to the dismissal of a number of New York City teachers. In 1949 the Board of Education began a new purge. From 1950 to early 1953, twenty-four teachers were fired and thirty-four resigned under investigation. By one estimate, over three hundred New York City teachers lost their jobs in the 1950s. SISS thus served to reinforce local activities with its 1952–53 hearings in New York City. The refusal by Teachers Union leaders to testify about their affiliations established grounds for their dismissal under Section 903 of the city charter.

Ultimately, the probers failed in their aim to expose Marxist-Leninist propagandizing in Gotham's classrooms. Bella Dodd, a former Communist and Teachers Union leader, claimed that Communist teachers who knew Party dogma "cannot help but slant their teaching in that direction." A Queens College professor said he knew a score of students whom the Communists had "ruined" and turned into "misfits." Yet aside from a few parents' complaints and "one case where I think we could prove it," the city's school superintendent had no evidence of indoctrination. Though Communists had obviously acquired great leverage in the Teachers Union, SISS located its best case of university subversion in a book about *China*.

HUAC quizzed educators too, but its scrutiny of the movie industry earned higher returns when it resumed its inquiry into Hollywood in 1951. By then the Hollywood Ten* were in prison, the film industry's opposition to HUAC was shattered, and the blacklist was growing. Fear washed through the movie lots. The economic distress visited on Hollywood by the growth of television further frazzled nerves. Said one witness, the renewed assault was "like taking a pot shot at a wounded animal." When subpoenaed, actress Gale Sondergaard asked the Screen Actors Guild for help, its board rebuffed her, likening her criticism of HUAC to the Communist line. The Screen Directors Guild made its members take a loyalty oath.

Yet few secrets were left to ferret out: the identity of Hollywood's Communists had long ceased to be a mystery. Early in the 1951 hearings, Congressman Francis Walter even asked why it was "material . . . to have the names of people when we already know them?" For HUAC, getting new information had become secondary to conducting ceremonies of exposure and penitence. Would the witness "name names" or not?

Of 110 witnesses subpoenaed in 1951, 58 admitted having had Party involvements. Some cogently explained why they had since disowned communism. Budd Schulberg recalled that while he was writing *What Makes Sammy Run,* the Party told him to submit an outline, confer with its literary authorities, and heed its artistic canons. *The Daily Worker* received his book favorably, but after being updated on Party aesthetics, the reviewer wrote a second piece thrashing the novel. One screenwriter recalled how the Party line on a studio painters' strike shifted perplexingly in 1945: we "could walk through the picket lines in February, and not in June."

Witnesses seeking to steer between punishment and fingering co-workers faced tearing ethical choices. Naming known Reds or those previously named might stave off harm, but this ploy was tinged with moral bankruptcy. Some soured ex-Communists did resist giving names, not wanting, in actor Larry Parks's phrase, to "crawl through the mud to be an informer." Some named each other; some said little, ducking quickly behind the Fifth Amendment. Others told all. The 155 names that writer Martin Berkeley gave set a record. Others gabbed freely. Parrying with humor the oft-asked question—would he defend America against the Soviets?—actor Will Geer, already middle-aged, cheerfully agreed to fight in his way: growing vegetables and entertaining the wounded. The idea of people his vintage shouldering arms amused him; wars "would be negotiated immediately."

In this as in all inquiries, witnesses trod a path set with snares. The courts disallowed the Hollywood Ten's use of the First Amendment to avoid testifying,

---

* [The Hollywood Ten were members of the film industry who refused to testify before Congress in 1947 about communist infiltration of the industry.—Ed.]

so a witness's only protection was the Fifth Amendment guarantee against self-incrimination. Even this route crossed minefields. *Blau v. U.S.* (1950) ruled that one might plead the Fifth legitimately to the question of Party membership. However, the 1950 case of *Rogers v. U.S.* dictated caution: one had to invoke the Fifth at the outset, not in the middle, of a line of questions inching toward incrimination. Having testified that she herself held a Party office, the court ruled, Jane Rogers had waived her Fifth Amendment privilege and could not then refuse to testify about others.

HUAC tried to quick-march Fifth-takers into pitfalls. One gambit was a logical fork: if answering would incriminate him, a witness might use the Fifth; but if innocent, he could not honestly do so. Thus, the committee held, the witness was either guilty or lying—even though the courts did not accept this presumption of guilt. However, a new odious category, the "Fifth-Amendment Communist," was born. Such witnesses, whether teachers, actors, or others, rarely hung onto their jobs.

Legal precedent also demanded care in testifying about associations. One witness pled the Fifth in response to the question of whether he was a member of the American Automobile Association. HUAC members enjoyed asking if witnesses belonged to the Ku Klux Klan, hoping to nettle them into breaking a string of refusals to answer. On their part, witnesses devised novel defenses like the so-called "diminished Fifth." A witness resorting to the "slightly diminished Fifth" would deny present CP membership but refuse to open up his past or that of others; those using the "fully diminished Fifth," on the other hand, testified about their own pasts but no one else's. (The "augmented Fifth" was like the slightly diminished Fifth, but the witness also disclaimed any sympathy for communism.)

The question of whether to testify freely or take the Fifth convulsed the higher precincts of American arts and letters. Writer Lillian Hellman, subpoenaed in 1952, took the bold step of writing HUAC's chairman that she would take the Fifth only if asked to talk about others. She realized that by answering questions about herself, she waived her privilege and was subject to a contempt citation, but better that than to "bring bad trouble" to innocent people. She simply would not cut her conscience "to fit this year's fashions." When she testified, she did invoke the Fifth but scored a coup with her eloquent letter and managed to avoid a contempt citation. In 1956 the playwright Arthur Miller also refused to discuss other people but, unlike Hellman, did not take the Fifth. (His contempt citation was later overturned.)

Art came to mirror politics. Miller had previously written *The Crucible,* whose hero welcomed death rather than implicate others in the seventeenth-century Salem witch trials. Admirers stressed the play's relevance to modern witch-hunts. In contrast, Elia Kazan, who had named names, directed the smash movie *On the Waterfront,* whose hero (Marlon Brando), implored by a fighting priest (Karl Malden) to speak out, agreed to inform against criminals in a longshoremen's union. None of these works dealt with communism, but their pertinence to current political issues was not lost. Among the arbiters of American culture, these moral choices prompted heated debate, which still reverberated in the 1980s.

The issues were not only philosophical. The sanctions were real. Noncooperative witnesses were blacklisted, their careers in Hollywood shattered. Many drifted into other lines of work. Many became exiles, moving to Europe, Mexico, or New York. Some suffered writer's block. Some families endured steady FBI surveillance and such vexations as sharply increased life insurance premiums (for an assertedly dangerous occupation). Being blacklisted so dispirited several actors that their health was impaired, and premature death resulted. Comedian Philip Loeb, blacklisted and unemployable, his family destroyed, committed suicide in 1955.

Even though several hundred members of the entertainment industry forfeited their livelihoods after HUAC appearances, the studios, networks, producers, and the committee itself did not admit publicly that a blacklist existed. (Privately, some were candid. "Pal, you're dead," a soused producer told writer Millard Lampell. "They told me that I couldn't touch you with a barge pole.") In this shadow world, performers and writers wondered if their talents had indeed eroded. Had one's voice sharpened, one's humor dulled?

For blacklisting to work, HUAC's hammer needed an anvil. It was duly provided by other groups who willingly punished hostile or reluctant witnesses. American Legion publications spread the word about movies whose credits were fouled by subversion; Legionnaires (and other local true believers) could pressure theatre owners, if necessary, by trooping down to the Bijou to picket offending films. The mere threat of such forces soon choked off the supply of objectionable pictures at the source. Indeed, Hollywood, responding to broad hints from HUAC and to its own reading of the political climate, began making anti-Communist potboilers. These low-budget "B" pictures did poorly at the box office. They provided insurance, not profits.

Though entertainment industry moguls justified screening employees' politics by citing the threat from amateur censors, usually professional blacklisters made the system work. Blacklisting opened up business vistas on the Right. In 1950 American Business Consultants, founded by three ex-FBI agents, published *Red Channels,* a compendium listing 151 entertainers and their Communist-front links. *Counterattack,* an ABC publication started in 1947, periodically offered the same type of information. In 1953 an employee left ABC to establish Aware, Inc., which sold a similar service. Companies in show biz subscribed to these countersubversive finding aids and paid to have the names of those they might hire for a show or series checked against "the files." Aware charged five dollars to vet a name for the first time, two dollars for rechecks. It became habit for Hollywood, radio and TV networks, advertisers, and stage producers (though blacklisting had its weakest hold on Broadway) not to employ entertainers whose names cropped up in such files.

A few found ways to evade total proscription. Writers could sometimes submit work under pseudonyms. Studios asked some writers on the blacklist to doctor ailing scripts authored by others. The blacklisted writers received no screen credits and were paid a pittance, but at least they were working. Ostracized actors did not have this option. Said comedian Zero Mostel: "I am a man of a thousand faces, all of them blacklisted." A TV producer once called a talent agent to ask, "Who have you got like John Garfield?" He had Garfield himself, the agent exclaimed; but, of course, the blacklisted Garfield was taboo.

Unlike actors, blacklisted writers could also find work in television, which devoured new scripts ravenously. As in film, some used assumed names. Others worked through "fronts" (whence came the title of Woody Allen's 1976 movie). They wrote, but someone else put his name to the script (and might demand up to half of the income). Mistaken-identity plot twists worthy of a Restoration comedy resulted. One writer using a pseudonym wrote a script that he was asked, under a second pseudonym, to revise. Millard Lampell submitted a script under a phony name; the producers insisted that the script's writer appear for consultation; told that he was away and unavailable, they went for a quick fix: they asked Lampell to rewrite his own (unacknowledged) script.

The obverse of blacklisting was "clearance." Desperate actors or writers could seek absolution from a member of the anti-Communist industry. Often, not surprisingly, the person to see was one who had played a part in creating the blacklist. Roy Brewer, the chief of the International Alliance of Theatrical Stage Employees, had redbaited the leftist craft guilds, but helped rehabilitate blacklistees, as did several conservative newspaper columnists. The American Legion, which issued lists of Hollywood's undesirables, also certified innocence or repentance. A listee might get by with writing a letter to the Legion. Or he might be made to list suspect organizations he had joined and to tell why he joined, when he quit, who invited him in, and whom he had enticed. Thus the written route to clearance might also require naming names.

To regain grace, some sinners had to repent publicly, express robust patriotism in a speech or article, or confess to having been duped into supporting leftist causes. Typically, a blacklistee had to be willing to tell all to the FBI or to HUAC. Even liberal anti-Communists were "graylisted," and some had to write clearance letters. Humphrey Bogart had bought trouble by protesting the 1947 HUAC hearings against the Hollywood Ten. In his article, "I'm No Communist," he admitted he had been a "dope" in politics. Actor John Garfield, whose appearance before HUAC sent his career and life into a tailspin, was at the time of his death about to publish an article titled "I Was a Sucker for a Left Hook."

Like teachers and entertainers, charitable foundations also triggered the suspicion of congressional anti-Communists. These products of capitalism plowed back into society some of the vast wealth of their Robber Baron founders, but conservatives found their philanthropic tastes too radical. In 1952 a special House committee led by Georgia conservative Eugene Cox inquired into the policies of tax-exempt foundations. Did not "these creatures of the capitalist system," asked Cox, seek to "bring the system into disrepute" and to assume "a socialistic leaning"? . . .

&0&

How deeply did anti-communism gouge the social and political terrain of the 1950s? With dissent defined as dangerous, the range of political debate obviously was crimped. The number of times that books were labeled dangerous, thoughts were scourged as harmful, and speakers and performers were rejected as outside the pale multiplied. Anti-Communist extremism and accompanying pressures toward conformity had impact in such areas as artistic expression, the labor movement, the cause of civil rights, and the status of minorities in American life.

For some denizens of the Right, threats of Communist influence materialized almost anywhere. For instance, Illinois American Legionnaires warned that the Girl Scouts were being spoonfed subversive doctrines. Jack Lait and Lee Mortimer's yellow-journalistic *U.S.A. Confidential* warned parents against the emerging threat of rock and roll. It bred dope use, interracialism, and sex orgies. "We know that many platter-spinners are hopheads. Many others are Reds, left-wingers, or hecklers of social convention." Not every absurdity owed life to the vigilantes, however. A jittery Hollywood studio cancelled a movie based on Longfellow's "Hiawatha" for fear it would be viewed as "Communist peace propaganda."

Books and ideas remained vulnerable. It is true that the militant Indiana woman who abhorred *Robin Hood*'s subversive rob-from-the-rich-and-give-to-the-poor message failed to get it banned from school libraries. Other locales were less lucky. A committee of women appointed by the school board of Sapulpa, Oklahoma, had more success. The board burned those books that it classified as dealing improperly with socialism or sex. A spokesman claimed that only five or six "volumes of no consequence" were destroyed. A librarian in Bartlesville, Oklahoma, was fired for subscribing to the *New Republic, Nation,* and *Negro Digest.* The use of UNESCO [United Nations Educational, Scientific, and Cultural Organization] materials in the Los Angeles schools became a hot issue in 1952. A new school board and superintendent were elected with a mandate to remove such books from school libraries.

Local sanctions against unpopular artists and speakers often were effective. In August 1950, a New Hampshire resort hotel banned a talk by Owen Lattimore after guests, apparently riled by protests of the Daughters of the American Revolution and others, remonstrated. Often local veterans—the American Legion and Catholic War Veterans—initiated pressures. The commander of an American Legion Post in Omaha protested a local production of a play whose author, Garson Kanin, was listed in *Red Channels.* A founder of *Red Channels* warned an American Legion anti-subversive seminar in Peoria, Illinois, that Arthur Miller's *Death of a Salesman,* soon to appear locally, was "a Communist-dominated play." Jaycees and Legionnaires failed to get the theatre to cancel the play, but the boycott they mounted sharply curbed the size of the audience.

Libraries often became focal points of cultural anxieties. Not every confrontation ended like those in Los Angeles or Sapulpa, but librarians felt they were under the gun. "I just put a book that is complained about away for a while," said one public librarian. Occasionally, books were burned. "Did you ever try to burn a book?" asked another librarian. "It's *very* difficult." One-third of a group of librarians sampled in the late 1950s reported having removed "controversial" items from their shelves. One-fifth said they habitually avoided buying such books.

Academics, too, were scared. Many college and university social scientists polled in 1955 confessed to reining in their political views and activities.

Twenty-seven percent had "wondered" whether a political opinion they had expressed might affect their job security or promotion; 40 percent had worried that a student might pass on "a warped version of what you have said and lead to false ideas about your political views." Twenty-two percent had at times "refrained from expressing an opinion or participating in some activity in order not to embarrass" their institution. Nine percent had "toned down" recent writing to avoid controversy. One teacher said he never expressed his own opinion in class. "I express the recognized and acknowledged point of view." Some instructors no longer assigned *The Communist Manifesto.*

About a hundred professors actually lost jobs, but an even greater number of frightened faculty trimmed their sails against the storm. Episodes far short of dismissal could also have a chilling effect. An economist at a Southern school addressed a business group, his talk, titled "Know Your Enemy," assessed Soviet resources and strengths. He was denounced to his president as a Communist. Another professor was assailed for advocating a lower tariff on oranges. "If I'd said potatoes, I wouldn't have been accused unless I had said it in Idaho." Some teachers got in mild trouble for such acts as assigning Robert and Helen Lynds' classic sociological study, *Middletown,* in class or listing the Kinsey reports on human sexuality as recommended reading. A professor once sent students to a public library to read works by Marx because his college's library had too few copies. Librarians logged the students' names.

The precise effect of all this professed anxiety was fuzzy. Many liberals claimed that Americans had been cowed into silence, that even honest anti-Communist dissent had been stilled, and that basic freedoms of thought, expression, and association had languished. The worriers trotted out appropriate comparisons: the witch trials in Salem, the Reign of Terror in France, the Alien and Sedition Acts, Know-Nothingism, and the Palmer raids. Justice William O. Douglas warned of "The Black Silence of Fear." Prominent foreigners like Bertrand Russell and Graham Greene decried the pall of fear they observed in America. On July 4, 1951, a *Madison Capital-Times* reporter asked passersby to sign a paper containing the Bill of Rights and parts of the Declaration of Independence. Out of 112, only one would do so. President Truman cited the episode to show McCarthyism's dire effects. McCarthy retorted that Truman owed an apology to the people of Wisconsin in view of that paper's Communist-line policies. Some McCarthy allies upheld the wisdom of refusing to sign any statement promiscuously offered.

McCarthy's defenders ridiculed the more outlandish laments for vanished liberties. A New York rabbi who blamed "McCarthyism" for the current spree of college "panty raids" offered a case in point. Conservative journalist Eugene Lyons was amused by an ACLU spokesman, his tonsils flaring in close-up on television, arguing "that in America no one any longer dares open his mouth." Such talk, said Lyons, led to "hysteria over hysteria." In their apologia for McCarthy, William F. Buckley and L. Brent Bozell snickered at such silliness. They found it odd that, in a time when left-of-center ideas were supposedly being crushed, liberals seemed to monopolize symposia sponsored by the major universities, even in McCarthy's home state, and that Archibald MacLeish and Bernard De Voto, two of those who condemned the enervating climate of fear, had still managed to garner two National Book Awards and a Pulitzer Prize. To Buckley and Bozell, the only conformity present was a proper one—a consensus that communism was evil and must be fought wholeheartedly.

But did such an argument miss the point? The successes enjoyed by prominent, secure liberals were one thing; far more numerous were the cases of those less visible and secure who lost entertainment and lecture bookings, chances to review books, teaching posts, even assembly-line jobs. The fight over the Communist menace had gone far beyond roistering debate or asserting the right of those who disagree with a set of views not to patronize them. People, a great number of whom had committed no crime, were made to suffer.

POSTSCRIPT

Did Communism Threaten America's Internal Security After World War II?

The "Venona Transcripts" represent only one set of sources depicting the Soviet spy apparatus in the United States. The Venona papers were not released to the public until 1995. Haynes and Klehr have also collaborated on two documentary collections based on the archives of the American Communist Party, which had been stored for decades in Moscow and were opened to foreign researchers in 1992. See *The Secret World of American Communism* (Yale University Press, 1995) and *The Soviet World of American Communism* (Yale University Press, 1998), both of which contain useful collections of translated Russian documents, which are virtually impossible to access. Haynes and Klehr's work also substantiates charges made by Allen Weinstein and his translator, former KGB agent Alexander Vassiliev, in *The Haunted Wood: Soviet Espionage in America— The Stalin Era* (Random House, 1999).

According to Fried, 24 teachers from New York City were fired and 34 resigned while under investigation between 1950 and early 1953. According to one estimate, over 300 teachers in the city lost their jobs because of their political beliefs. Similar dismissals also took place in public universities and colleges across the country. Book burnings were rare, but many public libraries discarded pro-Communist books or put them in storage. In Bartlesville, Oklahoma, in 1950, librarian Ruth Brown was fired from her job after 30 years ostensibly for circulating magazines like *The New Republic* and *The Nation,* which were deemed subversive. Actually, many agree that she was fired for supporting civil rights activism, a fact that the American Library Association left out in defending her. See Louise S. Robinson, *The Dismissal of Miss Ruth Brown: Civil Rights, Censorship, and the American Library* (University of Oklahoma Press, 2000).

Four books represent a good starting point for students: M. J. Heale, *American Anticommunism: Combating the Enemy Within, 1830–1970* (Johns Hopkins University Press, 1990) extends Americans' fears of subversion back to the Jackson years; Ellen Schrecker, *The Age of McCarthyism: A Brief History With Documents* (Bedford Books, 1994) blames both parties for the excesses of the anti-Communist assault against radicals who were fighting against status quo race relations in the 1930s and 1940s; John Earl Haynes, *Red Scare or Red Menace? American Communism and Anticommunism in the Cold War Era* (Ivan R. Dee, 1996), which argues that anticommunism was a reasonable response to a real threat; and Richard Gid Powers, *Not Without Honor: The History of American Anticommunism* (Free Press, 1995), which portrays anticommunism as a mainstream political movement with many variations.

ISSUE 3

Should President Truman Have Fired General MacArthur?

YES: John S. Spanier, from "The Politics of the Korean War," in Phil Williams, Donald M. Goldstein, and Henry L. Andrews, Jr., eds., *Security in Korea: War, Stalemate, and Negotiation* (Westview Press, 1994)

NO: D. Clayton James with Anne Sharp Wells, from *Refighting the Last War: Command and Crisis in Korea, 1950–1953* (Free Press, 1993)

ISSUE SUMMARY

YES: Professor of political science John S. Spanier argues that General Douglas MacArthur was fired because he publicly disagreed with the Truman administration's "Europe first" policy and its limited war strategy of containing communism in Korea.

NO: Biographer D. Clayton James and assistant editor Anne Sharp Wells argue that General MacArthur was relieved of duty because there was a lack of communication between the Joint Chiefs of Staff and the headstrong general, which led to a misperception over the appropriate strategy in fighting the Korean War.

On June 25, 1950, North Korea launched a full-scale attack against South Korea. President Harry S. Truman assumed that the Russians were behind the attack and that they wanted to extend communism into other parts of Asia. The United Nations Security Council unanimously passed a resolution condemning North Korea's well-planned, concerted, and full-scale invasion of South Korea and asked for a halt to the invasion and a withdrawal back to the 38th parallel.

The South Koreans, meanwhile, sent Truman a desperate appeal for help, and the president responded quickly. He bypassed Congress and did not ask for an official declaration of war. Instead he responded to the UN resolutions and ordered General Douglas MacArthur to use American naval and air forces to attack North Korean military targets south of the 38th parallel.

It soon became clear that South Korean ground troops could not withstand North Korea's well-coordinated attack. In response, Truman increased

America's military presence by ordering a naval blockade of North Korea and air attacks north of the 38th parallel. Sixteen nations sent troops, but South Korea and the United States contributed 90 percent of the ground troops, and the United States alone supplied 93 percent of the air forces and 85 percent of the naval forces. By September there were 210,000 American ground forces, and MacArthur was the UN commander.

At first the war went badly for the UN forces. The inexperienced South Korean and American troops were nearly pushed off the peninsula until they established a strong defensive perimeter near the southeastern tip of Korea. Then MacArthur launched an amphibious attack on Inchon, near the western end of the 38th parallel, which caught the North Koreans by surprise. Thousands surrendered and others fled across the 38th parallel chased by UN troops.

The attempt to unify the Korean peninsula under a pro-Western, anticommunist government was short-lived. MacArthur had assured Truman at their only face-to-face meeting in mid-October that the Chinese Communists would not enter the war. The general was mistaken. In late November contingents of "Chinese volunteers" entered North Korea and attacked the overextended UN forces. Instead of going home for Christmas as MacArthur had predicted, UN troops were soon pushed back into South Korea. Seoul, the capital of South Korea, was again captured by the Communists in January 1951. By the spring of 1951, however, UN troops had successfully pushed the Chinese Communists back across the 38th parallel.

As early as December 1950, the Truman administration had decided to shift its policy in Korea back to its original goal: contain communist expansion in Korea and restore the status quo prior to the North Korean attack of June 25. Since UN troops were in control of South Korea by the spring of 1951, Truman decided that the UN command would issue a statement that it was ready to arrange a cease-fire. No concessions were made to the Chinese, but it held out the possibility of negotiating broader issues in Asia.

The announcement proposing a truce was never made. When the Joint Chiefs of Staff informed MacArthur of the State Department's proposal, he undercut Truman by issuing his own directive to the Chinese, threatening to expand the war to the "coastal areas and intern bases" of China unless the enemy's commander-in-chief met with MacArthur to end the war and fulfill "the political objectives" of the UN forces in Korea.

Truman boiled over. He relieved MacArthur of all his duties in the Far East. It would be two years and three months before the new president, Dwight D. Eisenhower, would sign the truce accords ending the Korean War.

Should President Truman have fired General MacArthur? In the following selections, John S. Spanier provides a strong defense of Truman's limited war policy. He maintains that MacArthur should have been fired for his public disagreement with this policy of containing communism in Korea. D. Clayton James and Anne Sharp Wells argue that MacArthur was relieved because there was a lack of communication between the Joint Chiefs of Staff and the headstrong general and a misperception over the appropriate strategy in fighting the Korean War.

 **YES**

The Politics of the Korean War

Introduction

Prior to June 25, 1950, Korea was outside the U.S. defense perimeter. On June 25, however, the defense of South Korea rose from low to highest priority as U.S. policy-makers considered the consequences of North Korea's aggression, aggression that they believed could not have occurred without Soviet instigation or support.

There were several reasons for this. First, South Korea, while not a U.S. ally, was an American protégé; Washington had helped the South Korean government with economic and military aid and had a responsibility toward the regime it had created.

Second, had the North Koreans gained control over the entire peninsula, they would, in the metaphor used by the Japanese, have "pointed the Korean dagger straight at Japan's heart." After Nationalist China's collapse in 1949, the United States needed Japan as an ally. It thus had to defend South Korea; otherwise, Japan might have chosen a neutral stance in the Cold War, which, with the attack on South Korea, had spread from Europe to Asia.

A third reason for the U.S. intervention was to preserve the recently established North Atlantic Treaty Organization (NATO). In the absence of a strong response in Korea, the United States commitment to Western Europe would have had no credibility.

Finally, the United States sought to achieve a broader milieu goal. President Truman recalled that, during the 1930s, the democracies, working through the League of Nations, had failed to react to the aggressions of Italy, Japan, and Germany. This failure had encouraged further aggression, destroyed the League, and eventually resulted in World War II. The United States wanted a post-war world free from aggression: the United Nations (UN) was still new and was widely perceived as a symbol of a more peaceful world. A failure to act in South Korea, therefore, would not only whet the appetite of the Soviet Union, but would also undermine the UN.

The resulting defense of South Korea was America's first experience with limited war. The interests at stake were compatible with the restoration of the status quo ante; the total defeat of North Korea, the unconditional surrender of

From John S. Spanier, "The Politics of the Korean War," in Phil Williams, Donald M. Goldstein, and Henry L. Andrews, Jr., eds., *Security in Korea: War, Stalemate, and Negotiation* (Westview Press, 1994). Copyright © 1994 by Westview Press, a member of the Perseus Books Group, LLC. Reprinted by permission. Notes omitted.

its armed forces, and the elimination of its government were not, as in World War II, a prerequisite for the achievement of American objectives. A limited war was the rational response to a less than total challenge. It would have made little sense for the United States to defend South Korea by attacking the Soviet Union because it believed Moscow to be the source of aggression. That would have been irrational; countries do not risk their existence for limited, although very important, interests.

This was particularly so in the nuclear era. It was no longer "a question of *whether* to fight a limited war, but of *how* to avoid fighting any other kind." Limited war would allow the United States to escape the all-or-nothing alternative —inaction or attacking the Soviet Union (later, as the U.S. and Soviet nuclear arsenals grew, referred to as suicide-or-surrender alternatives)—ensuring the walls of containment would not be breached and allowing the United States to pursue containment at an acceptable risk and cost without risking a war with the Soviet Union. . . .

The Drive to the Yalu

By definition, the key problem in a limited war is escalation. Escalation may, of course, be a perfectly acceptable, even desirable, course of action under certain circumstances as, for instance, in cease-fire negotiations. Attacking certain targets previously left as "privileged sanctuaries," for example, could provide the extra incentive needed for the adversary to be more conciliatory and end hostilities. However, it should be the political leaders who weigh the military and political risks and costs of escalation. Escalation should be a deliberate, conscious choice, not a quick response to a battlefield decision taken by the theater commander. To grant the theater commander the freedom to conduct the military campaign as he sees fit is to surrender this critical control.

The war, after the American-led forces crossed the thirty-eighth parallel, was a model of how *not* to fight a limited war. Beginning in late October, there were increasing reports of clashes between Chinese troops and South Korean and then American forces. In early November, MacArthur, in his flamboyant style, denounced the Chinese Communist intervention as one of the most flagrant violations of international law in history. Just as soon as he made this announcement, however, the Chinese Communist forces disengaged, arousing considerable speculation about the purpose of the Chinese intervention in Korea. Was it to protect the hydroelectric dams on the Yalu River? Was it to establish a deeper buffer zone, ranging from the narrow neck above Pyongyang, North Korea's capital, to the Yalu River frontier in order to keep U.S. troops at some distance and ensure they would not cross into China? Was it to drive American forces back to the thirty-eighth parallel, restoring the status quo ante? Or was it the total defeat of the coalition forces, unifying all of Korea in the process, the original North Korean objective?

No one really knew. The most likely aim seemed to be some sort of buffer. The initial intervention, followed by the breakoff, might have been intended to communicate to the American government not to approach the Chinese frontier with non-South Korean troops; or perhaps it was for all UN forces to stay south of a buffer area. In any event, the Chinese disengagement may have been intended to explore political solutions that would either preclude Chinese intervention altogether or limit it to northern-most Korea.

Even if it was only a ruse to gain time and build up Chinese forces for a drive to push the Americans into the sea, it is doubtful Chinese leaders were in full agreement about the desirability of a war with the world's most powerful country at a time when the Chinese hold on the mainland was not yet secure and the new regime faced mounting economic problems. Had diplomacy yielded an acceptable alternative that would have provided the new regime with security, a massive Chinese intervention with all its consequences might have been avoided.

Perhaps Truman's decision to pick his general and then let him determine how best to wage the war would have been workable with a general more in sympathy with administration objectives (like Matthew Ridgway, MacArthur's successor) or a less prestigious and politically powerful general, even if he were not particularly sympathetic to administration goals (like Mark Clark). Unfortunately, it proved impossible with MacArthur, the American viceroy in Tokyo.

Although MacArthur enthusiastically endorsed the President's decision in June and swore total loyalty, it was not long before the surface unity between Washington and Tokyo started to come apart. In late July, instead of sending one of his generals to gather information for the Joint Chiefs of Staff about the defensibility of Formosa, MacArthur decided personally to visit the island. At the end of his visit, MacArthur issued a statement warmly praising Chiang, who returned the compliment in a statement that referred not only to plans for the joint defense of Formosa, but talked of having laid the foundation for "Sino-American military cooperation." This suggestion of broader Nationalist-MacArthur (rather than U.S.) cooperation must have concerned the mainland regime, already upset by the second U.S. intervention in the Chinese civil war. MacArthur dismissed criticisms of his visit when he declared the purpose of his trip, which had been strictly military, had been "maliciously misrepresented to the public by those who invariably in the past have propagandized a policy of defeatism and appeasement in the Pacific."

Then, instead of leaving well enough alone, MacArthur sent a long message to the annual conference of the Veterans of Foreign Wars. He elaborated on the strategic significance of Formosa and declared that United States policy on Formosa came from defeatists and appeasers who did not "understand the Orient... (and) Oriental psychology," a specialty he had long claimed for himself. When the administration, the target of these verbal attacks, already irritated by MacArthur's visit to Formosa, learned of MacArthur's message, he was ordered to withdraw it—although by then it was too late to stop its widespread dissemination because it had been sent to press associations, newspapers, and magazines.

These were early indications that MacArthur was an uncontrollable force. His position, however, was strengthened when, on the day the Chinese forces broke off contact, the Republicans in the mid-term election increased their Senate representation by five to forty-seven and House representation by twenty-eight to 199 (with the Democrats holding 235 seats). Even more notable still was the defeat of several senior Democratic senators, like Scott Lucas, the majority leader, Millard Tydings, chairman of the Senate Armed Services Committee, and Francis Myers, the Democratic Whip (the first two were targets of Senator McCarthy). Reelected were Republican conservatives Robert Taft (now the party's leading presidential candidate for 1952), Eugene Milliken, Homer Capehart, and Alexander Wiley. Also elected on the Republican side were such pro-Nationalist and pro-McCarthy figures as Nixon and Dirksen.

The election was clearly overshadowed by McCarthy's tactics, McCarthy's charges and McCarthy's imitators. The upshot was to enhance McCarthy's influence in the Senate and the country and strengthen MacArthur's hand in the conduct of the Korean War as the Republicans stepped up their attacks of appeasement and "softness on Communism" on an administration that, by any objective standards, had repeatedly demonstrated its tough anti-Communist foreign policy. The political price for Truman to take on MacArthur had gone up. MacArthur must have felt virtually untouchable; he certainly acted as if he were.

His orders as he advanced into North Korea were quite specific: he was to destroy the Communist forces, provided that there were no signs of impending or actual Chinese or Soviet intervention; as a matter of policy, he was to use only South Korean troops near the Chinese and Soviet frontiers in order to eliminate any possibility of provocation. Secretary of Defense George Marshall sent him a directive stating he was to feel unhampered tactically and strategically in proceeding north of the parallel, words intended to apply to the crossing of the parallel, but which MacArthur interpreted to mean that he could wage the campaign as he saw fit.

Thus, in late October, MacArthur authorized the use of all ground forces in the drive toward the Yalu, despite the earlier orders against sending any but South Korean forces to the Chinese frontier. The Secretary of Defense and the Joint Chiefs, all junior officers when MacArthur was already a general, handled MacArthur with great solicitousness. The Secretary of State called their approach "timorous."

Perhaps MacArthur had sound reasons for issuing his authorization to proceed north, the JCS said; they "would like information of these reasons since the action contemplated was a matter of concern to them." MacArthur fired back that it was a matter of "military necessity" because of the inadequacies of the South Korean Army. The Army Chief of Staff, General Joseph L. (Lighting Joe) Collins, finding this explanation incredible, considered MacArthur's action a clear violation of his orders and was concerned MacArthur might fail to consult the JCS in a more serious situation.

A second clash between the JCS and MacArthur occurred on the 7th of November, the day after MacArthur had informed the world about the Chinese intervention, when he ordered a bombing attack on the Korean ends of the bridges across the Yalu. When his air component commander Far East Air Force Commander Lieutenant General George E. Stratemeyer checked this order with Washington, the Joint Chiefs were upset. They were concerned that some of the bombs might land on Chinese soil at the very moment when a UN meeting on the Chinese intervention was about to take place and the United States wanted support for a resolution calling on the Chinese to halt their aggression. Bombing along the Yalu would only intensify China's antagonism. While the President was willing to authorize the bombing if there were an immediate and serious threat to U.S. forces, MacArthur had sent no such message. His last message to the JCS on November 4 had been optimistic. He had doubted the Chinese intervention was a full-scale one; the message's tone was one of "don't worry." MacArthur was therefore reminded of previous orders that no bombing closer than five miles to the Chinese frontier was permitted.

MacArthur, furious, shot back a message that men and materiel were "pouring" across all bridges over the Yalu from Manchuria, not just jeopardizing, but threatening "the ultimate destruction" of UN forces. Every hour the bombing was postponed "will be paid for dearly in American and other United Nations blood." Stating he could not accept responsibility for the major calamity that would follow if he were not permitted to bomb the bridges, he demanded the chiefs bring this matter to the President's attention. Truman, seeking to avoid trouble if the issue became public, permitted the bombing to proceed, warning MacArthur again of the danger of escalating the conflict.

Thus, MacArthur, appealing over his military superiors' heads to the Commander in Chief himself, was allowed to do what he had initially intended to do through a fait accompli. He then followed this with a public message that the Chinese had not only grossly violated international law by their intervention, but that more Chinese forces were in reserve in the "privileged sanctuary" of Manchuria. He hinted that this privilege might not last. The chairman of the Joint Chiefs, General Omar Bradley, wrote afterwards that "this night we committed the worst possible error. . . . Right then—that night—the JCS should have taken the firmest control of the Korean War and dealt with MacArthur bluntly." The chiefs were concerned, however, that if they ordered him to a more defensible line across North Korea's "narrow waist," there would be "another burst of outrage, perhaps a tumultuous resignation and angry public charges of appeasement" just as the voters were showing up at the polls.

The climax in this tug of war between Washington and the general came over his decision to launch a "home by Christmas" offensive on November 24 with his forces on the left separated from those on the right (permitting the Chinese to drive through this center). In the weeks leading up to this, disaster might have been averted had MacArthur been ordered to take up defensive positions. The difficulty was that he would have claimed Washington was denying him victory and he might have had to be relieved. Consequently, everyone hesitated and wavered and lost the opportunity to ward off a catastrophe. General Ridgway thought the JCS held MacArthur in "almost superstitious awe" as a "larger than life military figure who had so often been right when everyone else had been wrong." Thus, they were afraid to challenge him and give him a flat order not to advance forward and split his thinly spread armies when Chinese intervention appeared probable and imminent. "Why don't the Joint Chiefs send orders to MacArthur and tell him what to do?" Ridgway asked one of the JCS members. "He wouldn't obey the orders. What can we do?" he was told in reply.

Recent evidence suggests the Chinese may have intended a full-scale intervention from the beginning. Nevertheless, it is clear that by not exploring alternatives to the advance to the Yalu and, above all, not restraining MacArthur in order to avoid domestic turmoil, the administration ensured an escalation that prolonged the war to 1953 and only postponed the inevitable clash with its head-strong theater commander.

MacArthur's Dismissal

When, on November 24, MacArthur launched his offensive and the Chinese launched theirs, the UN Command faced what the general called a "new war." MacArthur called for new guidelines. His recommendations were: a naval blockade of the Chinese coast; air bombardment of China's industrial complex, communication network, supply depots, and troop assembly points; the reinforcement of UN troops with Chinese Nationalist troops; and diversionary actions with a possible second front on the mainland facing Formosa.

There is also some evidence MacArthur recommended the use of atomic weapons, although he denied it publicly. These measures MacArthur assured the JCS, would not only win in Korea, but "severely cripple and largely neutralize China's capability to wage aggressive war" and thereby "save Asia from the engulfment otherwise facing it." While publicly claiming his prescription was a formula for victory in Korea, MacArthur had a broader objective, namely, to take advantage of Communist China's intervention to wage a preventive war. Ridgway, who took over the retreating army in Korea and was MacArthur's eventual successor, believed that MacArthur's concept of victory "was no less than the global defeat of communism."

MacArthur also made clear that, if his recommendations were rejected his command would have to be evacuated or be subjected to steady attrition. He could not defeat the Chinese forces unless the restraints imposed by Washington—which were "without precedent in history"—were lifted. Either Washington should let him conduct the war as he saw fit—and then he would win—or the United States should withdraw from Korea altogether.

This either-or position was very suspect in Washington. There was an underlying sense that MacArthur was deliberately exaggerating his predicament in order to compel the administration to accept his recommendations. Indeed, to Ridgway, MacArthur's suggestion of throwing in the towel without putting up any fight and his failure to go to Korea and use some of his famous rhetoric to rally his troops were disgraceful. Bradley wondered why an army with superior ground firepower and complete air superiority could not stem the Chinese advance, especially as Chinese logistical lines became longer and more vulnerable to air strikes.

Truman, in addition, felt MacArthur was trying to allay responsibility for the failure of his offensive by saying "he would have won the war except for the fact that we (in Washington) would not let him have his way ... I should have relieved General MacArthur then and there." The reason Truman did not do this, he said, was he did not wish it to appear that MacArthur was being fired because the offensive had failed. "I have never believed in going back on people when luck is against them . . ."

The administration therefore did two things. It sent MacArthur a directive, addressed to all officials, that foreign and military policy statements were not to be released until cleared by the State or Defense Departments. It also sent General Collins to Korea. In December, while UN forces were still retreating, Collins reported back to the JCS that the situation was not as critical as MacArthur had pictured it and Korea could be held. MacArthur however, persisted in his demand that the limitations be lifted and his forces be reinforced or evacuated.

When Collins returned to Korea in January 1951, along with the Air Force Chief of Staff, General Hoyt S. Vandenberg, they discovered General Ridgway, who had been there less than a month, had revitalized the army. From that point, Washington:

> Looked beyond MacArthur to Ridgway for reliable military assessments and guidance. Although we continued to address JCS messages and directives to MacArthur, there was a feeling that MacArthur had been 'kicked upstairs' to chairman of the board and was, insofar as military operations were concerned, mainly a prima donna figurehead who had to be tolerated.

The Republicans, however, did not share the administration's assessment. The Republican right, true to its pre-war isolationism with its twin traditions of rejecting entangling alliances with European states and favoring unilateralism in Asia, opposed sending troops to Europe because that might provoke the Soviets whose manpower the United States could not match. It did so while supporting MacArthur's course of action, even though this would deepen the U.S. involvement in a war with Communist China, which also had vastly superior manpower resources.

The shock of Chinese intervention and the headlong U.S. retreat led the Truman Administration to reject MacArthur's military prescriptions. There were several reasons for this. First, the JCS doubted that air and naval power and the imposition of blockade could bring the conflict to an early conclusion. The successful implementation of MacArthur's strategy would require, contrary to the general's assessment, large reinforcements. Indeed, General Omar N. Bradley, the Chairman of the Joint Chiefs of Staff, thought the only way to gain a decisive result would be to fight an all-out war with China, which would be a lengthy affair and require a large commitment of U.S. forces.

A second concern was that MacArthur's recommendations might bring the Soviet Union into the conflict. The Soviet Union could no more afford to see Communist China defeated than China could tolerate the defeat of North Korea. Indeed, the Soviet Union, not Communist China, was America's principal and most powerful enemy. Therefore, the United States had to concentrate its focus and resources on Western Europe, which, as two world wars had amply demonstrated, was America's "first line of defense." The country could not afford to squander its huge, but nonetheless finite resources in what General Bradley described as "the wrong war, at the wrong place, at the wrong time, and with the wrong enemy." If there was a right war in the right place, it would have been with the Soviet Union, the primary enemy, fought in Europe, the area of primary security interest. However, the United States did not think it was ready for such a conflict in 1950 and 1951. Ever since the Soviet atomic explosion in 1949, Washington believed that, until the United States had built up its nuclear strength, in part to balance Soviet conventional superiority, it was imperative to avoid confrontation with Moscow.

Third, the European allies strongly opposed MacArthur for the same reasons as the administration: his prescription, if followed, would divert U.S. attention and power away from Europe and risk war with the Soviet Union. The allies were also dismayed by Washington's inability to control or discipline MacArthur. The result was a declining confidence in American political leadership and judgment. Moreover, the European members of NATO sought to counter the pressure exercised on the administration from the right. They were reluctant to condemn China and impose sanctions, in part because they felt MacArthur was not blameless in provoking China's intervention and in part because they feared a condemnation of China would strengthen those forces in the United States that wanted a war with China. The administration, caught in the middle, ultimately managed to obtain support in the UN for a resolution condemning Communist China, but at a price: no follow-up military action.

Thus, the unity of the Atlantic alliance was preserved. MacArthur and the Republicans threatened the cohesion of the alliance, one of the key reasons for the administration's defense of South Korea. Indeed, the United States could not simultaneously "go it alone" in Asia, as MacArthur and his supporters wanted, and pursue a policy of collective security in Europe.

After the Chinese intervention, the Administration took seriously the principles of crisis management, such as presidential control of military options, avoiding options likely to motivate the enemy to escalate, pauses in military operations, and coordinating military moves with political-diplomatic action. The administration also reverted to its initial objective of protecting only the security of South Korea. Without ever explicitly admitting it had made a mistake in crossing the thirty-eighth parallel, the administration recognized that the attempt to reunite Korea and eliminate Communist North Korea had led to a dangerous escalation. Ending the war could only be achieved by restoring the status quo ante on the Korean peninsula.

Further clashes with MacArthur were inevitable, as he was unwilling to reconcile himself to a war limited to Korea and the defense of only South Korea. As MacArthur saw the issue, the only way to prevent future Chinese Communist military expansion was by destroying its capability to wage war now. Negotiations to end the war on the basis of the status quo ante would leave China's war potential intact and, therefore, had to be prevented. The administration's assessment was very different. As UN forces approached the thirty-eighth parallel once more, after having imposed very heavy casualties upon the Chinese, the administration, unwilling to attempt forced reunification a second time, sought to explore the possibilities of ending hostilities on the basis of the prewar partition of the country. Washington believed that if made without threat or recrimination, such an offer might be well received in Beijing.

MacArthur was informed on March 20 that the President, after consultation with the allies, would announce his willingness to discuss suitable terms for concluding the war. On March 24, the general issued his own statement. Pointing out China's failure to conquer all of Korea despite its numerical superiority and the restrictions placed upon him, MacArthur suggested that the enemy "must by now be painfully aware that a decision of the United Nations to depart from its tolerant effort to contain the war to the area of Korea, through expansion of our military operations to his coastal areas and interior bases would doom Red China to the risk of imminent military collapse." He then offered to confer with the Chinese military commander about ending the fighting and achieving the UN objectives without being burdened by such "extraneous matters" as Formosa and China's seat in the UN.

By delivering this virtual ultimatum, asking Beijing to admit that it had lost the war or face an expansion of the conflict and total defeat, MacArthur sought to undercut the administration's effort to achieve a cease-fire and start negotiations to end the war. In a letter to the Republican Minority Leader in the House, Representative Joseph W. Martin, Jr., written on the 19th of March, but not released until April 5, the general elaborated that the restrictions imposed upon him were not in accord with "the conventional pattern of meeting force with maximum counter-force," which "we never failed to do in the past." He said Martin's view of allowing Chiang to open a second front on the Chinese mainland was "in conflict with neither logic nor tradition." The war in Asia must be met with "determination and not half-measures," for it was in Asia that the critical battle was being fought; if this battle was lost, Europe's fall would be inevitable.

The President was furious. MacArthur was continuing to challenge the principle of civilian authority. Not surprisingly, therefore, Truman fired MacArthur. It probably should have been done months earlier, but politically it was a risky and unpopular thing to do. MacArthur himself had finally left Truman with no option. Nevertheless, given the political situation in the United States, it took great courage for the President to fire the General. Indeed, the dismissal created a political furor.

Whether the dismissal of MacArthur encouraged the Chinese to begin cease-fire negotiations shortly afterwards is not known, but it had to reassure them that China itself would not be attacked and that U.S. aims no longer included the forceful unification of Korea. This was reaffirmed by the administration in the congressional hearings held after MacArthur returned triumphantly home. To the degree that there were internal differences in the Chinese leadership about the terms on which to settle the war, MacArthur's firing and administration statements may have strengthened those who—as in the U.S. government —were willing to settle on the basis of the pre-war division. The Soviets also appeared ready to explore the ending of hostilities; it was their UN representative who, responding to U.S. feelers, publicly declared (somewhat obliquely) in June that the Soviet people believed peace was possible.

It is also unknown to what extent the situation on the battlefield contributed to the Chinese and Soviet willingness to negotiate. Ridgway had not only rallied his demoralized and retreating army, but honed it into a deadly fighting force. He stopped repeated Chinese offensives in early 1951 by inflicting immense casualties on Chinese troops through the effective use of artillery and air power. Having suffered about a half million casualties in the eight months since the intervention and, with their May offensive broken, the Chinese were demoralized, unable to resist Ridgway's offensive, and placed on the defensive as their long logistical lines were exposed to constant air attacks and the supply situation became desperate.

Had the administration been willing to continue the offensive, the Chinese would have been in danger of being driven back, perhaps to North Korea's narrow neck. This might have encouraged China to conclude the war before their armies were ripped apart. Instead, when the Soviets and Chinese suggested that they were willing to talk about a cease-fire, the administration immediately agreed and halted the offensive. Pressured by public opinion to end the war and unsure that it could count on domestic support for such a tough bargaining strategy, the administration was unwilling to sacrifice more American lives in order to end the war at lines slightly north of where it had begun. The expectation was of a fairly rapid conclusion to the war. Thus, the cost of the Truman Administration's political weakness and inability to coordinate policy and strategy, so characteristic of the American belief that the two were divorced and that diplomacy would follow the use of force, was very high.

In the event, the negotiations dragged on until 1953. In stopping the offensive, the administration had inadvertently ensured the continuation of the war. The Chinese, reinforced, continued to resist, delaying a settlement while seeking to improve the terms for ending the war at little cost to themselves. During that time, 20,000 Americans were killed, more than in the first year of the war; among all UN forces, the figure of those who died in battle was about twice that of the earlier period.

The tragic irony was that the final terms President Eisenhower accepted were little different from those proposed by the UN early in the negotiations; but Eisenhower could accept terms that Truman could not. The Republican President, a moderate who had opposed Senator Taft for the nomination, was immune to charges by his party's right wing of appeasement and "coddling Communism" (not that it did not try, but finally, forced to fight, Eisenhower destroyed McCarthy). However, Harry Truman, a Democrat, despite his staunch record of anti-Communism in Europe and the containment of Soviet power, was vulnerable to such scurrilous charges even though the United States could have done little to prevent Chiang's regime from committing political suicide. Harry Truman, who had succeeded Franklin Roosevelt when he died, could have run for a second term in 1952. Instead, he chose not to run.

**D. Clayton James with
Anne Sharp Wells**

 **NO**

MacArthur's Dare Is Called

Differences in Strategy

The dismissal of General [Douglas] MacArthur in April 1951 is a watershed in the history of American strategic direction in the Korean conflict. For the ensuing two years and three months of hostilities and truce negotiations no major challenge would be offered to the Truman administration's manner of limiting the war except for a few Allied leaders who urged more compromises with the communists at Panmunjom than the American wished to make for the sake of a quicker end to the fighting. With the removal of MacArthur, moreover, the post-1945 trend of increasing input by the State Department of military policy was accelerated. By the bellicose nature of his criticism of the Truman administration's direction of the war, MacArthur had placed himself in the position of championing a military solution in Korea in the American tradition of preferring strategies of annihilation, instead of attrition. He left the scene as an uncompromising warrior, though, in actuality, his differences with Truman were not as simplistic as they appeared. During World War II, as in the Korean conflict, for instance, he had argued for a balanced global strategy that accorded high priorities to not only Europe but also Asia and the Pacific. In view of the sites where American boys have died in combat since 1945, perhaps that and other arguments of the fiery old general need not have been dismissed so lightly.

Contrary to popular accounts, the strategic aspect of the Truman–MacArthur controversy was not based on the President's advocacy of limited war and the general's alleged crusading for a global war against communism. MacArthur wanted to carry the war to Communist China in air and sea operations of restricted kinds, but he never proposed expanding the ground combat into Manchuria or North China. Both Washington and Tokyo authorities were acutely aware that the Korean struggle could have escalated into World War III if the Soviet Union had gone to war, but at no time did MacArthur wish to provoke the USSR into entering the Korean War. He predicted repeatedly that none of his actions would lead to Soviet belligerency, which, he maintained steadfastly, would be determined by Moscow's own strategic interests and its own timetable.

From D. Clayton James with Anne Sharp Wells, *Refighting the Last War: Command and Crisis in Korea, 1950-1953* (Free Press, 1993). Copyright © 1993 by D. Clayton James. Reprinted by permission of The Free Press, an imprint of Simon & Schuster Adult Publishing Group. Notes omitted.

Yet there were significant strategic differences between Truman and MacArthur. The "first war," against North Korea, did not produce any major collisions between the general and Washington except on Formosa policy, which did not reach its zenith until the Communist Chinese were engaged in Korea. The strategic plans of MacArthur for a defensive line at the Naktong, for an amphibious stroke through Inchon and Seoul, and for a drive north of the 38th parallel all had the blessings of the President and the Joint Chiefs before they reached their operational stages. Even the Far East commander's plans for separate advances by the Eighth Army and the X Corps into North Korea and for an amphibious landing at Wonsan, though they raised eyebrows in Washington, did not draw remonstrances from his superiors, who viewed such decisions as within the purview of the theater chief. Sharp differences between MacArthur and Washington leaders only emerged after the euphoric days of October 1950 when it seemed the North Korean Army was beaten and the conflict was entering its mopping-up phase. Perhaps because of the widespread optimism that prevailed most of that month, neither Tokyo nor Washington officials were aware of a strategic chasm developing between them....

Perhaps it might not have been too late to avert war with Communist China if the Joint Chiefs [JCS] had focused less on MacArthur's impudence toward them and more on the strategic consequence at stake in the Far East commander's move, namely, the escalation of the war by Communist China rather than by the USSR. While MacArthur had largely discounted the possibility of the Soviet Union's entry into the war, he had not seemed greatly concerned about Communist China's possible belligerency. As he had cockily assured the President at Wake, his air power would decimate the Chinese Communist Forces if they tried to advance south of the Yalu. The aggressive move up to the border with American troops in the lead was imprudent adventurism on MacArthur's part, but, on the other hand, the Joint Chiefs' timidity toward him and their priority on his effrontery to them at such a critical strategic juncture left them fully as liable as he was for the decisive provocation of Peking....

While the Great Debate was heating up on Capitol Hill, the beginning of MacArthur's end occurred when [Army Chief of Staff General Joseph L.] Collins, his Army superior and the executive agent for the JCS in Far East matters, visited Tokyo and the Korean front on January 15–17, accompanied by Vandenberg, the Air Force chief. Their trip had been precipitated by a false dilemma MacArthur had posed to his superiors the previous week: As Truman saw it, the Tokyo commander declared the only alternatives were to "be driven off the peninsula, or at the very least suffer terrible losses." Collins reported that during their meeting at MacArthur's GHQ [general headquarters] in Tokyo, MacArthur again appealed for the four divisions. Upon visiting Ridgway [MacArthur's eventual successor] and his troops in Korea, however, Collins found a renovated force preparing to go on the offensive. He was able to return to Washington with the good news, backed by Vandenberg's findings also, that MacArthur was not only uninformed about the situation at the front but also deceitful in posing the false dilemma of evacuation or annihilation if they did not approve his proposals and troop requests. Ridgway's counsel, rather than MacArthur's, was thereafter increasingly sought by the Joint Chiefs and the President.

MacArthur had been found wanting in both strategy and stratagem. Far more crucial, the U.S. government had reaffirmed its foremost global priority to be the security of its Atlantic coalition. Similar to his plight during the Second World War, MacArthur again was arguing in futility for greater American strategic concern about Asia and the Pacific against a predominantly Europe-first leadership in Washington. Having spent over twenty-five years of his career in the Far East, MacArthur may have been biased in speaking out for a higher priority on American interests in that region. There is little question, however, that communist expansionism was mounting in East and Southeast Asia and that American leaders knew little about the susceptibilities of the peoples of those areas. To MacArthur, his struggle to get Washington's attention focused on the Pacific and Asia must have seemed as frustrating as the efforts by him and Fleet Admiral Ernest King to get more resources allocated to the war against Japan.

Despite the warmongering allegations leveled against him, MacArthur never proposed resorting to nuclear weapons while he was Far East chief. In December 1952, he did suggest in a private talk with Eisenhower and Dulles, the President-elect and the next secretary of state, that a line of radioactive waste materials be air-dropped along the northern border of North Korea, to be followed by conventional amphibious assaults on both coasts as well as atomic bombing of military targets in North Korea to destroy the sealed-off enemy forces. He saw this as "the great bargaining lever to induce the Soviet [Union] to agree upon honorable conditions toward international accord." It must be remembered, however, that he had been out of command for twenty months, and, besides, Eisenhower and Dulles scorned his counsel and never sought it again.

In truth, Presidents Truman and Eisenhower, not MacArthur, both considered the use or threat of nuclear force in the Korean War. On November 30, 1950, Truman remarked at a press conference that use of the atomic bomb was being given "active consideration," but Allied leaders, with British Prime Minister Clement R. Attlee in the forefront, exhibited such high states of anxiety over his comment that the President never openly discussed that option again. In January 1952, however, he confided in his diary that he was considering an ultimatum to Moscow to launch atomic raids against Soviet cities if the USSR did not compel the North Koreans and Red Chinese to permit progress in the Korean truce negotiations. "This means all out war," he wrote angrily but wisely reconsidered the next day. In the spring of 1953, President Eisenhower tried to intimidate the Chinese and North Koreans into signing an armistice on UN terms by threatening to use nuclear weapons, which by then included hydrogen bombs. MacArthur had nothing to do with these nuclear threats. Nevertheless, the canard of MacArthur as a warmonger who was eager to employ nuclear weapons in the Korean conflict has persisted in popular and scholarly writings over the years.

A Threat to Civil-Military Relations?

MacArthur's record of arrogant and near-insubordinate conduct during the previous decade on the world stage was well known to the leaders in Washington in 1950–1951. During World War II, President Roosevelt and General Marshall, the Army chief of staff, had been greatly annoyed when he attempted to get Prime Ministers Churchill and Curtin to press for more American resources to be allocated to the Southwest Pacific theater in 1942. MacArthur appeared to encourage anti-Roosevelt groups in American politics who tried in vain to stir up a draft of him for the Republican presidential nomination in 1944. As for defiance of his military superiors, MacArthur launched a number of amphibious operations prior to obtaining authorization from the Joint Chiefs. Admiral Morison observes that "the J.C.S. simply permitted MacArthur to do as he pleased, up to a point" in the war against Japan.

On several occasions during the early phase of the occupation of Japan, MacArthur defied Truman's instructions for him to come to Washington for consultations, the general pleading his inability to leave "the extraordinarily dangerous and inherently inflammable situation" in Japan. Truman was so irked that he quoted two of the general's declinations in his memoirs written nearly a decade afterward. In 1948, MacArthur again appeared willing to run against his commander in chief, but his right-wing supporters were unable to secure the Republican nomination for him. His dissatisfaction with Washington directives during the later phases of the occupation almost led to his replacement by a civilian high commissioner. His growing alienation from administration policies during the first eight months of the Korean fighting gave rise to speculation that he might head an anti-Truman ticket in the 1952 presidential race.

The administration officials who testified at the Senate hearings on MacArthur's relief clearly indicated that they viewed his attitude and conduct as insubordinate and a threat to the principle of civilian supremacy over the military. Secretary of Defense Marshall, probably the most admired of the witnesses representing the administration, was adamant about MacArthur's unparalleled effrontery toward his superiors:

> It is completely understandable and, in fact, at times commendable that a theater commander should become so wholly wrapped up in his own aims and responsibilities that some of the directives received by him from higher authorities are not those that he would have written for himself. There is nothing new about this sort of thing in our military history. What is new, and what had brought about the necessity for General MacArthur's removal, is the wholly unprecedented situation of a local theater commander publicly expressing his displeasure at and his disagreement with the foreign and military policies of the United States.
>
> It became apparent that General MacArthur had grown so far out of sympathy with the established policies of the United States that there was a grave doubt as to whether he could any longer be permitted to exercise the authority in making decisions that normal command functions would assign to a theater commander. In this situation, there was no other recourse but to relieve him.

The evidence accumulated in the Senate investigation of May and June 1951 demonstrates that virtually all of his transgressions fell under the category of disobedience of the President's "muzzling directives" of December 6, 1950. The general's responses, in turn, had revealed his deep opposition to administration policies. The press had widely publicized his blasts; indeed, many of his missives had gone to national news magazines and major newspapers by way of interviews with and correspondence to their publishers and senior editors or bureau chiefs. His false dilemma about evacuation or annihilation, which was rankling enough to his superiors since he seemed to pass responsibility to them, was a frequent theme in his flagrantly defiant public statements. McCarthyism had already left the national press in a feeding frenzy, so it was natural for reporters eager to exploit the popular hostility against Truman and [Dean] Acheson to give lavish attention to the antiadministration barbs of one of the nation's greatest heroic figures of World War II.

Most heinous to Commander in Chief Truman were the general's ultimatum to the head of the Chinese Communist Forces [CCF] on March 24 and his denunciation of administration policy read in the U.S. House of Representatives on April 5. The general had been told that Truman would soon announce a new diplomatic initiative to get a Korean truce before Ridgway's army advanced across the 38th parallel again. MacArthur arrogantly and deliberately wrecked this diplomatic overture by issuing his own public statement directed to the CCF leader, which scathingly criticized Red China's "complete inability to accomplish by force of arms the conquest of Korea," threatened "an expansion of our military operations to its coastal areas and interior bases [that] would doom Red China to the risk of imminent military collapse," and offered "at any time to confer in the field with the commander-in-chief of the enemy forces in the earnest effort to find any military means whereby realization of the political objectives of the United Nations in Korea... might be accomplished without further bloodshed."

In sixteen or more instances in the previous four months the volatile Far East chief had made statements sharply chastising the administration for its errors or absence of policy in the Far East. MacArthur was bent now upon some dramatic gesture to salvage his waning stature. By late March, the UN commander became so paranoid that he believed that he had ruined a plot created by some in the United Nations, the State Department, and high places in Washington to change the status of Formosa and the Nationalists' seat in the UN.

Upon reading MacArthur's shocking statement of the 24th, the President firmly but secretly decided that day to dismiss him; only the procedure and the date had to be settled. Truman heatedly remarked to an assistant that the general's act was "not just a public disagreement over policy, but deliberate, premeditated sabotage of US and UN policy." Acheson described it as "defiance of the Chiefs of Staff, sabotage of an operation of which he had been informed, and insubordination of the grossest sort to his Commander in Chief." Astoundingly, however, the President, through the JCS, sent him a brief and mildly worded message on March 25 reminding him of the directives of December 6 and telling him to contact the Joint Chiefs for instructions if the Chinese commander asked for a truce.

The message from Washington on March 20 alerting him to the impending peace move also set off MacArthur's second climatic act of self-destruction in his endeavor to redirect American foreign and military policies to a greater focus on Asia's significance to the self-interests of the United States. That same day the general wrote Representative Joseph W. Martin, Jr., the House minority leader and a strong Asia-first and Nationalist China crusader. Martin had asked for comments on a speech by the congressman hitting Truman's weak support of Formosa, his limited-war strategy in Korea, and his plans to strengthen NATO. In his letter, MacArthur endorsed his friend Martin's views with enthusiasm but offered nothing new, even admitting that his positions "have been submitted to Washington in most complete detail" and generally "are well known." What made the general's comments different this time were their coincidence with the sensitive diplomatic maneuvering, Martin's dramatic reading of the letter on the floor of the House, and the front-page headlines MacArthur's words got. . . .

At the Senate hearings, MacArthur claimed the letter to Martin was "merely a routine communication." On the other hand, Truman penned in his diary on April 6: "MacArthur shoots another political bomb through Joe Martin. . . . This looks like the last straw. Rank insubordination. . . . I call in Gen. Marshall, Dean Acheson, Mr. Harriman and Gen. Bradley before Cabinet [meeting] to discuss situation." Acheson exclaimed that the Martin letter was "an open declaration of war on the Administration's policy." When Truman conferred with the above "Big Four," as he called them, he did not reveal that his mind had been made up for some time; instead, he encouraged a candid discussion of options and expressed his desire for a unanimous recommendation from them as well as the three service chiefs, Collins, Sherman, and Vandenberg.

Over the weekend Truman talked to key members of the Cabinet to solicit their opinions, while top State and Defense officials met in various groupings to discuss the issue. At the meeting of the President and the Big Four on Monday, April 9, the relief of General MacArthur was found to be the unanimous verdict of the President, the Big Four, and the service chiefs. . . .

MacArthur was the first to testify at the Senate hearings [in early May], and when he expounded on the harmonious relationship and identity of strategic views between him and his military superiors, he seems to have believed this sincerely, if naively. One by one, Marshall, Bradley, Collins, Sherman, and Vandenberg would later tell the senators that they were not in accord with MacArthur on matters of the direction of the war, relations with civilian officials, the value of the European allies, and the priority of the war in the global picture, among other differences. Not aware of how united and devastating against him his uniformed superiors would be, MacArthur set about describing a dichotomy in the leadership of the war from Washington, with Truman, Acheson, Harriman, and other ranking civilians of the administration, especially the State Department, which tended to have unprecedented input in military affairs

by 1950–1951, being responsible for the policy vacuum, indecisiveness, and protracted, costly stalemate. On the other hand, he and the Pentagon leaders, along
with most of the other senior American officers of the various services, wanted
to fight in less limited fashion and gain a decisive triumph in order to deter
future communist aggression.

MacArthur, thinking he spoke for his military colleagues, told the senators that Truman and his "politicians" favored "the concept of a continued and
indefinite campaign in Korea . . . that introduces into the military sphere a political control such as I have never known in my life or have ever studied." He
argued that "when politics fails, and the military takes over, you must trust the
military." Later he added: "There should be no non-professional interference in
the handling of troops in a campaign. You have professionals to do that job and
they should be permitted to do it." As for his recommendations for coping with
the entry of the Red Chinese onto the battlefield, he maintained that "most" of
them, "in fact, practically all, as far as I know—were in complete accord with
the military recommendations of the Joint Chiefs of Staff, and all other commanders." Referring to a JCS list of sixteen courses of action that were under
consideration on January 12, which included three of the four he had recommended on December 30, he claimed with some hyperbole, "The position of
the Joint Chiefs of Staff and my own, so far as I know, were practically identical." He pictured his ties with the JCS as idealistic, indeed, unrealistic; "The
relationships between the Joint Chiefs of Staff and myself have been admirable.
All members are personal friends of mine. I hold them individually and collectively in the greatest esteem." It was a desperate endeavor to demonstrate that
the basic friction lay between the civilian and the military leadership, not between him and the Pentagon, but it became a pathetic revelation of how out of
touch he was with the Joint Chiefs. For want of conclusive proof as to his motivation, however, leeway must be allowed for MacArthur's wiliness, which had
not altogether abandoned him: He may have been trying to exploit tensions between the State and Defense departments, with few uniformed leaders holding
Acheson and his lieutenants in high regard.

Fortunately for MacArthur, Marshall and the Joint Chiefs, who had chafed
over Acheson's obvious eagerness to see the proud MacArthur fall, felt an affin-
ity with this senior professional in their field who had long commanded with
distinction. They could not bring themselves to court-martial him. Further,
Truman's terrible ratings in the polls—worse than Nixon's at the ebb of Watergate—and the firestorm that McCarthyism had produced for him and Acheson
weakened him so politically that a court-martial of MacArthur would have
been foolhardy in the extreme. During the first five days after MacArthur's relief, a White House staff count showed that Truman received almost thirteen
thousand letters and telegrams on the issue, of which 67 percent opposed the
President's action. By the end of the Senate hearings on the general's relief,
much of the public, Congress, and the press had lost interest in the inquiry,
though polls indicated that a majority of those who cared enough to give an
opinion now were against MacArthur. The notion that he might have touched
off World War III was on its way to becoming one of the more unfortunate
myths about the general.

Insubordination, or defiance of authority, was the charge most frequently leveled against MacArthur at the time and later by high-ranking officials of the Truman administration, including those in uniform. Of course, there was no doubt of his insubordination in the minds of the two chief architects of his dismissal, Truman and Acheson. On numerous occasions during his days of testimony before the Senate committees, it will be recalled, MacArthur himself said that the nation's commander in chief was empowered to appoint and dismiss his uniformed leaders for whatever reason, which surely included rank insubordination. There was no serious question about Truman's authority to relieve MacArthur, but the President and the Joint Chiefs found such great difficulty in dismissing him because there was no genuine threat to the principle of civilian supremacy over the military in this case. MacArthur was not an "American Caesar" and held very conservative views of the Constitution, the necessity of civilian control, and the traditions and history of the American military. When the President finally decided to gird his loins and dismiss MacArthur, the action was swift and Ridgway replaced him smoothly and effectively in short order. All the President had to do was issue the order to bring about the change in command, and it was clear that his power as commander in chief was secure and unchallenged. The President and his Far East commander had differed over strategic priorities and the direction of the war, but their collision had not posed a serious menace to civilian dominance over the military in America.

Breakdowns in Command and Communication

A significant and often overlooked reason for the termination of MacArthur's command was a breakdown in communications between him and his superiors. During the Second World War, MacArthur and the Joint Chiefs of Staff sometimes differed in ways that indicated misconceptions more than strategic differences, but the two sides and their key lieutenants had personal ties between them that were lacking between the Tokyo and Washington leaders of 1950–1951. During the Korean War, the camps of Truman and MacArthur strongly influenced each man's perception of the other. This is not to say that on their own Truman and MacArthur would have become cordial friends. But their lieutenants undoubtedly were important in molding their judgments. Their only direct contact had been a few hours at Wake Island on October 15, 1950, of which a very small portion had been spent alone. Despite the fact that they had never met before and were never to talk again, they would go to their graves implacable enemies.

If the Truman-MacArthur personal relationship was limited to one brief encounter, the personal links between the Far East leader and the seven men who were the President's principal advisers on the Korean War—the Big Four and the service chiefs—were almost nil. Acheson never met him. Marshall visited him once during World War II while going to Eisenhower's headquarters numerous times. Bradley and Harriman had no personal ties with MacArthur at all prior to June of 1950, although each traveled to Tokyo to confer with him after the Korean hostilities commenced. None of the Big Four was an admirer of MacArthur's flamboyant leadership style, yet Marshall, who had been his military superior in World War II, had treated him with commendable fairness despite the Southwest Pacific commander's sometimes difficult ways. All of the Big Four were strongly committed to the security of West Europe, and all had considerable experience and friends there.

None of the service chiefs had any personal contacts with MacArthur of any importance prior to the outbreak of war in Korea, whereupon they made a number of trips to Tokyo to meet with him and his senior commanders and staff leaders. Collins was on the faculty of the United States Military Academy during MacArthur's last year as superintendent (1921–1922), and Vandenberg was a cadet for the three years (1919–1922) of his tenure. Neither of them, however, really got to know the aloof superintendent, though both knew much about him, especially his hero image from the battlefields of France and his efforts to bring reforms to the school despite faculty and alumni resistance. Collins and Vandenberg achieved their senior commands in the Second World War in the European theater; the former had seen combat first in the Solomons, which was not in MacArthur's theater. When he was on Admiral Chester W. Nimitz's staff during the war in the Pacific, Sherman conferred with MacArthur at three or more intertheater planning sessions. Sherman, who had the most significant pre-1950 personal contact with MacArthur, was his strongest supporter of the seven men on a number of his ideas and plans, notably the Inchon assault. On the other hand, Marshall, the oldest of the seven (like MacArthur, born in 1880), and the officer with seniority in the service, was the last of the group to be persuaded that MacArthur should be relieved of his commands.

Of these key advisers to the President, Acheson stands out for his vituperativeness toward the Tokyo commander. In a bitter exchange of press statements in the autumn of 1945 contradicting each other over estimated troop strength needed in occupied Japan, Acheson and MacArthur seemed to exhibit a deep and natural incompatibility. Acheson blamed MacArthur in part for trouble in getting his approval as under secretary of state passed by the Senate that fall. When he was secretary of state later, he visited Europe often but never Japan, and in 1949 he was behind the move to oust the general as head of the Allied occupation. Certainly as proud and arrogant as MacArthur, Acheson could be invidious. Writing nearly two decades after the dismissal, Acheson still harbored deep wrath: "As one looks back in calmness, it seems impossible to overestimate the damage that General MacArthur's willful insubordination and incredibly bad judgment did to the United States in the world and to the Truman Administration in the United States." Acheson was the abiding voice in Truman's ear from 1945 onward urging him to dump "the Big General," and it was he who primarily continued to stoke the long-cold coals even after most of his cohorts had let the fire die as far as public statements were concerned.

The sorry spectacle of MacArthur testifying at the Senate hearings about his harmonious relations with the Joint Chiefs not only exposed his ignorance of the situation but also pointed up how poorly the JCS had communicated their doubts and anxieties, as well as their anger, to the theater commander. It was an invitation to trouble to place him in the UN command in the first place because of both his prior record of defying authority and his long career of distinction and seniority in comparison to theirs. It should have been understood from the beginning of the Korean War that his past achievements gave him no claim to special privileges in obeying orders and directives, especially in such an unprecedented limited conflict that could quickly become a third world war. Time after time, especially after the Red Chinese intervention, the Joint Chiefs retreated from the policy guidance and new directives they should have given MacArthur and should have demanded his obedience. Instead, his intimidation of the Joint Chiefs led them to appease him.

On the other hand, MacArthur discovered that he could not awe or intimidate Truman. Indeed, at the end, the President dismissed him so abruptly and crudely that the general heard of it first from a commercial radio broadcast. Speaking as a professional, MacArthur later said, "No office boy, no charwoman, no servant of any sort would have been dismissed with such callous disregard for the ordinary decencies." For MacArthur, his erroneous image of Truman as a fox terrier yapping at his heels instead of a tough, decisive commander in chief was a costly failure in communication.

If the Joint Chiefs had been more responsible in keeping MacArthur on a short leash, perhaps the collision course between the President and the general might have been averted. The absurd spectacle of the Senate investigation into the general's relief, which bestowed upon Pyongyang, Peking, and Moscow an abundance of data on American strategy in the midst of war, surely could have been avoided. While MacArthur's career was terminated by the confrontation, Truman's also was cut short, the controversy mightily affecting his chances for reelection. Truman won over MacArthur, but it was a Pyrrhic victory politically.

MacArthur's relief was, in part, a legacy of World War II and the strategic priorities of that conflict. Roosevelt and his Joint Chiefs of Staff had early agreed to the British priority on the defeat of Germany because the Atlantic community of nations was vital to American national security and the threat by Japan was more distant. In the midst of another Asian war, MacArthur was sacrificed by a different President and his Defense and State advisers, who did not consider American strategic interests as menaced in East Asia as in Europe. It remains to be seen whether a century hence the Far East will loom as important to American self-interests as MacArthur predicted.

POSTSCRIPT

Should President Truman Have Fired General MacArthur?

In 1950 MacArthur's disagreements with Truman were twofold. First, he disliked the Truman administration's Europe-oriented policy of "containment" of Russian expansionism; second, he detested the defensive strategy that was implied in fighting a limited war under a containment policy.

MacArthur's sympathies lay with those who blamed the Truman administration for the "loss of China" to the Communists and hoped that the UN forces would push the Communists out of a reunified Korea. On his visit to Formosa on August 2, 1950, he embarrassed the Truman administration with his remarks that plans had been developed for the effective coordination of Chinese and American forces in case of an attack on the island. A few weeks later he was nearly fired after he sent a long message to the national commander of the Veterans of Foreign Wars, which stated, "Nothing could be more fallacious than the threadbare argument by those who advocate appeasement and defeatism in the Pacific that if we defend Formosa we alienate continental Asia."

Spanier contends that MacArthur stretched orders from the Defense Department and Joint Chiefs of Staff well beyond their original intent. Particularly upsetting to Truman was MacArthur's public statement asking Beijing to admit it lost the war or face expansion of the war into parts of China and risk total defeat. This pronouncement, says Spanier, "undercut the administration's effort to achieve a cease-fire and start negotiations to end the war." It also convinced the president that he had to fire the general. The Joint Chiefs of Staff agreed.

James is the author of a three-volume biography of MacArthur. The third volume—*Triumph and Disaster, 1945–1964* (Houghton Mifflin, 1985)—covers in greater detail MacArthur's role in post–World War II Asia. James admits that MacArthur was arrogant and at times difficult to deal with but asserts that the Joint Chiefs of Staff might have prevented MacArthur's firing if they had exerted more control over him.

Spanier agrees with James that the Joint Chiefs of Staff were timorous in dealing with MacArthur. This was likely because many of the Joint Chiefs were much younger than MacArthur, who was then 70 years old, and were afraid to challenge a "living legend." Furthermore, MacArthur had proven to a highly skeptical Joint Chiefs and Defense Department that his tactical abilities were still sharp, given the success of the surprise landing behind the lines of the enemy at Inchon.

Spanier and James agree that a more aggressive military policy might have ended the war two years earlier. Could UN field commander Matthew Ridgeway or MacArthur have forced the Chinese and North Koreans to accept a divided

Korea if they had pushed the Chinese to North Korea's narrow neck? Was the Truman administration too politically weak to do this? Was the administration's policy and strategy poorly coordinated? Could MacArthur have been persuaded to accept a compromise-negotiated settlement?

Students who wish to learn more should start with Richard Lowitt, ed., *The Truman-MacArthur Controversy* (Rand McNally, 1984). Walter Karp explores the aftermath of the controversy in "Truman vs. MacArthur," in *American Heritage* (April/May 1984). There are three books that cover the controversy in detail and are supportive of Truman's decision. Many consider the best to be John W. Spanier, *The Truman-MacArthur Controversy and the Korean War* (W. W. Norton, 1959, 1965). See also Trumball Higgins, *Korea and the Fall of MacArthur: A Precis in Limited War* (Oxford University Press, 1960) and Richard H. Rovere and Arthur Schlesinger, Jr., *The MacArthur Controversy and American Foreign Policy* (Transaction Books, 1992), which was originally published at the height of the controversy in 1951. Other defenses include *Memoirs by Harry S. Truman: Years of Trial and Hope, vol. 2* (Signet Paperback, 1956, 1965) and former secretary of state Dean Acheson's caustic *Present at the Creation* (W. W. Norton, 1969). More recent criticism of MacArthur's vision comes from retired brigadier general Roy K. Flint, former head of the history department at West Point, in "The Truman-MacArthur Conflict: Dilemma of Civil-Military Relationships in the Nuclear Age," in Richard H. Kohn, ed., *The United States Military Under the Constitution of the United States, 1789–1989* (New York University Press, 1991).

MacArthur's defense of his policies and anger over his firing can be found in his *Reminiscences* (McGraw-Hill, 1964) and in Charles A. Willoughby and John Chamberlain, *MacArthur: 1941–1951* (McGraw-Hill, 1954). Willoughby was an intelligence officer on MacArthur's staff.

For a good short history of the war, students should see Burton I. Kaufman, *The Korean War: Challenges in Crisis, Credibility and Command,* 2d ed. (McGraw-Hill, 1997). Kaufman has also edited *The Korean Conflict* (Greenwood Press, 1999), an excellent compendium of chronologies, biographical sketches, and bibliography. Two starting points for all the recent research in Soviet archives pertaining to the Korean War are Rosemary Foot, "Making Known the Unknown War: Policy Analysis of the Korean Conflict Since the Early 1980's" and Robert J. McMahon, "The Cold War in Asia: The Elusive Synthesis." Both are essays from *Diplomatic History* that have been reprinted in Michael J. Hogan, ed., *America in the World: The Historiography of American Foreign Relations Since 1941* (Cambridge University Press, 1995).

ISSUE 4

Were the 1950s America's "Happy Days"?

YES: Melvyn Dubofsky and Athan Theoharis, from *Imperial Democracy: The United States Since 1945*, 2d ed. (Prentice Hall, 1988)

NO: Douglas T. Miller and Marion Nowak, from *The Fifties: The Way We Really Were* (Doubleday, 1977)

ISSUE SUMMARY

YES: Professor of history and sociology Melvyn Dubofsky and professor of history Athan Theoharis argue that throughout the 1950s, the U.S. economy dominated much of the globe and created a period of unprecedented growth and prosperity for the percentage of the American population that made it into the middle class.

NO: Professor of history Douglas T. Miller and journalist Marion Nowak argue that the nostalgia craze, which re-creates the 1950s as a sweet, simple, golden age of harmony, masks the fact that the decade was an era of conformity in which Americans feared the bomb, Communists, crime, and the loss of a national purpose.

Since the mid-1970s Americans have used the 1950s as the standard by which all future successes and failures are measured. Cable television replays old shows espousing the family values that Americans most admire. But what were the 1950s really like? Was the period truly America's "Happy Days"?

Most people agree that America in the 1950s reflected the title of economist John Kenneth Gailbraith's book *The Affluent Society* (Houghton Mifflin, 1958). Because the United States was physically untouched during World War II, it was instrumental in rebuilding the economies of the major noncommunist countries in Europe and Asia through the use of the Marshall Plan, Point Four Program, and other foreign aid programs.

At home the expected postwar recession and depression never occurred. Controlling inflation while stabilizing employment became the primary concern of the economists. During the war American workers had built up over $140 billion in savings. Hungry for consumer goods they had been unable to acquire from 1942 through the middle of 1945, Americans went on a massive consumer buying spree—one that has continued to the present day.

There were, however, some disturbing economic trends in the 1950s. Poverty was still widespread among many nonwhite groups and the displaced coal miners in Appalachia. Large corporations were buying up smaller ones, and individual farms were coming under the control of agribusinesses. Income inequality also increased: In 1949 the top 1 percent of the population owned 19 percent of the nation's wealth; by 1960 it owned 33 percent.

If the rich got richer, so did millions of other Americans. As Michael W. Schuyler points out in his article "The 1950s: A Retrospective View," *Nebraska History* (Spring 1996), "Average family income, which was $3,000 in 1947, increased dramatically to $5,400 in 1959. The gross national product increased from $318 billion in 1950 to $440 billion in 1960. Between 1945 and 1960 the real earning power of the average wage earner increased by 22 percent."

In spite of this pleasant lifestyle, America became an anxiety-ridden society in the 1950s. World War II ended in the defeat of fascism, but a cold war developed against America's former ally the Soviet Union, which seemed bent on spreading communism not only throughout Eastern Europe but also across the entire world. The United States extended economic and military assistance to Greece and Turkey in 1947 and two years later formed the first peacetime alliance in history—the North Atlantic Treaty Organization (NATO)—in order to contain the spread of communism. Although Western Europe stood fast, leaks sprang up in other parts of the world.

Crime, corruption, and communism seemed rampant in the 1950s. The news was spread by television. In 1946 there were only 7,000 television sets in the entire country; by 1960 they numbered over 50 million. Politicians filled the void on daytime television with an endless parade of hearings. Juvenile delinquency, it was argued, resulted from a moral breakdown in the home and community. Comic books and rock and roll were held to be the culprits, and the city council of Jersey City solved the problem by banning rock and roll at all school dances. Meanwhile, Senator Joseph McCarthy continued his search for Communists in the government but overreached himself when he bullied high-level military officials in his senatorial investigation of the army in 1954. Eisenhower's powerful chief of staff, Sherman Adams, resigned amidst allegations that he received gifts from a contractor. The government panicked when the Russians launched the Earth-orbiting *Sputnik I* satellite into space in October 1957. Could Ivan read better than Johnny? Had America lost its moral leadership and prestige in the eyes of the world, as two government reports indicated in 1960?

In the first of the following selections, Melvyn Dubofsky and Athan Theoharis argue that throughout the 1950s, the United States dominated much of the world's economy. They also hold that the country experienced a period of unprecedented growth and prosperity for nearly two-thirds of its population, which made it into the middle class. In the second selection, Douglas T. Miller and Marion Nowak assert that the decade was an era dominated by the need to conform and by feelings of fear about the bomb, Communists, crime, and the loss of a national purpose.

Melvyn Dubofsky and
Athan Theoharis

 **YES**

Imperial Democracy:
The United States Since 1945

Economic Growth and a Consumer Society

Throughout the 1950s the United States economy dominated much of the globe. Though less dependent on foreign trade for economic growth than most other industrial nations, the relatively small percentages of United States domestic production and capital that entered international trade had an enormous impact on the economies of smaller, less productive nations. Despite the fact that America's gross national product expanded relatively more slowly than other rapidly industrializing societies, the United States' productive base was so immense that between 1949 and 1960 absolute real GNP increased from $206 billion to over $500 billion, a rise of nearly 150 percent. Such economic power, especially in relation to weaker, less industrialized societies, allowed the United States to set the terms of trade. Thus American corporations during the 1950s purchased raw materials cheaply and sold manufactured goods dearly. As America grew wealthier, raw material-producing nations in Latin America, Africa, and Asia became relatively poorer....

The New Growth Industries

During the 1950s some of the old standbys of industrial America—railroads, coal mining, textiles, and shoe manufacturing—continued a decline that had begun in the 1920s. Railroad freight traffic fell steadily before the inroads of highway trucking, and passengers discarded long-distance trains in favor of more rapid air or cheaper bus transportation. By the end of the 1960s nearly the entire rail network in the Northeast, including the giant Penn-Central, had gone bankrupt. Coal found itself unable to compete with oil, natural gas, nuclear power, and water power; the nearly 600,000 miners employed at the end of World War II had fallen to about 100,000 by 1970. Cotton and woolen manufacture succumbed to synthetic fibers and domestic production to cheaper foreign manufactures. The shoe industry wrote an equally sorry chapter. Endicott-Johnson, the world's largest shoe manufacturer, had employed about 28,000 production workers in its New York Southern Tier factories in the late 1940s; by 1970 the

From Melvyn Dubofsky and Athan Theoharis, *Imperial Democracy: The United States Since 1945*, 2d ed. (Prentice Hall, 1988). Copyright © 1988 by Prentice Hall, Inc. Reprinted by permission of Pearson Education, Inc., Upper Saddle River, NJ. Notes omitted.

production force had dipped below 4,000, the company began to dismantle its mills, and it even purchased shoes from Rumania for sale in its American retail outlets. Such instances of economic decline caused permanent depression in many New England towns and Appalachian coal patches. Again in the 1950s, as in the 1920s, economic sores festered on a generally healthy economic body.

If parts of New England and Appalachia declined economically, other regions of the nation prospered as never before. Wherever chemicals, business machines, electronics, and computers were manufactured the economy boomed, for these were the postwar growth industries par excellence. They were the new industries fit for survival in a "new society." Their economic growth based on technological and scientific advances, electronic-chemical firms stressed research and development programs (almost half of which were financed by the federal government), hired thousands of new graduates from the nation's universities, and served as the employers for a technocratic-scientific elite.

E. I. DuPont de Nemours & Co., Dow, and Monsanto prospered by manufacturing the synthetic goods that increasingly transformed the United States into a plastic society. Women wore their nylon stockings, people cooked on their Teflon pots and pans, men donned Dacron suits and Orlon shirts, and cars rolled on synthetic tires. Electronics, the child of wartime technological innovations, transistorized the postwar world. As tiny transistors replaced bulky tubes, teenagers walked everywhere holding the ubiquitous portable radio, and homebodies carried small TVs from room to room and house to patio. It was a society in which stereophonic sound replaced high fidelity phonographs only to be displaced in turn by quadraphonic sound. The electronics industry promised to turn every home into a private concert hall; indeed, some new houses were built with sound systems wired into every room. And electric eyes now opened and shut garage doors.

Meantime, automation and its associated business machines produced still greater profits and affected the economy more substantially than plastics and electronics. What Ford and General Electric symbolized in the 1920s, IBM and Xerox personified in post-World War II America. Ever since the industrial revolution, machinery had been replacing human labor in manufacturing. But where humans once operated the new machines, in the postwar era of automation such companies as IBM produced machines that controlled themselves as well as other machines. Automation, based on the same simple feedback principle that operated home thermostats, controlled steel strip mills, auto assembly lines, and entire petrochemical complexes. Computers, the next stage in the process of automation and first introduced commercially in 1950, had the ability to remember, sort materials, and make decisions; computers could also write poetry, compose music, play chess, and simulate strategy in a football game. So varied were the computer's uses that they were utilized by hotel chains, insurance companies, banks, airlines, and even universities (by the 1960s college students were identified by their IBM numbers) to simplify increasingly complex paper transactions. Where automation once threatened only blue-collar industrial workers, it now endangered the job security of millions of white-collar clerks. Even politicians, eager to predict beforehand the results of elections, worshipped at the shrine of the high-speed mainframe computer.....

One reason for the success of the new growth industries was their close link to the Department of Defense, postwar America's largest single business contractor. The Pentagon supplied a lavish market for electronic and chemical manufacturers, as its deadly nuclear missiles with their elaborate guidance systems relied on synthetics, transistorized modules, and advanced computers. Even the more mundane hardware used by infantry, artillery, and nonnuclear aircraft depended heavily on electronic components and computerized guidance. NASA too provided an economic bonanza for the world of electronics. Without transistors, computers, and chemical fuels, there would have been no flight in space, no man on the moon. Between government contracts and consumer demand for household appliances (household use of electricity tripled in the 1950s), the growth industries prospered enormously.

American agriculture changed as well in the postwar era. Farming became a big business. Agricultural productivity rose more rapidly than demand for foodstuffs for most of the first two postwar decades, forcing millions of smaller farmers off the land; and large farmers prospered as a result of government subsidy programs and their own efficiency. Because production rose so rapidly, prices for agricultural goods declined, and profits could be made only by lowering unit costs of production through intensive application of fertilizers, use of costly new farm machinery, and introduction of sophisticated managerial techniques. Smaller farms simply lacked the resources and the capital to purchase fertilizer, acquire new machinery, and hire costly managerial experts. They also lacked enough land to make the use of expensive new machinery profitable or to join the soil bank, a program intended to promote soil conservation by paying farmers cash subsidies to let some of their land lie fallow. In other words, because most federal farm programs and subsidies were directly proportional to farm size and productivity, large farmers received proportionately more benefits than small farmers. The beneficiaries of federal largesse, the big farmers also possessed the land, capital, and knowledge necessary to grow food and fibers most efficiently. Consequently the percentage of owner-operated farms rose, and the size of the typical farm increased substantially. Cotton production shifted away from the South, where it remained profitable only on the extremely large plantation, to the immense corporate, irrigated farms of Texas, Arizona, and southern California. Farming in such prosperous agricultural states as California, Arizona, and Florida was justly labeled "agribusiness." In some cases industrial corporations, Tenneco among others, purchased large farms.....

Affluence and Consumption

The stability of the American political and economic system as well as the absence of working-class discontent and militancy flowed from the successful creation of a mass consumer society. The car in every garage and chicken in every pot which Hoover and the Republicans had promised Americans in

1928 arrived in the 1950s. And now it also included beefsteaks, color television, stereophonic sound, and suburban split-levels.

Mass consumption depended on constantly rising real wage levels, a condition the United States economy sustained between 1945 and 1960. By 1956 the real income of the average American was more than 50 percent greater than it had been in 1929, and by 1960 it was 35 percent higher than it had been in the last year of World War II.

How typical Americans spent their increased earnings was determined as much by external factors as by intrinsic, real personal needs. Indeed, the larger the income an individual earned the more choice he or she had in its disposal. As growing numbers of citizens satisfied their need for food and shelter, the manufacturers of attractive but nonessential goods competed lustily for the consumer's dollar.

To sell the autos, refrigerators, dishwashers, stereo sets, and other appliances that rolled off production lines, manufacturers resorted to Madison Avenue and intensive advertising. Between 1946 and 1957 expenditures on advertising increased by almost 300 percent, rising to over $10 billion annually. Not only did the money devoted to advertising rise significantly, but the lords of Madison Avenue also developed more sophisticated selling tactics. Successful advertising was complicated when consumers had to select from among breakfast cereals and cars that differed neither in price nor utility and also had to be convinced to buy products never before manufactured. Employing all the tools of normal (and abnormal) psychology, advertisers alerted consumers to the psychic benefits of larger cars, sweeter-smelling underarms, striped toothpaste, and Marlboro—the man's cigarette. Brighter teeth, Madison Avenue implied, guaranteed every wallflower a desirable husband, and the cigarillo won every man a buxom and accommodating female. Able to allocate money and talent to the one-minute television spot, advertisers bombarded viewers with irresistible commercials. Madison Avenue sales campaigns got such good results in the marketplace that in time many candidates for public office substituted the one-minute television spot for the half-hour platform speech. By the 1960s, Madison Avenue sold presidents as well as Pontiacs, congressmen as well as Cadillacs.

More than advertising was required to create the postwar consumer society. Regardless of the reality of rising wages, millions of citizens still lacked income sufficient to satisfy their demand for goods. A 1950 Census Bureau survey of over 7,000 families, for example, showed that 60 percent having earnings of $4,000 or less spent more than they earned. Even those workers whose incomes exceeded their current expenses seldom had a margin of savings adequate to sustain the cash purchase of such costly durables as autos and large home appliances. Only by borrowing money on the assumption that higher future earnings would render repayment painless could most citizens satisfy their desire for cars and dishwashers.

As advertising stimulated the demand for consumer goods, the nation's financial institutions financed their purchase. Between 1946 and 1957, private indebtedness increased by 360 percent—in contrast, total public debt rose by only 11 percent and the federal debt actually declined. More remarkable still was the rise in consumer installment indebtedness; the estimated annual installment credit outstanding soared from just over $4 billion in 1946 to over $34 billion in 1957. Automobile installment credit alone rose from under $1 billion to in excess of $15 billion. The propensity to buy now and pay later made the cash registers ring. Detroit produced over five million new cars in 1949 and in the peak year of 1955 sold nearly eight million autos, a record unsurpassed until the late 1960s.

For those individuals whose earnings rose annually, consumer credit and installment buying provided a relatively easy means to achieve rapid material affluence. But for those Americans whose income failed to rise, or rose only haltingly, installment buying became more an economic trap than an avenue to comfort. Unable to save sufficient cash to underwrite their purchases, these unfortunate consumers frequently failed to earn enough to pay the interest as well as the principal on their installment contract. In some cases, credit costs effectively increased the original purchase price by one third or more.

The consumption craze took many shapes in the 1950s. Such economists as Walt W. Rostow suggested that when men and women in America's "high mass consumption society" satisfied their desire for cars and appliances, they invested surplus income in babies. Whatever the precise cause no one could doubt that a population explosion took place from 1945 through the 1950s. Medical science and improved nutrition lengthened life spans, and the multiple (three or more) child household became commonplace. The public philosophy of the 1950s, as proclaimed by psychologists, TV comedians, preachers, and politicians, sanctified the home and woman's place in it. The ideal female married young and well, bore a large brood, and remained home to create the perfect environment for keeping the American family together. The sanctification of the family and the idealization of the woman as mother and homemaker further promoted the growth of a consumer society. Larger families required bigger houses with more appliances to simplify "mom's" work and increased purchases to provide for the children. Before long many one-car families would become two-, three-, and in rare instances even four-car households.

If affluence enabled many Americans to enjoy unsurpassed material comforts, millions of citizens still struggled to make ends meet. If new recruits joined the "jet set" and flew to vacations in Rio, Biarritz, and Monaco, many workers, like the Bronx couple that *New York Times* reporter A. H. Raskin investigated, who lived half an hour by subway from Times Square, saw "less of [the] Great White Way than the average farmer from Pumpkin Corners." John K. Galbraith lamented in *The Affluent Society* the ubiquity of public squalor amidst America's opulence and hinted at the persistence of poverty. Nonetheless, regardless of how unequally and inequitably the fruits of affluence were distributed, many of those Americans who did not share fully still felt themselves more comfortable in the 1950s than they had been in the 1930s and more fortunate than non-Americans. As Raskin's Bronx worker remarked: "We're a lot better off than we would be anywhere else in the world. We may not get everything we want, but at least we can choose what to do with our money. In other countries they don't even have a choice. No matter how bad things are, we're better off than they are."

The Triumph of the Suburbs

The emergence of an affluent mass consumer society saw the reassertion of a pattern of residential mobility and settlement that had been retarded by depression and war. In the 1950s, as also had happened in the 1920s, millions of citizens deserted the cities for the suburbs. Except in the South and Southwest where urban population continued to grow as a result of the annexation of adjacent land, the bulk of metropolitan population growth occurred in the suburbs. By 1960 in most northern metropolises, suburban residents outnumbered central city occupants, and as people fled the urban core, so, too, did businesses, trades, and professions. The "Miracle Mile" in Manhasset on Long Island's North Shore brought Fifth Avenue to the suburbs, just as similar suburban shopping centers elsewhere attracted downtown's most prestigious retailers to new locations with ample parking space and affluent consumers.

Suburban development stimulated a housing boom of unprecedented dimensions. As of 1960, one fourth of all the housing in the nation had been constructed in the previous decade, during which annual new-housing starts regularly exceeded the growth of new households. In the 1950s, for the first time in history, more Americans owned their homes, albeit usually with heavy mortgages, than rented dwelling space.

The reasons for this exodus to suburbia might have remained constant from the 1920s to the 1950s; after 1945, however, the opportunity to flee the city had expanded significantly. The desire for a private home with a lawn and garden in a suburban arcadia had long been an integral aspect of popular culture. The economic costs and occupational impracticality of suburban life, however, had put it beyond the reach of most Americans. All this changed in the postwar world, as federal credit and highway policies, technological innovations, and a mass consumer society reshaped metropolitan America.

In the postwar world, as automobile ownership became general, Americans had been liberated from dependence on mass public transit. The possession of a private car snapped the link that hitherto had connected the individual's home to his place of work via public transit. Through federal and state highway programs funded by fuel taxes, limited access highways were constructed that linked new suburbs and older central cities. The prospect of smooth, unimpeded traffic flow on safe, modern highways and in private cars led passengers to abandon subways, trolleys, and buses and to move from the city to the suburbs. Americans were now free to reside wherever their incomes allowed, and suburbia was also opening up to a wider range of incomes.

Federal policies enlarged the suburban housing market by providing generous mortgage loans to World War II veterans and by insuring the mortgages marketed by private lending agencies. The self-amortizing mortgage, whereby the homeowner paid back his original loan at a fixed monthly rate (comparable to rent) over a 20- to 30-year-term, became the common means to home ownership. Federal tax policy also stimulated suburban expansion, for citizens received a generous income tax deduction for the interest charges and real estate taxes paid on their homes. The availability of long-term credit and the inducement of tax advantages drew well-to-do middle-class Americans to suburbia. Working-class citizens needed a further inducement, the chance to purchase a home within their means. Here the firm of Arthur Levitt and Sons provided one solution, doing for the housing market what Ford had done for autos. Just as Ford offered a basic car in a single color at a low price, Levitt sold a standardized dwelling unit in one color—white—at a price within the reach of thousands of working-class Americans. His original "little boxes" constructed in the first Levittown in central Long Island soon had counterparts in New Jersey and Pennsylvania.

Suburbia in general and Levittown in particular occasioned a new image of American society, one consonant with the concept of a mass consumer public. Suburbia, in the words of social critic and planner Lewis Mumford, offered the prospect of

> a multitude of uniform, identifiable houses, lined up inflexibly, at uniform distances, on uniform roads, in a treeless communal waste, inhabited by people of the same class, the same income, the same age group, witnessing the same television performances, eating the same tasteless pre-fabricated foods, from the same freezers, conforming in every outward and inward respect to a common mold.

In the "little boxes made of ticky tacky," about which Pete Seeger sang, lived William F. Whyte's "organization men" who in their haste to adjust smoothly to their fellow junior executives became as undifferentiated as the houses in which they dwelled.

Critics of suburbia mounted a contradictory attack against the emerging character of national life. On the one hand, they charged suburban residents with uniformity, dullness, and unthinking accommodation to neighborhood mores. On the other hand, they indicted suburbanites, as did John Keats in *The Crack in the Picture Window*, for alcoholism, adultery (wife-swapping was said to be the favorite indoor suburban sport), and juvenile delinquency. Whatever the substance of the criticism, it seemed to miss the mark, for suburban growth proceeded unabated.

In fact most social criticism portrayed a fictional suburbia, not its reality. By the late 1950s American suburbs contained as many differences as similarities; there was no single ideal-type suburban community. Communities of upwardly mobile young executives who preferred accommodation to conflict, uniformity to individualism, such as William F. Whyte located in Chicago's environs, did exist. So, too, did communities of wealthy senior executives and rentiers, whose incomes and security enabled them to experiment with architecture and engage in eccentric behavior. At the other end of the suburban spectrum, one could find working-class developments whose residents had moved from the city but had scarcely altered their life style; they still voted Democratic, preferred baseball to ballet, and the company of relatives to that of neighbors. Even the allegedly undifferentiated, standardized world of Levittown contained, as the sociologist Herbert Gans discovered, a universe of strikingly individualized homes. Levittowners wasted no time in applying personal touches and preferences to the standardized homes and creating a society in which, according to Gans, they felt very much at home and comfortable....

Mass Culture and Its Critics

The affluence of the 1950s and 1960s laid the basis for what came to be known as "mass culture." Never before had so much music, drama, and literature been accessible to so many people as a result of fundamental changes in the presentation of entertainment and enlightenment. Television, the long-playing record, improved sound-reproduction equipment, and paperback books brought a plethora of cultural forms within reach of the great mass of Americans.

Once again, as had happened during the 1920s, Americans celebrated their exceptional prosperity. A new hedonism symbolized by oversized, overpowered cars crammed with options and adorned outside with two-tone color patterns, vinyl tops, and fins captivated consumers. Americans relished a culture of consume, enjoy, and dispose. We were, in the words of the historian David Potter, "people of plenty."

Not everyone, to be sure, joined in the American celebration. Some critics raised questions about the quality of life. Whereas once left-wing intellectuals had lamented the ubiquity of poverty and exploitation, they now bewailed a consumer society in which shoppers had become as indistinguishable from each other as the merchandise they purchased.

A few critical voices cried out in the wilderness. The industrial sociologist William F. Whyte portrayed in scholarly detail the culture of the prototypical success story of the 1950s, the rising young corporate executive, the hero of best-selling novelist Sloan Wilson's *The Man in the Gray Flannel Suit*. Whyte showed these young executives as insecure, status-driven people who lived transitorily in suburban developments housing only their own kind, and as "organization men" who molded their personalities to suit the corporate image. The radical and idiosyncratic scholar C. Wright Mills discerned a bleak future in his 1951 book, *White Collar*. He described a society of men and women who worked without autonomy or direction, who strived only for status, and who lived as dependent beings, not free citizens. In *White Collar*, one glimpsed an American mass potentially susceptible to producing fascism, as their Italian and German likes had in the 1920s and 1930s.

David Riesman, the premier critic of mass society, early on diagnosed the new American disease in *The Lonely Crowd* (1950). Americans once, he wrote, had been an inner-directed people, men and women who could distinguish right from wrong, who could chart their own directions and goals in life. Now, Americans had become an other-directed people, who lacked their own internal moral compasses. The great mass of postwar Americans lost themselves in a "lonely crowd" to which they looked for values and personal decisions. The independent democratic citizen had become a cypher in the clutches of an anonymous mass society.

Such tendencies toward mass society caused a minority of Americans to worry that the nation had lost its sense of purpose amidst a flood of consumer goods. They wondered if mass society could rise above the level of a car dealer's showroom.

But the great mass of Americans shared no such worries. Those who could consumed as never before, and those who could not aspired to do the same....

The Culture of Consensus

The hard edges of the Cold War and the tensions of McCarthyism had been softened in the United States of the late 1950s by the smiles, platitudes, and tranquility of the Eisenhower era. It was a time to consume, to achieve, and to celebrate.

Intellectuals and writers who for much of the twentieth century had been at war with a materialistic, bourgeois America now also joined the celebration. *Partisan Review*, a literary intellectual journal which had served at the end of the 1930s as a voice for non-Stalinist Marxists, in the 1950s sponsored a symposium entitled "Our Country and Our Culture." In it one contributor declared, "For the first time in the history of the modern intellectual, America is not to be conceived of as a priori the vulgarest and stupidest nation of the world."

Indeed, the America of the 1950s was a country in which private foundations generously subsidized free-lance intellectuals and many of those same intellectuals gladly served such government agencies as the Central Intelligence Agency through the Congress for Cultural Freedom. Cultural anticommunism united intellectuals, trade unionists, and such socialists as Norman Thomas in a common front with corporate executives and federal officials.

What had happened to American intellectuals and social critics was aptly caught in the substance and title of *Commentary* editor Norman Podhoretz's 1968 autobiography. The son of Jewish-immigrant parents, himself born and bred in the Brownsville, Brooklyn, ghetto, Podhoretz had made his way to Columbia University and from there to the apex of the New York literary intellectual universe. His journey through life was surely, as he titled it, a case of *Making It* in America.

Formal academic works reflected a similar influence. Where once history books stressed have-nots versus haves, farmers versus bankers, section versus section, and city versus country, in the 1950s they spoke of consensus and shared values. David Potter perceived abundance as the single most influential factor in the American experience, and he entitled his interpretive history of America *People of Plenty*. In 1956 Richard Hofstadter won the Pulitzer Prize for a study, *The Age of Reform*, which emphasized the relative absence of class conflict, the priority of status over class, and the basic American commitment to private property, the profit motive, and capitalist institutions.

Economists, too, saw social harmony and material abundance as the new reality. In their view, the Keynesian economic revolution had given them the tools to fine tune the economy in order to maintain full employment and price stability. Students no longer had to look to classical economics or its Marxist repudiation for solutions to contemporary problems.

None celebrated America's success more lustily than political scientists and sociologists. Both academic groups saw democracy, especially in America, as a completed, successful experiment. Full democratic rights were in place, all adults had basic citizenship, and all were formally legal before the law. No single, unified group ruled or dominated society to the detriment of others. Instead, a variety of equally balanced interest groups competed with each other for public favors and influence with the state, which acted as an honest broker among them. This system came to be known as pluralism to distinguish it from authoritarianism and totalitarianism.

According to the political sociologists, pluralism was not a belief system comparable to socialism, communism, or fascism. It was rather a simple practice of balancing harmoniously competing claims and rights in an affluent, democratic society, which had, as the sociologist Seymour Martin Lipset claimed in his book *Political Man*, abolished all class politics based on irreconcilable "isms." Indeed, as Daniel Bell proclaimed in a collection of essays published in 1960, the United States had seen *The End of Ideology*. One essay in the collection analyzed trade unionism as "The Capitalism of the Proletariat," and another, "Crime as an American Way of Life," dissected criminal activities as an ethnic version of "making it." The passions which had generated mass socialist parties, the Bolshevik Revolution, fascism in Italy, and nazism in Germany, Bell proclaimed as dead. The new generation, he wrote, "finds itself... within a framework of political society that has rejected ... the old apocalyptic and chiliastic visions."

John F. Kennedy's election as president symbolized the marriage of "new generation" intellectuals to the power of the American state. The new president invited Robert Frost to read a poem at the inauguration. The historian Arthur Schlesinger, Jr., served as White House scholar-in-residence; the economic historian Walt W. Rostow acted as a foreign-policy planner; the economist John Kenneth Galbraith went to India as ambassador; and the historians Samuel Eliot Morison and Henry Steele Commager sang the praises of "Camelot" on the Potomac.

Not that voices of dissent and criticism were silent in the 1950s. Not at all. The *New Republic* and *Nation* magazines maintained their long traditions of left-liberal social and political commentary. In the 1950s a group of anti-Stalinist Social Democrats founded *Dissent*, a journal which tried to keep alive in America the perspectives associated with Western European labor and social democratic parties. For the more orthodox on the left, there was always *Monthly Review*, in which Paul Baran and Paul Sweezy subjected contemporary American and world developments to the scrutiny of Marxist economics and theory. But in the 1950s and early 1960s their audiences were relatively small and their sometimes strident criticism of affluent America no more than tiny voices in the wilderness.

It was this reality that led C. Wright Mills to cry out as early as 1951 that "political expression is banalized, political theory is barren administrative detail, history is made behind men's backs."

In reality, the affluent mass culture of the 1950s that bred a quiet generation of organization men lost in the void of a "lonely crowd" was more ephemeral than it first appeared. Indeed it was shot through with unseen cracks and flaws. John Kenneth Galbraith may have bemoaned the widespread public squalor amidst the private affluence; for more than 30 million Americans even affluence was beyond reach. Rural life decayed apace, urban ghettos spread and festered, nonwhite Americans remained at best second-class citizens and at worst the hapless victims of social and economic discrimination, and most wage workers, regardless of skin color, endured as objects of external authority. Wealth and poverty, the ideal of equality versus the reality of inequality, and authority against freedom remained inextricably at war in affluent America. During the 1960s, the social tinder represented by poverty and racialism ignited in the form of urban race riots and the impassioned militancy of the New Left and the radical feminist movements.

Before then, however, the presidency of Dwight David Eisenhower made affluence and harmony appear to be the rule. Unprecedented economic growth, rising real incomes, and the new mass culture promoted by television laid the foundation for the relative quiescence of the Eisenhower era. Eisenhower's ability to dampen old political feuds, to legitimate the New Deal "revolution" as he castigated overgrown government and "creeping socialism," his success at softening the harsher aspects of the Cold War, and his taming of the worst excesses of McCarthyism reinforced the aura of complacency associated with the 1950s. Ike's mid-American, small-town origins, his wide, winning grin, and his placidity assured most Americans that all was well at home and abroad.

The Fifties: The Way We Really Were

Hula hoops, bunny hops, 3-D movies. Davy Crockett coonskins, chlorophyll toothpaste, 22 collegians stuffed into a phone booth. Edsels and tail-finned Cadillacs. Greasy duck's-ass hairdos, leather jackets, souped-up hot rods, dragging, cruising, mooning. Like crazy, man, dig? Kefauver hearings, Howdy Doody, Kukla, Fran and Ollie, Bridey Murphy, Charles Van Doren, Francis Gary Powers. *The Catcher in the Rye, The Power of Positive Thinking; Howl, On the Road.* Patti Page, Pat Boone, Vic Damone; Little Richard, Chuck Berry, Elvis Presley; The Platters, The Clovers, The Drifters; Bill Haley and the Comets, Danny and the Juniors. Mantle, Mays, Marciano. Pink shirts, gray flannels, white bucks. I LIKE IKE.

THE FABULOUS FIFTIES!—or so 1970s nostalgia would lead one to believe. A 1972 issue of *Newsweek*, complete with Marilyn Monroe cover, explored this phenomenon under the heading "Yearning for the Fifties: The Good Old Days." "It was a simple decade," *Newsweek* writers recalled, "when hip was hep, good was boss." That same year *Life* magazine reminisced about "The Nifty Fifties"— "it's been barely a dozen years since the '50s ended and yet here we are again, awash in the trappings of that sunnier time."

This wistful view of the fifties first became evident about 1971 and 1972. It quickly exploded into a national craze that still pervades the popular images of the mid-century era. Numerous examples of fifties nostalgia exist in the seventies. It was the theme of movies like *American Graffiti, The Last Picture Show, Let the Good Times Roll*, and *The Way We Were*. Television shows "Happy Days" and "Laverne and Shirley" recreated an idyllic fifties world of youth and innocence. The TV show "M*A*S*H" even managed to make people a little homesick for the Korean War. By February 1976, the fifties rock-and-roll parody *Grease* began its fifth season. It had become Broadway's longest running show by far, and this despite the fact that it never had name stars, hit songs, or a high budget.

Popular music in this post-Beatles period also saw a major revival of fifties rock. By the mid-seventies Elvis Presley, Chuck Berry, Rick Nelson, Fats Domino, Little Richard, and Bill Haley again were drawing mass audiences. Record companies were reissuing fifties hits on special golden-oldies LPs, and many radio

From Douglas T. Miller and Marion Nowak, *The Fifties: The Way We Really Were* (Doubleday, 1977). Copyright © 1977 by Douglas T. Miller. Reprinted by permission. Notes omitted.

stations were devoting several hours daily to an oldies format. The fifties musical revival spawned contemporary groups such as Sha-Na-Na, Flash Cadillac and the Continental Kids, and Vince Vance and the Valiants. These groups not only sang the oldies, they also revived the greaser look. Vince Vance even got himself arrested while attempting to steal an Edsel hubcap. Nightclubs too have cashed in on nostalgia. Across the country, clubs have featured old music and special trivia nights with questions such as "Who played James Dean's girlfriend in *Rebel Without a Cause*?"

Another sign of the fifties fad has been in clothing. Leather motorcycle jackets, picture sweaters, pedal pushers, pleated skirts, and strapless evening dresses have been hot items in the last few years. In 1973, Monique, the New York *Daily News* fashion reporter, announced: "the feeling of the fifties that will rule a large part of the fashion next fall is already apparent." A year earlier Cyrinda Foxe, a Marilyn Monroe look-alike modeling a dress from a fifties collection, claimed that "people just go crazy when I walk down the street! The fifties were so much sexier."

What does all this nostalgia mean? Periods of intense longing for an earlier era indicate that people are discontented with the present. Excessive, sentimental nostalgia generally occurs during times of perceived crisis. Such has been the case in the seventies. The rise of the fifties enthusiasm coincided with widespread disillusionment and a growing conservatism. For many people the 1950s came to symbolize a golden age of innocence and simplicity, an era supposedly unruffled by riots, racial violence, Vietnam, Watergate, assassinations. People numbed by the traumas of the sixties and seventies, desiring to forget the horrors of presidential crime, soaring prices, Cambodian bombings, Kent State, My Lai, the Manson case, the Chicago Convention, the murder of two Kennedys, Martin Luther King, and Malcolm X, yearned for a quieter time. As a Cleveland oldies-but-goodies disc jockey put it, "my audience wants to forget its problems and return to—or at least recall—those happy high-school times—the prom, no wars, no riots, no protests, the convertibles and the drive-in." Another DJ even saw the fifties music revival as a way to bridge the generation gap. "I get the feeling that through this music some of the kids are finding a backdoor way of getting together with their parents." Nostalgia, then, is a pleasant distraction. One imagines the past, and so overlooks the present.

Additionally, since we live in a society that prizes youth over age, there is a natural tendency for nostalgia on the part of the aging generation. For those who grew up in the fifties, the happy images of that decade are a positive reassurance—a reclaiming of fading youth. Then too in the mid-seventies the general realization that energy, prosperity, and growth are not limitless undoubtedly makes Americans a more retrospective, nostalgic people. We may die tomorrow, but we wish to remember it as a good world while it lasted.

But whatever the reasons for the fifties revival, the image of that decade conveyed by current nostalgia is badly distorted. The artifacts of the fifties are still with us. The facts are less clear. Looking back on that period, people today see it as a time of fun and innocence, a soda-shop world with youth as its only participants. They recall Bo Diddley and Buddy Holly, but ignore Joe McCarthy and John Foster Dulles. Nostalgia is highly selective. No one is staging a House

Un-American Activities Committee revival, or longing for the good old days of nuclear brinksmanship and the deadly H-bomb tests.

Certainly, there was some fun in the fifties—the Coasters' songs, Lenny Bruce's nightclub routines, Sid Caesar's TV antics. But in retrospect it was essentially a humorless decade, one in which comic Mort Sahl could raise national ire by cracking a single J. Edgar Hoover joke. Much of what strikes observers as quaint now—Nixon's Checkers speech, Norman Vincent Peale's homilies, or tail-finned Cadillacs—were grotesque realities at the time. It was more an era of fear than fun. The bomb, communists, spies, and Sputnik all scared Americans. And fear bred repression both of the blatant McCarthyite type and the more subtle, pervasive, and personal daily pressures to conform.

Astute social critics have found the fifties anything but the good old days. To the late Paul Goodman it was an "extraordinarily senseless and unnatural" time. American society, in his words, was "a Closed Room with a Rat Race as the center of fascination, powerfully energized by fear of being outcasts." To Michael Harrington the decade "was a moral disaster, an amusing waste of life." Norman Mailer bluntly described the fifties as "one of the worst decades in the history of man." ...

"Meet the Typical American," announced a 1954 *Reader's Digest* article. "The average American male stands five feet nine inches tall, weighs 158 pounds, prefers brunettes, baseball, beefsteak and French fried potatoes, and thinks the ability to run a home smoothly and efficiently is the most important quality in a wife." The average American woman, the article continued, "is five feet four, weighs 132, can't stand an unshaven face." This typical female preferred marriage to a career. As the average weights of men and women might suggest, many Americans were on the heavy side. The prevalent styles encouraged this. Women in pleated skirts falling a few inches below the knees were expected to be shapely in a plump sort of way. Bikinis were largely limited to the girlie magazines. But big breasts, symbols of motherhood, were definitely in vogue. For men, excess flab was easily concealed beneath baggy pleated pants, suits and shirts that did not follow body lines, boxer shorts and bathing trunks, Bermudas with knee-length socks. So in this decade of suburban prosperity, many people carried paunches as if they were symbols of success.

The goals of these "average" Americans were not radical. What George Meany said of organized labor in the mid-fifties would have applied to most groups: "We do not seek to recast American society. We do seek an ever-rising standard of living by which we mean not only more money but more leisure and a richer cultural life."

Leisure and culture—Americans took to these as never before. About one sixth of all personal income was spent on leisure pursuits. In record force people painted-by-numbers, drank, gardened, watched TV, traveled, listened to music, hunted and fished, read *Reader's Digest* condensed books. Doing-it-oneself became a national fad. Everything from home permanents to boat building had millions of amateur practitioners. In 1954 it was reported that 70 per cent of all wallpaper bought was hung by novices, while some 11 million weekend carpenters drilled, sawed, and sanded some 180 square miles of plywood with their

25 million power tools. In California, the Pan Pacific Do-It-Yourself Show even exhibited separate pieces of fur that could be assembled into a do-it-yourself mink coat. For persons of a more sedentary nature, American industry produced quantities of amusing junk—cigarette lighters that played "Smoke Gets in Your Eyes," whisky-flavored toothpaste, mink-trimmed clothespins, Venus toothpicks, Jayne Mansfield hot-water bottles.

Americans could do just about anything. Or so at least they were told in hundreds of books purportedly revealing the secrets of how to make love, how to tap one's secret source of strength, how to mix a good martini, how to get thin or fat, how to be popular, powerful, famous, rich.

But it was *Culture* that American boosters boasted of most. "Once in a great while a society explodes in a flood of new ideas, new tastes, new standards," claimed Fenton Turck in a 1952 *Reader's Digest* article. "A fresh and exciting age emerges, alive with expanding opportunities. Today's Americans are living in one of these extraordinary periods." Turck talked of a great flowering of culture. As evidence of this he cited such things as increased attendance at concerts, opera, and theater. Art museums, opera companies, and symphony orchestras all multiplied in the fifties, as did the sale of quality paperbacks and classical records.

Culture had status appeal and an increased portion of the population had both the leisure and money to dabble in it. Perhaps the apogee of the era's culture boom was reached in April 1960, when the Parke-Bernet Galleries held a huge art auction to benefit the Museum of Modern Art. The New York City auction room was linked via closed-circuit TV to similar rooms in Chicago, Dallas, and Los Angeles. The auction was a great success; an Utrillo went to a Dallas millionaire for $20,000, a Cézanne to a New York collector for $200,000. Bidding on a Hans Hartung had reached the $10,000 level before anyone noticed it was hung upside down. "We're ready for our renaissance," claimed poet Louis Untermeyer at mid-decade. "Westward the course of culture!"

In addition to celebrating American culture and living standards, many people saw the United States in the middle of the twentieth century as having a peculiar and providential mission. "We are living in one of the great watershed periods of history," asserted Democratic presidential nominee Adlai Stevenson in the 1952 campaign. This era "may well fix the pattern of civilization for many generations to come. God has set for us an awesome mission: nothing less than the leadership of the free world." The editors of *Fortune* felt the same. "There come times in the history of every people," they wrote, "when destiny knocks on their door with an iron insistence." In American history, as they read it, destiny had so knocked three times: "Once when we faced the seemingly impossible odds of British power to gain our independence: once at Fort Sumter, when we faced the bloody task of preserving our union: and it is knocking today [1951].... Our outlook is the same as it was at the time of the Revolution, and again at the time of the Civil War: the shape of things to come depends on us: our moral decision, our wisdom, our vision, and our will."

That America would succeed in fulfilling its God-given mission few doubted. The future was bright. "Our spiritual road map," predicted philosopher Morris Ernst, "will carry the direction pointers: 1976—This Way—Energy, Leisure, Full Rich Life."

Yet despite the varied and frequent versions of "America the Beautiful," doubts and anxieties were also present. The fifties was a time of tensions and insecurities. Early in the decade the usually optimistic Norman Vincent Peale spoke of an "epidemic of fear and worry" in the United States. "All doctors," he declared, "are having cases of illness which are brought on directly by fear, and aggravated by worry and a feeling of insecurity." For some Americans the greatest anxieties stemmed from the cold war. "Our nation," warned a late-fifties civil defense pamphlet, "is in a grim struggle for national survival and the preservation of freedom in the world." And of course there was the constant threat of nuclear destruction which left people, in the words of one mid-fifties observer, "in a state of suspension, waiting to see whether the Bomb is going to fall or not."

For other people, the speed of social and economic change generated un-certainties and cast doubts on old certitudes. The new prosperity and changing lifestyles, while materially benefiting many, caused insecurities. Traditional eth-nic neighborhoods were breaking down as newly prosperous people fled to suburbia. Yet this very mobility created rootlessness. Many people simply dis-covered that abundance was not enough. In any case Americans became quite self-critical and made best sellers of books telling them of their shortcomings.

In this light, some of the most important social and cultural phenom-ena of the fifties are more understandable. The overwhelming emphasis on the family gave people a sense of place and personal identity. The massive return to religion provided individuals with a sense of security; it reassured them that the traditional moral verities were still valid. Sustained and successful attacks against progressive education were another manifestation of the search for tra-ditional, absolute values. So too was the intellectual emphasis on consensus. Historians, sociologists, and other social scientists played down conflict and instead stressed the harmonious and enduring nature of American democratic values. Blacks and other nonwhites, who did not share equally in America's bounty, were assured by the white media that they never had it so good. Gen-erally speaking, neither racial nor economic classes were recognized. Critics of this celebrated consensus, whether from right or left, tended to be treated as psychological deviants suffering from such cliché ills as status anxiety or authoritarian personality. Nonconformists and rebels were subject to harsh con-formist pressures. No wonder then that bipartisan banality flourished. Both major political parties clung tenaciously to the same center, maintaining the status quo while mouthing provincial Protestant platitudes and preparing for Armageddon....

If one were attempting a precise periodization, the fifties could well be divided into three parts: 1948–53, 1954–57, 1958–60. These three periods might then be labeled "The Age of Fear," "The Era of Conservative Consensus," and "The Time of National Reassessment."

The age of fear: The post-World War II era really begins around 1948. By then the nation had essentially adjusted to a peacetime economy; depression had not recurred and people were coming to believe in the possibility of perpetual prosperity. At the same time, the cold war had become a debilitating reality. A chronology of terror began unfolding. In 1948 a communist coup was successful in Czechoslovakia and the Soviets blockaded western access to Berlin. That same year in the United States, talk of treason and communist infiltration became commonplace, especially after a former New Deal State Department official, Alger Hiss, was accused by Whittaker Chambers of having passed secrets to the Russians. The following year, 1949, the Soviets exploded their first atomic bomb and Mao Tse-tung's communist forces were victorious in China. Early in 1950 President Harry S. Truman announced plans to begin development of a hydrogen bomb (it was perfected by 1952); Senator Joseph McCarthy added the loudest voice to the already sizable outcry of anticommunist witch hunters. Nineteen fifty also saw the conviction of Alger Hiss for perjury, the arrest and trial of Ethel and Julius Rosenberg as atomic spies (they were executed in 1953), the outbreak of the Korean War, and Senator Estes Kefauver's televised criminal investigations that dramatically revealed the extent and power of organized crime.

Such events shocked and frightened people, and the last years of Truman's presidency proved a trying time—a period of suspicions, accusations, loyalty oaths, loathings, extreme chauvinistic Americanism. Republicans, attempting to regain power, were not averse to charging the Democrats with being "soft on communism," though in reality both parties were excessively anticommunist. Tensions raised by Korean fighting, supposed communist infiltration, spy trials, loyalty investigations, inflation, crime, and the bomb reached near hysteric proportions in the early fifties. Dissent was suppressed, conformity demanded. With the exception of a few legitimate espionage cases, none of which really endangered national security, *most victims of the anti-red mania were guilty of little more than holding unpopular opinions.* Not only the national government, but thousands of local communities as well felt obliged to search out and destroy suspected subversive views. Teachers, government workers, entertainers, and many others were dismissed. Textbooks were censored and libraries closed.

Yet such fear and repression, plus prosperity, also made Americans seem united under a national faith. Seeing the world in dualistic terms of good versus evil, people celebrated the United States as the bastion of freedom, democracy, and "people's capitalism." Intellectuals defended America and searched for enduring consensual values of the country's past and present. A noncritical conservative consensus emerged offering hope and reassurance during this age of fear. The widespread emphasis on religion and the family gave further solace. The combined anxiety and hope of this period is well illustrated in the title of a 1950 song—"Jesus Is God's Atomic Bomb."

The era of conservative consensus: The conservative consensus and celebration of America continued into the mid-fifties, and fortunately for national nerves the fears and anxieties began to ebb. Several factors contributed to this: the death of Stalin and the end of the Korean War in 1953; the downfall of Senator McCarthy in 1954; the Geneva summit conference with the Soviets in 1955; the lack of new spy sensations after 1950; continued prosperity; and, above all, the election of Eisenhower to the presidency.

When Ike was first elected in 1952, one Pennsylvania housewife remarked: "It's like America has come home." And so it seemed to millions. While politics traditionally means conflict, Ike appeared to people as above politics. He was the heroic general come to unite the nation in peace and prosperity as he had defended it earlier in war. Democratic presidents Roosevelt and Truman had for 20 years emphasized a politics of class strife and crisis. With Eisenhower came the appearance at least of a politics of unity and classlessness. His boyish grin and downhome homely face, his simple sincere platitudes about home, mother, and heaven, his circumlocutions when difficult issues came up, all these things endeared him to millions and made him a symbol, not of party, but of national consensus. Americans, tired of constant crises and the hysteria of the age of fear, found in Ike a symbol of hope and confidence.

And so, by the mid-fifties there came a brief happy moment—the quintessential fifties—prosperous, stable, bland, religious, moral, patriotic, conservative, domestic, buttoned-down. Huge tail-finned cars sold in record numbers, *The Power of Positive Thinking* and *The Man in the Gray Flannel Suit* sat atop the best-seller lists, and the "Spirit of Geneva" seemed to diffuse itself over the globe. Domestically no problem appeared more pressing than the specter of juvenile delinquency, though in reality young people overwhelmingly accepted the values of their elders and dedicated themselves to the bourgeois goals of security, sociability, domesticity. They went steady, married young, had lots of children, lived the conforming life of "togetherness."

Crises still existed. Poverty, racism, sexism, and militarism all threatened America. But Eisenhower and most citizens tried to ignore such ills. The sting seemed gone from the times, and a cheerful nation overwhelmingly re-elected Eisenhower in 1956. Just before that election, David Riesman and Stewart Alsop visited a new suburb south of Chicago to poll voters. They found people vague about politics but liking Ike. "Most of the people we spoke to were young housewives, often interrupted in their midday television program...." They were educated but complacent. "As one looked over that flat Illinois prairie at all the signs of prosperity," generalized Riesman, "it was not hard to see why these people were so bland politically and responded to the same qualities in Ike.... These people were not self-made men who remembered their struggles against hardship but, rather, a society-made generation who could not believe society would let them down...." These were the model fifties figures—suburbanized, bureaucratized, smug, secure.

The time of national reassessment: Eisenhower's second term quickly revealed how precarious the mid-fifties plateau of repose actually was. Even before that new term began, America's foreign relations suffered major setbacks. Just prior to the 1956 elections, fighting broke out in Egypt and Hungary. In late October, Anglo-French-Israeli forces invaded the Suez region of Egypt in an attempt to regain the canal which Egyptian leader Gamal Abdel Nasser earlier had nationalized. Third World anticolonial resentment and threatened Soviet intervention convinced the Eisenhower administration that the invasion must be ended. America pressured Britain, France, and Israel to withdraw. They did so. However, these nations' humiliation embittered them toward the United States. Western unity seemed seriously weakened. During these same tense days of late October and early November 1956, the Soviet Union, taking advantage of the dissent among the Western powers, harshly crushed an anticommunist uprising in Hungary that had broken out only a week before the Suez war. For a few weeks the world hovered on the brink of nuclear war. And while both crises were over at about the same time as Eisenhower's November re-election, they greatly intensified international tensions. Suez and Hungary clearly revealed the 1955 Geneva summit to be only a temporary thaw in the cold war.

Less than a year later, the domestic tranquillity of the mid-fifties was also disrupted. In September 1957, American racism was shockingly unveiled when the school-integration issue reached crisis proportions in Little Rock. Eisenhower, who was not sympathetic to the civil rights movement, reluctantly was forced to send troops into that city to insure compliance with the Supreme Court's 1954 desegregation decision. But the ugly scenes in front of Central High School laid bare for Americans and the world this nation's deep-seated racial tensions.

Then a month later in October 1957, the Soviets launched Sputnik I, the world's first earth-orbiting satellite. Americans were profoundly shocked. National self-confidence seemed shattered in the light of this demonstrated Soviet superiority in space science. Calls for an expanded arms race accelerated. American affluence, once the nation's pride, now was blamed for enfeebling the populace. Progressive education, which had been on the defensive throughout the decade, was quickly demolished as people demanded intellectual discipline with more emphasis on science, mathematics, and language.

Sputnik clearly struck the major blow against mid-fifties tranquillity. But other developments in the last three years of Eisenhower's presidency added to American doubts and increased the national penchant for soul-searching. At about the same time as the Soviet space successes, the American economy began to slump. By the spring of 1958, a major recession existed; unemployment had climbed to 7.7 per cent of the total labor force, the highest rate since 1941. That same year congressional committees disclosed conflict-of-interest violations by presidential appointees and charges of influence-peddling by Vice-President Nixon's former campaign manager. Even Ike's closest, most trusted and influential adviser, Sherman Adams, was dismissed for taking bribes. Adams, it was revealed, had accepted expensive gifts from Bernard Goldfine, a wealthy businessman with cases pending before the government. On tour in Latin America that year, Nixon was spat upon, jeered, and stoned. A year later, Charles Van Doren, a handsome young instructor from Columbia University, scion of an eminent literary family, revealed to investigators that the brilliance he had displayed in winning vast sums on a TV quiz show was fake. The show had been rigged. At about the same time famed disc jockey Alan Freed, the self-appointed father of rock and roll, became involved in a payola scandal. Among other revelations were exposés of widespread cheating in schools and of a group of New York cops working for a burglary ring.

By May 1960, when the Soviets announced that Francis Gary Powers had been shot down in a U-2 spy plane over Russian territory, the American propensity for critical self-evaluation had become obsessive. A presidential Commission on National Goals, which Eisenhower had established after Sputnik, produced a ponderous report, *Goals for Americans*. The Rockefeller Brothers Fund issued their own version, *Prospect for America*. *Life, Look*, the New York *Times* and other mass-circulation publications featured articles and whole issues discussing national purpose and the future role of America. Leading social and political writers began turning out books with titles like *America the Vincible* and *What Ivan Knows and Johnny Doesn't*.

Much of the national debate focused on dissatisfaction with the quality of American life. Conformity and materialism, critics argued, had dulled Americans into a complacent averageness. "Our goal has become a life of amiable sloth," complained *Time* editor Thomas Griffith in 1959. "We are in danger of becoming a vibrating and mediocre people." "Looking at some of the institutions we nourish and defend," Robert Heilbroner noted, early in 1960, "it would not be difficult to maintain that our society is an immense stamping press for the careless production of underdeveloped and malformed human beings, and that, whatever it may claim to be, it is not a society fundamentally concerned with moral issues, with serious purposes, or with human dignity." Such laments swelled into a national chorus of self-reproach as Americans once more showed themselves to be an anxious, self-conscious people.

Yet there remained an underlying note of hope in this intramural abuse. Most doubters viewed their disparagements as enterprises of self-correction. "America the Beautiful" would soar once more if only we could speed up economic growth, put a man on the moon, develop a more flexible military establishment, rekindle a spirit of national self-sacrifice, and so on and so on. John F. Kennedy's 1960 campaign epitomized the schizophrenic national mood of doubt and hope. In this, many others concurred. Walter Lippmann stated in July 1960, "We're at the end of something that is petering out and aging and about finished." He was not unhappy about this; rather he sensed that a new and better day was coming. Arthur Schlesinger, Jr., already active with Kennedy people, also lamented the late fifties but foretold "a new epoch" of "vitality," "identity," and "new values... straining for expression and for release."

The fifties, then, is not a neat single unit. The decade began with terror and affluence uniting a people under a national faith. The mid-fifties, desperately tired of crises, continued that faith in a more casual and relaxed manner. Yet by 1960, that mask of faith was drawn aside to reveal a changing face: regretful, doubting, yet also looking in hope to a rebirth.

POSTSCRIPT

Were the 1950s America's "Happy Days"?

The period after World War II was one of both affluence and anxiety for most Americans. Dubofsky and Theoharis emphasize the affluent side. The American economy not only brought prosperity to its increasing white-collar and stable blue-collar workers at home, but it also revived the economies of the Western European nations and noncommunist Asian countries. The increased wealth of the American worker in the 1950s brought about a consumption craze. Installment buying for automobiles and appliances and single-family homes purchased with long-term mortgages, financed in many cases at low interest rates by the government on behalf of the veterans, were the order of the day.

There were cracks in the economy, to be sure. Dubofsky and Theoharis point out that most nonwhites, especially blacks and Hispanics, did not share in the general prosperity. Some of "the old standbys of industrial America—railroads, coal mining, textiles, and shoe manufacturing—continued a decline that had begun in the 1920s." Labor union membership in general dropped, and individual farms fell into the hands of agribusinesses. Finally, many poor people, especially those with incomes under $4,000 per year, were spending more than they earned.

Miller and Nowak focus on the negative side mentioned in passing by Dubofsky and Theoharis. They point out that in a society "that prizes youth over age," there is a tendency on the part of the older generation to re-create through television, movies, and books a nostalgic past that never really existed. Americans, say Miller and Nowak, lost their motives and became anxious as they moved to their "little boxes" in the suburbs. They became overweight, were obsessed with their status, and were afraid that Communists might overthrow the American government.

Both readings can be criticized for giving an unbalanced assessment of the 1950s, although Dubofsky and Theoharis do mention the cracks in the affluent society. However, blacks did push their demands for school desegregation, which the Supreme Court ordered in the *Brown v. Board of Education of Topeka, Kansas,* decisions of 1954 and 1955, and demonstrated successfully for political and legal equality in the 1960s.

There is an enormous bibliography on the 1950s. A sympathetic overview is Michael W. Schuyler, "The 1950s: A Retrospective View," *Nebraska History* (Spring 1996), which summarizes the major social and economic currents of the 1950s. Also supportive of the absence of extremes is Stephen J. Whitfield's "The 1950s: The Era of No Hard Feelings," *South Atlantic Quarterly* (Summer 1975). Alan Ehrenhalt's "Learning From the Fifties," *Wilson Quarterly* (Summer 1995) is a brilliant case study of Chicago, Illinois, that points out the high price some people in the 1950s paid to enjoy the good life. The starting point for the critical cultural studies of television, film, and literature is Guile McGregor, "Domestic Blitz: A Revisionist History of the Fifties," *American Studies* (Spring 1993).

There are a number of excellent monographs on the 1950s. Eric F. Goldman, *The Crucial Decade and After: America, 1945–1960* (Random House, 1960) remains a great read and pushes the view that Americans had developed "a broad concern about the public issues of the day."

In a class by themselves are Paul A. Carter's *Another Part of the Fifties* (Columbia University Press, 1983) and journalist David Halberstam's *The Fifties* (Willard Books, 1993), a book that is eminently readable in its portraits of 1950s heroes, such as Charles Van Doren, Marlon Brando, and Bill Russell. Some of the same material is covered from a more conservative viewpoint by Jeffrey Hart, ed., *When the Going Was Good: Life in the Fifties* (Crown, 1982).

President Dwight D. Eisenhower dominated the politics of the 1950s in the same way that one of his predecessors, Franklin D. Roosevelt, did the depression decade and World War II. In the 1950s the public loved Eisenhower, but the intellectuals did not. Early assessments of him as an ineffectual old man who let his staff make the decisions can be found in Dean Alberton's collection of articles *Eisenhower as President* (Hill & Wang, 1963). Revisionists who have researched through the private papers and diaries of the president and his staff have concluded that he really was in charge. See Fred I. Greenstein, *The Hidden Hand Presidency* (Johns Hopkins University Press, 1994). Past revisionist arguments that he was in charge but fumbled anyway are assessed in the chapter entitled "Vicissitudes of Presidential Reputations: Eisenhower," in Arthur M. Schlesinger, Jr., *The Cycles of American History* (Houghton Mifflin, 1986). A major biography that is sympathetic to its subject is Stephen A. Ambrose's *Eisenhower: Soldier and President* (Simon & Schuster, 1990).

Other worthy books on a variety of 1950s topics include Thomas C. Reeves, ed., *McCarthyism*, 3rd ed. (Robert E. Krieger, 1989); Harold G. Vatter, *The U.S. Economy in the 1950s* (University of Chicago Press, 1985); James Gilbert, *A Cycle of Outrage: America's Reaction to the Juvenile Age* (Oxford University Press, 1986); and Karal A. Marling, *As Seen on TV: The Visual Culture of Everyday Life in the 1950s* (Harvard University Press, 1994).

ISSUE 5

Did Lee Harvey Oswald Kill President Kennedy by Himself?

YES: President's Commission on the Assassination of President John F. Kennedy, from *The Warren Report: Report of the President's Commission on the Assassination of President John F. Kennedy* (September 24, 1964)

NO: Michael L. Kurtz, from *Crime of the Century: The Kennedy Assassination From a Historian's Perspective,* 2d ed. (University of Tennessee Press, 1993)

ISSUE SUMMARY

YES: The President's Commission on the Assassination of President John F. Kennedy argues that Lee Harvey Oswald was the sole assassin of President Kennedy and that he was not part of any organized conspiracy, domestic or foreign.

NO: Professor of history Michael L. Kurtz argues that the Warren commission ignores evidence of Oswald's connections with organized criminals and with pro-Castro and anti-Castro supporters, as well as forensic evidence that points to multiple assassins

On November 22, 1963, at 12:30 p.m., President John F. Kennedy was shot while riding in a motorcade with his wife, Jacqueline, and Governor and Mrs. John Connally through the western end of downtown Dallas, Texas. After Secret Service agent Roy Kellerman noticed that the president was shot, he ordered the car to proceed as quickly as possible to Parkland Hospital. At one o'clock the president was pronounced dead. A stunned nation mourned for five days. Yet nearly 40 years later many questions remain unanswered. Did Lee Harvey Oswald kill President Kennedy? How many shots were fired? Was there a second or third shooter? Was Oswald set up, or was he part of a grand conspiracy? Did Jack Ruby kill Oswald on the way to his arraignment because he was distraught over the president's death or because he was ordered by the Mafia to kill Oswald?

A belief in conspiracies has been a common thread throughout American history. "The script has become familiar," according to professor of history

Robert Alan Goldberg. "Individuals and groups, acting in secret, move and shape recent American history. Driven by a lust for power and wealth, they practice deceit, subterfuge, and even assassination brazenly executed. Nothing is random or the matter of coincidence."

Popular views on American foreign policy, for example, are strewn with conspiracies. Here is a partial list: munitions makers led America into World War I; President Franklin D. Roosevelt deliberately exposed the fleet at Pearl Harbor to a Japanese attack in order to get the United States into World War II; Roosevelt sold out Eastern Europe to the Soviets at the Yalta Conference because he was pro-Russian; the Communists infiltrated the State Department and foreign service, which permitted the Communists to take over China in 1949; and the "seven sisters"—the big oil companies—deliberately curtailed the flow of oil in 1974 in order to jack up gasoline prices.

Assassinations—the overthrow of an opponent through murder—are not as common in American politics as they have been in other countries. Only four presidents have been assassinated in the United States—Abraham Lincoln, James Garfield, William McKinley and John F. Kennedy. All the assassins were identified as white males who were somewhat delusional or, at best, loners promoting a cause. The best known is John Wilkes Booth, a famous actor who killed Lincoln because the president had destroyed slavery and the Old South. Garfield was murdered by a disappointed office seeker, McKinley by an anarchist, and Kennedy supposedly by a disgruntled Marxist.

The Lincoln and Kennedy assassinations are unique because the deaths of both presidents are linked with conspiracies. Most Lincoln scholars reject the theory that Secretary of War Edward Stanton plotted with Booth to kill the president. But the Kennedy assassination has produced an enormous quantity of literature, if not all of first-rate quality, arguing that Kennedy was the victim of a conspiracy.

In the following selection, the President's Commission on the Assassination of President John F. Kennedy rejects the view that Lee Harvey Oswald was involved with any other person or group in a conspiracy to assassinate the president. The commission denies that Oswald was a foreign agent or was encouraged by any foreign government to kill the president. Nor was Oswald "an agent, employee, or informant of the FBI, CIA or any other governmental agency." In short, Oswald fit the profile of the brooding lone gunmen who killed Garfield and McKinley and set the tone for Arthur Bremmer, Squeaky Frome, and John Hinkley, who tried to kill presidential candidate George Wallace and Presidents Gerald Ford and Ronald Reagan, respectively.

In the second selection, Michael L. Kurtz questions the conclusions of the *Warren Report*. He argues that forensic evidence points to a possible second or third killer located at the grassy knoll in front of the motorcade in addition to the assassin who fired shots from the sixth floor of the Texas School Book Depository Building. Kurtz also contends that Oswald had connections with minor organized crime figures and with both pro-Castro and anti-Castro plotters, supporting the existence of a conspiracy.

President's Commission on the
Assassination of President
John F. Kennedy

 **YES**

The Warren Report

The Commission has... reached certain conclusions based on all the available evidence. No limitations have been placed on the Commission's inquiry; it has conducted its own investigation, and all Government agencies have fully discharged their responsibility to cooperate with the Commission in its investigation. These conclusions represent the reasoned judgment of all members of the Commission and are presented after an investigation which has satisfied the Commission that it: has ascertained the truth concerning the assassination of President Kennedy to the extent that a prolonged and thorough search makes this possible.

1. The shots which killed President Kennedy and wounded Governor Connally were fired from the sixth floor window at the southeast corner of the Texas School Book Depository. This determination is based upon the following:

(a) Witnesses at the scene of the assassination saw a rifle being fired from the sixth floor window of the Depository Building, and some witnesses saw a rifle in the window immediately after the shots were fired.

(b) The nearly whole bullet found on Governor Connally's stretcher at Parkland Memorial Hospital and the two bullet fragments found in the front seat of the Presidential limousine were fired from the 6.5-millimeter Mannlicher-Carcano rifle found on the sixth floor of the Depository Building to the exclusion of all other weapons.

(c) The three used cartridge cases found near the window on the sixth floor at the southeast corner of the building were fired from the same rifle which fired the above-described bullet and fragments, to the exclusion of all other weapons.

(d) The windshield in the Presidential limousine was struck by a bullet fragment on the inside surface of the glass, but was not penetrated.

(e) The nature of the bullet wounds suffered by President Kennedy and Governor Connally and the location of the car at the time of the shots establish that the bullets were fired from above and behind the

From President's Commission on the Assassination of President John F. Kennedy, *The Warren Report: Report of the President's Commission on the Assassination of President John F. Kennedy* (September 24, 1964). Washington, D.C.: U.S. Government Printing Office, 1964.

Presidential limousine, striking the President and the Governor as follows:

(1) President Kennedy was first struck by a bullet which entered at the back of his neck and exited through the lower front portion of his neck, causing a wound which would not necessarily have been lethal. The President was struck a second time by a bullet which entered the right-rear portion of his head, causing a massive and fatal wound.

(2) Governor Connally was struck by a bullet which entered on the right side of his back and traveled downward through the right side of his chest, exiting below his right nipple. This bullet then passed through his right wrist and entered his left thigh where it caused a superficial wound.

(f) There is no credible evidence that the shots were fired from the Triple Underpass, ahead of the motorcade, or from any other location.

2. The weight of the evidence indicates that there were three shots fired.

3. Although it is not necessary to any essential findings of the Commission to determine just which shot hit Governor Connally, there is very persuasive evidence from the experts to indicate that the same bullet which pierced the President's throat also caused Governor Connally's wounds. However, Governor Connally's testimony and certain other factors have given rise to some difference of opinion as to this probability but there is no question in the mind of any member of the Commission that all the shots which caused the President's and Governor Connally's wounds were fired from the sixth floor window of the Texas School Book Depository.

4. The shots which killed President Kennedy and wounded Governor Connally were fired by Lee Harvey Oswald. This conclusion is based upon the following:

(a) The Mannlicher-Carcano 6.5-millimeter Italian rifle from which the shots were fired was owned by and in the possession of Oswald.

(b) Oswald carried this rifle into the Depository Building on the morning of November 22, 1963.

(c) Oswald, at the time of the assassination, was present at the window from which the shots were fired.

(d) Shortly after the assassination, the Mannlicher-Carcano rifle belonging to Oswald was found partially hidden between some cartons on the sixth floor and the improvised paper bag in which Oswald brought the rifle to the Depository was found close by the window from which the shots were fired.

(e) Based on testimony of the experts and their analysis of films of the assassination, the Commission has concluded that a rifleman of Lee Harvey Oswald's capabilities could have fired the shots from the rifle used in the assassination within the elapsed time of the shooting. The Commission has concluded further that Oswald possessed the capability with a rifle which enabled him to commit the assassination.

(f) Oswald lied to the police after his arrest concerning important substantive matters.

(g) Oswald had attempted to kill Maj. Gen. Edwin A. Walker (Resigned, U.S. Army) on April 10, 1963, thereby demonstrating his disposition to take human life.

5. Oswald killed Dallas Police Patrolman J. D. Tippit approximately 45 minutes after the assassination. This conclusion upholds the finding that Oswald fired the shots which killed President Kennedy and wounded Governor Connally and is supported by the following:

(a) Two eyewitnesses saw the Tippit shooting and seven eyewitnesses heard the shots and saw the gunman leave the scene with revolver in hand. These nine eyewitnesses positively identified Lee Harvey Oswald as the man they saw.

(b) The cartridge cases found at the scene of the shooting were fired from the revolver in the possession of Oswald at the time of his arrest to the exclusion of all other weapons.

(c) The revolver in Oswald's possession at the time of his arrest was purchased by and belonged to Oswald.

(d) Oswald's jacket was found along the path of flight taken by the gunman as he fled from the scene of the killing.

6. Within 80 minutes of the assassination and 35 minutes of the Tippit killing Oswald resisted arrest at the theatre by attempting to shoot another Dallas police officer.

7. The Commission has reached the following conclusions concerning Oswald's interrogation and detention by the Dallas police:

(a) Except for the force required to effect his arrest, Oswald was not subjected to any physical coercion by any law enforcement officials. He was advised that he could not be compelled to give any information and that any statements made by him might be used against him in court. He was advised of his right to counsel. He was given the opportunity to obtain counsel of his own choice and was offered legal assistance by the Dallas Bar Association, which he rejected at that time.

(b) Newspaper, radio, and television reporters were allowed uninhibited access to the area through which Oswald had to pass when he was moved from his cell to the interrogation room and other sections of the building, thereby subjecting Oswald to harassment and creating chaotic conditions which were not conducive to orderly interrogation or the protection of the rights of the prisoner.

(c) The numerous statements, sometimes erroneous, made to the press by various local law enforcement officials, during this period of confusion and disorder in the police station, would have presented serious obstacles to the obtaining of a fair trial for Oswald. To the extent that the information was erroneous or misleading, it helped to create doubts, speculations, and fears in the mind of the public which might otherwise not have arisen.

8. The Commission has reached the following conclusions concerning the killing of Oswald by Jack Ruby on November 24, 1963:

(a) Ruby entered the basement of the Dallas Police Department shortly after 11:17 a.m. and killed Lee Harvey Oswald at 11:21 a.m.
(b) Although the evidence on Ruby's means of entry is not conclusive, the weight of the evidence indicates that he walked down the ramp leading from Main Street to the basement of the police department.
(c) There is no evidence to support the rumor that Ruby may have been assisted by any members of the Dallas Police Department in the killing of Oswald.
(d) The Dallas Police Department's decision to transfer Oswald to the county jail in full public view was unsound. The arrangements made by the police department on Sunday morning, only a few hours before the attempted transfer, were inadequate. Of critical importance was the fact that news media representatives and others were not excluded from the basement even after the police were notified of threats to Oswald's life. These deficiencies contributed to the death of Lee Harvey Oswald.

9. The Commission has found no evidence that either Lee Harvey Oswald or Jack Ruby was part of any conspiracy, domestic or foreign, to assassinate President Kennedy. The reasons for this conclusion are:

(a) The Commission has found no evidence that anyone assisted Oswald in planning or carrying out the assassination. In this connection it has thoroughly investigated, among other factors, the circumstances surrounding the planning of the motorcade route through Dallas, the hiring of Oswald by the Texas School Book Depository Co. on October 15, 1963, the method by which the rifle was brought into the building, the placing of cartons of books at the window, Oswald's escape from the building, and the testimony of eyewitnesses to the shooting.
(b) The Commission has found no evidence that Oswald was involved with any person or group in a conspiracy to assassinate the President, although it has thoroughly investigated, in addition to other possible leads, all facets of Oswald's associations, finances, and personal habits, particularly during the period following his return from the Soviet Union in June 1962.

(c) The Commission has found no evidence to show that Oswald was employed, persuaded, or encouraged by any foreign government to assassinate President Kennedy or that he was an agent of any foreign government, although the Commission has reviewed the circumstances surrounding Oswald's defection to the Soviet Union, his life there from October of 1959 to June of 1962 so far as it can be reconstructed, his known contacts with the Fair Play for Cuba Committee and his visits to the Cuban and Soviet Embassies in Mexico City during his trip to Mexico from September 26 to October 3, 1963, and his known contacts with the Soviet Embassy in the United States.

(d) The Commission has explored all attempts of Oswald to identify himself with various political groups, including the Communist Party, U.S.A., the Fair Play for Cuba Committee, and the Socialist Workers Party, and has been unable to find any evidence that the contacts which he initiated were related to Oswald's subsequent assassination of the President.

(e) All of the evidence before the Commission established that there was nothing to support the speculation that Oswald was an agent, employee, or informant of the FBI, the CIA, or any other governmental agency. It has thoroughly investigated Oswald's relationships prior to the assassination with all agencies of the U.S. Government. All contacts with Oswald by any of these agencies were made in the regular exercise of their different responsibilities.

(f) No direct or indirect relationship between Lee Harvey Oswald and Jack Ruby has been discovered by the Commission, nor has it been able to find any credible evidence that either knew the other, although a thorough investigation was made of the many rumors and speculations of such a relationship.

(g) The Commission has found no evidence that Jack Ruby acted with any other person in the killing of Lee Harvey Oswald.

(h) After careful investigation the Commission has found no credible evidence either that Ruby and Officer Tippit, who was killed by Oswald, knew each other or that Oswald and Tippit knew each other.

Because of the difficulty of proving negatives to a certainty the possibility of others being involved with either Oswald or Ruby cannot be established categorically, but if there is any such evidence it has been beyond the reach of all the investigative agencies and resources of the United States and has not come to the attention of this Commission.

10. In its entire investigation the Commission has found no evidence of conspiracy, subversion, or disloyalty to the U.S. Government by any Federal, State, or local official.

11. On the basis of the evidence before the Commission it concludes that Oswald acted alone. Therefore, to determine the motives for the assassination of President Kennedy, one must look to the assassin himself. Clues to Oswald's motives can be found in his family history, his education or lack of it, his acts, his writings, and the recollections of those who had close contacts with him

throughout his life. The Commission has presented with this report all of the background information bearing on motivation which it could discover. Thus, others may study Lee Oswald's life and arrive at their own conclusions as to his possible motives.

The Commission could not make any definitive determination of Oswald's motives. It has endeavored to isolate factors which contributed to his character and which might have influenced his decision to assassinate President Kennedy. These factors were:

(a) His deep-rooted resentment of all authority which was expressed in a hostility toward every society in which he lived;

(b) His inability to enter into meaningful relationships with people, and a continuous pattern of rejecting his environment in favor of new surroundings;

(c) His urge to try to find a place in history and despair at times over failures in his various undertakings;

(d) His capacity for violence as evidenced by his attempt to kill General Walker;

(e) His avowed commitment to Marxism and communism, as he understood the terms and developed his own interpretation of them; this was expressed by his antagonism toward the United States, by his defection to the Soviet Union, by his failure to be reconciled with life in the United States even after his disenchantment with the Soviet Union, and by his efforts, though frustrated, to go to Cuba.

Each of these contributed to his capacity to risk all in cruel and irresponsible actions.

12. The Commission recognizes that the varied responsibilities of the President require that he make frequent trips to all parts of the United States and abroad. Consistent with their high responsibilities Presidents can never be protected from every potential threat. The Secret Service's difficulty in meeting its protective responsibility varies with the activities and the nature of the occupant of the Office of President and his willingness to conform to plans for his safety. In appraising the performance of the Secret Service it should be understood that it has to do its work within such limitations. Nevertheless, the Commission believes that recommendations for improvements in Presidential protection are compelled by the facts disclosed in this investigation.

(a) The complexities of the Presidency have increased so rapidly in recent years that the Secret Service has not been able to develop or to secure adequate resources of personnel and facilities to fulfill its important assignment. This situation should be promptly remedied.

(b) The Commission has concluded that the criteria and procedures of the Secret Service designed to identify and protect against persons considered threats to the President, were not adequate prior to the assassination.

(1) The Protective Research Section of the Secret Service, which is responsible for its preventive work, lacked sufficient trained personnel and the mechanical and technical assistance needed to fulfill its responsibility.

(2) Prior to the assassination the Secret Service's criteria dealt with direct threats against the President. Although the Secret Service treated the direct threats against the President adequately, it failed to recognize the necessity of identifying other potential sources of danger to his security. The Secret Service did not develop adequate and specific criteria defining those persons or groups who might present a danger to the President. In effect, the Secret Service largely relied upon other Federal or State agencies to supply the information necessary for it to fulfill its preventive responsibilities, although it did ask for information about direct threats to the President.

(c) The Commission has concluded that there was insufficient liaison and coordination of information between the Secret Service and other Federal agencies necessarily concerned with Presidential protection. Although the FBI, in the normal exercise of its responsibility, had secured considerable information about Lee Harvey Oswald, it had no official responsibility, under the Secret Service criteria existing at the time of the President's trip to Dallas, to refer to the Secret Service the information it had about Oswald. The Commission has concluded, however, that the FBI took an unduly restrictive view of its role in preventive intelligence work prior to the assassination. A more carefully coordinated treatment of the Oswald case by the FBI might well have resulted in bringing Oswald's activities to the attention of the Secret Service.

(d) The Commission has concluded that some of the advance preparations in Dallas made by the Secret Service, such as the detailed security measures taken at Love Field and the Trade Mart, were thorough and well executed. In other respects, however, the Commission has concluded that the advance preparations for the President's trip were deficient.

(1) Although the Secret Service is compelled to rely to a great extent on local law enforcement officials, its procedures at the time of the Dallas trip did not call for well-defined instructions as to the respective responsibilities of the police officials and others assisting in the protection of the President.

(2) The procedures relied upon by the Secret Service for detecting the presence of an assassin located in a building along a motorcade route were inadequate. At the time of the trip to Dallas, the Secret Service as a matter of practice did not investigate, or cause to be checked, any building located along the motorcade route to be taken by the President. The responsibility for observing windows in these buildings during the motorcade was divided between local police personnel stationed on

the streets to regulate crowds and Secret Service agents riding in the motorcade. Based on its investigation the Commission has concluded that these arrangements during the trip to Dallas were clearly not sufficient.

(e) The configuration of the Presidential car and the seating arrangements of the Secret Service agents in the car did not afford the Secret Service agents the opportunity they should have had to be of immediate assistance to the President at the first sign of danger.

(f) Within these limitations, however, the Commission finds that the agents most immediately responsible for the President's safety reacted promptly at the time the shots were fired from the Texas School Book Depository Building.

Michael L. Kurtz

 **NO**

Some Questions

When a historian investigates a past event, he usually begins by asking questions about that event. Innumerable questions about the Kennedy assassination have been raised. Some of them are worth considering, for they touch upon the most critical features of the assassination mysteries. The available evidence does not permit definitive answers to all those questions, but they do deserve attention.

1. Who killed President Kennedy?

This, of course, remains the central mystery in the entire assassination saga. Unfortunately, we do not know the answer. That more than one individual fired shots at the president cannot seriously be doubted. Their identities, however, are unknown.

2. Did Lee Harvey Oswald fire any of the shots?

The evidence against Oswald is impressive: the discovery of his rifle bearing his palmprint on the sixth floor of the Book Depository building; the testimony of eyewitness Howard Brennan; Oswald's prints on the cartons and paper sack at the window; the discovery of three cartridge cases from his rifle by the window; the discovery of two bullet fragments fired from his rifle in the limousine; his departure from the building soon after the shooting.

On the other side of the coin, the evidence in Oswald's favor is equally impressive: eyewitness identification of him on the second floor of the Depository building fifteen minutes before the assassination and two minutes after it; the lack of his prints on the outside of the rifle; the questions as to whether the cartridge cases had actually been fired from the rifle during the assassination; the extremely difficult feat of marksmanship an assassin firing from the window faced; the lack of corroboration for Brennan's contradictory and confused identification.

3. How did Lee Harvey Oswald escape the scene of the assassination?

From Michael L. Kurtz, *Crime of the Century: The Kennedy Assassination From a Historian's Perspective*, 2d ed. (University of Tennessee Press, 1993). Copyright © 1982 by University of Tennessee Press. Reprinted by permission. Notes omitted.

There is no evidence to support the claim of the Warren Commission that Oswald walked out through the front door of the Book Depository building at 12:33. With the exception of the bus transfer allegedly found in Oswald's pocket, neither is there any evidence to support the commission's claim that Oswald caught a bus and a taxi. Replete with contradictions, the testimony of Mary Bledsoe and William Whaley hardly prove that the bus and taxi ride took place.

In contrast, the eyewitness and photographic evidence strongly supports Deputy Sheriff Roger Craig's testimony that he saw Oswald run from the rear of the building about fifteen minutes after the assassination and enter a station wagon driven by a dark-skinned man. Eyewitness Helen Monaghan saw Oswald in an upper floor of the building five to ten minutes after the shots. Eyewitnesses Helen Forrest and James Pennington corroborated Craig's story, for they, too, saw Oswald flee the building and enter the station wagon. While not conclusive, this evidence very solidly supports the conspiracy theory.

4. Was Oswald's gun fired at President Kennedy and Governor Connally?

The fact that two large bullet fragments, ballistically proven traceable to Oswald's rifle, were found in the front seat of the presidential limousine supplies very strong evidence that the rifle was fired once, although the possibility that the fragments were planted in the car cannot be disproven.

No other evidence proves that the rifle was fired more than once. Even if they could be proven beyond question to have been fired from Oswald's rifle, the three empty cartridge cases found on the floor by the sixth-floor window of the Depository building provide no indication that they were fired from the weapon on 22 November 1963. Obviously, the possibility exists that they were fired previously and dropped there to implicate Oswald. Even if the rifle was one of the assassination weapons, there is no proof that Oswald fired it.

5. Are the backyard photographs of Oswald holding a rifle authentic?

Because of several apparent discrepancies between the man pictured in the photographs and known pictures of the real Oswald, many Warren Commission critics questioned the authenticity of the backyard photographs. The panel of photographic experts appointed by the House Select Committee did exhaustive tests on the photographs and negatives and concluded that they were authentic.

For all of the commotion about the photographs, their relevance to the assassination is obscure. They were taken in April 1963, seven months before the assassination. Photographs of Oswald holding a weapon at that time hardly prove or disprove that he discharged that weapon seven months later.

6. How many shots were fired?

The Warren Commission based its three-shot theory primarily on the three cartridge cases, and the House Committee based its four-shot theory primarily on the Dallas police tape. The earwitnesses provide little assistance, for their accounts of the number of shots range from none to seven. Nor do the wounds on Kennedy and Connally provide an answer. Connally's wounds could have been caused by as few as one and as many as three shots, while Kennedy's may have been caused by from two to four shots. The bulk of the evidence points to four shots, three from the rear and one from the front.

7. How many shots struck President Kennedy?

On the surface, the two bullet wounds in the rear of Kennedy's body and the two in front suggest four as the answer to the question. However, the possibility that the two front holes were exit wounds for the rear holes demands close analysis. The rear holes of entrance in the head and back are positive evidence of two shots. As we have seen, the huge, gaping wound in the right front of the president's head could not simply have been an exit hole from one of Oswald's bullets. Almost certainly, it was also an entrance wound caused by a "dum-dum" or exploding bullet fired from the Grassy Knoll. The front wound in Kennedy's throat was probably *not* caused by a separate bullet. The answer, therefore, is at least three.

8. What caused the tiny bullet hole in President Kennedy's throat?

The Warren Commission's and House Committee's claim that this hole was the exit hole for the bullet that entered Kennedy's back is not supported by the evidence. The wound in the president's throat was round, clean, and encircled by a ring of bruising. Moreover, it was extremely small, smaller than the diameter of most bullets. The Forensic Pathology Panel's assertion that the buttoned collar of Kennedy's shirt caused his skin to stretch taut, thus resulting in a small exit wound, appears erroneous. Ordinarily, bullets exiting through taut skin cause large exit wounds because the bullets push tissue and matter through the skin causing it to explode outward, much as a paper bag filled with air will expand and rupture in an uneven, jagged manner as the air rushes out.

If the throat wound were an entrance wound, as some critics have charged, there would have to be some evidence of its path through the body. Since there is none, this explanation can likewise be discounted.

The most plausible explanation for the wound is that it was caused by a fragment of bone or bullet from the head shot. No hole in the neck is visible in enlargements of individual frames of the Zapruder film and in other visual records. This virtually eliminates both the exit and entrance wound theories. The most reasonable explanation, then, is that a fragment was forced through the skull cavity by the tremendous cranial pressure of the head shot and exited through the president's neck.

9. Was Bullet 399 a genuine assassination bullet?

The overwhelming weight of the evidence indicates that Bullet 399 played no role in the Kennedy assassination. The bullet's almost intact condition precludes it as the cause of Governor Connally's wounds. The removal of bullet fragments from the governor's wrist, the extensive damage to his rib and wrist, and the wounds ballistics tests results all argue persuasively against Bullet 399 as having caused any of Connally's injuries.

A bullet was discovered on a hospital stretcher that had no connection with the assassination. Darrell Tomlinson and O. P. Wright, the only two witnesses who saw the bullet on the stretcher, refused to believe that Bullet 399 was the one they saw. Nor would the two Secret Service officials who handled the stretcher bullet agree that Bullet 399 was the one they handled.

Although Bullet 399 was fired from Oswald's rifle, there is no evidence whatsoever to suggest that it caused any of the wounds on Kennedy and Connally. The Warren Commission and the House Committee assumed that Bullet 399 was the infamous single bullet, primarily because it could be traced to Oswald's rifle. Both bodies, however, failed to investigate the possibility that the bullet was planted in order to implicate Oswald.

It is possible that Bullet 399 entered Kennedy's back, penetrated only a couple of inches into the body, and did not exit—later falling out during external cardiac massage. This, in fact, was the original impression of the autopsy pathologists. If this is the case, we do not know how it wound up on a hospital stretcher that had no connection with the assassination.

Because of the incomplete information available, we still do not know when Bullet 399 was fired or how it came into the possession of the FBI as an item of ballistic evidence.

10. Did an assassin fire shots from the Grassy Knoll?

Yes. The huge, gaping hole in the right front of President Kennedy's head was almost certainly caused by an exploding bullet fired from the knoll. The rapid backward and leftward movement of Kennedy's head, as well as the backward and leftward spray of brain tissue, skull bone, and blood are very strong indicators of a shot from the right front. Assuming that it is authentic, the acoustical tape actually recorded the sound of a knoll shot.

Eye and earwitness testimony furnishes further evidence of a shot from the knoll. Almost three-quarters of the witnesses who testified heard shots from the knoll during the shooting, and three people saw a flash of light there. Five witnesses smelled gunpowder in the knoll area. A witness saw a man fleeing the knoll immediately after the shooting, and two law enforcement officials encountered phony "Secret Service" men in the parking lot behind the knoll within minutes after the gunfire.

11. If a shot came from the Grassy Knoll, why was no physical evidence of it discovered?

The answer to this question, so frequently asked by defenders of the *Warren Report,* is as simple as it is obvious. Common sense should be sufficient to explain that anyone taking the risk of killing the President of the United States would also have taken the precautions necessary to avoid leaving physical evidence of his guilt. The peculiar part of this aspect of the assassination case is not the lack of physical evidence on the knoll, but the plethora of evidence scattered all over the sixth floor of the Book Depository building. The two government investigations insist that Lee Harvey Oswald did not even bother to pick up the three cartridge cases and paper bag near the sixth-floor window but, in the process of descending the building stairs, paused for the refreshment of a Coke before departing the building.

An assassin with even the slightest concern with making a successful escape would hardly have selected the sixth floor of the Depository Building for his firing site. He would have been trapped on an upper floor of the building. His only means of escape would have been to descend six flights of stairs and then weave his way through the crowd of spectators and police to freedom.

The Grassy Knoll, on the other hand, provided a natural and ideal sniper's position. The six-foot-high wooden fence and the abundance of shrubbery concealed him from the crowd, yet gave him an undisturbed line of fire at the president. The parking lot right behind the knoll gave him quick access to a getaway vehicle.

12. Who were the "Secret Service" men encountered on the knoll right after the shots?

We know that they were not genuine Secret Service agents since all agents remained with the motorcade during its dash to Parkland Hospital. The men who flashed "Secret Service" credentials to Officer Smith and Constable Weizman, therefore, were imposters, and their identities have never been discovered. It need hardly be mentioned that the Warren Commission made no attempt to investigate this obviously serious matter.

13. Who were the three "tramps" arrested in the railroad yards behind the Grassy Knoll?

The theory that two of the three men were E. Howard Hunt and Frank Sturgis may be dismissed as unwarranted speculation. However, their true identities have never been determined. The Dallas police must have had some reason for arresting them but destroyed the records of the arrest. It is unlikely that the police would have suspended their search for the president's assassin to look for vagrants. However, as with so many other aspects of this case, the incomplete evidence does not permit an answer to the question.

14. Were two men seen together on an upper floor of the Texas School Book Depository building?

Yes. Witnesses Carolyn Walther, Richard Carr, Ruby Henderson, Arnold Rowland, and Johnny L. Powell saw two men, one of them dark-complected, together on the sixth floor. The Hughes and Bronson films of the assassination apparently show two men near the sixth-floor window.

15. Why did the Secret Service fail to respond to the initial gunshots and attempt to protect President Kennedy?

The Zapruder and other films and photographs of the assassination clearly reveal the utter lack of response by Secret Service agents Roy Kellerman and James Greer, who were in the front seat of the presidential limousine. After the first two shots, Greer actually slowed the vehicle to less than five miles an hour. Kellerman merely sat in the front seat, seemingly oblivious to the shooting. In contrast, Secret Service Agent Rufus Youngblood responded instantly to the first shot, and before the head shots were fired, had covered Vice-President Lyndon Johnson with his body.

Trained to react instantaneously, as in the attempted assassinations of President Gerald Ford by Lynette Fromme and Sara Jane Moore and of President Ronald Reagan by John Warnock Hinckley, the Secret Service agents assigned to protect President Kennedy simply neglected their duty. The reason for their neglect remains one of the more intriguing mysteries of the assassination.

16. Why have so many important witnesses in the assassination case met strange deaths?

It is true that certain key individuals in the Kennedy assassination case have met with sudden death under rather unusual circumstances. Among these are Lee Harvey Oswald, David Ferrie, and Jimmy Hoffa. Oswald was gunned down by Jack Ruby in the presence of seventy armed policemen. Ferrie died of natural causes after typing two suicide notes. Hoffa mysteriously disappeared.

The deaths of these and other persons connected with the case have prompted some assassination researchers to speculate that certain sinister forces responsible for Kennedy's murder are responsible for these deaths. However, there is no concrete evidence linking any of the deaths with the assassination itself. Unless such evidence is produced, all attempts to establish such a connection must remain in the realm of conjecture.

17. Was a paper bag found on the floor by the sixth-floor window?

The *Warren Report* claims that it was. However, the bag was not photographed in place, and Dallas law enforcement officers Luke Mooney, Roger Craig, and Gerald Hill, the first three policemen to reach the "sniper's nest," testified that they did *not* see the 38-inch-long sack, which, according to the *Report*, lay only two feet from the window. Three officers who arrived later remember seeing a bag there.

Once again, we are faced with conflicting evidence, and the reader has to decide for himself which appears more reliable.

18. Were all the eyewitnesses to the assassination interviewed?

No. Incredibly, the Dallas police did not seal off Dealey Plaza right after the assassination. They permitted traffic to proceed on Elm Street, just as if nothing had happened there. Over half the eyewitnesses simply left and went home without ever being questioned. Many inmates in the Dallas County Jail watched the motorcade from their prison cells. Even though these men literally constituted a captive audience, none was ever interrogated.

19. Did the Dallas police mishandle the physical evidence?

Yes. The paper bag allegedly found near the sixth-floor window was not photographed in place. The three empty cartridge cases were placed in an envelope, with no indication of the precise location in which each case was found. The police mishandled the book cartons around the window so badly that while only three of Oswald's prints were found on the nineteen cartons, twenty-four prints of policemen were found. The police permitted the press to enter the Depository building shortly after the discovery of the rifle. Before a thorough search of the building had taken place, the press roamed all over it, conceivably destroying evidence. The Dallas police neglected to mark and seal each item of physical evidence, e. g., the rifle, the revolver, the cartridge cases, thus separating each from the others. Instead, they put all the evidence in a large box, an action that resulted in their needlessly touching each other. The police, moreover, gave the Warren Commission three separate and contradictory versions of the transcription of the police radio calls at the time of the assassination. The Dallas police also produced four different, contradictory versions of the way in which the boxes by the window were stacked.

20. Why did the authorities change the motorcade route?

The original route, published in the *Dallas Morning-News* on 22 November 1963, called for the motorcade to proceed directly on Main Street through the triple underpass, *without* making the cumbersome turns onto Houston and Elm streets. The motorcade, however, did make the turn onto Elm, so it could take the Elm Street ramp to Stemmons Freeway. This was not the most direct route to President Kennedy's destination, the Trade Mart building. It would have been quicker and safer for the caravan to go straight on Main Street to Industrial Boulevard, where the Trade Mart is located. We do not know why the change was made.

21. Why did Officer Tippit stop Oswald?

It is difficult to accept the Warren Commission's claim that Tippit stopped Oswald because Oswald fitted the description of the suspect in the Kennedy assassination. That description was so general that it could have described thousands of individuals. Since Tippit had a view only of Oswald's rear, one wonders how he could have matched him with the suspect. Furthermore, if Tippit really suspected Oswald, he almost surely would have drawn his revolver against such a dangerous suspect. Yet, according to the commission's star eyewitness, Helen Markham, Tippit not only made no attempt to make the arrest of a lifetime, he engaged him in friendly conversation.

Neither the Warren Commission nor the House Select Committee on Assassinations tried to explore the unusual circumstances surrounding Tippit's presence in the area. Almost every other police officer in Dallas was ordered to proceed to Dealey Plaza, Parkland Hospital, or Love Field Airport. Tippit alone received instructions to remain where he was, in the residential Oak Cliffs section, where no suspicion of criminal activity had been raised. The police dispatcher also ordered Tippit to "be at large for any emergency that comes in," most unusual instructions, since the primary duty of all policemen is to "be at large" for emergencies.

22. Did Oswald murder J. D. Tippit?

The evidence against Oswald is strong. Eyewitness Helen Markham identified Oswald as the murderer. The House Select Committee located another eyewitness, Jack Tatum, who also identified Oswald as the killer. Six other witnesses saw Oswald fleeing the murder scene, and four cartridge cases fired from Oswald's revolver were found at the scene.

On the other hand, eyewitnesses Aquila Clemmons and Frank Wright saw two men kill Tippit. A witness, questioned by the FBI but never called before the Warren Commission, saw a man who did not resemble Oswald kill Tippit. The bullets removed from Tippit's body were too mutilated to permit identification of them with Oswald's revolver. Moreover, the cartridge cases and the bullets did not match, the cases coming from different manufacturers than the bullets.

Clearly, the proper channel for resolving this conflicting evidence was a court of law, but Oswald's death made this impossible. As noted, neither the commission nor the committee conducted its inquiry under the adversary process to help settle such issues. The question, therefore, must remain unanswered.

23. Why was Officer Tippit patrolling an area outside his assigned district when he was shot?

Only J. D. Tippit could answer that question, and he is dead. At 12:45 P.M., fifteen minutes after the assassination, the Dallas police dispatcher ordered Tippit to proceed to the "central Oak Cliffs area," which is outside his regularly assigned district. The original Dallas police version of the police tape contains no reference to Tippit. The second version, transcribed five months later, contains the order to Tippit. J. D. Tippit was the only policeman in Dallas who was given instructions to patrol a quiet residential area, where no crime had been committed. Every available police officer was ordered to proceed immediately to Dealey Plaza or to Parkland Hospital. The last known location of Officer Tippit was Lancaster and Eighth, about eight blocks from the murder scene. Tippit reported this location at 12:54, twenty-one minutes before he was shot. The Warren Commission would have us believe that Tippit was so careful and methodical in his duties that it took him twenty-one minutes to travel eight blocks. This is a speed of about two miles an hour, slower than a normal walking pace. Obviously, this is yet another matter requiring further investigation.

24. Why did it take Oswald thirty minutes to run from the scene of the Tippit murder to the Texas theater only five blocks away?

Officer Tippit was killed at 1:15 P.M. and Oswald ran into the Texas Theater at 1:45. Clearly, it did not take him a half-hour to run five blocks. Neither the Warren Commission nor the House Select Committee produced any evidence to indicate what Oswald did during that time span.

25. How many shots were fired at Officer Tippit?

The official Tippit autopsy report states that four bullets were recovered from Tippit's body. Four bullets now form part of the physical evidence in the case. Yet, as with so many other parts of the Kennedy assassination, some of the circumstances underlying the discovery of this evidence appear strange and indeed mysterious.

The original Dallas police inventory of evidence turned over to the FBI lists "bullet [*sic*] recovered from body of Officer J. D. Tippit." The other three bullets did not turn up until four months after the murder, when they were discovered in a file cabinet at Dallas police headquarters (the same cabinet that contained the tape?).

On 11 December 1963, Secret Service agents Edward Moore and Forrest Sorrels reported their conversation with Dallas medical examiner Dr. Earl Rose: "only three of the four bullets penetrated into Tippit's body. The fourth apparently hit a button on the officer's coat. . . . When the examination [autopsy] was performed, three bullets were removed from the body and turned over to the Police Crime Lab." The police homicide report confirms this. According to that report, Tippit was shot "once in the right temple, once in the right side of the chest, and once in center of stomach." The actual autopsy, however, states that three bullets struck Tippit in the chest and one struck him in the head. A letter from J. Edgar Hoover to J. Lee Rankin notifies the commission that the FBI did not receive the "three [*sic*] bullets until late March 1964, four months after the assassination. Yet Secret Service agents Moore and Sorrels reported on 11 December, only three weeks after the murder, that the bullets "are now in the possession of the FBI."

The obvious contradictions in the evidence leave unanswered the questions of whether three or four shots struck Tippit and what happened to the bullets. Considering the fact that three of the bullets were Remingtons and one was a Winchester, while two of the cartridge cases found at the Tippit murder scene were Remingtons and two were Winchesters, it is not unreasonable to conclude that the Tippit murder requires clarification.

26. Why did Jack Ruby kill Lee Harvey Oswald?

The Warren Commission's claim that Ruby wanted to spare Mrs. Kennedy the personal ordeal of a trial seems flimsy. When Earl Warren interviewed Ruby in the Dallas jail, Ruby pleaded with the chief justice to let him testify in

Washington, where he would tell the real story behind the whole assassination controversy. Inexplicably, Warren denied Ruby's request.

While it is possible to imagine numerous motives for Ruby's act, there is no reliable, independent evidence to substantiate such speculation. Whatever Ruby's reasons, they remain unknown.

27. How did Ruby gain access to the heavily guarded basement of Dallas police headquarters?

The House Select Committee on Assassinations uncovered evidence that indicated the likelihood that a Dallas police officer assisted Ruby in entering the basement.

The fact that Ruby managed to walk past seventy armed law enforcement officials and gun down Oswald obviously raises suspicions of a conspiracy in this murder. The available evidence, however, does not permit a conclusive determination either of the nature or extent of that conspiracy.

28. Did Jack Ruby and Lee Harvey Oswald know each other?

Over a dozen reliable witnesses claim to have seen the two men together during the four months prior to the assassination. Six separate eyewitnesses saw Ruby and Oswald in Ruby's Carousel Club in November 1963. Those witnesses included three employees and three patrons of the club. The author has interviewed a journalist who saw a photograph of Ruby and Oswald together.

The other witnesses included a lady who saw Ruby and Oswald together in New Orleans in the summer of 1963. While the FBI dismissed her account, Ruby, in fact, did visit New Orleans during that period.

Again, the evidence is not conclusive, but it does strongly suggest that Ruby and Oswald may very well have known each other before the assassination.

29. Did the Dallas police violate Lee Harvey Oswald's legal rights while they held him in custody?

Despite the Warren Commission's disclaimer, the answer is a decided affirmative. At his midnight press conference on 22 November, Oswald told newsmen that he was "not allowed legal representation" and requested "someone to come forward to give me legal assistance." The Dallas police chief, Jesse Curry, admitted that "we were violating every principle of interrogation." . . . [T]he police lineups appeared rigged to make identification of Oswald almost certain. He was the only suspect with a bruised and cut face and with disheveled clothing. He was dressed differently from the other men in the lineup. He was put in a lineup with three teenagers. At least one witness was persuaded by the police to sign an affidavit identifying Oswald *before* he viewed the lineup. The search warrant authorizing the search of Oswald's room did not specify the objects being sought by the police.

30. Did Oswald drive an automobile?

The Warren Commission claims that he did not, but there is substantial evidence to the contrary. Albert Bogard, a Dallas new car salesman, swore that he took Oswald for a test drive of a car less than two weeks before the assassination. Edith Whitworth and Gertrude Hunter saw Oswald driving a blue 1957 Ford about two weeks before the assassination. One of the lodgers in Oswald's rooming house at 1026 North Beckley Avenue let him drive his blue Ford sedan. Two service station operators recalled Oswald's driving a car and having it serviced. Journalists attempting to trace Oswald's route from Laredo, Mexico, to Dallas interviewed numerous service station operators, cafe owners, and other proprietors who recalled Oswald's stopping at their establishments.

31. With whom did Oswald associate during his stay in New Orleans in the spring and summer of 1963?

Although the Warren Commission concluded that Oswald's Marxist, pro-Castro views led him to various activities promoting those views, it failed to demonstrate that Oswald contacted even one individual of similar views during his New Orleans stay. The evidence, in fact, demonstrated that *all* of Oswald's known associations were with individuals of right-wing persuasion. The author's extensive research into this topic has produced much new evidence of Lee Harvey Oswald's right-wing activities in New Orleans.

On numerous occasions, Oswald associated with Guy Bannister, an ex-FBI official and a private investigator. Militantly anti-Castro and rabidly segregationist, Bannister was well known in the New Orleans area for his extremist views. Twice, Bannister and Oswald visited the campus of Louisiana State University in New Orleans and engaged students in heated discussions of federal racial policies. During these discussions, Oswald vehemently attacked the civil rights policies of the Kennedy administration.

Another right-wing extremist with whom Oswald associated was David William Ferrie. A defrocked Eastern Orthodox priest, an expert pilot, a research chemist, and a sexual deviate, Ferrie also actively participated in anti-Castro organizations and smuggled supplies to anti-Castro rebels in Cuba. Once, Ferrie and Oswald attended a party, where they discussed the desirability of a *coup d'état* against the Kennedy administration. On another occasion, Oswald and Ferrie were seen at Ponchartrain Beach, a New Orleans amusement park. Oswald and Ferrie also frequented the Napoleon House bar, a popular hangout for college students. There they often debated Kennedy's foreign policy with the students. Accompanied by two "Latins," Ferrie and Oswald were observed in Baton Rouge, where they openly denounced Kennedy's foreign and domestic policies.

One of the most significant eyewitness observations was of Ferrie, Oswald, and numerous Cubans, all dressed in military fatigues and carrying automatic rifles, conducting what appeared to be a "military training maneuver." This event took place near Bedico Creek, a swampy inland body of water near Lake Ponchartrain, about fifty miles north of New Orleans. This occurred in early

September 1963, two months after the final government raid on anti-Castro guerrilla camps in the United States.

The night of 22 November, David Ferrie drove 250 miles from New Orleans to Galveston, Texas, in a blinding thunderstorm. At Galveston, Ferrie received and made several long-distance telephone calls. The following day, he drove to Houston, then Alexandria, Louisiana, and then to Hammond, where he spent the night in the dormitory room of a friend who was a student at a local college. Then he returned to New Orleans, where he underwent questioning by the FBI. Shortly after the assassination, Ferrie deposited over seven thousand dollars in his bank account, even though he did not have a steady job.

Obviously, these New Orleans activities of Oswald's warrant further investigation. The House Select Committee on Assassinations appreciated the significance of Oswald's New Orleans activities but failed to investigate them properly. Instead, it devoted much attention to such irrelevant matters as Ferrie's tenuous link to Carlos Marcello and the bookmaking activities of Oswald's uncle.

What relationship these matters have to the assassination of President Kennedy is unclear. As we have seen, the evidence does not permit a definitive statement about Oswald's role in the Kennedy murder. As far as David Ferrie and Guy Bannister are concerned, there is no evidence at all to link them to the crime. The New Orleans evidence, however, does demonstrate that Oswald's public image as a pro-Castro Marxist was a facade masking the anti-Castro and anti-Communist agitator beneath.

32. How significant was the Garrison investigation?

In February 1967, New Orleans District Attorney Jim Garrison announced that his office was investigating the assassination. This sensational news aroused a storm of controversy and publicity. The Garrison investigation resulted in the arrest and trial of New Orleans businessman Clay Shaw for conspiracy to murder John F. Kennedy. The 1969 trial resulted in Shaw's acquittal.

During the two-year investigation, Garrison made many irresponsible statements about the FBI, CIA, and other government agencies and about assassins firing from manholes and escaping through underground sewers. However, he did reveal the large extent to which the federal government had suppressed evidence about the assassination, demonstrated the relationship between Oswald and Bannister and Ferrie, and brought out much new information about the Zapruder film, the Kennedy autopsy, and ballistics evidence.

33. Did Oswald work for an intelligence agency of the United States government?

No. The evidence clearly shows that Oswald had no direct relationship with United States intelligence. After his defection to the Soviet Union, both the FBI and CIA maintained dossiers on Oswald, but these files contain no information pertinent to the assassination. Those writers who have suggested that

Oswald's sojourn in the U.S.S.R., his trip to Mexico City, or his contacts with FBI Agent James Hosty proved significant to the assassination have failed to substantiate their theories.

34. Was an imposter buried in Lee Harvey Oswald's grave?

Differences of up to three inches in reports of Oswald's height, plus minor variations in the reports of certain physical marks on Oswald's body (wrist scars, mastoidectomy scar, etc.) have led some critics, most notably Michael Eddowes, a British investigator, to call for a disinterrment of Oswald's coffin and an exhumation autopsy on the body in it.

Eddowes's theory that while he was in the Soviet Union, Oswald was eliminated by the KGB and his place taken by a trained imposter is far-fetched. Oswald lived with his wife for over a year after they left the U.S.S.R. Oswald's mother, brother, and other relatives all saw him and had close contact with him and did not notice anything unusual about him.

35. Is vital evidence in the Kennedy assassination missing from the National Archives collection of assassination materials?

Numerous items of critical significance are indeed missing: the president's brain, tissue slides of his wounds, several autopsy photographs and X-rays, some bullet fragments originally tested by the FBI, and miscellaneous documents and other materials. The lack of these materials obviously presents a formidable obstacle to any attempt to answer some of the key questions about the assassination. Why they are missing is not known.

36. Why did the FBI and CIA withhold information from the Warren Commission?

As far as the FBI is concerned, it seems that the main reason was J. Edgar Hoover's precipitous decision that there was no assassination conspiracy and his almost paranoid desire not to tarnish the bureau's public image. Hoover tried to dissuade Lyndon Johnson from appointing a presidential commission to investigate the assassination, but Johnson bowed to public pressure. One of Hoover's top assistants, William Sullivan, stated that Hoover regarded the Warren Commission as an adversary and even periodically leaked information to the press to force the commission to conduct its inquiry along the lines of the already completed FBI report. The acting attorney general Nicholas deB. Katzenbach, testified that if the FBI had come across evidence of a conspiracy, "what would have happened to that information, God only knows." The 125,000 pages of FBI assassination files, many of them marked by Hoover himself, contain much information that the bureau never shared with the commission.

The CIA, too, failed to share all of its information with the Warren Commission. But its refusal to do so stemmed from the nature of the agency itself. The purpose of the CIA is to gather intelligence, a function that requires secrecy.

The agency investigated the assassination only as it related to foreign activities. It appointed Richard Helms as its liaison with the Warren Commission, and Helms gave the commission only information that did not compromise the CIA's extensive network of agents. It is true that the CIA did not inform the Warren Commission about various matters, but in almost all instances, the information withheld had only an indirect connection with the assassination.

37. In his book Best Evidence, *David Lifton asserted that the body of President Kennedy was altered to conceal evidence of shots from the front. How valid is Lifton's theory?*

In his book, Lifton asserted that an unidentified group of conspirators planned, executed, and concealed the assassination of President Kennedy. Even though the Zapruder film and certain other evidence indicated gunfire from the Grassy Knoll, the "best evidence" in the case and the evidence that would be given the most credence in a court of law was the official autopsy. Therefore, the conspirators altered the body of President Kennedy to make it appear he had been shot from behind.

When the president was rushed into the emergency room at Parkland Hospital, the doctors noticed a tiny hole in the throat. They all believed that this hole was clearly a wound of entrance, as the remarks to the press by the Parkland physicians indicated. Furthermore, the Dallas doctors stated, both in their written medical reports and in their testimony before the Warren Commission, that there was a very large wound of exit in the rear of the president's head. These observations were substantiated by those of laboratory and X-ray technicians, photographers, and physicians at Bethesda Naval Hospital who saw the body before the autopsy began.

To assure the success of their scheme, the plotters had to change the nature of the wounds on the body in order to make it appear that it contained only evidence of rear-entry wounds. The conspirators, therefore, carried out an elaborate plot of what Lifton calls "deception and disguise," a fantastic plot that entailed altering the body of John Kennedy.

From interviews with witnesses at Bethesda and from other sources, Lifton concludes that the body was removed from its bronze coffin while the presidential party was aboard Air Force One on the trip from Dallas to Washington. As the television cameras focused on the removal of the bronze coffin from the plane, the conspirators put the body in a helicopter and flew it to Bethesda. There they arranged various means, including two ambulances, to deceive the official party awaiting the arrival of the bronze coffin.

As this deception took place, his body was altered to give it the appearance of having been struck from the rear. The conspirators removed the brain and "reconstructed" the skull, eradicating all signs of the massive exit hole in the back of the head. They also placed small entrance holes in the upper back and in the rear of the head. When the actual autopsy was performed, the pathologists inspected a body that gave the appearance of being hit twice from behind. Lifton quotes the Sibert-O'Neill FBI autopsy report that "surgery of the head area" had been performed prior to the start of the postmortem. This, Lifton believes, was the alteration done on the original head wounds.

David Lifton's theory is not only novel, but it presents a startling account of an assassination plot conceived, executed, and disguised by the executive branch of the federal government. David Lifton has a reputation as one of the most thorough assassination researchers. His work is well documented and displays a careful attention to detail. For these reasons, and because of the sensational nature of Lifton's theory, an analysis of his main points will now be presented.

The documentary record substantiates Lifton's contention that medical descriptions of the Kennedy head wounds vary widely. Most of the Dallas doctors did testify that they saw a large exit wound in the back of the head, whereas the autopsy describes a small entrance wound in the back of the head and a large exit wound to the front. Lifton, however, ignored the fact that not all the Dallas doctors saw a large wound in the rear of the head. Dr. Charles Baxter stated that he saw a wound in the "temporal parietal plate of bone" in the side of the head. Dr. Adolph Giesecke noted the absence of skull from the top of the head to the ear, and from the browline to the back of the head. Dr. Kenneth Salyer observed a wound of the right temporal region on the side of the head. And Dr. Marion Jenkins mentioned "a great laceration of the right side of the head." Lifton quoted only those Dallas physicians who saw the large hole in the rear of the head and thus presented a misleading impression to his readers.

More significantly, Lifton ignored a vital aspect of the evidence. Throughout the emergency room treatment, President Kennedy lay on his back, with the back of his head resting on the mattress of the emergency cart. As Dr. Malcolm Perry told the Warren Commission, "He was lying supine [on his back] on the emergency cart." At no time was he turned over. If there was one point on which all the Dallas doctors agreed, it was that they never saw the president's back, including the rear of his head.

During the twenty minutes in which they worked to save President Kennedy's life, the Parkland physicians did not even attempt to treat the head wound. Their efforts at resuscitation centered on the tracheotomy and on closed chest massage. Busy with these emergency measures, the doctors did not examine the head wound closely. During the time in which they were in the emergency room, the Dallas doctors glanced at the head wound and saw blood and brain tissue oozing out and two large flaps of scalp covering much of the hair and exposing the cranial cavity. They did not see the head after it was cleaned, and they took no measurements to record the exact nature of the wounds. As one of the Dallas physicians remarked to the author, the reason he and his colleagues mentioned a large wound in the rear of the head is that from their brief glances at the head, it looked like a rear wound. However, after seeing the Zapruder film and the autopsy drawings, he was perfectly satisfied that the would was indeed in the right front of the head.

Another omission in Lifton's theory is his belief that the conspirators inflicted wounds on the body over six hours after the assassination. Although he claims to have read widely in textbooks on forensic pathology, Lifton apparently did not notice one of the most elementary principles of autopsy procedure: damage inflicted on a body after death is easily distinguishable from that inflicted on a living body. If the conspirators had reconstructed Kennedy's skull and produced two entrance wounds on the body, the Bethesda pathologists would have recognized the postmortem changes. By the time of the autopsy, the body was in the beginning stages of rigor mortis and exhibited signs of livor mortis and algor mortis (three of the stages a corpse undergoes after death). Any damage inflicted on that body would have displayed definite pathological signs of alteration, and the entrance wounds in the back and the head would not have shown microscopic indications of "coagulation necrosis," since the blood had long since ceased circulating.

Lifton claims that John Kennedy was shot in the front of the head by gunfire from the Grassy Knoll, thus causing the large exit wound in the rear observed by the Dallas doctors. Yet he fails to account for the fact that no one at Dallas or Bethesda saw an entrance wound in the front of the head. If the Dallas doctors were so observant as to see an exit wound in the rear of the head while the president lay face-up on the cart, why did they not see the entrance wound also?

Instead of the contradictory recollections of the Dallas doctors, we possess the objective evidence of the Zapruder film. Frames Z314–335 clearly depict the very large wound on the right front side of John Kennedy's head. The film also shows that the rear of the head remains intact throughout the assassination. Lifton argues that the CIA must have "doctored" the film to produce a false image. In addition to producing no evidence whatsoever to support this speculation, Lifton ignored the fact that the film graphically shows the violent backward movement of the head, hardly evidence of a rear-entering shot.

The autopsy X-rays and photographs depict the entrance holes in the back and in the rear of the head and also the huge, gaping wound in the right front of the head. According to Lifton, the photographs and X-rays were taken after the reconstruction of the body, so they would corroborate the autopsy findings. As we have seen, the photographs and X-rays do not provide irrefutable evidence of wounds inflicted only from the rear. The very large wound on the right side of the head depicted in these visual records could have been made by the explosion of a "dum-dum" bullet fired from the right front. In addition, through dental identification and precise comparisons of certain anatomical features, experts hired by the House Select Committee on Assassinations positively identified the X-rays and photographs as authentic and the body depicted in them as that of John F. Kennedy. If the skull were "reconstructed," as Lifton claims, the X-rays would not contain the anatomical features essential to proper authentication.

In his work, Lifton quotes extensively from the FBI agents present at the autopsy and from laboratory technicians. FBI Agents Sibert and O'Neill, for example, stated that "surgery of the head area" had been performed prior to the autopsy. To Lifton, this is proof that the conspirators had reconstructed the skull. In fact, the Sibert-O'Neill report was written by the agents the day after the autopsy. It is neither a verbatim record of the proceedings nor a detailed medical recounting of the events that took place. The laboratory technicians and other witnesses to the autopsy provided widely divergent accounts of the wounds. By quoting only those that supported his thesis, Lifton provided a very misleading account to his readers, as he did with the Dallas doctors.

Another of Lifton's arguments is that during the autopsy, Dr. Humes removed the brain from the cranial vault without recourse to the surgical procedures normally required. To Lifton, this was evidence that the brain had been removed prior to the autopsy by the conspirators in order to alter it. This argument has little basis. The autopsy protocol, as well as the testimony of the pathologists, attest to the enormous damage done to the head. The skull was shattered. Almost three-quarters of the right half of the brain had been blown out of the head. When Dr. Humes began his examination of the head, pieces of the skull came apart in his hands, vivid testimony to the explosive impact of the bullet. All of the damage to the head that Lifton details as unusual can be explained as the result of an exploding bullet literally blowing the head apart.

Lifton believes that the autopsy photographs showing the large, gaping wound in the right front of President Kennedy's head were deliberately altered to make the wound appear as an exit wound. That it was an exit wound is precisely what the autopsy pathologists believed and what all subsequent medical inspections of the photographs concluded. However, the wound is not necessarily one of exit. An exploding bullet fired from the right front could have caused that wound. In the first volume of the House Select Committee on Assassinations hearings on the murder of Martin Luther King, drawings made from autopsy photographs of Dr. King clearly show a huge hole almost four inches long and two inches wide on the lower right side of the face, just above the jaw. According to the committee's Forensic Pathology Panel, this huge wound in Dr. King's face was an *entrance* wound caused by the explosion of a soft-nosed 30.06 bullet. Dr. Michael Baden, the chairman of the panel, told the committee that "the injuries seen on Dr. King with the bursting explosive-like injury to the face" were "entirely consistent" with an entrance wound of an exploding bullet.

David Lifton's theory, as sensational as it may appear, simply does not stand verified by the objective evidence. As detailed here, the autopsy left much room for criticism, and the fact that certain items of the medical evidence are missing obviously raises suspicions of a possible cover-up. The questions surrounding the death of President Kennedy are numerous, many of them still unanswered. Those posed by David Lifton, however, do not fall into this category.

POSTSCRIPT

Did Lee Harvey Oswald Kill President Kennedy by Himself?

Since the Kennedy assassination, more than 3,000 books, articles, fictional films, documentaries, plays, television programs, and newsletters on the subject have been released. One book that summarizes and critically analyzes the literature, provides an interpretation of the assassination, and contains an extensive bibliographical listing is Robert Alan Goldberg, *Enemies Within: The Culture of Conspiracy in Modern America* (Yale University Press, 2001). Also see Bob Callahan, *Who Shot JFK? A Guide to the Major Conspiracy Theories* (Simon & Schuster, 1993), which features pointed and humorous illustrations by Mark Zingarelli in addition to a lively text that provides welcome relief from the more sober accounts.

Could a single bullet have wounded Governor Connally *and* killed Kennedy? Dennis Brio supports the single-bullet theory in a series of articles in the May and October 1992 issues of the *Journal of the American Medical Association*. Critics' dissenting letters appear in the October 1992 issue, and John Lattimer responds in the March 1993 issue. The single-bullet theory is also supported by Gerald Posner in chapter 14 of *Case Closed: Lee Harvey Oswald and the Assassination of JFK* (Random House, 1993). Posner's argument relies upon computer enhancements of the Zapruder film (the only one to record the entire shooting) by Michael West and the Failure Analysis Associates, a firm specializing in computer reconstruction for lawsuits. But John Nichols, a forensic pathologist, and Charles Wilber, a forensic scientist, have conducted studies that indicate that major bullet no. 399 could not have inflicted all the damage to Connally. See their presentations in the video *Reasonable Doubt: The Single Bullet Theory* (White Star Productions, 1988).

Conspiracy theories about the Kennedy assassination abound. Organized crime might have played a part for a number of reasons. For example, Attorney General Robert Kennedy, the president's brother, had been investigating alleged racketeering in Jimmy Hoffa's Teamster's Union, which he began doing for a Senate committee in the 1950s. Also, John H. Davis, in *The Kennedy Contract: The Mafia Plot to Assassinate the President* (Harper Paperbacks, 1993) and *Mafia Kingfish: Carlos Marcello and the Assassination of John F. Kennedy* (McGraw-Hill, 1989), contends that New Orleans Mafia chieftain Carlos Marcello ordered a hit on the president because Kennedy had reneged on his promise to go easy on organized crime after the Mob delivered the deciding vote from Illinois from the west side of Chicago in the close presidential election of 1960.

On the Internet . . .

Civil Rights: A Status Report

Kevin Hollaway is the author of this detailed history of black civil rights, from the discovery of the New World to the present. In his own words, "It is not my intent to complain about the present state of Black America, nor to provide excuses. My intent is [to] provide an unbiased picture of Black American history; something that is often missing from many classrooms in America."

http://www.ghgcorp.com/hollaway/civil.htm

National Committee to Preserve Social Security and Medicare

The National Committee to Preserve Social Security and Medicare was founded in 1982 to serve as an advocate for the landmark federal programs Social Security and Medicare and for all Americans who seek a healthy, productive, and secure retirement.

http://www.ncpssm.org

Vietnam: Yesterday and Today

The purpose of this Web site, which has been created primarily for students and teachers, is to point those who are interested in studying and teaching about the Vietnam War to materials that will be useful.

http://servercc.oakton.edu/~wittman/

Vietnam War.net

This site offers a variety of educational, entertainment, and research material relevant to the study of the Vietnam War.

http://www.vietnamwar.net

National Women's History Project

The National Women's History Project is a nonprofit corporation, founded in Sonoma County, California, in 1980. The organization provides numerous links to sites on women's history under such categories as The Women's Rights Movement, Politics, African-American Women, and Peace and War.

http://www.nwhp.org

The American Presidency: Richard M. Nixon Biography

This Grolier Online page provides a detailed biography of Richard Nixon, including his early political career, the "Nixon fund," his foreign and domestic affairs policies, and his resignation from the presidency. Also included are links to Grolier Online pages on related topics, such as the Watergate affair and Spiro Agnew, and suggested sources for further reading.

http://www.grolier.com/presidents/ea/bios/37pnixo.html

PART 2

From Liberation Through Watergate:
1963–1974

*T*he 1960s have become stereotyped like the roaring twenties. However, there is much truth in the stereotype. John F. Kennedy, the youngest
person ever elected president, promised to get the country moving again.
He did, but in some ways he did not intend. Poverty was to be attacked by
educating and retraining those groups that were left behind by the New
Deal, middle-class reforms. At the same time, African Americans and
women rose up and demanded that they be granted their civil, political,
and economic rights as first-class citizens.

Foreign affairs ended the decade on a sour note. "Containment"
went berserk in Vietnam. Lyndon Johnson escalated American participation to 550,000 troops by 1968 and then tried to negotiate a peace
settlement. His successor, Richard M. Nixon, tried to withdraw American troops and at the same time not lose Vietnam to the Communists.
In the long term Nixon failed on two counts: Vietnam was captured by
the Communists in 1975; but Nixon was long gone by then—pressured to
resign because of the Watergate fiasco.

- Was Martin Luther King, Jr.'s Leadership Essential to the Success
  of the Civil Rights Revolution?

- Did the Great Society Fail?

- Was the Americanization of the War in Vietnam Inevitable?

- Has the Women's Liberation Movement Been Harmful to
  American Women?

- Will History Forgive Richard Nixon?

ISSUE 6

Was Martin Luther King, Jr.'s Leadership Essential to the Success of the Civil Rights Revolution?

YES: Adam Fairclough, from "Martin Luther King, Jr. and the Quest for Nonviolent Social Change," *Phylon* (Spring 1986)

NO: Clayborne Carson, from "Martin Luther King, Jr.: Charismatic Leadership in a Mass Struggle," *Journal of American History* (September 1987)

ISSUE SUMMARY

YES: Professor of history Adam Fairclough argues that Martin Luther King, Jr., was a pragmatic reformer who organized nonviolent direct action protests in strategically targeted local communities, which provoked violence from his opponents, gaining publicity and sympathy for the civil rights movement.

NO: Professor of history Clayborne Carson concludes that the civil rights struggle would have followed a similar course of development even if King had never lived because its successes depended upon mass activism, not the actions of a single leader.

T he modern civil rights movement goes back to the Reconstruction era (1865–1877), when blacks were granted freedom, citizenship, and voting rights. By the end of the nineteenth century, however, black Americans had been legally segregated in public facilities, which included schools, parks, swimming pools, and municipal and state offices. At the same time the southern states had disenfranchised blacks or intimidated them into not voting. The black middle class, led by Booker T. Washington, had accepted legal segregation as a trade-off for limited economic opportunities in their segregated communities.

The black community entered the twentieth century determined to regain its rights as American citizens. During the opening years of the twentieth century, a group of northern black professionals, led by its most prominent intellectual W. E. B Du Bois, joined with white progressives and formed the National Association for the Advancement of Colored People (NAACP). The main objective of the NAACP was to eradicate the accomodationist policies of Booker T. Washington and the acceptance of segregation through the "separate but equal principle," which the Supreme Court had written into the legal system. This was accomplished in 1896 when the Court ruled in *Plessy v. Ferguson* that segregating blacks and whites into separate railroad cars was permissible provided both facilities were equal.

Realizing that no civil rights legislation could pass through the committee chaired in Congress by southern white conservatives, the NAACP decided to attack the separate but equal principle established in the *Plessy* case through the courts. The concept of separate but equal was challenged in a series of court cases in which it was argued that segregation violated the equal protection clause of the Fourteenth Amendment.

The legal system moves very slowly, but protest movements often speed up changes. As early as the 1930s blacks picketed stores in Harlem when they were refused service. In 1947 there were protests at Palisades Amusement Park in northern New Jersey when blacks were not allowed to purchase tickets to the swimming pool.

The first big step in the nonviolence resistance phase of the civil rights movement came in 1956 with the Montgomery Bus Boycott. On December 1, 1955, Rosa Parks, a middle-aged black seamstress, refused to give up her seat to a white passenger as required by Alabama law. E. B. Nixon, an officer with the all-black Brotherhood of Sleeping Car Porters and local head of the NAACP, bailed his friend and fellow worker Parks out of jail. She then gave Nixon permission to use her arrest to mount a one-day bus boycott.

On the day of the boycott Nixon asked Martin Luther King, Jr., a 27-year-old son of a prominent Atlanta minister and a newcomer to Montgomery, to deliver the keynote address at a mass rally of the Montgomery Improvement Association (MIA). King appeared an unlikely candidate to challenge the status quo on race relations. He grew up comfortably, was middle class, was educated at the black Atlanta University complex, and received a master's degree at Crozier Theological Seminary at Boston University. Though King had never been politically active before, he delivered a memorable address to an overflow audience at a local Baptist church.

The Montgomery Bus Boycott led to a Supreme Court ruling that declared unconstitutional a Montgomery ordinance that required segregated city buses. The boycott provided a number of lessons for civil rights leaders. First, it made many black southerners more assertive in their demands for full citizenship in spite of a white backlash of bomb threats and Ku Klux Klan (KKK) rallies. Second, it propelled King into the spotlight. Third, it captured the attention of the nation's news media and gained sympathetic coverage of its causes. Finally, the boycott produced a new set of tactics, which speeded up the pace of desegregation for the black community.

In the selections that follow, Adam Fairclough demonstrates the importance of King's leadership to the civil rights movement, while Clayborne Carson plays down the mythical image of King, arguing that King is a product of a movement that would have occurred even if King had never lived.

Adam Fairclough

 **YES**

Martin Luther King, Jr. and the Quest for Nonviolent Social Change

The Alabama cities of Birmingham and Selma have given their names to the most effective campaigns of nonviolent protest in recent history. The Birmingham demonstrations paved the way for the 1964 Civil Rights Act, which swept away segregation in public accommodations. The Selma protests of 1965 engendered the Voting Rights Act, a measure that cut away the political basis of white supremacy by ending the disfranchisement of blacks. Together, this legislation amounted to a "Second Reconstruction" of the South, restoring to black Southerners rights that had been formally granted after the Civil War but stripped away after the Compromise of 1877.

Understanding of this historical breakthrough, however, is far from perfect. It is beyond doubt that the man who led the Birmingham and Selma protests, Martin Luther King, Jr., made a mighty contribution. But more needs to be known about the dynamics of social change in the 1960s and about the political world in which King and his followers operated. King's biography, much of it hagiographic in character, has tended to simplify these dynamics and neglect the wider political context. There has been inadequate appreciation, too, of the hard-headed calculation that entered into King's strategy, the political sophistication of his advisers, and the importance of his organizational base, the Southern Christian Leadership Conference (SCLC). Nevertheless, some historians and political scientists have begun to analyze critically the campaigns of nonviolent direct action undertaken by King and SCLC. Implicitly or explicitly, their work has cast doubt on many commonly held assumptions about the civil rights movement and raised important questions. Why, if most whites disapproved of it so strongly, could nonviolent protest succeed in generating political support for the civil rights movement? Was nonviolent direct action a means of persuasion, or did it depend for its effectiveness upon pressure and coercion? To what extent, if any, did King seek deliberately to provoke violence by whites? How much support did King's tactics command among blacks? Did he create a truly "mass" movement, or were his victories achieved in spite of limited backing? This essay explores the evolution, execution, and political im-

From Adam Fairclough, "Martin Luther King, Jr. and the Quest for Nonviolent Social Change," *Phylon*, vol. 47, no. 1 (Spring 1986). Copyright © 1986 by *Phylon*. Notes omitted.

pact of King's methods in an attempt to explain the dynamics of nonviolent direct action.

In the most systematic study of King's techniques to date, political scientist David J. Garrow argued that the evolution of King's strategy fell into two phases. During the first, from his emergence as a leader in 1956 to the Albany protests of 1961–62, King conceived of direct action as a means of persuading Southern whites of the moral injustice of segregation and discrimination. When the Albany campaign failed, however, King abandoned this approach as unrealistic and, according to Garrow, adopted a strategy of "nonviolent coercion." Instead of trying to convince their adversaries of the rightness of their goals, King and SCLC sought to pressure the federal government into curbing white supremacists through legislation. Implemented with great success in Birmingham and Selma, this new strategy mobilized Northern public opinion behind the civil rights movement through dramatic confrontations that publicized segregationist violence. Since it invited violent opposition, this strategy, Garrow believes, "bordered on nonviolent provocation."

Garrow is not alone in detecting a distinct shift from persuasion to coercion in the way King conducted nonviolent direct action, with the coercive elements very much to the fore by the time of the 1963 Birmingham campaign. Elliott M. Zashin earlier had advanced a similar argument in his study, *Civil Disobedience and Democracy* (1972). Their experience in the deep South, Zashin contended, convinced most black activists that nonviolent protest had virtually no effect on white racists: its only value lay in its utility as a pressure tactic. By 1964, few entertained the notion that direct action could change the values of the adversary. King, Zashin believed, came to a similar conclusion and although, for reasons of diplomacy, he downplayed the coercive nature of his tactics, SCLC's leader "clearly . . . recognized the pressure involved in direct action." As he admitted in his celebrated "Letter From Birmingham City Jail," nonviolent protest sought to "create such a crisis and foster such a tension that a community which has constantly refused to negotiate is forced to confront the issue."

Before examining this argument, it is necessary to recognize that the historical analysis of King's thought presents a number of problems. First, King never expounded his theory of nonviolence in a systematic way, nor did he record a detailed account of his tactics. In addition, many of his books, articles and speeches were partly or wholly "ghosted," and it is not always easy to determine exactly what King did write. Third it must be borne in mind that King's writings and speeches were public statements designed to persuade and convince, and many of them were tailored to white audiences. Finally, King did not live in an intellectual vacuum: he had a wide circle of friends, colleagues and advisers with whom he debated tactics and strategy. His thinking was never fixed and rigid. Indeed, it would be astonishing if King's perception of the world remained static in view of the turbulent era in which he lived. Without doubt, he became more hard-headed and politically astute as a result of age and experience. In "Letter From Birmingham City Jail," for example, he expressed profound disappointment that the civil rights movement had failed to attract more support from white Southerners. There is no reason to suppose that this disillusionment was insincere.

It is doubtful, however, that King's strategy underwent a basic shift in emphasis of the kind posited by Zashin and Garrow. There is little evidence that King ever believed that nonviolent protest functioned solely, or even mainly, as a form of moral persuasion. Quite the contrary; in his earliest public writings he equated nonviolence with struggle and resistance organized through a militant mass movement. Philosophically and in practice, he explicitly rejected the notion that oppressed groups could overcome their subjection through ethical appeals and rational argument; they also needed an effective form of pressure. The assertion that King failed to appreciate the necessity for "black power" is simply erroneous. "A mass movement exercising nonviolence," he wrote in 1957, "is an object lesson in power under discipline." Having recently led a successful year-long economic boycott supported by 50,000 black people, he surely knew what he was talking about. A *New York Times* profile in March, 1956 noted that King stressed the Hegelian concept of "struggle as a law of growth," and that he regarded the bus boycott "as just one aspect of a world-wide revolt of oppressed peoples."

The intentions of the people who created SCLC underline this point. Bayard Rustin, Stanley Levison and Ella Baker were seasoned political activists who moved in the circles of the New York Left. Steeped in Marxist and socialist ideas, they regarded nonviolent direct action in political, not moral, terms. "The basic conception of SCLC," said Baker, "was that it would capitalize on what was developed in Montgomery in terms of mass action." In Levison's words, the subject was "to reproduce that pattern of mass action, underscore mass, in other cities and communities." It is unlikely that King viewed SCLC in any other way.

To emphasize King's political realism is not to deny his underlying idealism. For him, nonviolence was an ethical imperative, and his commitment to it was absolute and consistent. Moreover, he did sometimes imply that nonviolent protest worked partly through persuasion, by "awakening a sense of moral shame in the opponent." Nonviolent resisters, he explained, touched the hearts and consciences of their adversaries, converting oppressors into friends. But the significance of such statements should not be exaggerated. He admitted that "when the underprivileged demand freedom, the privileged first react with bitterness and resistance;" nonviolence could not change the "heart" of the oppressor until the social structure that perpetuated injustice and false ideology had been destroyed. His verbal characterizations of nonviolence must also be read in context. In sermons, for example, he frequently likened nonviolence to a kind of supranatural power—a "Soul Force" that could defeat physical force. Of course, such descriptions were not meant to be taken literally: King was simplifying complex ideas and communicating them in a way that black Southerners —poorly educated, politically inexperienced, but imbued with a deep religious sensibility—could grasp easily. King's belief that some adversaries might still be touched by the suffering and goodwill of nonviolent resisters was genuine, although in Bayard Rustin's opinion it "was often very confusing—and frustrating—to his followers." But this belief was marginal to his strategy of protest.

When King spoke of "converting" oppressors, he was thinking of a long-term historical process rather than an immediate personal response.

There was, therefore, an underlying continuity in King's conception of nonviolent direct action. It envisaged a mass movement opposed to white supremacy and which operated primarily through direct pressure. It assumed that racism was a Southern anachronism and that a growing majority of whites sympathized with the goal of integration and equality. It regarded the federal government as a potential ally, and it believed that the nonviolent protesters attracted support if their opponents responded with violence. The notion of a pre-1963 "persuasive" strategy aimed at winning over Southern whites and a post-1963 "coercive" strategy designed to provoke federal intervention is misleading. King consistently followed the two-pronged strategy of exerting pressure on Southern whites and seeking to involve the federal government.

Federal involvement comprised a crucial element in SCLC's strategy as early as 1961, when King called upon President Kennedy to issue a "Second Emancipation Proclamation"—an Executive Order banning segregation and discrimination. King was not alone, of course, in appreciating the importance of federal action: with the election of a Democratic President whose platform included a strong civil-rights plank, black leaders sensed a golden opportunity to mobilize federal support for their goals. They knew that political considerations made Kennedy reluctant to meddle in the South's "local" affairs. But the daring Freedom Rides of May–August 1961 demonstrated that nonviolent protest could spur the government to action, even against its will, by creating a crisis of law and order to which it had to respond.

SCLC's protests in Albany, Georgia, represented King's first major effort to implement the two-pronged strategy outlined above. On the one hand he exerted pressure on local whites, through demonstrations, sit-ins and economic boycotts, to negotiate over the demands of blacks. On the other hand, by creating a serious local crisis and generating public concern, he tried to induce the federal government to intervene in some way. That he failed on both counts does not mean that the strategy was unsound or that it differed in essentials from the one successfully pursued in Birmingham. King failed in Albany for tactical reasons, notably inadequate planning and poor choice of target, rather than over-reliance on "nonviolent persuasion." The significance of Birmingham is not that King finally discovered the necessity for pressure, but that he at last discovered how to make that pressure effective.

If the strategy was clear, the tactics had to be developed and refined through trial and error and the experience of others. From the founding of SCLC in 1957 to the Birmingham campaign of 1963, King was speculating, experimenting and learning, attempting to adapt a theory that both to political realities and to the practical considerations that constrained black Southerners.

King learned two vital tactical lessons during these years. The first was that he would have to make do with limited numbers. SCLC's architects had anticipated that the Montgomery bus boycott would spark a wave of similar protests throughout the South. For a variety of reasons, however, this did not happen. Many blacks were skeptical of boycotts. More radical tactics like sit-ins and demonstrations evoked still deeper misgivings: they set back orderly progress; they alienated white moderates and provoked a "backlash;" they were wasteful and ineffective. Jail often spelt economic disaster, and individuals thought twice about volunteering for arrest if their families might suffer as a consequence. True, the sit-in movement of 1960 showed that students and young people, free from the economic burdens and family responsibilities that constrained their elders, would willingly act as "foot soldiers" in direct action campaigns. The sit-ins also demonstrated how direct action itself tended to promote unity and support among blacks, rendering the conservatism of older leaders less troublesome. Even so, the number of "foot soldiers" was limited; the concept, much in vogue in 1960–1964, of a "nonviolent army" that would steamroll the opposition through sheer weight of numbers turned out to be unrealistic. Albany taught King that no more than 5 percent of a given black population could be persuaded to volunteer for jail. He learned to frame his tactics accordingly.

The second tactical lesson was that, to quote Bayard Rustin, "protest becomes an effective tactic to the degree that it elicits brutality and oppression from the power structure." The government's conduct during the Freedom Rides—intervening in Alabama, where Klan mobs had been permitted to run amok, but adopting a "hands-off" policy towards Mississippi, where the police had kept order and carried out "peaceful" arrests—sent a coded but clear message to Southern segregationists; federal intervention could be avoided if the authorities kept violence in check. Albany's Chief of Police, Lauri Pritchett, applied this lesson with intelligence and skill, out-maneuvering the protesters. First, he trained his men to arrest demonstrators courteously and without unnecessary force. "For a period of four to five months," he reported to the city commission, "members of the Albany Police Department was [sic] indoctrinated to this plan of nonviolence. . . . At each roll call [they] were lectured and shown films on how to conduct themselves." Second, anticipating a "jail-in," Pritchett secured ample prison space in the surrounding counties. Finally, to protect the City's legal flank he charged demonstrators with such offenses as breach of the peace and unlawful assembly rather than with violation of the segregation laws. His plan worked to perfection: blacks went to jail by the thousands—King himself went three times—but the City adamantly refused to negotiate and the federal government did virtually nothing.

However much King and SCLC deplored Pritchett's self-serving definition of "nonviolence," they had to accept that victory had eluded them. Clearly, SCLC needed to be much more careful in its choice of target. In Birmingham, King elected to confront an adversary with a clear record of brutality, gambling on a violent response which, publicized by a violence-fixated press, would galvanize public opinion and jolt the federal government into action. In 1951 the reporter Carl Rowan had described Birmingham as "the world's most race-conscious city . . . a city of gross tensions, a city where the color line is drawn in every conceivable place [and where] Eugene "Bull" Connor, white-supremacist police commissioner, sees that no man, white or black, crosses the line." Connor was still police commissioner in 1963, and SCLC calculated that this man, notorious for his Klan connections and violence toward blacks, would react to nonviolent protests in a manner very different from Pritchett's. It disclaimed any intent to "provoke" violence. Nevertheless, as local black leader Fred Shut-tlesworth put it, "the idea of facing 'Bull' Connor was the thing." Acting as predicted by SCLC, Connor's response to the protests of early May—the mass arrest of children, the use of fire-hoses and police-dogs—was publicized the world over.

But did the protests really achieve anything? The desegregation agreement which King won with the help of federal mediators has often been denigrated. One of the most widely read texts on black history describes it as "token concessions that were later not carried out." At the time, Southern whites argued that orderly change was already on the way; the protests merely hindered that process. It is surely no coincidence, however, that the first small steps in the direction of desegregation occurred precisely when King's campaign climaxed. Few blacks believed that the city's businessmen would have accepted desegregation but for the double pressure of the demonstrations and the economic boycott of downtown stores. Conservative blacks like A. G. Gaston, who had initially opposed direct action, changed their minds when they saw that the white merchants were bending: "The demonstrations gave us a wedge we never had before to use at the bargaining table." Narrow as it was, the agreement of May 10, 1963, represented the city's first substantive break with its white supremacist past. In the most thorough available study of the negotiations, historian Robert Corley concluded that "the end of segregation was dramatically hastened because King and his demonstrators threatened chaos in a city whose leaders were now desperate for order."

What of its impact on federal policy: did Birmingham produce the Civil Rights Act, as King and Shuttlesworth liked to claim? Garrow thinks not, pointing to the gap between SCLC's protests and the introduction of the Bill, as well as the long delay in its becoming law. He suggests that the lack of a clear goal in Birmingham, plus the black rioting of early May, might explain why there was "no widespread national outcry, no vocal reaction by the nation's clergy, and no immediate move by the administration to propose salutary legislation." Birmingham, he concludes, was far less successful than SCLC's later campaign in Selma.

Comparisons between Birmingham and Selma, however, must be treated with caution. It is true, as Garrow notes, that Birmingham produced a relatively muted response from Congress; Selma prompted nearly two hundred sympathetic speeches, Birmingham a mere seventeen. But a simple statistical comparison is misleading for the political context in 1963 was very different from that of 1965. Congressmen were far more wary about speaking out on civil rights in 1963. Most regarded it as a sure "vote-loser," and Northern Democrats were anxious to avoid a damaging intra-party dispute that would redound to the benefit of the Republican party. But in 1965, with the Republicans routed in the elections of the previous year, Northern Democrats felt politically less inhibited. In addition, by 1965 the nation had become more accustomed to the idea that the government should combat racial discrimination; far fewer people still maintained that the South's racial problems could be solved through local, voluntary action. Finally, by 1965 the civil rights movement enjoyed greater legitimacy and respectability. To compare the Congressional response to Birmingham with the reaction to Selma two years later is to compare like with unlike.

The impact of Birmingham should not be judged by its effect on Congress: the initiative for the Civil Rights Bill came from the Executive, not the Legislative branch. And by all accounts, SCLC's protests were pivotal in persuading the Kennedy administration to abandon its executive-action strategy in favor of legislation. Robert Kennedy was the driving force behind the Bill. For two years he had tried to deal with each racial crisis on an ad hoc basis. However, Birmingham convinced him that crises would recur, with increasing frequency and magnitude, unless the government adopted a more radical approach. According to Edwin Guthman, who served under Attorney General Kennedy, the violence in Birmingham "convinced the President and Bob that stronger federal civil rights laws were needed."

Did the rioting in Birmingham detract from the effectiveness of SCLC's campaign? SCLC did everything possible to minimize the likelihood of counterviolence by blacks. But King and his advisers realized that the Kennedy administration was not simply responding to the moral outrage evoked by Connor's tactics; it was far more perturbed by the threat of chaos and bloodshed. Birmingham raised the specter of retaliation by blacks and the prospect of a violent revolt by them, leading to uncontrollable racial warfare, began to haunt John and Robert Kennedy. Much as he deplored violence by his followers, King consciously exploited this anxiety for the sake of furthering his goals. In "Letter From Birmingham City Jail" he buttressed his appeal for support by whites by warning that without major concessions "millions of Negroes will . . . seek solace in black-nationalist ideologies—a development that would inevitably lead to a frightening racial nightmare." Thus did he redefine nonviolence as an alternative to, or defense against, violence by blacks. This argument reached its target: the Civil Rights Bill was in large measure designed to get blacks off the streets, to obviate the threat of violence, and to strengthen the influence of "responsible" black leaders.

In Birmingham, King broke the political logjam and delivered a hammerblow against white supremacy. Mass movements did not come made-to-order, however; their success hinged upon sound planning, intelligent leadership, and a fortuitous situation. King had the advantage in Birmingham of a strong local base created by Fred Shuttlesworth, meticulous planning by Wyatt Walker, and a civic elite that was amenable to change. His next campaign, in St. Augustine, Florida (March–July 1964), went awry because the local movement was weak, the planning poor, and opposition by whites intransigent. Largely ineffective, the St. Augustine protests also suffered from lack of clarity in goals; because of this confusion, SCLC's tactics tended to cancel out each other. It is easy to see why King targeted St. Augustine. Heavily dependent on the tourist industry, the city's economy could be seriously damaged by demonstrations. Second, SCLC's chances of engineering a dramatic confrontation were excellent: Northern Florida was Ku Klux Klan country. A branch had been organized in the St. Augustine area in the summer of 1936, and it had close ties with the city and county police. From King's point of view, the Klan presence made St. Augustine doubly attractive. Demonstrations would flush the Klan into the open, thus compelling the state authorities or, failing these, the federal government to suppress it. The nature of SCLC's strategy was evident from its use of the night march. Adopted at the instance of Hosea Williams, who had pioneered this tactic in Savannah, the night march invited attack. The resulting Klan violence showed the police in their true colors, exposing the inadequacy of local law enforcement.

By publicizing the Klan menace King did succeed, with help from U.S. District Judge Bryan Simpson, in making Governor Farris Bryant crack down on white troublemakers. The strategy of forcing the Klan out of the woodwork, however, hampered the achievement of desegregation, SCLC's publicly stated goal. Moreover, in light of the imminent passage of the Civil Rights Bill, SCLC's demonstrations against segregated motels and restaurants seemed pointless. King reasoned that when whites accepted desegregation under legal compulsion they could avoid making any admission that blacks were not treated fairly. "This is morally wrong," he insisted. "We want them to admit that segregation is evil and take it upon themselves to rid this city of it." Yet it made little difference in practice if they abandoned segregation under the pressure of direct action rather than the compulsion of the law, and in any event, the Civil Rights Act, backed up by legal action from the NAACP Legal Defense Fund, desegregated St. Augustine's public accommodations.

In the Selma campaign (January–April 1965), everything went right. The local movement, built up by The Student Nonviolent Coordinating Committee (SNCC), was solidly entrenched. The strategy of the protests had been carefully thought out by James Bevel. SCLC's preparatory staff work was thorough. Above all, the campaign had a single clear, attainable goal—federal voting rights legislation—to which both the target and the tactics were directly relevant. With justice, Selma has been singled out as the most effective application of nonviolent direct action in the history of the civil rights movement.

The notes which he penned in Selma jail give a fascinating insight into King's tactics. In detailed written instructions to Andrew Young, SCLC's executive director, King orchestrated the protests from his cell with masterly finesse. Perhaps the most telling lines were those chiding Young for cancelling a demonstration in response to a favorable court decision. "Please don't be too soft," he wrote his lieutenant. "We have the offensive. It was a mistake not to march today. In a crisis we must have a sense of drama. . . . We may accept the restraining order as a partial victory, but we can't stop." Not until SCLC triggered the violent confrontation of March 7—"Bloody Sunday"—did King feel his goal securely within reach.

The efficacy of King's tactics at Selma flowed from the fact that, to quote Zashin, "people were shocked by the segregationists' violence, not because the self-suffering of the demonstrators was saliently impressive." Garrow came to the same conclusion, adding that the non-controversial nature of SCLC's goal, the right to vote, and the complete absence of violence by blacks both helped to make the campaign a success.

The fact that SCLC designed its tactics to elicit violence might appear callous and irresponsible. Yet the assertion that SCLC deliberately "provoked" violence by whites has to be qualified. If their nonviolent efforts to secure basic

Constitutional rights met with violence from racist whites, King argued, then law, logic and morality required society to punish the perpetrators of violence, not condemn its victims. It might seem paradoxical that King invited racist violence but denied in any sense provoking it. But he could also argue that violence was intrinsic to white supremacy and that nonviolent protesters merely brought that violence to the public's attention. In some notes he prepared for a press conference, he anticipated the question "Does your movement depend on violence?" by writing, "When you give witness to an evil you do not cause that evil but you oppose it so it can be cured." The violence of March 7, he added, "brought into every home the terror and brutality that Negroes face every day."

Nevertheless, SCLC's tactics exposed King to the charge that he manipulated local blacks, offering his followers as targets for the aggression of whites. Although undeniably manipulative, nobody could justifiably accuse SCLC of disguising to its followers the dangers they faced. "There can be no remission of sin without the shedding of blood," wrote King. SCLC's claim to leadership rested on the fact that its staff shared the same risks as the rank-and-file demonstrators. Thus King came under the sharpest criticism when he seemed to be avoiding the perils that he asked his followers to brave.

By staging its protests in carefully contrived, highly publicized situations, SCLC tried to evoke violence by whites while keeping casualties to a minimum. The news media played a crucial, if unwitting, role in this strategy. "The presence of reporters," wrote Paul Good, "not only publicized their cause but also acted as a deterrent in places where officials feared bad publicity." Television crews and photographers had an especially inhibiting effect; as Bayard Rustin put it, "Businessmen and chambers of commerce across the South dreaded the cameras." Even in Birmingham, and to some extent in Selma as well, extensive press coverage caused law enforcement officials to proceed with caution. As another of King's advisers, Stanley Levison, pointed out, "the fact that the demonstrations focused public attention from all over the country . . . restrained even the most vicious elements from moving out too freely." When the police did resort to violence, they usually stopped short of lethal force; in all of SCLC's demonstrations in the South, only two deaths resulted from police attacks. SCLC realized moreover, that the news value of racist violence depended as much on the ability of the press to report it as on the gravity of the violence itself. Snarling German Shepherds, gushing fire-hoses, and club-wielding state troopers could have a greater impact on the public consciousness than murders and bombings if reporters and film crews were present at the scene. Nonviolent protest, wrote King, "dramatized the essential meaning of the conflict and in magnified strokes made clear who was the evildoer and who was the undeserving victim." SCLC tried to evoke dramatic violence rather than deadly violence, and King, as August Meier pointed out in 1965, constantly retreated "from situations that might result in the deaths of his followers."

Despite his enormous popularity and prestige, King learned never to take support of blacks for granted. Leadership and tactics, not numbers, were the key ingredients in King's successes. In the teeming cities of the North, one-twentieth of the black population amounted to a small army. The potential for nonviolent direct action seemed immense. If the team that had organized

Selma were turned loose on Chicago, Andrew Young speculated, SCLC would have numbers enough—perhaps 100,000—to bring the city to a standstill. The sheer power of numbers in the North was "awesome," he thought. "I tremble to think what might happen if it is not organized and disciplined in the interests of positive social change." Even as Young spoke, a devastating riot was unfolding in Los Angeles, which, after five days of violence, left thirty-one blacks and three whites dead. On the heels of the Watts riot King, previously so cautious about leaving the South, insisted that SCLC move North and move fast; "The present mood dictates that we cannot wait." Thus it was with a mixture of self-confidence and pessimistic urgency that SCLC embarked on its first Northern campaign.

The anticipated numbers, however, failed to materialize. Chicago had a black population of a million, but it stayed on the sidelines. Barely 50,000 people attended the biggest mass rally: King's demonstrations attracted, at most, twenty-five hundred, at least half of whom were white. King, it has been argued, was out of tune with the mood, culture, and problems of the Northern ghetto. The product of a cocooned middle-class environment, he was not attuned to the cynicism and defeatism that so often prevailed among the black urban poor. His bourgeois emphasis on thrift and self-help obscured him to the realities of their plight; his goal of integration (expressed in Chicago by the demand for "open housing") was marginal, at best, to their immediate concerns. There is a scintilla of truth in this argument. Yet there were many sound reasons for attacking housing segregation, the most visible and far-reaching expression of white racism. Exposure to the Chicago slums, moreover, soon brought home to King the poverty and degradation of the urban ghetto, rapidly disabusing him of his more simplistic assumptions about the efficacy of "bootstrap" economics.

The fact remained, nevertheless, that only a tiny minority acted on King's message. By 1966, in fact, King was becoming increasingly isolated as an advocate of nonviolent direct action. The concept of independent action by blacks in opposition to the white majority—a concept popularized by SNCC's slogan, "Black Power"—was fast gaining ground among intellectuals and activists. But the opposite strategy of seeking political change in coalition with whites was also winning converts. Articulated most persuasively by Bayard Rustin, the coalition strategy envisaged little role for nonviolent direct action on the grounds that economic problems simply were not susceptible to marches and demonstrations. Indeed, Rustin argued that in the post-Watts era, with rioting and repression feeding off each other, direct action had become counterproductive, alienating whites and "breeding despair and impotence" among blacks. Reflecting on SCLC's decline from the perspective of the mid-1970s, Rustin concluded that King persisted in the tactics of protest long after their usefulness had been exhausted.

The disturbed political climate of the late 1960s made doubtful the success of any strategy of blacks. King assessed "Black Power" as a confused, impractical doctrine, and he deplored its connotations of violence and separatism. Yet Rustin's coalitionism struck him as only slightly less unrealistic. In practice, it boiled down to giving blanket support to the Johnson administration—a line rendered both morally repugnant and politically futile by Johnson's grow-ing obsession with the war in Vietnam. The defeat of the 1966 Civil Rights Bill and the Republicans gains in the November elections signalled the dis-integration of the informal, bi-partisan "coalition of conscience" which had sustained the civil rights movement in 1963–65. King accurately sensed that it would be impossible—and, in light of the conservatism and hawkishness of most trade unions, undesirable—to resurrect it. Yet he could offer no al-ternative strategy with any conviction. Indeed, political trends plus his own experiences in Chicago persuaded him that he had badly underestimated the force of white racism. Blacks were not confronting a regional minority but a national majority. It was a shattering conclusion and it drove him to despair.

During the last two years of his life, King was torn between his old faith in the capacity of liberal democracy for enlightened reform, and a Marxian view of the state as an engine of capitalist exploitation. That he became more radical is certain; the need for a thoroughgoing redistribution of wealth and power was a consistent theme of his public and private statements. Occasionally, in his darkest moments, he feared that America was drifting irreversibly toward facsism. Yet King could never forget that the federal government had been his ally. He wanted to believe the current reactionary trend was a passing phase, the irrational spin-off of rioting and war. Although shaken by Chicago and alienated from the President, he convinced himself that public opinion was malleable and the government still susceptible to the right kind of pressure. Nonviolent protest could still work, he insisted to his somewhat skeptical staff. "If it hasn't worked in the North, it just hasn't been tried enough."

King's last project, the "Poor People's Campaign," is sometimes described as revolutionary. To some it recalled the "nonviolent army" idea of the early 1960s. King himself spoke of "class struggle" and threatened massive civil dis-obedience on a scale that could bring Washington to a grinding halt. Behind the radical rhetoric, however, the strategy and tactics of the campaign closely re-sembled the pattern of Birmingham and Selma. Although he spoke of creating a new radical coalition, the groups King looked to for support were, by and large, the same that had comprised the "coalition of conscience" in the earlier period. He envisaged a "Selma-like movement" which, if "powerful enough, dramatic enough, and morally appealing enough," would mobilize "the churches, labor, liberals, intellectuals," as well as the new breed of "Black Power" militants and "New Left" white radicals. Far from raising a "nonviolent army," King planned to bring only three thousand demonstrators to Washington—about the number who had gone to jail in Birmingham and Selma. "We aren't going to close down the Pentagon," he told SCLC's board of directors. "Anybody talking about clos-ing down the Pentagon is just talking foolishness. We can't close down Capitol Hill." The aim was not to "coerce" the federal government, but to generate a sympathetic response from the people of the nation. King's demands were moderate, he believed, and he wanted to promote consensus, not conflict.

Had he lived, King might well have achieved at least a partial success. The political situation in 1968 was volatile and fluid; the election of Richard Nixon, and the years of "benign neglect," was not a foregone conclusion. Perhaps King would have cancelled or postponed the Poor People's Campaign, reasoning that a Hubert Humphrey or Robert Kennedy presidency would give him more room for maneuver. In terms of influence and accomplishment, King outstripped all other black leaders and would-be leaders. His capacity to adapt to rapidly changing circumstances would surely have been tested to the limit, but a healthy and astute pragmatism had always been part of his outlook. "I am still searching myself," he told his staff. "I don't have all the answers, and I certainly have no claim to omniscience." There was no magic formula for social change; the dynamics of direct action could only be discovered in struggle, in resistance, even in defeat.

Martin Luther King, Jr.: Charismatic Leadership in a Mass Struggle

The legislation to establish Martin Luther King, Jr.'s birthday as a federal holiday provided official recognition of King's greatness, but it remains the responsibility of those of us who study and carry on King's work to define his historical significance. Rather than engaging in officially approved nostalgia, our remembrance of King should reflect the reality of his complex and multifaceted life. Biographers, theologians, political scientists, sociologists, social psychologists, and historians have given us a sizable literature of King's place in Afro-American protest tradition, his role in the modern black freedom struggle, and his electic ideas regarding nonviolent activism. Although King scholars may benefit from and may stimulate the popular interest in King generated by the national holiday, many will find themselves uneasy participants in annual observances to honor an innocuous, carefully cultivated image of King as a black heroic figure.

The King depicted in serious scholarly works is far too interesting to be encased in such a didactic legend. King was a controversial leader who challenged authority and who once applauded what he called "creative maladjusted nonconformity." He should not be transformed into a simplistic image designed to offend no one—a black counterpart to the static, heroic myths that have embalmed George Washington as the Father of His Country and Abraham Lincoln as the Great Emancipator.

One aspect of the emerging King myth has been the depiction of him in the mass media, not only as the preeminent leader of the civil rights movement, but also as the initiator and sole indispensible element in the southern black struggles of the 1950s and 1960s. As in other historical myths, a Great Man is seen as the decisive factor in the process of social change, and the unique qualities of a leader are used to explain major historical events. The King myth departs from historical reality because it attributes too much to King's exceptional qualities as a leader and too little to the impersonal, large-scale social factors that made it possible for King to display his singular abilities on a national stage. Because the myth emphasizes the individual at the expense of the

From Clayborne Carson, "Martin Luther King, Jr.: Charismatic Leadership in a Mass Struggle," *Journal of American History*, vol. 74 (September 1987). Copyright © 1987 by The Organization of American Historians. Reprinted by permission.

black movement, it not only exaggerates King's historical importance but also distorts his actual, considerable contribution to the movement.

A major example of this distortion has been the tendency to see King as a charismatic figure who single-handedly directed the course of the civil rights movement through the force of his oratory. The charismatic label however, does not adequately define King's role in the southern black struggle. The term *charisma* has traditionally been used to describe the godlike, magical qualities possessed by certain leaders. Connotations of the term have changed, of course, over the years. In our more secular age, it has lost many of its religious connotations and now refers to a wide range of leadership styles that involve the capacity to inspire—usually through oratory—emotional bonds between leaders and followers. Arguing that King was not a charismatic leader, in the broadest sense of the term, becomes somewhat akin to arguing that he was not a Christian, but emphasis on King's charisma obscures other important aspects of his role in the black movement. To be sure, King's oratory was exceptional and many people saw King as a divinely inspired leader, but King did not receive and did not want the kind of unquestioning support that is often associated with charismatic leaders. Movement activists instead saw him as the most prominent among many outstanding movement strategists, tacticians, ideologues, and institutional leaders.

King undoubtedly recognized that charisma was one of many leadership qualities at his disposal, but he also recognized that charisma was not a sufficient basis for leadership in a modem political movement enlisting numerous self-reliant leaders. Moreover, he rejected aspects of the charismatic model that conflicted with his sense of his own limitations. Rather than exhibiting unwavering confidence in his power and wisdom, King was a leader full of self-doubts, keenly aware of his own limitations and human weaknesses. He was at times reluctant to take on the responsibilities suddenly and unexpectedly thrust upon him. During the Montgomery bus boycott, for example, when he worried about threats to his life and to the lives of his wife and child, he was overcome with fear rather than confident and secure in his leadership role. He was able to carry on only after acquiring an enduring understanding of his dependence on a personal God who promised never to leave him alone.

Moreover, emphasis on King's charisma conveys the misleading notion of a movement held together by spellbinding speeches and blind faith rather than by a complex blend of rational and emotional bonds. King's charisma did not place him above criticism. Indeed, he was never able to gain mass support for his notion of nonviolent struggle as a way of life, rather than simply a tactic. Instead of viewing himself as the embodiment of widely held Afro-American racial views, he willingly risked his popularity among blacks through his steadfast advocacy of nonviolent strategies to achieve radical social change.

He was a profound and provocative public speaker as well as an emotionally powerful one. Only those unfamiliar with the Afro-American clergy would assume that his oratorical skills were unique, but King set himself apart from other black preachers through his use of traditional black Christian idiom to advocate unconventional political ideas. Early in his life King became disillusioned with the unbridled emotionalism associated with his father's religious fundamentalism, and, as a thirteen year old, he questioned the bodily resurrection of Jesus in his Sunday school class. His subsequent search for an intellectually satisifying religious faith conflicted with the emphasis on emotional expressiveness that pervades evangelical religion. His preaching manner was rooted in the traditions of the black church, while his subject matter, which often reflected his wide-ranging philosophical interests, distinguished him from other preachers who relied on rhetorical devices that manipulated the emotions of the listeners. King used charisma as a tool for mobilizing black communities, but he always used it in the context of other forms of intellectual and political leadership suited to a movement containing many strong leaders.

Recently, scholars have begun to examine the black struggle as a locally based mass movement, rather than simply a reform movement led by national civil rights leaders. The new orientation in scholarship indicates that King's role was different from that suggested in King-centered biographies and journalistic accounts. King was certainly not the only significant leader of the civil rights movement, for sustained protest movements arose in many southern communities in which King had little or no direct involvement.

In Montgomery, for example, local black leaders such as E. D. Nixon, Rosa Parks, and Jo Ann Robinson started the bus boycott before King became the leader of the Montgomery Improvement Association. Thus, although King inspired blacks in Montgomery and black residents recognized that they were fortunate to have such a spokesperson, talented local leaders other than King played decisive roles in initiating and sustaining the boycott movement.

Similarly, the black students who initiated the 1960 lunch counter sit-ins admired King, but they did not wait for him to act before launching their own movement. The sit-in leaders who founded the Student Nonviolent Coordinating Committee (SNCC) became increasingly critical of King's leadership style, linking it to the feelings of dependency that often characterize the followers of charismatic leaders. The essence of SNCC's approach to community organizing was to instill in local residents the confidence that they could lead their own struggles. A SNCC organizer failed if local residents became dependent on his or her presence; as the organizers put it, their job was to work themselves out of a job. Though King influenced the struggles that took place in the Black Belt regions of Mississippi, Alabama, and Georgia, those movements were also guided by self-reliant local leaders who occasionally called on King's oratorical skills to galvanize black protestors at mass meetings while refusing to depend on his presence.

If King had never lived, the black struggle would have followed a course of development similar to the one it did. The Montgomery bus boycott would have occurred, because King did not initiate it. Black students probably would have rebelled—even without King as a role model—for they had sources of tactical and ideological inspiration besides King. Mass activism in southern cities and voting rights efforts in the deep South were outgrowths of large-scale social and political forces, rather than simply consequences of the actions of a single leader. Though perhaps not as quickly and certainly not as peacefully nor with as universal a significance, the black movement would probably have achieved its major legislative victories without King's leadership, for the southern Jim

Crow system was a regional anachronism, and the forces that undermined it were inexorable.

To what extent, then, did King's presence affect the movement? Answering that question requires us to look beyond the usual portrayal of the black struggle. Rather than seeing an amorphous mass of discontented blacks acting out strategies determined by a small group of leaders, we would recognize King as a major example of the local black leadership that emerged as black communities mobilized for sustained struggles. If not as dominant a figure as sometimes portrayed, the historical King was nevertheless a remarkable leader who acquired the respect and support of self-confident, grass-roots leaders, some of whom possessed charismatic qualities of their own. Directing attention to the other leaders who initiated and emerged from those struggles should not detract from our conception of King's historical significance; such movement-oriented research reveals King as a leader who stood out in a forest of tall trees.

King's major public speeches—particularly the "I Have a Dream" speech—have received much attention, but his exemplary qualities were also displayed in countless strategy sessions with other activists and in meetings with government officials. King's success as a leader was based on his intellectual and moral cogency and his skill as a conciliator among movement activists who refused to be simply King's "followers" or "lieutenants."

The success of the black movement required the mobilization of black communities as well as the transformation of attitudes in the surrounding society, and King's wide range of skills and attributes prepared him to meet the internal as well as the external demands of the movement. King understood the black world from a privileged position, having grown up in a stable family within a major black urban community; yet he also learned how to speak persuasively to the surrounding white world. Alone among the major civil rights leaders of his time, King could not only articulate black concerns to white audiences, but could also mobilize blacks through his day-to-day involvement in black community institutions and through his access to the regional institutional network of the black church. His advocacy of nonviolent activism gave the black movement invaluable positive press coverage, but his effectiveness as a protest leader derived mainly from his ability to mobilize black community resources.

Analyses of the southern movement that emphasize its nonrational aspects and expressive functions over its political character explain the black struggle as an emotional outburst by discontented blacks, rather than recognizing that the movement's strength and durability came from its mobilization of black community institutions, financial resources, and grass-roots leaders. The values of southern blacks were profoundly and permanently transformed not only by King, but also by involvement in sustained protest activity and community-organizing efforts, through thousands of mass meetings, workshops, citizenship classes, freedom schools, and informal discussions. Rather than merely accepting guidance from above, southern blacks were resocialized as a result of their movement experiences.

Although the literature of the black struggle has traditionally paid little attention to the intellectual content of black politics, movement activists of the 1960s made a profound, though often ignored, contribution to political thinking. King may have been born with rare potential, but his most significant leadership attributes were related to his immersion in, and contribution to, the intellectual ferment that has always been an essential part of Afro-American freedom struggles. Those who have written about King have too often assumed that his most important ideas were derived from outside the black struggle—from his academic training, his philosophical readings, or his acquaintance with Gandhian ideas. Scholars are only beginning to recognize the extent to which his attitudes and those of many other activists, white and black, were transformed through their involvement in a movement in which ideas disseminated from the bottom up as well as from the top down.

Although my assessment of King's role in the black struggles of his time reduces him to human scale, it also increases the possibility that others may recognize his qualities in themselves. Idolizing King lessens one's ability to exhibit some of his best attributes or, worse, encourages one to become a debunker, emphasizing King's flaws in order to lessen the inclination to exhibit his virtues. King himself undoubtedly feared that some who admired him would place too much faith in his ability to offer guidance and to overcome resistance, for he often publicly acknowledged his own limitations and mortality. Near the end of his life, King expressed his certainty that black people would reach the Promised Land whether or not he was with them. His faith was based on an awareness of the qualities that he knew he shared with all people. When he suggested his own epitaph, he asked not to be remembered for his exceptional achievements—his Nobel Prize and other awards, his academic accomplishments; instead, he wanted to be remembered for giving his life to serve others, for trying to be right on the war question, for trying to feed the hungry and clothe the naked, for trying to love and serve humanity. "I want you to say that I tried to love and serve humanity." Those aspects of King's life did not require charisma or other superhuman abilities.

If King were alive today, he would doubtless encourage those who celebrate his life to recognize their responsibility to struggle as he did for a more just and peaceful world. He would prefer that the black movement be remembered not only as the scene of his own achievements, but also as a setting that brought out extraordinary qualities in many people. If he were to return, his oratory would be unsettling and intellectually challenging rather than remembered diction and cadences. He would probably be the unpopular social critic he was on the eve of the Poor People's Campaign rather than the object of national homage he became after his death. His basic message would be the same as it was when he was alive, for he did not bend with the changing political winds. He would talk of ending poverty and war and of building a just social order that would avoid the pitfalls of competitive capitalism and repressive communism. He would give scant comfort to those who condition their activism upon the appearance of another King, for he recognized the extent to which he was a product of the movement that called him to leadership.

The notion that appearances by Great Men (or Great Women) are necessary preconditions for the emergence of major movements for social change reflects not only a poor understanding of history, but also a pessimistic view of the possibilities for future social change. Waiting for the Messiah is a human weakness that is unlikely to be rewarded more than once in a millennium. Studies of King's life offer support for an alternative optimistic belief that ordinary people can collectively improve their lives. Such studies demonstrate the capacity of social movements to transform participants for the better and to create leaders worthy of their followers.

POSTSCRIPT

Was Martin Luther King, Jr.'s Leadership Essential to the Success of the Civil Rights Revolution?

Fairclough delivers an important portrait of King. He challenges not only the mythical views about King but also the portraits that a number of his biographers have written. First of all, he places King within the context of the dynamics of the social changes of the 1960s. Fairclough disagrees with those who see King primarily as a great orator and a symbolic leader of the movement. He argues that King was a flexible and practical revolutionary who understood that power, not moral suasion, lay at the heart of the civil rights protest movements. Consequently, Fairclough disputes David J. Garrow's contention in *Bearing the Cross: Martin Luther King, Jr. and the Southern Christian Leadership Conference* (Morrow/Avon, 1999) that King's belief about nonviolence was originally viewed as a form of moral suasion. When the demonstrations failed to convert white southerners or even attract white moderates, says Garrow, King finally realized that mass protests would only work as a pressure tactic that was needed to evoke a violent response from the oppressors.

Fairclough denies that King ever made such an ideological shift. King, in his view, was a realist who understood that nonviolence was a tactic used in a struggle to achieve power. While he may have been disappointed that only a few white southerners converted to the movement, the Montgomery Bus Boycott of 1956 was only the first phase of a worldwide revolt of oppressed people.

Carson might seem to underestimate the uniqueness of King. He admits that King could speak persuasively to the white community and at the same time "mobilize black community resources." These ideas were first articulated by the historian August Meier, who described King as a conservative militant in his widely reprinted article "On the Role of Martin Luther King," *New Politics* (Winter 1965). King not only bridged the black and white power structures, but he also acted as a broker between the more militant protest groups, such as the Student Nonviolent Coordinating Committee (SNCC) and the more conservative, legal-oriented NAACP.

The literature on King is enormous. An interpretive short biography is Adam Fairclough, *Martin Luther King, Jr.* (University of Georgia Press, 1995). Older interpretations are nicely summarized in C. Eric Lincoln, ed., *Martin Luther King, Jr.: A Profile* (Hill & Wang, 1970), which includes Meier's classic essay. Peter J. Albert and Ronald Hoffman have edited a more recent symposium, *We Shall Overcome: Martin Luther King, Jr. and the Black Freedom Struggle* (Da Capo Press, 1990). Stephen B. Oates, *Let the Trumpet Sound: The Life of Martin*

Luther King, Jr. (Harper & Row, 1982) uses King's papers but is mainly descriptive. Also see Oates, "Trumpet of Conscience: A Portrait of Martin Luther King, Jr.," *American History Illustrated* (April 1988); David Garrow, "Martin Luther King, Jr. and the Cross of Leadership," *Peace and Change* (Fall 1987); and "The Intellectual Development of Martin Luther King, Jr.: Influences and Commentaries," *Union Seminary Quarterly* (vol. 40, 1986), pp. 5–20. A well-written early biography is David L. Lewis, *King: A Critical Biography* (Praeger, 1970). See also Lewis's "Martin Luther King, Jr. and the Promise of Nonviolent Populism," in John Hope Franklin and August Meier, eds., *Black Leaders of the Twentieth Century* (University of Illinois Press, 1982). Two volumes that defy description are Taylor Branch's sprawling *Parting the Waters* (Simon & Schuster, 1988) and *Pillar of Fire* (Simon & Schuster, 1998), which takes the reader through the King years up to 1965. A third volume has yet to be published.

The literature of the civil rights movement is also enormous. Two of the best overviews written for students are John A. Salmond, *My Mind Set on Freedom: A History of the Civil Rights Movement, 1954–1968* (Ivan R. Dee, 1997), a survey in the American Ways series; and Peter B. Levy, *The Civil Rights Movement* (Greenwood Press, 1998), which is part of the Greenwood Press Guides to Historic Events of the Twentieth Century series. Two excellent collections of essays are Charles W. Eagles, ed., *The Civil Rights Movement in America* (University Press of Mississippi, 1986), a symposium held at the University of Mississippi in 1985 among several of the most important civil rights historians, and Paul Winters, ed., *The Civil Rights Movement* (Greenhaven Press, 2000), which contains a number of useful topical articles. Three more detailed studies are Jack M. Bloom's theoretical *Class, Race, and the Civil Rights Movement* (Indiana University Press, 1987); Harvard Sitkoff, *The Struggle for Black Equality, 1954–1992*, rev. ed. (Hill & Wang, 1993); and David R. Goldfield, *Black, White, and Southern: Race Relations and Southern Culture, 1940 to the Present* (Louisiana State University Press, 1990). The best film series on the civil rights movement is Henry Hampton's 14-hour *Eyes on the Prize: America's Civil Rights Years, 1954–1965*. Two excellent primary source anthologies came from this series: Clayborne Carson et al., eds., *Eyes on the Prize: Civil Rights Reader* (Penguin Books, 1991) and Henry Hampton and Steve Fayer, eds., *Voice of Freedom: An Oral History of the Civil Rights Movement From the 1950s Through the 1980s* (Bantam Books, 1990).

Local studies that de-emphasize the national movement covered so well by the contemporary press and most American history texts include William Chafe, *Civilities and Civil Rights: Greensboro, North Carolina, and the Black Struggle for Freedom* (Oxford University Press, 1981), which castigates the white moderates for using southern charm to avoid the racial divide; Adam Fairclough, *Race and Democracy: The Civil Rights Struggle in Louisiana, 1915–1972* (University of Georgia Press, 1995); Charles M. Payne, *I've Got the Light of Freedom: The Organizing Tradition and the Mississippi Freedom Struggle* (University of California Press, 1995); and John Dittmer, *Local People: The Struggle for Civil Rights in Mississippi* (University of Illinois, 1994).

ISSUE 7

Did the Great Society Fail?

YES: Charles Murray, from "The Legacy of the 60's," *Commentary* (July 1992)

NO: Joseph A. Califano, Jr., from "How Great Was the Great Society?" in Barbara C. Jordan and Elspeth D. Rostow, eds., *The Great Society: A Twenty Year Critique* (LBJ Library and LBJ School of Public Affairs, 1986)

ISSUE SUMMARY

YES: Conservative social critic Charles Murray argues that not only did the Great Society's retraining, anticrime, and welfare programs not work, but they actually contributed to the worsening plight of U.S. inner cities.

NO: Joseph A. Califano, Jr., a former aide to President Lyndon Johnson, maintains that the Great Society programs brought about positive revolutionary changes in the areas of civil rights, education, health care, the environment, and consumer protection.

Now that the twentieth century has ended, historians can look back at the era's three major political reform movements: Progressivism (1900–1917); the New Deal (1933–1938); and the Great Society (1963–1965). There were a number of similarities among the three movements. They were all led by activist, Democratic presidents—Woodrow Wilson, Franklin Roosevelt, and Lyndon Johnson. Top-heavy Democratic congressional majorities were created, which allowed the reform-minded presidents to break through the gridlock normally posed by an unwieldy Congress and to pass an unusual amount of legislation in a short time span. Finally, all three reform currents came to a sudden stop when America's entrance into war diverted the nation's physical and emotional resources away from reform efforts at home.

Progressivism, the New Deal, and the Great Society also had to grapple with the social and economic problems of a nation where the majority of people lived in cities with populations of 100,000 or more and worked for large corporations. In order to solve these problems, government could no longer be a passive observer of the Industrial Revolution. Reformers believed that government would have to intervene in order to make capitalism operate fairly. Two approaches were used: (1) regulating the economy from the top down and (2) solving social problems from the bottom up.

World War II, the subsequent cold war, a world economy that was dominated by the United States until the late 1960s, and a general prosperity that prevailed in the economic cycle kept reform efforts at a minimum during the Truman (1945–1953) and Eisenhower (1953–1961) presidencies.

In 1960, when Democrat John F. Kennedy defeated Republican Richard Nixon, there were two major social and economic problems that remained unresolved by the New Deal: (1) the failure to integrate blacks into the mainstream of American society and (2) the failure to provide a decent standard of living for the hard-core poor, the aged, the tenant farmers, the migrant workers, the unemployed coal miners and mill workers, and the single mothers of the inner city. Early in Kennedy's administration, Congress passed the Area Redevelopment Act of 1961, which provided close to $400 million in federal loans and grants for help to 675 "distressed areas" of high unemployment and low economic development. The president had plans for a more comprehensive attack on poverty, but his assassination on November 22, 1963, prevented implementation.

Kennedy's successor, Lyndon Johnson, took advantage of the somber mood of the country after Kennedy's assassination and of his landslide election victory in 1964, which created top-heavy Democratic congressional majorities of 295 to 140 in the House of Representatives and 68 to 32 in the Senate. Johnson believed that the Great Society and its programs were to be the completion of the New Deal. The Civil Rights Act of 1964 and the Voting Rights Act of 1965 introduced blacks into the mainstream of American society. Medicare and Medicaid tied health care for the elderly and poor people to the social security system. And the Elementary Secondary Education and the Higher Education Acts of 1965 provided funds for low-income local school districts and scholarships and subsidized low-interest loans for needy college students.

In January 1964 Johnson called for an "unconditional war on poverty." Later that year the Economic Opportunity Act was passed. This created an Office of Economic Opportunity (OEO), which set up a variety of community action programs for the purpose of expanding the educational, health care, housing, and employment opportunities in poor neighborhoods. Between 1965 and 1970 the OEO operated on the cheap, establishing such Community Action Programs (CAPs) as the Job Corps, which trained lower-class teenagers and young adults for employment, and Head Start, whose purpose was to give underprivileged preschool children skills that they could use when they attended regular elementary schools.

In the first of the following selections, Charles Murray argues that the liberal Great Society retraining, anticrime, and welfare programs not only did not work but contributed to the worsening plight of U.S. inner cities. In the second selection, Joseph A. Califano, Jr., argues that the Great Society programs brought about positive revolutionary changes in the areas of civil rights, education, health care, the environment, and consumer protection.

The Legacy of the 60's

Is President Bush hinting that the Peace Corps destroyed the moral fiber of poor people?" asked Albert Shanker, the president of the American Federation of Teachers, responding to the claim by the White House spokesman, Marlin Fitzwater, that the failed social programs of the 1960's were responsible for the Los Angeles riot. For Senator Daniel Patrick Moynihan, Attorney General William Barr's assertion that the Great Society caused the breakdown of family structure was "one of the most depraved statements I have ever heard from an American official." Even Republican campaign strategists were having none of the administration line, the New York *Times* reported. "Next," one of them was quoted as saying, "Marlin [Fitzwater] will blame the savings-and-loan crisis on Woodrow Wilson."

Speaking of blame, I must take a share of it for the ridicule heaped on the administration, for in 1984 I published a book called *Losing Ground* which concluded that the reforms of social policy in the 60's directly made things worse for the American poor. And, ineptly as the administration went about pressing its point, I agree with Fitzwater's more ambitious thesis. The conditions in South-Central Los Angeles in 1992 that produced the riot *are* importantly a product of those reforms of a quarter-century ago....

The post–L.A. received wisdom seems to have three components. First, since the Republicans have been in power for twelve years, current social policy is their social policy. Second, the plight of black America got worse in the 80's. Third, we know by this time that some programs worked, with Head Start and Job Corps heading the list, so it is time to hitch up our pants and start doing the things that we know how to do.

All three of these contentions are wrong—with qualifications, of course, but still wrong.

❧

For most of affluent America, the social policies of the 60's are over and done with. Most of these people have long since sent their children to private schools or moved to suburbs where the public schools are run as the parents wish. Most live in communities where the cops roust suspicious people, the Supreme Court

From Charles Murray, "The Legacy of the 60's," *Commentary* (July 1992). Copyright © 1992 by Charles Murray. Reprinted by permission of *Commentary* and the author. Notes omitted.

be damned, and crime is low; or they live in urban enclaves where (within the enclave) crime is low. As for the rules about welfare and food stamps and social services, these never affected the affluent.

Within the inner city, however, especially among the poor, and most especially among the black poor, the 60's remain in full flower. An adolescent on the streets of an inner city as of 1992 lives in a governmental and policy environment only marginally different from the one that had evolved by the early 70's.

The schools work much as they did then. The reforms of the 60's saw an elaborate social agenda laid on the schools, the imposition of restrictions on how schools could deal with problem students (and, indirectly, how effectively they could educate gifted students), and. layers of bureaucracy and books of rules that went along with vastly expanded federal assistance.

Suburban schools jettisoned much of this nonsense in the 80's. But the reforms of the 60's dove-tailed nicely with the propensity of big-city school bureaucracies to become ever more immobile, for the teachers' unions to hedge their responsibilities ever more restrictively, and for big-city pressure groups to use the schools as a political football. A few cities such as Chicago are making desperate attempts to break out of this bind, but with little success. Whatever was wrong with the training and the social signals being given by the educational system to an inner-city adolescent in the early 70's is still wrong today, and the reforms of the 60's still bear important responsibility for that.

Welfare remains more generous than it was during the heyday of the 60's reforms. I know this conflicts with the endlessly repeated claim that the purchasing power of welfare benefits has fallen so much that we are back to the levels of the 50's. But this argument is always expressed in terms of the purchasing power of the Aid to Families with Dependent Children (AFDC) benefits. If instead one includes all the major elements in the welfare package —adding in food stamps, Medicaid, and housing subsidies—then benefits increased rapidly during the decade from 1965 to 1974, retreated modestly in real value throughout the rest of the 70's, and rose during the 80's.

Being more precise involves getting into the question of how Medicaid and housing benefits are to be valued. But throughout the range of the accepted methods, it remains true that the value of the welfare package in 1992 is higher than it was when Ronald Reagan took office, and that it is at the level of the early 70's, just below the peak. Furthermore, these statements are based on calculations that do not include Women, Infants, and Children (WIC) benefits, school-lunch programs, and the many special funds and services for welfare recipients that are part of the package in most major cities.

In short, the assertion that the situation facing a potential welfare mother in 1992 is significantly different from the situation that has faced her ever since the end of the 60's reforms is simply wrong. The key point about welfare is this: in 1960, it was so meager that only a small set of young women at the very bottom layer of society could think it was "enough" to enable a woman to keep a baby without a husband. By 1970, it was "enough" both in the resources it provided and in the easier terms under which it could be obtained, to enable a broad stratum of low-income women to keep a baby without a husband. That remains true today.

The changes during the Reagan years consisted of the amendments to the Omnibus Budget Reconciliation Act (OBRA) in 1981, which tightened the eligibility rules for receiving AFDC payments, and the welfare reform bill of 1988. The OBRA amendments represented a significant change, moving away from the assumptions of the 60's, and it produced a reduction in the welfare rolls. Had there been another half-dozen reforms with the same weight and vector, the Reagan administration could properly claim to have had its own welfare policy. But the OBRA amendments were an isolated exception, and their effects were limited to potential recipients who possessed substantial independent income— not the heart of the welfare problem.

The only other significant change in the welfare system, in 1988, went in the opposite direction. The rhetoric was new, reflecting the principle that society expects welfare recipients to work. But the work and training aspects of the bill were deferred and indefinite. The immediate effect was to expand benefits by granting AFDC women a year of Medicaid coverage and child-care benefits after leaving the rolls. As in the reforms of the 60's, the intent was to give women on welfare an incentive to get jobs, but, again as in the reforms of the 60's, the legislation ignored the effects on women who were not on welfare.

Since 1988, the AFDC rolls have broken out of the narrow range within which they had been moving for a decade and have been climbing steadily. Some blame it on the recession, even though welfare rolls have not previously tracked with unemployment. It seems more likely that we are observing the replay of an old phenomenon: whenever Congress has legislated a new incentive for women to leave welfare, the unintended downward pull into the welfare system has outweighed the intended upward push out.

⟡

With regard to crime, the situation in the 90's compared to the 60's is mixed. The 60's gave the nation a fundamentally new stance toward law enforcement and punishment. The number of prisoners dropped during the 60's—not just prisoners in proportion to arrests, but the raw number. Meanwhile, the Supreme Court was handing down the decisions—*Miranda, Mapp,* and the rest of the usual suspects—that are notorious for restricting the police. The administration of justice during the 60's became more haphazard, with wider use of plea bargains, longer delays between arrest and trial, trial and sentencing, sentencing and execution of judgment, along with other changes that reduced the swiftness and certainty of punishment for crime. It also happened that crime increased by an astonishing amount during the 60's.

What is different today? Yes, everyone now favors law and order, including the Supreme Court. But the major decisions of the 60's have been narrowed only at the margins, not reversed. The rules of the game remain essentially the same as they were at the end of the reform period. If you get picked up today for a felony in a big city, chances are you will be back on the street tomorrow, even if you have a prior record. If your case is pursued at all (many are not), chances are you will be able to plea-bargain it down to a much lesser charge. Unless you have a long prior record, chances are you will do no jail time. All of these procedures will probably take months to transpire.

In one respect, policy has unquestionably changed. The prison population more than doubled during the 80's, indicating that the risks of going to prison if caught were raised. To that extent, those who say that the Republicans established their own policy and are accountable for it have a point. There are, however, three bottom lines in the crime game. The first is your chance of being punished if you get caught, and that has indeed gone up. But the second is the chance of getting caught at all, and that has either remained steady since the end of the reform period or dropped. The third is opportunities to make money from crime, and this has remained at least constant and, in the drug trade, expanded.

It is unclear how these conflicting trends might balance out in the eyes of an adolescent standing on a streetcorner contemplating whether to get involved in a hustle. It is certainly a mistake to think that the law-and-order years of the Republicans have made a major difference in that adolescent's perception of how the criminal-justice system works. The system of 1992 is still essentially the system that was shaped by the reform period.

None of this discussion is intended to imply that we could return to the pre-reform levels of crime or illegitimacy if we repealed a few laws and reversed a few Supreme Court decisions. On the contrary, the social dynamics of the inner city have taken on a life of their own, and I think it is unlikely that anything short of radical changes will produce much of an effect on the behaviors associated with the underclass. But if the question is how the social policy of the 60's can be responsible for the problems of the 90's, the answer is straightforward: the reform period set those dynamics in motion and, with minor exceptions, the policies it produced are still in effect.

The next question is whether the 80's saw blacks lose ground, thereby producing the "rage and frustration" that are said to have caused the Los Angeles riot. Unquestionably, some things did get worse, principally antagonism between the races. But racial hostility is one thing; the facts regarding black progress and regression during the 80's are another. (All the [relevant] data . . . may be found in the basic statistical compendia of the Bureau of the Census, the National Center for Health Statistics, and the Departments of Labor and Education.) . . .

What is one to make of [the] heterogeneous set of indicators and results? Partisans of both sides will seize upon the indicators that suit them, but the pattern is probably susceptible to a few generalizations. One is that black status improved in both the 70's and 80's on things that primarily reflect external conditions or behaviors by the black middle class. Infant mortality drops as medical technology improves; black enrollment in college expands with financial help and affirmative action; white-collar employment grows among blacks who have taken advantage of educational opportunities.

The second general comment is that the deterioration in black status is concentrated in the mainsprings of the underclass: dropout from the labor force among young males and births to single young women, both of which continued to grow in the 80's, though more slowly than in the 70's. As long as these behaviors continue, the plight of the black inner city will deepen.

The final general comment is that the 80's come out of the comparison much better than the day-to-day media accounts would lead one to expect. People who want to indict the 80's as a decade of neglect must find other data. I am unaware of any major surprises that lurk in such other measures, but perhaps they exist. If anyone finds them, I suggest only that the presenter follow [this] procedure...: show the figures for 1960 and 1970 along with those for 1980 and 1990, and focus on indicators that represent how people's lives have changed, not how government spending has changed.

ᴇ⁄ᴏᴦᴏ

So far as government spending goes, there is now almost a mantra: "We know Head Start works. We know Job Corps works." Other programs sometimes make the list, but these are the stars. Commentary on the problems of the black inner city also has recently begun to assume that certain solutions will work, if only we do the obvious thing and try them.

Thus one often reads op-ed columns in which it is assumed that of course black teenage girls would have fewer babies if only they had access to better sex education, or that of course the unemployment rate among teenage black males would go down if only jobs were made available. This self-assurance is invincibly ignorant of history. The effects of such programs have been assessed, we have a rich and reasonably consistent body of results, and those results are not encouraging.

Head Start is a striking example. Let me begin by saying that I think a good preschool is generally a good thing for the same reason that kindergarten is a good thing, and I am in favor of providing good preschools for disadvantaged children. Head Start, however, is not being discussed just as a nice thing to do for children, but as an example of how we can make progress in the inner city.

The reality is that no program of the 60's has been more often evaluated, more thoroughly, than Head Start—a synthesis published in 1983 annotated 1,500 studies. This work has produced a few broad conclusions. One is that Head Start programs, properly implemented, can enhance some aspects of social development and school performance. But these effects are spotty, and when they occur they fade, disappearing altogether after about three years. All in all, Head Start is not exactly a failure (it is still a nice thing to do for kids), but neither is there any reason to believe that anything will change in the inner city if only Congress fully funds Head Start.

But surely we know that Head Start reduces delinquency and unemployment and pregnancies in later life? No. We have a handful of experimental programs that have made such claims with varying degrees of evidence to back them up, but none of them bears much resemblance to Head Start.

By far the best known of these is the Perry Preschool Program from Ypsilanti, Michigan, which had 58 youngsters and a control group of 65. (Let us pause for a moment and consider what would happen to someone who tried to claim that an intervention strategy did *not* work on the basis of one program with 58 youngsters.) Perry Preschool had four teachers each year, and in any one year these four teachers together were dealing with no more than a total of 24 children—a 1:6 ratio. The teachers were handpicked, highly trained and motivated. They received further extensive training in the special curriculum adopted for the program. In addition to the daily preschool time, the program included an hour-and-a-half home visit to each mother each week.

The first salient point is thus that Perry Preschool was a handcrafted little jewel that the federal government cannot conceivably replicate nationwide— not because there is not enough money (though that is part of it), but because of the nature of large programs. Bureaucracies give you Head Starts, not Perry Preschools.

The other salient point has to do with outcomes. Perry Preschool is the chief source of the claim that preschool intervention can reduce high-school dropout, unemployment, delinquency, and pregnancies. Yet when the program's 58 children were assessed at age nineteen, 33 percent had dropped out of high school, 41 percent were unemployed, 31 percent had been arrested, and the 25 girls had experienced 17 pregnancies. All of these numbers were evidence of success because the rates for the control group were even worse, but it is not the sort of success that the advocates of Head Start can afford to describe explicitly.

⌘

Like Head Start, the Job Corps has been evaluated many times over the years. When the results have been aggregated over all centers, they have usually shown modest gains in average earnings—a matter of a few hundred dollars per year. When evaluators examine individual centers, anecdotal evidence indicates that some are more effective than others. The best ones have a demanding work load, strict rules of behavior, and strict enforcement (which means that many of the entrants never finish the course).

In other words, the Job Corps works for young people who are able to get up every morning, stick with a task, accept a subordinate relationship, and work hard. These people also tend to do well without the Job Corps. Not even the best of the Job Corps centers has a good track record with young people who cannot make themselves get up every morning, who get discouraged easily, get mad when someone tells them what to do, and take a nap when no one is watching. But the latter are among the characteristics of the chronically unemployed.

We have a great deal of experience with job programs that try to deal with the chronically unemployed and the inner-city youth who has never held a job. After twelve years in which social programs have been unpopular, it is easy to forget how massive those job programs were. At their height in the late 70's, the programs under the Comprehensive Employment and Training Act (CETA) had nearly four million first-time entrants in a single year and an annual budget equivalent to $19 billion in 1990 dollars. The evaluations of CETA came in, and the consensus conclusion was that it had some positive impact on women, but not on men. This is consistent with findings from other, small-scale demonstration projects such as those conducted by the Manpower Demonstration Research Corporation and early results from the evaluation of the Job Training Partnership Act.

Unfortunately, the failure to affect males is decisive, for a core problem in the inner city is that males are not assuming their role in the community as husbands, fathers, and providers. If job programs are to be the answer for the 90's, what is it that we propose to do differently this time around?

More generally, attempts to solve the problems of the inner city have a consistent record. The failures vastly outnumber the successes. The claimed successes tend to evaporate when an independent evaluator assesses them. The handful of successes that survive scrutiny are local, small-scale, initiated and run by dedicated people, and operated idiosyncratically and pragmatically—all the things that large-scale federal programs inherently cannot be. Nor, as the government has found after many attempts, can the successes be franchised like a McDonald's, for the idiosyncratic capabilities of the founders turn out to be crucial to the success of the original.

Ever since the conclusion that "nothing works" was advanced in the 80's, the advocates of new programs have tried to show why it is an exaggeration. They have been able to do so, insofar as some problems (such as poverty among the elderly) can be cured by writing enough checks, a task at which the federal government excels. But when it comes to programs that will change the behavior of adolescents and young adults, the record of federal social programs (and most state and municipal social programs) remains dismal. The resurgence of optimism about social programs represents a mismatch between the actual nature of the underclass and the way people want it to be, and a mismatch between the actual way that large-scale programs are implemented and the way each new generation of reformers thinks it can implement them.

❦

These observations are out of season. It is a time for lighting candles. But there is a case to be made for cursing the darkness. South-Central Los Angeles and inner cities throughout America did not need to evolve the way they have done. Until the last few decades, poor communities throughout American history had been able to function as communities, despite objective deprivation and oppression far greater than any community faces in 1992. Then, in the space of a few years, just as we were finally lifting the objective elements of deprivation and oppression, we inadvertently undercut the pilings on which communities rest.

It turns out that communities survive by socializing their young to certain norms of behavior. They achieve that socialization with the help of realities to which parents can point—you have to work, or you won't eat; if you don't have a husband, you won't be able to take care of your children; if you commit crimes, you will go to jail. From this raw material, communities fashion the gentler rewards and penalties of social life that constrain unwanted behaviors and foster desired ones. Outside the inner city, we are busily reconstructing the damage done to the social fabric during the reform period of the 60's, with considerable success. Inside the inner city, that fabric has become so tattered that it is difficult to see any external means of restoration.

I will therefore refrain from concluding with my own ten-point plan. All we can be sure of is that authentic solutions will be radical ones. There are essentially two alternatives. One is authoritarian, treating the inner city as occupied territory and its citizens as wards to be tutored and manipulated by the wise hand of the state. The other, and in my view the only choice that American democracy can live with, is to take seriously the old aphorism that the only way to make a man trustworthy is to trust him. The only way that inner-city communities will again begin to function as communities is if the individuals within them are again permitted and required to engage in that most Jeffersonian of enterprises, self-governance.

Joseph A. Califano, Jr.    **NO**

How Great Was the Great Society?

Historians should make no mistake in judging the Johnson administration. What Lyndon Johnson and the Great Society were about twenty years ago was revolution.

President Johnson came to office in an America where the economy had been stagnant for several years; an America where movie theaters and restaurants within a short walk of our nation's Capitol were still segregated, for whites only; an America of unparalleled abundance and prosperity in which more than 20 percent of the people lived in poverty.

It was also an America feeling the birth pains of urbanization and the world's first postindustrial society, a nation becoming a lonely crowd, troubled by the organization men in gray flannel suits, the beat generation, and everything getting bigger than life.

The modern age that had brought America unprecedented material riches had also brought an assault on the individuality of the human spirit. The loneliness of the large city was replacing the friendliness of the rural hamlet. Chain stores with anonymous clerks and thousands of products were turning the neighborhood grocer, haberdasher, and druggist into Norman Rockwell antiques. Computers were replacing people as bill collectors. The mass production of automobiles exceeded our ability to construct and repair roads. Real estate was owned and being traded by people who never saw it. Products were sold and money lent by distant corporations, far away from buyers and borrowers across America. Television was nationalizing culture and taste, reshaping politics and entertainment, and bringing bad news into living rooms every night.

The task of preserving personal identity and human dignity was difficult enough for the affluent middle class of America; it was impossible for the poor who struggled in a supersociety that threatened to engulf the individual with its supermarketplace, superuniversities, overcrowded urban schools and courts, big unions, big corporations, big governments.

Against this backdrop, it's not surprising that Lyndon Johnson's historic University of Michigan commencement speech described the Great Society which he aspired to create as "a place where men are more concerned with the quality of their goals than the quantity of their goods... a challenge constantly renewed; beckoning us toward a destiny where the meaning of our lives

From Joseph A. Califano, Jr., "How Great Was the Great Society?" in Barbara C. Jordan and Elspeth D. Rostow, eds., *The Great Society: A Twenty Year Critique* (LBJ Library and LBJ School of Public Affairs, 1986). Copyright © 1986 by Joseph A. Califano, Jr. Reprinted by permission of the author.

matches the marvelous products of our labor." President Johnson voiced the hope that in the future men would look back and say: "It was then, after a long and weary way, that man turned the exploits of his genius to the full enrichment of his life."

How much of Johnson's hope did the Great Society realize? Was it good or bad for America?

The cornerstone of the Great Society was a robust economy. With that, the overwhelming, majority of the people could get their fair share of America's prosperity. A growing economic pie also allowed the affluent to take bigger pieces, even as we committed a larger portion to the public sector.

Despite a growing economy, some citizens needed special help. There were those who needed the sort of support most of us got from our mothers and fathers: a decent place to live, clothing, health care, an education to develop their talents. Great Society programs like elementary and secondary education, financial aid for college, job training, and much of the health care effort were designed to put them on their own feet, not on the taxpayer's back.

There were also Americans who, largely through no fault of their own, were unable to take care of themselves. For them, the Great Society sought to provide either money or the services that money could buy, so they could live at a minimum level of human dignity. Among these were the poor children, the permanently disabled, and the elderly.

Did the Great Society programs fail? Many who come at them with the political hindsight of the contemporary right think so. But—

Ask the 11 million students who have received loans for their college education whether the Higher Education Act failed.

Ask the 4 million blacks who registered to vote in eleven Southern states and the 6,000 blacks who held elective public office in 1984 whether the Voting Rights Act failed.

Ask the 8 million children who have been through Head Start whether the Poverty Program failed.

Ask the millions of Americans who have enjoyed the 14,000 miles of scenic trails, 7,200 miles of scenic rivers, 45 new national parks, 83 million acres of wilderness areas, and 833 endangered species of plants, animals, and birds that have been preserved—ask them whether the 278 conservation and beautification laws, including the Wilderness Act of 1964, the Endangered Species Preservation Act of 1966, and the Scenic Trails System and Wild and Scenic Rivers Acts of 1968 failed.

Ask the 2 million senior citizens who were raised above the poverty level by the minimum payment requirements of the Social Security Act amendments of 1966 whether that legislation failed.

Ask the millions of visitors whether the laws establishing the Kennedy Center and Hirschorn Museum failed.

Ask the 400 professional theater companies, the 200 dance companies, and the 100 opera companies that have sprung up since 1965 whether the National Endowments for the Arts and Humanities failed.

Ask San Franciscans that use BART, Washingtonians that use Metro, Atlantans that use MARTA, and cities and counties that use the 56,000 buses purchased since 1966—the equivalent of our entire national fleet—whether the Urban Mass Transit Act failed.

Ask the millions of workers who gained new skills through the Manpower Development and Training Act, the Job Corps, and the National Alliance for Businessmen, whether those programs failed.

Ask the 10 million Americans living in the 3 million housing units funded by federal aid whether the Great Society Housing Acts of 1964 and 1968 failed.

What would America be like if there had been no Great Society programs?

Perhaps no better examples exist than the changes brought about by health laws, civil rights statutes, and consumer legislation.

Health.   Without Medicare and Medicaid; the heart, cancer and stroke legislation; and forty other health bills, life expectancy would be several years shorter, and deaths from heart disease, stroke, diabetes, pneumonia, and influenza would be much higher. Since 1962, life expectancy has jumped five years, from seventy to seventy-five. Life expectancy for blacks has risen even more, with a stunning eight-year improvement for black women. This year, for the first time in America, a black baby girl at birth has a life expectancy greater than that of a white baby boy.

Civil rights.   In 1965, when the Voting Rights Act was passed, there were 79 black elected officials in the South; now there are nearly 3,000. Nationally, the percentage of blacks registered to vote has grown from less than 30 percent to almost 60 percent. Before the Civil Rights Act of 1964, black people in large parts of this country could not sleep in most hotels, eat in most restaurants, try on clothes at department stores, or get a snack at a lunch counter. Today, this seems a foreign and distant memory. Black enrollment in higher education has tripled, and the proportion of blacks holding professional, technical, and management jobs has more than doubled.

Consumer protection.   The Great Society's consumer legislation sought to give the individual a fair chance in the world of products sold with the aid of the best designers and marketers, money lent on notes prepared by the shrewdest lawyers and accountants, meat and poultry from chemically fed animals, thousands of products from baby cribs that choked to refrigerator doors that couldn't be pushed open from the inside. So the Great Society gave birth to the Truth in Packaging, Truth in Lending, Wholesome Meat, Wholesome Poultry, and Product Safety Acts. And if you want to know why it's so hard to open a Tylenol bottle, blame the Great Society's child safety legislation. Auto and Highway Safety Acts gave us seat belts, padded dash boards, and a host of automobile design changes.

Has America changed?

- When Lyndon Johnson spoke at the University of Michigan in 1964, he noted that 8 million adult Americans had not finished five years of school, 20 million had not finished eight years, and 54 million had not completed high school. Today, only 3 million have not completed five years, 8 million have not completed 8 years, and 28 million have not completed high school.

- Infant mortality has been cut by more than half, from 26 deaths per 1,000 live births in 1963 to 10.9 in 1983.
- More than 30,000 schools have received funds under the Elementary and Secondary Education Act to teach remedial math and reading to disadvantaged students.
- Thanks to Highway Beautification, 600,000 billboards have been removed from highways and 10,000 junkyards have been cleaned up.

And what of the overall impact of the Great Society on poverty in America? In 1960, 22 percent of the American people lived below the official poverty level. When Lyndon Johnson left office in 1969, that had dropped to 13 percent. Despite the relatively flat economy of the 1970s, the official poverty level did not rise. Indeed, by 1979 it was still about 12 percent. But, and this is a but we must repeat again and again, if we count the income effects of the Great Society service programs, such as those for health care, job training, aid to education, and rehabilitation for the handicapped, by the mid-1970s the poverty rate had been reduced to less than 7 percent. The early 1980s have sadly seen the rate rise up again.

And the Great Society has been invaluable to President Reagan, not just as a political whipping boy, but as the key to his attack on inflation. President Reagan was able to drive down inflation with a sledgehammer because of the cushions Lyndon Johnson's Great Society provided: liberalization of welfare, food stamps and unemployment compensation; Medicaid and Medicare; community health centers; work training; housing; and a host of other programs. Ronald Reagan taught us that we can rapidly wring inflation out of the economy because the remnants of a compassionate, interventionist government are there not only to keep the mobs off the streets, but to keep most needy families at a minimum living standard and adequately fed.

I've always felt that Lyndon Johnson died convinced that the civil rights programs, notably the Voting Rights Act, marked his administration's finest hours. He certainly spent his political capital generously to enact these programs. To me, the Great Society's achievements with older Americans have also been remarkable. The combination of Medicare, Medicaid's support of nursing homes (forty-three cents of each Medicaid dollar goes to them), minimum Social Security benefits, senior citizen centers and food programs, and improved Veterans Administration benefits, along with private-sector retirement plans, virtually eliminated poverty among the elderly in America. As LBJ used to say, much remains to be done; I believe a great deal of our energies and resources in the future must be devoted to poor children and single-parent families.

I've given many examples of the successes of the Great Society. What of its shortcomings?

Did we legislate too much? Perhaps. We seemed to have a law for everything. Fire safety. Water safety. Pesticide control for the farm. Rat control for the ghetto. Bail reform. Immigration reform. Medical libraries. Presidential disability. Juvenile delinquency. Safe streets. Tire safety. Age discrimination. Fair housing. Corporate takeovers. International monetary reform. Sea grant colleges. When we discovered that poor students needed a good lunch, we devised legislation for a school lunch program. When we later found out that breakfast helped them learn better, we whipped up a law for a school breakfast program. When a pipeline exploded, we proposed the Gas Pipeline Safety Act. When my son Joe swallowed a bottle of aspirin, President Johnson sent Congress a Child Safety Act. When it was too hard for citizens to get information out of the government, we drafted a Freedom of Information Act. When we needed more doctors, or nurses, or teachers, we legislated programs to train them.

Did we stub our toes? Of course.

We made our mistakes, plenty of them. In health, our Great Society quest to provide access to health care for the elderly and the poor led us to accede to the demands of hospitals and physicians for open-ended cost-plus and fee-for-service payments. As a result, with Medicare and Medicaid, we adopted inherently wasteful and inefficient reimbursement systems. Incidently, we recognized the danger of exploding health care costs in 1968, but Congress denied President Johnson's request to change Medicare's payment system.

There were too many narrow categorical grant programs created in health, education, and social services. It's one thing to embark upon a program to help states educate millions of poor children, or to provide scholarships so that any American with the brains and talent can go to college. It's quite another to set curriculum priorities from Washington with funds that must be spent on specific subjects of education, such as environmental or ethnic studies or metric education.

The struggle for civil rights left us deeply and often unjustifiably suspicious of the motives and intentions of institutional and middle America. It influenced our attitudes about consumer safety, occupational health, environmental protection, and transportation. It undermined our trust in the states.

As a result, many federal laws were written in far too much detail. And regulation writers cast aside the great American common-law principle that every citizen is presumed to obey, the law. Quite the contrary, we wrote laws and regulations on the theory that each citizen would seek to circumvent them. We became victims of the self-defeating and self-fulfilling premise that, unless we were protected by a law or regulation, we were vulnerable. As regulations got into too many nooks and crannies of American life, they created testy resistance and needlessly invited ridicule. But we should remember that the massive influx of regulations that so irritated Americans came not during the Johnson years, but the decade that followed. It was the seventies, not the sixties, that brought us 6,000 schedule codes under Medicare, pages and pages of regulations under the Occupational Health and Safety legislation, hundreds of pages of education regulations.

At times we may have lost sight of the fact that these laws—hundreds of them—were not an end in themselves. Often we did not recognize that government could not do it all. And, of course, there were overpromises. But they were based on high hopes and great expectations and fueled by the frustration of seeing so much poverty and ignorance and illness amidst such wealth. We simply could not accept poverty, ignorance, and hunger as intractable, permanent features of American society. There was no child we could not feed; no adult we could not put to work; no disease we could not cure; no toy, food, or appliance we could not make safer; no air or water we could not clean. But it was all part of asking "not how much, but how good; not only how to create wealth, but how to use it, not only how fast we (were) going, but where we [were] headed."

This twentieth anniversary of the Great Society is not a time for giving up on those precious goals to which so many of us devoted so much of our energy and our lives. It is not even a time for hunkering down. The Great Society is alive and well—in Medicare and Medicaid; in the air we breathe and the water we drink, in the rivers and lakes we swim in; in the schools and colleges our students attend; in the medical miracles from the National Institutes of Health; in housing and transportation and equal opportunity. We can build on the best of it, and recognize our mistakes and correct them.

We must once again join our talents and experience to make our government a responsive servant of the people. For a democratic government to respond means to lead, to forge the claims of narrow groups on the anvil of government to serve the needs of all of our people, to know the special importance of protecting the individual in the modern bureaucracy, to recognize the fundamental right of each person to live in human dignity.

That was what the Great Society at its best did. It converted the hopes and aspirations of all kinds of Americans into a political force that brought out much of the good in each of us. The result was a social revolution in race relations that even a bloody civil war could not achieve; a revolution in education that opened college to any American with the ability and ambition to go; a revolution in health that provided care for all the elderly and many of the poor; a sea change in the relationship of consumers to big corporate sellers and lenders; a born-again respect for our land and air and water that is still gaining momentum.

The achievements of the Great Society did not come easily. As everyone in this room knows, that kind of work in government is hard, often frustrating, sometimes exasperating. But the rewards are far greater for those in a democracy who work persistently to build and shape government to serve the people, than for those who tear it apart or lash out in despair and frustration because the task is too much for them. I deeply believe that the Great Society teaches that we can succeed in that work of building and shaping. Like G. K. Chesterton, "I do not believe in a fate that befalls people however they act. But I do believe in fate that befalls them unless they act."

Too many of us, including many of our young Americans and some in government, don't try because the tasks seem too difficult, sometimes impossible. Of course those who govern will make mistakes, plenty of them. But we must not fear failure. What we should fear above all is the judgment of God and history if we, the most affluent people on God's earth, free to act as we wish, choose not to govern justly, not to distribute our riches fairly, and not to help the most vulnerable among us—or worse if we choose not even to try. Whatever historians of the Great Society say twenty years later, they must admit that we tried, and I believe they will conclude that America is a better place because we did.

Note

1. Some statistics in this address are taken from papers prepared for this conference by professionals in fields on which the Great Society touched: Donald M. Baker, Counsel for Labor, Committee on Education and Labor, U.S. House of Representatives, and General Counsel. Office of Economic Opportunity, 1964–1969; Michael C. Barth, Vice President, ICF Incorporated, a Washington, D.C., consulting firm, an expert in economics and income maintenance programs; Livingston Biddle, former Chairman of the National Endowment For the Arts; Ernest L. Boyer, former U.S. Commissioner of Education and now President of the Carnegie Foundation for the Advancement of Teaching; Richard Cotton, an attorney with the Washington office of Dewey, Ballantine, Bushby, Palmer & Wood and an expert in environmental and energy issues; Karen Davis, economist and Chair, Department of Health Policy and Management at the Johns Hopkins University School of Public Health; Representative Henry B. Gonzalez, Chairman, Subcommittee on Housing and Community Development, Committee on Banking, Finance, and Urban Affairs, U.S. House of Representatives; Representative James J. Howard, Chairman, Committee on Public Works and Transportation, U.S. House of Representatives; David Swankin, a public-interest attorney in the Washington, D.C. law firm of Swankin and Turner and former Executive Director of the President's Committee on Consumer Interests, forerunner to the White House Office of Consumer Affairs; Ray Marshall, professor of economics at the LBJ School of Public Affairs and Secretary of Labor during the Carter administration, and William L. Taylor, Director of the Center for National Policy Review at Catholic University and David Tatel, attorney with the Washington, D.C., law firm of Hogan and Hartson and director of the HEW Office for Civil Rights during the Carter administration, both experts in civil rights. The text of the speech represents the views of Mr. Califano, for which he assumes complete responsibility.

POSTSCRIPT

Did the Great Society Fail?

$\mathbf{M}$urray is one of best known conservative social policy intellectuals in the United States. His *Losing Ground: American Social Policy,* 1950–1980 (Basic Books, 1984) was sponsored into a best-seller by the Manhattan Institute (a right-wing think tank) and became required reading for the Reagan administration staffers. The book uses statistical evidence to demonstrate that the Great Society welfare programs made the situation worse for the American underclass. Like President George Bush's press secretary, Marlin Fitzwater, Murray argues that the conditions in south central Los Angeles that produced the 1992 riots were "a product of the reforms of a quarter century ago."

Murray is not without his critics. Christopher Jencks disputes Murray's analysis in *Rethinking Social Policy: Race, Poverty and the Underclass* (Harvard University Press, 1992). Jencks argues, for example, that a single parent may provide a more desirable environment for raising children than a welfare mother who has been forced into an unreliable marriage. But Murray holds that only through a tight-knit nuclear family will the social problems of a poverty-ridden underclass be resolved.

While conservatives believe that the Great Society has gone too far, and while radicals argue that the reforms never extended beyond surface changes, a third group (liberals) defends both the thrust and the outcome of President Johnson's social programs. Califano gives a spirited defense of the Great Society's accomplishments, listing the hundreds of bills pouring forth from Congress concerning mass transportation, public housing, the environment, education, consumer protection, health care, and civil rights programs.

Did the Great Society succeed? Certainly Califano is correct in arguing that Johnson's programs benefited many middle-class families in the areas of health, education, and consumer protection. The elderly also got big boosts in social security payments and an improved health care package. Finally, where would African Americans be today without the Voting Rights Act of 1965?

Where Califano and Murray disagree is in the efforts of the job-training and welfare programs to eliminate hard-core poverty in the large cities. Murray contends that these programs created new problems. But Califano defends the goals and accomplishments of the Great Society.

Three books are essential to the understanding of the Johnson years: Nicholas Lemann, *The Promised Land: The Great Black Migration and How It Changed America* (Alfred A. Knopf, 1991); Allen J. Matusow, *The Unraveling of America: A History of Liberalism in the 1960's* (Harper & Row, 1984); and John Morton Blum, *Years of Discord: American Politics and Society, 1961–1974* (W. W. Norton, 1991).

ISSUE 8

Was the Americanization of the War in Vietnam Inevitable?

YES: Brian VanDeMark, from *Into the Quagmire: Lyndon Johnson and the Escalation of the Vietnam War* (Oxford University Press, 1991)

NO: H. R. McMaster, from *Dereliction of Duty: Lyndon Johnson, Robert McNamara, the Joint Chiefs of Staff, and the Lies That Led to Vietnam* (HarperCollins, 1997)

ISSUE SUMMARY

YES: Professor of history Brian VanDeMark argues that President Lyndon Johnson failed to question the viability of increasing U.S. involvement in the Vietnam War because he was a prisoner of America's global containment policy and because he did not want his opponents to accuse him of being soft on communism or endanger support for his Great Society reforms.

NO: H. R. McMaster, an active-duty army tanker, maintains that the Vietnam disaster was not inevitable but a uniquely human failure whose responsibility was shared by President Johnson and his principal military and civilian advisers.

At the end of World War II, imperialism was coming to a close in Asia. Japan's defeat spelled the end of its control over China, Korea, and the countries of Southeast Asia. Attempts by the European nations to reestablish their empires were doomed. Anti-imperialist movements emerged all over Asia and Africa, often producing chaos.

The United States faced a dilemma. America was a nation conceived in revolution and was sympathetic to the struggles of Third World nations. But the United States was afraid that many of the revolutionary leaders were Communists who would place their countries under the control of the expanding empire of the Soviet Union. By the late 1940s the Truman administration decided that it was necessary to stop the spread of communism. The policy that resulted was known as *containment*.

Vietnam provided a test of the containment doctrine in Asia. Vietnam had been a French protectorate from 1885 until Japan took control of it during World War II. Shortly before the war ended, the Japanese gave Vietnam its independence, but the French were determined to reestablish their influence in the area. Conflicts emerged between the French-led nationalist forces of South Vietnam and the Communist-dominated provisional government of the Democratic Republic of Vietnam (DRV), which was established in Hanoi in August 1945. Ho Chi Minh was the president of the DRV. An avowed Communist since the 1920s, Ho had also become the major nationalist figure in Vietnam. As the leader of the anti-imperialist movement against French and Japanese colonialism for over 30 years, Ho managed to tie together the communist and nationalist movements in Vietnam.

A full-scale war broke out in 1946 between the communist government of North Vietnam and the French-dominated country of South Vietnam. After the Communists defeated the French at the battle of Dien Bien Phu in May 1954, the latter decided to pull out. At the Geneva Conference that summer, Vietnam was divided at the 17th parallel, pending elections.

The United States became directly involved in Vietnam after the French withdrew. In 1955 the Republican president Dwight D. Eisenhower refused to recognize the Geneva Accord but supported the establishment of the South Vietnamese government. In 1956 South Vietnam's leader, Ngo Dinh Diem, with U.S. approval, refused to hold elections, which would have provided a unified government for Vietnam in accordance with the Geneva Agreement. The Communists in the north responded by again taking up the armed struggle. The war continued for another 19 years.

Both President Eisenhower and his successor, John F. Kennedy, were anxious to prevent South Vietnam from being taken over by the Communists, so economic assistance and military aid were provided. Kennedy's successor, Lyndon Johnson, changed the character of American policy in Vietnam by escalating the air war and increasing the number of ground forces from 21,000 in 1965 to a full fighting force of 550,000 at its peak in 1968.

The next president, Richard Nixon, adopted a new policy of "Vietnamization" of the war. Military aid to South Vietnam was increased to ensure the defeat of the Communists. At the same time, American troops were gradually withdrawn from Vietnam. South Vietnamese president Thieu recognized the weakness of his own position without the support of U.S. troops. He reluctantly signed the Paris Accords in January 1973 only after being told by Secretary of State Henry Kissinger that the United States would sign them alone. Once U.S. soldiers were withdrawn, Thieu's regime was doomed. In spring 1975 a full-scale war broke out, and the South Vietnamese government collapsed.

In the following selection, Brian VanDeMark argues that President Johnson failed to question the viability of increasing U.S. involvement in Vietnam because he was a prisoner of America's global containment policy and because he did not want his opponents to accuse him of being soft on communism. In the second selection, H. R. McMaster argues that the Vietnam disaster was not inevitable but a uniquely human failure whose responsibility was shared by Johnson and his civilian and military advisers.

 **YES**

Into the Quagmire

Vietnam divided America more deeply and painfully than any event since the Civil War. It split political leaders and ordinary people alike in profound and lasting ways. Whatever the conflicting judgments about this controversial war—and there are many—Vietnam undeniably stands as the greatest tragedy of twentieth-century U.S. foreign relations.

America's involvement in Vietnam has, as a result, attracted much critical scrutiny, frequently addressed to the question, "Who was guilty?"—"Who led the United States into this tragedy?" A more enlightening question, it seems, is "How and why did this tragedy occur?" The study of Vietnam should be a search for explanation and understanding, rather than for scapegoats.

Focusing on one important period in this long and complicated story—the brief but critical months from November 1964 to July 1965, when America crossed the threshold from limited to large-scale war in Vietnam—helps to answer that question. For the crucial decisions of this period resulted from the interplay of longstanding ideological attitudes, diplomatic assumptions and political pressures with decisive contemporaneous events in America and Vietnam.

Victory in World War II produced a sea change in America's perception of its role in world affairs. Political leaders of both parties embraced a sweepingly new vision of the United States as the defender against the perceived threat of monolithic communist expansion everywhere in the world. This vision of American power and purpose, shaped at the start of the Cold War, grew increasingly rigid over the years. By 1964–1965, it had become an ironbound and unshakable dogma, a received faith which policymakers unquestionably accepted—even though the circumstances which had fostered its creation had changed dramatically amid diffused authority and power among communist states and nationalist upheaval in the colonial world.

Policymakers' blind devotion to this static Cold War vision led America into misfortune in Vietnam. Lacking the critical perspective and sensibility to reappraise basic tenets of U.S. foreign policy in the light of changed events and local circumstances, policymakers failed to perceive Vietnamese realities accurately and thus to gauge American interests in the area prudently. Policymakers, as a consequence, misread an indigenous, communist-led nationalist

From Brian VanDeMark, *Into the Quagmire: Lyndon Johnson and the Escalation of the Vietnam War* (Oxford University Press, 1991). Copyright © 1991 by Brian VanDeMark. Reprinted by permission of Oxford University Press, Inc., and the author. Notes omitted.

movement as part of a larger, centrally directed challenge to world order and stability; tied American fortunes to a non-communist regime of slim popular legitimacy and effectiveness; and intervened militarily in the region far out of proportion to U.S. security requirements.

An arrogant and stubborn faith in America's power to shape the course of foreign events compounded the dangers sown by ideological rigidity. Policymakers in 1964–1965 shared a common postwar conviction that the United States not only should, but could, control political conditions in South Vietnam, as elsewhere throughout much of the world. This conviction had led Washington to intervene progressively deeper in South Vietnamese affairs over the years. And when—despite Washington's increasing exertions —Saigon's political situation declined precipitously during 1964–1965, this conviction prompted policymakers to escalate the war against Hanoi, in the belief that America could stimulate political order in South Vietnam through the application of military force against North Vietnam.

Domestic political pressures exerted an equally powerful, if less obvious, influence over the course of U.S. involvement in Vietnam. The fall of China in 1949 and the ugly McCarthyism it aroused embittered American foreign policy for a generation. By crippling President Truman's political fortunes, it taught his Democratic successors, John Kennedy and Lyndon Johnson [LBJ], a strong and sobering lesson: that another "loss" to communism in East Asia risked renewed and devastating attacks from the right. This fear of reawakened McCarthyism remained a paramount concern as policymakers pondered what course to follow as conditions in South Vietnam deteriorated rapidly in 1964–1965.

Enduring traditions of ideological rigidity, diplomatic arrogance, and political vulnerability heavily influenced the way policymakers approached decisions in Vietnam in 1964–1965. Understanding the decisions of this period fully, however, also requires close attention to contemporary developments in America and South Vietnam. These years marked a tumultuous time in both countries, which affected the course of events in subtle but significant ways.

Policymakers in 1964–1965 lived in a period of extraordinary domestic political upheaval sparked by the civil rights movement. It is difficult to overstate the impact of this upheaval on American politics in the mid-1960s. During 1964–1965, the United States—particularly the American South—experienced profound and long overdue change in the economic, political, and social rights of blacks. This change, consciously embraced by the liberal administration of Lyndon Johnson, engendered sharp political hostility among conservative southern whites and their deputies in Congress—hostility which the politically astute Johnson sensed could spill over into the realm of foreign affairs, where angry civil rights opponents could exact their revenge should LBJ stumble and "lose" a crumbling South Vietnam. This danger, reinforced by the memory of McCarthyism, stirred deep political fears in Johnson, together with an abiding aversion to failure in Vietnam.

LBJ feared defeat in South Vietnam, but he craved success and glory at home. A forceful, driving President of boundless ambition, Johnson sought to harness the political momentum created by the civil rights movement to enact a far-reaching domestic reform agenda under the rubric of the Great Society. LBJ would achieve the greatness he sought by leading America toward justice and opportunity for all its citizens, through his historic legislative program.

Johnson's domestic aspirations fundamentally conflicted with his uneasy involvement in Vietnam. An experienced and perceptive politician, LBJ knew his domestic reforms required the sustained focus and cooperation of Congress. He also knew a larger war in Vietnam jeopardized these reforms by drawing away political attention and economic resources. America's increasing military intervention in 1964–1965 cast this tension between Vietnam and the Great Society into sharp relief.

Johnson saw his predicament clearly. But he failed to resolve it for fear that acknowledging the growing extent and cost of the war would thwart his domestic reforms, while pursuing a course of withdrawal risked political ruin. LBJ, instead, chose to obscure the magnitude of his dilemma by obscuring America's deepening involvement as South Vietnam began to fail. That grave compromise of candor opened the way to Johnson's eventual downfall.

Events in South Vietnam during 1964–1965 proved equally fateful. A historically weak and divided land, South Vietnam's deeply rooted ethnic, political, and religious turmoil intensified sharply in the winter of 1964–1965. This mounting turmoil, combined with increased communist military attacks, pushed Saigon to the brink of political collapse.

South Vietnam's accelerating crisis alarmed American policymakers, driving them to deepen U.S. involvement considerably in an effort to arrest Saigon's political failure. Abandoning the concept of stability in the South *before* escalation against the North, policymakers now embraced the concept of stability *through* escalation, in the desperate hope that military action against Hanoi would prompt a stubbornly elusive political order in Saigon.

This shift triggered swift and ominous consequences scarcely anticipated by its architects. Policymakers soon confronted intense military, political, and bureaucratic pressures to widen the war. Unsettled by these largely unforeseen pressures, policymakers reacted confusedly and defensively. Rational men, they struggled to control increasingly irrational forces. But their reaction only clouded their attention to basic assumptions and ultimate costs as the war rapidly spun out of control in the spring and summer of 1965. In their desperation to make Vietnam policy work amid this rising tide of war pressures, they thus failed ever to question whether it could work—or at what ultimate price. Their failure recalls the warning of a prescient political scientist, who years before had cautioned against those policymakers with "an infinite capacity for making ends of [their] means."

The decisions of 1964–1965 bespeak a larger and deeper failure as well. Throughout this period—as, indeed, throughout the course of America's Vietnam involvement—U.S. policymakers strove principally to create a viable noncommunist regime in South Vietnam. For many years and at great effort and cost, Washington had endeavored to achieve political stability and competence in Saigon. Despite these efforts, South Vietnam's political disarray persisted and deepened, until, in 1965, America intervened with massive military force to avert its total collapse.

Few policymakers in 1964–1965 paused to mull this telling fact, to ponder its implications about Saigon's viability as a political entity. The failure to re-examine this and other fundamental premises of U.S. policy—chief among them Vietnam's importance to American national interests and Washington's ability to forge political order through military power—proved a costly and tragic lapse of statesmanship. . . .

⟡

The legacy of Vietnam, like the war itself, remains a difficult and painful sub-ject for Americans. As passions subside and time bestows greater perspective, Americans still struggle to understand Vietnam's meaning and lessons for the country. They still wonder how the United States found itself ensnared in an ambiguous, costly, and divisive war, and how it can avoid repeating such an ordeal in the future.

The experience of Lyndon Johnson and his advisers during the decisive years 1964–1965 offers much insight into those questions. For their decisions, which fundamentally transformed U.S. participation in the war, both reflected and defined much of the larger history of America's Vietnam involvement.

Their decisions may also, one hopes, yield kernels of wisdom for the fu-ture; the past, after all, can teach us lessons. But history's lessons, as Vietnam showed, are themselves dependent on each generation's knowledge and under-standing of the past. So it proved for 1960s policymakers, whose ignorance and misperception of Southeast Asian history, culture, and politics pulled America progressively deeper into the war. LBJ, [Secretary of State Dean] Rusk, [Robert] McNamara, [McGeorge] Bundy, [Ambassador Maxwell] Taylor—most of their generation, in fact—mistakenly viewed Vietnam through the simplistic ideolog-ical prism of the Cold War. They perceived a deeply complex and ambiguous regional struggle as a grave challenge to world order and stability, fomented by communist China acting through its local surrogate, North Vietnam.

This perception, given their mixture of memories—the West's capitula-tion to Hitler at Munich, Stalin's postwar truculence, Mao's belligerent rhetoric —appears altogether understandable in retrospect. But it also proved deeply flawed and oblivious to abiding historical realities. Constrained by their mem-ories and ideology, American policymakers neglected the subtle but enduring force of nationalism in Southeast Asia. Powerful and decisive currents—the deep and historic tension between Vietnam and China; regional friction among the Indochinese states of Vietnam, Laos, and Cambodia; and, above all, Hanoi's fa-natical will to unification—went unnoticed or unweighed because they failed to fit Washington's worldview. Although it is true, as Secretary of State Rusk once said, that "one cannot escape one's experience," Rusk and his fellow poli-cymakers seriously erred by falling uncritical prisoners of their experience.

Another shared experience plagued 1960s policymakers like a ghost: the ominous specter of McCarthyism. This frightful political memory haunted LBJ and his Democratic colleagues like a barely suppressed demon in the national psyche. Barely ten years removed from the traumatic "loss" of China and its devastating domestic repercussions, Johnson and his advisers remembered its consequences vividly and shuddered at a similar fate in Vietnam. They talked about this only privately, but then with genuine and palpable fear. Defense Secretary McNamara, in a guarded moment, confided to a newsman in the spring of 1965 that U.S. disengagement from South Vietnam threatened "a disastrous political fight that could... freeze American political debate and even affect political freedom."

Such fears resonated deeply in policymakers' minds. Nothing, it seemed, could be worse than the "loss" of Vietnam—not even an intensifying stalemate secured at increasing military and political risk. For a President determined to fulfill liberalism's postwar agenda, Truman's ordeal in China seemed a powerfully forbidding lesson. It hung over LBJ in Vietnam like a dark shadow he could not shake, an agony he would not repeat.

McCarthyism's long shadow into the mid-1960s underscores a persistent and troubling phenomenon of postwar American politics: the peculiar vulnerability besetting liberal Presidents thrust into the maelstrom of world politics. In America's postwar political climate—dominated by the culture of anti-communism—Democratic leaders from Truman to Kennedy to Johnson remained acutely sensitive to the domestic repercussions of foreign policy failure. This fear of right-wing reaction sharply inhibited liberals like LBJ, narrowing what they considered their range of politically acceptable options, while diminishing their willingness to disengage from untenable foreign commitments. Thus, when Johnson did confront the bitter choice between defeat in Vietnam and fighting a major, inconclusive war, he reluctantly chose the second because he could not tolerate the domestic consequences of the first. Committed to fulfilling the Great Society, fearful of resurgent McCarthyism, and afraid that disengagement meant sacrificing the former to the latter, LBJ perceived least political danger in holding on.

But if Johnson resigned never to "lose" South Vietnam, he also resigned never to sacrifice his cherished Great Society in the process. LBJ's determination, however understandable, nonetheless led him deliberately and seriously to obscure the nature and cost of America's deepening involvement in the war during 1964–1965. This decision bought Johnson the short-term political maneuverability he wanted, but at a costly long-term political price. As LBJ's credibility on the war subsequently eroded, public confidence in his leadership slowly but irretrievably evaporated. And this, more than any other factor, is what finally drove Johnson from the White House.

It also tarnished the presidency and damaged popular faith in American government for more than a decade. Trapped between deeply conflicting pressures, LBJ never shared his dilemma with the public. Johnson would not, or felt he dare not, trust his problems with the American people. LBJ's decision, however human, tragically undermined the reciprocal faith between President and public indispensable to effective governance in a democracy. Just as tragically, it fostered a pattern of presidential behavior which led his successor, Richard Nixon, to eventual ruin amid even greater popular political alienation.

Time slowly healed most of these wounds to the American political process, while reconfirming the fundamental importance of presidential credibility in a democracy. Johnson's Vietnam travail underscored the necessity of public trust and support to presidential success. Without them, as LBJ painfully discovered, Presidents are doomed to disaster.

Johnson, in retrospect, might have handled his domestic dilemma more forthrightly. An equally serious dilemma, however, remained always beyond his —or Washington's—power to mend: the root problem of political disarray in South Vietnam. The perennial absence of stable and responsive government in Saigon troubled Washington policymakers profoundly; they understood, only too well, its pivotal importance to the war effort and to the social and economic reforms essential to the country's survival. Over and over again, American officials stressed the necessity of political cooperation to their embattled South Vietnamese allies. But to no avail. As one top American in Saigon later lamented, "[Y]ou could tell them all 'you've got to get together [and stop] this haggling and fighting among yourselves,' but how do you make them do it?" he said. "How do you make them do it?"

Washington, alas, could not. As Ambassador Taylor conceded early in the war, "[You] cannot order good government. You can't get it by fiat." This stubborn but telling truth eventually came to haunt Taylor and others. South Vietnam never marshaled the political will necessary to create an effective and enduring government; it never produced leaders addressing the aspirations and thus attracting the allegiance of the South Vietnamese people. Increasing levels of U.S. troops and firepower, moreover, never offset this fundamental debility. America, as a consequence, built its massive military effort on a foundation of political quicksand.

The causes of this elemental flaw lay deeply imbedded in the social and political history of the region. Neither before nor after 1954 was South Vietnam ever really a nation in spirit. Divided by profound ethnic and religious cleavages dating back centuries and perpetuated under French colonial rule, the people of South Vietnam never developed a common political identity. Instead, political factionalism and rivalry always held sway. The result: a chronic and fatal political disorder.

Saigon's fundamental weakness bore anguished witness to the limits of U.S. power. South Vietnam's shortcomings taught a proud and mighty nation that it could not save a people in spite of themselves—that American power, in the last analysis, offered no viable substitute for indigenous political resolve. Without this basic ingredient, as Saigon's turbulent history demonstrated, Washington's most dedicated and strenuous efforts will prove extremely vulnerable, if not futile.

This is not a happy or popular lesson. But it is a wise and prudent one, attuned to the imperfect realities of an imperfect world. One of America's sagest diplomats, George Kennan, understood and articulated this lesson well when he observed: "When it comes to helping people to resist Communist pressures, . . . no assistance . . . can be effective unless the people themselves have a very high degree of determination and a willingness to help themselves. The moment they begin to place the bulk of the burden on us," Kennan warned, "the whole situation is lost." This, tragically, is precisely what befell America in South Vietnam during 1964–1965. Hereafter, as perhaps always before—*external* U.S. economic, military, and political support provided the vital elements of stability and strength in South Vietnam. Without that *external* support, as events following America's long-delayed withdrawal in 1973 showed, South Vietnam's government quickly failed.

Washington's effort to forge political order through military power spawned another tragedy as well. It ignited unexpected pressures which quickly overwhelmed U.S. policymakers, and pulled them ever deeper into the war. LBJ and his advisers began bombing North Vietnam in early 1965 in a desperate attempt to spur political resolve in South Vietnam. But their effort boomeranged wildly. Rather than stabilizing the situation, it instead unleashed forces that soon put Johnson at the mercy of circumstances, a hostage to the war's accelerating momentum. LBJ, as a result, began steering with an ever looser hand. By the summer of 1965, President Johnson found himself not the controller of events but largely controlled by them. He had lost the political leader's "continual struggle," in the words of Henry Kissinger, "to rescue an element of choice from the pressure of circumstance."

LBJ's experience speaks powerfully across the years. With each Vietnam decision, Johnson's vulnerability to military pressure and bureaucratic momentum intensified sharply. Each step generated demands for another, even bigger step—which LBJ found increasingly difficult to resist. His predicament confirmed George Ball's admonition that war is a fiercely unpredictable force, often generating its own inexorable momentum.

Johnson sensed this danger almost intuitively. He quickly grasped the dilemma and difficulties confronting him in Vietnam. But LBJ lacked the inner strength—the security and self-confidence—to overrule the counsel of his inherited advisers.

Most of those advisers, on the other hand—especially McGeorge Bundy and Robert McNamara—failed to anticipate such perils. Imbued with an overweening faith in their ability to "manage" crises and "control" escalation, Bundy and McNamara, along with Maxwell Taylor, first pushed military action against the North as a lever to force political improvement in the South. But bombing did not rectify Saigon's political problems; it only exacerbated them, while igniting turbulent military pressures that rapidly overwhelmed these advisers' confident calculations.

These advisers' preoccupation with technique, with the application of power, characterized much of America's approach to the Vietnam War. Bundy and McNamara epitomized a postwar generation confident in the exercise and efficacy of U.S. power. Despite the dark and troubled history of European intervention in Indochina, these men stubbornly refused to equate America's situation in the mid-1960s to France's earlier ordeal. To them, the United States possessed limitless ability, wisdom, and virtue; it would therefore prevail where other western powers had failed.

This arrogance born of power led policymakers to ignore manifest dangers, to persist in the face of ever darkening circumstances. Like figures in Greek tragedy, pride compelled these supremely confident men further into disaster.

They succumbed to the affliction common to great powers throughout the ages —the dangerous "self-esteem engendered by power," as the political philosopher Hans Morgenthau once wrote, "which equates power and virtue, [and] in the process loses all sense of moral and political proportion."

Tradition, as well as personality, nurtured such thinking. For in many ways, America's military intervention in Vietnam represented the logical fulfillment of a policy and outlook axiomatically accepted by U.S. policymakers for nearly two decades—the doctrine of global containment. Fashioned at the outset of the Cold War, global containment extended American interests and obligations across vast new areas of the world in defense against perceived monolithic communist expansion. It remained the lodestar of America foreign policy, moreover, even as the constellation of international forces shifted dramatically amid diffused authority and power among communist states and nationalist upheaval in the post-colonial world.

Vietnam exposed the limitations and contradictions of this static doctrine in a world of flux. It also revealed the dangers and flaws of an undiscriminating, universalist policy which perceptive critics of global containment, such as the eminent journalist Walter Lippmann, had anticipated from the beginning. As Lippmann warned about global containment in 1947:

> Satellite states and puppet governments are not good material out of which to construct unassailable barriers [for American defense]. A diplomatic war conducted as this policy demands, that is to say conducted indirectly, means that we must stake our own security and the peace of the world upon satellites, puppets, clients, agents about whom we can know very little. Frequently they will act for their own reasons, and on their own judgments, presenting us with accomplished facts that we did not intend, and with crises for which we are unready. The "unassailable barriers" will present us with an unending series of insoluble dilemmas. We shall have either to disown our puppets, which would be tantamount to appeasement and defeat and loss of face, or must support them at an incalculable cost....

Here lay the heart of America's Vietnam troubles. Driven by unquestioning allegiance to an ossified and extravagant doctrine, Washington officials plunged deeply into a struggle which itself dramatized the changed realities and complexities of the postwar world. Their action teaches both the importance of re-examining premises as circumstances change and the costly consequences of failing to recognize and adapt to them.

Vietnam represented a failure not just of American foreign policy but also of American statesmanship. For once drawn into the war, LBJ and his advisers quickly sensed Vietnam's immense difficulties and dangers—Saigon's congenital political problems, the war's spiraling military costs, the remote likelihood of victory—and plunged in deeper nonetheless. In their determination to preserve America's international credibility and protect their domestic political standing, they continued down an ever costlier path.

That path proved a distressing, multifaceted paradox. Fearing injury to the perception of American power, diminished faith in U.S. resolve, and a conservative political firestorm, policymakers rigidly pursued a course which ultimately injured the substance of American power by consuming exorbitant lives and resources, shook allied confidence in U.S. strategic judgment, and shattered liberalism's political unity and vigor by polarizing and paralyzing American society.

Herein lies Vietnam's most painful but pressing lesson. Statesmanship requires judgment, sensibility, and, above all, wisdom in foreign affairs—the wisdom to calculate national interests prudently and to balance commitments with effective power. It requires that most difficult task of political leaders: "to distinguish between what is desireable and what is possible, . . . between what is desireable and what is essential."

This is important in peace; it is indispensable in war. As the great tutor of statesmen, Carl von Clausewitz, wrote, "Since war is not an act of senseless passion but is controlled by its political object, the value of this object must determine the sacrifices to be made for it in *magnitude* and also in *duration*. Once the expenditure of effort exceeds the value of the political object," Clausewitz admonished, "the object must be renounced. . . ." His maxim, in hindsight, seems painfully relevant to a war which, as even America's military commander in Vietnam, General William Westmoreland, concluded, "the vital security of the United States was not and possibly could not be clearly demonstrated and understood. . . ."

LBJ and his advisers failed to heed this fundamental principle of statesmanship. They failed to weigh American costs in Vietnam against Vietnam's relative importance to American national interests and its effect on overall American power. Compelled by events in Vietnam and, especially, coercive political pressures at home, they deepened an unsound, peripheral commitment and pursued manifestly unpromising and immensely costly objectives. Their failure of statesmanship, then, proved a failure of judgment and, above all, of proportion.

NO

H. R. McMaster

Dereliction of Duty

$\mathbf{T}$he Americanization of the Vietnam War between 1963 and 1965 was the product of an unusual interaction of personalities and circumstances. The escalation of U.S. military intervention grew out of a complicated chain of events and a complex web of decisions that slowly transformed the conflict in Vietnam into an American war.

Much of the literature on Vietnam has argued that the "Cold War mentality" put such pressure on President Johnson that the Americanization of the war was inevitable. The imperative to contain Communism was an important factor in Vietnam policy, but neither American entry into the war nor the manner in which the war was conducted was inevitable. The United States went to war in Vietnam in a manner unique in American history. Vietnam was not forced on the United States by a tidal wave of Cold War ideology. It slunk in on cat's feet.

Between November 1963 and July 1965, LBJ made the critical decisions that took the United States into war almost without realizing it. The decisions, and the way in which he made them, profoundly affected the way the United States fought in Vietnam. Although impersonal forces, such as the ideological imperative of containing Communism, the bureaucratic structure, and institutional priorities, influenced the president's Vietnam decisions, those decisions depended primarily on his character, his motivations, and his relationships with his principal advisers.

Most investigations of how the United States entered the war have devoted little attention to the crucial developments which shaped LBJ's approach to Vietnam and set conditions for a gradual intervention. The first of several "turning points" in the American escalation comprised the near-contemporaneous assassinations of Ngo Dinh Diem and John F. Kennedy. The legacy of the Kennedy administration included an expanded commitment to South Vietnam as an "experiment" in countering Communist insurgencies and a deep distrust of the military that manifested itself in the appointment of officers who would prove supportive of the administration's policies. After November 1963 the United

From H. R. McMaster, *Dereliction of Duty: Lyndon Johnson, Robert McNamara, the Joint Chiefs of Staff, and the Lies That Led to Vietnam* (HarperCollins, 1997). Copyright © 1997 by H. R. McMaster. Reprinted by permission of HarperCollins Publishers, Inc. Notes omitted.

States confronted what in many ways was a new war in South Vietnam. Having deposed the government of Ngo Dinh Diem and his brother Nhu, and having supported actions that led to their deaths, Washington assumed responsibility for the new South Vietnamese leaders. Intensified Viet Cong activity added impetus to U.S. deliberations, leading Johnson and his advisers to conclude that the situation in South Vietnam demanded action beyond military advice and support. Next, in the spring of 1964, the Johnson administration adopted graduated pressure as its strategic concept for the Vietnam War. Rooted in Maxwell Taylor's national security strategy of flexible response, graduated pressure evolved over the next year, becoming the blueprint for the deepening American commitment to maintaining South Vietnam's independence. Then, in August 1964, in response to the Gulf of Tonkin incident, the United States crossed the threshold of direct American military action against North Vietnam.

The Gulf of Tonkin resolution gave the president carte blanche for escalating the war. During the ostensibly benign "holding period" from September 1964 to February 1965, LBJ was preoccupied with his domestic political agenda, and McNamara built consensus behind graduated pressure. In early 1965 the president raised U.S. intervention to a higher level again, deciding on February 9 to begin a systematic program of limited air strikes on targets in North Vietnam and, on February 26, to commit U.S. ground forces to the South. Last, in March 1965, he quietly gave U.S. ground forces the mission of "killing Viet Cong." That series of decisions, none in itself tantamount to a clearly discernable decision to go to war, nevertheless transformed America's commitment in Vietnam.

⦁⟡⦁

Viewed together, those decisions might create the impression of a deliberate determination on the part of the Johnson administration to go to war. On the contrary, the president did not want to go to war in Vietnam and was not planning to do so. Indeed, as early as May 1964, LBJ seemed to realize that an American war in Vietnam would be a costly failure. He confided to McGeorge Bundy, " . . . looks like to me that we're getting into another Korea. It just worries the hell out of me. I don't see what we can ever hope to get out of this." It was, Johnson observed, "the biggest damn mess that I ever saw. . . . It's damn easy to get into a war, but . . . it's going to be harder to ever extricate yourself if you get in." Despite his recognition that the situation in Vietnam demanded that he consider alternative courses of action and make a difficult decision, LBJ sought to avoid or to postpone indefinitely an explicit choice between war and disengagement from South Vietnam. In the ensuing months, however, each decision he made moved the United States closer to war, although he seemed not to recognize that fact.

The president's fixation on short-term political goals, combined with his character and the personalities of his principal civilian and military advisers, rendered the administration incapable of dealing adequately with the complexities of the situation in Vietnam. LBJ's advisory system was structured to achieve consensus and to prevent potentially damaging leaks. Profoundly insecure and distrustful of anyone but his closest civilian advisers, the president viewed the JCS [Joint Chiefs of Staff] with suspicion. When the situation in Vietnam seemed to demand military action, Johnson did not turn to his military advisers to determine how to solve the problem. He turned instead to his civilian advisers to determine how to postpone a decision. The relationship between the president, the secretary of defense, and the Joint Chiefs led to the curious situation in which the nation went to war without the benefit of effective military advice from the organization having the statutory responsibility to be the nation's "principal military advisers."

What Johnson feared most in 1964 was losing his chance to win the presidency in his own right. He saw Vietnam principally as a danger to that goal. After the election, he feared that an American military response to the deteriorating situation in Vietnam would jeopardize chances that his Great Society would pass through Congress. The Great Society was to be Lyndon Johnson's great domestic political legacy, and he could not tolerate the risk of its failure. McNamara would help the president first protect his electoral chances and then pass the Great Society by offering a strategy for Vietnam that appeared cheap and could be conducted with minimal public and congressional attention. McNamara's strategy of graduated pressure permitted Johnson to pursue his objective of not losing the war in Vietnam while postponing the "day of reckoning" and keeping the whole question out of public debate all the while.

McNamara was confident in his ability to satisfy the president's needs. He believed fervently that nuclear weapons and the Cold War international political environment had made traditional military experience and thinking not only irrelevant, but often dangerous for contemporary policy. Accordingly, McNamara, along with systems analysts and other civilian members of his own department and the Department of State, developed his own strategy for Vietnam. Bolstered by what he regarded as a personal triumph during the Cuban missile crisis, McNamara drew heavily on that experience and applied it to Vietnam. Based on the assumption that carefully controlled and sharply limited military actions were reversible, and therefore could be carried out at minimal risk and cost, graduated pressure allowed McNamara and Johnson to avoid confronting many of the possible consequences of military action.

Johnson and McNamara succeeded in creating the illusion that the decisions to attack North Vietnam were alternatives to war rather than war itself. Graduated pressure defined military action as a form of communication, the object of which was to affect the enemy's calculation of interests and dissuade him from a particular activity. Because the favored means of communication (bombing fixed installations and economic targets) were not appropriate for the mobile forces of the Viet Cong, who lacked an infrastructure and whose strength in the

South was political as well as military, McNamara and his colleagues pointed to the infiltration of men and supplies into South Vietnam as proof that the source and center of the enemy's power in Vietnam lay north of the seventeenth parallel, and specifically in Hanoi. Their definition of the enemy's source of strength was derived from that strategy rather than from a critical examination of the full reality in South Vietnam—and turned out to be inaccurate.

Graduated pressure was fundamentally flawed in other ways. The strategy ignored the uncertainty of war and the unpredictable psychology of an activity that involves killing, death, and destruction. To the North Vietnamese, military action, involving as it did attacks on their forces and bombing of their territory, was not simply a means of communication. Human sacrifices in war evoke strong emotions, creating a dynamic that defies systems analysis quantification. Once the United States crossed the threshold of war against North Vietnam with covert raids and the Gulf of Tonkin "reprisals," the future course of events depended not only on decisions made in Washington but also on enemy responses and actions that were unpredictable. McNamara, however, viewed the war as another business management problem that, he assumed, would ultimately succumb to his reasoned judgment and others' rational calculations. He and his assistants thought that they could predict with great precision what amount of force applied in Vietnam would achieve the results they desired and they believed that they could control that force with great precision from halfway around the world. There were compelling contemporaneous arguments that graduated pressure would not affect Hanoi's will sufficiently to convince the North to desist from its support of the South, and that such a strategy would probably lead to an escalation of the war. Others expressed doubts about the utility of attacking North Vietnam by air to win a conflict in South Vietnam. Nevertheless, McNamara refused to consider the consequences of his recommendations and forged ahead oblivious of the human and psychological complexities of war.

Despite their recognition that graduated pressure was fundamentally flawed, the JCS were unable to articulate effectively either their objections or alternatives. Interservice rivalry was a significant impediment. Although differing perspectives were understandable given the Chiefs' long experience in their own services and their need to protect the interests of their services, the president's principal military advisers were obligated by law to render their best advice. The Chiefs' failure to do so, and their willingness to present single-service remedies to a complex military problem, prevented them from developing a comprehensive estimate of the situation or from thinking effectively about strategy.

When it became clear to the Chiefs that they were to have little influence on the policy-making process, they failed to confront the president with their objections to McNamara's approach to the war. Instead they attempted to work within that strategy in order to remove over time the limitations to further action. Unable to develop a strategic alternative to graduated pressure, the Chiefs became fixated on means by which the war could be conducted and pressed for an escalation of the war by degrees. They hoped that graduated pressure would evolve over time into a fundamentally different strategy, more in keeping with their belief in the necessity of greater force and its more resolute application. In so doing, they gave tacit approval to graduated pressure during the critical period in which the president escalated the war. They did not recommend the total force they believed would ultimately be required in Vietnam and accepted a strategy they knew would lead to a large but inadequate commitment of troops, for an extended period of time, with little hope for success.

❦

McNamara and Lyndon Johnson were far from disappointed with the joint Chiefs' failings. Because his priorities were domestic, Johnson had little use for military advice that recommended actions inconsistent with those priorities. McNamara and his assistants in the Department of Defense, on the other hand, were arrogant. They disparaged military advice because they thought that their intelligence and analytical methods could compensate for their lack of military experience and education. Indeed military experience seemed to them a liability because military officers took too narrow a view and based their advice on antiquated notions of war. Geopolitical and technological changes of the last fifteen years, they believed, had rendered advice based on military experience irrelevant and, in fact, dangerous. McNamara's disregard for military experience and for history left him to draw principally on his staff in the Department of Defense and led him to conclude that his only real experience with the planning and direction of military force, the Cuban missile crisis, was the most relevant analogy to Vietnam.

While they slowly deepened American military involvement in Vietnam, Johnson and McNamara pushed the Chiefs further away from the decision-making process. There was no meaningful structure through which the Chiefs could voice their views—even the chairman was not a reliable conduit. NSC meetings were strictly *pro forma* affairs in which the president endeavored to build consensus for decisions already made. Johnson continued Kennedy's practice of meeting with small groups of his most trusted advisers. Indeed he made his most important decisions at the Tuesday lunch meetings in which Rusk, McGeorge Bundy, and McNamara were the only regular participants. The president and McNamara shifted responsibility for real planning away from the JCS to ad hoc committees composed principally of civilian analysts and attorneys, whose main goal was to obtain a consensus consistent with the president's pursuit of the middle ground between disengagement and war. The products of those efforts carried the undeserved credibility of proposals that had been agreed on by all departments and were therefore hard to oppose. McNamara and Johnson endeavored to get the advice they wanted by placing conditions and qualifications on questions that they asked the Chiefs. When the Chiefs' advice was not consistent with his own recommendations, McNamara, with the aid of the chairman of the Joint Chiefs of Staff, lied in meetings of the National Security Council about the Chiefs' views.

Rather than advice McNamara and Johnson extracted from the JCS acquiescence and silent support for decisions already made. Even as they relegated the Chiefs to a peripheral position in the policy-making process, they were careful to preserve the facade of consultation to prevent the JCS from opposing the administration's policies either openly or behind the scenes. As American involvement in the war escalated, Johnson's vulnerability to disaffected senior military officers increased because he was purposely deceiving the Congress and the public about the nature of the American military effort in Vietnam. The president and the secretary of defense deliberately obscured the nature of decisions made and left undefined the limits that they envisioned on the use of force. They indicated to the Chiefs that they would take actions that they never intended to pursue. McNamara and his assistants, who considered communication the purpose of military action, kept the nature of their objective from the JCS, who viewed "winning" as the only viable goal in war. Finally, Johnson appealed directly to them, referring to himself as the "coach" and them as "his team." To dampen their calls for further action, Lyndon Johnson attempted to generate sympathy from the JCS for the great pressures that he was feeling from those who opposed escalation.

The ultimate test of the Chiefs' loyalty came in July 1965. The administration's lies to the American public had grown in magnitude as the American military effort in Vietnam escalated. The president's plan of deception depended on tacit approval or silence from the JCS. LBJ had misrepresented the mission of U.S. ground forces in Vietnam, distorted the views of the Chiefs to lend credibility to his decision against mobilization, grossly understated the numbers of troops General Westmoreland had requested, and lied to the Congress about the monetary cost of actions already approved and of those awaiting final decision. The Chiefs did not disappoint the president. In the days before the president made his duplicitous public announcement concerning Westmoreland's request, the Chiefs, with the exception of commandant of the Marine Corps Greene, withheld from congressmen their estimates of the amount of force that would be needed in Vietnam. As he had during the Gulf of Tonkin hearings, Wheeler lent his support to the president's deception of Congress. The "five silent men" on the Joint Chiefs made possible the way the United States went to war in Vietnam.

Several factors kept the Chiefs from challenging the president's subterfuges. The professional code of the military officer prohibits him or her from engaging in political activity. Actions that could have undermined the administration's credibility and derailed its Vietnam policy could not have been undertaken lightly. The Chiefs felt loyalty to their commander in chief. The Truman-MacArthur controversy during the Korean War had warned the Chiefs about the dangers of overstepping the bounds of civilian control. Loyalty to their services also weighed against opposing the president and the secretary of defense. Harold Johnson, for example, decided against resignation because he thought he had to remain in office to protect the Army's interests as best he could. Admiral McDonald and Marine Corps Commandant Greene compromised their views on Vietnam in exchange for concessions to their respective services. Greene achieved a dramatic expansion of the Marine Corps, and McDonald ensured that the Navy retained control of Pacific Command. None of the Chiefs had sworn an oath to his service, however. They had all sworn, rather, to "support and defend the Constitution of the United States."

General Greene recalled that direct requests by congressmen for his assessment put him in a difficult situation. The president was lying, and he expected the Chiefs to lie as well or, at least, to withhold the whole truth. Although the president should not have placed the Chiefs in that position, the flag officers should not have tolerated it when he had.

Because the Constitution locates civilian control of the military in Congress as well as in the executive branch, the Chiefs could not have been justified in deceiving the peoples' representatives about Vietnam. Wheeler in particular allowed his duty to the president to overwhelm his obligations under the Constitution. As cadets are taught at the United States Military Academy, the JCS relationship with the Congress is challenging and demands that military officers possess a strong character and keen intellect. While the Chiefs must present Congress with their best advice based on their professional experience and education, they must be careful not to undermine their credibility by crossing the line between advice and advocacy of service interests.

Maxwell Taylor had a profound influence on the nature of the civil-military relationship during the escalation of American involvement in Vietnam. In contrast to Army Chief of Staff George C. Marshall, who, at the start of World War II, recognized the need for the JCS to suppress service parochialism to provide advice consistent with national interests, Taylor exacerbated service differences to help McNamara and Johnson keep the Chiefs divided and, thus, marginal to the policy process. Taylor recommended men for appointment to the JCS who were less likely than their predecessors to challenge the direction of the administration's military policy, even when they knew that that policy was fundamentally flawed. Taylor's behavior is perhaps best explained by his close personal friendship with the Kennedy family; McNamara; and, later, Johnson. In contrast again to Marshall, who thought it important to keep a professional distance from President Franklin Roosevelt, Taylor abandoned an earlier view similar to Marshall's in favor of a belief that the JCS and the president should enjoy "an intimate, easy relationship, born of friendship and mutual regard."

◆

The way in which the United States went to war in the period between November 1963 and July 1965 had, not surprisingly, a profound influence on the conduct of the war and on its outcome. Because Vietnam policy decisions were made based on domestic political expediency, and because the president was intent on forging a consensus position behind what he believed was a middle policy, the administration deliberately avoided clarifying its policy objectives and postponed discussing the level of force that the president was willing to commit to the effort. Indeed, because the president was seeking domestic political consensus, members of the administration believed that ambiguity in the objectives for fighting in Vietnam was a strength rather than a weakness. Determined to prevent dissent from the JCS, the administration concealed its development of "fall-back" objectives.

Over time the maintenance of U.S. credibility quietly supplanted the stated policy objective of a free and independent South Vietnam. The principal civilian planners had determined that to guarantee American credibility, it was not necessary to win in Vietnam. That conclusion, combined with the belief that the use of force was merely another form of diplomatic communication, directed the military effort in the South at achieving stalemate rather than victory. Those charged with planning the war believed that it would be possible to preserve American credibility even if the United States armed forces withdrew from the South, after a show of force against the North and in the South in which American forces were "bloodied." After the United States became committed to war, however, and more American soldiers, airmen, and Marines had died in the conflict, it would become impossible simply to disengage and declare America's credibility intact, a fact that should have been foreseen. The Chiefs sensed the shift in objectives, but did not challenge directly the views of civilian planners in that connection. McNamara and Johnson recognized that, once committed to war, the JCS would not agree to an objective other than imposing a solution on the enemy consistent with U.S. interests. The JCS deliberately avoided clarifying the objective as well. As a result, when the United States went to war, the JCS pursued objectives different from those of the president. When the Chiefs requested permission to apply force consistent with their conception of U.S. objectives, the president and McNamara, based on their goals and domestic political constraints, rejected JCS requests, or granted them only in part. The result was that the JCS and McNamara became fixated on the means rather than on the ends, and on the manner in which the war was conducted instead of a military strategy that could connect military actions to achievable policy goals.

Because forthright communication between top civilian and military officials in the Johnson administration was never developed, there was no reconciliation of McNamara's intention to limit the American military effort sharply and the Chiefs' assessment that the United States could not possibly win under such conditions. If they had attempted to reconcile those positions, they could not have helped but recognize the futility of the American war effort.

The Joint Chiefs of Staff became accomplices in the president's deception and focused on a tactical task, killing the enemy. General Westmoreland's "strategy" of attrition in South Vietnam, was, in essence, the absence of a strategy. The result was military activity (bombing North Vietnam and killing the enemy in South Vietnam) that did not aim to achieve a clearly defined objective. It was unclear how quantitative measures by which McNamara interpreted the success and failure of the use of military force were contributing to an end of the war. As American casualties mounted and the futility of the strategy became apparent, the American public lost faith in the effort. The Chiefs did not request the number of troops they believed necessary to impose a military solution in South Vietnam until after the Tet offensive in 1968. By that time, however, the president was besieged by opposition to the war and was unable even to consider the request. LBJ, who had gone to such great lengths to ensure a crushing defeat over Barry Goldwater in 1964, declared that he was withdrawing from the race for his party's presidential nomination.

Johnson thought that he would be able to control the U.S. involvement in Vietnam. That belief, based on the strategy of graduated pressure and Mc-Namara's confident assurances, proved in dramatic fashion to be false. If the president was surprised by the consequences of his decisions between November 1963 and July 1965, he should not have been so. He had disregarded the advice he did not want to hear in favor of a policy based on the pursuit of his own political fortunes and his beloved domestic programs.

The war in Vietnam was not lost in the field, nor was it lost on the front pages of the *New York Times* or on the college campuses. It was lost in Washington, D.C., even before Americans assumed sole responsibility for the fighting in 1965 and before they realized the country was at war; indeed, even before the first American units were deployed. The disaster in Vietnam was not the result of impersonal forces but a uniquely human failure, the responsibility for which was shared by President Johnson and his principal military and civilian advisers. The failings were many and reinforcing: arrogance, weakness, lying in the pursuit of self-interest, and, above all, the abdication of responsibility to the American people.

POSTSCRIPT

Was the Americanization of the War in Vietnam Inevitable?

The book from which VanDeMark's selection was excerpted is a detailed study of the circumstances surrounding the decisions that President Lyndon Johnson made to increase America's presence in Vietnam via the bombing raids of North Vietnam in February 1965 and the introduction of ground troops the following July. VanDeMark agrees with McMaster that Johnson did not consult the Joint Chiefs of Staff about the wisdom of escalating the war. In fact, Johnson's decisions of "graduated pressure" were made in increments by the civilian advisers surrounding Secretary of Defense Robert McNamara. The policy, if it can be called such, was to prevent the National Liberation Front and its Viet Cong army from taking over South Vietnam. Each service branch fought its own war without coordinating with one another or with the government of South Vietnam. In VanDeMark's view, U.S. intervention was doomed to failure because South Vietnam was an artificial and very corrupt nation-state created by the French and later supported by the Americans. It was unfortunate that the nationalist revolution was tied up with the Communists led by Ho Chi Minh, who had been fighting French colonialism and Japanese imperialism since the 1920s—unlike Korea and Malaysia, which had alternative, noncommunist, nationalist movements.

Why did Johnson plunge "into the quagmire"? For one thing, Johnson remembered how previous democratic presidents Franklin D. Roosevelt and Harry S. Truman had been charged with being soft on communism and accused of losing Eastern Europe to the Russians after the Second World War and China to the Communists in the Chinese Civil War in 1949. In addition, both presidents were charged by Senator Joseph McCarthy and others of harboring Communists in U.S. government agencies. If Johnson was tough in Vietnam, he could stop communist aggression. At the same time, he could ensure that his Great Society social programs of Medicare and job retraining, as well as the impending civil rights legislation, would be passed by Congress.

As an army officer who fought in the Persian Gulf War, McMaster offers a unique perspective on the decision-making processes used by government policymakers. McMaster spares no one in his critique of what he considers the flawed Vietnam policy of "graduated pressure." He says that McNamara, bolstered by the success of America during the Cuban Missile Crisis, believed that the traditional methods of fighting wars were obsolete. Johnson believed in McNamara's approach, and the president's own need for consensus in the decision-making process kept the Joint Chiefs of Staff out of the loop.

Unlike other military historians, who generally absolve the military from responsibility for the strategy employed during the war, McMaster argues that the Joint Chiefs of Staff were responsible for not standing up to Johnson and telling him that his military strategy was seriously flawed. McMaster's views are not as new as some reviewers of his book seem to think. Bruce Palmer, Jr., in *The Twenty-Five Year War: America's Military Role in Vietnam* (University Press of Kentucky, 1984), and Harry G. Summers, Jr., in *On Strategy: A Critical Analysis of the Vietnam War* (Presidio Press, 1982), also see a flawed strategy of war. Summers argues that Johnson should have asked Congress for a declaration of war and fought a conventional war against North Vietnam.

One scholar has claimed that over 7,000 books about the Vietnam War have been published. The starting point for the current issue is Lloyd Gardner and Ted Gittinger, eds., *Vietnam: The Early Decisions* (University of Texas Press, 1997). See also Larry Berman, *Planning a Tragedy: The Americanization of the War in Vietnam* (W. W. Norton, 1982) and *Lyndon Johnson's War* (W. W. Norton, 1989); David Halberstam, *The Best and the Brightest* (Random House, 1972); and Lloyd C. Gardner, *Pay Any Price: Lyndon Johnson and the Wars for Vietnam* (Ivan R. Dee, 1995). Primary sources can be found in the U.S. Department of State's two-volume *Foreign Relations of the United States, 1964–1968: Vietnam* (Government Printing Office, 1996) and in the relevant sections of one of the most useful collections of primary sources and essays, *Major Problems in the History of the Vietnam War*, 2d ed., by Robert J. McMahon (Houghton Mifflin, 2000).

The bureaucratic perspective can be found in a series of essays by George C. Herring entitled *LBJ and Vietnam: A Different Kind of War* (University of Texas Press, 1995). Herring is also the author of the widely used text *America's Longest War: the United States and Vietnam* (Alfred A. Knopf, 1986). A brilliant article often found in anthologies is by historian and former policymaker James C. Thomson, Jr., "How Could Vietnam Happen? An Autopsy," *The Atlantic Monthly* (April 1968). An interesting comparison of the 1954 Dien Bien Phu and 1965 U.S. escalation decisions is Fred I. Greenstein and John P. Burke, "The Dynamics of Presidential Reality Testing: Evidence From Two Vietnam Decisions," *Political Science Quarterly* (Winter 1989–1990). A nice review essay on Vietnam's impact on today's military thinking is Michael C. Desch's "Wounded Warriors and the Lessons of Vietnam," *Orbis* (Summer 1998).

ISSUE 9

Has the Women's Liberation Movement Been Harmful to American Women?

YES: F. Carolyn Graglia, from *Domestic Tranquility: A Brief Against Feminism* (Spence, 1998)

NO: Jo Freeman, from "The Women's Liberation Movement: Its Origins, Structure, Activities, and Ideas," in Jo Freeman, ed., *Women: A Feminist Perspective,* 3rd ed. (Mayfield, 1984)

ISSUE SUMMARY

YES: Writer and lecturer F. Carolyn Graglia argues that women should stay at home and practice the values of "true motherhood" because contemporary feminists have discredited marriage, devalued traditional homemaking, and encouraged sexual promiscuity.

NO: Feminist Jo Freeman argues that in the late 1960s activists challenged the notion of women's inferior status in society through lawsuits and through "consciousness-raising" sessions to develop egalitarian and liberation values.

In 1961 President John F. Kennedy established the Commission on the Status of Women to examine "the prejudice and outmoded customs that act as barriers to the full realization of women's basic rights." Two years later Betty Friedan, a closet leftist from suburban Rockland County, New York, wrote about the growing malaise of the suburban housewife in her best-seller *The Feminist Mystique* (W. W. Norton, 1963).

The roots of Friedan's "feminine mystique" go back much earlier than the post–World War II "baby boom" generation of suburban America. Woman historians have traced the origins of the modern family to the early nineteenth century. As the nation became more stable politically, the roles of men, women, and children became segmented in ways that still exist today. Dad went to work, the kids went to school, and Mom stayed home. Women's magazines, gift books, and the religious literature of the period ascribed to these women a role that professor Barbara Welter has called the "Cult of True Womanhood." She describes the ideal woman as upholding four virtues—piety, purity, submissiveness, and domesticity.

In nineteenth-century America most middle-class white women stayed home. Those who entered the workforce as teachers or became reformers were usually extending the values of the Cult of True Womanhood to the outside world. This was true of the women reformers in the Second Great Awakening and the peace, temperance, and abolitionist movements before the Civil War. The first real challenge to the traditional values system occurred when a handful of women showed up at Seneca Falls, New York, in 1848 to sign the Women's Declaration of Rights.

It soon became clear that if they were going to pass reform laws, women would have to obtain the right to vote. After an intense struggle the Nineteenth Amendment was ratified on August 26, 1920. Once the women's movement obtained the vote there was no agreement on future goals. The problems of the Great Depression and World War II overrode women's issues.

World War II brought about major changes for working women. Six million women entered the labor force for the first time, many of whom were married. "The proportion of women in the labor force," writes Lois Banner, "increased from 25 percent in 1940 to 36 percent in 1945. This increase was greater than that of the previous four decades combined." Many women moved into high-paying, traditionally men's jobs as policewomen, firefighters, and precision toolmakers. Steel and auto companies that converted over to wartime production made sure that lighter tools were made for women to use on the assembly lines. The federal government also erected federal child-care facilities.

When the war ended in 1945 many working women lost their nontraditional jobs. The federal day-care program was eliminated, and the government told women to go home even though a 1944 study by the Women's Bureau concluded that 80 percent of working women wanted to continue in their jobs after the war.

Most history texts emphasize that women did return home, moved to the suburbs, and created a baby boom generation, which reversed the downward size of families between 1946 and 1964. What is lost in this description is the fact that after 1947 the number of working women again began to rise. By 1951 the proportion had reached 31 percent. Twenty-two years later, at the height of the women's liberation movement, it reached 42 percent.

When Friedan wrote *The Feminine Mystique* in 1963, both working-class and middle-class, college-educated women experienced discrimination in the marketplace. When women worked they were expected to become teachers, nurses, secretaries and airline stewardesses—the lowest-paying jobs in the workforce. In the turbulent 1960s this situation was no longer accepted.

In the following selection, F. Carolyn Graglia defends the traditional role of women in contemporary America. Women, she contends, should stay at home and practice the values of "true womanhood." Contemporary feminists, she argues, have devalued traditional homemaking, encouraged sexual promiscuity, and discredited marriage as a career for women. In the second selection, Jo Freeman argues that society needs to raise its consciousness to admit the equality of the sexes and restructure the economy so that men's work and women's work are of equal value.

F. Carolyn Graglia

 **YES**

Domestic Tranquility

Introduction

Since the late 1960s, feminists have very successfully waged war against the traditional family, in which husbands are the principal breadwinners and wives are primarily homemakers. This war's immediate purpose has been to undermine the homemaker's position within both her family and society in order to drive her into the work force. Its long-term goal is to create a society in which women behave as much like men as possible, devoting as much time and energy to the pursuit of a career as men do, so that women will eventually hold equal political and economic power with men. . . .

Feminists have used a variety of methods to achieve their goal. They have promoted a sexual revolution that encouraged women to mimic male sexual promiscuity. They have supported the enactment of no-fault divorce laws that have undermined housewives' social and economic security. And they obtained the application of affirmative action requirements to women as a class, gaining educational and job preferences for women and undermining the ability of men who are victimized by this discrimination to function as family breadwinners.

A crucial weapon in feminism's arsenal has been the status degradation of the housewife's role. From the journalistic attacks of Betty Friedan and Gloria Steinem to Jessie Bernard's sociological writings, all branches of feminism are united in the conviction that a woman can find identity and fulfillment only in a career. The housewife, feminists agree, was properly characterized by Simone de Beauvoir and Betty Friedan as a "parasite," a being something less than human, living her life without using her adult capabilities or intelligence, and lacking any real purpose in devoting herself to children, husband, and home.

Operating on the twin assumptions that equality means sameness (that is, men and women cannot be equals unless they do the same things) and that most differences between the sexes are culturally imposed, contemporary feminism has undertaken its own cultural impositions. Revealing their totalitarian belief that they know best how others should live and their totalitarian willingness to force others to conform to their dogma, feminists have sought to modify our social institutions in order to create an androgynous society in which male

From F. Carolyn Graglia, *Domestic Tranquility: A Brief Against Feminism* (Spence, 1998). Copyright © 1998 by F. Carolyn Graglia. Reprinted by permission of Spence Publishing Company. Notes omitted.

and female roles are as identical as possible. The results of the feminist juggernaut now engulf us. By almost all indicia of well-being, the institution of the American family has become significantly less healthy than it was thirty years ago.

Certainly, feminism is not alone responsible for our families' sufferings. As Charles Murray details in *Losing Ground*, President Lyndon Johnson's Great Society programs, for example, have often hurt families, particularly black families, and these programs were supported by a large constituency beyond the women's movement. What distinguishes the women's movement, however, is the fact that, despite the pro-family motives it sometimes ascribes to itself, it has actively sought the traditional family's destruction. In its avowed aims and the programs it promotes, the movement has adopted Kate Millett's goal, set forth in her *Sexual Politics,* in which she endorses Friedrich Engels's conclusion that "the family, as that term is presently understood, must go"; "a kind fate," she remarks, in "view of the institution's history." This goal has never changed: feminists view traditional nuclear families as inconsistent with feminism's commitment to women's independence and sexual freedom.

Emerging as a revitalized movement in the 1960s, feminism reflected women's social discontent, which had arisen in response to the decline of the male breadwinner ethic and to the perception—heralded in Philip Wylie's 1940s castigation of the evil "mom"—that Western society does not value highly the roles of wife and mother. Women's dissatisfactions, nevertheless, have often been aggravated rather than alleviated by the feminist reaction. To mitigate their discontent, feminists argued, women should pattern their lives after men's, engaging in casual sexual intercourse on the same terms as sexually predatory males and making the same career commitments as men. In pursuit of these objectives, feminists have fought unceasingly for the ready availability of legal abortion and consistently derogated both motherhood and the worth of full-time homemakers. Feminism's sexual teachings have been less consistent, ranging from its early and enthusiastic embrace of the sexual revolution to a significant backlash against female sexual promiscuity, which has led some feminists to urge women to abandon heterosexual sexual intercourse altogether.

Contemporary feminism has been remarkably successful in bringing about the institutionalization in our society of the two beliefs underlying its offensive: denial of the social worth of traditional homemakers and rejection of traditional sexual morality. The consequences have been pernicious and enduring. General societal assent to these beliefs has profoundly distorted men's perceptions of their relationships with and obligations to women, women's perceptions of their own needs, and the way in which women make decisions about their lives.

Traditional Homemaking Devalued

The first prong of contemporary feminism's offensive has been to convince society that a woman's full-time commitment to cultivating her marriage and rearing her children is an unworthy endeavor. Women, assert feminists, should treat marriage and children as relatively independent appendages to their life of full-time involvement in the workplace. To live what feminists assure her is the only life worthy of respect, a woman must devote the vast bulk of her time and energy to market production, at the expense of marriage and children. Children, she is told, are better cared for by surrogates, and marriage, as these feminists perceive it, neither deserves nor requires much attention; indeed, the very idea of a woman's "cultivating" her marriage seems ludicrous. Thus spurred on by the women's movement, many women have sought to become male clones.

But some feminists have appeared to modify the feminist message; voices —supposedly of moderation—have argued that women really are different from men. In this they are surely right: there are fundamental differences between the average man and woman, and it is appropriate to take account of these differences when making decisions both in our individual lives and with respect to social issues. Yet the new feminist voices have not conceded that acknowledged differences between the sexes are grounds for reexamining women's flight from home into workplace. Instead, these new voices have argued only that these differences require modification of the terms under which women undertake to reconstruct their lives in accordance with the blueprint designed by so-called early radicals. The edifice erected by radical feminism is to remain intact, subject only to some redecorating. The foundation of this edifice is still the destruction of the traditional family. Feminism has acquiesced in women's desire to bear children (an activity some of the early radicals discouraged). But it continues steadfast in its assumption that, after some period of maternity leave, daily care of those children is properly the domain of institutions and paid employees. The yearnings manifested in women's palpable desire for children should largely be sated, the new voices tell us, by the act of serving as a birth canal and then spending so-called quality time with the child before and after a full day's work.

Any mother, in this view, may happily consign to surrogates most of the remaining aspects of her role, assured that doing so will impose no hardship or loss on either mother or child. To those women whose natures make them less suited to striving in the workplace than concentrating on husband, children, and home, this feminist diktat denies the happiness and contentment they could have found within the domestic arena. In the world formed by contemporary feminism, these women will have status and respect only if they force themselves to take up roles in the workplace they suspect are not most deserving of their attention. Relegated to the periphery of their lives are the home and personal relationships with husband and children that they sense merit their central concern.

Inherent in the feminist argument is an extraordinary contradiction. Feminists deny, on the one hand, that the dimension of female sexuality which engenders women's yearning for children can also make it appropriate and satisfying for a woman to devote herself to domestic endeavors and provide her children's full-time care. On the other hand, they plead the fact of sexual difference to justify campaigns to modify workplaces in order to correct the effects of male influence and alleged biases. Only after such modifications, claim feminists, can women's nurturing attributes and other female qualities be adequately expressed in and truly influence the workplace. Manifestations of these female qualities, feminists argue, should and can occur in the workplace once it has been modified to blunt the substantial impact of male aggression and competitiveness and take account of women's special requirements.

Having launched its movement claiming the right of women—a right allegedly denied them previously—to enter the workplace on an *equal* basis with men, feminism then escalated its demands by arguing that female differences require numerous changes in the workplace. Women, in this view, are insufficiently feminine to find satisfaction in rearing their own children but too feminine to compete on an equal basis with men. Thus, having taken women out of their homes and settled them in the workplace, feminists have sought to reconstruct workplaces to create "feminist playpens" that are conducive to female qualities of sensitivity, caring, and empathy. Through this exercise in self-contradiction, contemporary feminism has endeavored to remove the woman from her home and role of providing daily care to her children—the quintessential place and activity for most effectively expressing her feminine, nurturing attributes.

The qualities that are the most likely to make women good mothers are thus redeployed away from their children and into workplaces that must be restructured to accommodate them. The irony is twofold. Children—the ones who could benefit most from the attentions of those mothers who do possess these womanly qualities—are deprived of those attentions and left only with the hope of finding adequate replacement for their loss. Moreover, the occupations in which these qualities are now to find expression either do not require them for optimal job performance (often they are not conducive to professional success) or were long ago recognized as women's occupations—as in the field of nursing, for example—in which nurturing abilities do enhance job performance.

Traditional Sexual Morality Traduced

The second prong of contemporary feminism's offensive has been to encourage women to ape male sexual patterns and engage in promiscuous sexual intercourse as freely as men. Initially, feminists were among the most dedicated supporters of the sexual revolution, viewing female participation in casual sexual activity as an unmistakable declaration of female equality with males. The women in our society who acted upon the teachings of feminist sexual revolutionaries have suffered greatly. They are victims of the highest abortion rate in the Western world. More than one in five Americans is now infected with a viral sexually transmitted disease which at best can be controlled but not cured and is often chronic. Sexually transmitted diseases, both viral and bacterial, disproportionately affect women because, showing fewer symptoms, they often go untreated for a longer time. These diseases also lead to pelvic infections that cause infertility in 100,000 to 150,000 women each year.

The sexual revolution feminists have promoted rests on an assumption that an act of sexual intercourse involves nothing but a pleasurable physical sensation, possessing no symbolic meaning and no moral dimension. This is an understanding of sexuality that bears more than a slight resemblance to sex as depicted in pornography: physical sexual acts without emotional involvement. In addition to the physical harm caused by increased sexual promiscuity, the denial that sexual intercourse has symbolic importance within a framework of moral accountability corrupts the nature of the sex act. Such denial necessarily makes sexual intercourse a trivial event, compromising the act's ability to fulfill its most important function after procreation. This function is to bridge the gap between males and females who often seem separated by so many differences, both biological and emotional, that they feel scarcely capable of understanding or communicating with each other.

Because of the urgency of sexual desire, especially in the male, it is through sexual contact that men and women can most easily come together. Defining the nature of sexual intercourse in terms informed by its procreative potentialities makes the act a spiritually meaningful event of overwhelming importance. A sexual encounter so defined is imbued with the significance conferred by its connection with a promise of immortality through procreation, whether that connection is a present possibility, a remembrance of children already borne, or simply an acknowledgment of the reality and truth of the promise. Such a sex act can serve as the physical meeting ground on which, by accepting and affirming each other through their bodies' physical unity, men and women can begin to construct an enduring emotional unity. The sexual encounter cannot perform its function when it is viewed as a trivial event of moral indifference with no purpose or meaning other than producing a physical sensation through the friction of bodily parts.

The feminist sexual perspective deprives the sex act of the spiritual meaningfulness that can make it the binding force upon which man and woman can construct a lasting marital relationship. The morally indifferent sexuality championed by the sexual revolution substitutes the sex without emotions that characterizes pornography for the sex of a committed, loving relationship that satisfies women's longing for romance and connection. But this is not the only damage to relationships between men and women that follows from feminism's determination to promote an androgynous society by convincing men and women that they are virtually fungible. Sexual equivalency, feminists believe, requires that women not only engage in casual sexual intercourse as freely as men, but also that women mimic male behavior by becoming equally assertive in initiating sexual encounters and in their activity throughout the encounter. With this sexual prescription, feminists mock the essence of conjugal sexuality that is at the foundation of traditional marriage.

Marriage as a Woman's Career Discredited

Even academic feminists who are considered "moderates" endorse doctrines most inimical to the homemaker. Thus, Professor Elizabeth Fox-Genovese, regarded as a moderate in Women's Studies, tells us that marriage can no longer be a viable career for women. But if marriage cannot be a woman's career, then despite feminist avowals of favoring choice in this matter, homemaking cannot be a woman's goal, and surrogate child-rearing must be her child's destiny. Contrary to feminist claims, society's barriers are not strung tightly to inhibit women's career choices. Because of feminism's very successful efforts, society encourages women to pursue careers, while stigmatizing and preventing their devotion to child-rearing and domesticity.

It was precisely upon the conclusion that marriage cannot be a viable career for women that *Time* magazine rested its Fall 1990 special issue on "Women: The Road Ahead," a survey of contemporary women's lives. While noting that the "cozy, limited roles of the past are still clearly remembered, sometimes fondly," during the past thirty years "all that was orthodox has become negotiable." One thing negotiated away has been the economic security of the homemaker, and *Time* advised young women that "the job of full-time homemaker may be the riskiest profession to choose" because "the advent of no-fault and equitable-distribution divorce laws" reflect, in the words of one judge, the fact that "[s]ociety no longer believes that a husband should support his wife."

No-fault divorce laws did not, however, result from an edict of the gods or some force of nature, but from sustained political efforts, particularly by the feminist movement. As a cornerstone of their drive to make women exchange home for workplace, and thereby secure their independence from men, the availability of no-fault divorce (like the availability of abortion) was sacrosanct to the movement. *Time* shed crocodile tears for displaced homemakers, for it made clear that women must canter down the road ahead with the spur of no-fault divorce urging them into the workplace. Of all *Time*'s recommendations for ameliorating women's lot, divorce reform—the most crying need in our country today—was not among them. Whatever hardships may be endured by women who would resist a divorce, *Time*'s allegiance, like that of most feminists, is clearly to the divorce-seekers who, it was pleased to note, will not be hindered in their pursuit of self-realization by the barriers to divorce that their own mothers had faced.

These barriers to divorce which had impeded their own parents, however, had usually benefited these young women by helping to preserve their parents' marriage. A five-year study of children in divorcing families disclosed that "the overwhelming majority preferred the unhappy marriage to the divorce," and many of them, "despite the unhappiness of their parents, were in fact relatively happy and considered their situation neither better nor worse than that of other families around them." A follow-up study after ten years demonstrated that children experienced the trauma of their parents' divorce as more serious and long-lasting than any researchers had anticipated. *Time* so readily acquiesced in the disadvantaging of homemakers and the disruption of children's lives because the feminist ideological parameters within which it operates have excluded marriage as a *proper* career choice. Removing the obstacles to making it a *viable* choice would, therefore, be an undesirable subversion of feminist goals.

That *Time* would have women trot forward on life's journey constrained by the blinders of feminist ideology is evident from its failure to question any feminist notion, no matter how silly, or to explore solutions incompatible with the ideology's script. One of the silliest notions *Time* left unexamined was that young women want "good careers, good marriages and two or three kids, and they don't want the children to be raised by strangers." The supposed realism of this expectation lay in the new woman's attitude that "I don't want to work 70 hours a week, but I want to be vice president, and *you* have to change." But even if thirty hours were cut from that seventy-hour workweek, the new woman would still be working the normal full-time week, her children would still be raised by surrogates, and the norm would continue to be the feminist version of child-rearing that *Time* itself described unflatteringly as "less a preoccupation than an improvisation."

The illusion that a woman can achieve career success without sacrificing the daily personal care of her children—and except among the very wealthy, most of her leisure as well—went unquestioned by *Time*. It did note, however, the dissatisfaction expressed by Eastern European and Russian women who had experienced as a matter of government policy the same liberation from home and children that our feminists have undertaken to bestow upon Western women. In what *Time* described as "a curious reversal of Western feminism's emphasis on careers for women," the new female leaders of Eastern Europe would like "to reverse the communist diktat that all women have to work." Women have "dreamed," said the Polish Minister of Culture and Arts, "of reaching the point where we have the choice to stay home" that communism had taken away. But blinded by its feminist bias, *Time* could only find it "curious" that women would choose to stay at home; apparently beyond the pale of respectability was any argument that it would serve Western women's interest to retain the choice that contemporary feminism—filling in the West the role of communism in the East—has sought to deny them.

Now was its feminist bias shaken by the attitudes of Japanese women, most of whom, *Time* noted, reject "equality" with men, choosing to cease work after the birth of a first child and later resuming a part-time career or pursuing hobbies or community work. The picture painted was that of the 1950s American suburban housewife reviled by Betty Friedan, except that the American has enjoyed a higher standard of living (particularly a much larger home) than has the Japanese. In Japan, *Time* observed, being "a housewife is nothing to be ashamed of." Dishonoring the housewife's role was a goal, it might have added, that Japanese feminists can, in time, accomplish if they emulate their American counterparts.

Japanese wives have broad responsibilities, commented *Time,* because most husbands leave their salaries and children entirely in wives' hands; freed from drudgery by modern appliances, housewives can "pursue their interests in a carefree manner, while men have to worry about supporting their wives and children." Typically, a Japanese wife controls household finances, giving her husband a cash allowance, the size of which, apparently, dissatisfies one-half of the men. Acknowledging that Japanese wives take the leadership in most homes, one husband observed that "[t]hings go best when the husband is swimming in the palm of his wife's hand." A home is well-managed, said one wife, "if you make your men feel that they're in control when they are in front of others, while in reality you're in control." It seems like a good arrangement to me.

Instead of inquiring whether a similar carefree existence might appeal to some American women, *Time* looked forward to the day when marriage would no longer be a career for Japanese women, as their men took over household and child-rearing chores, enabling wives to join husbands in the workplace. It was noted, however, that a major impediment to this goal, which would have to be corrected, was the fact that Japanese day-care centers usually run for only eight hours a day. Thus, *Time* made clear that its overriding concern was simply promoting the presence of women in the work force. This presence is seen as a good *per se,* without any *pro forma* talk about the economic necessity of a second income and without any question raised as to whether it is in children's interest to spend any amount of time—much less in excess of eight hours a day —in communal care....

The Awakened Brünnhilde

... Those who would defend anti-feminist traditionalism today are like heretics fighting a regnant Inquisition. To become a homemaker, a woman may need the courage of a heretic. This is one reason that the defense of traditional women is often grounded in religious teachings, for the heretic's courage usually rests on faith. The source of courage I offer is the conviction, based on my own experience, that contemporary feminism's stereotypical caricature of the housewife did not reflect reality when Friedan popularized it, does not reflect reality today, and need not govern reality.

Feminists claimed a woman can find identity and fulfillment only in a career; they are wrong. They claimed a woman can, in that popular expression, "have it all"; they are wrong—she can have only some. The experience of being a mother at home is a different experience from being a full-time market producer who is also a mother. A woman can have one or the other experience, but not both at the same time. Combining a career with motherhood requires a woman to compromise by diminishing her commitment and exertions with respect to one role or the other, or usually, to both. Rarely, if ever, can a woman adequately perform in a full-time career if she diminishes her commitment to it sufficiently to replicate the experience of being a mother at home.

Women were *never* told they could *not* choose to make the compromises required to combine these roles; within the memory of all living today there were always some women who did so choose. But by successfully degrading the housewife's role, contemporary feminism undertook to force this choice upon all women. I declined to make the compromises necessary to combine a career with motherhood because I did not want to become like Andrea Dworkin's spiritual virgin. I did not want to keep my being intact, as Dworkin puts it, so that I could continue to pursue career success. Such pursuit would have required me to hold too much of myself aloof from husband and children: the invisible "wedge-shaped core of darkness" that Virginia Woolf described as being oneself would have to be too large, and not enough of me would have been left over for them.

I feared that if I cultivated that "wedge-shaped core of darkness" within myself enough to maintain a successful career, I would be consumed by that career, and that thus desiccated, too little of me would remain to flesh out my roles as wife and mother. Giving most of myself to the market seemed less appropriate and attractive than reserving myself for my family. Reinforcing this decision was my experience that when a woman lives too much in her mind, she finds it increasingly difficult to live through her body. Her nurturing ties to her children become attenuated; her physical relationship with her husband becomes hollow and perfunctory. Certainly in my case, Dr. James C. Neely spoke the truth in *Gender: The Myth of Equality:* "With too much emphasis on intellect, a woman becomes 'too into her head' to function in a sexual, motherly way, destroying by the process of thought the process of feeling her sexuality."

Virginia Woolf never compromised her market achievements with motherhood; nor did the Brontë sisters, Jane Austen, or George Eliot. Nor did Helen Frankenthaler who, at the time she was acknowledged to be the most prominent living female artist, said in an interview: "We all make different compromises. And, no, I don't regret not having children. Given my painting, children could have suffered. A mother must make her children come first: young children are helpless. Well, paintings are objects but they're also helpless." I agree with her; that is precisely how I felt about the briefs I wrote for clients. Those briefs were, to me, like helpless children; in writing them, I first learned the meaning of complete devotion. I stopped writing them because I believed they would have been masters too jealous of my husband and my children.

Society never rebuked these women for refusing to compromise their literary and artistic achievements. Neither should it rebuke other kinds of women for refusing to compromise their own artistry of motherhood and domesticity. Some women may agree that the reality I depict rings truer to them than the feminist depiction. This conviction may help them find the courage of a heretic. Some others, both men and women, may see enough truth in the reality I depict that they will come to regret society's acquiescence in the status degradation of the housewife. They may then accept the currently unfashionable notion that society should respect and support women who adopt the anti-feminist perspective.

It is in society's interest to begin to pull apart the double-bind web spun by feminism and so order itself as not to inhibit any woman who *could* be an awakened Brünnhilde. Delighted and contented women will certainly do less harm—and probably more good—to society than frenzied and despairing ones. This is not to suggest that society should interfere with a woman's decision to follow the feminist script and adopt any form of spiritual virginity that suits her. But neither should society continue to validate destruction of the women's pact by the contemporary feminists who sought to make us all follow their script. We should now begin to dismantle our regime that discourages and disadvantages the traditional woman who rejects feminist spiritual virginity and seeks instead the very different delight and contentment that she believes best suits her.

NO

Jo Freeman

The Women's Liberation Movement

Sometime during the 1920s, feminism died in the United States. It was a premature death—feminists had just obtained that long-sought tool, the vote, with which they had hoped to make an equal place for women in this society—but it seemed irreversible. By the time the suffragists' granddaughters were old enough to vote, social mythology had firmly ensconced women in the home, and the very term *feminist* had become an insult.

Social mythology, however, did not always coincide with social fact. Even during the "feminine mystique" era of the 1940s and 1950s, when the relative numbers of academic degrees given to women were dropping, the absolute numbers of such degrees were rising astronomically. Women's participation in the labor force was also rising, even while women's position within it was declining. Opportunities to work, the trend toward smaller families, plus a change in preferred status symbols from a leisured wife at home to a second car and a color television set, helped transform the female labor force from one of primarily single women under twenty-five, as it was in 1940, to one of married women and mothers over forty, as it was by 1950. Simultaneously, the job market became even more rigidly sex-segregated, except for traditionally female professional jobs such as teaching and social work, which were flooded by men. Women's share of professional and technical jobs declined by a third, with a commensurate decline in women's relative income. The result of all this was the creation of a class of highly educated, underemployed, and underpaid women.

Origins of the Movement in the 1960s

In the early 1960s, feminism was still an unmentionable, but it was slowly awakening from the dead. The first sign of new life was President Kennedy's establishment of a national Commission on the Status of Women in 1961. Created at the urging of Esther Petersen of the Women's Bureau, the short-lived commission thoroughly documented women's second-class status. It was followed by the formation of a citizen's advisory council and fifty state commissions. Many of the people involved in these commissions, dissatisfied with the lack of progress made on their recommendations, joined with Betty Friedan in 1966 to found the National Organization for Women (NOW).

From Jo Freeman, "The Women's Liberation Movement: Its Origins, Structure, Activities, and Ideas," in Jo Freeman, ed., *Women: A Feminist Perspective,* 3rd ed. (Mayfield, 1984). Copyright © 1984 by Mayfield Publishing Company. Reprinted by permission of The McGraw-Hill Companies.

NOW was the first new feminist organization in almost fifty years, but it was not the sole beginning of the organized expression of the movement. The movement actually had two origins, from two different strata of society, with two different styles, orientations, values, and forms of organization. In many ways there were two separate movements. Although the composition of both branches was predominantly white, middle-class, and college-educated, initially the median age of the activists in what I call the older branch of the movement was higher. It also began first. In addition to NOW, this branch generated such organizations as the National Women's Political Caucus (NWPC), Women's Equity Action League (WEAL), Federally Employed Women (FEW), and almost 100 different organizations and caucuses of professional women. Their style of organization is traditionally formal, with elected officers, boards of directors, bylaws, and the other trappings of democratic procedure. All started as top-down organizations lacking a mass base. Only NOW and the NWPC subsequently developed a mass base, though not all wanted to.

In 1967 and 1968, unaware of and unknown to NOW or to the state commissions, the other branch of the movement was taking shape. While it did not begin on the campuses, its activators were on the younger side of the generation gap. Although few were students, all were under thirty and had received their political education as participants in or concerned observers of the social action projects of the preceding decade. Many came directly from new left and civil rights organizations, where they had been shunted into traditional roles and faced with the contradiction of working in a freedom movement but not being very free. Others had attended various courses on women in the multitude of free universities springing up around the country during those years.

During 1967 and 1968 at least five groups formed spontaneously and independently in five different cities—Chicago, Toronto, Detroit, Seattle, and Gainesville, Florida. They arose at a very auspicious moment. The blacks had just kicked the whites out of the civil rights movement, student power had been discredited by Students for a Democratic Society (SDS), and the organized new left was on the wane. Only draft-resistance activities were on the rise and this movement more than any other of its time exemplified the social inequities of the sexes. Men could resist the draft; women could only counsel resistance.

There had been individual temporary caucuses and conferences of women as early as 1964 when Stokely Carmichael of the Student Nonviolent Coordinating Committee (SNCC) made his infamous remark that "the only position for women in SNCC is prone." But it was not until 1967 that the groups developed a determined, if cautious, continuity and began to expand. In 1968 they held a national conference, attended by over 200 women from around this country and Canada on less than a month's notice. For the next few years they expanded exponentially.

This expansion was more amoebic than organized, because the younger branch of the movement prided itself on its lack of organization. Eschewing structure and damning leadership, it carried the concept of "everyone doing her own thing" almost to its logical extreme. The thousands of sister chapters around the country were virtually independent of each other, linked only by journals, newsletters, and cross-country travelers. Some cities had a coordinating committee that tried to maintain communication among local groups and to channel newcomers into appropriate ones, but none of these committees had any power over the activities, let alone the ideas, of the groups it served.

One result of this style was a very broadly based, creative movement, to which individuals could relate as they desired, with no concern for orthodoxy or doctrine. Another result was political impotence. It was impossible for this branch of the movement to organize a nationwide action, even if there could have been agreement on issues. Fortunately, the older branch of the movement had the structure necessary to coordinate such actions and was usually the one to initiate them.

Activities

The activities of the two branches were significantly different. In general, the older branch stayed with the traditional forms, creating national organizations that used the legal, political, and media institutions of the country with great skill. As a result of their activities the Equal Employment Opportunity Commission changed many of its originally prejudicial attitudes toward women. Numerous lawsuits were filed under the sex provision of Title VII of the 1964 Civil Rights Act. The Equal Rights Amendment passed Congress twice. The Supreme Court legalized some abortions. Complaints were filed against several hundred colleges and universities, as well as many businesses, charging sex discrimination. Articles on feminism appeared in virtually every news medium, and a host of new laws were passed prohibiting sex discrimination in a variety of areas.

The younger branch was more experimental. Its most prevalent innovation was the development of the "rap group." Essentially an educational technique, it spread far beyond its origins and became a major organizational unit of the whole movement. From a sociological perspective, the rap group is probably the most valuable contribution by the women's liberation movement to the tools for social change. As such it deserves some extended attention here.

The rap group serves two main functions. One is simply bringing women together in a situation of structured interaction. It has long been known that people can be kept down as long as they are kept divided from each other, relating more to their social superiors than to their social equals. It is when social development creates natural structures in which people can interact with one another and compare their common concerns that social movements take place. This is the function that the factory served for workers, the church for the southern civil rights movement, the campus for students, and the ghetto for urban blacks. Women have generally been deprived of structured interaction and been kept isolated in their individual homes, relating more to men than to each other. Natural structures for interaction are still largely lacking, although they have begun to develop. But the rap group provided an artificial structure that does much the same thing.

The second function of the rap group is as an actual mechanism for social change. It is a structure created specifically for the purpose of altering the participants' perceptions and conceptions of themselves and of society at large. The process is known as "consciousness raising" and is very simple. Women come together in groups of five to fifteen and talk to one another about their personal problems, personal experiences, personal feelings, and personal concerns. From this public sharing of experiences comes the realization that what each thought was individual is in fact common, that what each considered a personal problem has a social cause and probably a political solution. Women see how social structures and attitudes have limited their opportunities and molded them from birth. They ascertain the extent to which women have been denigrated in this society and how they have developed prejudices against themselves and other women.

This process of deeply personal attitude change makes the rap group a powerful tool. The need for any movement to develop "correct consciousness" has long been known. But usually this consciousness is not developed by means intrinsic to the structure of the movement and does not require such a profound resocialization of one's self-concept. This experience is both irreversible and contagious. Once women have gone through such a resocialization, their views of themselves and the world are never the same again even if they stop participating actively in the movement. Those who do drop out rarely do so without spreading feminist ideas among their own friends and colleagues. All who undergo consciousness raising feel compelled themselves to seek out other women with whom to share the experience.

There are several personal results from this process. The initial one is a decrease in self- and group-depreciation. Women come to see themselves and other women as essentially worthwhile and interesting. With this realization, the myth of the individual solution explodes. Women come to believe that, if they are the way they are because of society, they can change their lives significantly only by changing society. These feelings in turn create in each a consciousness of herself as a member of a group and the feeling of solidarity so necessary to any social movement. From this awareness comes the concept of "sisterhood."

The need for group solidarity explains why men have been largely excluded from women's rap groups. Sisterhood was not the initial goal of these groups, but it has been one of the more beneficial by-products. Originally, the idea of exclusion was borrowed from the black power movement, which was much in the public consciousness when the women's liberation movement began. It was reinforced by the unremitting hostility of most of the new left men at the prospect of an independent women's movement not tied to radical ideology. Even when this hostility was not evident, women in virtually every group in the United States, Canada, and Europe soon discovered that, when men were present, traditional sex roles reasserted themselves regardless of the good intentions of the participants. Men inevitably dominated the discussion and usually would talk only about how women's liberation related to men, or how men were oppressed by sex roles. In all-female groups, women found the discussions more open, honest, and extensive. They could learn how to relate to other *women,* not just to men.

While the male exclusion policy arose spontaneously, the rap group did not develop without a struggle. The political background of many of the early feminists of the younger branch predisposed them against the rap group as "un-political," and they would condemn discussion meetings that "degenerated" into "bitch sessions." This trend was particularly strong in centers of new left activity. Meanwhile, other feminists, usually with a civil rights or apolitical background, saw that the "bitch sessions" obviously met a basic need. They seized upon it and created the consciousness raising rap group. Developed initially in New York and Gainesville, the idea soon spread throughout the country, becoming the paradigm for most movement organization.

NOW and NWPC

Two national organizations, NOW and NWPC, continue to function primarily as pressure groups within the limits of traditional political activity. Diversification in the older branch of the movement has been largely along occupational lines and primarily within the professions. This branch has stressed using the tools for change provided by the system, however limited these may be. It emphasizes short-range goals and does not attempt to place them within a broader ideological framework. . . .

The Small Groups

The younger branch of the women's movement has had an entirely different history and faces different prospects. It was able to expand rapidly in the beginning because it could capitalize on the new left's infrastructure of organizations and media and because its initiators were skilled in local community organizing. Since the primary unit was the small group and no need for national cooperation was perceived, multitudinous splits increased its strength rather than drained its resources. Such fission was often "friendly" in nature and, even when not, served to bring ever-increasing numbers of women under the movement's umbrella.

Unfortunately, these newly recruited masses lacked the organizing skills of the initiators, and, because the very ideas of "leadership" and "organization" were in disrepute, they made no attempt to acquire them. They did not want to deal with traditional political institutions and abjured all traditional political skills. Consequently, the growth of movement institutions did not go beyond the local level, and they were often inadequate to handle the accelerating influx of new people into the movement. Although these small groups were diverse in kind and responsible to no one for their focus, their nature determined both the structure and the strategy of the movement. The major, though hardly exclusive, activities of the younger branch were organizing rap groups, putting on conferences, putting out educational literature, running service projects such as bookstores and health centers, and organizing occasional marches against pornography or to "Take Back the Night." This branch contributed more in the impact of its ideas than in its activities. It developed several ideological perspectives, much of the terminology of the movement, an amazing number of publications and counterinstitutions, numerous new issues, and even new techniques for social change.

Nonetheless, its loose structure was flexible only within certain limits, and the movement never transcended them. The rap groups were excellent for changing individual attitudes, but they were not very successful in dealing with social institutions. Their loose, informal structure encouraged participation in discussion, and their supportive atmosphere elicited personal insight; but neither was very efficient for handling specific tasks. Thus, although the rap groups were of fundamental value to the development of the movement, the more structured groups were more politically effective.

Individual rap groups tended to flounder when their members exhausted the virtues of consciousness raising and decided they wanted to do something more concrete. The problem was that most groups were unwilling to change their structure when they changed their tasks. They accepted the ideology of structureless without recognizing the limits on its uses.

Because structurelessness provided no means of resolving political disputes or carrying on ideological debates, the younger branch was racked by several major crises during the early seventies. The two most significant ones were an attempt by the Young Socialist Alliance (YSA), youth group of the Socialist Workers' Party (SWP), to take over the movement, and the so-called gay/straight split. The Trotskyist YSA saw the younger branch of the movement as a potential recruiting ground for socialist converts and directed its members to join with that purpose in mind. Although YSA members were never numerous, their enormous dedication and their contributions of time and energy enabled them to achieve positions of power quickly in many small groups whose lack of structure left no means of resisting. However, many new left women had remained within the younger branch, and their past experience with YSA predisposed them to mistrust it. Not only did they disagree with YSA politics but they also recognized that, because YSA members owed their primary allegiance to a centralized national party, those members had the potential to control the entire movement. The battle that ensued can euphemistically be described as vicious, and it resulted in YSA being largely driven from the younger branch of the movement. (Several years later, in their SWP guise, YSA members began to join NOW, but NOW's structure made it more difficult to control.) However, the alienation and fragmentation this struggle left in its wake made the movement ill prepared to meet its next major crisis.

The gay/straight split occurred not because of the mere presence of lesbians in feminist groups but because a vocal group of those present articulated lesbianism as the essential feminist idea. It was argued first that women should identify with, live with, and associate with women only, and eventually that a woman who actually slept with a man was clearly consorting with the enemy and could not be trusted. When this view met the fear and hostility many straight women felt toward homosexuality, the results were explosive.

The gay/straight struggle raged for several years and consumed most of the time and energy of the younger branch. By the time the tensions eased, most straight women had either become gay or left the younger branch. Some joined NOW, some rejoined the new left, and many simply dropped out of women's groups altogether. After gay women predominated (by about four to one) in the small groups, their anger toward straight women began to moderate. However, the focus of both the gay and the straight women remaining was no longer directed at educating or recruiting nonfeminists into the movement but rather at building a "women's culture" for those that remained. While a few groups engaged in outreach through public action on issues of concern to all women (e.g., rape) or even on issues concerning straight women exclusively (e.g., wife beating), most of the small groups concerned themselves with maintaining a comfortable niche for "women-identified women" and with insulating themselves from the damnation of the outside world. Consequently, while the small groups still exist throughout the country, most are hard for the uninitiated to locate and thus their impact on the outside world is now limited.

Their impact on the organizations of the older branch is also limited, because the networks that formerly existed were largely demolished by these crises. A major impetus for NOW's movement in a more radical direction during the early seventies was the pressure it received from the small groups, which frequently accused it of being part of the establishment. The insurgent faction that took control of NOW in the mid-seventies did so on the platform of "out of the mainstream and into the revolution." Once this faction attained power, however, it proceeded to go in the opposite direction, becoming more concerned with respectability, in order to gain support for the ERA from a wide spectrum of women, and less concerned with developing a consistent feminist interpretation on issues. Without pressure from the younger branch, NOW found the mainstream more appealing than revolution.

Ideas

Initially, there was little ideology in the movement beyond a gut feeling that something was wrong. NOW was formed under the slogan "full equality for women in a truly equal partnership with men," and in 1967 the organization specified eight demands in a Bill of Rights. It and the other organizations of the older branch have largely concluded that attempts at a comprehensive ideology have little to offer beyond internal conflict.

In the younger branch a basic difference of opinion developed quite early. It was disguised as a philosophical difference, was articulated and acted on as a strategic one, but was actually more of a political disagreement than anything else. The two sides involved were essentially the same ones that differed over the rap groups, but the split endured long after those groups became ubiquitous. The original issue was whether the fledgling women's liberation movement should remain a branch of the radical left movement or become an independent women's movement. Proponents of the two positions became known as "politicos" and "feminists," respectively, and traded arguments about whether the enemy was capitalism or male-dominated social institutions and values. They also traded a few epithets; politicos called feminists politically unsophisticated and elitist, and in turn were accused of subservience to the interests of left-wing men. With the influx of large numbers of previously apolitical women, an independent, autonomous women's liberation movement became a reality instead of an argument. The spectrum shifted toward the feminist direction, but the basic difference in orientation remained until wiped out by the debate over lesbian feminism. Those women who maintained their allegiance to the left then created their own socialist feminist groups or united in feminist caucuses within left organizations.

Socialist feminism and lesbian feminism are just two of the many different interpretations of women's status that have been developed. Some are more sophisticated than others, and some are better publicized, yet there is no single comprehensive interpretation that can accurately be labeled *the* women's liberationist, feminist, neofeminist, or radical feminist analysis. At best one can say there is general agreement on two theoretical concerns. The first is the feminist critique of society, and the second is the idea of oppression.

The traditional view of society assumes that men and women are essentially different and should serve different social functions; their diverse roles and statuses simply reflect these essential differences. The feminist perspective starts from the premise that women and men are constitutionally equal and share the same human capabilities; observed differences therefore demand a critical analysis of the social institutions that cause them. Since these two views start from different premises, neither can refute the other in logical terms.

The term *oppression* was long avoided by feminists out of a feeling that it was too rhetorical. But there was no convenient euphemism, and *discrimination* was inadequate to describe what happens to women and what they have in common with other disadvantaged groups. As long as the word remained illegitimate, so did the idea, and that was too valuable to lose. Oppression is still largely an undeveloped concept in which the details have not been sketched, but it appears to have two aspects, related much as the two sides of a coin are —distinct yet inseparable. The sociostructural aspect is easily visible because its manifestations are reflected in the legal, economic, social, and political institutions. The sociopsychological aspect is often intangible—hard to grasp and hard to alter. Group self-hate and distortion of perceptions to justify a preconceived interpretation of reality are just some of the factors being teased out.

Sexism is the word used to describe the particular kind of oppression that women experience. Starting from the traditional belief in the difference between the sexes, sexism embodies two core concepts. The first is that men are more important than women—not necessarily superior (we are far too sophisticated these days to use that tainted term) but more important, more significant, more valuable, more worthwhile. This presumption justifies the idea that it is more important for a man, the "breadwinner," to have a job or a promotion, to be paid well, to have an education, and in general to have preference over a woman. It is the basis of men's feeling that if women enter a particular occupation they will degrade it and that men must then leave it or be themselves degraded. It is also at the root of women's feeling that they can raise the prestige of their professions by recruiting men, which they can do only by giving men the better jobs. From this value come the attitudes that a husband must earn more than his wife or suffer a loss of personal status and that a wife must subsume her interests to his or be socially castigated. The first core concept of sexist thought, then, is that men do the important work in the world, and the work done by men is what is important.

The second core concept is that women are here for the pleasure and assistance of men. This is what is implied when women are told that their role is complementary to that of men, that they should fulfill their natural "feminine" functions, that they are different from men and should not compete with them. From this concept comes the attitude that women are and should be dependent on men for everything, especially their identities, the social definition of who they are. It defines the few roles for which women are socially rewarded—wife, mother, mistress (all pleasing or beneficial to men)—and leads directly to the pedestal theory that extols women who stay in their place as good helpmates to men.

This attitude stigmatizes women who do not marry or who do not devote their primary energies to the care of men and their children. Association with a man is the basic criterion for a woman's participation in this society, and a woman who does not seek her identity through a man is a threat to the social values. Similarly this attitude causes women's liberation activists to be labeled *manhaters* for exposing the nature of sexism. People feel that a woman not devoted to looking after a man must either hate men or be unable to "catch" one. The effect of this second core concept of sexist thought, then, is that women's identities are defined by their relationship to men, and their social value is determined by that of the men they are related to.

The sexism of our society is so pervasive that we are not even aware of all its manifestations. Unless a person has developed a sensitivity to its workings, by adopting a self-consciously contrary view, she or he accepts those workings with little question as "normal" and justified. People are said to "choose" what in fact they have never thought about. A good example of sexism is what happened during and after World War II. The sudden onslaught of the war radically changed the whole structure of American social relationships as well as the American economy. Men were drafted into the army and women into the labor force. Now desperately needed, working women had their wants met by society, as the wants of the boys at the front were met. Federal financing of day-care centers in the form of the Lanham Act passed Congress in a record two weeks. Special crash training programs were provided to give the new women workers skills they were not previously thought capable of exercising. Women instantly assumed positions of authority and responsibility unavailable to them only the year before.

But what happened when the war ended? Both men and women had heeded their country's call to duty to bring the struggle to a successful conclusion. Yet men were rewarded for their efforts and women punished for theirs. The returning soldiers were given the GI Bill and other veterans' benefits. They got their old jobs back and a disproportionate share of the new ones created by the war economy. Women, on the other hand, saw their child-care centers dismantled and their training programs cease. They were fired or demoted in droves and often found it difficult to enter colleges flooded with ex-GIs matriculating on government money. Is it any wonder that they heard the message that their place was in the home? Where else could they go?

The eradication of sexism, and of sexist practices like those described above, is obviously one of the major goals of the women's liberation movement. But it is not enough to destroy a set of values and leave a normative vacuum. The old values have to be replaced with something. A movement can begin by declaring its opposition to the status quo, but eventually, if it is to succeed, it has to propose an alternative.

I cannot pretend to be definitive about the possible alternatives contemplated by the numerous participants in the women's liberation movement. Yet from the plethora of ideas and visions that feminists have thought, discussed, and written about, I think two predominant ideas have emerged. I call these the egalitarian ethic and the liberation ethic. They are closely related and merge into what can only be described as a feminist humanism.

The egalitarian ethic means that the sexes are equal; therefore sex roles must go. Our history has proved that institutionalized *difference* inevitably means *inequality*, and sex-role stereotypes have long since become anachronistic. Strongly differentiated sex roles were rooted in the ancient division of labor; their basis has been torn apart by modern technology. Their justification was rooted in the subjection of women to the reproductive cycle. That has already been destroyed by modern pharmacology. The cramped little boxes of personality and social function to which society assigns people from birth must be broken open so that all people can develop independently, as individuals. This means that there will be an integration of the social functions and life-styles of men and women as groups until, ideally, one cannot tell anything relevant about a person's social role by knowing that person's sex. But this greater similarity of the two groups also means more options for individuals and more diversity in the human race. No longer will there be men's work and women's work. No longer will humanity suffer a schizophrenic personality desperately trying to reconcile its "masculine" and "feminine" parts. No longer will marriage be an institution in which two half-people come together in hopes of making a whole.

The liberation ethic says this is not enough. Not only the limits of the roles but also their content must be changed. The liberation ethic looks at the kinds of lives currently being led by men as well as women and concludes that both are deplorable and neither is necessary. The social institutions that oppress women as women also oppress people as people and can be altered to make a more human existence for all. So much of our society is hung upon the framework of sex-role stereotypes and their reciprocal functions that the dismantling of this structure will provide the opportunity for making a more viable life for everyone.

It is important to stress that these two ethics must work in tandem. If the first is emphasized over the second, then we have a women's rights movement, not one of women's liberation. To seek for equality alone, given the current male bias of the social values, is to assume that women want to be like men or that men are worth emulating; it is to demand that women be allowed to participate in society as we know it, to get their piece of the pie, without questioning whether that society is worth participating in. Most feminists today find this view inadequate. Those women who are personally more comfortable in what is considered the male role must realize that that role is made possible only by the existence of the female role—in other words, only by the subjugation of women. Therefore women cannot become equal to men without the destruction of those two interdependent, mutually parasitic roles. To fail to recognize that the integration of the sex roles and the equality of the sexes will inevitably lead to basic structural changes is to fail to seize the opportunity to decide the direction of those changes.

It is just as dangerous to fall into the trap of seeking liberation without due concern for equality. This is the mistake made by many left radicals. They find the general human condition to be so wretched that they feel everyone should devote her or his energies to the millennial revolution in the belief that the liberation of women will follow naturally the liberation of people.

However, women have yet to be defined as people, even among the radicals, and it is erroneous to assume that their interests are identical to those of men. For women to subsume their concerns once again is to ensure that the promise of liberation will be a spurious one. There has yet to be created or conceived by any political or social theorist a revolutionary society in which women were equal to men and their needs equally considered. The sex-role structure has never been comprehensively challenged by male philosophers, and the systems they have proposed have all presumed the existence of a sex-role structure.

Exclusive emphasis on the liberation ethic can also lead to a sort of radical paradox. This is the situation in which the new left women frequently were caught during the early days of the women's movement. They did not want to pursue "reformist" issues that might be achieved without altering the basic nature of the system, because, they felt, these reforms would only strengthen the system. However, their search for a sufficiently radical action or issue came to naught. They then found themselves unable to do anything, out of fear that it might be counterrevolutionary. Inactive revolutionaries are much more innocuous than active reformists.

But, even among those who are not rendered impotent, the unilateral pursuit of liberation can take its toll. Some radical women have been so appalled at the condition of most men, and the possibility of becoming even partially what men are, that they have clung to the security of the role they know while waiting for the revolution to liberate everyone. Some men, fearing that role reversal is a goal of the women's liberation movement, have taken a similar position. Both have failed to realize that the abolition of sex roles must be a part of any radical restructuring of society and thus have failed to explore the possible consequences of such role integration. The goal they advocate may be one of liberation, but it does not involve women's liberation.

Separated from each other, the egalitarian ethic and the liberation ethic can be crippling, but together they can be a very powerful force. Separately they speak to limited interests; together they speak to all humanity. Separately, they afford only superficial solutions; together they recognize that sexism not only oppresses women but also limits the potential of men. Separately, neither will be achieved, because both are too narrow in scope; together, they provide a vision worthy of our devotion. Separately, these two ethics liberate neither women nor men; together, they can liberate both.

POSTSCRIPT

Has the Women's Liberation Movement Been Harmful to American Women?

Graglia's critique of contemporary feminism is a throwback to women of the late nineteenth and early twentieth century who opposed the women social workers and suffragettes who entered the man's world. Her book is a modern restatement of Barbara Welter's classic and widely reprinted article "The Cult of True Womanhood," *American Quarterly* (Summer 1996).

Graglia argues that contemporary feminism ignores women's primary role in raising the children and preserving the moral character of the family. She blames contemporary feminism along with the Great Society's social programs for promoting a sexual revolution that has destroyed the American family by fostering sexually transmitted diseases and a high divorce rate.

Both the antifeminist Graglia and the profeminist Freeman have been critiqued by moderate feminists like Elizabeth Fox-Genovese and Cathy Young, who contend that contemporary feminists have not spoken to the concerns of married women, especially women from poor or lower-middle-class families who must work in order to help support the family. Fox-Genovese's *Feminism Is Not the Story of My Life: How Today's Feminist Elite Have Lost Touch With the Real Concerns of Women* (Doubleday, 1996) is peppered with interviews of white, African American, and Hispanic Americans of different classes and gives a more complex picture of the problems women face today. Young, author of *Cease Fire! Why Women and Men Must Join Forces to Achieve True Equality* (Free Press, 1999), asserts that Graglia denies the real discrimination women faced in the job market in the 1950s. Furthermore, Young says, Graglia's critique of the sexual revolution is an attempt to restore a view of female sexuality as essentially submissive.

In 1998 Harvard University Press reprinted Betty Friedan's two later books, which are critical of some of the directions that the women's movement took—*The Second Stage* and *It Changed My Life,* both with new introductions with suggestions for the twenty-first century. Other important books by activists with historical perspectives are Sara Evans, *Personal Politics: The Roots of Women's Liberation in the Civil Rights Movement and the New Left* (Vintage, 1979) and Jo Freeman, *The Politics of Women's Liberation* (Longman, 1975).

A comprehensive history of the movement is Flora Davis, *Moving the Mountain: The Women's Movement in America Since 1960* (Simon & Schuster, 1991). See also William Chafe, *The Paradox of Change: American Women in the Twentieth Century* (Oxford University Press, 1991) and Susan M. Hartmann, *From Margin to Mainstream: American Women and Politics Since 1960* (Alfred A. Knopf, 1989).

ISSUE 10

Will History Forgive Richard Nixon?

YES: Joan Hoff-Wilson, from "Richard M. Nixon: The Corporate Presidency," in Fred I. Greenstein, ed., *Leadership in the Modern Presidency* (Harvard University Press, 1988)

NO: Stanley I. Kutler, from "Et Tu, Bob?" *The Nation* (August 22–29, 1994)

ISSUE SUMMARY

YES: According to professor of history Joan Hoff-Wilson, the Nixon presidency reorganized the executive branch and portions of the federal bureaucracy and implemented domestic reforms in civil rights, welfare, and economic planning, despite its limited foreign policy successes and the Watergate scandal.

NO: Professor and political commentator Stanley I. Kutler argues that President Nixon was a crass, cynical, narrow-minded politician who unnecessarily prolonged the Vietnam War to ensure his reelection and implemented domestic reforms only when he could outflank his liberal opponents.

In late April 1994 former president Richard M. Nixon, age 81, died in a coma in a hospital in New York City. Twenty years before, Nixon became the only U.S. president forced to resign from office.

Richard Milhous Nixon was born in Yorba Linda in Orange County, California, on January 9, 1913, the second of five children. When he was nine his family moved to Whittier, California. His mother encouraged him to attend the local Quaker school, Whittier College, where he excelled at student politics and debating. He earned a tuition-paid scholarship to Duke University Law School and graduated third out of a class of 25 in 1937. He returned to Whittier and for several years worked with the town's oldest law firm.

Nixon had hopes of joining a bigger law firm, but World War II intervened. He worked in the tire rationing section for the Office of Price Administration in Washington, D.C., before joining the navy as a lieutenant, junior grade, where he served in a Naval Transport Unit in the South Pacific for the duration of the war. Before his discharge from active duty, Republicans asked him to run for a seat in California's 12th congressional district in the House of Representatives. He won the primary and defeated Jerry Vorhees, a New Deal Democratic incumbent, in the general election of 1946. In that year the Republicans gained control of Congress for the first time since 1930.

During Nixon's campaign against Vorhees, he accused Vorhees of accepting money from a communist-dominated political action committee. This tactic, known as "red-baiting," was effective in the late 1940s and early 1950s because the American public had become frightened of the communist menace. In 1950 Nixon utilized similar tactics in running for the U.S. Senate against Congresswoman Helen Gahagan Douglas. He won easily.

Young, energetic, a vigorous campaign orator, and a senator from the second largest state in the Union with impeccable anticommunist credentials, Nixon was chosen by liberal Republicans to become General Dwight D. Eisenhower's running mate in the 1952 presidential election. In the election Eisenhower and Nixon overwhelmed the Democrats. Nixon became the second-youngest vice president in U.S. history and actively used the office to further his political ambitions.

The 1960 presidential campaign was one of the closest in modern times. Nixon, who was considered young for high political office at that time, lost to an even younger Democratic senator from Massachusetts, John F. Kennedy. Out of 68 million votes cast, less than 113,000 votes separated the two candidates.

In 1962 Nixon was persuaded to seek the governorship of California on the premise that he needed a power boost to keep his presidential hopes alive for 1964. Apparently, Nixon was out of touch with state politics. Governor Pat Brown defeated him by 300,000 votes.

Nixon then left for New York City and became a partner with a big-time Wall Street legal firm. He continued to speak at Republican dinners, and he supported Barry Goldwater of Arizona for the presidency in 1964. After Goldwater's decisive defeat by Lyndon Johnson, Nixon's political fortunes revived yet again. In March 1968 Johnson announced that he was not going to run again for the presidency. Nixon took advantage of the opening and won the Republican nomination.

During the 1968 presidential campaign Nixon positioned himself between Democratic vice president Hubert Humphrey, the liberal defender of the Great Society programs, and the conservative, law-and-order, third-party challenger Governor George Wallace of Alabama. Nixon stressed a more moderate brand of law and order and stated that he had a secret plan to end the war in Vietnam. He barely edged Humphrey in the popular vote, but Nixon received 301 electoral votes to 191 for Humphrey. Wallace received nearly 10 million popular votes and 46 electoral college votes.

This background brings us to Nixon's presidency. Was Nixon an effective president? In the following selections, Joan Hoff-Wilson argues that Nixon achieved a number of domestic policy successes in the areas of civil rights, welfare, and economic planning, and in the reorganization of the executive branch and some federal agencies. Stanley I. Kutler maintains that President Nixon was a crass, cynical, narrow-minded bigot who implemented policy changes for strictly political reasons.

Joan Hoff-Wilson  **YES**

Richard M. Nixon:
The Corporate Presidency

Richard Milhous Nixon became president of the United States at a critical juncture in American history. Following World War II there was a general agreement between popular and elite opinion on two things: the effectiveness of most New Deal domestic policies and the necessity of most Cold War foreign policies. During the 1960s, however, these two crucial postwar consensual constructs began to break down; and the war in Indochina, with its disruptive impact on the nation's political economy, hastened their disintegration. By 1968 the traditional bipartisan, Cold War approach to the conduct of foreign affairs had been seriously undermined. Similarly, the "bigger and better" New Deal approach to the modern welfare state had reached a point of diminishing returns, even among liberals.

In 1968, when Richard Nixon finally captured the highest office in the land, he inherited not only Lyndon Johnson's Vietnam war but also LBJ's Great Society. This transfer of power occurred at the very moment when both endeavors had lost substantial support among the public at large and, most important, among a significant number of the elite group of decision makers and leaders of opinion across the country. On previous occasions when such a breakdown had occurred within policy- and opinion-making circles—before the Civil and Spanish American Wars and in the early years of the Great Depression—domestic or foreign upheavals had followed. Beginning in the 1960s the country experienced a similar series of failed presidents reminiscent of those in the unstable 1840s and 1850s, 1890s, and 1920s.

In various ways all the presidents in these transitional periods failed as crisis managers, often because they refused to take risks. Nixon, in contrast, "[couldn't] understand people who won't take risks." His proclivity for risk taking was not emphasized by scholars, journalists, and psychologists until after he was forced to resign as president. "I am not necessarily a respecter of the status quo," Nixon told Stuart Alsop in 1958; "I am a chance taker." Although this statement was made primarily in reference to foreign affairs, Nixon's entire political career has been characterized by a series of personal and professional crises and risky political policies. It is therefore not surprising that as president

From Joan Hoff-Wilson, "Richard M. Nixon: The Corporate Presidency," in Fred I. Greenstein, ed., *Leadership in the Modern Presidency* (Harvard University Press, 1988). Copyright © 1988 by The President and Fellows of Harvard College. Reprinted by permission of Harvard University Press. Notes omitted.

he rationalized many of his major foreign and domestic initiatives as crises (or at least as intolerable impasses) that could be resolved only by dramatic and sometimes drastic measures.

A breakdown in either the foreign or domestic policy consensus offers both opportunity and danger to any incumbent president. Nixon had more opportunity for risk-taking changes at home and abroad during his first administration than he would have had if elected in 1960 because of the disruptive impact of war and domestic reforms during the intervening eight years. Also, he inherited a wartime presidency, with all its temporarily enhanced extralegal powers. Although the Cold War in general has permanently increased the potential for constitutional violations by presidents, only those in the midst of a full-scale war (whether declared or undeclared) have exercised with impunity what Garry Wills has called "semi-constitutional" actions. Although Nixon was a wartime president for all but twenty months of his five and one-half years in office, he found that impunity for constitutional violations was not automatically accorded a president engaged in an undeclared, unsatisfying, and seemingly endless war. In fact, he is not usually even thought of, or referred to, as a wartime president.

Periods of war and reform have usually alternated in the United States, but in the 1960s they burgeoned simultaneously, hastening the breakdown of consensus that was so evident by the time of the 1968 election. This unusual situation transformed Nixon's largely unexamined and rather commonplace management views into more rigid and controversial ones. It also reinforced his natural predilection to bring about change through executive fiat. Thus a historical accident accounts in part for many of Nixon's unilateral administrative actions during his first term and for the events leading to his disgrace and resignation during his second.

The first few months in the Oval Office are often intoxicating, and a new president can use them in a variety of ways. But during the socioeconomic confusion and conflict of the late 1960s and early 1970s, some of the newly appointed Republican policy managers (generalists) and the frustrated holdover Democratic policy specialists (experts) in the bureaucracy unexpectedly came together and began to consider dramatic policy changes at home and abroad. Complex interactions between these very different groups produced several significant shifts in domestic and foreign affairs during the spring and summer of 1969. A radical welfare plan and dramatic foreign policy initiatives took shape.

The country had elected only one other Republican president since the onset of FDR's reform administrations thirty-six years earlier. Consequently, Nixon faced not only unprecedented opportunities for changing domestic policy as a result of the breakdown in the New Deal consensus, but also the traditional problems of presidential governance, exacerbated in this instance by bureaucratic pockets of resistance from an unusual number of holdover Democrats. Such resistance was not new, but its magnitude was particularly threatening to a distrusted (and distrustful) Republican president who did not control either house of Congress. Nixon's organizational recommendations for containing the bureaucracy disturbed his political opponents and the liberal press as much as, if not more than, their doubts about the motivation behind many of his substantive and innovative suggestions on other domestic issues such as welfare and the environment.

Because much of the press and both houses of Congress were suspicious of him, Nixon naturally viewed administrative action as one way of obtaining significant domestic reform. Moreover, some of his initial accomplishments in administratively redirecting U.S. foreign policy ultimately led him to rely more on administrative actions at home than he might have otherwise. In any case, this approach drew criticism from those who already distrusted his policies and priorities. Nixon's covert and overt expansion and prolongation of the war during this period reinforced existing suspicions about his personality and political ethics. In this sense, liberal paranoia about his domestic programs fueled Nixon's paranoia about liberal opposition to the war, and vice versa. By 1972, Nixon's success in effecting structural and substantive change in foreign policy through the exercise of unilateral executive power increasingly led him to think that he could use the same preemptive administrative approach to resolve remaining domestic problems, especially following his landslide electoral victory....

Foreign Policy Scorecard

It was clearly in Nixon's psychic and political self-interest to end the war in Vietnam as soon as possible. Although he came to office committed to negotiate a quick settlement, he ended up prolonging the conflict. As a result, he could never build the domestic consensus he needed to continue the escalated air and ground war (even with dramatically reduced U.S. troop involvement) and to ensure passage of some of his domestic programs. For Nixon (and Kissinger) Vietnam became a symbol of influence in the Third World that, in turn, was but one part of their geopolitical approach to international relations. Thus the war in Southeast Asia had to be settled as soon as possible so as not to endanger other elements of Nixonian diplomatic and domestic policy.

Instead, the president allowed his secretary of state to become egocentrically involved in secret negotiations with the North Vietnamese from August 4, 1969, to January 25, 1972 (when they were made public). As a result, the terms finally reached in 1973 were only marginally better than those rejected in 1969. The advantage gained from Hanoi's agreement to allow President Nguyen Van Thieu to remain in power in return for allowing North Vietnamese troops to remain in South Vietnam can hardly offset the additional loss of twenty thousand American lives during this three-year-period—especially given the inherent weaknesses of the Saigon government by 1973. On the tenth anniversary of the peace treaty ending the war in Vietnam, Nixon admitted to me that "Kissinger believed more in the power of negotiation than I did." He also said that he "would not have temporized as long" with the negotiating process had he not been "needlessly" concerned with what the Soviets and Chinese might think if the United States pulled out of Vietnam precipitately. Because Nixon saw no way in 1969 to end the war quickly except through overt massive bombing attacks, which the public demonstrated in 1970 and 1971 it would not tolerate, there was neither peace nor honor in Vietnam by the time that war was finally concluded on January 27, 1973; and in the interim he made matters worse by secretly bombing Cambodia.

The delayed ending to the war in Vietnam not only cast a shadow on all Nixon's other foreign policy efforts but also established secrecy, wiretapping, and capricious personal diplomacy as standard operational procedures in the conduct of foreign policy that ultimately carried over into domestic affairs. Despite often duplicitous and arbitrary actions, even Nixon's strongest critics often credit him with an unusual number of foreign policy successes.

Although fewer of his foreign policy decisions were reached in a crisis atmosphere than his domestic ones, Nixon's diplomatic legacy is weaker than he and many others have maintained. For example, the pursuit of "peace and honor" in Vietnam failed; his Middle Eastern policy because of Kissinger's shuttling ended up more show than substance; his Third World policy (outside of Vietnam and attempts to undermine the government of Allende in Chile) were nearly nonexistent; détente with the USSR soon foundered under his successors; and the Nixon Doctrine has not prevented use of U.S. troops abroad. Only rapprochement with China remains untarnished by time because it laid the foundation for recognition, even though he failed to achieve a "two China" policy in the United Nations. This summary is not meant to discredit Richard Nixon as a foreign policy expert both during and after his presidency. It is a reminder that the lasting and positive results of his diplomacy may be fading faster than some aspects of his domestic policies.

Outflanking Liberals on Domestic Reform

Presidents traditionally achieve their domestic objectives through legislation, appeals in the mass media, and administrative actions. During his first administration Nixon offered Congress extensive domestic legislation, most of which aimed at redistributing federal power away from Congress and the bureaucracy. When he encountered difficulty obtaining passage of these programs, he resorted more and more to reform by administrative fiat, especially at the beginning of his second term. All Nixonian domestic reforms were rhetorically linked under the rubric of the New Federalism. Most competed for attention with his well-known interest in foreign affairs. Most involved a degree of the boldness he thought necessary for a successful presidency. Most increased federal regulation of nondistributive public policies. Most were made possible in part because he was a wartime Republican president who took advantage of acting in the Disraeli tradition of enlightened conservatism. Most offended liberals (as well as many conservatives), especially when it came to implementing certain controversial policies with legislation. Many were also undertaken in a crisis atmosphere, which on occasion was manufactured by individual members of Nixon's staff to ensure his attention and action.

In some instances, as political scientist Paul J. Halpern has noted, Nixon's long-standing liberal opponents in Congress "never even bothered to get the facts straight" about these legislative and administrative innovations; the very people who, according to Daniel Moynihan, formed the "natural constituency" for most of Nixon's domestic policies refused to support his programs. It may well have been that many liberals simply could not believe that Nixon would ever do the right thing except for the wrong reason. Thus they seldom took the time to try to determine whether any of his efforts to make the 1970s a decade of reform were legitimate, however politically motivated. Additionally, such partisan opposition made Nixon all the more willing to reorganize the executive branch of government with or without congressional approval.

My own interviews with Nixon and his own (and others') recent attempts to rehabilitate his reputation indicate that Nixon thinks he will outlive the obloquy of Watergate because of his foreign policy initiatives—not because of his domestic policies. Ultimately, however, domestic reform and his attempts at comprehensive reorganization of the executive branch may become the standard by which the Nixon presidency is judged.

Environmental Policy

Although Nixon's aides cite his environmental legislation as one of his major domestic achievements, it was not high on his personal list of federal priorities, despite polls showing its growing importance as a national issue. White House central files released in 1986 clearly reveal that John Ehrlichman was initially instrumental in shaping the president's views on environmental matters and conveying a sense of crisis about them. Most ideas were filtered through him to Nixon. In fact Ehrlichman, whose particular expertise was in land-use policies, has been described by one forest conservation specialist as "the most effective environmentalist since Gifford Pinchot." Ehrlichman and John Whitaker put Nixon ahead of Congress on environmental issues, especially with respect to his use of the permit authority in the Refuse Act of 1899 to begin to clean up water supplies before Congress passed any "comprehensive water pollution enforcement plan."

"Just keep me out of trouble on environmental issues," Nixon reportedly told Ehrlichman. This proved impossible because Congress ignored Nixon's recommended ceilings when it finally passed (over his veto) the Federal Water Pollution Control Act amendments of 1972. Both Ehrlichman and Whitaker agreed then and later that it was "budget-busting" legislation designed to embarrass the president on a popular issue in an election year. Statistics later showed that the money appropriated could not be spent fast enough to achieve the legislation's stated goals. The actual annual expenditures in the first years after passage approximated those originally proposed by Nixon's staff.

Revamping Welfare

Throughout the 1968 presidential campaign Nixon's own views on welfare remained highly unfocused. But once in the Oval Office he set an unexpectedly fast pace on the issue. On January 15, 1969, he demanded an investigation by top aides into a newspaper allegation of corruption in New York City's Human Resources Administration. Nixon's extraordinary welfare legislation originated in a very circuitous fashion with two low-level Democratic holdovers from the Johnson administration, Worth Bateman and James Lyday. These two bureaucrats fortuitously exercised more influence on Robert Finch, Nixon's first secretary of health, education and welfare, than they had been able to on John W. Gardner and Wilbur J. Cohn, Johnson's two appointees. Finch was primarily responsible for obtaining Nixon's approval of what eventually became known as the Family Assistance Program (FAP).

If FAP had succeeded in Congress it would have changed the emphasis of American welfare from providing services to providing income; thus it would have replaced the Aid to Families with Dependent Children (AFDC) program, whose payments varied widely from state to state. FAP called for anywhere from $1,600 (initially proposed in 1969) to $2,500 (proposed in 1971) for a family of four. States were expected to supplement this amount, and in addition all able-bodied heads of recipient families (except mothers with preschool children) would be required to "accept work or training." However, if a parent refused to accept work or training, only his or her payment would be withheld. In essence, FAP unconditionally guaranteed children an annual income and would have tripled the number of children then being aided by AFDC.

A fundamental switch from services to income payments proved to be too much for congressional liberals and conservatives alike, and they formed a strange alliance to vote it down. Ironically, FAP's final defeat in the Senate led to some very impressive examples of incremental legislation that might not have been passed had it not been for the original boldness of FAP. For example, Supplementary Security Income, approved on October 17, 1972, constituted a guaranteed annual income for the aged, blind, and disabled.

The demise of FAP also led Nixon to support uniform application of the food stamp program across the United States, better health insurance programs for low-income families, and an automatic cost-of-living adjustment for Social Security recipients to help them cope with inflation. In every budget for which his administration was responsible—that is, from fiscal 1971 through fiscal 1975 —spending on all human resource programs exceeded spending for defense for the first time since World War II. A sevenfold increase in funding for social services under Nixon made him (not Johnson) the "last of the big spenders" on domestic programs.

Reluctant Civil Rights Achievements

Perhaps the domestic area in which Watergate has most dimmed or skewed our memories of the Nixon years is civil rights. We naturally tend to remember that during his presidency Nixon deliberately violated the civil rights of some of those who opposed his policies or were suspected of leaking information. Nixon has always correctly denied that he was a conservative on civil rights, and indeed his record on this issue, as on so many others, reveals as much political expediency as it does philosophical commitment. By 1968 there was strong southern support for his candidacy. Consequently, during his campaign he implied that if elected he would slow down enforcement of federal school desegregation policies.

Enforcement had already been painfully sluggish since the 1954 *Brown v. Board of Education* decision. By 1968 only 20 percent of black children in the South attended predominantly white schools, and none of this progress had occurred under Eisenhower or Kennedy. Moreover, the most dramatic improvement under Johnson's administration did not take place until 1968, because HEW deadlines for desegregating southern schools had been postponed four times since the passage of the 1964 Civil Rights Act. By the spring of 1968, however, a few lower court rulings, and finally the Supreme Court decision in *Green v. Board of Education,* no longer allowed any president the luxury of arguing that freedom-of-choice plans were adequate for rooting out racial discrimination, or that de facto segregation caused by residential patterns was not as unconstitutional as *de jure* segregation brought about by state or local laws.

Despite the real national crisis that existed over school desegregation, Nixon was not prepared to go beyond what he thought the decision in *Brown* had mandated, because he believed that de facto segregation could not be ended through busing or cutting off funds from school districts. Nine days after Nixon's inauguration, his administration had to decide whether to honor an HEW-initiated cutoff of funds to five southern school districts, originally scheduled to take place in the fall of 1968 but delayed until January 29, 1969. On that day Secretary Finch confirmed the cutoff but also announced that the school districts could claim funds retroactively if they complied with HEW guidelines within sixty days. This offer represented a change from the most recent set of HEW guidelines, developed in March 1968, which Johnson had never formally endorsed by signing.

At the heart of the debate over various HEW guidelines in the last half of the 1960s were two issues: whether the intent of the Civil Rights Act of 1964 had been simply to provide freedom of choice or actually to compel integration in schools; and whether freedom-of-choice agreements negotiated by HEW or lawsuits brought by the Department of Justice were the most effective ways of achieving desegregation. Under the Johnson administration the HEW approach, based on bringing recalcitrant school districts into compliance by cutting off federal funding, had prevailed. Nixon, on the other hand, argued in his First Inaugural that the "laws have caught up with our consciences" and insisted that it was now necessary "to give life to what is in the law." Accordingly, he changed the emphasis in the enforcement of school desegregation from HEW compliance agreements to Justice Department actions—a legal procedure that proved very controversial in 1969 and 1970, but one that is standard now.

Nixon has been justifiably criticized by civil rights advocates for employing delaying tactics in the South, and particularly for not endorsing busing to enforce school desegregation in the North after the April 20, 1971, Supreme Court decision in *Swann v. Charlotte-Mecklenburg Board of Education.* Despite the bitter battle in Congress and between Congress and the executive branch after *Swann,* the Nixon administration's statistical record on school desegregation is impressive. In 1968, 68 percent of all black children in the South and 40 percent in the nation as a whole attended all-black schools. By the end of 1972, 8 percent of southern black children attended all-black schools, and a little less than 12 percent nationwide. A comparison of budget outlays is equally revealing. President Nixon spent $911 million on civil rights activities, including $75 million for civil rights enforcement in fiscal 1969. The Nixon administration's budget for fiscal 1973 called for $2.6 billion in total civil rights outlays, of which

$602 million was earmarked for enforcement through a substantially strengthened Equal Employment Opportunity Commission. Nixon supported the civil rights goals of American Indians and women with less reluctance than he did school desegregation because these groups did not pose a major political problem for him and he had no similar legal reservations about how the law should be applied to them.

Mixing Economics and Politics

Nixon spent an inordinate amount of time on domestic and foreign economic matters. Nowhere did he appear to reverse himself more on views he had held before becoming president (or at least on views others attributed to him), and nowhere was his aprincipled pragmatism more evident. Nixon's failure to obtain more revenue through tax reform legislation in 1969, together with rising unemployment and inflation rates in 1970, precipitated an effort (in response to a perceived crisis) to balance U.S. domestic concerns through wage and price controls and international ones through devaluation of the dollar. This vehicle was the New Economic Policy, dramatically announced on August 15, 1971, at the end of a secret Camp David meeting with sixteen economic advisers. Largely as a result of Treasury Secretary Connally's influence, Nixon agreed that if foreign countries continued to demand ever-increasing amounts of gold for the U.S. dollars they held, the United States would go off the gold standard but would at the same time impose wage and price controls to curb inflation. The NEP perfectly reflected the "grand gesture" Connally thought the president should make on economic problems, and the August 15 television broadcast dramatized economic issues that most Americans, seldom anticipating long-range consequences, found boring.

When he was not trying to preempt Congress on regulatory issues, Nixon proposed deregulation based on free-market assumptions that were more traditionally in keeping with conservative Republicanism. The administration ended the draft in the name of economic freedom and recommended deregulation of the production of food crops, tariff and other barriers to international trade, and interest rates paid by various financial institutions. Except for wage and price controls and the devaluation of the dollar, none of these actions was justified in the name of crisis management. In general, however, political considerations made Nixon more liberal on domestic economic matters, confounding both his supporters and his opponents.

Nixon attributes his interest in international economics to the encouragement of John Foster Dulles and his desire as vice-president in the 1950s to create a Foreign Economic Council. Failing in this, he has said that his travels abroad in the 1950s only confirmed his belief that foreign leaders understood economics better than did American leaders, and he was determined to remedy this situation as president. Nixon faced two obstacles in this effort: Kissinger (because "international economics was not Henry's bag"), and State Department officials who saw "economic policy as government to government," which limited their diplomatic view of the world and made them so suspicious or cynical (or both) about the private sector that they refused to promote international commerce to the degree that Nixon thought they should. "Unlike the igno-ramuses I encountered among economic officers at various embassies in the 1950s and 1960s," Nixon told me, "I wanted to bring economics to the foreign service."

Because of Nixon's own interest in and knowledge of international trade, he attempted as president to rationalize the formulation of foreign economic policy. After 1962, when he was out of public office and practicing law in New York, he had specialized in international economics and multinational corpo-rations—definitely not Henry Kissinger's areas of expertise. In part because they were not a "team" on foreign economic policy and in part because Nixon by-passed the NSC almost entirely in formulating his New Economic Policy, Nixon relied not on his national security adviser but on other free-thinking outsiders when formulating foreign economic policy.

Next to John Connally, Nixon was most impressed with the economic views of Peter G. Peterson, who, after starting out in 1971 as a White House adviser on international economic affairs, became secretary of commerce in January 1972. Although Connally and Peterson appeared to agree on such early foreign economic initiatives as the NEP and the "get tough" policy toward Third World countries that nationalized U.S. companies abroad, as secretary of com-merce Peterson ultimately proved much more sophisticated and sensitive than the secretary of the treasury about the United States' changed economic role in the world. In a December 27, 1971, position paper defending Nixon's NEP, Peterson remarked that the new global situation in which the United States found itself demanded "shared leadership, shared responsibility, and shared burdens.... The reform of the international monetary systems," he said, must fully recognize and be solidly rooted in "the growing reality of a genuinely interdependent and increasingly competitive world economy whose goal is mu-tual, shared prosperity—not artificial, temporary advantage." At no point did Peterson believe, as Connally apparently did, that "the simple realignment of exchange rates" would adequately address the economic realignment problems facing the international economy.

In 1971 Nixon succeeded in establishing an entirely new cabinet-level Council on International Economic Policy (CIEP), headed by Peterson. This was not so much a reorganization of functions as it was an alternative to fill an existing void in the federal structure and to provide "clear top-level focus on international economic issues and to achieve consistency between interna-tional and domestic economic policy." For a variety of reasons—not the least of which was Kissinger's general lack of interest in, and disdain for, the unglam-orous aspects of international economics—the CIEP faltered and finally failed after Nixon left office. Its demise seems to have been hastened by Kissinger's recommendation to the Congressional Commission on Organization of Foreign Policy that it be eliminated, despite the fact that others, including Peterson, tes-tified on its behalf. The CIEP was subsequently merged with the Office of the Special Trade Representative.

Even with Nixon's impressive foreign and domestic record, it cannot be said that he would have succeeded as a managerial or administrative president had Watergate not occurred. Entrenched federal bureaucracies are not easily controlled or divested of power even with the best policy-oriented management strategies. That his foreign policy management seems more successful is also no surprise: diplomatic bureaucracies are smaller, more responsive, and easier to control than their domestic counterparts. Moreover, public concern (except for Vietnam) remained minimal as usual, and individual presidential foreign policy initiatives are more likely to be remembered and to appear effective than domestic ones. Nonetheless, the real importance of Nixon's presidency may well come to rest not on Watergate or foreign policy, but on his attempts to restructure the executive branch along functional lines, to bring order to the federal bureaucracy, and to achieve lasting domestic reform. The degree to which those Nixonian administrative tactics that were legal and ethical (and most of them were) became consciously or unconsciously the model for his successors in the Oval Office will determine his final place in history.

Although Nixon's corporate presidency remains publicly discredited, much of it has been privately preserved. Perhaps this is an indication that in exceptional cases presidential effectiveness can transcend popular (and scholarly) disapproval. What Nixon lacked in charisma and honesty, he may in the long run make up for with his phoenixlike ability to survive disaster. Nixon has repeatedly said: "No politician is dead until he admits it." It is perhaps an ironic commentary on the state of the modern presidency that Richard Nixon's management style and substantive foreign and domestic achievements look better and better when compared with those of his immediate successors in the Oval Office.

Et Tu, Bob?

There is nothing quite like H.R. Haldeman's diaries, published recently during the official period of mourning for Richard Nixon. They are repulsive almost beyond belief, yet therein lies their importance. Ostensibly designed to record the doings of a great man, they devastate Nixon's reputation. Truly Haldeman has proved Mark Antony's observation that the good that men do is buried with their bones; the evil they do lives long after them. The diaries appeared three weeks after Nixon's death as a nearly 700-page book, unveiled first on a two-part *Nightline* program, which predictably focused on Nixon's racial and ethnic slurs. Soon thereafter came the CD-ROM, which included a "complete" version of the diaries (60 percent more material than in the book) and some added attractions, including "home" movies (developed at government expense), photos, bios of key and bit players and an amazing apologia in the form of an unsent 40,000-plus-word letter to James Neal, who prosecuted Haldeman. Like Antony, Haldeman had motives other than praising Caesar.

The diaries reflect two men in an "intense one-on-one relationship," men who were not, according to Haldeman's widow, personal friends. Since Nixon had few close friends, this means very little. The two often dined alone on the presidential yacht and then went to the President's sitting room to chat. The President would drink his '57 Lafite-Rothschild and serve Haldeman the California "Beaulieu Vineyard stuff." And Haldeman would have to read aloud Nixon's *Who's Who* entry. Maybe he was supposed to savor that instead.

The tapes revealed Nixon's shabbiness; the diaries underline his shallowness. The recurring themes of the diaries are simple: getting re-elected, getting even. Nixon was consumed with P.R., constantly prodding Haldeman on how to spin stories, how to protect his image and, almost comically, how to deny that the President was interested in such things. Haldeman, the old advertising executive, usually relished the game, yet he must have found it tiresome as well. P.R., he noted, "would work a lot better if he would quit worrying . . . and just be President." Impossible; for Nixon it was all.

Altogether, the picture is not pretty. It is mostly warts and little face, and certainly not the one Nixon had in mind as he took his leave. Shortly after Haldeman died last fall, Nixon asked Haldeman's family to delay publication, ostensibly so as not to interfere with the promotion of his own book. What

From Stanley I. Kutler, "Et Tu, Bob?" *The Nation* (August 22–29, 1994). Copyright © 1994 by The Nation, Inc. Reprinted by permission.

a hoot it would have been if Nixon, appearing on the *Today* show, had had to confront some of the juicier items from his trusted aide's diaries. In any event, Haldeman said that he hoped his book—which fleshes out and expands the daily notes that have been available for some time—would "once and for all" put the Nixon years into perspective. It certainly helps, but probably not as he intended.

Nixon always knew that Haldeman's diaries were potential dynamite. Archibald Cox subpoenaed the files on May 25, 1973, but the President had taken control of the diaries and put them with his papers, which eventually went to the National Archives (over his protests, to be sure). In 1980, Haldeman cut a deal with the Archives, deeding the diaries to the public (meaning he always intended for them to be seen, contrary to *Nightline*'s and his wife's assertions) in exchange for the Archives' agreement to keep them closed for a decade, later extended for several more years. Haldeman then promptly filed suit against the government, claiming (falsely) that he had been unlawfully deprived of access to his property in the intervening years. But the court refused to get involved "in the niceties of Fifth Amendment doctrine" since the case revolved around one question: Why did Haldeman leave his diaries in the White House when he was dismissed on April 30, 1973?

The government nailed Haldeman when it introduced Oval Office conversations for May 2 and 9, 1973 (Haldeman had "left" the White House but he returned—to listen to tapes!), in which Nixon and Haldeman typically concocted a scenario for future spin. In brief, Nixon would claim the materials as his own and cloak them with executive privilege: "Your notes belong to the President," Nixon told him. Haldeman finished the thought: "And fortunately, they're ... in your possession; they're not in mine." In those days, we had few illusions about Nixon and his aide. District Judge John Garrett Penn said that Haldeman could have avoided the dispute had he claimed the diaries as his own at the outset, or had he made photocopies when he viewed the materials. The conflict, the judge ruled, was entirely Haldeman's fault. "He could have obviated this entire conflict; he chose another route solely for his own protection, and should not now be given a forum to complain that he did not choose wisely." He may not have chosen wisely as far as Nixon is concerned— but Haldeman will do well by his heirs.

Most reactions to the diaries have concentrated on long-familiar Nixon slanders of Jews and blacks. The reluctance to confront the policy and institutional concerns of the diaries is somewhat understandable, for if the mainstream media honestly surveyed this material, they would impeach themselves for their insipid attempts to peddle revisionist views of Nixon in the wake of his death. The diaries clearly reveal the President's extraordinary cynicism, as well as his lack of knowledge of both domestic and foreign policy. No single work so effectively exposes Nixon as a mean, petty, vindictive, insecure—even incompetent —man, and all this from one who professed to admire him; from a man Nixon even said he "loved." Could it have been intentional?

Haldeman himself spent the past two decades portraying himself as a self-less, self-effacing, dedicated servant to the President. But the myth of Haldeman as Stevens the butler in *Remains of the Day*—just a passive vessel for Nixon's commands—is misleading. Haldeman was an old-fashioned Southern California reactionary, weaned on his family's nativist and patriotic views and supported by a plumbing fortune. Nixon correctly perceived him as a "son-of-a-bitch" and used him as a "Lord High Executioner."

Unintentionally, I would guess, Haldeman has provided us with wonderful comic moments. After the Thomas Eagleton nomination fiasco in 1972, Spiro Agnew, either with inspired wit or sheer meanness, asked Dr. Joyce Brothers to second his own nomination—as if to receive psychological certification of his sanity. Nixon issued a presidential order directing Agnew to rescind the invitation. Then there are Great Moments of Protocol: Who would ride in the President's golf cart, Bob Hope or Frank Sinatra? Finally, Nixon wanted a White House reception to honor Duke Ellington and told Haldeman to invite other jazz notables, including Guy Lombardo. "Oh well," the knowing Haldeman sighed.

Haldeman's diaries show that he spent either hours or "all day" with the President. Sometimes Haldeman recorded Nixon's thoughts on substantive policy such as China or the settlement of the Vietnam War. But usually the subjects were relentlessly repetitive, as were the homilies that Nixon dispensed. And yet Haldeman faithfully recorded and preserved the President's words. During the 1972 campaign, Haldeman and John Ehrlichman spent inordinate amounts of time listening to the President repeatedly go over matters such as his prospects in every state, who would be dismissed, who would be moved and how enemies would be punished. Apparently even "two of the finest public servants," as Nixon characterized them when he dismissed them, could not abide the monotony of it all without sarcasm. "Why did he buzz me?" Haldeman asked Ehrlichman in a note written during one of the President's soliloquies. Like a schoolchild answering a passed message, Ehrlichman sketched several answers:

> "He had an itchy finger."

> "Also there was a chair unoccupied."

> "Also he has been talking about not just reordering the chaos,
> and he would like you to understand that point."

Supposedly, Nixon wanted someone to keep the "routine baloney" away from him; it "bores and annoys him," Haldeman noted. Yet Haldeman often wearily complained about the tedium, as when he noted that the "P had the morning clear, unfortunately, and called me ... for over four hours as he wandered through odds and ends...."

Aside from the President's behavior, the most significant revelations surround Henry Kissinger. From the outset, Nixon and Haldeman recognized Kissinger as a devious, emotionally unstable person. The President saw him as a rival for public acclaim, ever anxious to magnify himself for the contemporary and historical record. Nixon did not entirely trust Kissinger's briefings. Most surprising, however, was Haldeman's intimate involvement in the management of foreign policy as the President regularly shared his thoughts and views on Kissinger with his Chief of Staff.

In the pathology of the Nixon White House, perhaps the sickest subject involved what Haldeman repeatedly called the "K-Rogers flap," which he blamed equally on Kissinger's "unbelievable ego" and Secretary of State William Rogers's pique. We long have understood Kissinger's pre-inaugural coup that enabled him and Nixon to bypass the State Department bureaucracy; yet what Kissinger wanted was the place for himself. Haldeman relentlessly portrays Kissinger as a mercurial, temperamental infant, constantly concerned with his standing and status; Nixon considered Kissinger "obsessed beyond reason" with Rogers.

Nixon and Kissinger appear more as adversaries than as allies. In November 1972, miffed at Kissinger's media attempts to grab the lion's share of credit for the China opening, Nixon instructed Haldeman to tell Kissinger that he had tapes of their conversations! Nixon warned Haldeman that *Time* might "needle us [and] go for K as the Man of the Year, which would be very bad, so we should try to swing that around a different way." Students of Vietnam policy have an interesting task in sorting out responsibility for the protracted peace negotiations. Kissinger expressed to Haldeman his fear that Nixon wanted to "bug out" and not carry through on long-term negotiations. Kissinger well knew that message would get back to Nixon and steel him against any appearances of being "soft."

Haldeman's diaries substantially confirm the criticism of Kissinger's detractors, especially Seymour Hersh's biting analysis of the Nixon-Kissinger foreign policies in *The Price of Power*. Appearance was often substituted for substance, and at times, as in the SALT negotiations, Kissinger seemed entirely out of his element. What then does this say of the President of the United States—who similarly was unconcerned with substance and seemed most bent on preventing Kissinger from getting too much praise? Certainly, Adm. Elmo Zumwalt had it right when he said that two words did not apply to the Vietnam peace accords: peace and honor. Kissinger's frantic search for a Shanghai Communiqué in 1972 would have bordered on the comic had it not been so fraught with obsequiousness toward his new friends and cynicism toward Nixon's longtime Taiwanese patrons.

Everything had a political calculus. In December 1970, Nixon, Kissinger and Haldeman considered a Vietnam trip the next spring in which the President would make "the basic end of the war announcement." Kissinger objected, saying that if we pulled out in 1971 there could be trouble (ostensibly for the Thieu regime) that the Administration would have to answer for in the 1972 elections. Kissinger urged Nixon to commit only to withdrawing all troops by the end of 1972. Another year of casualties seemed a fair exchange for the President's electoral security.

Billy Graham's choicer remarks about Jews and their "total domination of the media" have been prominently reported. Let's take Graham at his word and agree that some of his best friends are Jews. In the guise of God's messenger, Graham was a Nixon political operative, dutifully reporting back to the White House on what Lyndon Johnson had said about George McGovern, George Wallace's intentions on resuming his presidential bid in 1972, Graham's efforts to calm down Martha Mitchell, plans to organize Christian youth for Nixon, his advice to Johnny Carson to be a little biased in Nixon's favor if he wanted to be helpful and the Shah of Iran's remark that the President's re-election had saved civilization. When Nixon's tapes were first revealed in April 1974, a chastened Graham complained about Nixon's "situational ethics" and lamented that he had been "used." Used once, used again, he could not resist the limelight of preaching at Nixon's funeral.

✑✿✑

John Ehrlichman has maintained that Nixon would be remembered as the great domestic policy President of the twentieth century. (Guess who was Nixon's domestic adviser?) That notion, too, is a chapter in the current drive for revisionism. Well, it won't wash, unless one accepts the view that whatever was accomplished happened in spite of Richard Nixon. His Administration publicly advocated policies that the President clearly didn't believe in. Consider:

- School desegregation: Haldeman noted that Nixon was "really concerned... and feels we have to take some leadership to try to reverse Court decisions that have forced integration too far, too fast." Nixon told Attorney General John Mitchell to keep filing cases until they got a reversal. Nixon proposed getting a right-wing demagogue into some tough race and have him campaign against integration—and he "might even win." He fired Leon Panetta, then a mid-level Health, Education and Welfare functionary, who was doing too much in behalf of school desegregation. (Panetta wouldn't quit, so Nixon announced his "resignation.")
- "[Nixon] was very upset that he had been led to approve the IRS ruling about no tax exemption for private schools, feels it will make no votes anywhere and will badly hurt private schools...."
- "About Family Assistance Plan, [President] wants to be sure it's killed by Democrats and that we make big play for it, but don't let it pass, can't afford it."
- "On welfare, we have to support HR 1 until the election. Afterward, we should not send it back to Congress." "On HR 1 there's some concern that if we hang too tight on the passage of it, that it may actually pass and defeat our Machiavellian plot. Our Congressional tactic overall has got to be to screw things up."
- "He's very much concerned about handling of the drug situation; wants the whole thing taken out of HEW. He makes the point that they're all on drugs there anyway."
- Nixon agreed to continue an I.B.M. antitrust action but urged Haldeman "to make something out of it so we can get credit for attacking business."

- "The P was also very upset about the DDT decision. Ruckleshaus has announced a ban on it. He [Nixon] thinks we should get this whole environment thing out of E and [John] Whitaker's hands because they believe in it, and you can't have an advocate dismantle something he believes in. He also wanted [Fred] Malek to check on who Ruckleshaus has on his staff in terms of left-wing liberals."
- Nixon "made the point that he feels deeply troubled that he's getting sucked in too much on welfare and environment and consumerism."

Liberals cringed in 1968 when Nixon promised to appoint judges who would favor the "peace forces" as opposed to the "criminal forces." Nixon, of course, like all Presidents, sought appointments to mirror his (and his constituency's) wishes. After the Senate rejected his nomination of G. Harrold Carswell for the Supreme Court in 1970, Nixon briefly flirted with nominating Senator Robert Byrd, knowing the Senate would be unlikely to reject one of its own. When Hugo Black resigned from the Court in 1971, Nixon, feverishly backed by Pat Buchanan, pushed for Virginia Congressman Richard Poff, once an ardent backer of segregation. Nixon happily recognized that this would only roil the waters again. Poff had the good sense to withdraw, whereupon Nixon raised Byrd's name again. Why not? Byrd was a former Klansman and "more reactionary than [George] Wallace," Nixon said, obviously relishing a chance to embarrass the Senate.

Following this, Nixon warmed to Mitchell's inspired concoction of nonentities: Herschel Friday (a fellow bond lawyer) and Mildred Lilley, an obscure local California judge who was meant only to be a sacrificial lamb. "The theory on the woman is that the ABA is not going to approve her, and therefore, he'll let her pass and blame them for it," Haldeman wrote. (This was the same American Bar Association committee that had endorsed the unqualified Carswell, Haldeman failed to note.) Nixon wanted Lewis Powell, but for the other open seat the White House tendered an offer to Senator Howard Baker, who called in his answer half an hour too late and was displaced by William Rehnquist in a coup led by Richard Moore, friend and aide to John Mitchell. A rare moment as the President caught Haldeman by surprise.

Everyone seemed happy, Nixon said, except his wife, who had been campaigning for a woman. That is the only time Haldeman recorded the President taking Mrs. Nixon seriously. The diaries are filled with Nixon and Haldeman's shared disdain for the First Lady; for example, Nixon could spare but a few moments for her 60th birthday party and then he hid out in his office.

◦◦◦◦◦

Almost from the day that Nixon assumed office, he was off and running for 1972. Teddy Kennedy preoccupied him; in 1969, Nixon and his staff saw the battle over the antiballistic missile as the opening salvo of the 1972 campaign against Kennedy. Even after Chappaquiddick, Nixon seriously believed that Kennedy was a threat. He instigated Ehrlichman's own investigation of the incident and repeatedly told Haldeman that they couldn't let the public forget Chappaquiddick. He encouraged Charles Colson, who had agents follow Kennedy in Paris and photograph him with various women.

Vietnam was small potatoes compared with the amount of time the President and his aide plotted strategy and dirty tricks against political enemies. The Boys of '72 knew their way around this territory without much help. In Nixon's 1962 gubernatorial campaign, they had established a bogus Democratic committee to mail cards to registered Democrats expressing concern for the party under Pat Brown. A Republican judge convicted them of campaign law violations and held that the plan had been "reviewed, amended and finally approved by Mr. Nixon personally," and that Haldeman similarly "approved the plan and the project."

In July 1969, Nixon directed Haldeman to establish a "dirty tricks" unit with the likes of Pat Buchanan and Lyn Nofziger. "Hardball politics," Haldeman later called it. Nixon regularly urged that the I.R.S. investigate Democratic contributors and celebrity supporters. He also wanted a review of the tax returns of all Democratic candidates "and start harassment of them, as they have done of us." He wanted full field investigations of Clark Clifford and other doves; he ordered mailings describing Edmund Muskie's liberal views to be sent throughout the South; and one basic line of his Watergate counteroffensive was to expose Democratic Party chairman Larry O'Brien's tax problems and his allegedly unsavory list of clients.

Alas, Haldeman has little new to offer on Watergate. He claims that the diaries are unexpurgated and complete on this score. That may be stretching the truth. The Watergate section contains long, discursive comments about the activities of many principals, but they are merely summaries Haldeman compiled from contemporary documents and his own choice memories. The entries focus on the complicity of just about everyone but H.R. Haldeman. When read together with the lengthy letter that Haldeman allegedly wrote (and did not send) in 1978 to the prosecutor, the implication is that he and Nixon were guilty only of a "political containment"—he was no party to a conspiracy to obstruct justice and he committed no perjury. He knew that the burglars had been given "hush money," but he insisted it was not a cover-up. It is a little late in the day for such a defense; furthermore, his own words demolish it.

The diaries expand on the finger-pointing that emerged from the tape revelations twenty years ago. Now we clearly see how Nixon, Haldeman and Ehrlichman sought to make Mitchell their fall guy, and how they coddled John Dean for so long to keep him in camp. In the letter to prosecutor James Neal, Haldeman turned from Mitchell to establish the outlines of a Dean conspiracy theory, one that has become fashionable among the former President's men in recent years.

From the outset, Haldeman knew the significance of the Watergate break-in. The day after, he called it "the big flap over the weekend," and he immediately knew that the Committee to Re-elect the President was involved. If so, that meant the White House, for John Mitchell and Jeb Magruder reported directly to Haldeman and his aides on campaign activity. Eventually, the True Campaign Chairman—the President himself—knew what happened there. Two days later,

Haldeman reported that Nixon "was somewhat interested" in the events. Interested enough that we have eighteen and a half minutes of deliberately erased tape. Later that same day, June 20, Haldeman noted that Watergate "obviously bothered" Nixon and they discussed it "in considerable detail." But he gives us none.

Haldeman is fudging here. Tapes released two years ago, which cover Watergate conversations for June 1972—we previously had only the notorious "smoking gun" tape of June 23—reveal extensive conversations, beginning with the first attempt to concoct a containment or cover-up scenario on June 20. (Once again, the media missed this story as they made much ado about Nixon's remark that Liddy was "a little nuts.") Using the C.I.A. to thwart the F.B.I. was not a one-time occurrence on June 23; the two men repeatedly tried to stifle the investigation under the cover of national security, even after C.I.A. Director Richard Helms ended his cooperation. In these tapes, Haldeman seems to sense the futility of their efforts: "We got a lid on it and it may not stay on," he told the President on June 28. For nearly a year—not just in his last month as Chief of Staff—Haldeman knew that Watergate was trouble.

Significantly, Haldeman omits any mention of the President's offer of cash to him and Ehrlichman in April 1973—after Ehrlichman ominously said, "I gotta start answering questions." When the President asked if they could use cash, Haldeman reacted with a blend of fury and sarcasm. "That compounds the problem," he said. "That really does." For good reason, Nixon needed their silence. But the President's insensitivity knew no bounds. After he announced Haldeman's resignation, he asked his departing aide to check out reaction to the speech. Probably for the only time, Haldeman refused a direct request. But in fact, he spent several more months listening to tapes to prepare for Nixon's defense.

The thousands of hours of taped conversations that Nixon fought so long to suppress will eventually be made public. Does anyone believe they will exonerate him or enhance his historical reputation? In the meantime, Haldeman's diaries take the lid off the Oval Office for the first four years of Nixon's presidency. What he has shown beyond dispute is that the Nixon of the Watergate years—furtive, manipulative and petty; often weak, sometimes comic and, above all, dishonest—was consistent with the behavior patterns of the earlier years. No Old Nixon; no New Nixon: There was one and only one.

POSTSCRIPT

Will History Forgive Richard Nixon?

Hoff-Wilson is one of the few professional historians to render a positive evaluation of President Nixon. She places him in the context of the late 1960s and early 1970s, when support for big government, New Deal, Great Society programs had dimmed and the bipartisan, anticommunist foreign policy consensus had been shattered by the Vietnam War. She gives him high marks for vertically restructuring the executive branch of the government and for attempting a similar reorganization in the federal bureaucracy.

Unlike most defenders of Nixon, Hoff-Wilson considers Nixon's greatest achievements to be domestic. Although he was a conservative, the welfare state grew during his presidency. In the area of civil rights, between 1968 and 1972 affirmative action programs were implemented, and schools with all black children in the southern states declined from 68 percent to 8 percent. Even on such Democratic staples as welfare, the environment, and economic planning, Nixon outflanked the liberals.

Hoff-Wilson has fleshed out her ideas in much greater detail in *Nixon Reconsidered* (Basic Books, 1994). British conservative cabinet minister and historian Jonathan Aitken has also written a favorable and more panoramic view of the former president entitled *Nixon: A Life* (Regnery Gateway, 1993).

Historian Stephen E. Ambrose's three-volume biography *Nixon* (Simon & Schuster, 1987–1991) also substantiates Hoff-Wilson's emphasis on Nixon's domestic successes. Ambrose's evaluation is even more remarkable because he was a liberal historian who campaigned for George McGovern in 1972 and had to be talked into writing a Nixon biography by his publisher. In domestic policy, Ambrose told the *Washington Post* on November 26, 1989, Nixon "was proposing things in '73 and '74 he couldn't even make the front pages with—national health insurance for all, a greatly expanded student loan operation, and energy and environmental programs." With regard to foreign policy, both Ambrose and Aitken disagree with Hoff-Wilson; they consider Nixon's foreign policy substantial and far-sighted. In the second volume of his biography, *Nixon: The Triumph of a Politician, 1962–1972* (Simon & Schuster, 1989), Ambrose concludes that the president was "without peer in foreign relations where 'profound pragmatic' vision endowed him with the potential to become a great world statesman."

Kutler accepts none of the revisionists' premises. In *The Wars of Watergate: The Last Crisis of Richard Nixon* (Alfred A. Knopf, 1990), Kutler focuses on both the negative side of Nixon's personality and his abuse of presidential power. In his review of *The Haldeman Diaries*, Kutler finds further substantiation for his view that Nixon was a narrow-minded, bigoted, self-calculating individual who took no action in his career that was not politically motivated. Unlike other writers who saw a "new" Nixon emerge as president, Kutler maintains that there was only one Nixon—a man possessed with a "corrosive hatred that decisively shaped" his behavior and career.

Neither Ambrose nor Kutler accept the view that Nixon was a corporate executive who reorganized government to enhance decision making. Both would agree that Nixon loved intrigue, conspiracies, and surprise. At the same time Kutler argues that Nixon went much further than any of his predecessors in abusing presidential power by siccing the Internal Revenue Service (IRS) on potential enemies, impounding funds so that the Democrat-controlled Congress could not implement its legislative programs, and finally covering up and lying for over two years about the Watergate scandal.

Clearly, historians will be disputing the Nixon legacy for a long time. Two works have tried to place Nixon within the context of his times. Liberal historian Herbert S. Parmet, the first to gain access to Nixon's prepresidential papers, published *Richard Nixon and His America* (Little, Brown, 1990). Less thoroughly researched in primary sources but more insightful is *New York Times* reporter Tom Wicker's *One of Us: Richard Nixon and the American Dream* (Random House, 1991).

In order to gain a real feel for the Nixon years, you should consult contemporary or primary accounts. Nixon himself orchestrated his own rehabilitation in *RN: The Memoirs of Richard Nixon* (Grosset & Dunlop, 1978); *The Real War* (Warner Books, 1980); *Real Peace* (Little, Brown, 1984); *No More Vietnams* (Arbor House, 1985); and *In the Arena: A Memoir of Victory, Defeat and Renewal* (Simon & Schuster, 1990). Nixon's own accounts should be compared with former national security adviser Henry Kissinger's memoirs *White House Years* (Little, Brown, 1979). *The Haldeman Diaries: Inside the Nixon White House* (Putnam, 1994), which is the subject of Kutler's review essay, is essential for any undertaking of Nixon. Haldeman's account fleshes out the daily tensions of life in the Nixon White House and adds important details to the Nixon and Kissinger accounts. Other primary accounts include Kenneth W. Thompson, ed., *The Nixon Presidency: Twenty-two Intimate Perspectives of Richard M. Nixon*, Portraits of American Presidents Series, vol. 6 (University Press of America, 1987), which contains a series of discussions with former officials of the Nixon administration conducted by the White Burkett Miller Center for the Study of Public Affairs at the University of Virginia.

Two of the best review essays on the new historiography about America's 37th president are "Theodore Draper: Nixon, Haldeman, and History," *The New York Review of Books* (July 14, 1994) and Sidney Blumenthal, "The Longest Campaign," *The New Yorker* (August 8, 1994).

On the Internet ...

Cold War Hot Links

This page contains links to Web pages on the cold war that a variety of people have created. They run the entire spectrum of political thought and provide some interesting views on the cold war and the state of national security.

http://www.stmartin.edu/~dprice/cold.war.html

The Gulf War

This FRONTLINE page is a comprehensive and critical analysis of the 1990–1991 Persian Gulf crisis.

http://www.pbs.org/wgbh/pages/frontline/gulf/

American Immigration Resources on the Internet

This site contains many links to American immigration resources on the Internet. It includes a site on children's immigration issues, the Immigration and Naturalization Service home page, and a forum on immigration.

http://www.immigration-usa.com/resource.html

POTUS: William Jefferson Clinton

This is the William Jefferson Clinton page of POTUS: Presidents of the United States, a publication of the Internet Public Library. It features biographical information on Clinton, information on many members of his presidential staff, his inaugural addresses, and audio files of the president himself.

http://www.ipl.org/div/potus/wjclinton.html

Sebago Associates: Notes on the Florida Vote in the 2000 Election

Sebago Associates, Inc., undertook a variety of preliminary analyses on the Florida Vote in the 2000 presidential election in the days immediately following November 7. Three notes resulting from these analyses are presented on this site along with links to other analyses.

http://www.sbgo.com/election.htm

National Council for Science and the Environment

The National Council for Science and the Environment (NCSE) has been working since 1990 to improve the scientific basis for environmental decision making. NCSE is supported by almost 500 academic, scientific, environmental, and business organizations.

http://www.cnie.org

PART 3

Postindustrial America and the End of the Cold War: 1974–2001

*A*merica continued to experience a series of highs and lows during *the last quarter of the twentieth century. President Ronald Reagan's tax cuts and increased defense spending stimulated the economy but created an enormous budget deficit. Historians will continue to debate whether supply-side economics ended the cold war by forcing the Russians to spend themselves into bankruptcy or whether the United States could have become prosperous with less defense spending and more attention paid to those groups left out of the "new prosperity." The reputations of President Reagan, the two George Bushes, and Bill Clinton are heavily dependent upon whether or not the United States remains or declines as the dominant power in the world in the twenty-first century. Three recurring problems are left over from the last half of the twentieth century. One problem is whether or not the creation of Israel in 1948 has permanently destabilized the Middle East. Will the United States have to fight a second Gulf War to stabilize the balance of power in the area and to maintain a steady supply of oil? Second, can America remain a nation of immigrants and still retain its core culture as well as be secure from terrorism? Finally, is a prosperous, growing economy compatible with a healthy environment?*

- Did President Reagan Win the Cold War?

- Did President George Bush Achieve His Objectives in the Gulf War?

- Should America Remain a Nation of Immigrants?

- Will History Consider William Jefferson Clinton a Reasonably Good Chief Executive?

- Did the Supreme Court Hijack the 2000 Presidential Election From Al Gore?

- Environmentalism: Is the Earth Out of Balance?

ISSUE 11

Did President Reagan Win the Cold War?

YES: John Lewis Gaddis, from *The United States and the End of the Cold War: Implications, Reconsiderations, Provocations* (Oxford University Press, 1992)

NO: Daniel Deudney and G. John Ikenberry, from "Who Won the Cold War?" *Foreign Policy* (Summer 1992)

ISSUE SUMMARY

YES: Professor of history John Lewis Gaddis argues that President Reagan combined a policy of militancy and operational pragmatism to bring about the most significant improvement in Soviet-American relations since the end of World War II.

NO: Professors of political science Daniel Deudney and G. John Ikenberry contend that the cold war ended only when Soviet president Gorbachev accepted Western liberal values and the need for global cooperation.

The term *cold war* was first coined by the American financial whiz and presidential adviser Bernard Baruch in 1947. Cold war refers to the extended but restricted conflict that existed between the United States and the Soviet Union from the end of World War II in 1945 until 1990. Looking back, it appears that the conflicting values and goals of a democratic/capitalist United States and a communist Soviet Union reinforced this state of affairs between the two countries. Basically, the cold war ended when the Soviet Union gave up its control over the Eastern European nations and ceased to be a unified country itself.

The Nazi invasion of Russia in June 1941 and the Japanese attack on America's Pacific outposts in December united the United States and the Soviet Union against the Axis powers during World War II. Nevertheless, complications ensued during the top-level allied discussions to coordinate war strategy. The first meeting between the big three—U.S. president Franklin Roosevelt, British prime minister Winston Churchill, and Soviet premier Joseph Stalin—took place in Teheran in 1943 followed by another at Yalta in February 1945. These high-level negotiations were held under the assumption that wartime harmony among Britain, the United States, and the Soviet Union would continue; that Stalin, Churchill, and Roosevelt would lead the postwar world as they had conducted the war; and that the details of the general policies and agreements would be resolved at a less pressing time.

But none of these premises were fulfilled. By the time the Potsdam Conference (to discuss possible action against Japan) took place in July 1945, Churchill had been defeated in a parliamentary election, Roosevelt had died, and President Harry S. Truman had been thrust, unprepared, into his place. Of the big three, only Stalin remained as a symbol of continuity. Details about the promises at Teheran and Yalta faded into the background. Power politics, nuclear weapons, and mutual fears and distrust replaced the reasonably harmonious working relationships of the three big powers during World War II.

By 1947 the Truman administration had adopted a conscious policy of containment toward the Russians. This meant maintaining the status quo in Europe through various U.S. assistance programs. The NATO alliance of 1949 completed the shift of U.S. policy away from its pre–World War II isolationist policy and toward a commitment to the defense of Western Europe.

In the 1960s the largest problem facing the two superpowers was controlling the spread of nuclear weapons. The first attempt at arms control took place in the 1950s. After Stalin died in 1953, the Eisenhower administration made an "open-skies" proposal. This was rejected by the Russians, who felt (correctly) that they were behind the Americans in the arms race. In the summer of 1962 Soviet premier Nikita Khrushchev attempted to redress the balance of power by secretly installing missiles in Cuba that could be employed to launch nuclear attacks against U.S. cities. This sparked the Cuban Missile Crisis, the high point of the cold war, which brought both nations to the brink of nuclear war before the Russians agreed to withdraw the missiles.

During the Leonid Brezhnev–Richard Nixon years, the policy of *détente* (relaxation of tensions) resulted in a series of summit meetings. Most important was the SALT I agreement, which outlawed national antiballistic missile defenses and placed a five-year moratorium on the building of new strategic ballistic missiles.

Soviet-American relations took a turn for the worse when the Soviets invaded Afghanistan in December 1979. In response, President Jimmy Carter postponed presenting SALT II to the Senate and imposed an American boycott of the 1980 Olympic Games, which were held in Moscow.

Détente remained dead during President Ronald Reagan's first administration. Reagan not only promoted a military budget of $1.5 trillion over a five-year period, he also was the first president since Truman to refuse to meet the Soviet leader. Major changes, however, took place during Reagan's second administration. In the following selections, John Lewis Gaddis argues that President Reagan combined a policy of militancy and operational pragmatism to bring about significant improvements in Soviet-American relations, while Daniel Deudney and G. John Ikenberry credit Soviet president Mikhail Gorbachev with ending the cold war because he accepted Western liberal values and the need for global cooperation.

John Lewis Gaddis

 **YES**

The Unexpected Ronald Reagan

The task of the historian is, very largely, one of explaining how we got from where we were to where we are today. To say that the Reagan administration's policy toward the Soviet Union is going to pose special challenges to historians is to understate the matter: rarely has there been a greater gap between the expectations held for an administration at the beginning of its term and the results it actually produced. The last thing one would have anticipated at the time Ronald Reagan took office in 1981 was that he would use his eight years in the White House to bring about the most significant improvement in Soviet-American relations since the end of World War II. I am not at all sure that President Reagan himself foresaw this result. And yet, that is precisely what happened, with—admittedly—a good deal of help from Mikhail Gorbachev.

The question of how this happened and to what extent it was the product of accident or of conscious design is going to preoccupy scholars for years to come. The observations that follow are a rough first attempt to grapple with that question. Because we lack access to the archives or even very much memoir material as yet, what I will have to say is of necessity preliminary, incomplete, and almost certainly in several places dead wrong. Those are the hazards of working with contemporary history, though; if historians are not willing to run these risks, political scientists and journalists surely will. That prospect in itself provides ample justification for plunging ahead.

The Hard-Liner

... President Reagan in March, 1983, made his most memorable pronouncement on the Soviet Union: condemning the tendency of his critics to hold both sides responsible for the nuclear arms race, he denounced the U.S.S.R. as an "evil empire" and as "the focus of evil in the modern world." Two weeks later, the President surprised even his closest associates by calling for a long-term research and development program to create defense against attacks by strategic missiles, with a view, ultimately, to "rendering these nuclear weapons impotent and obsolete." The Strategic Defense Initiative was the most fundamental challenge to existing orthodoxies on arms control since negotiations on that subject had begun with the Russians almost three decades earlier. Once again it

From John Lewis Gaddis, *The United States and the End of the Cold War: Implications, Reconsiderations, Provocations* (Oxford University Press, 1992). Copyright © 1992 by John Lewis Gaddis. Reprinted by permission of Oxford University Press, Inc. Notes omitted.

called into question the President's seriousness in seeking an end to—or even a significant moderation of—the strategic arms race.

Anyone who listened to the "evil empire" speech or who considered the implications of "Star Wars" might well have concluded that Reagan saw the Soviet-American relationship as an elemental confrontation between virtue and wickedness that would allow neither negotiation nor conciliation in any form; his tone seemed more appropriate to a medieval crusade than to a revival of containment. Certainly there were those within his administration who held such views, and their influence, for a time, was considerable. But to see the President's policies solely in terms of his rhetoric, it is now clear, would have been quite wrong.

For President Reagan appears to have understood—or to have quickly learned—the dangers of basing foreign policy solely on ideology: he combined militancy with a surprising degree of operational pragmatism and a shrewd sense of timing. To the astonishment of his own hard-line supporters, what appeared to be an enthusiastic return to the Cold War in fact turned out to be a more solidly based approach to detente than anything the Nixon, Ford, or Carter administrations had been able to accomplish.

The Negotiator

There had always been a certain ambivalence in the Reagan administration's image of the Soviet Union. On the one hand, dire warnings about Moscow's growing military strength suggested an almost Spenglerian gloom [reflecting the theory of philosopher Oswald Spengler, which holds that all major cultures grow, mature, and decay in a natural cycle] about the future: time, it appeared, was on the Russians' side. But mixed with this pessimism was a strong sense of self-confidence, growing out of the ascendancy of conservatism within the United States and an increasing enthusiasm for capitalism overseas, that assumed the unworkability of Marxism as a form of political, social, and economic organization: "The West won't contain communism, it will transcend communism," the President predicted in May, 1981. "It won't bother to . . . denounce it, it will dismiss it as some bizarre chapter in human history whose last pages are even now being written." By this logic, the Soviet Union had already reached the apex of its strength as a world power, and time in fact was on the side of the West.

Events proved the optimism to have been more justified than the pessimism, for over the next four years the Soviet Union would undergo one of the most rapid erosions both of internal self-confidence and external influence in modern history; that this happened just as Moscow's long and costly military buildup should have begun to pay political dividends made the situation all the more frustrating for the Russians. It may have been luck for President Reagan to have come into office at a peak in the fortunes of the Soviet Union and at a trough in those of the United States: things would almost certainly have improved regardless of who entered the White House in 1981. But it took more than luck to recognize what was happening, and to capitalize on it to the extent that the Reagan administration did.

Indications of Soviet decline took several forms. The occupation of Afghanistan had produced only a bloody Vietnam-like stalemate, with Soviet troops unable to suppress the rebellion, or to protect themselves and their clients, or to withdraw. In Poland a long history of economic mismanagement had produced, in the form of the Solidarity trade union, a rare phenomenon within the Soviet bloc: a true workers' movement. Soviet ineffectiveness became apparent in the Middle East in 1982 when the Russians were unable to provide any significant help to the Palestinian Liberation Organization during the Israeli invasion of Lebanon; even more embarrassing, Israeli pilots using American-built fighters shot down over eighty Soviet-supplied Syrian jets without a single loss of their own. Meanwhile, the Soviet domestic economy which [former Soviet premier Nikita] Khrushchev had once predicted would overtake that of the United States, had in fact stagnated during the early 1980s, Japan by some indices actually overtook the U.S.S.R. as the world's second largest producer of goods and services, and even China, a nation with four times the population of the Soviet Union, now became an agricultural exporter at a time when Moscow still required food imports from the West to feed its own people.

What all of this meant was that the Soviet Union's appeal as a model for Third World political and economic development—once formidable—had virtually disappeared, indeed as Moscow's military presence in those regions grew during the late 1970s, the Russians increasingly came to be seen, not as liberators, but as latter-day imperialists themselves. The Reagan administration moved swiftly to take advantage of this situation by funneling military assistance—sometimes openly sometimes covertly—to rebel groups (or "freedom fighters," as the President insisted on calling them) seeking to overthrow Soviet-backed regimes in Afghanistan, Angola, Ethiopia, Cambodia, and Nicaragua; in October, 1983, to huge domestic acclaim but with dubious legality Reagan even ordered the direct use of American military forces to overthrow an unpopular Marxist government on the tiny Caribbean island of Grenada. The Reagan Doctrine, as this strategy became known, sought to exploit vulnerabilities the Russians had created for themselves in the Third World: this latter-day effort to "roll back" Soviet influence would, in time, produce impressive results at minimum cost and risk to the United States.

Compounding the Soviet Union's external difficulties was a long vacuum in internal leadership occasioned by [President Leonid] Brezhnev's slow enfeeblement and eventual death in November, 1982; by the installation as his successor of an already-ill Yuri Andropov, who himself died in February 1984; and by the installation of his equally geriatric successor, Konstantin Chernenko. At a time when a group of strong Western leaders had emerged—including not just President Reagan but also Prime Minister Margaret Thatcher in Great Britain, President François Mitterrand in France, and Chancellor Helmut Kohl in West Germany—this apparent inability to entrust leadership to anyone other than party stalwarts on their deathbeds was a severe commentary on what the sclerotic Soviet system had become. "We could go no further without hitting the end," one Russian later recalled of Chernenko's brief reign. "Here was the General Secretary of the party who is also the Chairman of the Presidium of the Supreme Soviet, the embodiment of our country, the personification of the party and he could barely stand up."

There was no disagreement within the Reagan administration about the desirability under these circumstances, of pressing the Russians hard. Unlike several of their predecessors, the President and his advisers did not see containment as requiring the application of sticks and carrots in equal proportion; wielders of sticks definitely predominated among them. But there were important differences over what the purpose of wielding the sticks was to be.

Some advisers, like [Secretary of Defense Casper] Weinberger, [Assistant Secretary of Defense for International Security Policy Richard] Perle, and [chief Soviet specialist on the National Security Council Richard] Pipes, saw the situation as a historic opportunity to exhaust the Soviet system. Noting that the Soviet economy was already stretched to the limit, they advocated taking advantage of American technological superiority to engage the Russians in an arms race of indefinite duration and indeterminate cost. Others, including Nitze, the Joint Chiefs of Staff, career Foreign Service officer Jack Matlock, who succeeded Pipes as chief Soviet expert at the NSC, and—most important—[Secretary of State Alexander M.] Haig's replacement after June, 1982, the unflamboyant but steady George Shultz, endorsed the principle of "negotiation from strength": the purpose of accumulating military hardware was not to debilitate the other side, but to convince it to negotiate.

The key question, of course, was what President Reagan's position would be. Despite his rhetoric, he had been careful not to rule out talks with the Russians once the proper conditions had been met: even while complaining, in his first press conference, about the Soviet propensity to lie, cheat, and steal, he had also noted that "when we can, . . . we should start negotiations on the basis of trying to effect an actual reduction in the numbers of nuclear weapons. That would be real arms reduction." But most observers—and probably many of his own advisers—assumed that when the President endorsed negotiations leading toward the "reduction," as opposed to the "limitation," of strategic arms, or the "zero option" in the INF [intermediate-range nuclear forces] talks, or the Strategic Defense Initiative, he was really seeking to avoid negotiations by setting minimal demands above the maximum concessions the Russians could afford to make. He was looking for a way they believed, to gain credit for cooperativeness with both domestic and allied constituencies without actually having to give up anything.

That would turn out to be a gross misjudgment of President Reagan, who may have had cynical advisers but was not cynical himself. It would become apparent with the passage of time that when the Chief Executive talked about "reducing" strategic missiles he meant precisely that; the appeal of the "zero option" was that it really would get rid of intermediate-range nuclear forces; the Strategic Defense Initiative might in fact, just as the President had said, make nuclear weapons "impotent and obsolete." A simple and straightforward man, Reagan took the principle of "negotiation from strength" literally: once one had built strength, one negotiated.

The first indications that the President might be interested in something other than an indefinite arms race began to appear in the spring and summer of

1983. Widespread criticism of his "evil empire" speech apparently shook him: although his view of the Soviet system itself did not change, Reagan was careful, after that point, to use more restrained language in characterizing it. Clear evidence of the President's new moderation came with the Korean airliner incident of September, 1983. Despite his outrage, Reagan did not respond—as one might have expected him to—by reviving his "evil empire" rhetoric; instead he insisted that arms control negotiations would continue, and in a remarkably conciliatory television address early in 1984 he announced that the United States was "in its strongest position in years to establish a constructive and realistic working relationship with the Soviet Union." The President concluded this address by speculating on how a typical Soviet couple—Ivan and Anya—might find that they had much in common with a typical American couple—Jim and Sally: "They might even have decided that they were all going to get together for dinner some evening soon."

It was possible to construct self-serving motives for this startling shift in tone. With a presidential campaign under way the White House was sensitive to Democratic charges that Reagan was the only postwar president not to have met with a Soviet leader while in office. Certainly it was to the advantage of the United States in its relations with Western Europe to look as reasonable as possible in the face of Soviet intransigence. But events would show that the President's interest in an improved relationship was based on more than just electoral politics or the needs of the alliance: it was only the unfortunate tendency of Soviet leaders to die upon taking office that was depriving the American Chief Executive—himself a spry septuagenarian—of a partner with whom to negotiate.

By the end of September, 1984—and to the dismay of Democratic partisans who saw Republicans snatching the "peace" issue from them—a contrite Soviet Foreign Minister Andrei Gromyko had made the pilgrimage to Washington to re-establish contacts with the Reagan administration. Shortly after Reagan's landslide re-election over Walter Mondale in November, the United States and the Soviet Union announced that a new set of arms control negotiations would begin early the following year, linking together discussions on START [Strategic Arms Reduction Talks], INF, and weapons in space. And in December, a hitherto obscure member of the Soviet Politburo, Mikhail Gorbachev, announced while visiting Great Britain that the U.S.S.R. was prepared to seek "radical solutions" looking toward a ban on nuclear missiles altogether. Three months later, Konstantin Chernenko, the last in a series of feeble and unimaginative Soviet leaders, expired, and Gorbachev—a man who was in no way feeble and unimaginative—became the General Secretary of the Communist Party of the Soviet Union. Nothing would ever be quite the same again.

Reagan and Gorbachev

Several years after Gorbachev had come to power, George F. Kennan was asked in a television interview how so unconventional a Soviet leader could have risen to the top in a system that placed such a premium on conformity. Kennan's reply reflected the perplexity American experts on Soviet affairs have felt in seeking to account for the Gorbachev phenomenon: "I really cannot explain it." It seemed most improbable that a regime so lacking in the capacity for innovation, self-evaluation, or even minimally effective public relations should suddenly produce a leader who excelled in all of these qualities; even more remarkable was the fact that Gorbachev saw himself as a revolutionary—a breed not seen in Russia for decades—determined, as he put it, "to get out of the quagmire of conservatism, and to break the inertia of stagnation."

Whatever the circumstances that led to it, the accession of Gorbachev reversed almost overnight the pattern of the preceding four years: after March, 1985, it was the Soviet Union that seized the initiative in relations with the West. It did so in a way that was both reassuring and unnerving at the same time: by becoming so determinedly cooperative as to convince some supporters of containment in the United States and Western Europe—uneasy in the absence of the intransigence to which they had become accustomed—that the Russians were now seeking to defeat that strategy by depriving it, with sinister cleverness, of an object to be contained.

President Reagan, in contrast, welcomed the fresh breezes emanating from Moscow and moved quickly to establish a personal relationship with the new Soviet leader. Within four days of Gorbachev's taking power, the President was characterizing the Russians as "in a different frame of mind than they've been in the past.... [T]hey, I believe, are really going to try and, with us, negotiate a reduction in armaments." And within four months, the White House was announcing that Reagan would meet Gorbachev at Geneva in November for the first Soviet-American summit since 1979.

The Geneva summit, like so many before it, was long on symbolism and short on substance. The two leaders appeared to get along well with one another: they behaved, as one Reagan adviser later put it, "like a couple of fellows who had run into each other at the club and discovered that they had a lot in common." The President agreed to discuss deep cuts in strategic weapons and improved verification, but he made it clear that he was not prepared to forgo development of the Strategic Defense Initiative in order to get them. His reason —which Gorbachev may not have taken seriously until this point—had to do with his determination to retain SDI as a means ultimately of rendering nuclear weapons obsolete. The President's stubbornness on this point precluded progress, at least for the moment, on what was coming to be called the "grand compromise": Paul Nitze's idea of accepting limits on SDI in return for sweeping reductions in strategic missiles. But it did leave the way open for an alert Gorbachev, detecting the President's personal enthusiasm for nuclear abolition, to surprise the world in January, 1986, with his own plan for accomplishing that objective: a Soviet-American agreement to rid the world of nuclear weapons altogether by the year 2000.

It was easy to question Gorbachev's motives in making so radical a proposal in so public a manner with no advance warning. Certainly any discussion of even reducing—much less abolishing—nuclear arsenals would raise difficult questions for American allies, where an abhorrence of nuclear weapons continued to coexist uneasily alongside the conviction that only their presence could deter superior Soviet conventional forces. Nor was the Gorbachev proposal clear on how Russians and Americans could ever impose abolition, even if they themselves agreed to it, on other nuclear and non-nuclear powers. Still, the line between rhetoric and conviction is a thin one: the first Reagan-Gorbachev summit may not only have created a personal bond between the two leaders; it may also have sharpened a vague but growing sense in the minds of both men that, despite all the difficulties in constructing an alternative, an indefinite continuation of life under nuclear threat was not a tolerable condition for either of their countries, and that their own energies might very well be directed toward overcoming that situation.

That both Reagan and Gorbachev were thinking along these lines became clear at their second meeting, the most extraordinary Soviet-American summit of the postwar era, held on very short notice at Reykjavik, Iceland, in October, 1986. The months that preceded Reykjavik had seen little tangible progress toward arms control; there had also developed, in August, an unpleasant skirmish between intelligence agencies on both sides as the KGB, in apparent retaliation for the FBI's highly publicized arrest of a Soviet United Nations official in New York on espionage charges, set up, seized, and held *USNEWS* correspondent Nicholas Daniloff on trumped-up accusations for just under a month. It was a sobering reminder that the Soviet-American relationship existed at several different levels, and that cordiality in one did not rule out the possibility of confrontation in others. The Daniloff affair also brought opportunity though, for in the course of negotiations to settle it Gorbachev proposed a quick "preliminary" summit, to be held within two weeks, to try to break the stalemate in negotiations over intermediate-range nuclear forces in Europe, the aspect of arms control where progress at a more formal summit seemed likely. Reagan immediately agreed.

But when the President and his advisers arrived at Reykjavik, they found that Gorbachev had much more grandiose proposals in mind. These included not only an endorsement of 50 percent cuts in Soviet and American strategic weapons across the board, but also agreement not to demand the inclusion of British and French nuclear weapons in these calculations—a concession that removed a major stumbling block to START—and acceptance in principle of Reagan's 1981 "zero option" for intermediate-range nuclear forces, all in return for an American commitment not to undermine SALT I's ban on strategic defenses for the next ten years. Impressed by the scope of these concessions, the American side quickly put together a compromise that would have cut ballistic missiles to zero within a decade in return for the right, after that time, to deploy strategic defenses against the bomber and cruise missile forces that would be left. Gorbachev immediately countered by proposing the abolition of *all* nuclear weapons within ten years, thus moving his original deadline from the year 2000 to 1996. President Reagan is said to have replied: "*All* nuclear weapons? Well, Mikhail, that's exactly what I've been talking about all along.... That's always been my goal."

A series of events set in motion by a Soviet diplomat's arrest on a New York subway platform and by the reciprocal framing of an American journalist in Moscow had wound up with the two most powerful men in the world agreeing—for the moment, and to the astonishment of their aides—on the abolition of all nuclear weapons within ten years. But the moment did not last. Gorbachev went on to insist, as a condition for nuclear abolition, upon a ban on the laboratory testing of SDI, which Reagan immediately interpreted as an effort to kill strategic defense altogether. Because the ABM treaty does allow for some laboratory testing, the differences between the two positions were not all that great. But in the hothouse atmosphere of this cold-climate summit no one explored such details, and the meeting broke up in disarray, acrimony, and mutual disappointment.

It was probably just as well. The sweeping agreements contemplated at Reykjavik grew out of hasty improvisation and high-level posturing, not careful thought. They suffered from all the deficiencies of Gorbachev's unilateral proposal for nuclear abolition earlier in the year; they also revealed how susceptible the leaders of the United States and the Soviet Union had become to each other's amplitudinous rhetoric. It was as if Reagan and Gorbachev had been trying desperately to outbid the other in a gigantic but surrealistic auction, with the diaphanous prospect of a nuclear-free world somehow on the block....

Negotiations on arms control continued in the year that followed Reykjavik, however, with both sides edging toward the long-awaited "grand compromise" that would defer SDI in return for progress toward a START agreement. Reagan and Gorbachev did sign an intermediate-range nuclear forces treaty in Washington in December, 1987, which for the first time provided that Russians and Americans would actually dismantle and destroy—literally before each other's eyes—an entire category of nuclear missiles. There followed a triumphal Reagan visit to Moscow in May, 1988, featuring the unusual sight of a Soviet general secretary and an American president strolling amiably through Red Square, greeting tourists and bouncing babies in front of Lenin's tomb, while their respective military aides—each carrying the codes needed to launch nuclear missiles at each other's territory—stood discreetly in the background. Gorbachev made an equally triumphal visit to New York in December, 1988, to address the United Nations General Assembly: there he announced a *unilateral* Soviet cut of some 500,000 ground troops, a major step toward moving arms control into the realm of conventional forces.

When, on the same day Gorbachev spoke in New York, a disastrous earthquake killed some 25,000 Soviet Armenians, the outpouring of aid from the United States and other Western countries was unprecedented since the days of Lend Lease. One had the eerie feeling, watching anguished television reports from the rubble that had been the cities of Leninakan and Stipak—the breakdown of emergency services, the coffins stacked like logs in city parks, the mass burials—that one had glimpsed, on a small scale, something of what a nuclear war might actually be like. The images suggested just how vulnerable both super-powers remained after almost a half-century of trying to minimize vulnerabilities. They thereby reinforced what had become almost a ritual incantation pronounced by both Reagan and Gorbachev at each of their now-frequent summits: "A nuclear war cannot be won and must never be fought."

But as the Reagan administration prepared to leave office the following month, in an elegiac mood very different from the grim militancy with which it had assumed its responsibilities eight years earlier, the actual prospect of a nuclear holocaust seemed more remote than at any point since the Soviet-American nuclear rivalry had begun. Accidents, to be sure, could always happen. Irrationality though blessedly rare since 1945, could never be ruled out. There was reason for optimism, though, in the fact that as George Bush entered the White House early in 1989, the point at issue no longer seemed to be "how to fight the Cold War" at all, but rather "is the Cold War over?"

Ronald Reagan and the End of the Cold War

The record of the Reagan years suggests the need to avoid the common error of trying to predict outcomes from attributes. There is no question that the President and his advisers came into office with an ideological view of the world that appeared to allow for no compromise with the Russians; but ideology has a way of evolving to accommodate reality especially in the hands of skillful political leadership. Indeed a good working definition of leadership might be just this —the ability to accommodate ideology to practical reality—and by that standard, Reagan's achievements in relations with the Soviet Union will certainly compare favorably with, and perhaps even surpass, those of Richard Nixon and Henry Kissinger.

Did President Reagan intend for things to come out this way? That question is, of course, more difficult to determine, given our lack of access to the archives. But a careful reading of the public record would, I think, show that the President was expressing hopes for an improvement in Soviet-American relations from the moment he entered the White House, and that he began shifting American policy in that direction as early as the first months of 1983, almost two years before Mikhail Gorbachev came to power. Gorbachev's extraordinary receptiveness to such initiatives—as distinct from the literally moribund responses of his predecessors—greatly accelerated the improvement in relations, but it would be a mistake to credit him solely with the responsibility for what happened: Ronald Reagan deserves a great deal of the credit as well.

Critics have raised the question, though, of whether President Reagan was responsible for, or even aware of, the direction administration policy was taking. This argument is, I think, both incorrect and unfair. Reagan's opponents have been quick enough to hold him personally responsible for the failures of his administration; they should be equally prepared to acknowledge his successes. And there are points, even with the limited sources now available, where we can see that the President himself had a decisive impact upon the course of events. They include, among others: the Strategic Defense Initiative, which may have had its problems as a missile shield but which certainly worked in unsettling the Russians; endorsement of the "zero option" in the INF talks and real reductions in START, the rapidity with which the President entered into, and thereby legitimized, serious negotiations with Gorbachev once he came into office; and, most remarkably of all, his eagerness to contemplate alternatives to the nuclear arms race in a way no previous president had been willing to do.

Now, it may be objected that these were simple, unsophisticated, and, as people are given to saying these days, imperfectly "nuanced" ideas. I would not argue with that proposition. But it is important to remember that while complexity, sophistication, and nuance may be prerequisites for intellectual leadership, they are not necessarily so for political leadership, and can at times actually get in the way. President Reagan generally meant precisely what he said: when he came out in favor of negotiations from strength, or for strategic arms reductions as opposed to limitations, or even for making nuclear weapons ultimately irrelevant and obsolete, he did not do so in the "killer amendment" spirit favored by geopolitical sophisticates on the right; the President may have been conservative but he was never devious. The lesson here ought to be to beware of excessive convolution and subtlety in strategy, for sometimes simple-mindedness wins out, especially if it occurs in high places.

Finally President Reagan also understood something that many geopolitical sophisticates on the left have not understood: that although toughness may or may not be a prerequisite for successful negotiations with the Russians—there are arguments for both propositions—it is absolutely essential if the American people are to lend their support, over time, to what has been negotiated. Others may have seen in the doctrine of "negotiation from strength" a way of avoiding negotiations altogether, but it now seems clear that the President saw in that approach the means of constructing a domestic political base without which agreements with the Russians would almost certainly have foundered, as indeed many of them did in the 1970s. For unless one can sustain domestic support—and one does not do that by appearing weak—then it is hardly likely that whatever one has arranged with any adversary will actually come to anything.

There is one last irony to all of this: it is that it fell to Ronald Reagan to preside over the belated but decisive success of the strategy of containment George F. Kennan had first proposed more than four decades earlier. For what were Gorbachev's reforms if not the long-delayed "mellowing" of Soviet society that Kennan had said would take place with the passage of time? The Stalinist system that had required outside adversaries to justify its own existence now seemed at last to have passed from the scene; Gorbachev appeared to have concluded that the Soviet Union could continue to be a great power in world affairs only through the introduction of something approximating a market economy, democratic political institutions, official accountability, and respect for the rule of law at home. And that, in turn, suggested an even more remarkable conclusion: that the very survival of the ideology Lenin had imposed on Russia in 1917 now required infiltration—perhaps even subversion—by precisely the ideology the great revolutionary had sworn to overthrow.

I have some reason to suspect that Professor Kennan is not entirely comfortable with the suggestion that Ronald Reagan successfully completed the execution of the strategy he originated. But as Kennan the historian would be the first to acknowledge, history is full of ironies, and this one, surely, will not rank among the least of them.

Daniel Deudney and
G. John Ikenberry

 **NO**

Who Won the Cold War?

The end of the Cold War marks the most important historical divide in half a century. The magnitude of those developments has ushered in a wide-ranging debate over the reasons for its end—a debate that is likely to be as protracted, controversial, and politically significant as that over the Cold War's origins. The emerging debate over why the Cold War ended is of more than historical interest: At stake is the vindication and legitimation of an entire world view and foreign policy orientation.

In thinking about the Cold War's conclusion, it is vital to distinguish between the domestic origins of the crisis in Soviet communism and the external forces that influenced its timing and intensity, as well as the direction of the Soviet response. Undoubtedly, the ultimate cause of the Cold War's outcome lies in the failure of the Soviet system itself. At most, outside forces hastened and intensified the crisis. However, it was not inevitable that the Soviet Union would respond to this crisis as it did in the late 1980s—with domestic liberalization and foreign policy accommodation. After all, many Western experts expected that the USSR would respond to such a crisis with renewed repression at home and aggression abroad, as it had in the past.

At that fluid historic juncture, the complex matrix of pressures, opportunities, and attractions from the outside world influenced the direction of Soviet change, particularly in its foreign policy. The Soviets' field of vision was dominated by the West, the United States, and recent American foreign policy. Having spent more than 45 years attempting to influence the Soviet Union, Americans are now attempting to gauge the weight of their country's impact and, thus, the track record of U.S. policies.

In assessing the rest of the world's impact on Soviet change, a remarkably simplistic and self-serving conventional wisdom has emerged in the United States. This new conventional wisdom, the "Reagan victory school," holds that President Ronald Reagan's military and ideological assertiveness during the 1980s played the lead role in the collapse of Soviet communism and the "taming" of its foreign policy In that view the Reagan administration's ideological counter-offensive and military buildup delivered the knock-out punch to a system that was internally bankrupt and on the ropes. The Reagan Right's perspective is an ideologically pointed version of the more broadly held conventional

From Daniel Deudney and G. John Ikenberry, "Who Won the Cold War?" *Foreign Policy*, no. 87 (Summer 1992). Copyright © 1992 by The Carnegie Endowment for International Peace. Reprinted by permission of G. John Ikenberry.

wisdom on the end of the Cold War that emphasizes the success of the "peace-through-strength" strategy manifest in four decades of Western containment. After decades of waging a costly "twilight struggle," the West now celebrates the triumph of its military and ideological resolve.

The Reagan victory school and the broader peace-through-strength perspectives are, however, misleading and incomplete—both in their interpretation of events in the 1980s and in their understanding of deeper forces that led to the end of the Cold War. It is important to reconsider the emerging conventional wisdom before it truly becomes an article of faith on Cold War history and comes to distort the thinking of policymakers in America and elsewhere.

The collapse of the Cold War caught almost everyone, particularly hardliners, by surprise. Conservatives and most analysts in the U.S. national security establishment believed that the Soviet-U.S. struggle was a permanent feature of international relations. As former National Security Council adviser Zbigniew Brzezinski put it in 1986, "the American-Soviet contest is not some temporary aberration but a historical rivalry that will long endure." And to many hardliners, Soviet victory was far more likely than Soviet collapse. Many ringing predictions now echo as embarrassments.

The Cold War's end was a baby that arrived unexpectedly, but a long line of those claiming paternity has quickly formed. A parade of former Reagan administration officials and advocates has forthrightly asserted that Reagan's hardline policies were the decisive trigger for reorienting Soviet foreign policy and for the demise of communism. As former Pentagon officials like Caspar Weinberger and Richard Perle, columnist George Will, neoconservative thinker Irving Kristol, and other proponents of the Reagan victory school have argued, a combination of military and ideological pressures gave the Soviets little choice but to abandon expansionism abroad and repression at home. In that view, the Reagan military buildup foreclosed Soviet military options while pushing the Soviet economy to the breaking point. Reagan partisans stress that his dramatic "Star Wars" initiative put the Soviets on notice that the next phase of the arms race would be waged in areas where the West held a decisive technological edge.

Reagan and his administration's military initiatives, however, played a far different and more complicated role in inducing Soviet change than the Reagan victory school asserts. For every "hardening" there was a "softening": Reagan's rhetoric of the "Evil Empire" was matched by his vigorous anti-nuclearism; the military buildup in the West was matched by the resurgence of a large popular peace movement; and the Reagan Doctrine's toughening of containment was matched by major deviations from containment in East-West economic relations. Moreover, over the longer term, the strength marshaled in containment was matched by mutual weakness in the face of nuclear weapons, and efforts to engage the USSR were as important as efforts to contain it.

The Irony of Ronald Reagan

Perhaps the greatest anomaly of the Reagan victory school is the "Great Communicator" himself. The Reagan Right ignores that his anti-nuclearism was as strong as his anticommunism. Reagan's personal convictions on nuclear weapons were profoundly at odds with the beliefs of most in his administration. Staffed by officials who considered nuclear weapons a useful instrument of statecraft and who were openly disdainful of the moral critique of nuclear weapons articulated by the arms control community and the peace movement, the administration pursued the hardest line on nuclear policy and the Soviet Union in the postwar era. Then vice president George Bush's observation that nuclear weapons would be fired as a warning shot and Deputy Under Secretary of Defense T. K. Jones's widely quoted view that nuclear war was survivable captured the reigning ethos within the Reagan administration.

In contrast, there is abundant evidence that Reagan himself felt a deep antipathy for nuclear weapons and viewed their abolition to be a realistic and desirable goal. Reagan's call in his famous March 1983 "Star Wars" speech for a program to make nuclear weapons impotent and obsolete was viewed as cynical by many, but actually it expressed Reagan's heartfelt views, views that he came to act upon. As *Washington Post* reporter Lou Cannon's 1991 biography points out, Reagan was deeply disturbed by nuclear deterrence and attracted to abolitionist solutions. "I know I speak for people everywhere when I say our dream is to see the day when nuclear weapons will be banished from the face of the earth," Reagan said in November 1983. Whereas the Right saw anti-nuclearism as a threat to American military spending and the legitimacy of an important foreign policy tool, or as propaganda for domestic consumption, Reagan sincerely believed it. Reagan's anti-nuclearism was not just a personal sentiment. It surfaced at decisive junctures to affect Soviet perceptions of American policy. Sovietologist and strategic analyst Michael MccGwire has argued persuasively that Reagan's anti-nuclearism decisively influenced Soviet-U.S. relations during the early Gorbachev years.

Contrary to the conventional wisdom, the defense buildup did not produce Soviet capitulation. The initial Soviet response to the Reagan administration's buildup and belligerent rhetoric was to accelerate production of offensive weapons, both strategic and conventional. That impasse was broken not by Soviet capitulation but by an extraordinary convergence by Reagan and Mikhail Gorbachev on a vision of mutual nuclear vulnerability and disarmament. On the Soviet side, the dominance of the hardline response to the newly assertive America was thrown into question in early 1985 when Gorbachev became general secretary of the Communist party after the death of Konstantin Chernenko. Without a background in foreign affairs, Gorbachev was eager to assess American intentions directly and put his stamp on Soviet security policy. Reagan's strong antinuclear views expressed at the November 1985 Geneva summit were decisive in convincing Gorbachev that it was possible to work with the West in halting the nuclear arms race. The arms control diplomacy of the later Reagan years was successful because, as *Washington Post* journalist Don Oberdorfer has detailed in *The Turn: From the Cold War to a New Era* (1991), Secretary of State George Shultz picked up on Reagan's strong convictions and deftly side-stepped hard-line opposition to agreements. In fact, Schultz's success at linking presidential unease about nuclear weapons to Soviet overtures in the face of right-wing opposition provides a sharp contrast with John Foster Dulles's refusal to act on President Dwight Eisenhower's nuclear doubts and the opportunities presented by Nikita Khrushchev's détente overtures.

Reagan's commitment to anti-nuclearism and its potential for transforming the U.S-Soviet confrontation was more graphically demonstrated at the October 1986 Reykjavik summit when Reagan and Gorbachev came close to agreeing on a comprehensive program of global denuclearization that was far bolder than any seriously entertained by American strategists since the Baruch Plan of 1946. The sharp contrast between Reagan's and Gorbachev's shared skepticism toward nuclear weapons on the one hand, and the Washington security establishment's consensus on the other, was showcased in former secretary of defense James Schlesinger's scathing accusation that Reagan was engaged in "casual utopianism." But Reagan's anomalous anti-nuclearism provided the crucial signal to Gorbachev that bold initiatives would be reciprocated rather than exploited. Reagan's anti-nuclearism was more important than his administration's military buildup in catalyzing the end of the Cold War.

Neither anti-nuclearism nor its embrace by Reagan have received the credit they deserve for producing the Soviet-U.S. reconciliation. Reagan's accomplishment in this regard has been met with silence from all sides. Conservatives, not sharing Reagan's anti-nuclearism, have emphasized the role of traditional military strength. The popular peace movement, while holding deeply antinuclear views, was viscerally suspicious of Reagan. The establishment arms control community also found Reagan and his motives suspect, and his attack on deterrence conflicted with their desire to stabilize deterrence and establish their credentials as sober participants in security policy making. Reagan's radical anti-nuclearism should sustain his reputation as the ultimate Washington outsider.

The central role of Reagan's and Gorbachev's anti-nuclearism throws new light on the 1987 Treaty on Intermediate-range Nuclear Forces, the first genuine disarmament treaty of the nuclear era. The conventional wisdom emphasizes that this agreement was the fruit of a hard-line negotiating posture and the U.S. military buildup. Yet the superpowers' settlement on the "zero option" was not a vindication of the hard-line strategy. The zero option was originally fashioned by hardliners for propaganda purposes, and many backed off as its implementation became likely. The impasse the hard line created was transcended by the surprising Reagan-Gorbachev convergence against nuclear arms.

The Reagan victory school also overstates the overall impact of American and Western policy on the Soviet Union during the 1980s. The Reagan administration's posture was both evolving and inconsistent. Though loudly proclaiming its intention to go beyond the previous containment policies that were deemed too soft, the reality of Reagan's policies fell short. As Sovietologists Gail Lapidus and Alexander Dallin observed in a 1989 *Bulletin of the Atomic Scientists* article, the policies were "marked to the end by numerous zigzags and reversals, bureaucratic conflicts, and incoherence." Although rollback had long been a cherished goal of the Republican party's right wing, Reagan was unwilling and unable to implement it.

The hard-line tendencies of the Reagan administration were offset in two ways. First, and most important, Reagan's tough talk fueled a large peace movement in the United States and Western Europe in the 1980s, a movement that put significant political pressure upon Western governments to pursue far-reaching arms control proposals. That mobilization of Western opinion created a political climate in which the rhetoric and posture of the early Reagan administration was a significant political liability. By the 1984 U.S. presidential election, the administration had embraced arms control goals that it had previously ridiculed. Reagan's own anti-nuclearism matched that rising public concern, and Reagan emerged as the spokesman for comprehensive denuclearization. Paradoxically, Reagan administration policies substantially triggered the popular revolt against the nuclear hardline, and then Reagan came to pursue the popular agenda more successfully than any other postwar president.

Second, the Reagan administration's hard-line policies were also undercut by powerful Western interests that favored East-West economic ties. In the early months of Reagan's administration, the grain embargo imposed by President Jimmy Carter after the 1979 Soviet invasion of Afghanistan was lifted in order to keep the Republican party's promises to Midwestern farmers. Likewise, in 1981 the Reagan administration did little to challenge Soviet control of Eastern Europe after Moscow pressured Warsaw to suppress the independent Polish trade union Solidarity, in part because Poland might have defaulted on multibillion dollar loans made by Western banks. Also, despite strenuous opposition by the Reagan administration, the NATO allies pushed ahead with a natural gas pipeline linking the Soviet Union with Western Europe. That a project creating substantial economic interdependence could proceed during the worst period of Soviet-U.S. relations in the 1980s demonstrates the failure of the Reagan administration to present an unambiguous hard line toward the Soviet Union. More generally, NATO allies and the vocal European peace movement moderated and buffered hardline American tendencies.

In sum, the views of the Reagan victory school are flawed because they neglect powerful crosscurrents in the West during the 1980s. The conventional wisdom simplifies a complex story and ignores those aspects of Reagan administration policy inconsistent with the hardline rationale. Moreover, the Western "face" toward the Soviet Union did not consist exclusively of Reagan administration policies, but encompassed countervailing tendencies from the Western public, other governments, and economic interest groups.

Whether Reagan is seen as the consummate hardliner or the prophet of anti-nuclearism, one should not exaggerate the influence of his administration, or of other short-term forces. Within the Washington beltway, debates about postwar military and foreign policy would suggest that Western strategy fluctuated wildly, but in fact the basic thrust of Western policy toward the USSR remained remarkably consistent. Arguments from the New Right notwithstanding, Reagan's containment strategy was not that different from those of his predecessors. Indeed, the broader peace-through-strength perspective sees the Cold War's finale as the product of a long-term policy, applied over the decades.

In any case, although containment certainly played an important role in blocking Soviet expansionism, it cannot explain either the end of the Cold War or the direction of Soviet policy responses. The West's relationship with the Soviet Union was not limited to containment, but included important elements of mutual vulnerability and engagement. The Cold War's end was not simply a result of Western strength but of mutual weakness and intentional engagement as well.

Most dramatically, the mutual vulnerability created by nuclear weapons overshadowed containment. Nuclear weapons forced the United States and the Soviet Union to eschew war and the serious threat of war as tools of diplomacy and created imperatives for the cooperative regulation of nuclear capability. Both countries tried to fashion nuclear explosives into useful instruments of policy, but they came to the realization—as the joint Soviet-American statement issued from the 1985 Geneva summit put it—that "nuclear war cannot be won and must never be fought." Both countries slowly but surely came to view nuclear weapons as a common threat that must be regulated jointly. Not just containment, but also the overwhelming and common nuclear threat brought the Soviets to the negotiating table. In the shadow of nuclear destruction, common purpose defused traditional antagonisms.

A second error of the peace-through-strength perspective is the failure to recognize that the West offered an increasingly benign face to the communist world. Traditionally, the Soviets' Marxist-Leninist doctrine held that the capitalist West was inevitably hostile and aggressive, an expectation reinforced by the aggression of capitalist, fascist Germany. Since World War II, the Soviets' principal adversaries had been democratic capitalist states. Slowly but surely Soviet doctrine acknowledged that the West's behavior did not follow Leninist expectations, but was instead increasingly pacific and cooperative. The Soviet willingness to abandon the Brezhnev Doctrine in the late 1980s in favor of the "Sinatra Doctrine"—under which any East European country could sing, "I did it my way"—suggests a radical transformation in the prevailing Soviet perception of threat from the West. In 1990, the Soviet acceptance of the de facto absorption of communist East Germany into West Germany involved the same calculation with even higher stakes. In accepting the German reunification, despite that country's past aggression, Gorbachev acted on the assumption that the Western system was fundamentally pacific. As Russian foreign minister Andrei Kozyrev noted subsequently, that Western countries are pluralistic democracies "practically rules out the pursuance of an aggressive foreign policy." Thus the Cold War ended despite the assertiveness of Western hardliners, rather than because of it.

The War of Ideas

The second front of the Cold War, according to the Reagan victory school, was ideological. Reagan spearheaded a Western ideological offensive that dealt the USSR a death blow. For the Right, driving home the image of the Evil Empire was a decisive stroke rather than a rhetorical flourish. Ideological warfare was such a key front in the Cold War because the Soviet Union was, at its core, an ideological creation. According to the Reagan Right, the supreme vulnerability of the Soviet Union to ideological assault was greatly underappreciated by Western leaders and publics. In that view, the Cold War was won by the West's uncompromising assertion of the superiority of its values and its complete denial of the moral legitimacy of the Soviet system during the 1980s. Western military strength could prevent defeat, but only ideological breakthrough could bring victory.

Underlying that interpretation is a deeply ideological philosophy of politics and history. The Reagan Right tended to view politics as a war of ideas, an orientation that generated a particularly polemical type of politics. As writer Sidney Blumenthal has pointed out, many of the leading figures in the neoconservative movement since the 1960s came to conservatism after having begun their political careers as Marxists or socialists. That perspective sees the Soviet Union as primarily an ideological artifact, and therefore sees struggle with it in particularly ideological terms. The neoconservatives believe, like Lenin, that "ideas are more fatal than guns."

Convinced that Bolshevism was quintessentially an ideological phenomenon, activists of the New Right were contemptuous of Western efforts to accommodate Soviet needs, moderate Soviet aims, and integrate the USSR into the international system as a "normal" great power. In their view, the *realpolitik* strategy urged by George Kennan, Walter Lippmann, and Hans Morgenthau was based on a misunderstanding of the Soviet Union. It provided an incomplete roadmap for waging the Cold War, and guaranteed that it would never be won. A particular villain for the New Right was Secretary of State Henry Kissinger, whose program of détente implied, in their view, a "moral equivalence" between the West and the Soviet Union that amounted to unilateral ideological disarmament. Even more benighted were liberal attempts to engage and co-opt the Soviet Union in hopes that the two systems could ultimately reconcile. The New Right's view of politics was strikingly globalist in its assumption that the world had shrunk too much for two such different systems to survive, and that the contest was too tightly engaged for containment or Iron Curtains to work. As James Burnham, the ex-communist prophet of New Right anticommunism, insisted in the early postwar years, the smallness of our "one world" demanded a strategy of "rollback" for American survival.

The end of the Cold War indeed marked an ideological triumph for the West, but not of the sort fancied by the Reagan victory school. Ideology played a far different and more complicated role in inducing Soviet change than the Reagan school allows. As with the military sphere, the Reagan school presents an incomplete picture of Western ideological influence, ignoring the emergence of ideological common ground in stimulating Soviet change.

The ideological legitimacy of the Soviet system collapsed in the eyes of its own citizens not because of an assault by Western ex-leftists, but because of the appeal of Western affluence and permissiveness. The puritanical austerity of Bolshevism's "New Soviet Man" held far less appeal than the "bourgeois decadence" of the West. For the peoples of the USSR and Eastern Europe, it was not so much abstract liberal principles but rather the Western way of life—the material and cultural manifestations of the West's freedoms—that subverted the Soviet vision. Western popular culture—exemplified in rock and roll, television, film, and blue jeans—seduced the communist world far more effectively than ideological sermons by anticommunist activists. As journalist William Echikson noted in his 1990 book *Lighting the Night: Revolution in Eastern Europe,* "instead of listening to the liturgy of Marx and Lenin, generations of would-be socialists tuned into the Rolling Stones and the Beatles."

If Western popular culture and permissiveness helped subvert communist legitimacy, it is a development of profound irony. Domestically, the New Right battled precisely those cultural forms that had such global appeal. V. I. Lenin's most potent ideological foils were John Lennon and Paul McCartney, not Adam Smith and Thomas Jefferson. The Right fought a two-front war against communism abroad and hedonism and consumerism at home. Had it not lost the latter struggle, the West may not have won the former.

The Reagan victory school argues that ideological assertiveness precipitated the end of the Cold War. While it is true that right-wing American intellectuals were assertive toward the Soviet Union, other Western activists and intellectuals were building links with highly placed reformist intellectuals there. The Reagan victory school narrative ignores that Gorbachev's reform program was based upon "new thinking"—a body of ideas developed by globalist thinkers cooperating across the East-West divide. The key themes of new thinking—the common threat of nuclear destruction, the need for strong international institutions, and the importance of ecological sustainability—built upon the cosmopolitanism of the Marxist tradition and officially replaced the Communist party's class-conflict doctrine during the Gorbachev period.

It is widely recognized that a major source of Gorbachev's new thinking was his close aide and speechwriter, Georgi Shakhnazarov. A former president of the Soviet political science association, Shakhnazarov worked extensively with Western globalists, particularly the New York-based group known as the World Order Models Project. Gorbachev's speeches and policy statements were replete with the language and ideas of globalism. The Cold War ended not with Soviet ideological capitulation to Reagan's anticommunism but rather with a Soviet embrace of globalist themes promoted by a network of liberal internationalists. Those intellectual influences were greatest with the state elite, who had greater access to the West and from whom the reforms originated.

Regardless of how one judges the impact of the ideological struggles during the Reagan years, it is implausible to focus solely on recent developments without accounting for longer-term shifts in underlying forces, particularly the widening gap between Western and Soviet economic performance. Over the long haul, the West's ideological appeal was based on the increasingly superior performance of the Western economic system. Although contrary to the expectation of Marx and Lenin, the robustness of capitalism in the West was increasingly acknowledged by Soviet analysts. Likewise, Soviet elites were increasingly troubled by their economy's comparative decline.

The Reagan victory school argues that the renewed emphasis on free-market principles championed by Reagan and then British prime minister Margaret Thatcher led to a global move toward market deregulation and privatization that the Soviets desired to follow. By rekindling the beacon of laissez-faire capitalism, Reagan illuminated the path of economic reform, thus vanquishing communism.

That view is misleading in two respects. First, it was West European social democracy rather than America's more free-wheeling capitalism that attracted Soviet reformers. Gorbachev wanted his reforms to emulate the Swedish model. His vision was not of laissez-faire capitalism but of a social democratic welfare state. Second, the Right's triumphalism in the economic sphere is ironic. The West's robust economies owe much of their relative stability and health to two generations of Keynesian intervention and government involvement that the Right opposed at every step. As with Western popular culture, the Right opposed tendencies in the West that proved vital in the West's victory.

There is almost universal agreement that the root cause of the Cold War's abrupt end was the grave domestic failure of Soviet communism. However, the Soviet response to this crisis—accommodation and liberalization rather than aggression and repression—was significantly influenced by outside pressures and opportunities, many from the West. As historians and analysts attempt to explain how recent U.S. foreign policy helped end the Cold War, a view giving most of the credit to Reagan-era assertiveness and Western strength has become the new conventional wisdom. Both the Reagan victory school and the peace-through-strength perspective on Western containment assign a central role in ending the Cold War to Western resolve and power. The lesson for American foreign policy being drawn from those events is that military strength and ideological warfare were the West's decisive assets in fighting the Cold War.

The new conventional wisdom, in both its variants, is seriously misleading. Operating over the last decade, Ronald Reagan's personal anti-nuclearism, rather than his administration's hardline, catalyzed the accommodations to end the Cold War. His administration's effort to go beyond containment and on the offensive was muddled, counter-balanced, and unsuccessful. Operating over the long term, containment helped thwart Soviet expansionism but cannot account for the Soviet domestic failure, the end of East-West struggle, or the direction of the USSR'S reorientation. Contrary to the hard-line version, nuclear weapons were decisive in abandoning the conflict by creating common interests.

On the ideological front, the new conventional wisdom is also flawed. The conservatives' anticommunism was far less important in delegitimating the Soviet system than were that system's internal failures and the attraction of precisely the Western "permissive culture" abhorred by the Right. In addition, Gorbachev's attempts to reform communism in the late-1980s were less an ideological capitulation than a reflection of philosophical convergence on the globalist norms championed by liberal internationalists. And the West was more appealing not because of its laissez-faire purity, but because of the success of Keynesian and social welfare innovations whose use the Right resisted.

Behind the debate over who "won" the Cold War are competing images of the forces shaping recent history. Containment, strength, and confrontation—the trinity enshrined in conventional thinking on Western foreign policy's role in ending the Cold War—obscure the nature of these momentous changes. Engagement and interdependence, rather than containment, are the ruling trends of the age. Mutual vulnerability, not strength, drives security politics. Accommodation and integration, not confrontation, are the motors of change.

That such encouraging trends were established and deepened even as the Cold War raged demonstrates the considerable continuity underlying the West's support today for reform in the post-Soviet transition. Those trends also expose as one-sided and self-serving the New Right's attempt to take credit for the success of forces that, in truth, they opposed. In the end, Reagan partisans have been far more successful in claiming victory in the Cold War than they were in achieving it.

POSTSCRIPT

Did President Reagan Win the Cold War?

Now that the cold war is over, historians must assess why it ended so suddenly and unexpectedly. Did President Reagan's military buildup in the 1980s force the Russians into economic bankruptcy? Gaddis gives Reagan high marks for ending the cold war. By combining a policy of militancy and operational pragmatism, says Gaddis, Reagan brought about the most significant improvement in Soviet-American relations since the end of World War II. Deudney and Ikenberry disagree. In their view the cold war ended only when the Russians saw the need for international cooperation in order to end the arms race, prevent a nuclear holocaust, and liberalize their economy. It was Western global ideas and not the hard-line containment policy of the early Reagan administration that caused Gorbachev to abandon traditional Russian communism, according to Deudney and Ikenberry.

Gaddis has established himself as the leading diplomatic historian of the cold war period. His assessment of Reagan's relations with the Soviet Union is balanced and probably more generous than that of most contemporary analysts. It is also very useful because it so succinctly describes the unexpected shift from a hard-line policy to one of détente. Gaddis admits that not even Reagan could have foreseen the total collapse of communism and the Soviet empire. While he allows that Reagan was not a profound thinker, Gaddis credits him with the leadership skills to overcome any prior ideological biases toward the Soviet Union and to take advantage of Gorbachev's offer to end the arms race. While many of the president's hard-liners could not believe that the collapse of the Soviet Union was for real, Reagan was consistent in his view that the American arms buildup in the early 1980s was for the purpose of ending the arms race. Reagan, says Gaddis, accomplished this goal.

Deudney and Ikenberry give less credit to Reagan than to global influences in ending the cold war. In their view, Gorbachev softened his hard-line foreign policy and abandoned orthodox Marxist economic programs because he was influenced by Western European cosmopolitans who were concerned about the "common threat of nuclear destruction, the need for strong international institutions, and the importance of ecological sustainability." Deudney and Ikenberry agree that Reagan became more accommodating toward the Russians in 1983, but they maintain that the cold war's end "was not simply a result of Western strength but of mutual weakness and intentional engagement as well."

There is a considerable bibliography assessing the Reagan administration. Three *Washington Post* reporters have provided an early liberal and critical assessment of Reagan. Lou Cannon's *President Reagan: The Role of a Lifetime* (Simon & Schuster, 1991) is a perceptive account of a reporter who has closely followed Reagan since he was governor of California. Haynes Johnson's *Sleep-walking Through History: America in the Reagan Years* (W. W. Norton, 1991) is more critical than Cannon's biography, but it is a readable account of Reagan's presidency. Don Oberdorfer, a former Moscow correspondent for the *Washing-ton Post*, has written *The Turn: From the Cold War to a New Era: The United States and the Soviet Union, 1983–1990* (Poseidon Press, 1991). Oberdorfer credits Secretary of State George Schultz with Reagan's turnaround from a hard-line to a détente approach to foreign policy. Historian Michael R. Beschloss and *Time* magazine foreign correspondent Strobe Talbott interviewed Gorbachev for *At the Highest Levels: The Inside Story of the End of the Cold War* (Little, Brown, 1993), which carries the story from 1987 through the Bush administration.

Early evaluations of Reagan by historians and political scientists are useful, although any works written before 1991 are likely to be dated in their prognostications because of the collapse of the Soviet Union. Historian Michael Schaller, in *Reckoning With Reagan: America and Its President in the 1980s* (Oxford University Press, 1992), argues that Reagan created an illusion of national strength at the very time it was declining. Political scientist Coral Bell analyzes the disparity between Reagan's declaratory and operational policies in *The Reagan Paradox: U.S. Foreign Policy in the 1980s* (Rutgers University Press, 1989). A number of symposiums on the Reagan presidency have been published. Two of the best are David E. Kyvig, ed., *Reagan and the World* (Greenwood Press, 1990) and Dilys M. Hill, Raymond A. Moore, and Phil Williams, eds., *The Reagan Presidency: An Incomplete Revolution?* (St Martin's Press, 1990), which contains primarily discussions of domestic policy.

Not all scholars are critical of Reagan. Some of his academic and intellectual supporters include British professor David Mervin, in the admiring portrait *Ronald Reagan and the American Presidency* (Longman, 1990), and Patrick Glynn, in *Closing Pandora's Box: Arms Races, Arms Control, and the History of the Cold War* (Basic Books, 1992). A number of conservative magazines have published articles arguing that American foreign policy hard-liners won the cold war. Two of the most articulate essays written from this viewpoint are Arch Puddington, "The Anti–Cold War Brigade," *Commentary* (August 1990) and Owen Harries, "The Cold War and the Intellectuals," *Commentary* (October 1991).

Books on the end of the cold war will continue to proliferate. Michael J. Hogan has edited the earliest views of the major historians in *The End of the Cold War: Its Meaning and Implications* (Cambridge University Press, 1992). Michael Howard reviews five books on the end of the cold war in "Winning the Peace: How Both Kennan and Gorbachev Were Right," *Times Literary Supplement* (January 8, 1993).

ISSUE 12

Did President George Bush Achieve His Objectives in the Gulf War?

YES: Colin L. Powell, from *My American Journey* (Random House, 1995)

NO: Michael R. Gordon and Bernard E. Trainor, from *The Generals' War: The Inside Story of the Conflict in the Gulf* (Little, Brown, 1995)

ISSUE SUMMARY

YES: Secretary of State Colin L. Powell argues that the American armed forces successfully achieved their limited and specific objective in the Gulf War, which was to liberate Kuwait from the occupation army of Iraq.

NO: Journalist Michael R. Gordon and Bernard E. Trainor, a retired lieutenant general of the U.S. Marine Corps, argue that the Bush administration's lack of a clear political strategy for postwar Iraq allowed Saddam Hussein to remain in power with half of his important Republican Guard military tank units intact.

O n August 2, 1990, 140,000 Iraqi troops and 1,800 tanks roared into Kuwait and installed a provisional government after the ruling Kuwaiti al-Sabah family fled to Saudi Arabia.

Why did Iraqi leader Saddam Hussein invade Kuwait? No one knows for sure, but several reasons have been offered. First, Iraq emerged from the 1980–1988 war with Iran with a much stronger military presence in the area. Control over Kuwait would enable a land-locked Iraq to gain control over Kuwait's large natural harbor along with approximately 120 miles of Gulf coastline. Second, many Iraqis believe that Kuwait was historically part of ancient Iraq as well as part of the Ottoman Empire, which ruled the area from the middle of the sixteenth century until World War I. Third, Hussein believed that Kuwait and Saudi Arabia pumped too much oil and kept oil prices low by not adhering to the production quotas of the other oil exporting countries in the area. Kuwait also did not forgive Baghdad's war debts or loan it money for reconstructing its economy. An invasion of Kuwait would enable Iraq to solve its economic problems with money left over for arms purchases and the development of nuclear weapons.

Less than a week after the invasion, President George Bush announced that American troops were being dispatched to Saudi Arabia, saying

> First, we seek the immediate, unconditional, and complete withdrawal of all Iraqi forces from Kuwait. Second, Kuwait's legitimate government must be restored to replace the puppet regime. And third, my administration... is committed to the security and stability of the Persian Gulf. And fourth, I am determined to protect the lives of American citizens abroad.

Bush never deviated from his firm stance that Iraq must leave Kuwait. His speech began the policy of Operation Desert Shield, and by early November the president had sent 240,000 military personnel and close to 1,000 high-tech combat aircraft into Saudi Arabia.

Bush's policies against Iraq received support from the international community. Bush actually had more problems convincing some members of Congress and the American military that a U.S. attack against Iraq was necessary. A heated debate in Congress began on January 10, 1991. Two resolutions were proposed. Senators Sam Nunn (D-Georgia) and George Mitchell (D-Maine) sponsored a draft resolution in the Senate to use force only to enforce the embargo and to protect American forces. Critics of the Nunn-Mitchell resolution argued that Hussein, while hurt by the embargo, had introduced austerity measures in Iraq and was not going to withdraw from Kuwait. The House of Representatives voted 250–183 against the Nunn-Mitchell anti-war resolution, and the Senate did likewise 53–46. Both houses supported a resolution sponsored by Representatives Stephen Solarz (D-New York) and Robert Michel (R-Illinois), which authorized the president to use armed force if Iraq did not withdraw from Kuwait on or before January 15, in accordance with UN Security Council Resolution 678.

On Wednesday, January 16, phase one of Operation Desert Storm began. According to Steve A. Yetiv, a consultant to the United States Joint Forces Command, "The United States expended more than half of its total inventory of non-nuclear missiles." Eighty-two tons of high-explosive bombs were dropped. On February 22 phase two of Desert Storm began. The ground war lasted only 100 hours. Within that time the world's sixth largest air force was severely crippled, and Iraq's army was reduced by 50 percent.

Did President Bush achieve his objective in the Gulf War in 1990–1991? In the following selection, Colin L. Powell argues in the affirmative. American armed forces, he says, fought a limited war under UN auspices and, with a minimum loss of life, liberated Kuwait from the occupation army of Iraq. In the second selection, Michael R. Gordon and Bernard E. Trainor disagree, arguing that the Bush administration's lack of a clear political strategy for postwar Iraq allowed Hussein to remain in power with half of his important Republican Guard military tank units intact.

Colin L. Powell  **YES**

Every War Must End

$\mathbf{B}$y the third week in February, the air war had been going on uninterrupted for thirty-five days. I wanted to make sure the President understood that war was going to look a lot different once fighting began on the ground. I took advantage of one of our almost daily briefings to paint the contrast. "Once the ground war begins," I said, "we don't get these antiseptic videos of a missile with a target in the cross hairs. When a battalion runs into a firefight, you don't lose a pilot or two, you can lose fifty to a hundred men in minutes. And a battlefield is not a pretty sight. You'll see a kid's scorched torso hanging out of a tank turret while ammo cooking off inside has torn the rest of the crew apart. We have to brace ourselves for some ugly images." I also made sure that Cheney and the President understood that ground combat cannot be reported as quickly as air strikes. "There's going to be confusion. You won't know what is happening for a while. And so in the early hours, please don't press us for situation reports."

The cold bath of reality was important. Notwithstanding Panama, Cheney had never seen war on a grand scale. The President had, but only from the air during his own long-ago fighter pilot days.

As the bombing continued, one downside of airpower started to come into sharp focus, particularly what happened on February 13. That day, two of our aircraft scored direct hits on the Al Firdos bunker in Baghdad, which we regarded as a command and control site and which the Iraqis claimed was an air-raid shelter. Whatever use the structure served, a large number of civilians died in the strike, which the whole world witnessed on television as victims were hauled from the smoking rubble. Schwarzkopf and I discussed this tragedy. Did we still need to pound downtown Baghdad over a month into the war? How many times could you bomb the Baath Party headquarters, and for what purpose? No one was sitting there waiting for the next Tomahawk to hit. Schwarzkopf and I started reviewing targets more closely before each day's missions.

If nothing else, the Al Firdos bunker strike underscored the need to start the combined air/ground offensive and end the war. During a quick visit Cheney and I had made to the war zone between February 8 and 10, Schwarzkopf had told us that he would be ready to go by February 21. As soon as Cheney and

From Colin L. Powell with Joseph E. Persico, *My American Journey* (Random House, 1995). Copyright © 1995 by Colin L. Powell. Reprinted by permission of Random House, Inc.

I got back to Washington, we reported this date to an impatient George Bush. Three days later, however, Norm called and told me that the 21st was out.

"The President wants to get on with this," I said. "What happened?"

"Walt Boomer needs more time," Schwarzkopf answered. Boomer's 1st and 2nd Marine Divisions were deployed to drive head-on from the center of the line toward Kuwait City. But first they had to breach a savage complex of entrenchments that the Iraqis had spent months erecting. The Marines would have to penetrate belts of antipersonnel and antitank mines, tangled rolls of booby-trapped barbed wire, more minefields, and deep tank traps, and then climb twenty-foot-high berms and cross trenches filled with burning oil. All the while, they would be under fire from Iraqi troops and artillery. Boomer wanted time to shift his point of attack twenty miles to the west, where one Iraqi defensive position had been largely abandoned under air attack and another line farther back was incomplete. He also wanted more airstrikes to weaken the enemy defenses before his troops moved.

"It'll cost a few days," Norm said. He wanted to put off the ground offensive until February 24.

"Remember the strategy," I reminded him. The frontal assaults were intended only to tie down the entrenched Iraqis, and that included the Marines' mission. "If Boomer hits serious resistance, he's to stop," I said. Having engaged the enemy, his troops would have accomplished their mission by allowing VII Corps and XVIII Airborne Corps to pull off the left hook in the sparsely defended western desert. "We don't need to kill a bunch of kids singing 'The Marines' Hymn,'" I said.

One of my fundamental operating premises is that the commander in the field is always right and the rear echelon is wrong, unless proved otherwise. The field commander is on the scene, feeling the terrain, directing the troops, facing and judging the enemy. I therefore advised Cheney to accept Norm's recommendation. Cheney reluctantly went to the President and got a postponement to February 24.

I backed Norm, though I thought he was being overly cautious. Over the previous weeks, I had watched VII Corps, with its tens of thousands of troops and hundreds of tanks, pour into Saudi Arabia. We had secretly moved our armored and airborne forces to Iraq's exposed western flank, and we had been holding our breath to see if the Iraqis responded. All they did was send another undermanned division to that part of the desert. That's it, I told myself. They had been sucked in by our moves hinting at a major frontal assault and an amphibious landing on Kuwait from the Persian Gulf. They had shown us everything they had, and it was nowhere near enough to stop our left hook. Earlier we had worried that the desert soil on the western flank might not be able to support heavy armored vehicles. The engineers had tested the sands, however, and gave us a "Go." We questioned local Bedouins, and they confirmed the solidity of the terrain.

The offensive timetable was further clouded as Mikhail Gorbachev tried to play peacemaker. On February 18, the Iraqi foreign minister, Tariq Aziz, went to Moscow to hear a plan under which we would stop hostilities if the Iraqis withdrew from Kuwait. President Bush was in a bind. It was too late for this approach, he believed. After the expenditure of $60 billion and transporting half a million troops eight thousand miles, Bush wanted to deliver a knockout punch to the Iraqi invaders in Kuwait. He did not want to win by a TKO that would allow Saddam to withdraw with his army unpunished and intact and wait for another day. Nevertheless, the President could not be seen as turning his back on a chance for peace.

On February 20, Norm called saying he had talked to his commanders and needed still another delay, to the 26th. He had the latest weather report in hand, he said, and bad weather was predicted for the 24th and 25th, maybe clearing on the 26th. Bad weather equaled reduced air support, which equaled higher casualties. I was on the spot. So far, Cheney had accepted my counsel. But now I did not feel that Norm was giving me sufficiently convincing arguments to take back to Cheney and the President, first that Boomer needed to move his Marines, then that the Marines needed more air support, then that the weather was bad, and on still another occasion, that the Saudi army was not ready. What should I expect next, a postponement to the 28th?

"Look," I told Norm, "ten days ago you told me the 21st. Then you wanted the 24th. Now you're asking for the 26th. I've got a President and a Secretary of Defense on my back. They've got a bad Russian peace proposal they're trying to dodge. You've got to give me a better case for postponement. I don't think you understand the pressure I'm under."

Schwarzkopf exploded. "You're giving me political reasons why you don't want to tell the President not to do something militarily unsound!" He was yelling. "Don't you understand? My Marine commander says we need to wait. We're talking about Marines' lives." He had to worry about them, he said, even if nobody else cared.

That did it. I had backed Norm at every step, fended off his critics with one hand while soothing his anxieties with the other. "Don't you pull that on me!" I yelled back. "Don't you try to lay a patronizing guilt trip on me! Don't tell me I don't care about casualties! What are you doing, putting on some kind of show in front of your commanders?"

He was alone, Schwarzkopf said, in his private office, and he was taking as much heat as I was. "You're pressuring me to put aside my military judgment out of political expediency. I've felt this way for a long time!" he said. Suddenly, his tone shifted from anger to despair. "Colin, I feel like my head's in a vise. Maybe I'm losing it. Maybe I'm losing my objectivity."

I took a deep breath. The last thing I needed was to push the commander in the field over the edge on the eve of battle. "You're not losing it," I said. "We've just got a problem we have to work out. You have the full confidence of all of us back here. At the end of the day, you know I'm going to carry your message, and we'll do it your way." It was time to break off the conversation before one of us threw another match into the gasoline.

Within half an hour, Norm was back on the phone with the latest weather update. The 24th and 25th did not look too bad after all. "We're ready," he said. We had a go for the 24th.

It was not my custom to show up at the White House in a turtleneck sweater and sport jacket, but I had been summoned suddenly from home for a meeting at 10:30 on Thursday evening, February 21. I found the President in his study. He had just come from Ford's Theater, where he had seen a great play, he said, Leslie Lee's *Black Eagles,* about the Tuskegee Airmen, the black fighter pilots of World War II fame. Cheney showed up next, wearing a tux, fresh from a reception for the queen of Denmark. The others arrived, rounding out the Gang of Eight. We had to make a decision about Gorbachev's pending peace proposal. The Russian leader had called Bush about it earlier in the evening. The President's problem was how to say no to Gorbachev without appearing to throw away a chance for peace.

"You've got two options," Brent Scowcroft said. "One is to tell the Russians to butt out. The other is to get better conditions and accept."

I looked at Cheney, who was sitting on the arm of a chair. I knew what he was thinking. He disliked and distrusted the Russians and hated seeing them use world opinion to pressure us and then get credit for what might turn out to be a bad solution. He preferred to throw out the Iraqis forcibly.

I could hear the President's growing distress in his voice. "I don't want to take this deal," he said. "But I don't want to stiff Gorbachev, not after he's come this far with us. We've got to find a way out."

I raised a finger. The President turned to me. "Got something, Colin?"

"We don't stiff Gorbachev," I said. I pointed out that world opinion had supported the UN's January 15 deadline for Saddam to clear out of Kuwait. "So let's put a deadline on Gorby's proposal. We say, great idea, as long as they're completely on their way out by, say, noon Saturday. If they go, you get the Nobel Peace Prize, Mr. Gorbachev. If, as I suspect, they don't move, then the flogging begins."

The room was silent as everybody seemed to chew on the idea. "What about that?" the President asked. He quickly won agreement all around, except from Cheney. "What about you, Dick?" The President asked.

Cheney looked as if he had been handed a dead rat. "I guess it's okay," he said.

At 10:40 A.M. the next morning, President Bush stood before the cameras in the Rose Garden. "The coalition will give Saddam Hussein until noon Saturday to do what he must do," a grim-visaged Bush said, "begin his immediate and unconditional withdrawal from Kuwait."

At noon on Saturday, February 23, Saddam let the Russian withdrawal proposal go by and passed the last exit. At 4:00 A.M., Riyadh time, the following day, in darkness and cold rain, U.S. Marines and an Army tank brigade, followed by Saudi, Egyptian, Kuwaiti, Syrian, and other Arab troops, crossed the border into Kuwait. Far to the west, XVIII Airborne Corps jumped off with the 82d Airborne Division and a French light armored division covering the left flank. The 101st Airborne Division (Air Assault) and the 24th Infantry Division (Mechanized) moved straight north into Iraq, heading for the Euphrates River Valley. Between these forces, VII Corps, with the British 1st Armored Division, stood poised to launch the left-hook main attack as soon as it was clear that the supporting attacks were holding the Iraqis in place. The ground war had begun.

Too keyed up to sleep, I stayed in the office and took incoming reports from Tom Kelly and Mike McConnell. I also watched CNN so that I would know the picture the rest of the world was getting. The Marines, rather than merely pinning down the Iraqis, had broken through the enemy defenses and were already moving toward Kuwait City. The way had been prepared by Marine reconnaissance teams who, days before, had exposed themselves to terrifying risks, crawling through the barbed wire and over the oil-filled trenches to lay out cleared lanes for the assault troops to race through.

In the west, General Barry McCaffrey's 24th Infantry Division punched sixty miles into Iraqi territory on the first day. The initial penetrations were so swift and so deep that Schwarzkopf was able to move up the left-hook timetable by fifteen hours. In those twenty-four hours of land combat, ten thousand hungry, thirsty, exhausted Iraqi soldiers, stunned by thirty-eight days of air bombardment, surrendered. Gary Luck's XVIII Airborne Corps alone took 3,200 prisoners, while suffering one man wounded. Our total casualties the first day were eight dead, twenty-seven wounded.

By the morning of the second day, the 1st Marine Division was fighting in and around Kuwait City International Airport. The Marines would have fulfilled their mission even if they had only tied down Iraqi forces. Instead, by the end of the day, they had encircled Kuwait City. An amphibious feint off the Kuwaiti coast tied down more Iraqi units. XVIII Airborne Corps thrust deeper into Iraq. VII Corps, under Lieutenant General Fred Franks, had the master strategic role, the flanking attack from west to east to cut off the Iraqi army in Kuwait and kill it, particularly the vaunted Republican Guard. But VII Corps was not moving as fast as we expected.

On that second day, we suffered a heavy blow. A Soviet-made Scud missile slammed into a makeshift barracks near Dhahran, killing twenty-eight American soldiers. The casualty list presented a harsh reality of our modern army; women were among the victims.

On February 26, the third day, I called Schwarzkopf at about noon his time. I told him that I hated second-guessing field commanders, but I could not understand why VII Corps was still not fully engaged. "Can't you get Fred Franks moving faster?" I asked. Schwarzkopf himself had already been leaning hard on Franks, and was just as happy to pass along additional pressure from the chairman. He soon got back to me with word that VII Corps was finally in the thick of the fight. Franks's troops had almost completely destroyed one Republican Guard division and had driven two others into retreat.

U.S. Marines, U.S. Army Special Forces, and Saudi, Egyptian, Kuwaiti, and other Arab troops liberated Kuwait City. XVIII Airborne Corps was approaching the Euphrates River Valley. Our intelligence indicated that of forty-two Iraqi divisions in the war zone, twenty-seven had already been destroyed or overrun. We had taken 38,000 prisoners and more kept pouring in. Our casualties remained light, though we suffered disturbing losses from friendly fire. Overall, however, the casualty rate was far below even our most optimistic estimates, thanks largely to the constant pounding our air forces were inflicting on the Iraqis.

ᴇ◢◉ɢ

Before the war began, someone on my staff had given me a book entitled *Every War Must End,* by Fred Ikle. I had worked with Ikle when he was undersecretary of defense for policy and I was Cap Weinberger's military assistant. The theme of his book intrigued me, because I had spent two tours in a war that seemed endless and often pointless. Warfare is such an all-absorbing enterprise, Ikle wrote, that after starting one, a government may lose sight of ending it. As he put it:

> Thus it can happen that military men, while skillfully planning their intricate operations and coordinating complicated maneuvers, remain curiously blind in failing to perceive that it is the outcome of the war, not the outcome of the campaigns within it, that determines how well their plans serve the nation's interests. At the same time, the senior statesmen may hesitate to insist that these beautifully planned campaigns be linked to some clear ideas for ending the war....

As an example, Ikle mentioned the cunningly conceived attack on Pearl Harbor, as contrasted to the scant thought the Japanese had given to how the war they started would end. I was so impressed by Ikle's ideas that I had key passages photocopied and circulated to the Joint Chiefs, Cheney, and Scowcroft. We were fighting a limited war under a limited mandate for a limited purpose, which was soon going to be achieved. I thought that the people responsible ought to start thinking about how it would end.

On the afternoon of February 27, Otis Pearson drove me to the White House for the Gang of Eight's daily military briefing. The heavy armor-plated bulletproof Cadillac held the road with a reassuring hug, around the huge Pentagon parking lot, up Route 27 over the Memorial Bridge, and into Washington. As we rode along, words from Ikle's book ran through my mind: "... fighting often continues long past the point where a 'rational' calculation would indicate that the war should be ended."

I had already spoken to Norm Schwarzkopf earlier in the morning and told him I sensed we were nearing endgame. The prisoner catch was approaching seventy thousand. Saddam had ordered his forces to withdraw from Kuwait. The last major escape route, a four-lane highway leading out of Kuwait City toward the Iraqi city of Basrah, had turned into a shooting gallery for our fliers. The road was choked with fleeing soldiers and littered with the charred hulks of nearly fifteen hundred military and civilian vehicles. Reporters began referring to this road as the "Highway of Death."

I would have to give the President and the Secretary a recommendation soon as to when to stop, I told Norm. The television coverage, I added, was starting to make it look as if we were engaged in slaughter for slaughter's sake.

"I've been thinking the same thing," Norm said.

I asked him what he wanted. "One more day should do it," he answered. By then he would be able to declare that Iraq was no longer militarily capable of threatening its neighbors. And he added, "Do you realize, if we stop tomorrow night, the ground campaign will have lasted five days? How does that sound, the Five-Day War?"

Since that chipped one day off the famous victory of the Israelis over the Arab states in 1967, I said, "Not bad. I'll pass it along."

At about 2:00 P.M., I rode through the gate to the West Wing entrance of the White House. Otis let me out, parked, and then discreetly brought me a big black leather map case as I waited in the lobby. I went up the stairway to the left, past the Chief of Staff's office, to avoid going through the reception room. You never knew who you might run into there, from the Soviet ambassador to a Girl Scout delegation. An Air Force officer, Major Bruce Caughman, the President's personal assistant, helped me set up an easel in the Oval Office facing the fireplace.

George Bush was upbeat and relaxed. The Gang of Eight, plus Richard Haas, Scowcroft's Middle East specialist, formed the usual U in front of the fireplace. Someone joked about the President leaving the fire to the pros. At a briefing a couple of days before, Bush had lit the fire himself, without opening the flue. The Oval Office had instantly filled with smoke. Alarms rang. Secret Service agents ran around frantically, throwing doors open, while freezing February winds blew in from the Rose Garden.

This morning, I snapped on the laser pointer and began describing the positions: the Marines and Prince Khaled's Arab force in Kuwait City, VII Corps closing its noose around the Iraqi forces trying to flee Kuwait, with only the Republican Guard still offering any serious resistance. In the far west, XVIII Airborne Corps had driven deep into Iraq to the banks of the Euphrates. When I finished describing the military chessboard, I said, "Mr. President, it's going much better than we expected. The Iraqi army is broken. All they're trying to do now is get out."

Our forces had a specific objective, authorized by the UN, to liberate Kuwait, and we had achieved it. The President had never expressed any desire to exceed that mandate, in spite of his verbal lambasting of Saddam. We presently held the moral high ground. We could lose it by fighting past the "rational calculation" Fred Ikle had warned about. And, as a professional soldier, I honored the warrior's code. "We don't want to be seen as killing for the sake of killing, Mr. President," I said. "We're within the window of success. I've talked to General Schwarzkopf. I expect by sometime tomorrow the job will be done, and I'll probably be bringing you a recommendation to stop the fighting."

"If that's the case," the President said, "why not end it today?" He caught me by surprise. "I'd like you all to think about that," he added, looking around the room. "We're starting to pick up some undesirable public and political baggage with all those scenes of carnage. You say we've accomplished the mission. Why not end it?" He could go on the air and announce a suspension of hostilities this evening, he said.

"That's something to consider," I replied. "But I need to talk to Norm first." I excused myself and went into the President's small private study just off the Oval Office. I picked up a secure phone, and the White House military operator put me through to Riyadh.

"Norm," I said, "the President wants to know if we can end it now."

"When is now?" he asked.

"We're looking at this evening." Given the eight-hour time difference, that would mean stopping the war in the middle of the night in the Gulf region.

"I don't have any problem," Norm said. "Our objective was to drive 'em out, and we've done it. But let me talk to my commanders, and unless they've run into a snag I don't know about, I don't see why we shouldn't stop."

"Cheney and I have to go up to the Hill and brief Congress soon," I said. "We can talk again when I get back."

I did not anticipate any objection from Schwarzkopf's field commanders. Norm had just given a televised press conference from Riyadh at 1:00 P.M. Washington time, and in this now famous "mother of all briefings," he had said, "We've accomplished our mission, and when the decision-makers come to the decision that there should be a cease-fire, nobody will be happier than me." He had also said, regarding the fleeing Iraqi forces, "The gate is closed. There is no way out of here." Later, he amended this statement to: "When I say the gate is closed, I don't want to give the impression that absolutely nothing is escaping." Heavy tanks and artillery were not getting through, he said. "I'm talking about the gate that is closed on the war machine...."

I went back into the Oval Office and reported to the President that the proposal looked okay to Schwarzkopf and to me, but Norm wanted to check with his commanders. No one in the room disagreed with the tentative decision to stop the war. Jim Baker was concerned about the effect on world opinion of pointless killing. Brent Scowcroft thought that fighting beyond necessity would leave a bad taste over what was so far a brilliant military operation. Cheney said that what mattered was achieving the coalition's aims, not how many more tanks we knocked out. We would meet again, however, for one last discussion after Cheney and I returned from Capitol Hill.

Before heading for the Hill, I called the vice chairman, Dave Jeremiah, and told him to brief the chiefs on the President's tentative decision to bring the war to an end. Dave called me later and said that all the chiefs concurred.

Cheney and I briefed the Senate at 3:00 P.M. and the House at 4:30 P.M. Their respective hearing rooms were packed for both presentations. We gave the members essentially the same map-and-chart show we had put on for the President. But we mentioned nothing about the war possibly ending this day.

By 5:30 P.M. we were back at the White House, where we joined the President in the small office off the Oval Office. I took note of the time the President made his final decision to suspend hostilities, 5:57. It was the commander in chief's decision to make, and he had made it. Every member of his policymaking team agreed. Schwarzkopf and I agreed. And there is no doubt in my mind that if Norm or I had had the slightest reservation about stopping now, the President would have given us all the time we needed.

We moved into the Oval Office and started discussing the timing and content of the announcement President Bush would make to the American people that night. He also began calling his coalition partners. We initially considered having the President go on the air at 9:00 P.M. to announce a "suspension of hostilities" as of 0500, February 28, in Riyadh. The word "suspension" was picked deliberately to make clear that this was not a cease-fire negotiated with the Iraqis, but a halt taken on our own initiative. I said that I would like to give Norm a few more hours of daylight so that he could check the battlefield and clean up any loose ends, which prompted an inspiration from John Sununu. "Why not make it effective midnight our time? That'll make it the Hundred-Hour War," John said. The President agreed, and shortly after 6:00 P.M., I got on the phone again with Schwarzkopf. I told him the President would speak at 9:00 our time to announce that the fighting would stop at 8:00 A.M. the following morning Riyadh time. That would give Norm almost the one more day he had asked for in our conversation earlier in the morning.

The President and then Cheney came on the line to congratulate the CINC. "Helluva job, Norm," the President said.

Schwarzkopf was soon back on the phone with a cautionary note. The gate was still slightly open, he told me. Some Republican Guard units and T-72 tanks could slip away. I told him to keep hitting them, and I would get back to him. I passed Norm's report to the President and the others. Although we were all taken slightly aback, no one felt that what we had heard changed the basic equation. The back of the Iraqi army had been broken. What was left of it was retreating north. There was no need to fight a battle of annihilation to see how many more combatants on both sides could be killed. Obviously, the President would have preferred total capitulation, the way World War II had ended. And we knew, barring a lucky bomb hit, that Saddam would likely survive the war. We further accepted that we would face criticism from some quarters for not continuing the fight. However, we had a clear mandate, and it was being achieved. The President reaffirmed his decision to end the fighting. I then called Schwarzkopf again and relayed to him that the White House understood that there would be some leakage of Iraqi forces, but that this condition was acceptable.

At 9:02 P.M., the President spoke to the nation from the Oval Office. "Kuwait is liberated. Iraq's army is defeated. Our military objectives are met," he began. "I am pleased to announce that at midnight tonight, eastern standard time, exactly one hundred hours since ground operations commenced and six weeks since the start of Operation Desert Storm, all U.S. and coalition forces will suspend offensive combat operations."

After the President's speech, he and Mrs. Bush invited the group up to the residential quarters for a quiet celebration. The ushers passed drinks around, and I sipped my usual rum and Coke. The atmosphere was one of relief more than festivity. We had not given George Bush another V-E Day. Still, he said, "I'm comfortable. No second thoughts." We had done the right thing, he believed, and we had prevailed. Within an hour I was back at Quarters 6 at Fort Myer. I wanted to tell Alma that we had just won a war. But she was already asleep.

⚜

Over 130 years after the event, historians are still debating General George Meade's decision not to pursue General Robert E. Lee's forces after the Union victory at Gettysburg. A half century after World War II, scholars are still arguing over General Eisenhower's decision not to beat the Soviet armies to Berlin. And, I expect, years from now, historians will still ask if we should not have fought longer and destroyed more of the Iraqi army. Critics argue that we should have widened our war aims to include seizing Baghdad and driving Saddam Hussein from power, as we had done with Noriega and the Panama Defense Force in Panama. The critics include even Admiral Crowe, who testified in Congress for continued sanctions and against going to war; but in his memoirs he argues that we should have continued fighting and expanded the mission to go after Saddam Hussein.

Matters were not helped when, one month after the war's end, Norm Schwarzkopf appeared on a PBS program, *Talking with David Frost.* Regarding the decision to end the fighting, Norm first said, "I reported that situation to General Powell. And he and I discussed, have we accomplished our military objectives, the campaign objectives. And the answer is yes." But a moment later, Norm said, "Frankly, my recommendation had been, you know, continue the march. I mean, we had them in a rout and we could have continued, you know, to reap great destruction upon them."

The next morning the direct White House line on my console rang with that insistent shrillness that made me sit at attention. George Bush sounded more hurt than angered. What did Norm mean? He had certainly been consulted about stopping the fighting. The war would not have ended then if he had asked for more time. "I talked to Norm myself," the President said.

I shared the President's disappointment. In fact, I was mad as hell at what Schwarzkopf had told David Frost. I called Norm in Riyadh. "That story won't fly," I said. "You're saying the President made a mistake. You make it look as if you gave him a different recommendation, and he ignored it."

"That's not what I meant at all," Norm replied.

"That's what came across," I said. "And the media are beating up on him."

Norm Schwarzkopf was, deservedly, a national hero. And the criticism that the fighting had stopped too soon had chipped his pedestal. He did not like it. The President, ever loyal, learned that Norm was feeling abused and called him once again, telling him not to worry. Still, I felt it was important to keep the record straight. Schwarzkopf had been a party to the decision, and now he seemed to be distancing himself from it. I put out a public statement, after clearing it with Norm, that read: "General Schwarzkopf and I both supported terminating Desert Storm combat operations at 12:00 midnight, 27 February 1991 (EST), as did all the President's advisors.... There was no contrary recommendation. There was no disagreement. There was no debate."

Norm began to back off from his Frost statement, and in his book, *It Doesn't Take a Hero,* he explained his thinking:

> My gut reaction was that a quick cease-fire would save lives. If we continued to attack through Thursday, more of our troops would get killed, probably not many, but some. What was more, we'd accomplished our mission: I'd just finished telling the American people that there wasn't enough left of Iraq's army for it to be a regional military threat... we'd kicked this guy's butt, leaving no doubt in anybody's mind that we'd won decisively, and we'd done it with very few casualties. Why not end it? Why get somebody else killed tomorrow? That made up my mind.

Schwarzkopf was absolutely right. Yet, it is still hard to drive a stake through charges that the job was left unfinished. The truth is that Iraq began the war with an army of over a million men, approximately half of whom were committed to the Kuwait theater of operations, where they were mauled. Iraq took such a battering in the Gulf War that four years afterward, its army is half its original size. And within the Iraqi ranks, I am sure that horror stories are told about what it was like to endure the wrath from the skies and on the ground during Desert Storm. The remaining Iraqi army is hardly a force with a will to fight to the death.

In October 1994, Saddam Hussein sent twenty thousand Republican Guards toward the Kuwaiti border, a paltry attempt to look tough while trying to get relief from UN sanctions. Immediately, the cry went up from the simple-solutionists: if only Saddam had been polished off during the Gulf War, he would not be stirring up trouble now. On October 23, the *New York Times* printed on its front page a long excerpt from a book on the Gulf War coauthored by one of the paper's reporters. The book excerpt was headlined "How Iraq Escaped to Threaten Kuwait Again." In it, the authors stated that "much of Iraq's crack troops, the Republican Guard, had not been destroyed," and that was why Saddam could still wield threatening military power.

While the belief that Saddam pulled off some sort of Dunkirk at the end of Desert Storm may have a superficial attraction, I want to cut it off and kill it once and for all. It is true that more tanks and Republican Guard troops escaped from Kuwait than we expected. And yes, we could have taken another day or two to close that escape hatch. And yes, we could have killed, wounded, or captured every single soldier in the Republican Guard in that trap. But it would not have made a bit of difference in Saddam's future conduct. Iraq, a nation of twenty million people, can always pose a threat to its tiny neighbor, Kuwait, with only 750,000 people. With or without Saddam and with or without the Republic Guard, Kuwait's security depends on arrangements with its friends in the region and the United States. That is the strategic reality. The other reality is that in 1991 we met the Iraqi army in the field and, while fulfilling the United Nation's objectives, dealt it a crushing defeat and left it less than half of what it had been.

But why didn't we push on to Baghdad once we had Saddam on the run? Why didn't we finish him off? Or, to put it another way, why didn't we move the goalposts? What tends to be forgotten is that while the United States led the way, we were heading an *international* coalition carrying out a clearly defined UN mission. That mission was accomplished. The President even hoped to bring all the troops home by July 4, which would have been dramatic but proved logistically impossible. He had promised the American people that Desert Storm would not become a Persian Gulf Vietnam, and he kept his promise.

From the geopolitical standpoint, the coalition, particularly the Arab states, never wanted Iraq invaded and dismembered. Before the fighting, I received a copy of a cable sent by Charles Freeman, the U.S. ambassador to Saudi Arabia. "For a range of reasons," Freeman said, "we cannot pursue Iraq's unconditional surrender and occupation by us. It is not in our interest to destroy Iraq or weaken it to the point that Iran and/or Syria are not constrained by it." Wise words, Mr. Ambassador. It would not contribute to the stability we want in the Middle East to have Iraq fragmented into separate Sunni, Shia, and Kurd political entities. The only way to have avoided this outcome was to have undertaken a largely U.S. conquest and occupation of a remote nation of twenty million people. I don't think that is what the American people signed up for.

Of course, we would have loved to see Saddam overthrown by his own people for the death and destruction he had brought down on them. But that did not happen. And the President's demonizing of Saddam as the devil incarnate did not help the public understand why he was allowed to stay in power. It is naive, however, to think that if Saddam had fallen, he would necessarily have been replaced by a Jeffersonian in some sort of desert democracy where people read *The Federalist Papers* along with the Koran. Quite possibly, we would have wound up with a Saddam by another name.

Often, as I travel around the country, parents will come up to me and say, "General, we want you to know our son"—or daughter—"fought in the Gulf War." I am always a little apprehensive when I ask, "I hope everything turned out all right." They usually say yes and express their thanks that their soldier came home safely. One hundred and forty-seven Americans gave their lives in combat in the Gulf; another 236 died from accidents and other causes. Small losses as military statistics go, but a tragedy for each family. I have met some of these families, and their loss is heartbreaking. Sadly, their tragedy is compounded by the high incidence of casualties caused by friendly fire. I am relieved that I don't have to say to many more parents, "I'm sorry your son or daughter died in the siege of Baghdad." I stand by my role in the President's decision to end the war when and how he did. It is an accountability I carry with pride and without apology.

Not only did Desert Storm accomplish its political objective, it started to reverse the climate of chronic hostility in the Middle East. King Hussein of Jordan and Yasser Arafat, chairman of the PLO, were the only two major Arab leaders who showed any support for the Iraqi position during the Gulf War, and both were weakened by their stance. As a result, three years later, they were trying to reach accommodations with Israel and their other neighbors. The Madrid Middle East Peace Conference, following Desert Storm, started the process that resulted in the historic agreement between Arafat and Israeli Prime Minister Rabin in September 1993 and the peace treaty between King Hussein and Israel in October 1994. The United States today enjoys access to the region denied before Desert Storm. Even the hostages in Lebanon were released in the aftermath of the conflict. And Iraq remains weak and isolated, kept in check by UN inspectors. Not a bad bottom line.

I am content with the judgment rendered on Desert Storm by probably the world's foremost contemporary military historian, John Keegan. "The Gulf War, whatever it is now fashionable to say," Keegan has written, "was a triumph of incisive planning and almost faultless execution." It fulfilled the highest purpose of military action: "the use of force in the cause of order."

The Generals' War

T hree weeks after the war ended, Schwarzkopf went to visit Walt Boomer and the rest of the Marine high command for an off-the-record discussion.

The war was over, but a new battle for the public mind had begun. The CENTCOM chief had worked hard to shape the public's impression during the war. The press has been controlled and the Iraqi threat painted in the darkest hues. Schwarzkopf had even weighed the public relations factor in planning military operations: he had told the Marines that one drawback of a Marine raid on Faylakah Island was that the media might portray the quick insertion and withdrawal of an amphibious force as a defeat for the allies.

Now Schwarzkopf was determined to come out ahead in the public relations battles. The general recalled how the book writers and the journalists had dissected the Grenada operation and highlighted its faults.

"Watch out what you say. Why do I say that? Because we have people interviewing everyone they can get their hands on. They are out writing their books," Schwarzkopf warned, according to a transcript the Marines kept of the meeting. "Just think of the reputation of the United States military, what it is today, compared to what it was six months ago. I think we ought to be very proud of what we did here, and don't allow those bastards to rob us of that."[1]

With their place in the history books at stake, the commanders sought to shape the war's legacy. So did the military services, as they struggled over the declining military budget.

Having urged his commanders not to cooperate with authors, Schwarzkopf turned around and wrote a book, which gave himself the lion's share of the credit for the allies' success. He also told subordinates that he had not second-guessed his commanders once the war was under way, ignoring his upbraiding of Franks. "I am a centralized planner and a decentralized executor. Just that simple," Schwarzkopf boasted to Boomer and his staff. "You have to have confidence in your subordinates. If you don't have, you get rid of them, and get someone that does. You don't micromanage on the battlefield because nobody has a better idea than the guy fighting the battle."

But even with the benefit of reflection, Schwarzkopf's book failed to recognize the significance of the battle of Khafji and how it had challenged CENTCOM's basic assumption that the Iraqis would stand and fight. Nor did

From Michael R. Gordon and Bernard E. Trainor, *The Generals' War: The Inside Story of the Conflict in the Gulf* (Little, Brown, 1995). Copyright © 1995 by Michael R. Gordon and Bernard E. Trainor. Reprinted by permission of Little, Brown and Company, Inc.

it acknowledge how his plan to let the Marines launch an all-out attack to the gates of Kuwait City while holding back the main Army attack made it easier for the Iraqis to get away. Instead, he blamed Franks for the failure to complete the destruction of the Republican Guard.

For Powell, the Gulf War was a way to restore the prestige and status the American military had lost during the Vietnam War. After the war, Powell oversaw the publication of the Joint Chiefs of Staff manual on military doctrine that touted the Gulf War as a "triumph of joint operational art." Powell was right that there was much of which to be proud. But when embarrassing examples of problems began to surface, Powell privately cautioned one Pentagon-based general against revealing disputes within the military family.

Neither Powell nor Schwarzkopf, however, had the last word, and the plethora of competing accounts from within the military establishment soon produced a cacophony.

The Army responded to Schwarzkopf's criticisms in a book-length account, entitled *Certain Victory,* that defended Franks's generalship and suggested that any misunderstandings stemmed from Schwarzkopf's inability to grasp the complexity of the battlefield from his distant Riyadh command post.[2]

To Schwarzkopf's consternation, the Army ignored his recommendation that Waller, not Franks, later be made the four-star head of the Army's Training and Doctrine Command. ("History is being revised to cover up the fact that Franks was not a very aggressive commander," Schwarzkopf said later, referring to the official Army accounts of the war. "It makes you feel bad that the institution you are serving is stretching its integrity."[3])

In an attempt to magnify the Army's accomplishments and minimize its shortcomings, the Army study claimed that airpower had had little effect on the Republican Guard. The Army account also asserted that most of the Iraqi army was north of Basra before the XVIII Airborne and VII Corps had a chance to cut it off. But that analysis was contradicted by a comprehensive CIA assessment, based on surveillance photos, that showed that the bulk of the Iraqi force that escaped was still south of Basra and in the Army's path at war's end.

The Air Force, for its part, portrayed the war as a vindication of the long quest to achieve a victory through airpower, boasting that airpower had destroyed Iraq's weapons of mass destruction, severed its lines of communication, and cut off the Iraqi troops. Lt. Gen. Charles Horner also sought to burnish his own record. The Air Force commander, who had rebuffed John Warden's Instant Thunder plan, never acknowledged Warden's role as an architect of the air campaign. Horner also told Congress that he was not aware of any disputes within CENTCOM, overlooking his threat to have Steve Arnold evicted from the Kuwaiti theater because of his complaints that the Army-nominated targets were not being hit.

On the whole, however, the Air Force was much more forthright than the Army. Air Force Secretary Donald Rice commissioned an independent survey of the use of airpower during the war—the "Gulf War Air Power Survey"—which in a scholarly and analytical way dissected the lessons of the war and defined airpower's limits. The study's analysis of the problems in hunting Scud missiles, neutralizing the Iraqi command structure, and destroying Iraq's weapons of mass destruction were not welcome by everyone in the Air Force. In an April 1993 memo, the official Air Force historian, Richard Hallion, himself the author of a book touting the use of airpower in the Gulf, suggested that the report be withheld. But the Air Force leadership, to its credit, ignored Hallion's suggestion and published the lengthy critique.[4]

The Marines, whose success had surprised Schwarzkopf and unintentionally contributed to the unraveling of CENTCOM's plan, also engaged in a measure of self-criticism. In a series of unclassified after-action reports, the Marines discussed their problems in clearing minefields and acknowledged their limited ability to use precision-guided weapons. The tensions between the Marine commandant and the Corps's top commander in the Gulf, however, was kept under wraps.

Navy officials, resentful at being overshadowed by the Air Force, were quick to highlight the glitches in the centralized system the Air Force generals established for running the war. Still, the service quietly acted on the lessons of the Gulf conflict. Navy officials acknowledged that their decision to stay aloof from joint military operations and to command its Gulf force from sea, instead of from Riyadh, was a mistake. Soon after the war, the Navy moved its one-star representative to CENTCOM from Honolulu to Tampa. More significantly, it revised its doctrine, deciding to concentrate on littoral warfare instead of using its carriers primarily to mount strikes deep into the enemy homeland.

It was not only the military leaders who tried to shape history. The civilian leadership of the Pentagon oversaw the official Defense Department history of the war. The politic document steered clear of the war's sharpest controversies. All services were afforded equal billing in what was deemed to be an unqualified victory, and the report sidestepped the issue of whether the war was ended prematurely before the military objectives were reached. When a senior civilian official, I. Lewis Libby, interviewed Schwarzkopf, he pointedly avoided the issue of termination.

The American defense establishment was not alone in its concern with the verdict of history.

Prince Khalid also sought to embellish the history of the Arab members of the coalition. In a long statement—"The Gulf War: Setting the Record Straight" —Khalid rejected any claims of faint-heartedness by the Syrian members of the coalition, made by Schwarzkopf publicly and privately by other American officers, and claimed that CENTCOM failed to provide adequate air support during the battle of Khafji.[5]

In Iraq, Saddam Hussein sought to capitalize on his defeat, restoring the morale in his army with lavish pay and awards and blaming Iraq's deteriorating economy on the American-inspired sanctions, not on the war. Turning history on its head, the Iraqi leader held up the war as a victory, boasting that he fought a brilliant delaying action in Kuwait, thus preventing the allies from crossing the Euphrates into Iraq's interior. What other army but the Iraqi could have achieved such a feat? he boasted. In the face of over half a million enemies, Iraq's army was still intact and the nation was still under the leadership of Saddam Hussein.

Emboldened by his ability to hold on to power, Saddam Hussein also claimed in the months after the war that his principal mistake was that he was not audacious enough, citing his failure to invade Saudi Arabia to preempt the American military buildup and his failure to exploit the hostages. But those remarks showed that the Iraqi leader still failed to appreciated the extent of his miscalculation.

If Saddam Hussein had been less audacious and contented himself with seizing the Rumaila oil field or the Bubiyan and Warbah islands, he probably could have pressed the Kuwaitis into making financial concessions, intimidated Saudi Arabia, and undermined the United States' credibility in the Gulf while avoiding a direct confrontation with the American military, Schwarzkopf and other American officials acknowledged. But by seizing all of Kuwait he over-played his hand. He provoked Washington at an ideal time for U.S. forces. The American military had reached a high level of training and technological pro-ficiency to counter the Soviets only to see its enemy disappear, but had yet to undergo the deep cuts mandated by budgetary pressures in Washington.

Even the Russians sought to redefine the war. In their study of the war the Russian military vigorously assailed any suggestion that Iraq's Soviet-supplied weapons were ineffective as a "propaganda trick by the West" and blamed Iraqi incompetence for the defeat. The Russians acknowledged the value of the al-lies' high-tech weapons systems, surveillance planes, and spy satellites, but also underscored their limitations.

"Reconnaissance data did not always reflect the actual Iraqi armed forces losses and deceived the higher political leadership of the United States rela-tive to the level of Iraq's combat potential, which led to adoption of incorrect decisions," the Russian report stated. "Thus, basing itself on this very recon-naissance data concerning the 'unacceptable losses by Iraq in men and materiel,' U.S. President G. Bush made the decision to halt military actions on the ground, literally four days after they had begun. All this speaks to the underestima-tion of the capabilities of the enemy due to the low reliability of intelligence information."[6]

As for George Bush, he portrayed the Persian Gulf War as the prototype of the post–cold war conflict. Bush predicted that future adversaries who studied it would think twice before challenging the United States.

"I think because of what has happened, we won't have to use U.S. forces around the world," Bush said the day after the war. "I think when we say some-thing that is objectively correct, like don't take over a neighbor, or you're going to bear some responsibility, people are going to listen because I think out of all this will be a newfound—put it this way, a reestablished credibility for the United States of America."

To some extent, Bush was right. The respect for American military tech-nology and the quality of American troops was greatly enhanced.

In the Middle East, where the nations had the closest view of the fighting, the conflict had a profound influence on the region. As a consequence of the air and ground campaigns, and the regimen of United Nations inspections, postwar Iraq was no longer an imminent nuclear menace and a threat to its neighbors. The United States had sent a message that oil was the lifeblood of the modern world and that Washington would do whatever was necessary to make sure it flowed.

Still, the failure to topple the Saddam Hussein regime meant that Iraq was still a potential menace to the Kurds, whom Washington had promised to protect, and a daily threat to the Shiites, who were afforded only partial protection, and to other states in the region. Nearly four years after the war, the United Nations embargo on Iraq was coming under increasing challenge in the Security Council from Turkey, France, and Russia, who saw economic benefits in dealing with Baghdad. The difficulty in sustaining the embargo and the cadre of trained scientists in Iraq posed the risk that Baghdad might be able to revive its programs to build weapons of mass destruction.

And while American ties to the Persian Gulf states were strengthened, the resistance to an overt American role in the region continued. The Saudis blocked the Bush administration's plans to store a division's worth of American armor equipment at King Khalid Military City and declined to acknowledge publicly that American Air Force planes were launching patrols of southern Iraq from Saudi airfields. CENTCOM's plans to establish a forward headquarters in Bahrain or other Gulf states were quietly dropped.

More broadly, despite President Bush's hope that the Gulf War would send a message of American resolve to troublemakers around the world, the conflict has become an anomaly in a world dominated by small wars in Somalia, Bosnia, and other distant trouble spots in which American credibility has been an early casualty.

But the legacy of the Gulf War will be determined not only by the actions of its generals, but by its implications for the future. If the conflict in the Gulf was not the war to end all wars, it has had enduring consequences and offered military and political lessons. It was a laboratory for the American military's new weapons and fighting doctrines, a test of the services' abilities to work together, an object lesson in the failure of deterrence and in the problems of war termination.

Limitations of the Powell Doctrine

Shaped by the Vietnam experience, the American military fashioned a winning strategy. Overwhelming force would be used. The enemy would be given no sanctuary; nor would there by any diplomatic pauses to let enemy forces catch their breath. It would be the generals, not civilian targeteers in Washington, who would pick the targets. A decisive victory would be achieved and American forces would be quickly withdrawn so as not to become entangled in the war's messy aftermath.

American power, it was said, would be like a raging thunderstorm, not a steady shower. The doctrine was applied in the invasions of Panama and Grenada with good results. Powell and Schwarzkopf made sure that it was applied to the Gulf as well. There was much in the approach that contributed to the success in the Gulf. With their unrelenting air and ground attacks, the allies seized and maintained the initiative. The air strikes against Baghdad and other targets in central Iraq and the armor operations deep into the Iraqi desert surprised and confounded the Iraqis. The Iraqi military was defeated at an astoundingly small cost in allied lives.

But the iron link between the use of military force and a decisive outcome had its political costs. First, it inhibited the Bush administration in August 1990 from maneuvering military forces in the Arabian Sea and Persian Gulf to deter Iraqi attacks on Kuwait and contributed to the failure of deterrence. When civilians at the State Department and the Pentagon recommended such demonstrations of American power, Powell fended them off.

Second, the Powell doctrine contributed to the decision to bring the war to a premature close and to the muddled ending and left Washington without a means for influencing events in postwar Iraq.

The military impulse to end the war as soon as a "victory" was achieved, to get out as quickly as possible, and to view support of the insurgents in southern Iraq not as a way to squeeze the Saddam Hussein regime but as a snare limited American military power as an instrument for shaping and enforcing the peace. Powell's all-or-nothing doctrine of decisive force not only is insufficient for many of the smoldering conflicts the United States faces today, where the military is called on not to win a decisive "victory" but to support diplomacy, protect peacekeepers, or carry out humanitarian tasks, it also has its limitations when it comes to ending major "high-intensity" wars.

Unrealistic Expectations About Casualties

The Gulf conflict created new expectations for low casualties in warfare in the mind of the public and within the military establishment. Historically, the United States has been willing to shed considerable blood to win what it viewed as "wars of survival," such as World War II. Loss was incidental to the mission. The United States liberally sacrificed its own sons and had no compunction about destroying its enemies. But one question raised by the Gulf War is whether commanders can be ruthless enough to pursue the enemy to the limits in the television age when the stakes are less than national survival.

In overseeing the air and ground campaigns, Powell and the White House were concerned not only about holding down American losses and civilian casualties, but about limiting the destruction of enemy combatants, as was evident in Washington's concern over the press reports about the "Highway of Death" and the Bush administration's decision to end the ground war at 100 hours and abjure going to Baghdad. This decision helped the American public lose touch with the reality of war—a grim, ghastly, and bloody affair. The American military has become a victim of its own success.

Concern over holding down casualties—from enemy attack and friendly fire—has become a constant in American planning for war. The assumption in the Pentagon today is that any military incursion must be low in cost to be politically feasible. While low casualties are desirable, the expectation that losses will be minimal on a fluid battlefield may inhibit the future use of force as an instrument of national power.

The expectation of low casualties has also undermined President Bush's hope that the Gulf War would send a message of American resolve to troublemakers around the world. In Somalia, Gen. Mohammed Farah Aidid used Saddam Hussein's strategy of trying to draw out the confrontation, bleed the Americans, and wait for public opinion to turn against military involvement. With no oil supplies at stake and the Americans supporting the mission more out of charity than animus toward a third-world tyrant, Aidid's approach worked. In Bosnia, Serb forces tightened their hold on the territory they wrested from the Muslims, knowing that NATO would limit itself to episodic threats to launch air strikes.

The All-Volunteer Military Is a Success

The war confirmed the military's personnel policy of relying on a well-trained volunteer force. The power and effectiveness of American troops, weapons, and equipment was so impressive as to leave no doubt that the United States is the most powerful military nation on earth. The United States brought to the battlefield an integrated system of sensors, stealth, electronic suppression techniques, and precision munitions designed to counter Soviet-style warfare on the European continent. It proved its worth in the desert. High technology was key to American military dominance.

The other strong suit the United States brought to the battlefield was the quality of its armed forces. Never in the history of the republic has a more competent and proficient military been fielded. The high quality displayed by all the services is a function of four things: high-caliber personnel, professional education, realistic and continuous training, and leadership.

The United States military operates with a pyramidal organizational structure. But while the structure is rigid, the execution is flexible in that subordinates are expected to take the action necessary to meet the mission goals. This fosters innovation and creativity.

The effectiveness of this system was demonstrated in countless ways during the Gulf War as service personnel coped with the unexpected. Without such a system of leadership, even the best weaponry and equipment in the hands of well-trained troops would not have been brought to bear effectively. As the result of this system, the logistical and operational deficiencies that emerged during the course of the deployment and war were solved by the initiative of scores of unnamed, unknown, and frequently unrewarded enlisted men and women and junior officers.

Military Reforms to Encourage Joint Service Warfare Are Incomplete

"Jointness" became the military's mantra after the passage of the Goldwater-Nichols Act in 1986. There was no intent to erase the differences in service philosophies and cultures. The idea was that the unique characteristics and strengths of each service could be molded to complement one another so that the whole would be more than the sum of its parts.

The reforms also strengthened the role of the chairman of the JCS and of field commanders. As a result, Powell wielded power and influence beyond that exercised by previous chairmen. His fellow members of the Joint Chiefs were relegated to onlookers who simply provided the forces. As for Schwarzkopf, he was the king of his domain. During the war, no serious attempt was made by any of the services to go around Schwarzkopf. A service chief could not even visit the Gulf without his permission.

But the Gulf War showed there is much to be done if the services are to operate in a truly joint manner.

At the outset of the Gulf crisis, Schwarzkopf himself violated the spirit of jointness. He imported a special team of planners—the Jedis—to draw up the ground offensive strategy. They initially excluded a Marine representative, even though the Marines had almost all of their combat forces committed to the campaign, but they invited a British officer. It was not a deliberate slight, but an unconscious reflection of service culture. For decades, the Army had focused on Europe. It had more in common with a long-standing NATO ally than it did with a service with which it rarely associated.

The air war was also riddled with interservice tensions. To run the air war, a Joint Forces Air Component Commander was created. The Air Force dominated the process. Its planners believed in centralized control of airpower and attacks against targets critical to the overall campaign, but the Army, Marine Corps, and Navy were unhappy with the system. The Air Force believed it was weakening the enemy by hitting Iraqi forces at home and within the "kill boxes" it drew on battlefield maps, but the Army and Marines complained that specific targets were ignored that they wanted to be hit. With the services at odds, the Marines tried to cut some corners by withholding planes from the Air Force–run campaign. And in the final days of the war, the Air Force was frustrated when the Army moved the Fire Support Coordination Line, which defined the area in which air strikes could not be carried out without coordination of ground commanders, so far forward that aircraft could not freely attack targets fleeing from the advancing allied troops.

At sea, the Navy and the Marines had their differences. The Navy was oriented around the aircraft carrier and had little interest in planning amphibious operations. The Marines had to dispatch a special team of amphibious planners from the United States to get the Navy to think seriously about attacks from the sea.

Even within the Army, there were differences that influenced performance. Heavy in armor, the Germany-based VII Corps was organized, trained, and equipped to fight the Soviet Army. Meticulous planning and deliberate synchronization were its hallmarks. Based in the United States as a central reserve, the XVIII Corps was not NATO-oriented, but ready to go anywhere in the world against any enemy.

The cultural differences between the services and Schwarzkopf's decentralized command policy, which gave maximum freedom of action within the framework of his overall plan, combined to frustrate the allies' carefully crafted strategy to destroy the Republican Guard. The problem was compounded by Powell and Schwarzkopf's failure to see Khafji as the defining moment in the war and by the services' differing interpretations of the battle. The Air Force was convinced that Khafji showed the failure of the Iraqi army to maneuver on the battlefield in the face of allied air superiority. The Marines were convinced of it too. They had taken the measure of the Iraqis at Khafji. But the Army, and the CENTCOM staff, continued their preparations as if the Iraqis were determined to put up a stiff fight.

CENTCOM planners counted on the Marines holding the enemy in place in southern Iraq so that VII Corps could launch its planned seven-to-ten-day offensive on the following day. But the rapid Marine advance on the first day of the ground war knocked the VII Corps's timetable into a cocked hat. The Marine action should not have been a surprise given the commitment the Marines have to offensive operations. Either Schwarzkopf should not have yielded to the Marines' entreaty that they be allowed to undertake a major ground offensive against the Iraqi forces defending Kuwait, or the Marines should have been held back until the main Army offensive was under way.

Doctrinal differences among the services still exist and are frequently papered over. The services that depend most on support from their sister services —the Army is a prime example—champion jointness, at least as long as their central role is preserved. Services capable of semiautonomous action, like the Air Force, tend to go their separate ways. While the differences among the services are often an asset, it is not enough to let the services fight as they see fit. An effort must be made to harmonize their plans and operations.

The Potential and Limitations of Airpower

Since the dawn of military aviation, airpower advocates have sought victory through airpower. Appalled by the carnage of trench warfare, they looked to the airplane as the key to future warfare.

Conventional airpower played a critical but unfulfilled role in World War II and the Korean War. Airpower never severed supply lines during the Vietnam War. When it came to the Gulf War, however, airpower advocates claimed that technology had finally caught up with doctrine and that air warfare would finally make good on its potential. With the advent of new and precise systems to acquire and destroy targets with a single missile, Air Force theoreticians and strategists maintained that the war could be won entirely through the air. Billy Mitchell's dream would be fulfilled.

The air campaign was impressive. Even though the air traffic within the theater was extremely heavy, with different types of aircraft and helicopters from different services and countries flying to and fro, the airspace management systems were effective and remarkably, there were no mid-air collisions during the war.

The Air Force did deliver on its promise to make any ground offensive a walkover. Several factors contributed to the collapse of the Iraqi army, including poor leadership and lack of motivation in the face of the international coalition. Nonetheless, the air attacks made it impossible for the Iraqis to mount an effective defense. Airpower crippled the Iraqi war machine. It neutralized sophisticated air defense systems, destroyed bridges and road junctions, destroyed the Iraqi artillery, and made it difficult for Iraq to maneuver forces on the battle-field. While the success of the bombing campaign against the Iraqi forces varied from unit to unit, it delivered a devastating psychological blow. Airpower did this at negligible cost to itself. The ground war was won in four days; but it was preceded by five weeks of bombing.

But the air campaign was not perfect, and it did not fulfill the Air Force dream of victory through airpower. The Iraqis proved adept at deception and camouflage. An air campaign can be no better than the intelligence it is based on, and the intelligence community was unaware of the extent of Iraq's nuclear program and facilities. The same was true of its Scud inventory. And as it turned out, more damage was done to the economic infrastructure than was intended. Electrical systems that were critical to Saddam Hussein's command and control were also critical to civilized urban life.

More important, if war is an extension of politics, it should have achieved a political success comparable to the military one, defeating Saddam Hussein as well as his army. The air-war planners aimed at winning the war by destroying Iraq's governing infrastructure and causing Saddam Hussein's overthrow.

The air-war planners chafed under the restrictions imposed by Powell on bombing missions in Baghdad. Even so, the air campaign was much more in-tense and sustained than John Warden's Instant Thunder plan. Saddam Hussein survived the war with his political and security apparatus intact. The Gulf War confirmed the Air Force's ever-increasing ability to destroy military things and people. But airpower had not demonstrated an ability to change governments.

For Want of a Nail

In war, as in other human affairs, it is the little things that count. Benefit-ing from the Reagan military buildup, the military used the most advanced high technology against the Iraqis. It used F-117 stealth bombers, surveillance drones, cruise missiles, and "fire-finder" radars that pinpointed enemy artillery and diesel-powered tanks. The widespread use of handheld global positioning system devices enabled the Army to determine its position in the vast Iraqi desert, a feat that eluded the Iraqis.

The high-tech weapons were not perfect. Some "smart bombs" missed their targets. But they succeeded beyond any reasonable expectation and helped the allies trump their enemy. The criticism that America's weapons were too complex and fragile to work in war was dispelled.

But the weak side of the Reagan military buildup was also exposed. In its single-minded pursuit of high-tech weaponary, the military ignored some unglamorous but essential areas.

The Marines lacked the mine-clearing gear they needed to breach Iraqi for-tifications. Given the proliferation of mines around the world, it was a glaring deficiency and the Marines were forced to turn to the Israelis for help.

The Navy also lacked the capability to sweep mines at sea, which would have made it difficult to carry out an amphibious landing had one been re-quired. Its recommendation was to destroy the Iraq minesweepers before the mines were laid—a preemptive policy that was politically infeasible as a matter of coalition politics and was a poor substitute for counter-mine capability.

Nor did the Navy have a sufficient number of ships to rapidly transport American forces to the distant Gulf.

Air Force pilots lacked radios to communicate with search and rescue teams without giving away their positions. And pilots were captured as a result. Had the Gulf War occurred just a few years later, the service would have been without the F-4Gs that contributed mightily to the air campaign. The Air Force plan—since revised—was to retire the planes.

The Army had plenty of 5,000-gallon fueling trucks, but not enough HEMTTs, special vehicles that could plow through the desert to deliver fuel to thirsty divisions. Its communications were distressingly fragile for fast-paced armor operations.

Ever-declining military budgets raise the risk that deficiencies will be compounded, not fixed. Mundane areas of national defense, which do little to burnish the services' prestige and force structure during peacetime, are vital during war.

War Termination

The untidy end to the conflict showed that it is not enough to plan a war. Civilian and military officials must also plan for the peace that follows. Civilian policy-makers also had not given much thought to the possibility that Iraq might break apart, let alone to the prospect that Saddam Hussein's foes might call on the allies for protection. Their failure to anticipate the upheaval in Iraq, their ignorance of the Shiites, and the White House's ambivalence about committing itself to toppling Saddam Hussein reflected the administration's absence of a clear political strategy for postwar Iraq—all of which was reflected in the negotiations at Safwan.

The decision to end the war can be analyzed at several levels. In terms of CENTCOM's military objectives, the decision to terminate the ground war at 100 hours was too hastily made amid the confusing swirl of battlefield events. From the start, CENTCOM's objective was not just to defeat the Republican Guard, render it "combat ineffective," or chase it out of southern Iraq, but to destroy the force. But that goal was not fulfilled. Half of the Republican Guard got away.

Bush administration officials later explained the allied advance was halted to avoid—as Cheney put it—the spectacle of "piling on" and to hold down American casualties. American field commanders later said, however, they could have driven to the gates of Basra and cut off much of the Iraqi army without a wholesale slaughter. The Iraqis could also have been encouraged to abandon their vehicles and walk north if the word had been passed to them in time. Instead, one day's worth of news reports about the Iraqi soldiers caught on the "Highway of Death" helped persuade the Bush administration to end the war.

Some senior administration officials said that they would not have supported ending the war so soon had they been informed that half of the Republican Guard tanks were likely to escape. But obtaining accurate battle damage assessments had been a problem throughout the war when the Iraqi troops were hunkered down and even more of a problem once the American and Iraqi troops were on the move. Powell and the White House decided to end the war based on initial, fragmentary intelligence reports instead of waiting for a fuller accounting.

In terms of the administration's overall political strategy, the premature end to the war was defensible if the goal was restricted to liberating Kuwait, blunting Saddam Hussein's offensive power, and allowing his government to use his diminished military to prevent the breakup of the country. But if the administration's aim was also to undermine the Saddam Hussein regime and afford a measure of protection to the Shiites, two objectives Washington specifically embraced after the war, the failure to complete the destruction of the Republican Guard detracted from those goals since it gave Saddam Hussein more loyal troops to suppress his enemies.

The United States also erred in renouncing any intention of going to Baghdad, a reassurance aimed at our Arab allies. This self-denial simplified things for Saddam Hussein when the ground war got under way. A "survivor," he then knew that he did not have to worry about the allies toppling him. All he would have to deal with was any internal disturbance. This he could do if his political, military, and security infrastructure remained in place even if he did lose Kuwait. This dictated that he simply salvage as much of his field army as possible for use at home.

Importantly, the decisions on ending the war also highlighted the failure to keep political and military objectives in synch. In summoning the nation to war, Bush had described Saddam Hussein as "worse than Hitler" and painted the conflict as a Manichaean struggle between good and evil. But when it came to waging war against the new "Hitler" the allied armies, as it were, stopped at the Rhine. The Bush administration ruled out the occupation of Baghdad, stopped the Army and Air Force assault before it had completed its destruction of the Republican Guard, interrupted the air war in downtown Baghdad after the destruction of the Al Firdos bunker, and failed to protect the insurgents or arm the resistance.

The Bush administration's ambivalence over the postwar settlement was revealed when it took the position after the war that economic sanctions were to remain in place until Saddam Hussein was removed from power. Washington, in effect, made the removal of the Iraqi leader an explicit goal of its policy, but not until its military forces were being withdrawn. Then eighteen months after abandoning the Shiite insurgents in the south, the Bush administration reversed itself and established a no-flight zone in southern Iraq to protect them.

Bush may have made his generals more comfortable by exercising restraint. But he failed to exploit the benefits that accrue to those who exercise overwhelming power. It allows those who exercise it to set the agenda and the course of the future on their own terms.

Notes

1. "A Line in the Sand," prepared by the Marine Corps Combat Development Command and available from the Marine Corps Association, Quantico, Virginia.

2. *Certain Victory: The U.S. Army in the Gulf War*, Office of the Chief of Staff, United States Army, Washington, D.C., 1993, pp. 314–315.

3. Interview, Schwarzkopf.

4. Memorandum from Richard Hallion, the Air Force historian, April 30, 1993.
   The "Gulf War Air Power Survey" contradicted much of what Hallion wrote in his own book, *Storm Over Iraq* (Smithsonian Institution Press, 1992). In his memo, Hallion wrote that he was "increasingly concerned that the actual accomplishments of airpower in the Gulf War will be distorted or misinterpreted by the upcoming GWAPS report in much the same way that the lessons learned and the accomplishments of airpower in the Second World War were distorted by the Strategic Bombing Survey. Further there is the potentiality that even the positive statements that the GWAPS report states will be gradually lost in much the same way that those of the USSBS [U.S. Strategic Bombing Survey] were in the 1950's."
   Hallion urged that the Air Force "seriously consider the implications of releasing this report."

5. "The Gulf War: Setting the Record Straight," General Kahlid bin Sultan, 1992.

6. Soviet Analysis of Operation Desert Storm and Operation Desert Shield, translated by the Defense Intelligence Agency, p. 32.

POSTSCRIPT

Did President George Bush Achieve His Objectives in the Gulf War?

Powell makes a strong case for the manner in which President Bush fought the Gulf War. According to the Powell doctrine, the United States should use its well-trained troops in short wars with limited and specific goals. Powell's views on warfare are clearly influenced by his two stints in Vietnam—a war in which the battles appeared endless and the goals seemed unclear and constantly changing. The Gulf War, by contrast, was limited to 35 days of air strikes and 100 hours of land combat, with the goal of liberating Kuwait under the UN mandate successfully accomplished, in Powell's view.

Powell takes to task critics who argue that the war left unfinished business because Hussein, although forced to leave Kuwait, remained in power in Iraq with his major troops—the Republican Guard—still a viable military force. Powell contends that by 1996 Hussein's army was only half the size it was before the war started. His influence in the region has waned because his supporters, the late King Hussein of Jordan and Yasser Arafat, chairman of the PLO, "both were weakened" because they supported the war. Powell also maintains that Kuwait, a nation of 700,000 people, will always be threatened by Iraq, a nation of 20 million people. The country's security depends upon arrangements with other nations in the Middle East and the United States.

Powell agrees with President Bush's argument that the overthrow of Saddam Hussein "would not contribute to the stability we want in the Middle East to have Iraq fragmented into separate Sunni, Shia, and Kurd political entities. The only way to have avoided this outcome was to have undertaken a largely U.S. conquest and occupation of a remote nation of twenty million people. I don't think that is what the American people signed up for."

Powell states that if Hussein fell from power, he would not "necessarily have been replaced by a Jeffersonian in some sort of desert democracy where people read *The Federalist Papers* along with the Koran. Quite possibly, we would have wound up with a Saddam by another name." If this is true, how strong a case could Powell make for an invasion of Iraq today?

Gordon and Trainor are highly critical of the Powell doctrine. Powell's doctrine, they admit, worked well in Granada in 1983 and in Panama in 1989, where a quick strike by an overwhelmingly superior force could obtain its objectives. But they maintain that Powell's doctrine in the Gulf War was flawed for several reasons. For one thing, it caused the Bush administration to react too slowly in Kuwait. If the American navy had stationed military forces in the Persian Gulf in 1990, it might have prevented Hussein from invading Kuwait. Powell's doctrine also led to an early ending of the war in Kuwait because the

Bush administration did not want to risk the lives of more American soldiers and at the same time did not want to sustain the bad publicity of killing soldiers who were retreating to Iraq along the "highway of death." Most important, the early ending of the war prevented the administration from influencing events in postwar Iraq, where Hussein continued to rule with an iron fist.

Gordon and Trainor are also critical of a number of military policies and tactics that were used in the Gulf War. They maintain that General Norman Schwarzkopf was too slow in ordering the army to pursue the enemy, which had been softened up by the marines more quickly than expected. The air force had difficulty hunting Scud missiles, neutralizing the Iraqi command structure, and destroying Iraq's weapons of mass destruction. In addition, doctrinal differences continued to create interservice rivalries and inefficiencies in carrying out military operations, and the emphasis on high-tech weapons led to the lack of simpler but necessary equipment, such as mine-clearing gear, which the marines had to borrow from the Israelis in order to breach the Iraqi fortifications.

Even if one accepts Gordon and Trainor's critique of America's military and political policies, the question remains: Could Saddam Hussein have been removed from power without a full-scale American invasion of Iraq?

The bibliography on the Gulf War is quite large. Readers should begin with two review essays by Robert A. Divine that critically analyze 14 books written about the war. See "The Persian Gulf War Revisited: Tactical Victory, Strategic Failure," *Diplomatic History* (Winter 2000) and "Historians and the Gulf War," *Diplomatic History* (Winter 1995). In a class by itself is a collection of memoirs by George Bush and Brent Scowcroft, *A World Transformed* (Alfred A. Knopf, 1998), which is written with three voices: one passage by Bush, one passage by Scowcroft, and one passage written jointly.

Two useful sources provide a solid background to the events of the Middle East since 1945: James W. Harper, "The Middle East, Oil and the Third World," in John M. Carroll and George C. Herring, eds., *Modern American Diplomacy,* rev. and enl. ed. (Scholarly Resources, 1996) and several essays in Edward R. Drachman and Alan Shank, eds., *Presidents and Foreign Policy: Countdown to Ten Controversial Decisions* (State University of New York Press, 1997).

Two other works deserve mention. Roger J. Spiller, in "A War Against History," *American Heritage* (February/March 2001), takes a critical look at the official histories of the armed forces and the superficial memoirs of some of the participants. And Steven A. Yetiv, *The Persian Gulf Crisis* (Greenwood Press, 1997) is a highly useful compendium of a chronology, biographical sketches, primary documents, bibliography, and a 135-page narrative of key events.

ISSUE 13

Should America Remain a Nation of Immigrants?

YES: Tamar Jacoby, from "Too Many Immigrants?" *Commentary* (April 2002)

NO: Patrick J. Buchanan, from *The Death of the West: How Dying Populations and Immigrant Invasions Imperil Our Country and Civilization* (Thomas Dunne Books, 2002)

ISSUE SUMMARY

YES: Social scientist Tamar Jacoby maintains that the newest immigrants keep America's economy strong because they work harder and take jobs that native-born Americans reject.

NO: Syndicated columnist Patrick J. Buchanan argues that America is no longer a nation because immigrants from Mexico and other Third World Latin American and Asian countries have turned America into a series of fragmented multicultural ethnic enclaves that lack a common culture.

Historians of immigration tend to divide the forces that encouraged voluntary migrations from one country to another into push and pull factors. Historically, the major reason why people left their native countries was the breakdown of feudalism and the subsequent rise of a commercially oriented economy. Peasants were pushed off the feudal estates of which they had been a part for generations. In addition, religious and political persecution for dissenting groups and the lack of economic opportunities for many middle-class émigrés also contributed to the migrations from Europe to the New World.

America was attractive to settlers long before the American Revolution took place. While the United States may not have been completely devoid of feudal traditions, immigrants perceived the United States as a country with a fluid social structure where opportunities abounded for everyone. By the mid-nineteenth century, the Industrial Revolution had provided opportunities for jobs in a nation that had always experienced chronic labor shortages.

There were four major periods of migration to the United States: 1607–1830, 1830–1890, 1890–1925, and 1968 to the present. In the seventeenth and eighteenth centuries, the white settlers came primarily, though not entirely, from the British Isles. They were joined by millions of African slaves. Both groups lived in proximity to several hundred thousand Native Americans. In those years the cultural values of Americans were a combination of what history professor Gary Nash has referred to as "red, white, and black." In the 30 years before the Civil War, a second phase began when immigrants came from other countries in northern and western Europe as well as China. Two European groups dominated. Large numbers of Irish Catholics emigrated in the 1850s because of the potato famine. Religious and political factors were as instrumental as economic factors in pushing the Germans to America. Chinese immigrants were also encouraged to come during the middle and later decades of the nineteenth century in order to help build the western portion of America's first transcontinental railroad and to work in low-paying service industries like laundries and restaurants.

By 1890 a third period of immigration had begun. Attracted by the unskilled jobs provided by the Industrial Revolution and the cheap transportation costs of fast-traveling, steam-powered ocean vessels, immigrants poured in at a rate of close to 1 million a year from Italy, Greece, Russia, and other countries of southern and eastern Europe. This flood continued until the early 1920s, when fears of a foreign takeover led Congress to pass legislation restricting the number of immigrants into the United States to 150,000 per year.

For the next 40 years America was ethnically frozen. The restriction laws of the 1920s favored northern and western European groups and were biased against southern and eastern Europeans. The depression of the 1930s, World War II in the 1940s, and minimal changes in the immigration laws of the 1950s kept migrations to the United States at a minimum level.

In the 1960s the immigration laws were drastically revised. The civil rights acts of 1964 and 1965, which ended legal discrimination against African Americans, were also the impetus for immigration reform. The 1965 Immigration Act represented a turning point in U.S. history. But it had unintended consequences. In conjunction with the 1990 Immigration Act, discrimination against non-European nations was abolished and preferences were given to family-based migrants over refugees and those with special skills. Immigrants from Latin American and Asian countries have dominated the fourth wave of migration and have used the loophole in the legislation to bring into the country "immediate relatives," such as spouses, children, and parents of American citizens who are exempt from the numerical ceilings of the immigration laws.

Should the United States allow the current flow of immigrants into the country to continue? In the following selection, Tamar Jacoby asserts that the newest immigrants keep America's economy strong because they work harder and take jobs that native-born workers reject. Jacoby also maintains that the newest immigrants will assimilate into mainstream culture as earlier generations did once the immigration laws provide permanence and stability. In the second selection, Patrick J. Buchanan argues that the new immigrants from Mexico, other parts of Latin America, and Asia who have been entering America since 1968 are destroying the core culture of the United States.

Tamar Jacoby

 **YES**

Too Many Immigrants?

Of all the issues Americans have had to rethink in the wake of September 11, few seem more baffling than immigration. As polls taken in the following weeks confirmed, the attacks dramatically heightened people's fear of foreigners—not just Muslim foreigners, all foreigners. In one survey, fully two-thirds of the respondents said they wanted to stop any immigration until the war against terror was over. In Congress, the once marginal Immigration Reform Caucus quadrupled in size virtually overnight, and a roster of sweeping new proposals came to the fore: a six-month moratorium on all visas, shutting the door to foreign students, even militarizing our borders with troops and tanks.

In the end, none of these ideas came close to getting through Congress. On the issue of security, Republicans and Democrats, law-enforcement professionals and civilians alike agreed early on that it was critical to distinguish terrorists from immigrants—and that it was possible to protect the country without isolating it.

The Bush administration and Congress soon came up with similar plans based on the idea that the best defense was to intercept unwanted visitors before they reached the U.S.—when they applied for visas in their home country, were preparing to board a plane, or were first packing a lethal cargo shipment. A bipartisan bill now making its way through Congress calls for better screening of visa applications, enhanced intelligence-sharing among federal agencies, new tamper-proof travel documents with biometric data, and better tracking of the few hundred thousand foreign students already in the U.S.

But the security debate is only one front in a broader struggle over immigration. There is no question that our present policy is defective, and immigration opponents are hoping that the attacks will precipitate an all-out fight about overhauling it. Yet even if the goal is only to secure our borders, Americans are up against some fairly intractable realities.

In the aftermath of September 11, for example, there have been calls for tracking not just foreign students but all foreigners already in the country. This is not an unreasonable idea; but it would be next to impossible to implement. Even monitoring the entry and exit of visitors, as the Immigration and Naturalization Service (INS) has been charged with doing, has turned out to be a logistical nightmare—we are talking about a *half-billion* entries and probably an

From Tamar Jacoby, "Too Many Immigrants?" *Commentary* (April 2002). Copyright © 2002 by *Commentary*. Reprinted by permission of *Commentary* and the author.

equal number of exits a year. (Of the total, incidentally, by far the largest number are Canadian and Mexican daily commuters, a third are Americans, and only a tiny percentage—fewer than a million a year—are immigrants seeking to make a new life in the U.S.) If collecting this information is difficult, analyzing and acting on it are a distant dream. As for the foreign-born population as a whole, it now stands at 28 million and growing, with illegal aliens alone estimated at between seven and eight million. It would take years just to identify them, much less find a way to track them all.

To this, the more implacable immigration opponents respond that if we cannot keep track of those already here, we should simply deport them. At the very least, others say, we should move to reduce radically the number we admit from now on, or impose a five- or ten-year moratorium. In the months since September 11, a variety of more and less extreme restrictionists have come together in a loose coalition to push forward such ideas. Although the movement has so far made little headway in Washington, it has become increasingly vocal, gaining a wide audience for its views, and has found a forceful, nationally known spokesman in the former presidential candidate and best-selling author Patrick J. Buchanan.

꧁꧂

The coalition itself is a motley assemblage of bedfellows: liberals worried about the impact of large-scale immigration on population growth and the environment, conservatives exercised about porous borders and the shattering of America's common culture, plus a sizable contingent of outright racial demagogues. The best known organization pushing for restriction is the Federation for Immigration Reform, or FAIR, which provided much of the intellectual ammunition for the last big anti-immigration campaign, in the mid-1990's.

FAIR is still the richest and most powerful of the restrictionist groups. In the months since the attacks, a consortium it leads has spent some $300,000 on inflammatory TV ads in Western states where the 2002 mid-term elections will bring immigration issues to the fore; over pictures of the nineteen hijackers, the spots argue that the only way to keep America safe is to reduce immigration severely. But FAIR no longer dominates the debate as it once did, and newer groups are springing up around it.

On one flank are grassroots cells. Scrappier and more populist than FAIR, some consist of no more than an individual with a web page or radio show who has managed to accumulate a regional following; other local organizations have amassed enough strength to influence the politics of their states, particularly in California. On the other flank, and at the national level, FAIR is increasingly being eclipsed by younger, more media-savvy groups like the Center for Immigration Studies (CIS) in Washington and the writers associated with the website VDARE, both of which aim at swaying elite opinion in New York and Washington.

Different groups in the coalition focus on different issues, and each has its own style and way of presenting itself. One organization, Project USA, has devoted itself to putting up roadside billboards—nearly 100 so far, in a dozen states—with provocative messages like, "Tired of sitting in traffic? Every day, another 8,000 immigrants arrive. Every day!!" Those in the more respectable factions spend much energy distancing themselves from the more militant or fanatical, and even those with roughly the same mandate can seem, or sound, very different.

Consider CIS and VDARE. Created in 1985 as a fact-finding arm of FAIR, CIS is today arguably better known and more widely quoted than its parent. The group's executive director, Mark Krikorian, has made himself all but indispensable to anyone interested in immigration issues, sending out daily electronic compendiums of relevant news stories culled from the national press. His organization publishes scholarly papers on every aspect of the issue by a wide circle of respected academic researchers, many of whom would eschew any association with, say, FAIR's exclusionary politics. Along with his director of research, Steven Camarota, Krikorian is also a regular on Capitol Hill, where his restrained, informative testimony is influential with a broad array of elected officials.

VDARE, by contrast, wears its political views on its sleeve—and they are deliberately provocative. Founded a few years ago by the journalist Peter Brimelow, a senior editor at *Forbes* and the author of the best-selling *Alien Nation: Common Sense About America's Immigration Disaster* (1995), VDARE is named after Virginia Dare, "the first English child born in the New World." Kidnapped as an infant and never seen again, Virginia Dare is thought to have eventually married into a local Indian tribe, or to have been killed by it—almost equally unfortunate possibilities in the minds of VDARE's writers, who make no secret of their concern about the way America's original Anglo-Saxon stock is being transformed by immigration.

The overall strength of today's restrictionist movement is hard to gauge. But there is no question that recent developments—both September 11 and the flagging American economy—have significantly boosted its appeal. One Virginia-based organization, Numbers USA, claims that its membership grew from 5,000 to over 30,000 in the weeks after the attacks. Buchanan's *The Death of the West: How Dying Populations and Immigrant Invasions Imperil Our Country and Civilization*[1]—a deliberately confrontational jeremiad—shot to the top of Amazon.com's best-seller list within days of publication, then moved to a perch in the *New York Times* top ten. Nor does it hurt that the anti-immigrant cause boasts advocates at both ends of the political spectrum. Thus, leftists repelled by the likes of Buchanan and Brimelow could read a more congenial statement of the same case in a recent, much-discussed series in the *New York Review of Books* by the distinguished sociologist Christopher Jencks.

To be sure, immigration opponents have also had some significant setbacks. Most notably, the Republican party, which stood staunchly with them in the mid-1990's in California, is now firmly on the other side of the issue—if anything, George W. Bush has become the country's leading advocate for liberalizing immigration law. But there can be no mistaking the depth of public concern over one or another of the questions raised by the restrictionists, and in the event of more attacks or a prolonged downturn, their appeal could surely grow.

ᴇ◉ᴈ

In addition to national security, immigration opponents offer arguments principally about three issues: natural resources, economics, and the likelihood that today's newcomers will be successfully absorbed into American society. On the first, restrictionists contend not only that immigrants compete with us and consume our natural resources, to the detriment of the native-born, but that their numbers will eventually overwhelm us, choking the United States to death both demographically and environmentally.

Much of Buchanan's book, for example, is devoted to a discussion of population. As he correctly notes, birth rates in Europe have dropped below replacement level, and populations there are aging. By 2050, he estimates, only 10 percent of the world's people will be of European descent, while Asia, Africa, and Latin America will grow by three to four billion people, yielding "30 to 40 new Mexicos." As the developed countries "die out," huge movements of hungry people from the underdeveloped world will swamp their territory and destroy their culture. "This is not a matter of prophecy," Buchanan asserts, "but of mathematics."

Extrapolating from similar statistics, Christopher Jencks has predicted that the U.S. population may double in size over the next half-century largely as a result of the influx of foreigners. (This is a much faster rate of growth than that foreseen by virtually any other mainstream social scientist.) Jencks imagines a hellish future in which American cities will become all but unlivable and suburban sprawl will decimate the landscape. The effect on our natural resources will be devastating, as the water supply dwindles and our output of carbon dioxide soars. (To put his arguments in perspective, Jencks finds nothing new in this pattern. Immigration has always been disastrous to our ecology, he writes: the Indians who crossed the Bering Strait 13,000 years ago depleted the continent's fauna by overhunting, and many centuries later the germs brought by Europeans laid waste to the Indians.)

Not all the arguments from scarcity are quite so apocalyptic, but all begin and end with the assumption that the size of the pie is fixed, and that continued immigration can only mean less and less for the rest of us. A similar premise underlies the restrictionists' second set of concerns—that immigrants steal jobs from native-born workers, depress Americans' wages, and make disproportionate use of welfare and other government services.

Here, groups like FAIR and CIS focus largely on the portion of the immigrant flow that is poor and ill-educated—not the Indian engineer in Silicon Valley, but the Mexican farmhand with a sixth-grade education. "Although immigrants comprise about 12 percent of America's workforce," CIS reports, "they account for 31 percent of high-school dropouts in the workforce." Not only are poverty rates among these immigrants higher than among the native-born, but, the restrictionists claim, the gap is growing. As for welfare, Krikorian points out that even in the wake of the 1996 reform that denied means-tested benefits to many immigrants, their reliance on some programs—food stamps, for example —still exceeds that of native-born Americans.

The restrictionists' favorite economist is Harvard's George Borjas, the author of a widely read 1999 book, *Heaven's Door*.[2] As it happens, Borjas did not confirm the worst fears about immigrants: they do not, for example, steal Americans' jobs, and today's newcomers are no poorer or less capable than those who came at the turn of the 20th century and ultimately did fine in America. Still, in Borjas's estimation, compared with the native-born of their era, today's immigrants are *relatively* farther behind than, say, the southern Europeans who came a century ago, and even if they do not actually take work away from Americans, they may prompt the native-born to move to other cities and thus adversely affect the larger labor market.

As a result, Borjas contends, the presence of these newcomers works to lower wages, particularly among high-school dropouts. And because of the cost of the government services they consume—whether welfare or public schooling or hospital care—they impose a fiscal drain on a number of states where they settle. In sum, immigrants may be a boon to U.S. business and to the middle class (which benefits from lower prices for the fruit the foreigners pick and from the cheap lawn services they provide), but they are an unfair burden on ordinary working Americans, who must subsidize them with higher taxes.

Borjas's claims have hardly gone unchallenged by economists on either the Right or the Left—including Jagdish Bhagwati in a heated exchange in the *Wall Street Journal*—but he remains a much-quoted figure among restrictionists, who particularly like his appealing-sounding note of concern for the native-born black poor. Borjas's book has also greatly strengthened those who propose that existing immigration policy, which is based mainly on the principle of family unification, be changed to one like Canada's that admits people based on the skills they bring.

This brings us to the third issue that worries the anti-immigration community: the apparent failure, or refusal, of large numbers of newcomers to assimilate successfully into American society, to learn our language, adopt our mores, and embrace American values as their own. To many who harp on this theme—Buchanan, the journalist Georgie Anne Geyer, the more polemical VDARE contributors—it is, frankly, the racial makeup of today's influx that is most troublesome. "Racial groups that are different are more difficult to assimilate," Buchanan says flatly, painting a nightmarish picture of newcomers with "no desire to learn English or become citizens." Buchanan and others make much of the influence of multiculturalism and identity politics in shaping the priorities of the immigrant community; his chapter on Mexican immigrants, entitled "La Reconquista," quotes extensively from extremist Chicano activists who want, he says, to "colonize" the United States.

On this point, it should be noted, Buchanan and his followers are hardly alone, and hardly original. Any number of observers who are *favorably* disposed to continued immigration have likewise raised an alarm over the radically divisive and balkanizing effects of multiculturalism and bilingual education. Where they part company with Buchanan is over the degree of danger they perceive—and what should be done about it.[3]

About one thing the restrictionists are surely right: our immigration policy is broken. Not only is the INS one of the least efficient and most beleaguered agencies in Washington—at the moment, four million authorized immigrants are waiting, some for a decade or more, for their paperwork to be processed—but official policy, particularly with regard to Mexico, is a hypocritical sham. Even as we claim to limit the flow of migrants, and force thousands to wait their turn for visas, we look the other way as hundreds of thousands enter the country without papers—illegal but welcomed by business as a cheap, pliable labor force. Nor do we have a clear rationale for the selection we end up making from the vast pool of foreigners eager to enter the country.

But here precisely is where the restrictionists' arguments are the least helpful. Take the issue of scarcity. The restrictionists construct their dire scenarios by extrapolating from the current flow of immigrants. But as anyone who follows these matters is aware, nothing is harder to predict than who and how many will come in the future. It is, for example, as easy today as it ever was to migrate to the U.S. from Puerto Rico, and wages on the island still lag woefully behind wages here. But the net flow from Puerto Rico stopped long ago, probably because life there improved just enough to change the calculus of hope that had been prodding people to make the trip.

Sooner or later, the same thing will happen in Mexico. No one knows when, but surely one hint of things to come is that population growth is slowing in Mexico, just as it slowed earlier here and in Europe. Over the past three decades, the Mexican fertility rate has dropped from an average 6.5 children per mother to a startling 2.5.

Nor are demographic facts themselves always as straightforward in their implications as the restrictionists assume. True, population is still growing faster in the underdeveloped world than in developed countries. But is this an argument against immigration, or for it? If they are to remain strong, countries *need* population—workers, customers, taxpayers, soldiers. And our own openness to immigrants, together with our proven ability to absorb them, is one of our greatest advantages over Japan and Europe, which face a demographic crisis as their ratio of workers to retirees adversely shifts. The demographer Ben Wattenberg has countered Buchanan with a simple calculation: "If we keep admitting immigrants at our current levels, there will be almost 400 million Americans by 2050. That"—and only that, one might add—"can keep us strong enough to defend and perhaps extend our views and values."

⋯⟨◈⟩⋯

The argument from economics is equally unhelpful. The most commonly heard complaint about foreign workers is that they take jobs from Americans. Not only is this assertion untrue—nobody has found real evidence to support it—but cities and states with the largest immigrant populations (New York, Los Angeles, and others) boast far faster economic growth and lower unemployment than cities and states that do not attract immigrants. In many places, the presence of immigrants seems to reduce unemployment even among native-born blacks—probably because of the way immigrants stimulate economic growth.

Economists looking for a depressive effect on native-born wages have been nearly as disappointed: dozens of studies over the past two or three decades have found at most modest and probably temporary effects. Even if Borjas is right that a native-born black worker may take home $300 less a year as a result of immigration, this is a fairly small amount of money in the overall scheme of things. More to the point, globalization would have much the same effect on wages, immigrants or no immigrants. Pressed by competition from foreign imports, American manufacturers have had to change production methods and cut costs, including labor costs. If they did not, they would have to go out of business—or move to an underdeveloped country where wages are lower. In either case, the U.S. economy would end up being hurt far more than by the presence of immigrant workers—who expand the U.S. economic pie when they buy shoes and groceries and washing machines from their American neighbors and call American plumbers into their homes.

What about the costs imposed by immigrants, especially by their use of government services? It is true that many immigrants—though far from all—are poorer than native-born Americans, and thus pay less in taxes. It is also true that one small segment of the immigrant population—refugees—tends to be heavily dependent on welfare. As a result, states with large immigrant populations often face chronic fiscal problems.

But that is at the state level, and mostly in high-welfare states like California. If we shift the lens to the federal level, and include the taxes that immigrants remit to the IRS, the calculation comes out very differently: immigrants pay in more than they take out. This is particularly true if one looks at the picture over the course of an immigrant's lifetime. Most come to the U.S. as young adults looking for work—which means they were already educated at home, relieving us of a significant cost. More important, even illegal immigrants generally keep up with payroll taxes, contributing to Social Security though they may never claim benefits. According to Stephen Moore, an economist at the Cato Institute, foreign-born workers are likely to contribute as much as $2 trillion to Social Security over the next 70 years, thus effectively keeping it afloat.

The economic debate often comes down to this sort of war of numbers, but the victories on either side are rarely conclusive. After all, even 28 million immigrants form but a small part of the $12-trillion U.S. economy, and most of the fiscal costs and benefits associated with them are relatively modest. Besides, fiscal calculations are only a small part of the larger economic picture. How do we measure the energy immigrants bring—the pluck and grit and willingness to improvise and innovate?

Not only are immigrants by and large harder-working than the native-born, they generally fill economic niches that would otherwise go wanting. The term economists use for this is "complementarity." If immigrants were exactly like American workers, they would not be particularly valuable to employers. They are needed precisely because they are different: willing or able to do jobs few American workers are willing or able to do. These jobs tend to be either at the lowest rungs of the employment ladder (busboy, chambermaid, line worker in a meatpacking plant) or at the top (nurse, engineer, information-technology worker).

It is no accident that 80 percent of American farmworkers are foreign-born, or that, if there were no immigrants, hotels and restaurants in many cities would have to close their doors. Nor is it an accident that immigrants account for a third of the scientific workforce in Silicon Valley, or that Asian entrepreneurs run a quarter of the companies there. Today's supply of willing laborers from Mexico, China, India, and elsewhere matches our demand in these various sectors, and the result is good for just about everyone—business, workers, and American consumers alike.

☙❦❧

To be sure, what is good for business, or even for American consumers, may not ultimately be good for the United States—and this is where the issue of assimilation comes in. "What is a nation?" Buchanan asks. "Is America nothing more than an economic system?" If immigrants do not come to share our values, adopt our heroes, and learn our history as their own, ultimately the nation will not hold. Immigration policy cannot be a suicide pact.

The good news is that assimilation is not going nearly as badly as the restrictionists claim. Though many immigrants start out at the bottom, most eventually join the working poor, if not the middle class. And by the time they have been here twenty years, they generally do as well as or better than the native-born, earning comparable salaries and registering *lower* poverty rates.

Nor is it true that immigrants fail or refuse to learn English. Many more than in previous eras come with a working knowledge of the language—it is hard to avoid it in the world today. Despite the charade that is bilingual education, nearly all high-school students who have been educated in this country—nine out of ten of them, according to one study—prefer English to their native tongue. And by the third generation, even among Hispanics, who are somewhat slower than other immigrants to make the linguistic shift, only 1 percent say they use "more or only Spanish" at home.

Despite the handicaps with which many arrive, the immigrant drive to succeed is as strong as ever. According to one important study of the second generation, newcomers' children work harder than their U.S. classmates, putting in an average of two hours of homework a night compared with the "normal" 30 minutes. They also aspire to higher levels of educational achievement, earn better grades, drop out less frequently—and expect only the best of their new homeland. Nearly two-thirds believe that hard work and accomplishment can triumph over prejudice, and about the same number say there is no better country than the United States. As for the lure of identity politics, one of the most thorough surveys of Hispanics, conducted in 1999 by the *Washington Post*, reported that 84 percent believe it is "important" or "very important" for immigrants "to change so that they blend into the larger society, as in the idea of the melting pot."

There is also bad news. Immigrant America is far from monolithic, and some groups do worse than others both economically and culturally. While fewer than 5 percent of Asian young people use an Asian language with their friends, nearly 45 percent of Latinos sometimes use Spanish. Close to 90 percent of Chinese parents expect their children to finish college; only 55 percent of Mexicans do. Indeed, Mexicans—who account for about a quarter of the foreign-born—lag behind on many measures, including, most worrisomely, education. The average Mexican migrant comes with less than eight years of schooling, and though the second generation is outstripping its parents, it too falls well below American norms, either for other immigrants or for the native-born.

When it comes to absorbing the American common culture, or what has been called patriotic assimilation, there is no question that today's immigrants are at a disadvantage compared with yesterday's. Many Americans themselves no longer know what it means to be American. Our schools teach, at best, a travesty of American history, distorted by political correctness and the excesses of multiculturalism. Popular culture supplies only the crudest, tinniest visions of our national heritage. Even in the wake of September 11, few leaders have tried to evoke more than a fuzzy, feel-good enthusiasm for America. No wonder many immigrants have a hard time making the leap from their culture to ours. We no longer ask it of them.

Still, even if the restrictionists are right about all this, their remedy is unworkable. Given the global economy, given the realities of politics and law enforcement in the United States, we are not going to stop—or significantly re-duce—the flow of immigrant workers into the country any time soon. Businesses that rely on imported labor would not stomach it; as it is, they object vocif-erously whenever the INS tries to enforce the law. Nor are American citizens prepared to live with the kinds of draconian measures that would be needed to implement a significant cutback or time-out. Even in the wake of the attacks, there is little will to require that immigrants carry ID cards, let alone to erect the equivalent of a Berlin Wall along the Rio Grande. In sum, if many immi-grants among us are failing to adopt our common culture, we will have to look elsewhere than to the restrictionists for a solution.

⋄◈⋄

What, then, is to be done? As things stand today, American immigration pol-icy and American law are perilously out of sync with reality—the reality of the market. Consider the Mexican case, not the only telling one but the most dramatic.

People born in Mexico now account for roughly 10 percent of the U.S. workforce, and the market for their labor is a highly efficient one. Very few recent Mexican migrants are unemployed; even modest economic upturns or downturns have a perceptible impact on the number trying to enter illegally, as word quickly spreads from workers in California or Kansas back to home villages in Mexico. This precise coordination of supply and demand has been drawing roughly 300,000 Mexicans over the border each year, although, even including minors and elderly parents, the INS officially admits only half that many.

One does not have to be a free-market enthusiast to find this discrepancy absurd, and worse. Not only does it criminalize badly needed laborers and productive economic activity. It also makes an ass of the law and insidiously corrupts American values, encouraging illegal hiring and discrimination against even lawful Mexican migrants.

Neither a moratorium nor a reduction in official quotas would eliminate this thriving labor exchange—on the contrary, it would only exacerbate the mismatch. Instead, we should move in the opposite direction from what the restrictionists demand, bringing the number we admit more into line with the reality of the market. The rationale for whom we ought to let in, what we should encourage and reward, is work.

This, as it happens, is precisely the direction in which President Bush was moving before September 11. A package of reforms he floated in July, arrived at in negotiations with Mexican president Vicente Fox, would have significantly expanded the number of visas for Mexican workers. The President's impulse may have been partisan—to woo Latino voters—but he stumbled onto the basis for an immigration policy that would at once serve America's interests and reflect its values. He put the core idea plainly, and got it exactly right: "If somebody is willing to offer a job others in America aren't willing to do, we ought to welcome that person to the country."

Compared with this, any other criterion for immigration policy—family reunification, country of origin, or skill level—sinks into irrelevancy. It makes no sense at all that three-quarters of the permanent visas available today should be based on family ties, while only one-quarter are employment-related. As for the Canadian-style notion of making skill the decisive factor, admitting engineers and college professors but closing the door to farmworkers, not only does this smack of a very un-American elitism but it disregards our all too palpable economic needs at the low end of the labor market.

The problem is that there is at present virtually no legal path into the U.S. for unskilled migrant laborers; unless they have relatives here, they have no choice but to come illicitly. If we accept the President's idea that immigration policy should be based on work, we ought to enshrine it in a program that makes it possible for those who want to work, and who can find a job, to come lawfully. The program ought to be big enough to meet market needs: the number of visas available the first year should match the number of people who now sneak in against the law, and in future years it should follow the natural rise and fall of supply and demand. At the same time, the new regime ought to be accompanied by serious enforcement measures to ensure that workers use this pipeline rather than continuing to come illegally outside it.

⋅⟨◉⟩⋅

Such a policy makes sound economic sense—and also would provide a huge boost for immigrant absorption and assimilation. By definition, the undocumented are effectively barred from assimilating. Most cannot drive legally in the U.S., or, in many states, get regular care in a hospital. Nor, in most places, can they send their children to college. An indelible caste line separates them from other Americans—no matter how long they stay, how much they contribute, or how ardently they and their children strive to assimilate. If we want newcomers to belong, we should admit them legally, and find a fair means of regularizing the status of those who are already here illicitly.

But rerouting the illegal flow into legal channels will not by itself guarantee assimilation—particularly not if, as the President and Congress have suggested, we insist that workers go home when the job is done. In keeping with the traditional Republican approach to immigration, the President's reform package included a proposal for a guest-worker program, and before September 11, both Democrats and Republicans had endorsed the idea. If we want to encourage assimilation, however, such a system would only be counterproductive.

The cautionary model in this case is Germany, which for years admitted unskilled foreigners exclusively as temporary guest workers, holding out virtually no hope that either they or their children could become German citizens. As it happened, many of these migrants remained in Germany long after the work they were imported for had disappeared. But today, nearly 40 years later, most of them still have not assimilated, and they remain, poorly educated and widely despised, on the margins of German society. Clearly, if what we hope to encourage is the putting-down of roots, any new visa program must give participants a shot at membership in the American body politic.

But how we hand out visas is only the first step in a policy aimed at encouraging immigrant absorption. Other steps would have to include the provision of basic services like instruction in English, civics classes, naturalization programs—and also counseling in more practical matters like how to navigate the American banking system. (Many newcomers, even when they start making money, are at sea in the world of credit cards, credit histories, mortgage applications, and the like.) All these nuts-and-bolts services are as essential as the larger tasks, from overhauling the teaching of American history to eliminating counterproductive programs like bilingual education and ethnic entitlements that only breed separatism and alienation.

❧

There can be no gainsaying the risks America runs in remaining open to new immigrants. The security perils, though real enough, are the least worrisome. Legalizing the flow of needed workers and providing them with papers will help keep track of who is here and also help prevent those who wish to do us harm from entering in the first place. The more daring, long-term gamble lies in continuing to admit millions of foreigners who may or may not make it here or find a way to fit in. This is, as Buchanan rightly states, "a decision we can never undo."

Still, it is an experiment we have tried before—repeatedly. The result has never come out exactly as predicted, and the process has always been a wrenching one. But as experiments go, it has not only succeeded on its own terms; it has made us the wonder of the world. It can do so again—but only if we stop denying reality and resolve instead to meet the challenge head-on.

Notes

1. Dunne Books, 320 pp., $25.95.
2. Reviewed by Irwin M. Stelzer in the September 1999 COMMENTARY.
3. In COMMENTARY, see, for example, Linda Chavez's "Our Hispanic Predicament" (June 1998) and "What To Do About Immigration" (March 1995), and my own "In Asian America" (July-August 2000).

Patrick J. Buchanan  **NO**

La Reconquista

$\mathbf{A}$s the [immigrant] invasion rolls on, with California as the preferred destination, sociologist William Frey has documented an out-migration of African Americans and Anglo-Americans from the Golden State in search of cities and towns like the ones they grew up in. Other Californians are moving into gated communities. A country that cannot control its borders isn't really a country anymore, Ronald Reagan warned us some twenty years ago.

Concerns about a radical change in America's ethnic composition have been called un-American. But they are as American as Benjamin Franklin, who once asked, "Why should Pennsylvania, founded by the English, become a Colony of Aliens, who will shortly be so numerous as to Germanize us instead of our Anglifying them...?" Franklin would never find out if his fears were justified. German immigration was halted during the Seven Years War.

Former president Theodore Roosevelt warned, "The one absolutely certain way of bringing this nation to ruin, of preventing all possibility of its continuing to be a nation at all, would be to permit it to become a tangle of squabbling nationalities."

Immigration is a necessary subject for national debate, for it is about who we are as a people. Like the Mississippi, with its endless flow of life-giving water, immigration has enriched America throughout history. But when the Mississippi floods its banks, the devastation can be enormous. Yet, by the commands of political correctness, immigration as an issue is off the table. Only "nativists" or "xenophobes" could question a policy by which the United States takes in more people of different colors, creeds, cultures, and civilizations than all other nations of the earth combined. The river is rising to levels unseen in our history. What will become of our country if the levees do not hold?

In late 1999, this writer left Tucson and drove southeast to Douglas, the Arizona border town of eighteen thousand that had become the principal invasion corridor into the United States. In March alone, the U.S. Border Patrol had apprehended twenty-seven thousand Mexicans crossing illegally, half again as many illegal aliens crossing in one month as there are people in Douglas.

From Patrick J. Buchanan, *The Death of the West: How Dying Populations and Immigrant Invasions Imperil Our Country and Civilization* (Thomas Dunne Books, 2002). Copyright © 2002 by Patrick J. Buchanan. Reprinted by permission of St. Martin's Press, LLC. Notes omitted.

While there, I visited Theresa Murray, an eighty-two-year-old widow and a great-grandmother who lives in the Arizona desert she grew up in. Her ranch house was surrounded by a seven-foot chain-link fence that was topped with coils of razor wire. Every door and window had bars on it and was wired to an alarm. Mrs. Murray sleeps with a .32-caliber pistol on her bed table, because she has been burglarized thirty times. Her guard dogs are dead; they bled to death when someone tossed meat containing chopped glass over her fence. Theresa Murray is living out her life inside a maximum-security prison, in her own home, in her own country, because her government lacks the moral courage to do its duty and defend the borders of the United States of America.

If America is about anything, it is freedom. But as Theresa Murray says, "I've lost my freedom. I can't ever leave the house unless I have somebody watch it. We used to ride our horses clear across the border. We had Mexicans working on our property. It used to be fun to live here. Now, it's hell. It's plain old hell."

While Theresa Murray lives unfree, in hellish existence, American soldiers defend the borders of Korea, Kuwait, and Kosovo. But nothing is at risk on those borders, half a world away, to compare with what is at risk on our border with Mexico, over which pass the armies of the night as they trudge endlessly northward to the great cities of America. Invading armies go home, immigrant armies do not.

Who Killed the Reagan Coalition?

For a quarter of a century, from 1968 until 1992, the Republican party had a virtual lock on the presidency. The "New Majority," created by Richard Nixon and replicated by Ronald Reagan, gave the GOP five victories in six presidential elections. The key to victory was to append to the Republican base two Democratic blocs: Northern Catholic ethnics and Southern white Protestants. Mr. Nixon lured these voters away from the New Deal coalition with appeals to patriotism, populism, and social conservatism. Success gave the GOP decisive margins in the industrial states and a "Solid South" that had been the base camp of the Democratic party since Appomattox. This Nixon-Reagan coalition proved almost unbeatable. McGovern, Mondale, and Dukakis could carry 90 percent of the black vote, but with Republicans taking 60 percent of the white vote, which was over 90 percent of the total, the GOP inevitably came out on top.

This was the Southern Strategy. While the media called it immoral, Democrats had bedded down with segregationists for a century without similar censure. FDR and Adlai Stevenson had put segregationists on their tickets. Outside of Missouri, a border state with Southern sympathies, the only ones Adlai captured in 1956 were Dixiecrat states later carried by George Wallace.

Neither Nixon nor Reagan ever supported segregation. As vice president, Nixon was a stronger backer of civil rights than Senators John F. Kennedy or Lyndon Johnson. His role in winning passage of the Civil Rights Act of 1957 was lauded in a personal letter from Dr. Martin Luther King, who hailed Vice

President Nixon's "assiduous labor and dauntless courage in seeking to make Civil Rights a reality."

For a quarter century, Democrats were unable to pick the GOP lock on the presidency, because they could not shake loose the Republican grip on the white vote. With the exception of Lyndon Johnson's landslide of 1964, no Democrat since Truman in 1948 had won the white vote. What broke the GOP lock on the presidency was the Immigration Act of 1965.

During the anti-Soviet riots in East Berlin in 1953, Bertolt Brecht, the Communist playwright, quipped, "Would it not be easier... for the government to dissolve the people and elect another?" In the last thirty years, America has begun to import a new electorate, as Republicans cheerfully backed an immigration policy tilted to the Third World that enlarged the Democratic base and loosened the grip that Nixon and Reagan had given them on the presidency of the United States.

In 1996, the GOP was rewarded. Six of the 7 states with the largest numbers of immigrants—California, New York, Illinois, New Jersey, Massachusetts, Florida, and Texas—went for Clinton. In 2000, 5 went for Gore, and Florida was a dead heat. Of the 15 states with the most foreign-born, Bush lost 10. But of the 10 states with the smallest shares of foreign-born—Montana, Mississippi, Wyoming, West Virginia, South Dakota, South Carolina, Alabama, Tennessee, and Arkansas—Bush swept all 10.

Among the states with the most immigrants, only Texas has been reliably Republican, but now it is going the way of California. In the 1990s, Texas took in 3.2 million new residents as the Hispanic share of Texas's population shot from 25 percent to 33 percent. Hispanics are now the major ethnic group in four of Texas's five biggest cities: Houston, Dallas, San Antonio, and El Paso. "Non-Hispanic Whites May Soon Be a Minority in Texas" said a recent headline in the *New York Times.* With the Anglo population down from 60 percent in 1990 to 53 percent, the day when whites are a minority in Texas for the first time since before the Alamo is coming soon. "Projections show that by 2005," says the *Dallas Morning News,* "fewer than half of Texans will be white."

❧◈❧

America is going the way of California and Texas. "In 1960, the U.S. population was 88.6 percent white; in 1990, it was only 75.6 percent—a drop of 13 percentage points in thirty years.... [By 2020] the proportion of whites could fall as low as 61 per cent." So writes Peter Brimelow of *Forbes.* By 2050, Euro-Americans, the largest and most loyal share of the electorate the GOP has, will be a minority, due to an immigration policy that is championed by Republicans. John Stuart Mill was not altogether wrong when he branded the Tories "the Stupid Party."

❧◈❧

Hispanics are the fastest-growing segment of America's population. They were 6.4 percent of the U.S. population in 1980, 9 percent by 1990, and in 2000 over

12 percent. "The Hispanic fertility rates are quite a bit higher than the white or black population. They are at the levels of the baby boom era of the 1950s," says Jeffrey Passel, a demographer at the Urban Institute. At 35.4 million, Hispanics now equal African Americans in numbers and are becoming as Democratic in voting preferences. Mr. Bush lost the African-American vote eleven to one, but he also lost Hispanics two to one.

In 1996, when Clinton carried Latino voters seventy to twenty-one, he carried first-time Latino voters ninety-one to six. Aware that immigrants could give Democrats their own lock on the White House, Clinton's men worked relentlessly to naturalize them. In the year up to September 30, 1996, the Immigration and Naturalization Service swore in 1,045,000 immigrants as new citizens so quickly that 80,000 with criminal records—6,300 for serious crimes—slipped by. [Table 1 shows] the numbers of new citizens in each of the last five years.

Table 1

1996	1,045,000
1997	598,000
1998	463,000
1999	872,000
2000	898,315

California took a third of these new citizens. As non-Latino white registration fell by one hundred thousand in California in the 1990s, one million Latinos registered. Now 16 percent of the California electorate, Hispanics gave Gore the state with hundreds of thousands of votes to spare. "Both parties show up at swearing-in ceremonies to try to register voters," says Democratic consultant William Carrick. "There is a Democratic table and a Republican table. Ours has a lot of business. Theirs is like the Maytag repairman." With fifty-five electoral votes, California, home state of Nixon and Reagan, has now become a killing field of the GOP.

꧁◉꧂

Voting on referenda in California has also broken down along ethnic lines. In 1994, Hispanics, rallying under Mexican flags, opposed Proposition 187 to end welfare to illegals. In the 1996 California Civil Rights Initiative, Hispanics voted for ethnic preferences. In 1998, Hispanics voted to keep bilingual education. Anglo-Americans voted the other way by landslides.

Ron Unz, father of the "English for the Children" referendum that ended state-funded bilingual education, believes the LA riot of 1992 may have been the Rubicon on the road to the balkanization of California.

> The plumes of smoke from burning buildings and the gruesome television footage almost completely shattered the sense of security of middle-class

Southern Californians. Suddenly, the happy "multicultural California" so beloved of local boosters had been unmasked as a harsh, dangerous, Third World dystopia.... the large numbers of Latinos arrested (and summarily deported) for looting caused whites to cast a newly wary eye on gardeners and nannies who just weeks earlier had seemed so pleasant and reliable. If multicultural Los Angeles had exploded into sudden chaos, what security could whites expect as a minority in an increasingly nonwhite California?

ↄ⊙ↄ

Except for refugees from Communist countries like Hungary and Cuba, immigrants gravitate to the party of government. The obvious reason: Immigrants get more out of government—in free schooling for their kids, housing subsidies, health care—than they pay in. Arriving poor, most do not soon amass capital gains, estates, or incomes that can be federally taxed. Why should immigrants support a Republican party that cuts taxes they don't pay over a Democratic party that will expand the programs on which they do depend?

After Ellis Island, the Democratic party has always been the first stop for immigrants. Only after they have begun to move into the middle class do the foreign-born start converting to Republicanism. This can take two generations. By naturalizing and registering half a million or a million foreign-born a year, the Democrats are locking up future presidential elections and throwing away the key. If the GOP does not do something about mass immigration, mass immigration will do something about the GOP—turn it into a permanent minority that is home to America's newest minority, Euro-Americans.

As the ethnic character of America changes, politics change. A rising tide of immigration naturally shifts politics and power to the Left, by increasing the demands on government. The rapidly expanding share of the U.S. electorate that is of African and Hispanic ancestry has already caused the GOP to go silent on affirmative action and mute its calls for cuts in social spending. In 1996, Republicans were going to abolish the U.S. Department of Education. Now, they are enlarging it. As Hispanic immigration soars, and Hispanic voters become the swing voters in the pivotal states, their agenda will become America's agenda. It is already happening. In 2000, an AFL-CIO that had opposed mass immigration reversed itself and came out for amnesty for illegal aliens, hoping to sign up millions of illegal workers as dues-paying union members. And the Bush White House—in its policy decisions and appointments—has become acutely attentive to the Hispanic vote, often as the expense of conservative principles.

America's Quebec?

Harvard economist George Borjas, who studied the issue, found no net economic benefit from mass migration from the Third World. The added costs of schooling, health care, welfare, social security, and prisons, plus the added pressure on land, water, and power resources, exceeded the taxes that immigrants contribute. The National Bureau of Economic Research puts the cost of immigration at $80.4 billion in 1995. Economist Donald Huddle of Rice University estimates that the net annual cost of immigration will reach $108 billion by

2006. What are the benefits, then, that justify the risks we are taking of the balkanization of America?

Census 2000 revealed what many sensed. For the first time since statehood, whites in California are a minority. White flight has begun. In the 1990s, California grew by three million people, but its Anglo population actually "dropped by nearly half a million... surprising many demographers." Los Angeles County lost 480,000 white folks. In the exodus, the Republican bastion of Orange County lost 6 percent of its white population. "We can't pretend we're a white middle class state anymore," said William Fulton, research fellow at USC's Southern California Studies Center. State librarian Kevin Starr views the Hispanization of California as natural and inevitable:

> The Anglo hegemony was only an intermittent phase in California's arc of identity, extending from the arrival of the Spanish... the Hispanic nature of California has been there all along, and it was temporarily swamped between the 1880s and the 1960s, but that was an aberration. This is a reassertion of the intrinsic demographic DNA of the longer pattern, which is a part of the California-Mexican continuum.

The future is predictable: With one hundred thousand Anglos leaving California each year, with the Asian population soaring 42 percent in a single decade, with 43 percent of all Californians under eighteen Hispanic, America's largest state is on its way to becoming a predominantly Third World state.

No one knows how this will play out, but California could become another Quebec, with demands for formal recognition of its separate and unique Hispanic culture and identity—or another Ulster. As Sinn Fein demanded and got special ties to Dublin, Mexican Americans may demand a special relationship with their mother country, dual citizenship, open borders, and voting representation in Mexico's legislature. President Fox endorses these ideas. With California holding 20 percent of the electoral votes needed for the U.S. presidency, and Hispanic votes decisive in California, what presidential candidate would close the door to such demands?

"I have proudly proclaimed that the Mexican nation extends beyond the territory enclosed by its borders and that Mexican migrants are an important —a very important—part of this," said President Zedillo. His successor agrees. Candidates for president of Mexico now raise money and campaign actively in the United States. Gov. Gray Davis is exploring plans to have Cinquo de Mayo, the fifth of May, the anniversary of Juarez's 1862 victory over a French army at Puebla, made a California holiday. "In the near future," says Davis, "people will look at California and Mexico as one magnificent region." Perhaps we can call it Aztlan.

❦

America is no longer the biracial society of 1960 that struggled to erase divisions and close gaps in a nation 90 percent white. Today we juggle the rancorous and rival claims of a multiracial, multiethnic, and multicultural country. Vice President Gore captured the new America in his famous howler, when he translated our national slogan, "E Pluribus Unum," backward, as "Out of one, many."

Today there are 28.4 million foreign-born in the United States. Half are from Latin America and the Caribbean, a fourth from Asia. The rest are from Africa, the Middle East, and Europe. One in every five New Yorkers and Floridians is foreign-born, as is one of every four Californians. With 8.4 million foreign-born, and not one new power plant built in a decade, small wonder California faces power shortages and power outages. With endless immigration, America is going to need an endless expansion of its power sources—hydroelectric power, fossil fuels (oil, coal, gas), and nuclear power. The only alternative is blackouts, brownouts, and endless lines at the pump.

In the 1990s, immigrants and their children were responsible for 100 percent of the population growth of California, New York, New Jersey, Illinois, and Massachusetts, and over half the population growth of Florida, Texas, Michigan, and Maryland. As the United States allots most of its immigrant visas to relatives of new arrivals, it is difficult for Europeans to come, while entire villages from El Salvador are now here.

The results of the Third World bias in immigration can be seen in our social statistics. The median age of Euro-Americans is 36; for Hispanics, it is 26. The median age of all foreign-born, 33, is far below that of the older American ethnic groups, such as English, 40, and Scots-Irish, 43. These social statistics raise a question: Is the U.S. government, by deporting scarcely 1 percent of an estimated eleven million illegal aliens each year, failing in its constitutional duty to protect the rights of American citizens? Consider:

- A third of the legal immigrants who come to the United States have not finished high school. Some 22 percent do not even have a ninth-grade education, compared to less than 5 percent of our native born.
- Over 36 percent of all immigrants, and 57 percent of those from Central America, do not earn twenty thousand dollars a year. Of the immigrants who have come since 1980, 60 percent still do not earn twenty thousand dollars a year.
- Of immigrant households in the United States, 29 percent are below the poverty line, twice the 14 percent of native born.
- Immigrant use of food stamps, Supplemental Social Security, and school lunch programs runs from 50 percent to 100 percent higher than use by native born.
- Mr. Clinton's Department of Labor estimated that 50 percent of the real-wage losses sustained by low-income Americans is due to immigration.
- By 1991, foreign nationals accounted for 24 percent of all arrests in Los Angeles and 36 percent of all arrests in Miami.
- In 1980, federal and state prisons housed nine thousand criminal aliens. By 1995, this had soared to fifty-nine thousand criminal aliens, a figure that does not include aliens who became citizens or the criminals sent over by Castro in the Mariel boat lift.

- Between 1988 and 1994, the number of illegal aliens in California's prisons more than tripled from fifty-five hundred to eighteen thousand.

None of the above statistics, however, holds for emigrants from Europe. And some of the statistics, on low education, for example, do not apply to emigrants from Asia.

Nevertheless, mass emigration from poor Third World countries is "good for business," especially businesses that employ large numbers at low wages. In the spring of 2001, the Business Industry Political Action Committee, BIPAC, issued "marching orders for grass-roots mobilization." The *Wall Street Journal* said that the 400 blue-chip companies and 150 trade associations "will call for continued normalization of trade with China... and easing immigration restrictions to meet labor needs...." But what is good for corporate America is not necessarily good for Middle America. When it comes to open borders, the corporate interest and the national interest do not coincide, they collide. Should America suffer a sustained recession, we will find out if the melting pot is still working.

But mass immigration raises more critical issues than jobs or wages, for immigration is ultimately about America herself.

What Is a Nation?

Most of the people who leave their homelands to come to America, whether from Mexico or Mauritania, are good people, decent people. They seek the same better life our ancestors sought when they came. They come to work; they obey our laws; they cherish our freedoms; they relish the opportunities the greatest nation on earth has to offer; most love America; many wish to become part of the American family. One may encounter these newcomers everywhere. But the record number of foreign-born coming from cultures with little in common with Americans raises a different question: What is a nation?

Some define a nation as one people of common ancestry, language, literature, history, heritage, heroes, traditions, customs, mores, and faith who have lived together over time on the same land under the same rulers. This is the blood-and-soil idea of a nation. Among those who pressed this definition were Secretary of State John Quincy Adams, who laid down these conditions on immigrants: "They must cast off the European skin, never to resume it. They must look forward to their posterity rather than backward to their ancestors." Theodore Roosevelt, who thundered against "hyphenated-Americanism," seemed to share Adams's view. Woodrow Wilson, speaking to newly naturalized Americans in 1915 in Philadelphia, echoed T.R.: "A man who thinks of himself as belonging to a particular national group in America has yet to become an American." This idea, of Americans as a separate and unique people, was first given expression by John Jay in *Federalist 2:*

> Providence has been pleased to give this one connected country to one united people—a people descended from the same ancestors, speaking the same language, professing the same religion, attached to the same principles of government, very similar in their manners and customs, and who,

by their joint counsels, arms, and efforts, fighting side by side through-out a long and bloody war, have nobly established their general liberty and independence.

But can anyone say today that we Americans are "one united people"?

We are not descended from the same ancestors. We no longer speak the same language. We do not profess the same religion. We are no longer simply Protestant, Catholic, and Jewish, as sociologist Will Herberg described us in his *Essay in American Religious Sociology* in 1955. We are now Protestant, Catholic, Jewish, Mormon, Muslim, Hindu, Buddhist, Taoist, Shintoist, Santeria, New Age, voodoo, agnostic, atheist, humanist, Rastafarian, and Wiccan. Even the mention of Jesus' name at the Inauguration by the preachers Mr. Bush selected to give the invocations evoked fury and cries of "insensitive," "divisive," and "exclu-sionary." A *New Republic* editorial lashed out at these "crushing Christological thuds" from the Inaugural stand. We no longer agree on whether God exists, when life begins, and what is moral and immoral. We are not "similar in our manners and customs." We never fought "side by side throughout a long and bloody war." The Greatest Generation did, but it is passing away. If the rest of us recall a "long and bloody war," it was Vietnam, and, no, we were not side by side.

We remain "attached to the same principles of government." But common principles of government are not enough to hold us together. The South was "attached to the same principles of government" as the North. But that did not stop Southerners from fighting four years of bloody war to be free of their Northern brethren.

In his Inaugural, President Bush rejected Jay's vision: "America has never been united by blood or birth or soil. We are bound by ideals that move us beyond our background, lift us above our interests, and teach us what it means to be a citizen." In his *The Disuniting of America,* Arthur Schlesinger subscribes to the Bush idea of a nation, united by shared belief in an American Creed to be found in our history and greatest documents: the Declaration of Independence, the Constitution, and the Gettysburg Address. Writes Schlesinger:

> The American Creed envisages a nation composed of individuals making their own choices and accountable to themselves, not a nation based on in-violable ethnic communities. For our values are not matters or whim and happenstance. History has given them to us. They are anchored in our na-tional experience, in our great national documents, in our national heroes, in our folkways, our traditions, and standards. [Our values] work for us; and, for that reason, we live and die by them.

Bush Americans no longer agree on values, history, or heroes. What one-half of America sees as a glorious past the other views as shameful and wicked. Columbus, Washington, Jefferson, Jackson, Lincoln, and Lee—all of them heroes of the old America—are all under attack. Those most American of words, equal-ity and freedom, today hold different meanings for different Americans. As for our "great national documents," the Supreme Court decisions that interpret our Constitution have not united us; for forty years they have divided us, bitterly, over prayer in school, integration, busing, flag burning, abortion, pornography, and the Ten Commandments.

Nor is a belief in democracy sufficient to hold us together. Half of the nation did not even bother to vote in the presidential election of 2000; three out of five do not vote in off-year elections. Millions cannot name their congressman, senators, or the Supreme Court justices. They do not care.

Whether one holds to the blood-and-soil idea of a nation, or to the creedal idea, or both, neither nation is what it was in the 1940s, 1950s, or 1960s. We live in the same country, we are governed by the same leaders, but can we truly say we are still one nation and one people?

It is hard to say yes, harder to believe that over a million immigrants every year, from every country on earth, a third of them breaking in, will reforge the bonds of our disuniting nation. John Stuart Mill warned that "free institutions are next to impossible in a country made up of different nationalities. Among a people without fellow-feeling, especially if they read and speak different languages, the united public opinion necessary to the working of representative government cannot exist."

We are about to find out if Mill was right.

POSTSCRIPT

Should America Remain a Nation of Immigrants?

Buchanan argues that the new immigration since 1968 from Mexico, other parts of Latin America, and Asia is destroying the core culture of the United States. He maintains that the new immigrants are responsible for America's rising crime rate; the increase in the number of households that are below the poverty level; and the increase in the use of food stamps, Supplemental Social Security, and school lunch programs. Furthermore, maintains Buchanan, low-income Americans sustain real wage losses of 50 percent because of competition from legal and illegal immigration.

Buchanan also asserts that America is losing the cultural war. He holds that the Republican Party's white-based majority under Presidents Richard Nixon and Ronald Reagan has been undermined by an immigrant-based Democratic Party. He notes that the two biggest states—California and Texas—are beset with ethnic enclaves who do not speak English and whose political and cultural values are outside the American mainstream.

Although Buchanan expresses feelings that are felt by many Americans today, his analysis lacks historical perspective. Ever since Columbus encountered the first Native Americans, tensions between immigrants and native-born people have existed. During the four peak periods of immigration to the United States, the host group has felt overwhelmed by the newest groups entering the country. Buchanan quotes Benjamin Franklin's concern about the German immigrants' turning Pennsylvania into a "Colony of Aliens, who will shortly be so numerous as to Germanize us instead of our Anglifying them." But Buchanan does not carry his observation to its logical conclusion. German immigration into the United States did not halt during the Seven Years War, as Buchanan contends. It continued during the nineteenth and early twentieth centuries, and Germans today constitute the largest white ethnic group in the country.

Buchanan also ignores the hostility accorded his own Irish-Catholic relatives by white, Protestant Americans in the 1850s, who considered the Irish crime-ridden, lazy, drunken ignoramuses living in ethnic enclaves who were unassimilable because of their "Papist" religious ceremonies. Irish males, it was said, often did not work but lived off the wages of their wives, who worked as maids. When menial jobs were performed mostly by Irish men, they were accused of lowering the wages of other working-class Americans. One may question whether the newest immigrants are different from Buchanan's own ancestors.

Jacoby gives a spirited defense of the newest immigrants. She dismisses the argument for increased immigration restriction after the September 11 attacks on the World Trade Center and the Pentagon by distinguishing between a terrorist and an immigrant. She contends that the estimates about a future population explosion in the country might be exaggerated, especially if economic conditions improve in Third World countries when the global economy becomes more balanced.

Jacoby stresses the positive impact of the new immigrants. Many of them—particularly those from India and other Asian countries—have contributed their skills to the computer industry in the Silicon Valley and other high-tech industrial parks across America. Jacoby also argues that even if poorer immigrants overuse America's health and welfare social services, many of them contribute portions of their pay to the Social Security trust fund, including illegal immigrants who might never receive a government retirement check. Jacoby does allow that although today's immigrants may be no poorer than those who came in the third wave at the turn of the twentieth century, today's unskilled immigrants are relatively further behind than the southern and eastern Europeans who came around 1900. This is the view of sociologist George J. Borjas in *Heaven's Door: Immigration and the American Economy* (Princeton University Press, 1999).

Most experts agree that changes need to be made in the U.S. immigration laws. Some groups, such as the Federation for American Immigration Reform (FAIR), would like to see a huge cut in the 730,000 legal immigrants, 100,000 refugees, and 200,000 illegal immigrants (Borjas's numbers) who came into America each year in the 1980s and 1990s. Borjas would add a point system to a numerical quota, which would take into account age, work experience, fluency in English, educational background, work experience, and the quality of one's job. Jacoby also favors an immigration policy that gives preference to immigrants with key job-related skills over those who use the loopholes in the law to reunite the members of their families. Unlike Buchanan, Jacoby maintains that the newest immigrants will assimilate as earlier groups did but only when their legal status as citizens is fully established.

There is an enormous bibliography on the newest immigrants. A good starting point, which clearly explains the immigration laws and their impact on the development of American society, is Kenneth K. Lee, *Huddled Masses, Muddled Laws: Why Contemporary Immigration Policy Fails to Reflect Public Opinion* (Praeger, 1998). Another book that concisely summarizes both sides of the debate and contains a useful glossary of terms is Gerald Leinwand, *American Immigration: Should the Open Door Be Closed?* (Franklin Watts, 1995).

Because historians take a long-range view of immigration, they tend to weigh in on the pro side of the debate. See L. Edward Purcell, *Immigration: Social Issues in American History Series* (Oryx Press, 1995); Reed Ueda's *Postwar America: A Social History* (Bedford Books, 1995); and David M. Reimers, *Still the Golden Door: The Third World War Comes to America,* 2d ed. (Columbia University Press, 1997) and *Unwelcome Strangers: American Identity and the Turn Against Immigration* (Columbia University Press, 1998).

ISSUE 14

Will History Consider William Jefferson Clinton a Reasonably Good Chief Executive?

YES: Nicholas Thompson, from "Graduating With Honors: The Hits and Misses of a Protean President," *The Washington Monthly* (December 2000)

NO: James MacGregor Burns and Georgia J. Sorenson et al., from *Dead Center: Clinton-Gore Leadership and the Perils of Moderation* (Scribner, 1999)

ISSUE SUMMARY

YES: Journalist Nicholas Thompson argues that President Bill Clinton's governing style of simultaneously pushing and pulling in hundreds of directions led Americans to be better off in 2000 than they were when Clinton first took office eight years earlier.

NO: Political scientists James MacGregor Burns and Georgia J. Sorenson et al. argue that Clinton will not rank among the near-great presidents because he was a transactional broker who lacked the ideological commitment to tackle the big issues facing American society.

William Jefferson Clinton, born in Hope, Arkansas, on August 19, 1946, is the third-youngest president ever to hold the office. Similar to Abraham Lincoln, Clinton is considered a true embodiment of the "log cabin myth," which holds that anybody can become president. Both Lincoln and Clinton grew up in poor, dysfunctional southern families. Lincoln was born in Kentucky and was raised by a stepmother and a father whose unsuccessful ventures as a farmer caused the family to move four times before Lincoln was 21. Both had stepbrothers who were constantly in financial and legal trouble.

By the age of 16 Clinton knew he wanted to be a major professional politician. After graduating from Georgetown University in 1968 with an international affairs degree, Clinton won a Rhodes scholarship and studied for two years at Oxford University. Like a number of his liberal and conservative counterparts of the 1960s, Clinton avoided the draft and earned a law degree from Yale University in 1973. His first experience in politics was as the Texas coordinator of George McGovern's presidential campaign in 1972. Ironically, Clinton served briefly as a staff attorney for the House Judiciary Committee, a year before the committee became preoccupied with investigating charges of impeachment against President Richard Nixon.

In the early 1970s Clinton returned to his home state and briefly taught law at the University of Arkansas. But, like Lincoln, politics was his real ambition. In 1974 he made a strong showing against an entrenched Republican incumbent in the House of Representatives but fared better in 1976 when he ran Jimmy Carter's presidential campaign in his home state and was elected state attorney general. In 1978, at age 32, Clinton became one of the youngest governors ever elected to the office.

In his first term Clinton tried to govern as a New Deal Democrat. He upgraded the state's highways but was forced to raise taxes on gasoline and auto licensing fees to pay the costs. Meanwhile, riots by 18,000 Cuban refugees at Fort Chaffee, Arkansas, which he was forced to quell in conjunction with a perception that the governor and his staff exhibited a streak of arrogance and overambitiousness, hurt his bid for reelection in 1980. Carter's failed presidency and the taxpayer revolt, which started in California and spread to the rest of the nation, left Clinton unemployed.

Clinton was down but not out. He ostensibly practiced law, but his real goal was to get reelected as governor. He began his campaign on television with an apology to the voters for raising highway taxes, blamed his mistakes on "youthful ignorance," and toured the state in an effort to listen to the concerns of his citizens. This strategy paid off. Clinton defeated his Republican opponent by a wide margin in 1982 and was reelected on four more occasions with little opposition through 1992.

Clinton thought about running for president in 1988 but decided to wait until 1992. He was only 45 but it was a propitious time. President George Bush was extremely popular in the winter of 1991 because he had led UN forces to victory over the Iraqis in Kuwait. Prominent Democrats considered it futile to run against a popular incumbent president. The challengers were a group of lesser Democrats whom Clinton was able to defeat in the primaries. On November 3, 1992, Clinton received only 43 percent of the popular vote, Bush 38 percent, and H. Ross Perot 19 percent, which was the second-highest percentage in American history for a third-party candidate. The margin of victory was much wider in the electoral college—Clinton's 370 votes to Bush's 168. Clinton won the election running as a centrist Democrat from Arkansas. He got Reagan Democrats in the northeast and midwestern states to come back to the fold.

Will history rank Bill Clinton as a near-great, average, or below average president? In the following selection, Nicholas Thompson gives Clinton a solid B grade for his zig-zag governing style, which Thompson asserts made Americans better off in 2000 than they were eight years earlier. In the second selection, James MacGregor Burns and Georgia J. Sorenson et al. argue that Clinton will not rank among the near-great presidents because he lacked the ideological commitment and overall vision to tackle the big issues facing American society.

Nicholas Thompson

 **YES**

Graduating With Honors

When Bill Clinton took the oath of office in 1993, Serbian forces were running rampant in Bosnia. Villages were burning; men were being lined up behind their houses and shot. Civil war was spreading, but the new president was shackled by Colin Powell's doctrine that the United States should never enter battle without decisive force and clear objectives. So Clinton put his thumbs in his pockets and continued the dithering of the Bush administration for a year and a half until shame essentially forced the Dayton peace settlement.

Six years later, when Serbian forces cut loose in Kosovo, Clinton threw Powell's doctrine out the window. Obviously unclear about his goals, the president alienated Republican and Democratic traditionalists alike. The United States certainly didn't use decisive force, nor did we pursue a clear objective: Were we trying to force Milosevic from power, or just stop human-rights abuses? And what was going on with our relationship with the U.N.? Clinton limited his options by pledging at the outset not to commit ground troops. So he waged the battle exclusively from bombers 15,000 feet up, fully aware that no country had ever won a war that way. No matter. Genuflecting to public opinion while juggling new strategies worked. Milosevic threw down his cards, and the end game was a rout. The Serbian dictator has been forced out of power and, despite minor snafus, victory came without the sacrifice of a single American life.

Neither Bosnia nor Kosovo was the defining moment of the Man From Hope's eight years in the White House. But the essence of Clintonism can be found in the difference between his responses to the two crises. For eight years, whenever Clinton let himself become constrained by grand themes and conventional wisdom, he failed. When he stayed in motion and used his instincts like a political fox, he triumphed.

He abandoned large legislative ideas when his healthcare plan imploded and Newt Gingrich took over Congress. He ditched the public investment plans he had campaigned on soon after being sworn in. He tried half-heartedly and unsuccessfully to come up with a big foreign policy idea, and instead produced a mishmash that infuriates experts but works fine for everybody else. He sometimes argues that his presidency does have a central theme: stewarding

From Nicholas Thompson, "Graduating With Honors: The Hits and Misses of a Protean President," *The Washington Monthly* (December 2000). Copyright © 2000 by The Washington Monthly Publishing, LLC, 733 15th St., NW, Suite 1000, Washington, DC 20005. http://www.washingtonmonthly.com. Reprinted by permission.

the country from the industrial age to the information age. Then this brilliant communicator essentially discredits the very notion with each garbled explanation.

Still, by simultaneously pushing and pulling in hundreds of directions, and sticking by a series of evolving moderate themes, Bill Clinton has justifiably won enduring popularity. The country is far more prosperous, safer, and internationally strong than when he took office. He has failed frequently, sometimes succeeded through sheer dumb luck, and changed the culture of politics for the worse. But ultimately this protean and often-maddening president is a big factor in why we're so much better off today than we were eight years ago.

Running the Economy

Grade: A

Presidents don't run the economy. They don't drive delivery trucks or lay electronic switches in silicon. But they do have their hands on the various levers that push the economy forward. They send signals to business; they help set key economic indices; they determine much of our trade policies.

Running for office, Clinton vowed to concentrate "like a laser beam" on the economy. This was still the era when Japan seemed like the biggest bull in the barnyard, and Clinton's economic plan was modeled on their industrial policy: ramping up our investment in public infrastructure and taxing companies to set up worker training programs. As Clinton said during the final presidential debate, "My passion is to pass a jobs program."

Once in office, Clinton quickly tacked. He learned both that the economy was gaining steam and that the budget deficit was worse than anticipated —consequently, his top economic advisers argued that deficit reduction, which should reduce long-term interest rates, was the surest way out of the slump. Clinton listened carefully and decided that being right trumped being consistent with campaign rhetoric. So he rolled up his sleeves and started doing what he does best: molding a policy, brawling in the back rooms, and charming potential supporters.

He navigated through a protracted battle within the administration and Congress, and wrote a budget that mixed deficit reduction with progressive policy and second-best compromises. He sharply reduced the deficit by lowering spending and raising the federal gasoline tax along with taxes on the affluent. He hiked up funding for the Earned Income Tax Credit, a reverse income tax that gives money back to poor people who work. He abandoned an energy tax, dear to Vice President Gore, which seemed like a last-minute deal killer.

Clinton's budget bill received absolutely no Republican support. It passed the House by two votes and squeaked through the Senate when an anguished Senator Bob Kerrey finally voted for the bill, relenting to hours of presidential arm-twisting, and Gore swooped in to cast the tie-breaking vote. That budget, the fruit of endless hours of presidential labor, probably remains Clinton's most important accomplishment. It set the economy on the right track and laid the groundwork for the coming prosperity.

Boom!

Immediately after the bill passed, long-term interest rates dropped. Clinton had not only taken a strong swing at the exploding deficit of the past 12 years, he had convinced the financial markets that he was going to work in concert with [Federal Reserve Bank chairman Alan] Greenspan. Traditionally, presidents and Fed chairmen have worked at cross-purposes—one foot down on the accelerator, one pumping the brakes. Clinton broke that destructive cycle with his political and personal skills. He invited Greenspan to sit between Tipper Gore and Hillary during his first State of the Union address. More important, he stuck firmly to Greenspan's specific deficit goals, passed on covertly by Treasury Secretary Lloyd Bentsen. The role of the Federal Reserve is to take away the punch bowl before the party gets out of hand, but Clinton made it clear that he was serving everyone ice water. So the chairman kept short-term interests rates virtually constant and the markets soared.

Clinton also pushed free-trade agreements through Congress by mustering a bipartisan coalition. With the help of a team of seasoned veterans, he steered the United States through the firestorms that menaced the world economy in 1997 and 1998. Clinton even courageously defied public opinion in offering Mexico a $40 billion loan when the peso crashed in 1995.

He also, through an act of cunning, stymied the [Newt] Gingrich Congress' efforts to roll back taxes and revert to the trickle-down policies of the Reagan and Bush years. In his 1998 State of the Union address, he lyrically proclaimed that we should use surpluses to "save Social Security first." As Michael Waldman, then the president's chief speechwriter, writes in his recent book, *POTUS Speaks:* "The Democrats leapt to their feet, cheering. Gingrich paused for a discernible instant—then he, too, stood, applauding.... In that instant, a trillion dollars silently shifted on the budget ledger from the column marked 'tax cut' to the column marked 'Social Security.'"

Clinton's four-word phrase was misleading: No president or Congress can really lock revenues away from future politicians. In practical terms, Clinton had guaranteed that surplus money coming from the Social Security tax would pay down the debt. Clinton knew that the country needed increased savings, not tax cuts that could well push the needle of the fast-moving economy into the red. Once again, Clinton had outfoxed his opponents—almost certainly for the country's good.

Domestic Policy

Grade: B+

When Clinton ran for office, Democrats had lost five of the previous six presidential elections. Their policies were seen nationally as mushy or excessive: They favored welfare cheats and snail darters and opposed accountable schools and crime enforcement.

Clinton entered the country's spotlight as a New Democrat and during the '92 campaign he gained traction by disavowing old Democratic gospel, espousing positions ranging from the death penalty to requiring welfare recipients to work. Once elected, he moved left and stumbled trying to push a more traditional Democratic agenda. He was only saved, it seems, by the Republican takeover of Congress.

Like a jazz musician who can only play by ear, at his best, Clinton listened carefully and moved forward by snatching ideas from every side. On environmental protection, for example, Clinton seemed at a loss during his first two years as he worked to implement pent-up Democratic initiatives. He first tried to reform mining and grazing laws, but Western Senators chewed him up. Then they clobbered him for trying to elevate the EPA [Environmental Protection Agency] into a cabinet level agency. Defeated there, and punched out on his proposed energy tax, Clinton's first term passed with little success.

After the 1994 election, Clinton found his stride. He rhetorically battled down the Republican Congress for their sudden attempt to take hatchets to environmental law. He stopped every single one of Gingrich's major environmental reforms. Clinton then bypassed Congress, using executive orders in lieu of legislation, to push politically popular conservation initiatives, culminating last year with an order forestalling new roads in over 40 million acres of national forest.

Clinton, however, wasn't a demagogue or a strict partisan. His most important accomplishment was ending the public perception that there is a choice between environmental protection and economic growth. He broke the stalemate between loggers and environmentalists over the spotted owl in the Pacific Northwest—a conflict about which George Bush had said "It's time to make people more important than owls"—by developing a plan that conserved sensitive land while offering job retraining and economic aid to logging communities. Instead of mandating that polluters strictly limit their nitrous oxide emissions, Clinton allowed them to set up a market-based trading system. Companies that were able to greatly reduce emissions were allowed to sell the right to pollute to less efficient competitors—a scheme that encourages innovation and ultimately makes conservation far more efficient, even if it does have unfortunate side effects for some communities. Clinton also tried to write such tradable permit schemes into the tabled Kyoto global warming treaty and introduced the possibility into the Clean Water Act.

He Got Game

Clinton came to office famously promising to "end welfare as we know it" and, in so doing, put the issue on the table. But his obsession with health care blocked him from moving on welfare early, and Republicans used the issue as a political wedge to help win Congress in 1994. Clinton was forced into reactive mode, responding to Newt Gingrich's proposed reforms. The president vetoed the first two. Despite including the agreed-upon premise that people on welfare should work, the Gingrich legislation was loaded down with poison pills such as removing the federal guarantee of Medicaid and slashing Supplemental Social

Security Income benefits—a long-standing program of payments for the elderly and disabled poor.

The third Republican bill of 1995 included some punitive measures—most brutally revoking all welfare benefits for non-citizen immigrants—but Clinton defied most of his top advisers and signed it, promising to fix the immigrant provisions, as he later partially did. Largely as a result, welfare rolls have declined by more than 50 percent nationally. There might be serious problems when the next recession hits, and the bill has done little to help the great number of people who have led such troubled lives that they struggle to hold any sort of job. The reform though seems to have worked as well as its proponents boasted it would. There are hundreds of thousands of people who have benefited, and welfare reform has changed the political discussion of poverty in America. It's not a coincidence that this was the first presidential election in recent memory where one or the other candidate didn't use aid to the poor as a bogeyman, or use criticisms of poverty in inflammatory coded language for race.

Clinton employed the strategy of bouncing, co-opting, and sticking with modest ideas to earn success on other issues, most prominently crime and education. The Republican line on crime for decades has more or less been lock 'em down or string 'em up and the GOP consistently earned higher ratings from the public. George Bush had fried Michael Dukakis in 1988 with his Willie Horton ads that portrayed the Massachusetts governor as soft on crime. But Clinton was pro-death penalty and, in 1992, Bush was left stammering by the governor's proposal to put 100,000 policemen on the street using a new style of community policing. The only way the vice president could try to gain a toughness edge during the first debate was to declare that he "happen[ed] to think that we need stronger death penalties for those that kill police officers."

On education, Clinton also did a very good job of rubbing the belly of his inner politician. He pushed a few issues from the traditional left, like piling up money for university students through an alphabet soup of grant programs and tax credits. But his real success came from his own ideas and his ability to cut an original path through the teachers' unions on the far left and the education slashers on the right. Clinton helped charter schools move forward, improving school innovation in at least modest ways. He also created a program that grants loans directly from the Department of Education to college students, instead of routing them through politically powerful middlemen. Previously, loans were primarily granted by Sallie Mae, a tremendously profitable quasi-governmental organization, and backed up by the government. Sallie Mae, which was privatized in 1996, now has to compete with the Education Department, resulting in lower-interest loans and savings for students. Clinton was also the first Democrat to really push standards nationally, requiring them for all states receiving federal funding through Title I. Standards aren't the magic bullet for our education problems, but it's a pretty good indicator of Clinton's success that the presidential debate in 2000 wasn't over whether we should have standards—it was over how to make them tougher and fairer.

The Hillary Trap

Of course, Clinton's domestic policy has not been an unbroken string of successes. He initially and halfheartedly tried for campaign finance reform but, once stymied, decided to blow a hole in the system and cut every conceivable legal corner. He essentially invented soft-money ads during his 1996 presidential race and seemed to follow the prayer of St. Augustine: "Lord give me chastity and continency, just not now." The president talked about reform, but he reveled in thousand-dollar-a-plate fundraisers and spent more energy finding new loopholes than closing them.

Clinton's biggest problems have come when he hasn't given himself space to move. After flirting with Social Security reform, the president eschewed the small steps that could solidify the system: from raising the retirement age to means testing benefits to reducing and rationalizing cost-of-living adjustments. On health care, Clinton tried to pass an ambitious bill, but he gave the project to his wife and Ira Magaziner and they flamed out on the politics. They didn't listen to critics; they didn't scratch the backs of potential friends; and they scuttled potential coalitions. Afterwards, the president tried to play catch-up. He signed the Kennedy-Kassebaum Act allowing workers to keep health insurance after switching jobs, and he created the Children's Health Insurance Program. Although important, both bills fell short of what is needed. Since Clinton became president, the number of Americans without health insurance has climbed from 37 to 42 million.

Not coincidentally, the worst mistakes of the administration have come because of Clinton's inability to separate political reality from his relationship with Hillary. It's not that she was a fount of bad advice. But when Clinton dealt with her, he stopped listening to advisers and allowed Hillary's rigid instincts to wrestle his more flexible ones to the ground. This is what happened with health care. It's also what happened when *The Washington Post* asked Clinton to hand over all of the documents relating to Whitewater. According to both David Gergen and George Stephanopoulos, top Clinton advisers, the president wanted to hand everything over but insisted on first talking to Hillary.

She didn't want to do it. Hillary thought the attacks would continue indefinitely regardless and she didn't understand that stonewalling would only pour gasoline on the fire. Still feeling sheepish after the publication of long exposes of his infidelity in *The American Spectator* and *Los Angeles Times,* Clinton acquiesced and refused to give the documents over. The media were infuriated and started charging hard, forcing Clinton to appoint independent council Robert Fiske to investigate the matter. Fiske dove into the ultimately innocent nuances of Whitewater and continually expanded the probe, a trend continued in spades by his replacement, Ken Starr.

Four years later, confronted by the Monica Lewinsky story, Clinton again went into hunker-down mode, quite likely because of his fear of facing his wife with the truth about his abominable behavior. Breaking with the pattern that had brought him so much success, Clinton decided to stick with one tactic. In a sense he was pursuing the mirror image of the Powell doctrine, move as slowly as possibly and follow each provable accusation with an admission and nothing more. He parsed words and gradually retreated, like a hedgehog sticking up its spines and backing into the corner. The result was the greatest shame of his presidency.

Foreign Affairs

Grade: B

Clinton has never had the respect of the foreign policy elite. He campaigned for office, denigrating George Bush's fixation on foreign affairs and his first few months on the job were disastrous. American soldiers were murdered and dragged through the streets of Mogadishu; a ship bringing Americans to train a civilian police force was turned around at Haiti's port by menacing thugs; villages burned in Bosnia as Clinton thumbed through briefing papers.

For many, the first few months set the pattern for the administration. John McCain has said repeatedly that Clinton has followed a pattern of "strategic incoherence" that will come back to bite us. Richard Haass, director of foreign policy studies at the Brookings Institution, wrote in *Foreign Affairs* [in] May [2000] that Clinton's "foreign policy suffered from a lack of presidential interest, attention, and respect. It suffered, in short, from malign neglect."

It is true that Clinton never offered a sweeping vision. He never convinced the public that he knew where he was going to move his chess pieces, and there's no Clinton doctrine that high-school students can memorize off of note cards. He flummoxed his allies and, in large part because of his decision to skirt the draft during Vietnam, seemed to cower before anyone in uniform.

But, Clinton did have a set of notions, and he did know how to push them through. He was consistent in his efforts to enlarge the community of market democracies and equalize the importance of international economies and policy. Previous presidents have been willing to pay almost any price to prop up anti-Communist leaders, from the brutal Duvaliers to the malevolent Mobutu; Clinton has been willing to do almost anything to open foreign markets and to bring peace. He fought tooth and nail for NAFTA [North American Free Trade Agreement] and GATT [General Agreement on Tariffs and Trade] and many lesser trade agreements.

Clinton also, as always, reacted well to unpredictability and, aggravating experts irked by successful amateurs, was able to dance his way out of every quagmire. Even with China, the bugbear of much of the Republican Congress, Clinton seems to have played his cards just about right. As China emerged as the greatest challenger to American hegemony, Clinton didn't take a uniform line. He pushed hard rhetorically on issues of human rights and intellectual property piracy. At the same time, he worked to integrate China's booming economy with ours and eventually was able to obtain a permanent normal trade relationship agreement. He also played tough by calling out war ships when China threatened Taiwan. Partly as a result, relations between Taiwan and the mainland have improved, our companies are flying into Beijing, and there are even signs of fledgling democracy in China's outer provinces.

There is also, in part due to Clinton, increased peace in Northern Ireland, and although Molotov cocktails are presently flying in Jerusalem, Israel has been able to forge peace with Egypt and Jordan and, at least, smooth relations with Syria. And this isn't just because of luck and inherited policies. Clinton is a skillful, indefatigable negotiator. As King Hussein of Jordan said to him: "I have never—with all due respect and all the affection that I held for your predecessors—have known someone with your dedication, clear headedness, focus, and determination to help resolve this issue in the best way possible."

Dealing With Washington and the Government

Grade: C+

When Bill Clinton debated George Bush and Ross Perot in 1992, he boasted endlessly about his accomplishments in Arkansas. After the governor ran on a bit too long, Perot noted that "I could say, you know, that I ran a small grocery store on the corner, therefore I extrapolate that into the fact that I can run Wal-Mart. That's not true."

That may have been Perot's most prescient line. Clinton came to Washington confident that he could handle the sprawling bureaucracy, and he quickly bumped his head. He appointed his buddy Mack McLarty as chief of staff despite McLarty's lack of federal experience. He devoted far too much energy to drafting a cabinet that looked like America and dawdled over choosing a White House staff. Not surprisingly, he soon lost control over the confrontation between the FBI and Branch Davidians at Waco, spun in circles over gays in the military, and with the firing of the White House travel office, set off a conservative hunt that ultimately ended up finding him innocent of malice but guilty of incompetence.

Clinton also struggled with his staff, bouncing between the advice given to him by senior aides and his young campaign team. At the same time, Clinton was frequently pushed into reactive mode—not unlike previous administrations, but with an unprecedented level of chaos. According to senior adviser Bill Curry, "most White Houses are floating ad-hocracies. This one just happened to be a bit more so than others."

Dollar Bill

Clinton has always loved to make policy more than to carry it out. He wanted to pass bills, he was terrific at partisan battles, and he seemed able to master the intricacies of every issue. According to Mike Cohen, a senior education adviser to Clinton for the past 15 years, "From the first time I met him, to the last time we talked in the White House, I have never failed to be impressed that he is the smartest person around on education policy."

Despite this, or perhaps because of it, Clinton's interest wasn't as deep as it should have been. He could make a great case for why Medicaid shouldn't be block-granted with welfare, but once a bill was passed and the press conference chairs had been folded up, Clinton seemed to move on to the next thing in his inbox. He did request weekly memos from cabinet members and was constantly looking for cabinet-level initiatives to wrap up in red ribbon. But he delegated the entire effort to reinvent government to Gore and disengaged from the issue so much that aides were often reluctant to even bother him with discussions of government reform. According to chief of staff Leon Panetta, the president didn't want to look at restructuring government because it "seemed in the past that it was a wasted effort."

Clinton paid almost no attention to the IRS until Senate hearings in 1997, even though it was revealed in 1993 that, in just one regional office, more than 350 employees had been investigated for snooping through the tax returns of friends, relatives, and celebrities. That wasn't enough for Clinton to act. It was only after the appalling, if exaggerated, stories of the men and women who testified at infamous 1997 hearings that Clinton decided to lock the barn door. The testimony had been politically motivated and a bit overblown, but no one could deny there was a serious problem. So the president crafted a reform bill that, as Al Gore said, would create "an IRS that is not just taken off people's backs but put on their side." But by trying to come out with a response as soon as the problem hit the newspapers, Clinton's reform was seriously flawed. It solved the public relations problem: The IRS no longer harasses people. But the agency has been forced to overcompensate and enforcement has bottomed out. Seizure of property to pay back taxes, for example, has declined 98 percent since the law was passed two years ago.

When *The New York Times* was about to publish a scathing report on the administration's failures at inspecting imported food, the president quickly cobbled together a measure to allow the FDA [Food and Drug Administration] to ban food imports—making good press, if not good governance. When the National Academy of Sciences released a report saying that medical mistakes killed tens of thousands of patients annually, Clinton announced that he was shocked and prepared a defiant legislative response. Either he wasn't on top of a relatively well-known issue, or he was lying and should have acted well before the issue hit the front of *The Washington Post*.

The pattern also holds in ensuring that legislation is implemented effectively. Clinton's crime bill revolved around 100,000 cops being moved into local police forces. But the implementation effort was understaffed, and seven years after the bill passed, the Justice Department estimates that only about 60,000 policemen are actually on the streets. Numerous departments have received so-called police-equivalents, like laptops, a large part of the money is still to be doled out, and a 1999 Inspector General's report estimated that 40 percent of the grantees were using the money to supplant local funds. In a suburb of Chicago, an audit found that thousands of dollars in COPS [Community Oriented Policing Services] money helped bankroll dog-track gambling and trips to Florida and Arizona.

In fairness, there will always be some problems stemming from the complexity of the federal government: Agencies will disintegrate, space ships will crash and contractors somewhere will screw something up. But a president has to minimize mistakes, and the way to do that isn't to run an administration that seems to stop at the White House.

Bill's Excellent Adventure

If there is a central theme to the career of Bill Clinton it's that he always wanted to have his cake and eat it too. He wanted to balance the budget without sacrificing core government programs; he wanted clean air without cutting corporations off at the knees; he wanted welfare recipients to take personal responsibility without ending up on the streets; he wanted free trade with China without having to give in on Taiwan and human rights. And to his great credit, Clinton has been smart enough, and shown a deep enough love of policy, to get what he wanted almost every time he allowed himself space to move.

The results have been magnificent. Since Clinton has come to office, we've gone from having the biggest budget deficits in history to having the biggest surpluses, and the boom is spreading fairly equally across society. We now have the lowest recorded African American and Hispanic poverty rates in history, the lowest percentage of Americans on welfare since 1965, and even indicators like teen pregnancy rates are dropping. We are experiencing the longest continuous crime drop in history. We have basically open and positive relationships with all of our potential major allies and antagonists. Clinton doesn't deserve all the credit, but he surely deserves some.

It's hard not to wish that Bill Clinton hadn't been so absorbed in himself that he was willing to act personally reckless, and that his love of the bright lights kept him out of the dark corners where so much government reform is needed. Even so, he got most of the big things right. It's only fair to grade him well now that the era of Bill Clinton is over.

**James MacGregor Burns and
Georgia J. Sorenson et al.**

 **NO**

What Kind of Leadership?

At some point a two-term president begins to think more about his place in history and less about his standing in the polls and at the polls. His hope for eternal fame rises most acutely after his reelection, of course, but not only then. Presidents are now held responsible for leading their party to win in congressional elections; thus Clinton, and Hillary Rodham Clinton too, were blamed for the Republican takeover of Congress in 1994, then credited for some Democratic gains in 1998. A president is also expected to help his vice president succeed him, but in 2000 that will be Al Gore's responsibility.

During much of his life—and perhaps as early as seizing JFK's hand—Clinton aspired to be not only president but a "great" president. One of his most crushing reactions to the Monica S. Lewinsky revelations was that his behavior had relegated him to the standing of a run-of-the-mill president. He might even be downgraded to failure—a rating inexplicably accorded Jimmy Carter in one polling of presidential scholars.

What is greatness in the White House? For years scholars have been rating presidents without a clear and agreed-on set of criteria. In our view, the bottom-line answer is conviction and commitment, plus the courage and competence to act on beliefs and promises. The scholarly rating game shows some volatility over the years in the standings of presidents—Harry Truman improved the more we got to know some of his successors—but the continuing "greats" over the years are the committed leaders Washington, Lincoln, and Franklin Roosevelt, with Thomas Jefferson just behind.

Monuments are another form of rating, especially in Washington. There is a pecking order in those memorials. For a century or more Washington and Lincoln have had their monuments, joined by Jefferson a half century ago and by FDR in the past decade. Washington's is the most imposing, Lincoln's the most evocative, Jefferson's the most philosophical, and Roosevelt's the most revealing about himself and his First Lady. Then there is Mount Rushmore, with Washington, Jefferson, and Lincoln carved in mighty stone, along with Theodore Roosevelt. Mean-spirited people complained that TR got there only because he and the sculptor were friends, but admirers of this "near great" are satisfied that he made it on his own.

From James MacGregor Burns and Georgia J. Sorenson with Robin Gerber and Scott W. Webster, *Dead Center: Clinton-Gore Leadership and the Perils of Moderation* (Scribner, 1999). Copyright © 1999 by James MacGregor Burns and Georgia J. Sorenson. Reprinted by permission of Scribner, an imprint of Simon & Schuster Adult Publishing Group.

Could Clinton aspire to a monument in Washington? Of course every president now gets his home library, no matter how great or nongreat. But Clinton might want more. Could he even hope for Mount Rushmore? There appears to be an open spot next to TR. But Franklin Roosevelt idolators see two spots that could be reserved for FDR and—yes—Eleanor. Still, what if someday the South Dakotans might balance the present three easterners and one midwesterner with a famous southerner?

Of course all this is terribly elitist. Dozens of other presidents, along with hundreds of governors, congressmen, local politicos, judges, and even professors are memorialized in thousands of courthouses, libraries, parks, and schools across the country. The warp and woof of American leadership, they are portrayed holding swords, canes, bibles, scrolls, constitutions, the reins of horses. Not one, so far as we know, brandishes a balanced budget law.

The Price of Centrism

A contradiction lay at the heart of Clinton's leadership: if he truly aspired to presidential greatness, the strategy he had chosen ensured that he would never achieve it. Rather, long before his presidency he had resolved on a centrist path that called for the kind of transactional leadership that he would exercise in abundance, especially in foreign policy. As a master broker he raised the art of the deal to world-class levels. But he rejected the kind of transformational leadership that might have placed him among the historic "greats."

What form did their transformational leadership take? Washington consolidated a whole new constitutional system that he had helped create. Jefferson recognized that political parties were necessary to unify and democratize that system, and he, with James Madison, fashioned the first opposition party. Lincoln moved on from demanding union at any price to demanding emancipation at any price and established a moral leadership that would vitalize his country for more than a century. FDR's remarkable foresight in broadening the antigovernment Bill of Rights into an "economic bill of rights" provided a "people's charter" that helped Americans cope with the ravages of the Depression and inequality.

The huge successes of these and other presidents displayed their transformational leadership: creativity in fashioning new policies; the courage to press for reforms and other changes despite popular apathy and opposition; the conviction to stick to grand principles no matter how long their realization might take; the commitment to the people to fight for their welfare at any personal cost. What was required for "greatness," in short, was a lifelong struggle to help achieve real, intended, principled, and lasting change.

Clinton could claim that he was just as committed to centrism as those great leaders had been committed to liberalism or progressivism. But just what was Clinton's centrism? The confusion over the term was vividly dramatized when his and Rodham Clinton's health bill of 1993–94 came to be categorized as a radical departure from his centrism. In fact in most respects the health plan epitomized moderate "mainstream" thinking. Rejecting the Canadian plan, it sought to attain a liberal goal, universal health care, without alienating conservatives, such as highly paid doctors and insurance companies. It had no particular ideology; it was neither socialist nor laissez-faire.

Confusion on this score was understandable because there seemed to be several brands of centrism. To some it was a kind of shopping list including moderate, liberal, and indeed conservative policies, from which the White House could pick items almost at will to meet immediate political and legislative exigencies. For others it was a nice balancing act, choosing conservative stands such as the death penalty and matching it with a liberal position on, say, gun control, without much in the middle.

The White House itself seemed unable to clarify this new form of government, or how it fit into the broader political system. In the summer of 1995, in a speech at Georgetown University, Clinton lamented that politics had become more and more fractured, and "just like the rest of us, pluralized. It's exciting in some ways, but as we divide into more and more and more sharply defined organized groups around more and more and more stratified issues, as we communicate more and more with people in extreme rhetoric through mass mailings or sometimes semihysterical messages right before election on the telephone, or thirty-second ads designed far more to inflame than to inform, as we see politicians actually getting language lessons on how to turn their adversaries into aliens, it is difficult to draw the conclusion that our political system is producing the sort of discussion that will give us the kind of results we need." Clinton seemed less than certain that mere goodwill among elected officials could paint over deep cracks in the polity.

Again and again the President invoked symbols of common ground, national unity, middle-class values, political partnership. Again and again he fell into pieties, such as civility, good citizenship, "strong families and faith," provoking in the minds of some listeners the only response to such shibboleths: "Of course, and who's against them?"

At that point, the President occupied the middle of the middle ground—so tenaciously that the liberal press searched for a Rasputin and found him in Dick Morris, who had come back to advise Clinton in 1995 after having worked for such conservatives as Jesse Helms and Paula Hawkins. But Clinton did not really need an advisor or a speechwriter for the Georgetown address. He was speaking from his heart and mind about his present political lodging place. Still, even this speech, lengthy though it was, omitted vital questions.

What about the Republicans? Were they supposed to suspend their partisanship to join the President on some peaceful ground? Clinton did not seem to recognize that he was confronted by one of the most disciplined and doctrinaire parties in this century, or if he did, he still assumed he could make deals with it. But the Republicans had won in 1994 with a most forthright platform, the Contract with America. Why should they break their promises to the people in order to trade with the President? These Republicans could hardly forget that Clinton had defeated a GOP governor in Arkansas and later driven their own president out of the White House. Who was he to talk conciliation?

And what about the Democrats? The President did not once mention the words *Democrat* or *Democratic party* in his Georgetown speech, though he was still using the old party catchwords—justice, equality, compassion, the Jeffersonian pursuit of happiness. Two hundred years earlier Jefferson and Madison were busy founding the Democratic-Republican party that would pursue the ancient values of liberty, equality, and fraternity. Was the modern Democratic party to stand by impotent while Clinton dickered with Republicans on his newly rediscovered common ground?

"Centrism is fine when it is the result of competing interests," William Safire wrote in late 1997. "Thesis; antithesis; synthesis. But centrism is vapid when it is the suffocator of interests, seeking to please rather than trying to move. Clinton's approach, in most cases, has been to follow the primrose path of polling down the middle: his motto has become a firm 'there must be no compromise without compromise.'"

Clinton's major failure was his inability, during his centrist phases, to frame a coordinated policy program that would make of his centrism not just an electoral strategy but a vital center of change. He was not against a political strategy in principle—he would tell aides that he wanted a "strategy" for some undertaking, as though strategies could be ordered up like tractors from John Deere. He loved strategy so much, someone quipped, that he had several of them, often at the same time. Clinton still clung to his overarching values of fairness and justice, but furthering such values to the degree he wished called for a strategy of change. Would centrist politics produce the kind of transformation that Clinton had so often championed and still seemed to support?

Perhaps it would if Clinton pursued his brokering kind of leadership persistently and skillfully. But in his heart he was not content to be only a dealer—at times his lofty values summoned him to a higher, transforming level of leadership. Such leadership, however, called for steady commitment to values such as equality and justice, priorities among those values, capacity to mobilize support both in his party and in movements that could be linked with the party, tenacity in pursuing his long-run visions and goals. It was not enough to know Niccolò Machiavelli's famous distinction between the courageous lion and the wily fox. He also needed to remember another Machiavelli dictum, which he quoted to a group of *Washington Post* reporters: "It must be considered that there is nothing more difficult to carry out or more doubtful of success, nor dangerous to handle, than to initiate a new order of things." For reformers have enemies, Machiavelli explained, and only "lukewarm defenders."

Clinton had lost many of his liberal defenders within three years of his somewhere-left-of-center 1992 campaign for the presidency. But he had not won over his centrist supporters, who feared another lurch to the left. Close observers had been tracking Clinton's ambivalence. Bob Woodward noted how Clinton sought to placate conservative foes of the energy (BTU) tax, stating, "I've been fighting the wrong folks." Elizabeth Drew reported that the President's ambivalence was raising again the "character issue," which could be overcome only if Clinton could move forcefully ahead on his program. It was not the first time someone pronounced, "Clinton was in a race against himself."

"On the one hand, the President badly wants to look like a problem-solver who will work with anyone to overcome the barriers of party and ideology," E. J. Dionne Jr. wrote in mid-1995. But Clinton also understood that "the Republicans have been dominating the political debate, and to change that, Democrats need to take on the large questions, challenging the Republican view of government fundamentally, and with conviction."

But Clinton could not resort to venomous politics. He could not hate those who hated him—not even the House Republicans who were targeting his favorite programs for extinction. "The Republicans were unanimous in their hatred for me—and I welcome their hatred," Franklin Roosevelt cried out to a roaring Democratic crowd at the height of the 1936 election campaign, as he scorched "economic royalists" who occupied positions similar to those of the Gingrich Republicans sixty years later. Clinton could not speak in such tones. Facing an ideological party, he could not be ideological because he was a transactional broker who was not always persistent and skillful enough to make his dealing stick, and was a would-be transforming leader without the deep conviction necessary to that strategy. No wonder some Americans considered him neither a fox nor a lion, but a chameleon.

The clinching argument for centrism is simple: it works. While the ideologues are out there speechifying and pontificating, New Democrats are out there getting things done—not as fast as the "old" liberals would like, perhaps, but centrists get there step by step.

They have a point. The Clinton-Gore centrists can boast of hundreds of presidential and congressional acts leading to incremental progress. But the problem, as always, is not simply what the centrists have done. It is what they have done in comparison with the enormity of the problem and with the changes, some of them regressive, that others are fashioning. It is not only a battle of leaders but a battle of leaderships, economic and social and ideological as well as political.

"Government bureaucracies built a half or even a quarter century ago," Al From wrote in 1991, "are incapable of coping with the challenges of the 1990s—jobs lost to companies overseas, stagnant family incomes, a burgeoning underclass, homelessness, rampant drug abuse and crime and violence in our cities, crumbling roads and bridges, declining public schools, and a deterioration of moral and cultural values symbolized by the breakdown of the family. We need a new set of political innovations."

Eight years and trillions of dollars later, can we say that any of these fundamental problems have been solved? Some economic improvement, yes, but the problems still stare at us. Take education—a concern of Clinton and Rodham Clinton's from their earliest days in Arkansas and a key test of centrist strategy. "We have to be prepared to reform the systems we have made," Governor Bill Clinton told the Democratic Leadership Council in 1990. "As the governors' statement on national education goals says, we can't get there with the system we've got. That's why restructuring schools nationwide is so important."

Restructuring schools? Restructuring the educational *system*? In eight years we have seen a plethora of proposals and programs for federal loans, grants, testing (for teachers and students), school uniforms, aid to special education, recruiting volunteers to teach fourth-graders to read, the end of "social promotion" in schools, adding one hundred thousand new teachers in the primary grades—most of these worthy and helpful—but nothing that could be described as a transformation of our educational system. Centrism, with its incremental advances, cannot possibly achieve such a huge task. And education continues in crisis in the United States.

The centrists have an excuse—the intractability of the American political system. And one of the key arguments for centrism is that it is flexible enough to allow brokering within the interstices of the constitutional checks and balances. Still, it is the liberals, and the conservatives demanding systemic change, who have the main problem with all the veto traps and institutional blocks in the political system. But transformational leaders have learned that the system will respond if they work at it long enough and hard enough; and if this fails to work, they have ideas about rejuvenating the system. Centrists have hardly been forthcoming with ideas for "reconstruction": centrists don't do that sort of thing.

So, Clinton began his seventh year in office amid a political and institutional shambles. Indeed, as Alison Mitchell observed in the *New York Times,* when the 1997–98 Congress came to an end, "it stood identified less with any signature bill than with the paralysis of American politics near century's end." The lesson seemed clear; centrists can deal and bargain and transact from the center; they can gain incremental changes from the center; they cannot truly lead and transform from the center.

Thus, the cardinal question transcends Bill Clinton's or Al Gore's or Hillary Rodham Clinton's "greatness." It goes to core issues about the dynamics of progress, the role of conflict and consensus in democracy, the capacity of people to bring about far-reaching change, the requirements of leadership. It sharply poses the difference between the truly "vital center" that Arthur Schlesinger Jr. wrote about years ago and the mainstream, bipartisan, flaccid centrism of the 1990s.

The Myth of Presidential Virtue

While Clinton had been jibbing and yawing in his search for the political center, right, left, or middle, some close observers had been searching for a center in him, ethical, moral, or virtuous.

No words are more confused or abused than the language of good behavior. Dictionaries don't help; ours defines morality as ethics, ethics as morality, and virtue as both. But the distinctions are crucial. We define *virtue* as approved personal conduct, especially sexual; *ethical* as rectitude or right conduct, especially in nonprivate business or professional behavior; and *moral* as fidelity to the highest and broadest of national or community values, past and present, especially as proclaimed and continually reiterated in formal pronouncements such as presidential inaugural addresses over a long span of time.

The myth of the virtuous American president began early, with George Washington. The story of the cherry tree, although fabricated, symbolized the honesty and integrity that later ennobled the first president's leadership. Yet, he was succeeded, after the very proper John Adams, by his fellow Virginian Thomas Jefferson, who was shown many years later to have probably slept with his slave Sally Hemmings. This was not only unvirtuous but illegal as miscegenation under the laws of the day. But the myth survived and even flourished during the nineteenth century because the genteel press, though it might criticize a president's policies, would not conceive of investigating and exposing presidential peccadilloes, and even scholarly biographers rarely dug into sexual behavior.

Throughout the twentieth century, rumors drifted around about the extramarital sexual behavior—both before and during their presidencies—on the part of Harding, Franklin Roosevelt, Eisenhower, JFK, LBJ, and perhaps earlier of Woodrow Wilson. But the press was not yet so intrusive, or respectable biographers so bold, as to shatter the benign image of the virtuous president. Only years later did it become known, for example, that Harding had had sex with his young mistress in a White House "closet"; or that FDR had had a romance in his earlier Washington days with his wife's secretary or that the liaison was renewed in the White House during his final years; or that JFK had indulged in numerous trysts in the presidential mansion.

How long could the myth survive? Its destruction would require the combination of a reckless president, some bad luck, and rapacious journalists. This was the unintended feat of Bill Clinton. But when one strips away the exploitation of the "scandal" and considers the titillating specifics of the sexual behavior—the caressing, groping, undressing, and the rest—was there any difference between what literally went on in Harding's closet and in Bill and Monica's lovemaking? Only one differences so far as the myth was concerned—Harding's was never exposed in all its graphic detail by an independent prosecutor and sensationalized in the press.

Clinton was attacked not only for his sexual behavior, of course, but for lying about it. And few Americans would ever forget that indignant finger thrust out from the tube, as the President flatly denied the accusations against him. But the earlier transgressors had lied too—implicitly in the case of Jefferson, or with the covering-up by Harding and Kennedy, with the aid of a complicit press.

At issue is the president's right to privacy, including his right to protect it. Beginning with childhood, we all exercise that right, against intrusive parents, prying friends, interrogating employers. Whatever the law may say about the obstruction of justice, William Buckley Jr. wrote, "it is unrealistic to distinguish sharply between the offense of adultery and the offense of lying about it, inasmuch as the second offense goes hand in hand with the first. Anyone who commits adultery is expected to lie about it."

The right to privacy remains the issue. Perhaps presidents do not need it. Or perhaps they need it most of all.

❧◈❧

The tragedy of Monicagate was intensely personal—the horrendous invasions of the privacy of Monica S. Lewinsky herself at the hands of an alleged friend

[Linda Tripp], the privacy of Bill Clinton and countless others at the hands of a rampaging prosecutor, and the intense distress for Hillary Rodham Clinton and daughter Chelsea. Everything revolved around the definition of virtue as sex. The tragedy quickly became political, as a media frenzy turned the ethical lesson of Monicagate upside down, grotesquely overemphasizing sex in the Oval Office and ignoring the nonsexual ethical implications. As a result the whole era rivals the Age of McCarthy in its confused and perverted priorities. It ignored the great lesson of American history that ethical concerns must trump private virtue in the public realms.

To free a president from public accountability for behavior in the private realm does not free him from ethical responsibilities in the public realm. Rather, it is to pinion him all the more tightly to his public obligations. It is to confront him with the ethical standards that Americans learn from their parents, teachers, ministers, scoutmasters, coaches, indeed, from the lofty heritage of Christian and Judaic teachings. The standards are old-fashioned but eternally new—rectitude, integrity, compassion, loyalty, responsibility, trustworthiness, civility, respect for all regardless of status, race, gender, or age.

Both the political and economic demands of transactional leadership require a set of more specific but still significant qualities for brokers and mediators—honesty, accountability, reciprocity, credibility, and prudence. How well would the presidents of this century meet both the broader and narrower tests? The answer is difficult because qualities such as rectitude and credibility are not easily definable and certainly not quantifiable. But we do know that presidents lie, dissemble, cover up, break promises, but that they also show compassion, treat people with respect, work hard for their intended goals. As academics we would grade presidents of this century ethically at around a "gentleman's C," with Richard Nixon lowering the collective grade and Jimmy Carter raising it.

How would Bill Clinton fare in this ethical lineup? Measured by the presidential leadership we have studied, we would place him in the middle of the middle, on the basis of Clinton's promises not met, trust not given him, public integrity questioned, along with his incremental progress and his compassion and respect for Americans not sharing in the promise of America. His standing rises a bit when combined with the "straight arrow" of Hillary Rodham Clinton. These evaluations, anecdotal and impressionistic, may well be modified when the Clinton-Gore leadership is evaluated in longer perspective, and with more factual information.

A pressing question that allows a more easily measurable answer, based on extensive historical data, is whether presidential ethics have declined over two centuries, and if so, whether the deterioration will continue. From the lofty ethical standards of Washington and most of the other founders, those standards declined during the nineteenth century as our political system became more democratized and more subject to bossism and corruption. This tendency was balanced by relatively strong parties that could enforce a measure of discipline on individual miscreants in order to protect their national image and popular vote appeal. As parties have declined in the twentieth century, this kind of collective control has yielded to highly personalistic politics that encourages candidates and officeholders to set their own ethical standards, if any, free of external influence. Bill Clinton—far more a manipulator of the national Democratic party than a disciplined agent of it—well exemplifies this trend.

Will the apparent overall decline in presidential ethics continue in the twenty-first century? Probably yes, for two reasons, political and intellectual.

Increasingly our political institutions and practices are forcing office seekers and -holders to resort to manipulation and deception. Our constitutional checks and balances have long compelled our political executives and legislators to be extraordinarily skillful in threading their way through the devices that thwart collective action. In the absence of strong parties that can unify and empower the rank and file in Congress and the state legislatures, factional leaders within the parties pursue their narrower ends by mobilizing money, interest groups, and legions of lobbyists. Policy—or the blocking of policy—falls into the hands of "transactional opportunists."

Nothing suggests any improvement in this situation; on the contrary, the problem will only worsen, and with it the tendency of politicians, including presidents, to take ethical shortcuts, fueled by money. The Constitution cannot be reformed to make for more responsible and accountable collective action, and the power of corporate money is bound to increase. The sheer incapacity of Congress to pass any effective control of campaign finance is a symptom of the malaise. Nor can presidents solve this problem; increasingly they are part of it.

Behind these political forces lies a pervasive intellectual doctrine— pragmatism. It is ludicrous how often this pretentious term—which today means only expedient, narrow, and short-run self-interest—is used in the press to defend mediocre political actors. "Don't worry folks, Senator Smith, who might talk like a visionary, is really down-to-earth, a practical man. He coaches Little League and makes bookcases in his basement. He will not be carried away by his ideals or principles. He's okay—a pragmatist." This kind of pragmatism has come to mean, ethically, "anything goes, if you can get away with it." The test is "what immediately works?"—with no consideration of broader, long-term aspects.

Fashioned by Harvardmen William James and Charles Sanders Peirce and others a century ago, pragmatism was a philosophical theory about truth and a refreshing reaction against the heavy Anglo-Hegelian European dogmas that dominated philosophical teaching in America. Pragmatism called for fresh thinking, intellectual innovation, new truths, practical experience. James described his kind of pragmatist: he "turns away from abstraction and insufficiency, from verbal solutions, from bad *a priori* reasons, from fixed principles, closed systems, and pretended absolutes and origins. He turns toward concreteness and adequacy, toward facts, toward action and toward power." James did not flinch from mentioning pragmatism's "cash-value."

So analytically based was this kind of pragmatism, so clearheaded in clarifying different kinds of thought and action, so relevant to American politics and markets, that the new doctrine established a dominant role in American thought in the twentieth century. But during that century the doctrine has been both trivialized and barbarized. Trivialized in its application to almost any business or political act needing a positive spin. Barbarized in its use as "practicality" to defend ethically dubious persons or acts. Thus the FDR White

House joked about some of the disreputable city bosses who trafficked with it; the Kennedy White House admitted it made use of rascals, but these were "our rascals"; the Bush White House compromised with some of the most egregious Christian-right extremists.

So today's "pragmatism" is not an ethical test of political leadership—it is merely winning votes in the next election. Almost anything legal—and much that borders on the illegal—is justified as the "practical" thing to do. But the pragmatists ignore broader and more long-run aspects of elections. How is the contest being waged? What broader stakes than winning are involved? How will defeat or victory impact the future? Winning elections obviously calls for practicality—but what about the role of vision and idealism?

Above all today's pragmatism is anti-ideology. But the pragmatists have made an ideology of pragmatism.

Pragmatism encourages compartmentalization—the separation of self-serving acts from their ethical implications. Bill Clinton is said to deal with his varied problems by putting them into separate boxes—a personal relations box, a budget box, an election box, a Southern Baptist box, a civil rights box. Perhaps this is understandable since, in a broader sphere, our government itself is compartmentalized, as the constitutional separation of powers distributes authority and accountability among House, Senate, White House, and judiciary, and subdivisions thereof, even apart from the division of powers between the national and state governments.

As the most dynamic and innovative branch, can the presidency regain the moral leadership that certain administrations have displayed in the past?

The Real Test: Moral Leadership

"Are you having fun?" *Rolling Stone* reporters asked Bill Clinton. It was around the end of his first year in the White House.

"You bet," he answered. "I like it very much. Not every hour of the day is fun. The country is going through a period of change."

"But are you having fun in this job?"

"I genuinely enjoy it."

Later in the interview one of the reporters told Clinton of a young man who had been disappointed by the President's performance and had asked the reporter to pass on his question: What was Clinton "willing to stand up for and die for"?

The President furiously turned on the reporter, his face reddening as his voice rose.

"But that's the press's fault too, damn it. I have fought more damn battles here for more things than any President in the last twenty years." Clinton raged on: he had not "gotten one damn bit of credit for it from the knee-jerk liberal press, and I am sick and tired of it and you can put that in the damn article." He got up there "every day, and I work till late at night on everything from national service to the budget to the crime bill and all this stuff and you guys take it and you say, 'Fine, go on to something else, what else can I hit him about?' " Clinton ranted on and on. He was amazingly self-revealing, a bit paranoid, and wildly off the mark.

The "knee-jerk liberal press." All Democratic presidents—FDR, JFK, LBJ, Carter—were criticized by liberals farther to the left, sometimes unfairly. It came with the job.

"I have fought and fought and fought and fought." What had he fought about? He had pursued a number of policies tenaciously—as he would in the next five years—but he was hardly the image of the Andy Jackson fighting president.

"I..." "I..." "I..." Clinton was remarkably narcissistic, even for a president. In happier moments Clinton boasted of his "White House team." This was a time when the White House troika of Bill, Al, and Hillary was especially influential.

"So if you convince them I don't have any convictions, that's fine, but it's a damn lie. It's a lie." He pointed to a couple of his policies, such as tax reform. Already the most common criticism of the President was his "lack of principle." And again, this was a standard charge against presidents—it too came with the territory.

"Do I care if I don't get credit? No." Of course Clinton did care immensely—that's what the shouting was about. "And you get no credit around here for fighting and bleeding..." But Clinton had not fought and bled—he had brokered and negotiated and compromised on a wide range of policies.

And clearly he was not a happy president, at least at this point. Political psychologist Stanley Renshon noted his "bitter sense of futility," which suggested the active-negative character types. This was a reference to the distinction that presidential scholar James David Barber had drawn between active-positive presidents (FDR, Truman, JFK, Carter), who were the most psychologically healthy, and the active-negatives, who dutifully carried out their presidential chores (Wilson, Hoover, LBJ, Nixon) but gained little happiness on the job. Had the cheery, sunny Bill Clinton who had started office as an active-positive, but then, frustrated by Congress and criticism, turned active-negative?

Perhaps it signified something simpler, and even more significant—Clinton's dissatisfaction with himself. Over and beyond his centrist strategy, his endless brokerage, his incremental steps, perhaps he still visualized himself ideally as a principled and visionary leader. Would he ever be in a position to display that kind of political leadership?

In the next five years he became a more seasoned president, more resilient and self-assured. In part this resulted from the sheer experience of governing, and his winning in 1996 the most glorious prize of American politics, a second presidential term. His job satisfaction also rose, ironically, after the Republican sweep of Congress in 1994, forcing him to define and defend his own policies.

Then Monicagate. Anyone who had seen Clinton reveal his vulnerabilities in the *Rolling Stone* interview, or in other incidents where he had lost his cool, could understand Clinton's excruciating mortification later in the titillating revelations. And now he had no one to blame—no "knee-jerk liberals" or hostile press—for his troubles, only his own reckless behavior.

❦❧

At the beginning of his presidency Bill Clinton had preached and promised change—big change. His presidential leadership would be measured by the success of his economic and social reform. While he was vague on some details, his and Hillary Rodham Clinton's plans became clearer when they proposed a comprehensive new health program. Facing a Democratic Congress, still in his presidential honeymoon, the President reasonably expected that, like FDR and others, he would be granted support and leeway.

The reaction to the rejection of the health bill still remains a mystery. The rejection itself was understandable—the First Lady's plan, developed with Ira Magaziner, had significant flaws, including overelaborate details that evidently tried to anticipate the flood of executive and administrative orders that usually follow the presidential signing of a major bill. In the long history of reform, first efforts often fail; the measure is revived and the fight goes on. Not so with the health bill. The rejection by a centrist Congress triggered a vituperative reaction against the proposers in the White House, not the destroyers on the Hill. The proposal was not only a failure; it was an outrage.

The most important of the overreactors was the President himself. Of all politicians he should have recognized the enormity of the high-powered and heavily financed attack the pharmaceutical and other lobbies had launched in Congress. But the conservatives won a double victory—the killing of the bill and Clinton's return to the centrist, incremental strategy that he and his Democratic Leadership Council [DLC] colleagues had embraced in the late 1980s.

So gradualism was back in favor. And over the next few years Clinton offered scores and scores of policy bytes, most of them welcomed by the public as promising to address specific problems and deficiencies. Supported by his Vice President and First Lady, he was imaginative and indefatigable in pressing for these small but benevolent changes. But he was most firm, most willing to spend his political capital, not on controversial liberal policies but on such centrist, DLC-backed programs at NAFTA [North American Free Trade Agreement] and budget balancing.

The tragedy of the Clinton administration was its failure to tackle the big changes needed to overcome the most glaring deficiencies and inequalities in American society.

Consider education. Clinton had prided himself on being the Education Governor of Arkansas, but even with the indispensable help of Rodham Clinton and a number of initiatives, Arkansas was still near the bottom of state standings on education when he left Little Rock. Then he would be, above all, the Education President, on the premise that the states could not do the job without ample funding from Washington. Soon he was initiating a host of education policy bytes, most of them worthy. But no teacher or parent could enjoy the illusion in 1999 that public education as a whole had been dramatically improved.

A *New York Times* article reported "leaky school roofs, buckling auditorium floors, antiquated coal furnaces, and dangerously rotted window frames." This was not a depression town in the 1930s but booming New York City in

November 1998. Teachers and parents could report thousands and thousands of such situations across the country. Education was still in crisis.

Or remember an even more deep-seated problem—the grotesque income gap between the rich and the poor in America. Here again Clinton offered a host of proposals, some of which alleviated the direct symptoms of poverty. But income data told the real story. "Overall, from the late sixties to the midnineties," according to Douglas A. Hicks of the University of Richmond, "income inequality, measured by the standard indicator called the Gini coefficient, increased by over twenty percent for families, and by almost twenty percent for households." Seen another way—in terms of quintiles of the U.S. population—the top 20 percent of our income distribution now receives almost half of the total national income. This is a greater share than the middle 60 percent earns and thirteen times the share of the poorest 20 percent. Clinton failed to exhibit the moral outrage that could have put inequality at the top of the nation's agenda.

Or take the "environmental challenge," Al Gore's special bailiwick. Early administration initiatives were either junked in Congress, as with the proposed BTU energy tax, or drastically cut, as with the proposed boost of the gasoline tax. After 1994, Clinton's and Gore's main efforts were devoted to thwarting Republican attempts to reverse recent gains in environmental policy. That policy —really a cluster of policies—was so complicated by global, national, regional, and special interest (oil industry) politics as to defy easy generalization, but it can be noted that Clinton and Gore's second term neared its end with their old environmental comrades disenchanted by the administration's centrist and weak leadership in this area.

The great excuse of Clinton and Gore—as of all American leaders trying to fashion major change—was the intractability of a constitutional system that utterly fragmented policy. Yet previous presidents had confronted the two-hundred-year-old Constitution and managed somehow to bring off huge changes—Roosevelt's New Deal programs, JFK's economic policies, LBJ's civil rights achievements. Of course, they enjoyed Democratic Congresses, but consider Ronald Reagan's conservative programs. He faced mainly Democratic Congresses but he put through his right-wing policies. He had two big things going for him: conviction and consistency.

The blockage of Clinton-Gore policies in Congress might have tempted Gore to propose major changes in the constitutional and political system. After all, he was in charge of REGO, the exciting project of Reinventing Government. With his strong philosophical interests, his legal and religious education, and his hands-on experience in politics and journalism, he might have at least proposed some constitutional changes for consideration—most notably the abolition of the midterm congressional elections, which had regularly wreaked havoc on presidents no matter how well or poorly they were leading. But the Vice President limited himself to downsizing the huge federal bureaucracy and experimenting with some managerial improvements. Government was hardly reinvented.

So if it was Government Lite under Clinton and Gore, as critics contended, how could they judge the President's efforts, for all his tenacity and compassion, as anything more than Leadership Lite?

POSTSCRIPT

Will History Consider William Jefferson Clinton a Reasonably Good Chief Executive?

Burns and Sorenson et al. distinguish between *transformational* leaders who confront foes head-on and push the nation in new directions and *transactional* leaders who make deals with their foes in Congress in order to win incremental changes. Clinton, they charge, lacked an overall vision; consequently, when he did bargain with the enemy on proposals for tax reform, gun control, and international trade agreements with the North American Free Trade Agreement (NAFTA) he ended up losing control of Congress to the Republicans in 1994. As Robert Reich, Clinton's first-term labor secretary put it, "A baby-boom president who could charm snakes has tried to charm America and only infuriated the snakes."

Thompson argues that President Clinton's governing style did not allow him to come up with one big domestic or foreign policy idea. "Still," says Thompson, "by simultaneously pushing and pulling in hundreds of directions, and sticking by a series of evolving moderate themes, Bill Clinton... is a big factor in why we're so much better off today [December 2000] than we were eight years ago."

Because Clinton has not been out of office for very long, the perspective on his presidency is limited. Yet a lot happened in the two years since he left office. Should Clinton be held responsible for some of the events of his successor's first term? For example, should Clinton be blamed for the failure of U.S. intelligence agencies to thwart the terrorist bombings of the World Trade Center and the Pentagon on September 11, 2002? Considering that the economy entered a recession with high deficits over the two years since he left, does Clinton deserve the A grade that Thompson awards him for his management of the economy? Finally, would the country have been better off if Clinton had resigned?

A number of important works have been published since Clinton left office. Joe Klein, a long-time Clinton watcher and the admitted unknown author of the fictional *Primary Colors: A Novel of Politics* (Thorndike Press, 1996), has published *The Natural: The Misunderstood Presidency of Bill Clinton* (Doubleday, 2002). Ronald Brownstein critically reviews four books on the Clinton presidency in "State of the Debate," *The American Prospect* (February 25, 2002). Finally, David Halberstam weighs in with the comprehensive *War in a Time of Peace: Bush, Clinton, and the Generals* (Simon & Schuster, 2001).

ISSUE 15

Did the Supreme Court Hijack the 2000 Presidential Election From Al Gore?

YES: Stephen Holmes, from "Afterword: Can a Coin-Toss Election Trigger a Constitutional Earthquake?" in Jack N. Rakove, ed., *The Unfinished Election of 2000* (Basic Books, 2001)

NO: John C. Yoo, from "In Defense of the Court's Legitimacy," in Cass R. Sunstein and Richard A. Epstein, eds., *The Vote: Bush, Gore, and the Supreme Court* (University of Chicago Press, 2001)

ISSUE SUMMARY

YES: Professor of law Stephen Holmes maintains that the U.S. Supreme Court acted in a highly partisan and hypocritical fashion in the case of *Bush v. Gore* when it utilized the equal protection clause of the Fourteenth Amendment to prevent the Florida Supreme Court from ordering a recount of the election returns in certain disputed counties.

NO: Professor of law John C. Yoo argues that "rather than acting hypocritically and lawlessly, the Court's decision to bring the Florida election dispute to a timely, and final, end not only restored stability to the political system but was also consistent with the institutional role the Court has shaped for itself over the last decade."

The electoral college was a product of one of the many compromises that took place at the Constitutional Convention of 1787. The principle of the separation of powers meant that members of both houses of Congress, the Supreme Court, and the office of the president would be chosen in four different ways. The delegates ruled out both the direct election of the president or having Congress select the president. A third method was chosen by which voters in each state could select an independent slate of electors who would meet at their respective state capitals and cast their votes for president.

According to the Constitution, each state was granted a number of electors equal to the number of senators and representatives in the House in Congress. Thus, larger states like Massachusetts and New York would have more electors than smaller states like Delaware and Georgia. Members of the electoral college would be chosen by the states in a manner prescribed by their legislatures. Originally they would cast two ballots for president, but only one could be for a candidate from their own state. The candidate who received the highest number of votes became president and the candidate who received the second highest number of votes became vice president. Because of a tie in the electoral college for president and vice president in the 1800 election, the Twelfth Amendment, which dictated that the electors had to designate one vote for president and one vote for vice president, was passed.

With the emergence of political parties, the electoral college lost its power to choose the president. In each presidential election the parties would choose rival slates of electors in each state. Although the electors still have the power to choose any citizen over the age of 35 as president, they almost always vote for the candidate of their respective party.

One flaw in the system is that it is possible for a presidential candidate to win the popular vote but lose the election because he did not carry the electoral college. This has happened four times in U.S. history—in 1824, 1876, 1888, and 2000. In the presidential election of 2000, Vice President Al Gore squared off against Texas governor George W. Bush. The election was extremely close. Bush carried 28 states that extended from the Appalachian mountains to the Rockies and from the Canadian border to the Gulf of Mexico. Gore took most of the Northeast, the industrial states of the upper Midwest, and most of the West Coast. Gore also won 540,000 more popular votes than Bush.

As the election night wore on, it became clear that whoever carried Florida would win the election. The final tally gave Bush a 930-vote majority. The closeness of the election triggered an automatic recount. But Democrats maintained that the balloting had been distorted by irregularities. Several counties used punch cards that often left chads hanging from the holes in the cards, preventing the voting machines from scoring the votes. It was also reported that in Palm Beach County, several hundred voters who meant to vote for Gore mistakenly voted for Reform Party candidate Patrick Buchanan because they were confused by the two-column "butterfly ballot."

The election was contested for a month in a storm of press conferences, recounts, and lawsuits. The Democrats wanted manual recounts extended beyond the official date by which the votes were to be counted. The Bush campaign filed lawsuits to block the deadline but was overruled by the U.S. Supreme Court in a two-part ruling in the case of *Bush v. Gore*. By a vote of 7–2, the Court halted the recounts, agreeing with Bush's legal team that the recounts violated equal protection of the laws. By a 5–4 vote, a majority held that no legal recount could be completed before the electoral college was to meet to cast its votes. Shortly thereafter, Gore conceded the election to Bush.

Did the Supreme Court hijack the election from Gore through its ruling in *Bush v. Gore*? In the following selection, Stephen Holmes argues that the U.S. Supreme Court acted in a highly partisan and hypocritical fashion when it denied an order from the Florida Supreme Court to recount the votes in the disputed counties. In the second selection, John C. Yoo maintains that *Bush v. Gore* was consistent with the institutional role shaped by the Supreme Court over the past decades.

Stephen Holmes

 **YES**

Can a Coin-Toss Election Trigger a Constitutional Earthquake?

Electoral politics looks considerably more impressive when observed from a filmy distance than when examined under a microscope. American democracy's inherent disorders and defects, it turns out, extend beyond abysmally low turnout, candidates manufactured by advertising agencies, and campaign financing shenanigans. The 2000 presidential election, in particular, revealed that a virtual draw in a winner-take-all contest assigns ultimate decision-making power not only to untypical swing voters (an outcome that is undemocratic enough) but also to unavoidable inaccuracies in the tabulation of ballots. Even if the hand recounts in Florida had been conducted more scrupulously and thoroughly than they were, the difference in votes between the two candidates would have remained statistically meaningless, that is to say, would have been less than the margin of error. Where the electorate is evenly divided, the identity of the U.S. president, who happens to hold the fate of the world in his hands, can be settled only by the flip of a coin.

Imaginative attempts have been made... to attribute some deep meaning to this underlying fortuity. Partisans on both sides have treated the intense polarization of the post-election circus, culminating in *Bush v. Gore,* as if it mirrored the state of the polity more accurately than the mind-numbingly bland campaign that preceded it. And the post-election rekindling of the same partisan passions that, a year before, had inflamed the struggle over impeachment, where law was manifestly subordinated to politics, gives some plausibility to this search for a deeper level of significance. Did not partisan politicians, unable to prevail at the ballot box, once again resort to highly malleable law, wielding it as a weapon to rout political foes?

The most incendiary, and not entirely implausible, way to elevate the post-election contest into a portentous showdown between rival worldviews has been to interpret it as a reprise of the battle for and against black enfranchisement. No one can plausibly deny that a poor black man is less likely than a rich white one to receive a fair trial in the United States. Before Florida 2000, however, most Americans imagined that the battle to extend the franchise to African-Americans was a thing of the past, largely resolved by the passage of

From Stephen Holmes, "Afterword: Can a Coin-Toss Election Trigger a Constitutional Earthquake?" in Jack N. Rakove, ed., *The Unfinished Election of 2000* (Basic Books, 2001). Copyright © 2001 by Jack N. Rakove, John Milton Cooper, Jr., Henry E. Brady, Alexander Keyssar, Pamela S. Karlan, Larry D. Kramer, and Stephen Holmes. Reprinted by permission of Basic Books, a member of Perseus Books, LLC.

the Voting Rights Act of 1965. But the nearly forgotten struggle against racial restrictions on the suffrage resurfaced rudely in the 2000 election, and not only in the legally questionable scrubbing of "possible felons" from voter lists. Although only 11 percent of Florida voters are black, 54 percent of the spoiled ballots were cast by blacks.

Democrats make much of such statistics. They do so because the tendency of Republicans to glamorize private initiative and denigrate government is not as immaculately race-neutral as it initially seems. In practice, the Republican predilection for purchasing private prosperity at the price of public squalor implies not so much an across-the-board as a *selective* defunding of public institutions. In poor black counties with a small tax base, antiquated voting machinery effectively dilutes the power of voters to influence the electoral outcome. In the aftermath to the 2000 election, the exasperation of African-Americans at minor episodes of disenfranchisement was quickened by sarcastic Republican comments, uttered with a social Darwinist edge, to the effect that voters themselves are responsible if they fail to follow written instructions. In affluent white counties, superior machinery and more professional poll watchers alerted voters who did not follow instructions to correct their mistakes on the spot. This suggests that, rhetoric aside, partisan Republicans are fully aware that the exercise of individual rights, such as the right to vote, depends critically on public expenditures. The reason they deny this publicly may not be intellectual incoherence and ignorance of political theory, therefore. Rather, they may simply hope to benefit from public expenditures themselves while starving the public institutions that give reality to the rights of others, including black Americans, who overwhelmingly tend to vote for the opposite party. Their strategy, if this analysis has any merit, is fairly simple: to fortify the castle of the strong, it helps to enfeeble the siege equipment of the weak.

That diverse levels of spending on voting technology, which must be kept in good repair and up-to-date by public expenditures, may have a significant discriminatory effect, is one of the unexpected lessons of election 2000. Thus, in optical-scanner counties, only 1 percent of the ballots registered no presidential selection, whereas 4 percent of the ballots in punch-card counties registered no choice. Such a differential strongly suggests that the rate of ballot invalidation can be reduced by public investment in better equipment. Contrariwise, an existing asymmetry that broadly favors Republicans can be consolidated, intentionally or inadvertently, by "reducing spending to balance the budget." Exclusively local funding of vote-tabulating machinery turns out to promote the unequal distribution of American citizenship itself.

Skepticism about Republican motives, fueled by such observations, has been reinforced by the curious and still inadequately theorized satisfaction that Republicans seem to feel at having won the White House without securing a popular plurality. Their repeated claim that the United States is "a Republic" and not "a Democracy," often articulated in this context, implies that our old-fashioned institutions, such as the electoral college, serve as "bulwarks" against "raw populism." But what does such logic imply about old-fashioned and therefore vote-diluting equipment in the poor black counties of Florida?

Conceivably, after the routine electoral contest had turned into an astonishing stalemate, some panel of "elder statesmen" could have appeared on the scene and formulated a procedure for resolving the conflict that would have appeared fair to both sides. Instead, both parties mobilized former secretaries of state—Warren Christopher for the Democrats, James ("Consigliere") Baker for the Republicans, lawyers both—to take the lead in presenting the respective cases for and against further recounts. Absent nonpartisan intervention, the post-election contest quickly degenerated into a mutual filing and flinging of charges and countercharges, rival camps vilifying each other as unpatriotic liars, with virtually no attempts being made at democratic deliberation. The outcome that had not been decided according to clear rules known in advance, it soon became clear, was going to be decided by crafty maneuvering within and around the rules, which turned out to be remarkably vague and elastic, as rules usually are. More to the point, the winner was destined to be the party with the best back-channel connections to powerful institutions in a position to bend the rules to reach a univocal solution.

The most important of these institutions, needless to say, was the U.S. Supreme Court. The problem with its clamorous intervention was not that it crossed a sacred line or entered into the political thicket. What made it so bitterly controversial was that the majority's decision violated the fundamental legal principle that an arbiter cannot have a stake in the outcome. The fact that *Bush v. Gore* has a much weaker basis in jurisprudence than *Dred Scott v. Sandford* is deplorable but not exceptional. The scandal lies in an appearance of vulgar favoritism. The majority is very unlikely to have decided as it did if the parties had been reversed. This is not to deny that the majority, despite disclaimers about an "unsought responsibility," *also* desired to look decisive, to play an eye-catching role in a once-in-a-lifetime American drama. That is to say, the justices who voted to consider the case were also intoxicated by self-importance, which is obviously not the same as turning themselves into pliant tools of the litigants they happen to like.

But at the very least, they also created the appearance of deciding the case on extralegal grounds. In the end, the majority's holding seems less ideological than political. On its face, the decision appears to have been driven by considerations of expediency, with ad hoc rationalizations very loosely attached. This apparent triumph of expediency over principle was symbolized most remarkably by Justice Antonin Scalia's sensational declaration (in his concurring opinion justifying the stay order of December 9) that the Court had to act in haste to ensure "public acceptance" of the Bush presidency, as if he imagined himself to be some sort of spin doctor, with an unparalleled grasp of the conditions of "democratic stability," able to engineer the attitudes of his countrymen from his chambers. Worst of all, the conservative faction was, or appeared to be, attempting to protect the interests of George W. Bush to consolidate and perpetuate the dominance of conservative thinking in the jurisprudence of the Court. (A President Gore might have rained more moderate liberals on Scalia's anti-liberal parade.) Apparently unembarrassed at being perceived as black-robed operatives in James Baker's run-out-the-clock campaign, the conservative majority took ample advantage of the special status of the Supreme Court, a body unique in our polity because subject to no higher authority empowered to correct its trespasses. The culmination of the justices' unaccountable conceit came in the famous disclaimer: "Our consideration is limited to the present circumstances." Once they had poured candidate Gore down the drainpipe, they comforted us with assurances that no extra babies were in the bath water.

It is now said that the opportunism of the conservative majority was made plain by its willingness to abandon, in this unique case, its deep commitment to states' rights and its unswerving hostility to judicial activism and equal protection.[1] To elevate their man to the White House, critics assert, they were willing to traduce their own judicial philosophy. And there is a lot to be said for this claim. But we should not overestimate the role of steady adherence to principle in the current majority's thinking.

True, conservatives have often found it useful to defend states' rights as a means of defending the rights of certain social groups, most notably the rights of southern whites against the rights of southern blacks. The traditional association of states' rights rhetoric with arrangements designed to keep blacks down is well known. For its part, the current majority has consistently sided with the strong against the weak, smiling, say, on corporations while frowning on the disabled. And to put their preferences into effect, they have not hesitated to invoke states' rights. They have done so, for instance, to favor gun owners and disfavor the victims of discrimination.[2] As if to confirm liberal suspicions, the conservatives on the Court regularly defer to state courts in death penalty cases. This probably has as much to do with their support of the death penalty as with any piety toward residual state sovereignty, however. The proof is that the same conservative majority, well before *Bush v. Gore,* did not hesitate to override states' rights if the social groups it favors could be helped by so doing.

An instrumental attitude toward states' rights among American conservatives is not of recent vintage. Federal fugitive slave laws are often mentioned as the great precedent in this context. In the famous case *Lochner v. New York* (1905), the Court similarly expressed its fondness for employers by denying the right of state legislatures to experiment with the regulation of labor contracts in favor of workers. More recently, conservatives' championing of federal tort reform reveals their willingness to trample lesser rights (namely, the rights of states) to defend greater rights (the rights of business). A cynic might even say that the principal purpose of "the rule of law," according to American conservative thought, is to help rich people keep their money. To this higher norm—which is not necessarily immoral as a matter of policy—they hold unswervingly, exhibiting little or no opportunistic shifting back and forth. Their selective and sporadic tenderness for states' rights, by contrast, suggests that the latter is only a means, not an end. Whatever slogans they toss around, America's judicial conservatives do not view themselves as citizens of separate states but rather as members of an exclusive and obviously nationwide, not merely local, club.

This is one of the keys to *Bush v. Gore.* Whatever its other merits and demerits, it drove dramatically home, for the first time, the conservative majority's fundamentally instrumental attitude toward states' rights. But the members of the current majority have often preferred political opportunism to ideological consistency. As a result, *Bush v. Gore,* however weakly reasoned, does not represent a radical rupture with their previous approach to states' rights.

If the Florida Supreme Court was correct in its claim that, "These statutes established by the legislature govern our decisions today," there would have been no federal question and no grounds for Supreme Court intervention to save Bush. Thus, the three far-right members of the Court were driven to invoke Article II of the federal Constitution, which by their reading vests plenary authority over the conduct of presidential elections in the state legislatures. What is especially interesting about their Article II claim is less its weakness as a matter of law than its extraordinary coincidence with the disinformation campaign orchestrated by the Republican camp. Justices Rehnquist, Scalia, and Thomas knew perfectly well that "the rule of law" leaves considerable latitude for judicial discretion and prudence (one example: the majority vote in *Bush v. Gore*). But they apparently found it useful to bury this basic truth for propagandistic ends. According to them, the Florida Supreme Court violated Article II, § 1, cl. 2 of the federal Constitution by rewriting—rather than merely interpreting or making coherent—the Florida election code, without any "reasonable" grounds. This charge, on its face, reinforced strongly the Bush campaign's charge that Democrats were trying to change the rules for electing the president halfway through the game. (Because the rules of the game, as conventionally understood, produced no winner, both sides were naturally attempting to massage and interpret the rules to their own advantage.)

To claim that the Florida Supreme Court's interpretation of Florida law was flagrant and unreasonable, of course, required the U.S. Supreme Court to set itself up as the final arbiter of the meaning of Florida law, something the three most conservative justices would most certainly have refused to do had a Democratic candidate been the likely beneficiary. In the public relations battle, the Bush team invoked Article II to suggest that the Constitution had assigned decisive discretionary authority, activated when an election produced no clear winner, to the Republican-dominated Florida state legislature. But Article II stipulates that "Each State shall appoint, in such Manner as the Legislature thereof may direct, a Number of Electors," and it empowers Congress to fix the time when such electors must be appointed (which ever since 1845 has been the Tuesday following the first Monday in November). It does not imply that partisan majorities in state legislatures may, after the fact, rewrite the rules for selecting electors that they had set down beforehand.

The Florida legislature has given Florida courts the power to interpret Florida statutes. The Florida Supreme Court could therefore reasonably claim to be basing its decision to continue the hand recounts on the clear intention of the Florida legislature, which had also stipulated that "no vote shall be declared invalid or void if there is a clear indication of the intent of the voter as determined by the canvassing board." The Florida Supreme Court also assumed that that state's paramount interest in case of an electoral deadlock was correctly assessing the discernible intent of the voters and thereby identifying the rightful winner. If the Florida Supreme Court's claim to be acting on the commands of the Florida legislature were allowed to stand, of course, the Supreme Court's grounds for intervention in the case would have been considerably weakened.

The rules that the Florida state legislature had established *before* November 7 can be summarized as follows. In a presidential election, (1) all legally valid votes must be counted; (2) a legally valid vote is one in which the clear intent of the voter can be discerned, whether or not instructions were strictly followed; (3) if the outcome of the election is contested, recounts to determine the rightful winner shall be conducted; (4) courts shall play an important role in handling disputes arising from such recounts; (5) circuit court decisions are subject to appellate review; and (6) when faced with conflicting statutes and issues not explicitly covered by statute, courts have the power of "statutory construction," that is, the authority to identify solutions and methods of reconciliation compatible with fundamental state interests. That the Florida Supreme Court violated Article II of the federal Constitution by flagrantly ignoring the will of the Florida legislature—as set down in the foregoing six points —is not even remotely plausible. A much more powerful case can be made that the Supreme Court itself violated Article II by wantonly overriding the explicit will of the Florida legislature that, in close elections, recounts will be held to ensure that all legally valid votes are counted.

To bolster their claim that the electoral dispute in Florida raised a justiciable federal question, a majority of five justices appended an equal protection argument to their Article II claim. "Having once granted the right to vote on equal terms, the State may not, by later arbitrary and disparate treatment, value one person's vote over another." The second argument is now widely viewed as extremely tenuous, even by those who cheered the results of *Bush v. Gore*. What is worse, by heaping one argument on top of the other, the majority seemed to be replicating the strategy of Bush campaign operatives, namely to spew forth as many miscellaneous arguments as possible, in the hope that at least some would strike the target.

However preposterous as constitutional law, the majority's opportunistic invocation of the Equal Protection Clause of the Fourteenth Amendment was not as inconsistent with their previous approach as is sometimes alleged. The conservatives on the Court have long been willing to embrace equal protection in much the same way that they have supported states' rights, that is, instrumentally, on a case-by-case basis, whenever they could thereby defend the interests of groups they favor (as in cases involving reverse discrimination). If white Americans seek a remedy, the conservative majority is much more likely to see the relevance of the Equal Protection Clause than if black Americans seek a remedy. Thus, the way they invoked equal protection in *Bush v. Gore* may be blameworthy and unprincipled, but it is not especially innovative or unprecedented.

What is galling, instead, is the recklessness with which the majority implicitly declared unconstitutional important provisions in the Florida election code itself (and, in fact, cast doubt on settled electoral practice throughout the country). It declared the intent standard that the legislature had established for conducting recounts to be impermissibly vague, because allowing excessive variation from one county to the next in methods of recounting. Rather than merely invalidating an ostensibly aberrant decision of the Florida Supreme Court, the conservative majority's equal protection argument strikes directly at the Florida legislature. That is to say, it assigns the Equal Protection Clause of the Fourteenth Amendment precedence over Article II, which denies that a state legislature's power to regulate presidential elections as it sees fit may be judicially circumscribed. Their desperate search for a federal question that could be endorsed by at least five justices drew them into the trap, from which they tried ludicrously to extricate themselves by saying good-bye to *stare decisis,* peremptorily stating that their decision had no value as a precedent.

The comic quality of this line of argument should be plain. Conservatives who have been adamant about the importance of devolving power away from the federal government and back to localities suddenly discover that local decision making engenders variety instead of uniformity. That was apparently a revelation. Differently designed ballots are counted by different technologies and recounted by different officials in different counties. To declare such settled practice to be unconstitutional, however, is to flirt with electoral nihilism. What makes the argument unsavory rather than merely comic is the way it implicitly denigrates the noblest legacy of the Supreme Court, namely the invocation of equal protection to intervene in state elections on the side of black Americans. The Equal Protection Clause of the Fourteenth Amendment was written to protect former slaves and their descendants from discrimination and to guarantee them rights of citizenship equal to the rights of white Americans. *Bush v. Gore* does not merely turn this tradition on its head, it does so with nose-thumbing contempt, refusing to offer any remedy to the real inequities in the American system of voting. This contempt was most clearly visible in the last-minute suggestion by Justices Kennedy and O'Connor that a recount could have been conducted if the Florida Supreme Court had had time to set a fixed statewide standard disallowing any variation in the way voter intent was established. The lack of time to do so, of course, was at least partly due to the Supreme Court's own prior failure to notify the Florida Supreme Court that uniform standards would be a decisive issues.

Finally, some defenders of *Bush v. Gore* present it as an act of "statesmanship," even implying that the conservative majority willingly sacrificed some of its own prestige to save the country from political turmoil and perhaps even a train wreck of unforeseeable proportions. The country was staring into an abyss, we learn, and the Court saved us all from a looming constitutional crisis. Unfortunately, such a claim assumes that the Supreme Court is competent to make empirical predictions about the course of political events. Because it possesses no such competence, the "train wreck" argument looks like just another sophistical rationalization of a self-serving partisan gambit.

The evident feebleness of the jurisprudential basis for *Bush v. Gore* has tempted partisan Democrats into making all sorts of predictions of their own, most of them echoing Justice Stevens's claim that, "Preventing the recount from being completed will inevitably cast a cloud on the legitimacy of the election" and Justice Breyer's suggestion that the decision was "a self-inflicted wound—a wound that may harm not just the Court, but the Nation." This bungled decision will come back to haunt the right, critics have repeatedly alleged. Not only will the federal courts be flooded by lawsuits whenever there is a close election, but the Bush presidency itself will be illegitimate and tainted.

The Supreme Court is even said to have thrown away in an instant the social prestige it had painstakingly accumulated over decades. And, finally, the public's faith in the rule of law, as something distinct from partisan political maneuvering, has supposedly been shattered.

This is all a great exaggeration, however, especially since no one takes *Bush v. Gore* seriously as constitutional law. And what exactly does it mean for the Court's credibility to be destroyed? Will Congress and the states now begin defying the Court at will? That hardly seems likely. To understand why so many distinguished legal academics were nevertheless aghast and dismayed by *Bush v. Gore,* we need to focus on *the Dworkin illusion* from which many of them suffer. By "the Dworkin illusion" I mean the association of judicial review with socially progressive causes, as avowed most prominently in the writings of the legal philosopher, Ronald Dworkin. This unjustifiable pairing attains a superficial plausibility from the common tendency to misinterpret the historical anomaly of the Warren Court as a typical case that best illustrates the purpose and function of judicial review. Legal academics with a liberal bent were appalled by *Bush v. Gore* because, until now, they have stubbornly refused to recognize, despite mountains of historical evidence, that the judiciary is almost always a status quo power. By behaving true to form in such a high-profile case, the Supreme Court may finally have released liberals from their outdated fantasy that judicial review was created to protect the weak against the strong.

The legal academy's subjective perception of a constitutional upheaval is not shared by the wider public. Why not? One explanation is economic prosperity and political indifference. The country is doing too well economically to discover a constitutional crisis in electoral disarray. Another explanation is that the legitimacy of the Supreme Court (like that of the Federal Reserve) depends as much on opacity as on impartiality. The reasoning of the Court, whether sound or unsound, is too cryptic to have much of an impact on ordinary citizens. A third possibility is that most Americans harbor no liberal illusions about the Court that could be shattered theatrically by *Bush v. Gore.* But this is not the whole story.

Most politically conscious Americans understand quite well that the rules of the game, laid down before the 2000 election, produced no clear winner. An additional function of voting, alongside the filling of public offices, is to allow the electorate, at regular intervals, to paint its self-portrait. In 2000, the American electorate disclosed itself, to itself, as divided down the middle. In this case, although some decision obviously had to be made, neither candidate could possibly have enjoyed greater democratic legitimacy than the other. That would have been true even if the hand recounts had been conducted in the most orderly and exhaustive manner possible. Neither Bush nor Gore, in sum, could plausibly assert superior legal pedigree. The clock was ticking, and a patently tie vote somehow had to be alchemized into a victory and a defeat. A coin toss would have done perfectly well to decide between the two contenders because the next president, in any case, was going to accede to office by accident.

The fact that the presidency was awarded by flipping a *loaded* coin was not necessarily lost on public perception. Most Americans presumably recognize that the conservatives on the Court are partisan Republicans besting partisan

Democrats, not moral heroes salvaging morality from dishonorable liberals. But the unprincipled opportunism and self-serving bias of the Court was not viewed as the basis for a "legitimacy crisis" because the Gore team, for its part, had failed to offer any procedurally neutral method, fair to both sides, for choosing a winner. Because they did not promptly propose a procedure that, ex ante, would leave the eventual winner unknown, they looked like they were fishing for votes rather than standing up for the disenfranchised. After proposing manual recounts according to the loosest possible standards in heavily Democratic counties—not to mention floating the idea of a special election in Palm Beach county—the Gore camp was unable to protest credibly against loaded dice. And anyway, the real reason Gore failed to prevail in the election was the defectively designed ballot in Palm Beach. That was not the fruit of some vast right-wing conspiracy, however, but a sheer accident, the equivalent of the faulty horseshoe that led to the loss of a kingdom.

Although the Republicans won and the Democrats lost, the losers did not resort to defiance or a refusal to cooperate. Thus, "the system worked." This too helps to explain why the public does not feel that the United States is undergoing a constitutional crisis. Ordinary Americans apparently believe that achieving a vital purpose is more important than cleaving meticulously to formal procedures, especially when both sides in a conflict raise equally plausible arguments about "what the rule of law requires." They were therefore by and large satisfied that the process ended with closure. The outcome may have been bad luck for Gore, but it was not a constitutional cataclysm for the country. An additional reason for acquiescence in a Bush presidency is that Democrats know they will have a chance for a comeback in the next elections. African-Americans feel less forgiving precisely because they feel that their turn will never come.

If a crisis of legitimacy is in the cards, this has less to do with the way Bush became president than with the way he began to behave after he took office. That he is a feeble figure unable to articulate American interests with any force has nothing to do with the way the electoral deadlock was finally resolved. After John Kennedy squeaked to victory in 1960, he appointed several prominent Republicans to key posts in his cabinet, in effect establishing a coalition government as an acknowledgment that the electorate was basically evenly divided. Bush did nothing of the sort. Instead of splitting the difference with Democrats, he pursued one-party rule on the basis of a tie vote. His legitimacy problems have been exacerbated by the manifest conflict between his ideological message, emphasizing individual responsibility, and his own life history, where social promotion plainly played a prominent role. Because his family always protected him from suffering the worst consequences of his irresponsible behavior, he is personally not in a good position to invoke "moral hazard" as a reason to defund programs offering some modest security to the poor. For *Bush* to state publicly that safety nets kill gumption is an invitation to laughter. That he is willing to say such things is deeply discrediting, perhaps even delegitimating, but this has nothing at all to do with the turmoil of election 2000 or *Bush v. Gore.*

Finally, what can we say about proposals to abolish the electoral college, a vestige of the past that cannot easily be justified today in a way most citizens could accept or even understand? The critical role of this eighteenth-century relic in determining the outcome of the election was somewhat overshadowed by the intervention of the Supreme Court. And awareness that sparsely populated states are unlikely to accept the curtailment of their unjust privileges has by now put a damper on the idea of abolishing it. But historians have nevertheless been busy reminding us that the electoral college is a typical case of special-interest constitutionalism, designed to favor slave-holding states. The disappearance of slave-holding states has not made the origins of the institution seem politically irrelevant because Bush won the electoral vote by prevailing in the sagebrush country, while Gore's victory in the ethnically mixed melting pot along the coasts gave him a popular plurality but not a majority in the electoral college.

The tainted origins of the electoral college are not especially relevant to the current value (or lack of value) of the institution. The proof is that the disproportional Senate is now barely controlled by the Democrats while the proportional House remains narrowly in Republican hands. In other words, those who propose to abolish the electoral college have an unjustifiable confidence in their ability to predict the political consequences of a change in constitutional rules. The electoral college is unlikely to be abolished, given the vested interests of sparsely populated states. But that is not necessarily a harm to one party or the other. Revisions in the structural provisions of a constitution very often have unintended consequences. Out of respect for our own weak grasp of social causality, we should hesitate to make such changes unless the reasons are overwhelming.

Finally, is election 2000 really unfinished...? This is far from obvious. For one thing, it was a statistically extraordinary event that is very unlikely to repeat itself. Moreover, *Bush v. Gore* seems finally to have persuaded liberals to shed their last illusions about the progressive potential of judicial review. Mission accomplished, case closed. Admittedly, political partisans may have good reasons for continuing to revisit those frenzied thirty-six days. But should we not all be wary of law school generals who cannot stop fighting the last war?

Notes

1. Alan Dershowitz, *Supreme Injustice: How the High Court Hijacked Election 2000* (New York: Oxford University Press, 2001).
2. U.S. v. Lopez, 514 U.S. 549 (1995) and Printz v. United States, 521 U.S. 98 (1997); Seminole Tribe v. Florida, 517 U.S. 44 (1996).

In Defense of the Court's Legitimacy

Even as it brought the 2000 presidential election to conclusion, *Bush v Gore*[1] gave rise to a flurry of attacks on the legitimacy of the Supreme Court. Many scholars criticized the Court for its creation of a new Equal Protection Clause claim never before seen, for its sudden imposition of a deadline that foreclosed any remedy, for its apparent hypocrisy in intervening into a local election dispute, and for its intervention into an utterly partisan dispute. Criticism usually would come as no surprise—it is merely the standard discussion about the actions of the institution that is the focus of much of our work in academia.

While early opinion polls show that most Americans have decided to move on,[2] it seems that many academic critics of *Bush v Gore* have decided to go beyond the usual mulling over of Supreme Court opinions. In the weeks following the Court's decision, prominent legal academics have voiced a number of objections that question the Court's very legitimacy, and in some cases have urged the political system to attack the Court. Many have characterized the decision as partisan and ungrounded in law.[3] Some have even compared the justices to partisan lobbyists.[4] As a result, these critics have called upon the Senate to refuse to confirm any Supreme Court justices during President Bush's term,[5] while others have hit upon the idea of reducing the number of justices on the Court.[6] Some have even gone so far as to compare the Court's alleged loss of legitimacy today to the Court's decision in *Dred Scott,* with all of the dire consequences that it portended.[7]

Much of this inflamed rhetoric, while good for grabbing headlines, no doubt resulted from the heat of the moment rather than from careful reflection and thought. But even if this criticism is shallow, it is broad. At least 585 law professors took the unusual step of signing an ad published in the New York Times on January 13, 2001, decrying *Bush v Gore* as an illegitimate, political decision.[8] The ad flatly declared: "when a bare majority of the U.S. Supreme Court halted the recount of ballots under Florida law, the five justices were acting as political proponents for candidate Bush, not as judges."[9]

Heady words. Such extraordinary criticism raises some questions worth pursuing. Did the Supreme Court somehow render an "illegitimate" decision in *Bush v Gore?* Has the Court undermined the institutional legitimacy that allows

From John C. Yoo, "In Defense of the Court's Legitimacy," in Cass R. Sunstein and Richard A. Epstein, eds., *The Vote: Bush, Gore, and the Supreme Court* (University of Chicago Press, 2001). Copyright © 2001 by The University of Chicago. Reprinted by permission of University of Chicago Press.

it to play a central role in American politics and society? What is the real threat to the Court's legitimacy in the aftermath of *Bush v Gore?*

This essay will argue that concerns about the Court's legitimacy are overblown. While it is certainly too early to be sure, the Court's actions, and their impact on the political system, come nowhere close to approaching the circumstances that surrounded earlier, real threats to the Court's standing. The Court did not decide any substantive issues—on a par with abortion or privacy rights, for example—that call upon the Court to remain continually at the center of political controversy for years. Instead, the Court issued a fairly narrow decision in a one-of-a-kind case—the procedures to govern presidential election counts—that is not likely to reappear in our lifetimes. Rather than acting hypocritically and lawlessly, the Court's decision to bring the Florida election dispute to a timely, and final, end not only restored stability to the political system but was also consistent with the institutional role the Court has shaped for itself over the last decade.

I. Legitimacy as Public Opinion

Legitimacy is a word often used in our political debate, but seldom defined precisely. We can think of institutional "legitimacy" as the belief in the binding nature of an institution's decisions, even when one disagrees with them.[10] This sociological or even psychological definition of the term is concerned with whether people will think the Court's decision in *Bush v Gore* was legitimate, and as a result will obey it.[11] It is different from philosophical legitimacy, in which one is concerned with moral obligations to follow the law.[12] Our Weberian definition of legitimacy is also different from the manner in which Critical Legal Studies scholars use the phrase to argue that because the legal system is radically indeterminate, and produces unjust results, it is illegitimate.[13]

One way, then, to judge whether *Bush v Gore* has undermined the Court's institutional legitimacy in American society would be to examine public attitudes toward the Court. Studies have shown that public support for the Court and its role in society run high, even though many have little knowledge about the Court's day-to-day activities.[14] While this is not the place to conduct a detailed study,[15] we may perhaps draw some initial conclusions from recent Gallup polling data. Over the last decade, poll respondents have usually held more confidence in the Supreme Court than in the other two branches of government.[16] In June 2000, 47 percent of those polled said that they held either a "great deal" or "quite a lot" of confidence in the Supreme Court, versus 42 percent for the presidency and 24 percent for Congress.[17] Even in light of the usual caveats surrounding the use of polling data, the resiliency in the Court's public support has been relatively deep and wide,[18] even as it has rendered a series of controversial decisions ranging from affirmative action to abortion to civil rights to religion.

Bush v Gore has not changed those overall numbers significantly. According to the Gallup poll, 59 percent of adults in January 2001 approved of the way the Supreme Court was handling its job, down only slightly from 62 percent in late August 2000.[19] While the Court's overall approval ratings have barely changed, however, the partisan composition of those numbers may be cause for concern. Approval of the Supreme Court among Republicans jumped from 60 percent in August 2000 to 80 percent by January 2001; among Democrats, that number fell from 70 percent in August to 42 percent in January.[20] But what may be most important is independents; there the Court's approval ratings dropped marginally from 57 to 54 percent.[21] While it is too early to tell whether this partisan split in attitudes toward the Court will undermine the Court's legitimacy, I think it more likely that the drop in Democratic opinions toward the Court will prove to be a temporary blip, for the reasons that follow.

II. Legitimacy as History

A second way to approach the question of legitimacy would be to compare *Bush v Gore* to other historical periods in which the Court's authority has come into question. If the Court's actions today were similar in significant ways to earlier moments of challenge to judicial legitimacy, then we might predict that the changes in the immediate polling data may augur a more sustained attack on the Court. Evaluating *Bush v Gore* in light of earlier historical periods, however, suggests that any sustained assault on the Court's legitimacy is unlikely to arise. The Court's authority has come under serious question four times in our history: the Marshall Court, the Taney Court's decision in *Dred Scott,* the Court's early resistance to the New Deal, and the Warren Court's fight against segregation and its expansion of individual liberties. Close inspection of these periods show that they bear little resemblance to *Bush v Gore.*

The defining characteristic of several of these periods was the persistent, central role of the Court in the political disputes of the day. The New Deal period is perhaps the most obvious in this regard. In an effort to end the Great Depression, President Franklin Roosevelt and a Democratic Congress enacted economic regulatory legislation that sought to impose national solutions on the crisis. In cases such as *A.L.A. Schechter Poultry Corp v United States*[22] and *Carter v Carter Coal Co,*[23] the Court invalidated New Deal laws as beyond Congress's Commerce Clause power. These cases followed upon a series of decisions during the Progressive Era that also had restricted the scope of Congress's powers to regulate the economy.[24] By the time of the 1936 presidential election, the Court had struck down six federal laws that formed part of FDR's effort to bring about economic recovery. The Supreme Court came to be seen as one of the last obstacles. Similarly, during the Warren Court period, the Court not only decided *Brown v Board of Education,*[25] but also remained in the forefront of the public's attention with other desegregation cases.[26]

In both periods, the Court intervened into the most pressing substantive issues of the day—economic depression and race, among others—and did so repeatedly over a course of years. Even during the Marshall Court period, in which the decisions might be considered more structural—the existence of judicial review,[27] Congress's Necessary and Proper Clause power,[28] the Commerce Clause power[29]—than substantive, the Court remained at the center stage of national politics for several years. Only in *Dred Scott*[30] can the Court be said to have decisively acted only once to settle a national issue. In invalidating the

Missouri Compromise, however, that one intrusion represented the Court's effort to end a divisive national debate that had been the central issue in American politics for several generations.

The nature of the Court's interference in these issues almost inevitably sparked a response by the other actors in the political system. In the case of the Marshall Court, it was Jefferson's muttered threats to defy judicial orders.[31] With the Taney Court, it was Abraham Lincoln's attacks on *Dred Scott* and, ultimately, the coming of the Civil War.[32] With the New Deal Court, President Roosevelt responded by campaigning against the Court and introducing his famous Court-packing plan.[33] With the Warren Court, it was resistance throughout the southern states, criticism in Congress, and criticism from presidential candidates.[34] The response of the political branches or the states demonstrates that the Court had acted in a manner that threatened its own legitimacy. Because the Court had sought to foreclose society (or parts of it) from using the lawmaking process to achieve certain ends, and because those ends were of such intense importance to the people, the chief if not only way for the people (or interest groups, if one prefers a public choice approach to the political process) to pursue their policy preferences was to attack the Court. In other words, the other political actors had to undermine the Court's legitimacy as an institution so as to convince the electorate to support efforts to evade or overturn its decisions.

Contrast these periods with *Bush v Gore*. In *Bush v Gore*, the Court sought to resolve a narrow legal issue involving the selection of presidential electors. The question bears no constitutional implications for the resolution of any significant and ongoing social issues of today—abortion, race relations, education, social security, defense. The decision poses no bar to a society that seeks to use the democratic process to resolve any pressing social problems. While the Democratic party has reason to be dissatisfied with the outcome of *Bush v Gore*, it has no interest in challenging the legal reasoning of the decision in the future. It is highly unlikely that the Court will remain a central player in future presidential election contests. Indeed, the Court's members were last involved in a disputed presidential election more than a century ago. Further, in *Bush v Gore*, the Court was not truly deciding a question of constitutional substance on a par with the scope of abortion rights or the national government's power to enforce civil rights. Instead, it was only clarifying the rules of the game for selecting the only federal official elected by the whole nation. It is difficult to conceive of a constitutional question that is more of a pure question of constitutional structure, rather than of substantive constitutional rights. Indeed, the Court perhaps was best suited, as a rational decisionmaker, to settle questions involving rules of constitutional process that may stalemate the other branches of government.

III. Legitimacy as Impartiality

A third way to examine whether *Bush v Gore* is likely to undermine the Court's legitimacy is to look at current theories of the sources of the Court's authority. The Court itself has sought to give content to its "legitimacy" in *Planned*

Parenthood of Southeastern Pennsylvania v Casey.[35] In refusing to overrule *Roe v Wade,*[36] a plurality explained that reversing its precedent would undermine the Court's legitimacy, which it saw as the very source of the judiciary's authority. "As Americans of each succeeding generation are rightly told, the Court cannot buy support for its decisions by spending money and, except to a minor degree, it cannot independently coerce obedience to its decrees."[37] Thus, the judiciary's power is distinguished from the use of force or finances, which are the tools of the political branches. "The Court's power lies, rather, in its legitimacy, a product of substance and perception that shows itself in the people's acceptance of the Judiciary as fit to determine what the Nation's law means and to declare what it demands."[38] Without the sword or purse, the *Casey* plurality believes, the Court's authority derives from the public's acceptance of its power to interpret the Constitution.

How does the Court maintain this legitimacy? According to the *Casey* plurality, the Court receives its public support by "making legally principled decisions under circumstances in which their principled character is sufficiently plausible to be accepted by the Nation."[39] In other words, only by acting in a manner that suggests that its decisions are the product of law rather than politics can the Court maintain its legitimacy. Therefore, the Court must adhere to settled precedent, lest the public believe that the Court is merely just another political actor. "[T]o overrule under fire in the absence of the most compelling reason to reexamine a watershed decision would subvert the Court's legitimacy beyond any serious question."[40] Without this legitimacy, the Court would be unable to perform its role as interpreter of the Constitution, which at times may require the Court to act against the popular will in favor of individual rights.

Leading social scientists appear to agree with the *Casey* plurality's notion of judicial legitimacy. The Court's institutional legitimacy both enhances the legitimacy of particular decisions and increases the voluntary acceptance of unpopular decisions.[41] Valuable as it is, however, legitimacy is hard to come by. Political scientists have emphasized the limited ability of the federal courts to enforce their decisions, and hence have turned to the Court's legitimacy as an explanation for compliance.[42] The Court's standing is further complicated because it lacks any electoral basis for its legitimacy.[43] The way to acquire this legitimacy, many scholars seem to believe, is for the Court to appear to act neutrally,[44] objectively,[45] or fairly,[46] by following standards of procedural justice or by making decisions that follow principled rules.

Thus, the question for judging the Court's legitimacy is to evaluate claims that the Rehnquist Court was so intent on achieving partisan ends in *Bush v Gore* that it violated or ignored its own guiding principles. Two claims are prominently made to suggest that *Bush v Gore* was inconsistent with the Court's earlier decisions. First, the Court was acting out of character when it exercised federal power to intervene in the core state function of running elections. Second, a Court that has criticized judicial "activism" suddenly interfered in an especially political process, one fraught with partisanship, and imposed its own unappealable solution upon the problem. The rest of this essay will examine whether these claims of judicial hypocrisy ring true.

Federalism has become the defining issue of the Rehnquist Court. To the extent that the current Court has changed American constitutional law, its activities in redefining the balance of power between the national government and the states will likely prove to be what the Rehnquist Court is best known for. Much of the Court's recent activity has been in the sphere of state sovereignty—protecting states as institutions from federal judicial power through state immunity from damages actions in federal court[47] and from federal legislative power through anti-commandeering principles.[48] Last Term's *United States v Morrison*[49] underscored yet another element of the Court's federalism project. In invalidating portions of the Violence Against Women Act,[50] *Morrison* indicates that the Court is serious about limiting national power itself, regardless of a law's effect on states as institutions. While the Court has made some important decisions restricting Congress's powers to expand individual constitutional rights in ways that cannot be abrogated by states,[51] *Morrison* declares the Court's firm intention to restore limits on Congress's basic power to regulate interstate commerce as well.[52]

A principled adherence to federalism, however, does not require the Court to refuse to review the presidential election procedures used by the states. Federalism does not create a free-fire zone where states may do anything they please. Rather, federalism is about the appropriate balance of power between federal and state authority, so that neither government abuses its own power at the expense of the rights of the people.[53] By dividing power between the federal and state governments, and then subjecting each to the separation of powers, James Madison wrote in Federalist 51, "a double security arises to the rights of the people. The different governments will control each other; at the same time that each will be controuled by itself."[54]

This is nowhere truer than in the area of voting. The Constitution certainly accords substantial leeway to the states to manage voting in their own way. As we now know, Article II, Section I of the Constitution declares: "each State shall appoint, in such Manner as the Legislature Thereof May Direct, a Number of Electors."[55] Nonetheless, our constitutional system today permits substantial federal intervention into state elections. Congress, for example, has required states to use single-member districts for congressional elections since 1842.[56] The Fourteenth and Fifteenth Amendments to the Constitution guarantee the individual right of each citizen to vote on an equal basis and prohibit states from attempting to discriminate against protected groups by denying them access to the voting booth.[57] *Bush v Gore's* per curiam holding found that the Fourteenth Amendment's guarantee of equal treatment in voting applied not just to access to the ballot box, but also to a state's treatment of a vote after it is cast.[58]

Federal courts and the federal government have engaged in sweeping intervention into state voting procedures. In decisions such as *Baker v Carr*[59] and *Reynolds v Sims,*[60] the Court established the principle of one-person, one-vote. In its recent redistricting cases, such as *Shaw v Reno,*[61] the Court has held that states cannot use race as a primary factor in drawing voting districts. Congress has also gotten into the game. Today, in many areas of the nation, the Voting Rights Act of 1965 prevents states from changing *any* voting standard, practice, or procedure without the permission of the Attorney General or a federal court in Washington, D.C.[62] Under this mix of federal laws and judicial precedents, the Court will hear claims that states have engaged in "vote dilution," where election procedures or redistricting essentially gives more political power to some districts over others.[63]

Beyond the general federal involvement in state voting procedures, presidential elections specifically implicate a mix of federal and state laws. The Constitution overrides state constitutions and their allocation of functions by delegating to state legislatures, specifically, the power to establish the rules for choosing presidential electors.[64] Federal law establishes the date on which the presidential election will be held in every state,[65] it allows state legislatures to choose alternative methods if a choice is not made,[66] and federal law explains how Congress will count a state's electoral votes that undergo a challenge.[67] While a state may use judicial methods to resolve these disputes, they must proceed by rules enacted before the election (the essence of the *Bush* suit before the U.S. Supreme Court). Finally, Congress has established December 18 as the date that the electors must meet in each state and send their votes to Washington.

So federal judicial review of state election procedures is nothing new, not even to the Rehnquist Court. It is certainly not the direct threat to our federal system of government that some have claimed, unless they believe that national intervention into state electoral systems violates the basic structure of our federal system of government. Indeed, the Court's intervention in the presidential election dispute was not completely without precedent. While it is true that states have the discretion to set the manner of the state's appointment of presidential electors, electors are federal, not state, officials chosen in a federal, not a state, election. When states select officers that play a federal role, as the Supreme Court announced in *U.S. Term Limits v Thornton*,[68] they have a reduced ability to interfere with their activities or method of selection. In *Term Limits*, for example, the Court rejected arguments that a state's constitutional power to control the "Times, Places, and Manner" of holding congressional elections allowed it to prevent incumbents from appearing on the ballot.[69] This suggests that the state's power over the manner of the selection of presidential electors cannot go far beyond procedural matters such as when and where an election is to be held. Once a state began to use procedures, as in Florida, that may have advantaged one candidate over another, federal principles justified judicial preservation of the integrity of the electoral process.

Even if federalism principles did not prevent the Court from resolving *Bush v Gore,* some may criticize the justices because of their intervention into a deeply political dispute. If not by its deeds, certainly by its rhetoric, the Rehnquist Court has promoted the idea of judicial restraint. While yet another phrase that is often used but seldom defined, judicial restraint can be seen generally as a response to the countermajoritarian difficulty.[70] Because judges are not elected and legislators are, judges should exercise such an undemocratic power as sparingly as possible—how sparingly and on what subjects, of course, remains the subject of great debate.[71] The last paragraph of the *Bush v Gore* per curiam genuflects to this ideal. "None are more conscious of the vital limits on judicial

authority than are the members of this Court, and none stand more in admira-
tion of the Constitution's design to leave the selection of the President to the
people, through their legislatures, and to the political sphere."[72]

Of course, the majority ran right into the political thickets anyway. Proponents of judicial restraint might have found the Court's interference surprising,
if not wholly unjustified. The Court had available any number of opportunities
to exercise Alexander Bickel's "passive virtues"[73] to avoid deciding the case, including denying certiorari in the first Florida election case to come before it,[74]
or denying the stay and certiorari in *Bush v Gore*. Nonetheless, the Court invoked its duty to decide federal question cases as justification. According to the
Court, "[w]hen contending parties invoke the process of the courts, however, it
becomes our unsought responsibility to resolve the federal and constitutional
issues the judicial system has been forced to confront."[75] Unfortunately, this
statement is so vague as to carry almost no meaning, as it encompasses any
number of cases that the Rehnquist Court would be only too happy to dismiss
on grounds of standing[76] or the political question doctrine.[77]

Critics of *Bush v Gore*, however, should not have been surprised by the
Court's lack of restraint. This Court has done everything but hide behind the
passive virtues. It has reaffirmed the right to abortion[78] and has placed limits on
religion in the public sphere.[79] In the federalism area, it has invalidated a series
of federal laws in order both to protect state sovereignty and to limit the powers
of the national government. One of the laws, the Violence Against Women Act,
passed Congress by large majorities in both houses of Congress. In the race
area, the Court has invalidated affirmative action in federal contracting[80] and
struck down redistricting that sought to maximize minority representation.[81]
On the First Amendment, the Court has invalidated federal laws so as to expand
commercial speech[82] and to protect indecent or pornographic material.[83] It
has risked confrontation with the political branches by striking down federal
laws solely on the ground that they violate the separation of powers. Hence, the
Court has invalidated the Line Item Veto Act[84] and reversed an effort to expand
religious freedoms that the Court had cut back.[85] This Court has been anything
but shy in flexing its powers of judicial review to intervene in some of the most
contentious issues of the day.

What is important about the Court's recent track record is not just the
frequency of the uses of judicial review, but their quality. Initially, the Marshall
Court in *Marbury v Madison* grounded judicial review in the Court's unique
function in deciding cases or controversies that arise under federal law.[86] As
Thomas Jefferson argued, this basis for judicial review leaves ample room for
the coordinate branches of government to interpret the Constitution in the
course of performing their own constitutional functions.[87] Under the Rehnquist Court, this limited vision of judicial review has steadily been supplanted
by assertions of judicial supremacy—that the Supreme Court is not just *an*
interpreter of the Constitution, but *the* interpreter of the Constitution.[88] To
be sure, the Court's move toward claiming that its readings of the Constitution were final, and that they bound the other branches, truly began with the
Burger Court's decision in *United States v Nixon*,[89] if not before.[90] Under the
Rehnquist Court, however, the justices have rapidly expanded their claims to

supremacy. In *City of Boerne v Flores*,[91] the Court unanimously declared that Congress could not use its power to enforce Fourteenth Amendment rights inconsistently with the Court's interpretation of the scope of those rights. Several cases have followed that make clear the justices' intentions to stand by *Flores*'s core holding.[92]

Such assertions of judicial supremacy belie any notions that the Rehnquist Court generally has followed a course of restraint. If the Court is willing to go so far as to declare that its power to interpret the Constitution is supreme over the other branches, certainly it is no greater a step to intervene in a dispute about non-substantive, rarely-used election procedures. Nor should critics of *Bush v Gore* express dismay at the role the Court took upon itself in settling the presidential election dispute. Claims to judicial supremacy bespeak an arrogance that the Court has a special role in the American political system, one borne not just out of its unique function in deciding cases or controversies, but out of some vague vision of itself as a final resolver of national issues. The justices, in other words, have truly come to believe in Justice Jackson's famous aphorism that "[w]e are not final because we are infallible, but we are infallible only because we are final."[93] Judicial supremacy has led the Court to view itself not only as the final interpreter of the Constitution, but also—since as Tocqueville noted, many political disputes in America eventually become legal ones—as the nation's final oracle on divisive national controversies.

This should have been apparent from a close reading of *Casey*, the same case in which the plurality of Justices O'Connor, Kennedy, and Souter articulated their theory about the Court's own legitimacy. In declaring its refusal to overrule *Roe v Wade*, the plurality equated the Court's power to interpret the Constitution with the authority to end divisive national controversies. It is worth quoting the plurality on this point:

> Where, in the performance of its judicial duties, the Court decides a case in such a way as to resolve the sort of intensely divisive controversy reflected in *Roe* and those rare, comparable cases, its decision has a dimension that the resolution of the normal case does not carry. It is the dimension present whenever the Court's interpretation of the Constitution calls the contending sides of a national controversy to end their national division by accepting a common mandate rooted in the Constitution.[94]

As *Casey* suggests, the Court's drive for supremacy reveals an image of itself as a great healer of national divisions. One need only have replaced "abortion" with "presidential election" to see that the Court would intervene in *Bush v Gore*.

By reviewing the case, the Supreme Court believed that it could finally bring an end to the destructive partisan struggle over the presidential election, and could do it in a way that would allow the nation to accept the final winner's own legitimacy. A look at the alternatives shows that events threatened to spiral out of control. Any Bush victory that resulted from the intervention of the Florida legislature or Congress, while legal, would undoubtedly have been questioned as driven purely by partisanship. On the other hand, Republicans would have rejected a Gore victory as the result of ever-changing, subjective dimple-counting practices of a few local party hacks or the decisions of a political state judiciary. All of the institutions that could control the outcome of the election —the legislature, the Florida Secretary of State, the Florida Supreme Court, the local election officials and Congress—were subject to charges of partisan bias. Although these institutions are popularly elected, their partisan nature might have allowed the election process to drag on—certainly both Republicans and Democrats demonstrated a willingness in Florida to fight on through each stage of the electoral college process. No doubt the Court believed that only it could intervene so as to bring the national election controversy to an end in a manner that would be accepted by the nation, as indeed it has been.[95]

This is not to say that the precise reasoning of the per curiam was utterly correct. I vastly prefer the theory put forward by the Chief Justice's concurrence: Florida's judiciary had so rewritten the state's electoral laws that it had violated Article II's delegation of authority to the state legislatures to choose the method for selecting presidential electors.[96] Indeed, the per curiam's sudden introduction of the December 12 cutoff date for a remedy—based on the assumption that the Florida legislature intended to adopt the safe harbor date for the selection of presidential electors provided for by 3 USC § 5—makes almost no sense at all unless read in light of the concurrence's structural analysis. What all of this goes to show, rather, is that in deciding *Bush v Gore* the Court was not acting in a hypocritical or partisan fashion. Instead of contradicting its own cases on federalism or judicial restraint, the Court acted in keeping with the general trends of its own jurisprudence over the last decade. The Court's declaration of its role in *Casey* might even have made the justices' intervention in the election dispute somewhat predictable. Consistency of action constitutes a core feature of theories about the Court's legitimacy. The Court's adherence to its own principles makes it all the more difficult, then, to conclude that *Bush v Gore* will undermine the judiciary's legitimacy.

Conclusion

Many in legal academia welcomed *Planned Parenthood v Casey* when it first appeared.[97] I would hazard a guess that many of these same supporters of *Casey* have not rushed to embrace *Bush v Gore*. Yet, *Casey* contained the seeds —the claims to judicial supremacy and the aggrandized notions of the Court's role in American society—that would blossom in *Bush v Gore*. Indeed, one can even view the emergence of the per curiam opinion—clearly the work of Justices Kennedy and O'Connor—as evidence of an ultimately failed effort to rebuild the coalition that had produced the unprecedented *Casey* plurality. As in *Casey,* in *Bush v Gore* the Court sought to end a national debate that it feared was tearing the country apart. In fact, the Court's chances of success were much higher in the presidential contest, in which the political system needed a final decision on process rules, than in the abortion debate, which has remained a controversial issue of intense importance to many Americans for decades. It seems that if the Court could intervene into such a contentious political debate as abortion, and survive with its legitimacy more or less intact, then it could safely bring the election dispute to a final conclusion as well.

Notes

1. *Bush v Gore,* 121 S Ct 525 (2000) (per curiam).

2. Even though a bare majority of Americans initially agreed with the Court's ruling in *Bush v Gore,* 80 percent of respondents to a CNN/USA Today/Gallup poll conducted on December 13, 2000, accepted Bush as the legitimate winner of the 2000 presidential election. David W. Moore, *Eight in Ten Americans to Accept Bush as "Legitimate" President,* Gallup News Service (Dec 14, 2000), available online at <http://www.gallup.com/poll/releases/pro01214.asp> (visited Feb 22, 2001).

3. See, for example, Akhil Amar, *The Supreme Court: Should We Trust Judges?,* LA Times MI (Dec 17, 2000) ("[T]his is not the rule of law: It is the rule of subjective sensibility.").

4. See, for example, Bruce Ackerman, *The Court Packs Itself,* Am Prospect 48 (Feb 12, 2001), available online at <http://www.prospect.org/print/V12/3/ackerman-b.html> (visited March 29, 2001).

5. See Id.

6. Neal Katyal, *Politics Over Principle,* Wash Post A35 (Dec 14, 2000).

7. Id, discussing *Scott v Sanford,* 60 US 393 (1857).

8. On the problems with academics participating in such groups letters or ads, see Neal Devins, *Bearing False Witness: The Clinton Impeachment and the Future of Academic Freedom,* 148 U Pa L Rev 165, 185–90 (1999) (warning of irrelevancy, loss of academic freedom, and reduced funding resulting from politically motivated letter writing).

9. Dave Zweifel, *Court Decision Still Rankles Law Profs,* Capital Times 6A (Jan 24, 2001) (reprinting text of ad).

10. Legitimacy in this sense is composed of both a belief that an institution's command is obligatory, and an action in compliance. See Max Weber, I *Economy and Society* 31–33 (Bedminster 1968). See also Alan Hyde, *The Concept of Legitimation in the Sociology of Law,* 1983 Wisc L Rev 379, 381–82 (discussing Weber's analysis of "legitimacy").

11. See Tom R. Tyler and Gregory Mitchell, *Legitimacy and the Empowerment of Discretionary Legal Authority: The United States Supreme Court and Abortion Rights,* 43 Duke L J 703, 711 n 25 (1994) (comparing sociological and philosophical notions of legitimacy).

12. See, for example, Ronald Dworkin, *Law's Empire* 190–215 (Belknap 1986); Joseph Raz, *The Authority of Law: Essays on Law and Morality* 1–27 (Clarendon 1979).

13. See Ken Kress, *Legal Indeterminacy,* 77 Cal L Rev 283, 285 (1989).

14. See, for example, Walter F. Murphy and Joseph Tanenhaus, *Publicity, Public Opinion, and the Court,* 84 Nw U L Rev 985, 1019 (1990) ("[A]nalyses show there is no necessary connection between knowledge and support for the Court.").

15. Political scientists have conducted several excellent studies about the relationship between public opinion and the Supreme Court. See, for example, Thomas R. Marshall, *Public Opinion and the Supreme Court* (Unwin Hyman 1989); Gregory A. Caldeira, *Public Opinion and the U.S. Supreme Court: FDR's Court-Packing Plan,* 81 Am Pol Sci Rev 1139 (1987).

16. *Confidence in Institutions,* available online at <http://www.gallup.com/poll/indicators/indconfidence.asp> (visited Feb 23, 2001).

17. Id.

18. Over the past ten years, the percentage of respondents who indicated that they had a "great deal" or "quite a lot" of confidence averages to 45.8 percent, with a low of 39 percent, and a high of 50 percent. Id.

19. Wendy W. Simmons, *Election Controversy Apparently Drove Partisan Wedge into Attitudes Towards Supreme Court,* available online at <http://www.gallup.com/poll/releases/pro10116.asp> (visited Feb 23, 2001).

20. Id.

21. Id. A tentative study of public opinion on the Supreme Court and the 2000 election conducted by political scientists reaches similar conclusions. They find that a majority of Americans approve of the Court's decision and believe it to have been fair. They also find that Democrats are far more likely to disapprove of the Court's decision and to view it as unfair than Republicans. See James L. Gibson, Gregory A. Caldeira, and Lester K. Spence, *The Supreme Court and the 2000 Presidential Election,* unpublished manuscript, available online at <http://artsci.wustl.edu/~legit/research.html> (visited Apr 27, 2001). Another study of the same authors finds that the Court has not damaged its legitimacy with *Bush v Gore.* After the Court's decision, they find that more than 80 percent of the public remains supportive of the Court, that more than 75 percent believe the Court can be trusted, and that about 85 percent would obey the Court even if they disagreed with its decisions. The authors compared their data to 1987 and 1995 polls and found that, if anything, support among the public for the Court has increased. See James L. Gibson, Gregory A. Caldeira, and Lester K. Spence, *The Legitimacy of the U.S. Supreme Court,* unpublished manuscript, available online at <http://artsci.wustl.edu/~legit/research.html> (visited Apr 27, 2001). As these political scientists conclude from the polling data, "support for the Court does not seem to have been depressed by its involvement in the 2000 presidential election." Id.

22. 295 US 495 (1935).

23. 298 US 238 (1936).

24. See, for example, *Hammer v Dagenhart,* 247 US 251 (1918).

25. 347 US 483 (1954).

26. *Brown v Board of Education ("Brown II"),* 349 US 294 (1955); *Bolling v Sharpe,* 347 US 497 (1954); *Cooper v Aaron,* 358 US 1 (1958); *Griffin v County School Board,* 377 US 218 (1964); *Green v County School Board,* 391 US 430 (1968).

27. *Marbury v Madison,* 5 US (1 Cranch) 137 (1803).

28. *M'Culloch v Maryland,* 17 US (4 Wheat) 316 (1819).

29. *Gibbons v Ogden,*] 22 US (9 Wheat) 1 (1824).

30. *Scott v Sanford ("Dred Scott"),* 60 US 393 (1857).

31. For my own discussion of one instance during this period, see John C. Yoo, *The First Claim: The Burr Trial,* United States v. Nixon, *and Presidential Power,* 83 Minn L Rev 1435, 1451 (1999).

32. See, for example, *The Dred Scott Decision: Speech at Springfield, Illinois, June 26, 1857,* in Roy P. Basler, ed, *Abraham Lincoln: His Speeches and Writings* 354-65 (World 1946).

33. William E. Leuchtenburg, *The Supreme Court Reborn: The Constitutional Revolution in the Age of Roosevelt* 82-162 (Oxford 1995).

34. Such resistance prevented school desegregation from taking hold in the South for more than a decade after *Brown.* See Gerald Rosenberg, *The Hollow Hope: Can Courts Bring About Social Change?* 74-93 (Chicago 1991). Recent work suggests that

the Warren Court did not act out of step with the political branches. See Lucas A. Powe, *The Warren Court and American Politics* 160–78 (Harvard 2000).

35. 505 US 833 (1992) (plurality opinion).

36. 410 US 113 (1973).

37. *Casey,* 505 US at 865).

38. Id.

39. Id at 866.

40. Id at 867.

41. Tyler and Mitchell, 43 Duke L J at 723 (cited in note 11).

42. See, for example, Murphy and Tanenhaus, 84 Nw U L Rev at 992 (cited in note 14).

43. Gregory A. Caldeira and James L. Gibson, *The Etiology of Public Support for the Supreme Court,* 36 Am J Pol Sci 635, 635 (1992).

44. Marshall, *Public Opinion* at 133 (cited in note 15) ("Justices are viewed as fair, neutral, and even-handed.").

45. Owen M. Fiss, *Objectivity and Interpretation,* 34 Stan L Rev 739, 744–45 (1982) (questioning "whether any judicial interpretation can achieve the measure of objectivity required by the idea of law").

46. Tyler and Mitchell, 43 Duke L J at 746 (cited in note 11) ("[T]he key factor affecting the perceived legitimacy of authorities is procedural fairness.").

47. See, for example, *Alden v Maine,* 527 US 706 (1999) (holding that the Eleventh Amendment gives states immunity from suits in state court arising under federal law issued pursuant to Congress's Article I powers); *Seminole Tribe v Florida,* 517 US 44 (1995) (holding that the previously established congressional power to abrogate state immunity is limited to implementation of the Fourteenth Amendment).

48. See, for example, *Printz v United States,* 521 US 898 (1997) (striking down a portion of the Brady Bill on grounds that it conscripted state officials to execute federal law); *New York v United States,* 505 US 144 (1992) (overturning a law that required the states either to enact radioactive waste legislation or take title to the waste).

49. 120 S Ct 1740 (2000).

50. Pub L No 103–322, 108 Stat 1941, codified at 42 USC § 13981 (1994).

51. See, for example, *Kimel v Florida Board of Regents,* 528 US 62 (2000) (holding that states were not subject to the Age Discrimination in Employment Act under the Eleventh Amendment); *College Savings Bank v Florida Prepaid Postsecondary Education Expense Board,* 527 US 666 (1999) (limiting Congress's power to unilaterally abrogate states' sovereign immunity through legislation designed to remediate or prevent constitutional violations under Section 5 of the Fourteenth Amendment); *City of Boerne v Flores,* 521 US 507 (1997) (invalidating the Religious Freedom Restoration Act as impermissibly expanding the scope of Fourteenth Amendment protections).

52. While the Court in *United States v Lopez,* 514 US 549 (1995), struck down a law on Commerce Clause grounds, many commentators were unsure whether this was to be a one-time event, given certain deficiencies in the federal law at issue there.

53. See John C. Yoo, *The Judicial Safeguards of Federalism,* 70 S Cal L Rev 1311, 1402–4 (1997).

54. Federalist 51 (Madison), in Jacob E. Cooke, ed, *The Federalist* 351 (Wesleyan 1961).

55. US Const Art II, § 1.

56. Act of June 25, 1842 § 2, 5 Stat 491, codified at 2 USC § 2c (1994).

57. US Const Amend XIV–XV.

58. 121 S Ct at 530.

59. 369 US 186 (1962).

60. 377 US 533 (1964).

61. 509 US 630 (1993).

62. Voting Rights Act, 42 USC §§ 1973 et seq (1994).

63. *Shaw*, 509 US at 641.

64. *McPherson v Blacker*, 146 US 1, 27 (1892).

65. 3 USC § I (1997).

66. Id § 2.

67. Id §§ 5, 15.

68. 514 US 779 (1995).

69. Id at 829.

70. For well-known efforts to define and grapple with the countermajoritarian difficulty, see generally Jesse H. Choper, *Judicial Review and the National Political Process: A Functional Reconsideration of the Role of the Supreme Court* (Chicago 1980); John Hart Ely, *Democracy and Distrust: A Theory of Judicial Review* (Harvard 1980); Alexander M. Bickel, *The Least Dangerous Branch: The Supreme Court at the Bar of Politics* (Yale 2d ed 1986).

71. For a discussion and criticism of the leading theories, see Terri Jennings Peretti, *In Defense of a Political Court* 36–54 (Princeton 1999).

72. *Bush v Gore*, 121 S Ct at 533.

73. Bickel, *Least Dangerous Branch* at 111–98 (cited in note 70).

74. *Bush v Palm Beach County Canvassing Board*, 121 S Ct 471 (2000) (per curiam).

75. *Bush v Gore*, 121 S Ct at 533.

76. See *Lujan v Defenders of Wildlife*, 504 US 555, 573–78 (1992).

77. *Nixon v United States*, 506 US 224, 228 (1993).

78. *Casey*, 505 US 833.

79. *Lee v Weisman*, 505 US 577, 592–93 (1992). The Court, however, also has sought to give religious groups an equal footing in its participation in government aid programs. *Mitchell v Helms*, 530 US 793 (2000) (holding that taxpayer money could be used to buy computers and other instructional materials for religious schools); *Agostini v Felton*, 521 US 203 (1997) (allowing publicly paid teachers to be provided to parochial schools to assist disabled students with remedial, secular education).

80. *Adarand Constructors, Inc v Pena*, 515 US 200 (1995).

81. *Shaw v Reno*, 509 US 630 (1993).

82. See, for example, *44 Liquormart, Inc v Rhode Island*, 517 US 484 (1996).

83. See, for example, *United States v Playboy Entertainment Group*, 120 S Ct 1878, 1893 (2000); *Reno v American Civil Liberties Union*, 521 US 844 (1997).

84. *Clinton v New York*, 524 US 417 (1998).

85. *Flores*, 521 US 507.

86. 5 US (1 Cranch) 137, 176 (1803). See also Robert Lowry Clinton, Marbury v. Madison *and Judicial Review* 15–17 (University Press of Kansas 1989); Christopher Wolfe, *The Rise of Modern Judicial Review: From Constitutional Interpretation to Judge-Made Law* 80–89 (Basic 1986).

87. See, for example, Letter from Thomas Jefferson to Abigail Adams, Sept 11, 1804, in Paul L. Ford, ed, 10 *Works of Thomas Jefferson* 89 n 1 (G. P. Putnam's Sons 1905).

88. For my account of this development, see John C. Yoo, Book Review, *Choosing Justices: A Political Appointments Process and the Wages of Judicial Supremacy,* 98 Mich L Rev 1436, 1458–61 (2000).

89. 418 US 683 (1974). For sharp criticism of this vision of judicial review, see Michael Stokes Paulsen, *The Most Dangerous Branch: Executive Power to Say What the Law Is,* 83 Georgetown L J 217, 228–38, 255–62 (1994).

90. Some might argue that the Court first proclaimed its supremacy in *Cooper v Aaron,* 358 US 1 (1958), in which the Court declared that not only were the Court's opinions the "supreme Law of the Land," but that the Court was "supreme in the exposition" of the Constitution. Id at 18. *Cooper,* however, was aimed not at the other branches of government, but at forcing state officials to follow federal interpretation of the Constitution. See Daniel A. Farber, *The Supreme Court and the Rule of Law:* Cooper v. Aaron *Revisited,* 1982 U Ill L Rev 387, 398–403.

91. 521 US 507 (1997).

92. See, for example, *Dickerson v United States,* 530 US 428 (2000) (holding Congress could not alter *Miranda* rights); *Morrison,* 120 S Ct 1740 (striking down the Violence Against Women Act); *Kimel,* 528 US 62 (preventing enforcement of the ADA against the states); *Florida Prepaid Postsecondary Education Expense Board v College Savings Bank,* 527 US 627 (1999) (holding Congress cannot abrogate state sovereign immunity from patent claims).

93. *Brown v Allen,* 344 US 443, 540 (1953) (Jackson concurring).

94. *Casey,* 505 US at 866–67.

95. On December 10, CNN reported that 61 percent of those polled preferred that the United States Supreme Court make the final decision on the selection of the next President, as compared to 17 percent who believed Congress should make the final decision, 9 percent who believed that the Florida State Supreme Court should make the final decision, and only 7 percent who believed the Florida legislature should make the final decision. See <http://www.cnn.com/2000/ALLPOLITICS/stories/12/10/cnn.poll> (visited Feb 24, 2001).

96. *Bush v Gore,* 121 S Ct at 533–35.

97. See, for example, Kathleen Sullivan, *The Supreme Court, 1991 Term Forward: The Justices of Rules and Standards,* 106 Harv L Rev 22, 24–25 (1992).

POSTSCRIPT

Did the Supreme Court Hijack the 2000 Presidential Election From Al Gore?

Holmes takes a dim view of the Supreme Court's decisions in the 2000 election. He argues that the Court misinterpreted Article II of the U.S. Constitution, which provides for the establishment of the electoral college and the rules by which the Senate and, if necessary, the House counts the votes. The Court exceeded its mandate by claiming that the Florida Supreme Court violated Article II by "ignoring the will of the Florida legislature" in trying to enforce the rules it established before November 7 to ensure that all votes were counted.

Holmes is also critical of liberals who fail to recognize that the U.S. Supreme Court is generally a "status quo" institution. He asserts that states rights, the equal protection clause of the Fourteenth Amendment (originally designed to protect the rights of the newly freed blacks in the 1860s), and the principle of judicial review are usually used to protect the rights of the more privileged groups in society.

Yoo makes the case that the Supreme Court was interpreting the proper mix of the federal government's relationship with the states in determining the role of the electoral college in the presidential election of 2000. Unlike most scholars, he justifies the federal Supreme Court's decision to strike down the Florida Supreme Court's order for a recount. The Supreme Court, says Yoo, should have stressed Chief Justice William H. Rehnquist's assertion that the Florida judiciary had rewritten the state's electoral college laws and violated the state legislature's authority to choose the method for selecting electors.

Yoo contends that the Supreme Court's decision in *Bush v. Gore* did not set any precedents. Yet many would contend that Yoo is wrong to argue that *Bush v. Gore* was primarily concerned with resolving "a narrow legal issue involving the selection of presidential electors." The Court knew that when it issued its decision, George W. Bush became the new president of the United States.

The bibliography on the 2000 election is already enormous. The starting point is the anthology *Bush v. Gore: The Court Cases and the Commentary* edited by E. J. Dionne, Jr., and William Kristol (Brookings Institution Press, 2001). Two other useful collections of essays about the Court's decisions are Jack N. Rakove, ed., *The Unfinished Election of 2000* (Basic Books, 2001) and Cass R. Sunstein and Richard A. Epstein, eds., *The Vote: Bush, Gore and the Supreme Court* (University of Chicago Press, 2001). Gary Rosen, "Reconsidering 'Bush v. Gore,' " *Commentary* (November 2001) summarizes the literature on the Court's decision. Several newspapers weighed in with their chronology of the events. The best is *Deadlock: The Inside Story of America's Closest Election* by the political staff of the *Washington Post* (PublicAffairs, 2001).

ISSUE 16

Environmentalism: Is the Earth Out of Balance?

YES: Otis L. Graham, Jr., from "Epilogue: A Look Ahead," in Otis L. Graham, Jr., ed., *Environmental Politics and Policy, 1960s–1990s* (Pennsylvania State University Press, 2000)

NO: Bjorn Lomborg, from "Yes, It Looks Bad, But...," "Running on Empty," and "Why Kyoto Will Not Stop This," *The Guardian* (August 15, 16, & 17, 2001)

ISSUE SUMMARY

YES: Otis L. Graham, Jr., a professor emeritus of history, maintains that the status of the biophysical basis of our economies, such as "atmospheric pollution affecting global climate, habitat destruction, [and] species extinction," is negative and in some cases irreversible in the long run.

NO: Associate professor of statistics Bjorn Lomborg argues that the doomsday scenario for earth has been exaggerated and that, according to almost every measurable indicator, mankind's lot has improved.

Historically, Americans have not been sympathetic to preserving the environment. For example, the first European settlers in the sixteenth and seventeenth centuries were awed by the abundance of land in the New World. They abandoned their Old World custom of practicing careful agricultural husbandry on their limited lands and instead solved their agricultural problems in North America by constantly moving to virgin land. The pioneers believed that the environment must be conquered, not protected or preserved.

The first real surge in the environmental movement occurred during the Progressive Era of the early twentieth century. Reformers were upset about the changes seen in America since the Civil War, such as an exploding population, massive immigration, political corruption, and the end of the frontier (as proclaimed by the 1890 census). The remedy for these problems, said the reformers, lay in strong governmental actions at the local, state, and national levels.

Environmentalists agreed that the government had to take the lead and stop the plundering of the remaining frontier before it was too late. But the movement split into two groups—conservationists and preservationists—a division that has continued in the movement to this day.

The Nixon administration pushed through the most important piece of environment regulation ever passed by the government: the National Environmental Policy Act of 1969, which established the Council for Environmental Quality (CEQ) for the purpose of coordinating all federal pollution control programs. This legislation empowered the Environmental Protection Agency (EPA) to set standards and implement CEQ policies on a case-by-case basis. The EPA thus became the centerpiece of the emerging federal environmental regulatory system.

In the late 1970s and early 1980s a new urban-oriented environmentalism emerged. The two major concerns surrounded the safety of nuclear power and the sites where toxic wastes were dumped. For years proponents of atomic power proclaimed that the technological benefits of nuclear power far outweighed the risks. Now the public began to have doubts.

More dangerous and more mysterious were the dangers from hazardous waste and pollutants stored improperly and often illegally across the country. The first widely known battle between local industry and the public occurred at Love Canal, near Niagara Falls, New York. In the 1950s a working-class neighborhood was constructed around a canal that was being used as a dump site for waste by Hooker Chemical, a local company. Although the local government denied it, cancers and birth defects in the community reached epic proportions. On August 2, 1978, the New York State health commissioner declared Love Canal a great and imminent peril to the health of the general public. President Jimmy Carter declared the Hooker Chemical dump site a national emergency, and by the following spring, 237 families had been relocated. Controversies such as Love Canal made the public aware that toxic waste dumps and the accompanying fallout were nationwide problems. Congress passed several laws in the 1980s to deal with this issue. The Superfund Act of 1980 created a $1.6 billion fund to clean up toxic wastes, and the Nuclear Waste Policy Act of 1982 directed a study of nine potential sites where the radioactive materials left over from the creation of nuclear energy could be permanently stored.

In spite of the lax enforcement of the laws under the Reagan administration, the public became alarmed again in 1988 when Representative Mike Synar (D-Oklahoma) chaired a congressional subcommittee on the environment that uncovered contamination of 4,611 sites at 761 military bases, a number of which threatened the health of the nearby communities. Many of these sites still need to be cleaned up.

Is the environmental crisis real? In the following selections, Otis L. Graham, Jr., contends that the problems of global warning, habitat destruction, and species extinction are probably irreversible and unsolvable. Bjorn Lomborg argues that the doomsday scenario for the earth has been exaggerated and that, by almost every measurable indicator, mankind's lot has improved.

Otis L. Graham, Jr.

A Look Ahead

Environmental policy is about fixing a problem—a large, complex, foundational problem. From the 1960s to the end of the century, the United States engaged this problem on a wider scale and with more energy than ever before, as a part of a global, multinational effort in this direction. Seen from our experience and vantage, what are the prospects ahead of humanity and nature in the ongoing negotiation of our relationship?

Serious thought on this question usually begins not with historical inquiry but with reports from technology and the natural and social sciences, disciplines that habitually project events and trends ahead. But projecting likely futures also turns out to involve history, since formulating education guesses about what lies ahead requires us to estimate what momentum and direction we have already established strongly enough to shape that future. The two broad schools of opinion on tomorrow have been called the Cornucopian and the Malthusian, labels that exaggerate the bias of the extreme ends of debate. Let us use the terms eco-optimists, people who wind up cheerful after they concede that there are a few problems, and eco-pessimists, people who see bad outcomes but still believe that something can be done or they would not be speaking.

The conviction that the American environment offered an inexhaustible resource was of course the primal assumption shaping our national history. Pessimism about using things up came later, the chief voices including George Perkins Marsh (*Man And Nature,* 1864), Frederick Jackson Turner's thoughts on the implications of the discovery in the Census of 1890 that the era of the frontier was over, the warnings of Teddy Roosevelt, Gifford Pinchot, and others in the first and second Conservation movements (who were usually optimists at bottom). The alarm-sounding books by Vogt and Osborn in 1948 and Walter Prescott Webb's *The Great Frontier* (1952) touched on the United States only as part of a global crisis of population pressing upon depleting resources, and were influential among a limited readership. The Sixties cranked up virtually every concern to a higher volume and larger audiences, and the reception of Stanford University biologist Paul Ehrlich's *The Population Bomb* (1968)—selling over a million copies in paperback, Ehrlich being interviewed in *Playboy* magazine and receiving wide media attention—gave the message of ecocrisis a mass audience. "The battle to feed all of humanity is over," Ehrlich wrote, predicting

From Otis L. Graham, Jr., "Epilogue: A Look Ahead," in Otis L. Graham, Jr., ed., *Environmental Politics and Policy, 1960s–1990s* (Pennsylvania State University Press, 2000). Copyright © 2000 by Pennsylvania State University. Reprinted by permission. Notes omitted.

the deaths of hundreds of millions of people in famines across the 1970s and mounting pressure upon resources and environment even in affluent societies like the United States. The Club of Rome's best-selling *The Limits to Growth* (1972), written by a team of MIT scholars led by Dennis L. Meadows, offered a melancholy projection of population pressure, resource depletion, and pollution that described a grim global slide over the next three decades into "a dismal and depleted existence," a miserable condition they called "overshoot and collapse." Eight years later the U.S. government came out in broad agreement. *Global 2000,* an interagency report commissioned by President Jimmy Carter and published in 1980, reported that "if present trends continue, the world in 2000 will be more crowded, more polluted, less stable ecologically, and more vulnerable to disruption than the world we live in now."

A counterattack against this strong current of eco-pessimism was predictable. Offer an idea that receives wide public attention in America and people will piggy-back into the limelight by providing an opposite view. Further, optimism runs deep in American history, and tends to assert itself when gloom is expressed. More important, one implication of the forecasts of ecocrisis was criticism of and demands for curbs on growth, a sentiment fundamentally and deeply alarming to the business community and other elements of American society. Another reason for stiff resistance to the very idea of eco-pessimism is its implication that there must be a larger role for government in regulating resource uses, waste disposal, and even procreation. "Mutual coercion mutually agreed upon" in the area of human fertility was the recommendation, and "freedom in a commons brings ruin to all" a memorable line, in University of California biologist Garrett Hardin's widely discussed and reprinted 1968 article, "The Tragedy of the Commons." "Free market" loyalists sensed dangerous implications—government intrusion into land and resource use, perhaps even the bedroom. A final factor attracting criticism was that the pessimists sometimes predicted with too much specificity and enthusiasm, and some of the bad things forecast did not happen, or did not happen on anything like the scale predicted or as soon as foreseen. "The Prophet Paul," as one writer dubbed Ehrlich, had indeed said in a magazine interview that "our large polluting population is responsible for air pollution that could very easily lead to massive starvation in the U.S. within the next two decades," and "I believe we're facing the brink because of population pressures." And Paul and William Paddock did predict mass starvation in China "within five or ten years" in their *Famine— 1975!*

To all of this the eco-optimists responded with a spirited critique and rebuttal. One of the earliest to emerge was to become a polarizing figure who went beyond skeptical questioning of the eco-pessimists to assert an almost religious belief that more growth and more people were the formula not for disaster but for a rosy future. This was Julian Simon, a professor of marketing at the University of Illinois until, "in the midst of a depression of unusual duration," he found healing in a conversion to the cause of "having more children and taking in more immigrants." He then moved to Washington, D.C., and began a productive and influential career as the leading eco-optimist. In a cascade of essays, public appearances, and books (principally *The Ultimate Re-*

source [1981]), Simon reversed every argument of the environmentalists. What was needed was more population, which would bring us more Mozarts and Einsteins, building the knowledge and genius sufficient to solve environmental problems. "There is no meaningful physical limit—even the commonly mentioned weight of the Earth—to our capacity to keep growing forever," was one of Simon's most reprinted remarks, as well as his paraphrase of the *Global 2000* conclusion: "If present trends continue, the world in 2000 will be less crowded, less polluted, more stable ecologically and less vulnerable to resource-supply disruption than the world we live in now."

The eco-optimist point of view had many more voices, often located in think tanks such as the Heritage Foundation or the Cato Institute whose support came from pro-capitalist foundations, corporations, and individuals. But the vulnerability of some of the language and predictions of the pessimists drew many and independent rebuttals. Journalist Gregg Easterbrook's *A Moment on the Earth* (1995) brought together an immense literature on environmental problems which he interpreted to mean that we were in fact winning the battle to preserve the environment. The air was cleaner, pollution is shrinking and will soon end, global warming is "almost certain to be avoided," and doomsday thinking "is nonsensical." Environmentalists should stop "proclaiming emergencies that do not exist." . . .

To this writer, at the end of the 1990s, the worriers have the most convincing scenarios, globally and even in the United States, as I am obliged to explain.

⋯◉⋯

There would be no debate if there were not facts and arguments on both sides. Optimists point out that global population-growth projections are slightly improving, the UN Population Division now seeing the likelihood (if current trends persist, always the fundamental qualifier) of a world population reaching (this is the middle of five projections) 10.8 billion by 2050, stabilizing at 11 billion persons around 2100. Earlier estimates in the middle range for 2050 had been closer to 12 billion, with responsible demographers fearing 16 billion (or more). Population growth rates have been declining more broadly than earlier projected. This is good news, depending on how you look at it. Is ending up with the smallest bad scenario therefore good news?

In Europe, the population worry has actually veered around to a very different, "birth dearth" anxiety. Most European nations began reporting below-replacement fertility rates in the 1970s, giving rise to fears that a shrinkage of nations lay ahead. Rising immigration rates into the prosperous nations of the European Union have ensured that nations will not shrink but will give rise to a more volatile concern over national identity. Will Italy, for example, with the lowest birth rates in the world and ever recorded, still be Italy in one hundred years, when it is populated by Muslim immigrants from Albania, Algeria, and elsewhere?

Thus the world faces two demographic problems: unprecedented population growth in the poorer and underdeveloped regions where most humans live, and stabilized and even potentially shrinking nationalities (not populations, which are replenished by immigration) in Europe, Australia, and the fastest growing industrialized nation since it permitted mass immigration with a 1965 law, the United States. To simplify, the global population is going to double (not triple, as we feared two decades ago), and nations whose fertility choices lead to shrinking populations will be put back on the growth path by immigration, welcome and legal or neither. (Japan will not permit immigration, and, as probably the only nation in the world that retains control over its demographic destiny, will have to decide very shortly how much to shrink.) Out of this mixed picture, some people make doubling rather than tripling into good news, the lesser of two disasters.

The enormity of the demographic upheaval whose final century we now enter should not be trivialized by calculations that trim a couple of billion off at the end. As Bill McKibben pointed out in 1998, "The *increase* in human population in the 1990s has exceeded the *total* population in 1960. The population has grown more since 1950 than it did during the previous four million years."

While this awesome event is at the core of our difficulties, we must know much more than whether "the population bomb" will in the end be judged as earthquake at Richter 6.5 or 7.0. The first question is food supplies, then the constellation of measures of human well-being that extend from mere survival. Here I will argue that much of the apparent good news is being misinterpreted.

As the Simon–Ehrlich bets show, we move through an era in which those who measure progress in the conventional ways—looking at measures of human well-being such as food production per capita, the prices (and thus availability) of basic commodities, life expectancy, including infant mortality, automobile or home or telephone ownership, and, in most societies in the second half of the century with Africa as a major exception, per capita income—can report impressive gains, and win Simonite bets. Even measurements of "natural resources" such as timber or fossil fuels, or environmental "quality" as defined in the environmental protection statutes since the 1960s, contain some ground for optimism, a sense of winning momentum. As eco-optimist writer Gregg Easterbrook said in 1995, there has been in the United States an "astonishing, and continuing, record of success" in improving water and air quality that humans use, more recycling of wastes, expanding acreage of forests—all of this at less cost than business and anti-environmental lobbies predicted. He might have mentioned gasoline dropping briefly in 1999 to $1 per gallon in the United States decisive evidence of a "natural resource shortage" that did not, to date, follow the scenario of the Malthusians.

But shift the focus from these conventional accounting categories in measuring human welfare to measures of ecosystem health—from the economists' evidence that humans are consuming more and living better (on the whole) to the ecologists' evidence that the ecosystem foundations are eroding—and the future takes on a worrier's look. Complacency, wrote an international team of scientists in *Science* in 1998, persists because "conventional indicators of the standard of living pertain to commodity production, not to the natural resource base on which all production depends." We Americans (and Canadians, Europeans, Asians, Australians, New Zealanders, most Latin Americans) are still "making progress," enlarging our consumption and numbers—while drawing down our basic capital, the ecological foundations of the earth's limited capacity to sustain humans. Economists are accustomed to report on our well-being measured in Gross Domestic Product (GDP), but "Ecolate" (Garrett Hardin's term, meant to go along with Literate and Numerate) natural scientists are desperately trying to get the public's attention for another category of reporting: the status of the biophysical basis of our economies. Ehrlich and his colleagues offered in the second bet to measure some of these—atmospheric pollution affecting global climate, habitat destruction, species extinction—knowing the trends to be negative.

Wherever one samples the trends, they signal the depletion of ecological capital, some of it surely irreversible. Arable soil acreage shrinks by erosion, salinization, and urban development. Habitat mutilation or disturbance, and invasive species, accelerate species extinction, shrinking the range and potential benefits of biodiversity. Human pollution and harvesting sterilize the oceans. And that most temporary piece of good fortune, humanity's wonderful energy bonanza of fossil fuels, when burned, sends skyward a global blanket warming the earth and stressing every ecosystem upon it.

A powerful new conception of this capital draw-down has emerged in the phrase "ecosystem services." Described in Paul and Anne Ehrlich, *Extinction* (1981), Gretchen Daily et al., *Nature's Services* (1997), and in a lead article in *Nature* in 1997 by Robert Costanza and associates, ecosystem services are the free goods drawn upon by the human economy and taken for granted, but now rapidly contracting: pollinating crops and natural vegetation, controlling potential agricultural pests, filtering and decomposing wastes, forming soil and maintaining fertility, maintaining the gaseous composition of the atmosphere. In the *Nature* article, Costanza and his associates, in an effort to gain the attention of policymakers and public, estimated the value of ecosystem services at $33 trillion a year, or twice the world's annual GDP.

Teddy Roosevelt thought we were running out of vital resources—forests, petroleum, wildlife, places of natural beauty. He was not wrong, but we now see more deeply into the problem. Ecosystems and their services are wounded and shrink, both because of overharvesting and conversion to agricultural or urban uses, and because "what we are running out of is what the scientists call 'sinks,'" in the words of Bill McKibben, places to dump our garbage at no (apparent) cost.

As the century comes to a close, Americans cruise into more and more affluence on a remarkable economic roll, not the best climate in which to absorb the complex news of the melancholy trends in our ecological bank accounts. That side of our situation is difficult to see. Economists, journalists, and law-trained policymakers are looking in another direction, measuring conventional things with prices on them. And the vast majority of us, woefully uneducated by our schools, universities, churches, and media, have only a dim understanding of the erosion of the often distant ecological foundations of our livelihood. We have no idea of where or how our "ecological footprint" is felt. Ecological footprint—a helpful concept in the hands of ecologists who hope to measure and visualize the far-flung impacts of our urbanized communities, "the 'load' imposed by given population on nature," in the words of Mathis Wackernagel and William Rees, authors of *Our Ecological Footprint* (1996). Seen in this way, Chicago may have (let us say) cleaned up its air and wastes and restored fish to the Chicago River. All appears well locally. But to discover that city's ecological footprint requires calculation of the ecological goods and services appropriated from far away—from distant agricultural land, from oceanic and forest carbon sinks absorbing atmospheric carbon dioxide, from waterways asked to dilute and break down wastes, from fisheries and forests harvested. The calculations have not been made not only because they are immensely complicated but also because no one has fixed a price for these ecosystem disturbances or knows who or how to charge. But whatever the calculation, we can be certain that Chicagoans, and all Americans in this perspective, are, due to their affluence, "larger" (and thus their footprint larger) than people from Brazil, some of whom are clear-cutting the Amazonian rain forests and thus have a much larger footprint than the residents of the Bangladesh flood plain. Where and how the footprint disturbs nature is out of sight and off the account books of our households. But to better foresee the human future requires an accounting that reaches across jurisdictional borders and is not confined to things already assigned pricetags.

⋘◉⋙

Three decades ago, alarmed writers about the future such as Paul Ehrlich, Barry Commoner, and the Club of Rome *Limits to Growth* authors occasionally used words like "bomb," "collapse," "descent into barbarism," "the death of the planet." Scientists all, they wished to gain attention, and did. But this occasional language, along with an underestimation of the role of human ingenuity, gave them the Parson Malthus problem: the disasters did not arrive on time. A generation later, lookers-ahead who come to pessimistic conclusions report with more sophistication, allow more complexity and perplexity to come through, and do not specify the date of the next famine. In *The Population Explosion* (1990), the Ehrlichs agree with T. S. Eliot that while the world might end with a "bang," it is more likely to end in a "whimper," the slow breakdown of both natural and agricultural ecosystems, with disease outbreaks, water shortages, and rising social disorder. This scenario, like most, looks to the experiences humans may expect, but there is a holocaust of sorts ahead for plant and animal life. Writer David Quammen surveyed paleontologists and found them convinced that "we are entering another mass extinction, a vale of biological impoverishment" in which "somewhere between one third and two thirds of all species" will become extinct. The resulting world will still have wildlife, of course, but only those who survived the ecological mauling by 10 billion humans. "Wildlife will consist of the pigeons and the coyotes," Quammen writes, "the black rats and the brown rats," rodents, cockroaches, house sparrows and geckos "and the barn cats and the skinny brown feral dogs . . . a Planet of Weeds."

This upcoming cascade of ecological breakdowns was increasingly seen as arriving regionally rather than uniformly around the globe. Many observers foresaw escalating problems ahead for the fast-growing giant, China, adding 13 million people a year, her thin soils eroding and cities choked with traffic, garbage, and heavily polluted air from coal combustion. In *Who Will Feed China?* (1995), Lester Brown warned that a combination of droughts and depletion of groundwater acquifers meant an imminent decline in the supply of water for Chinese farmers. Taken with conversion of farmland for urban uses, floods and erosion, agricultural production would fail to keep pace with a growing population, throwing that formerly food-sufficient nation of 1.2 billion onto world grain markets. The ripple effects would include rising grain prices and shortages in poor nations, a formula for famine and political instability.

It is the latter that increasingly draws attention. The world's poor will suffer as their numbers press ever harder upon degraded resources, but they cannot be expected always and everywhere to suffer patiently. Human conflicts between the globes' rich and poor seem likely to be a core dynamic of the difficulties ahead. Journalist Robert Kaplan caught President Clinton's attention with a 1996 article reporting on his travels along an arc of countries from Africa through the Middle East, where he found repeated examples of ecological collapse intensifying tribal and civil wars with several "failed states" losing control over national borders. In a sophisticated look out toward *The World in 2020* (1994), Hamish MacRae sees water shortages, a tightening of oil supplies, relentless habitat destruction, and unavoidable international conflict as China replaces the United States as the world's chief air polluter and thus driver of global warming. Even that Texas optimist Walt Rostow, in his recent look ahead at the twenty-first century, sees the period from the 1990s to 2025 as "a period of maximum strain on resources and the environment when global population is still expanding" and there might be, starting first in certain regions, "a global crisis of Malthusain consequences."

Rostow shares with most other forecasters a relaxed optimism about oil, not having checked lately with geologists. "With so much to worry about," Rostow writes, "why worry about energy," especially since massive new oil reserves are under development in the Caspian Sea region of central Asia?

But the time of troubles that he sees ahead in at least the first half of the twenty-first century will apparently include the next and final oil crunch. Some time in the first decade of that century, geologists are now arguing, world oil production will begin to decline and prices will rise. Whether or not political instability in the Middle East brings artificial shortages, oil production will soon begin falling behind demand, which is growing at 2 percent a year to double in 34 years. "The Petroleum Interval" for human-kind began about 140 years ago when Colonel Drake drilled oil in Pennsylvania, points out Walter Youngquist in *Geodestinies,* and will be more than 300 years from that event, "a brief bright blip on the screen of human history." No, says *Science* magazine, there is quickly gathering a consensus among geologists that "mankind will consume it all in a 2-century binge of profligate energy use." The time available to come up with alternatives is much shorter than anticipated.

Thus there seemed a shift across a broad front in the direction of eco-pessimist anticipation, laced here and there (as they had not been in the 1960s–1970s) with a qualified optimism about the possibility of technological leaps over or around some of the problems. Perhaps the decisive factor making for an overall sense of crisis was the evolving understanding of climate change. In the 1990s the scenario of global warming moved from a widely disputed hypothesis to an assumption about the planetary future, at least at the broad center of scientific and governmental opinion, augmented by some business converts, which included British Petroleum. Earth may surprise us, all admit, and not warm as predicted. But at century's end the added factor of almost certain warming and climatic instability seems like the draw of the game-killing black Queen in a game of Hearts. What will the "period of maximum strain" feel like, if greenhouse warming comes upon our overcrowded world as expected (all agree that no policy changes in any country can slow or reverse it until the second half of the . . . century)? Writer Bill McKibben imagined it "stormier" than before, both wetter and drier; spring coming earlier, summers hotter and longer; glacier meltings and retreat, rising oceans, altered ocean currents bringing abrupt climate change on shore; crop failures; millions of environmental refugees. "The next fifty years are a special time," he concluded in language suggesting difficulty in finding the right adjective but not wanting to use any of the common terms of alarm. Clearly it would not on the whole be a nice time, when wishing you to have a nice day will be enough. "The single most special thing about it may be that we are now apparently degrading the most basic functions of the planet."

From this perspective, Americans at the end of the twentieth century are enjoying an Indian Summer before the arrival of what Harvard biologist E. O. Wilson calls in understated terms "The Century of the Environment." Pleasant news and prospects surround us, by standard measures. Our own national economy as of this writing (1999) seems the only healthy, inflation-free, full-employment, steadily growing stock market booming large economy in a world of mixed performances, including the utter collapse of the system of our former rival. U.S. environmental policies and private-sector responses have produced welcome improvements in some measures of environmental and human health, and impressive institutional learning. As a people we are overweight and living longer than ever.

Yet a time of troubles looms ahead, in the view of most natural scientists and a growing number of other observers, one that will spare no country and respect no borders. Environmental problems and policy will push to the front of national and international agendas, and laterally inject themselves further into policy realms like national defense, trade, and public health. We cannot imagine how another symposium of this sort thirty years from now might assess U.S. environmental politics and policy. But since the anticipated problems a generation out into the doubling of human numbers are sure to be more formidable than the oil spills and pesticide warnings that launched in the Sixties a new era of environmental concern, our resources are also greater. It is well to briefly take stock of them.

Thirty years of serious pollution fighting has collected an impressive scientific, technological, and analytical base in American governments, universities, research centers, and corporations. Public support for environmental protection holds at high levels, even if the public is confused and misinformed about some things—relative risks of various hazards, and the basic demography of the United States and the planet. The "Brownlash" against environmentalism... did considerable damage but also forced some hard thinking about policy alternatives. At century's end there seems more long-term wind in the Green sails than in the Brown. Simonite denial of environmental decline is found only on the journalistic fringes, untenable any longer in the science-respecting mainstream. A steady boost in public environmental concern and education can be expected as we go to school amid future episodes of crisis—mammoth oil spills, local famine, epidemics, extreme weather disasters. The same can be said of the daily existence of Americans living amid intensifying pressures of urban congestion and suburban sprawl driven by the developed world's fastest population growth rate. These conditions will worsen and bring environmental matters to the foreground. The Green persuasion has already spread beyond its largely affluent, WASP social base and put down roots among ethnic and racial minorities in both urban and rural settings, and gathers new recruits from American religious communities, as well as from a surprisingly vigorous animal rights movement. The "business community," if that phrase has any meaning, has moved from solid hostility toward costly environmental regulations to an unevenly "Greened" or pro-active ally in lightening our ecological footprints. Environmental grassroots activism is invigorated and given intellectual and political leverage in the 1990s by the Internet, where millions of citizens exchange information and encouragement, quickly mobilize constituencies and focus political pressure.

Still, these and other assets applied to environmental repair will not be enough, for they have not yet been enough. One could read the history of environmental effort during the last four decades of the twentieth century as exposing a core defect in the campaign to realign humanity's relationship to the natural world. Environmentalism aims at what in the end? "Clean air" and "clean water" are useful phrases for media releases and legislation. But environmentalists have not communicated a compelling national goal, a vision of a future on the other side of the struggles to contain the succession of crises that growth produced. If thinking is not strategic, then it becomes tactical, and we clean up the nearby creek—but the growth path is never challenged. Americans, and apparently all others, still march to the equivalent of the Bible's injunction from Genesis 1:28: "Be fruitful, and multiply, and replenish the earth... and subdue it."

For a brief time in the penumbra of the Sixties, the audacious idea of realigning the purpose of American life away from perpetual national expansion seemed to make headway, as Beck and Kolankiewicz relate. "Limits to growth" was a book title and much-volleyed phrase in the early 1970s, and an intellectual high watermark in the search for a larger strategy for environmentalism came in 1972 when the Commission on Population and the American Future concluded that "no substantial benefits would result from continued growth of the nation's population" and that the nation should welcome and plan for stabilization. This was the sine qua non, a foundation on which could be built a more complete vision of what Franklin D. Roosevelt liked to call "a permanent country."

But the effort to re-aim America away from the growth path toward something else—the "stationary state" of John Stuart Mill?—foundered under intense and emotional opposition. Critics of the Rockefeller Commission's recommendation of population stabilization were quick to attach to that idea the scent of government intrusion into procreation, and to mobilize against one recommended tactic in particular, abortion rights. Then the media learned that demographers were reporting that replacement-level fertility had already been reached in the United States, a finding widely misunderstood to mean that U.S. population growth was over. Author Ben Wattenberg, among others, began to warn of a "birth dearth," and public discussion of population growth and goals slipped into a hopeless confusion through the Reaganite 1980s in which governmental policy actually aligned itself with the expansionist position of the Vatican.

By the 1990s those still concerned about population growth within the United States knew that the nation's growth rate was the fastest among industrialized nations, adding 3 million people a year (which meant a doubling time for the national population of 60–70 years), growth driven increasingly by the massive immigration released by the Immigration Act of 1965. As Beck and Kolankiewicz describe, a few environmental groups still called for U.S. (and world) population stabilization (one, Negative Population Growth, for a reduction) as one objective among many others. But most avoided the issue to sidestep the extra controversy thought to come with it. Members of the Sierra Club in 1998 forced a referendum to commit the Club to population stabilization and the reduction of immigration levels required to achieve that, and were turned back on a 60–40 percent vote by board and staff opposition, arguing not that the facts were wrong but that any position on immigration would attract criticism from ethnic spokespersons and create negative image problems.

Thus in the four decades under review, the first strategic goal on the way to "a permanent country"—population stabilization—was for a while endorsed from a presidential commission down through environmental intellectuals to the grassroots. Then it slid quietly to the margins until in 1998 the goal of capping population growth even if it required immigration limits could not carry a vote in the Sierra Club. As U.S. population surged ahead, the effort to put stabilization back on the American political agenda was blocked because it required immigration reduction, and that was not politically correct among the leadership of most environmental organizations. The entire period after the Sixties thus takes on the aspect of a vigorous and expanding environmental movement that somewhat puzzlingly lost its earlier grip on a key component of a larger strategic purpose, turning increasingly to tactical battles over this redwood grove or that city's air quality. The commitment to global as well as domestic family planning of the Kennedy-Johnson years, even Nixon's brief interest in population questions, gave way to a broad resignation about and a growing ignorance of global and especially national demographic trends. This was a part of the larger acquiescence by mainstream environmentalists in the Growth Path, after the Club of Rome had briefly stimulated a debate about establishing limits.

Of course, to redesign human values and institutions so that "growth"—in most material things, but not, as Mill pointed out, in matters of the mind and spirit—would meet limits involved a hellishly complicated set of trade-offs and calculations that only a priestly few wanted to discuss, let alone begin. American history marshals a long heritage of open frontiers and individualism against it. "Don't go to limited access!" shouted an agitated New England fisherman at a hearing on the shrinking stocks of bluefin tuna: "I don't want to be limited! That's not American!"

The easiest path of such a tectonic shift in social outlook on growth and limits, however, would be to end population growth. Indeed, in places it began to happen without a law, national policy, or much debate. Voluntarily, European, American, and some Asian women began to choose smaller families or no offspring at all, so that by the end of the 1990s some sixty countries (the United States was in the group until 1995, when immigration pushed fertility rates again above 2.1) had reached or moved below replacement-level fertility, prevented from absolute population shrinkage only by immigration from still-growing societies. At the 1994 UN Conference on Population in Cairo, 179 nations established (not unanimously; several Roman Catholic and Islamic nations objected) a plan to cap global population at 9.8 billion by 2050, an objective thought optimistic but not beyond reach. This would leave the earth swarming with 10 billion increasingly industrialized humans, and international discussion of how to reduce that burden would lead to bitter disputes over very hard choices.

One new feature of the landscape of international environmental politics, however, may force all nations to debate these choices. This is global warming. The ongoing international negotiations launched in Kyoto require all developed nations to accept binding limits on their CO_2 and other greenhouse gas emissions, and eventually all nations will in one way or another come under such pressure. For the United States, our permanent ceiling, absent some scientific recalculation, has been determined to be 7 percent below 1990 emissions. A limit has finally been set, a firm number! We hope to reach it by technological innovation and conservationist discipline, and these will be indispensable. But another logic is at work. In making our reductions to get within specified levels and then in staying there, each additional person in a nation's population—by excess of births over deaths, or by immigration—reduces the allowable amount to be divided among that population. Population growth, and some forms of economic growth, now have a new and formidable opponent, the zero-sum game of Greenhouse emission containment. One could again at least imagine that time called for by the 1972 Population Commission, when the environmental restoration project could aim at goalposts that are not forever moved outward by mounting human numbers.

As to what the ultimate goal should be, the idea of calculating the earth's "carrying capacity" was years ago lifted out of population biology and used as a basis for discussing ideal human population limits and lifestyles. The concept stimulated some fresh thinking, but it had at least the disadvantage of appearing to assume that the goal was mere physical survival of the largest number of humans at any given time. Then in 1987 the World Commission on Environment and Development, or the Brundtland Commission Report, *Our Common Future,* finally brought together the global discussions of economic development and the environment that had been on separate and sometimes hostile tracks since Third World countries at Stockholm in 1972 had forced developed countries to concede that development came first and must not be impeded by environmental concerns. *Our Common Future* attempted to reconcile and join economic and environmental goals, defining "sustainable development" as "development that meets the needs of the present without compromising the ability of future generations to meet their own needs."

Those vague words devised in an attempt to bridge the perspectives of First and Third worlds boosted "sustainable development" into a position at the end of the century as "a mantra that launched a thousand conferences," in the words of one participant in such global discussions. But perhaps Sustainable Development will be more than a short-lived topic at conferences. It affirms that it is possible to reconcile environmental and economic objectives, and therefore it is necessary. It has at least the advantage over Carrying Capacity that it changes our accounting by emphasizing intergenerational equity, the passing on of not only a viable ecological base to the next generation. And the word "needs" implies a menu of human wants that goes beyond mere resources sufficient for survival to include a need for nature's spaces and vistas and textures, even for sustainable hunting and fishing. In any event, the "thousand conferences" appear to be having some results. "Indicators of Sustainability" have begun to be developed to keep track of the state of ecological and socioeconomic systems, changes in them, and cause-and-effect relationships. Canada published sustainability indicators in 1993, President Clinton's Council on Sustainable Development began a series of reports in 1994 that includes 32 indicators, the European Union has an indicators program, and the city of Seattle launched a sustainability program in 1990 that has proposed 40 indicators of the "long-term health" of the environment, population, and community. Much is unclear and ill-defined in all this activity. But the process of debating and then monitoring sustainability indicators involves, and educates, hundreds—in a city like Seattle, thousands—of participants. A "buzz word" to enhance reports and project proposals, Sustainable Development seems at this stage also a promising conception of how humans might clarify their goals, match them to the long-term viability of ecosystems, and begin to honor their obligations to posterity. Fifty or a hundred years ago, when a now forgotten word was viable, this would have been called Planning—for a different and better future than the stressful one dead ahead.

 **NO**

Commentary of Bjorn Lomborg

Yes, It Looks Bad, But...

We are all familiar with the litany of our ever-deteriorating environment. It is the doomsday message endlessly repeated by the media, as when *Time* magazine tells us that "everyone knows the planet is in bad shape", and when the *New Scientist* calls its environmental overview "self-destruct".

We are defiling our Earth, we are told. Our resources are running out. The population is ever-growing, leaving less and less to eat. Our air and water is more and more polluted. The planet's species are becoming extinct in vast numbers—we kill off more than 40,000 each year. Forests are disappearing, fish stocks are collapsing, the coral reefs are dying. The fertile topsoil is vanishing. We are paving over nature, destroying the wilderness, decimating the biosphere, and will end up killing ourselves in the process. The world's ecosystem is breaking down. We are fast approaching the absolute limit of viability.

We have heard the litany so often that yet another repetition is, well, almost reassuring. There is, however, one problem: it does not seem to be backed up by the available evidence. We are not running out of energy or natural resources. There is ever more food, and fewer people are starving. In 1900, we lived for an average of 30 years; today we live for 67. According to the UN, we have reduced poverty more in the last 50 years than we did in the preceding 500, and it has been reduced in practically every country.

Global warming is probably taking place, though future projections are overly pessimistic and the traditional cure of radical fossil-fuel cutbacks is far more damaging than the original affliction. Moreover, its total impact will not pose a devastating problem to our future. Nor will we lose 25–50% of all species in our lifetime—in fact, we are losing probably 0.7%. Acid rain does not kill the forests, and the air and water around us are becoming less and less polluted.

In fact, in terms of practically every measurable indicator, mankind's lot has improved. This does not, however, mean that everything is good enough. We can still do even better.

Take, for example, starvation and the population explosion. In 1968, one of the leading environmentalists, Dr Paul R Erlich, predicted in his bestselling

From Bjorn Lomborg, "Yes, It Looks Bad, But...," "Running on Empty," and "Why Kyoto Will Not Stop This," *The Guardian* (August 15, 16, & 17, 2001). Copyright © 2001 by Bjorn Lomborg. Reprinted by permission of *The Guardian*.

book, *The Population Bomb,* that "the battle to feed humanity is over. In the course of the 1970s, the world will experience starvation of tragic proportions— hundreds of millions of people will starve to death."

This did not happen. Instead, according to the UN, agricultural production in the developing world has increased by 52% per person. The daily food intake in developing countries has increased from 1,932 calories in 1961—barely enough for survival—to 2,650 calories in 1998, and is expected to rise to 3,020 by 2030. Likewise, the proportion of people going hungry in these countries has dropped from 45% in 1949 to 18% today, and is expected to fall even further, to 12% in 2010 and 6% in 2030. Food, in other words, is becoming not scarcer but ever more abundant. This is reflected in its price. Since 1800, food prices have decreased by more than 90%, and in 2000, according to the World Bank, prices were lower than ever before.

Erlich's prediction echoed that made 170 years earlier by Thomas Malthus. Malthus claimed that, unchecked, human population would expand exponentially, while food production could increase only linearly by bringing new land into cultivation. He was wrong. Population growth has turned out to have an internal check: as people grow richer and healthier, they have smaller families. Indeed, the growth rate of the human population reached its peak of more than 2% a year in the early 1960s. The rate of increase has been declining ever since. It is now 1.26%, and is expected to fall to 0.46% by 2050. The UN estimates that most of the world's population growth will be over by 2100, with the population stabilising at just below 11bn.

Malthus also failed to take account of developments in agricultural technology. These have squeezed ever more food out of each hectare of land. It is this application of human ingenuity that has boosted food production. It has also, incidentally, reduced the need to take new land into cultivation, thus reducing the pressure on biodiversity.

The issues on food, population and air pollution covered here all contradict the litany. Yet opinion polls suggest that many people—in the rich world, at least—nurture the belief that environmental standards are declining. Four factors cause this disjunction between perception and reality.

The first is the lopsidedness built into scientific research. Scientific funding goes mainly to areas with many problems. That may be wise policy, but it will also create an impression that many more potential problems exist than is the case.

A second source of misperception is the self-interest of environmental groups. Though these groups are run overwhelmingly by selfless folk, they nevertheless share many of the characteristics of other lobby groups. They need to be noticed by the mass media. They also need to keep the money that sustains them rolling in. The temptation to exaggerate is surely there, and sometimes, indulged in.

In 1997, for example, the World Wide Fund for Nature issued a press release entitled Two-thirds of the World's Forests Lost Forever. The truth turned out to be nearer 20%. This would matter less if people applied the same degree of scepticism to environmental lobbying as they do to other lobby groups.

But while a trade organisation arguing for, say, weaker pollution controls is instantly seen as self-interested, a green organisation opposing such a weakening is seen as altruistic—even if a dispassionate view of the controls might suggest they are doing more harm than good.

A third source of confusion is the attitude of the media. People are clearly more curious about bad news than good, and newspapers and broadcasters give the public what it wants. That can lead to significant distortions of perception: an example was America's encounter with El Niño in 1997 and 1998. This climatic phenomenon was accused of wrecking tourism, causing allergies, melting ski slopes and causing 22 deaths by dumping snow in Ohio. Disney even blamed El Niño for a fall in share prices.

A more balanced view comes from a recent article in the *Bulletin of the American Meteorological Society*. It estimated the damage caused by the 1997–98 Niño at $4bn, but the benefits amounted to some $19bn. These came from higher winter temperatures (which saved an estimated 850 lives, reduced heating costs and diminished spring floods caused by meltwaters), and from the well-documented connection between past Niños and fewer Atlantic hurricanes. In 1998, America experienced no big Atlantic hurricanes and thus avoided huge losses. These benefits were not reported as widely as the losses.

The fourth factor is poor individual perception. People worry that the endless rise in the amount of stuff everyone throws away will cause the world to run out of places to dispose of waste. Yet even if UK waste production increases at the same rate as that in the US (surely an overestimate, since the British population does not increase as fast), the total landfill area needed for 21st-century UK waste would be a meagre 100ft tall and eight miles square—an area equivalent to 28% of the Isle of Man.

Knowing the real state of the world is important because fear of largely imaginary environmental problems can divert political energy from dealing with real ones. The Harvard University centre for risk analysis has carried out the world's largest survey of the costs of life-saving public initiatives. Only initiatives whose primary stated political goal is to save human lives are included. Thus, the many environmental interventions which have little or no intention to save human lives, such as raising oxygen levels in rivers, improving wetlands and setting up natural reservations, are not considered here. We only compare those environmental interventions whose primary goal is to save human lives (as in toxin control) with life-saving interventions from other areas.

There are tremendous differences in the price to be paid for extra life-years by means of typical interventions: the health service is quite low-priced, at $19,000 per median price to save a life for one year, but the environment field stands out with a staggeringly high cost of $4.2m.

This method of accounting shows the overall effectiveness of the American public effort to save human life. Overall, information exists about the actual cost of 185 programmes that account for an annual expenditure of $21.4bn, which saves around 592,000 life-years. The Harvard study shows that, had the spending been used in the most cost-efficient way, 1,230,000 life-years could have been saved for the same money. Without further costs, it would have been possible to save around 600,000 more life-years or, at 10 years per life, 60,000 more human beings.

When we fear for our environment, we seem easily to fall victim to short-term, feel-good solutions that spend money on relatively trifling issues and thus hold back resources from far more important ones. When we realise that we can forget about imminent breakdown, we can see that the world is basically heading in the right direction and that we can help to steer this development process by focusing on and insisting on reasonable prioritisation. When the Harvard study shows that we forgo saving 60,000 lives every year, this shows us the cost we pay for worrying about the wrong problems—too much for the environment and too little in other areas.

This does not mean that rational environmental management and environmental investment is not often a good idea—only that we should compare the costs and benefits of such investments to similar investments in all the other important areas of human endeavour. And to ensure that sensible, political prioritisation, we need to abandon our ingrained belief in a mythical litany and start focusing on the facts—that the world is indeed getting better, though there is still much to do.

Running on Empty?

It was an axiom of the early environmentalists that we were running out of resources, and that fear underlies much of the movement's thinking on recycling, on the belief that small is beautiful, and on the need to restructure society away from its obsession with resource-consuming production. The idea has held powerful sway during 30 years of popular thinking—despite the fact that it has been clearly shown to be incorrect. Scare stories of resource depletion still turn up in the media every so often, but many environmentalists today have disavowed their earlier fears.

For many people, the 1973 oil crisis was the first evidence of finite resources. But we have long worried about running out of all kinds of materials: in antiquity, grave concerns were voiced about the future of copper and tin. The 1972 bestseller *Limits to Growth*, by the so-called Club of Rome, picked up on the old worry, claiming that gold would run out in 1981, silver and mercury in 1985, and zinc in 1990. It hasn't happened, and yet the idea held an almost magical grip on intellectuals in the 70s and 80s; and even today most discussions are predicated on the logic of Limits to Growth.

Only the economists begged to differ. One of them, Julian Simon, grew so frustrated that in 1980 he issued a challenge to the environmentalists. Since increased scarcity would mean higher prices, he bet $10,000 that any given raw material—to be picked by his opponents—would have dropped in price at least one year later. Stanford University environmentalists Paul Ehrlich, John Harte and John Holdren, stating that "the lure of easy money can be irresistible", took him on.

The environmentalists put their money on chromium, copper, nickel, tin and tungsten, and they picked a time frame of 10 years. By September 1990, each of the raw materials had dropped in price: chromium by 5%, tin by a whopping 74%. The doom-mongers had lost.

The truth is that they could not have won. Ehrlich and co would have lost, whatever they had bet on: petroleum, foodstuffs, sugar, coffee, cotton, wool, minerals, phosphates—they had all become cheaper.

Today, oil is the most important and most valuable commodity of international trade, and its value to our civilisation is underlined by the recurrent worry that we are running out of it. In 1914, the US Bureau of Mines estimated that supplies would last only 10 more years. In 1939, the US department of the interior predicted that oil would last only 13 more years. In 1951, it made the same projection: oil had only 13 more years. As Professor Frank Notestein of Princeton said in his later years: "We've been running out of oil ever since I was a boy."

Again, measuring scarcity means looking at the price. Even if we were to run out of oil, this would not mean that oil was completely unavailable, only that it would be very, very expensive. The oil-price hike from 1973 to the mid-80s was caused by an artificial scarcity, as Opec introduced production restraints. Likewise, the present high price is caused by adherence to Opec-agreed production cutbacks in the late 90s. It is expected that the price will again decline from $27 a barrel to the low $20s by 2020, bringing it well within the $17-$30 suggested by eight other recent international forecasts.

The long-term trend is unlikely to deviate much from these levels because high prices deter consumption and encourage the development of other sources of oil—and forms of energy supply. Likewise, low prices have the opposite effect.

In fact, the price of petrol at US pumps, excluding tax, stood at $1.10 in early 2001—comparable with the lowest prices before the oil crisis. This is because most of the price consists of the costs of refining and transportation, both of which have experienced huge efficiency increases.

At the same time, we have had an ever-rising prediction of the number of years' worth of oil remaining (years of consumption), despite increasing consumption. This is astounding. Common sense dictates that if we had 35 years' consumption left in 1955, we should have had 34 years' supply left the year after—if not less, because we consumed more oil in 1956 than in 1955. But the chart shows that in 1956 there were more years of reserves available.

The development for non-fuel resources has been similar. Cement, aluminium, iron, copper, gold, nitrogen and zinc account for more than 75% of global expenditure on raw materials. Despite a two- to 10-fold increase in consumption of these materials over the past 50 years, estimates of the number of years it will take to run out of them have grown. And the increasing abundance is reflected in price: the Economist's price index for raw materials has dropped by 80% since 1845.

So how can we have used ever more, and still have ever more left? The answers provide three central arguments against the limited resources approach:

1. *"Known resources" is not a finite entity.*

It is not that we know all the places with oil, and now just need to pump it up. We explore new areas and find new oil. But since searching costs money, new searches will not be initiated too far in advance of production. Consequently, new oil fields will be added as demand rises.

It is rather odd that anyone could have thought that known resources pretty much represented what was left, and therefore predicted dire problems when these had run out. It is like glancing into my refrigerator and saying: "Oh, you've only got food for three days. In four days you will die of starvation." But in two days I will go to the supermarket and buy more food. The point is that oil will come not only from the sources we already know, but also from many sources of which we do not yet know. The US Geological Survey has regularly made assessments of the total undiscovered resources of oil and gas, and stated in March 2000: "Since 1981, each of the last four of these assessments has shown a slight increase in the combined volume of identified reserves and undiscovered resources."

2. We become better at exploiting resources.

We use new technology to extract more oil from known oilfields, become better at finding new oilfields, and can start exploiting oilfields that were previously too expensive and/or difficult to exploit. An initial drilling typically exploits only 20% of the oil in the reservoir. Even with the most advanced techniques using water, steam or chemical flooding to squeeze out extra oil, more than half the resource commonly remains in the ground. It is estimated that the 10 largest oilfields in the US will still contain 63% of their original oil when production closes down. Consequently, there is still much to be reaped in this area. According to the latest US Geological Survey assessment, such technical improvements are expected to increase the amount of available oil by 50%.

At the same time, we have become better at exploiting each litre of oil. Since 1973, the average US car has improved its mpg by 60%. Home heating in Europe and the US has improved by 24-43%. Many appliances have become much more efficient—dishwashers and washing machines have cut energy use by about 50%.

Most nations now exploit energy with increasing efficiency: we use less and less energy to produce each dollar, euro or yen in our gross national products. Since 1880, the UK has almost tripled its production per energy use; worldwide, the amount of wealth produced per energy unit doubled between 1971 and 1992.

We also exploit other raw materials better: today, a car contains only half as much metal as a car produced in 1970. Super-thin optical fibres carry the same number of telephone calls as 625 copper wires did 20 years ago. Newspapers are printed on ever-thinner paper, because paper production has been improved. Bridges contain less steel, because steel has become stronger and because we can calculate specifications more accurately. Moreover, information technology has changed our consumption—we buy fewer things and more bits. Programs worth several hundred dollars will fit on a CD-rom made from two cents' worth of plastic.

3. We can substitute.

We do not demand oil as such, but rather the services it can provide. Mostly we want heating, energy or fuel, and this we can obtain from other sources, if they prove to be better or cheaper. This happened in England around 1600 when wood became increasingly expensive (because of local deforestation and bad infrastructure), prompting a gradual switch to coal. During the latter part of the 19th century, a similar move from coal to oil took place.

In the short run, it would be most obvious to substitute oil with other commonly known fossil fuels such as gas and coal. For both, estimates of the number of years' supply remaining have increased. Moreover, shale oil could cover a large part of our longer-term oil needs. At $40 a barrel (less than one-third above the current world price of crude), shale oil can supply oil for the next 250 years at current consumption; in total, there is enough shale oil to cover our total energy consumption for 5,000 years.

In the long run, renewable energy sources could cover a large part of our needs. Today, they make up a vanishingly small part of global energy production, but this will probably change.

The cost of solar energy and wind energy has dropped by 94-98% over the past 20 years, and have come much closer to being strictly profitable. Renewable energy resources are almost incomprehensibly large. The sun could potentially provide about 7,000 times our own energy consumption—in principle, covering just 2.6% of the Sahara desert with solar cells could supply our entire needs.

It is likely that we will eventually change our energy uses from fossil fuels towards other, cheaper energy sources—maybe renewables, maybe fusion, maybe some as yet unthought-of technology. As Sheikh Yamani, Saudi Arabia's former oil minister and a founding architect of Opec, has pointed out: "The stone age came to an end not for a lack of stones, and the oil age will end, but not for a lack of oil." We stopped using stone because bronze and iron were superior materials; likewise, we will stop using oil when other energy technologies provide superior benefits.

Why Kyoto Will Not Stop This

[Recently] in Bonn, most of the world's nations (minus the US) reached an agreement to cut carbon emissions. Generally, the deal was reported as almost saving the world. This is not only untrue in the scientific sense—the deal will do almost no good—but it also constitutes a very poor use of our resources to help the world.

Global warming is important: environmentally, politically and economically. There is no doubt that mankind is increasing atmospheric concentrations of carbon dioxide and that this will increase temperatures. I basically accept the models and predictions from the 2001 report of the UN's intergovernmental panel on climate change (IPCC). But in order to make the best choices for our future, we need to separate hyperbole from reality.

The IPCC bases its warning that the world might warm up by 5.8C over the coming century on an enormous variety of projections and models, a kind of computer-aided storytelling. The high-emission scenarios seem plainly unlikely. Reasonable analysis suggests that renewable energy sources—especially solar power—will be competitive with, or even outcompeting, fossil fuels by the middle of the century. This means carbon emissions are much more likely to follow the low-emission scenarios, causing a warming of about 2-2.5C.

Moreover, global warming will not decrease food production; nor is it likely to increase storminess, the frequency of hurricanes, the impact of malaria, or, indeed, cause more deaths. It is even unlikely that it will cause more flooding, because a much richer world will protect itself better.

However, global warming will have serious costs—estimated by Yale University's Professor William Nordhaus to be about $5 trillion. Such estimates are inevitably uncertain, but derive from models assessing the cost of global warming in a wide variety of areas, including agriculture, forestry, fisheries, energy, water supply, infrastructure, hurricane damage, drought damage, coastal protection, land loss caused by a rise in sea level, loss of wetlands, loss of species, loss of human life, pollution and migration. The consequences of global warming will hit developing countries hardest (primarily because they are poor and have less capacity to adapt), while the industrialised nations may benefit from a warming lower than 2-3C.

Despite our intuition that we need to do something drastic about global warming, we are in danger of implementing a cure that is more costly than the original affliction: economic analyses clearly show that it will be far more expensive to cut carbon dioxide emissions radically than to pay the costs of adaptation to the increased temperatures.

All models agree that the effect of the Kyoto protocol on the climate will be minuscule (even more so after the negotiations in Bonn). One model, by a leading author of the 1996 IPCC report, shows us how an expected temperature increase of 2.1C by 2100 will be diminished by the protocol to an increase of 1.9C. To put it more clearly, the temperature that we would have experienced in 2094 has been postponed to 2100. In essence, the Kyoto protocol does not negate global warming, but merely buys the world six years.

If Kyoto is implemented with anything but global emissions trading, it will not only be almost inconsequential for the climate, but it will also constitute a poor use of resources. The cost of such a pact, just for the US, would be higher than the cost of solving the single most pressing global problem—providing the entire world with clean drinking water and sanitation. It is estimated that the latter would avoid 2m deaths every year, and prevent half a billion people becoming seriously ill annually. If no trading mechanism is implemented for Kyoto, the costs could approach $1 trillion, almost five times the cost of worldwide water and sanitation coverage. In comparison, total global aid today is about $50bn a year.

If we were to go even further and curb global emissions to the 1990 level, the net cost would escalate to about $4 trillion extra—comparable almost to the cost of global warming itself. Likewise, a temperature increase limit would cost anything from $3 to $33 trillion extra.

Basically, global warming will be expensive ($5 trillion) and there is very little we can do about it. Even if we were to handle global warming as well as possible—cutting emissions a little, far into the future—we would save a minimal amount (about $300bn). However, if we enact Kyoto or even more ambitious programmes, the world will lose.

So is it not curious that the typical reporting on global warming tells us all the bad things it will cause, but few or none of the negative effects of overly zealous regulation? And why are discussions on global warming rarely a considered meeting of opposing views, but instead dogmatic and missionary in tone?

The problem is that the discussion is not just about finding the best economic path for humanity; it has much deeper political roots. This is clear in the 2001 IPCC report, which tells us that we should build cars and trains with lower top speeds, extols the qualities of sailing ships and bicycles, and proposes regionalised economies to alleviate transport demands.

Essentially, the IPCC is saying that we need to change individual lifestyles, move away from consumption and focus on sharing resources (eg through co-ownership). Because of climate change, we have to remodel our world.

The problem, as the IPCC puts it, is that "the conditions of public acceptance of such options are not often present at the requisite large scale". It goes as far as suggesting that the reason why we are unwilling to accept slower (or no) cars, and regionalised economies with bicycles but no international travel, is that we have been indoctrinated by the media, where we see TV characters as reference points for our own lives, shaping our values and identities. Consequently, the media could also help form the path towards a more sustainable world: "Raising awareness among media professionals of the need for greenhouse gas mitigation and the role of the media in shaping lifestyles and aspirations could be an effective way to encourage a wider cultural shift."

While using global warming as a springboard for wider policy goals is entirely legitimate, such goals should be made explicit: it is problematic to have an organisation which gathers important scientific data on global warming also promoting a political agenda.

Thus the lessons of the global warming debate are fivefold. First, we have to realise what we are arguing about—do we want to handle global warming in the most efficient way, or do we want to use global warming as a stepping stone to other political projects? I believe that in order to think clearly, we should try to separate the issues, not least because trying to solve all problems at one go may result in bad solutions for all areas. So I try to address just the issue of global warming.

Second, we should not spend vast amounts of money to cut a tiny slice off the global temperature increase when this constitutes a poor use of resources, and when we could probably use these funds far more effectively in the developing world. This connection between the use of resources on global warming and aiding the third world goes much deeper because the developing world will experience by far the most damage. When we spend resources to mitigate global warming, we are helping future inhabitants in the developing world; however, if we spend the same money directly in the third world, we are helping present inhabitants, and thus their descendants.

Since the inhabitants of the third world are likely to be much richer in the future, and since the return on investments in developing countries is much higher than those in global warming (about 16% to 2%), the question really boils down to: do we want to help better-off inhabitants in the third world 100 years from now a little, or do we want to help poorer inhabitants in the present third world much more?

To give an indication of the size of the problem, the Kyoto protocol is likely to cost at least $150bn a year, possibly much more. Unicef estimates that just $70-80bn a year could give all third world inhabitants access to the basics, such as health, education, water and sanitation. More important still is that if we could muster such a massive investment in the present-day developing countries, this would also put them in a much better future position, in terms of resources and infrastructure, from which to manage a future global warming.

Third, since cutting back carbon dioxide emissions quickly turns very costly and easily counterproductive, we should focus more of our efforts on finding ways of reducing the emission of greenhouse gases in the long term. Partly, this means that we need to invest much more in the research and development of solar power, fusion and other likely power sources. Given the current US investment in renewable energy research and development of just $200m, a considerable increase would seem a promising investment to achieve a possible conversion to renewable energy towards the latter part of the century.

This also means we should be more open to other techno-fixes (so-called geo-engineering). These range from fertilising the ocean (making more algae bind carbon when they die and fall to the ocean floor) and putting sulphur particles into the stratosphere (cooling the earth) to capturing carbon dioxide from fossil fuel use and returning it to storage in geological formations..

Fourth, we ought to look at the cost of global warming in relation to the total world economy. Analysis shows that even if we chose the less efficient programmes to cut carbon emissions, it would defer growth at most by a couple of years by the middle of the century. In this respect, global warming is still a limited and manageable problem.

Finally, this also underscores that global warming is not nearly the most important problem in the world. What matters is making the developing countries rich and allowing the citizens of developed countries even greater opportunities.

There are four main scenarios from the 2001 IPCC report. If we choose a world focused on economic development within a global setting, the total income over the coming century will be some $900 trillion. However, should we go down a path focusing on the environment, even if we stay within a global setting, humanity will lose some $107 trillion, 12% of the total potential income. And should we choose a more regional approach to solving the problems of the 21st century, we will stand to lose $140-274 trillion. Moreover, the loss would mainly be to the detriment of the developing countries. Again, this should be seen in the light of a total cost of global warming of about $5 trillion, and the fact that the optimal global warming policy can save us just $300bn.

If we want to leave a planet with the most possibilities for our descendants, both in the developing and developed world, it is imperative that we focus primarily on the economy and solving our problems in a global context, rather than focusing on the environment in a regionalised context. Basically, this puts the spotlight on securing economic growth, especially in the third world, while ensuring a global economy—both tasks which the world has set itself within the framework of the World Trade Organisation (WTO).

If we succeed, we could increase world income by $107-274 trillion, whereas even if we achieve the absolutely most efficient global warming policies, we can increase wealth by just $300bn. To put it squarely, what matters to our and our children's future is not primarily decided within the IPCC framework, but within the WTO framework.

POSTSCRIPT

Environmentalism: Is the Earth Out of Balance?

$\mathbf{G}$raham provides a reasonably objective account of the battle between those who believe that our resources are being irrevocably depleted and those who deny that such a crisis exists and who argue that, with the exception of Africa, long-term environmental and economic trends should improve the quality of life in the future. Although he takes a more moderate stance than most writers about the environment, Graham lines up with the pessimists. According to Graham, 30 years of environmental laws have given scientists a great deal of information about the scientific problems and limits of governmental actions, and they have even provided society "with a qualified optimism about the possibility of technological leaps over or around some of the problems," such as improvements in air quality and limiting population growth. But Graham maintains that we may be "enjoying an Indian Summer" before we are overwhelmed by the more severe biophysical problems that are affecting the global climate.

Lomborg takes issue with the doomsday forecasts of the pessimists. He denies he has a conservative agenda even if his conclusions coincide with studies from right-wing think tanks such as the CATO Institute and the American Enterprise Institute (AEI). In fact, Lomborg calls himself a leftist who once belonged to Greenpeace and remains an environmentalist. A statistician by profession, Lomborg began his study of the environment in a seminar with 10 of his sharpest students at the University of Arthurs in Denmark. There he tried to refute the statistical critique of Julian Simon, whose articles and books tore apart the statistics of Paul Ehrlich and other prophets of doom. When he finished the seminar, Lomborg concluded that "a large amount of [Simon's] points stood up to scrutiny and conflicted with what we believed ourselves to know."

Miguel A. Santos, *The Environmental Crisis* (Greenwood Press, 1999) is a good starting point for examining this issue. The best historical overviews of the controversy are Hal K. Rothman's *Saving the Planet: The American Response to the Environment in the Twentieth Century* (Ivan R. Dee, 2000) and *The Greening of a Nation? Environmentalism in the United States Since 1945* (Harcourt Brace, 1998). Two excellent articles on the issue are Stewart L. Udall, "How the West Was Won," *American Heritage* (February/March 2000) and John Steele Gordon, "The American Environment," *American Heritage* (October 1993). Finally, two interesting books that reverse the traditional stances of liberals and conservatives on the environment are Gregg Easterbrook, *A Moment on the Earth: The Coming Age of Environmental Optimism* (Viking, 1995) and Peter Huber, *Hard Green: Saving the Environment From the Environmentalists: A Conservative Manifesto* (Basic Books, 1999).

Contributors to This Volume

EDITOR

LARRY MADARAS is a professor of history and political science at Howard Community College in Columbia, Maryland. He received a B.A. from the College of the Holy Cross in 1959 and an M.A. and a Ph.D. from New York University in 1961 and 1964, respectively. He has also taught at Spring Hill College, the University of South Alabama, and the University of Maryland at College Park. He has been a Fulbright Fellow and has held two fellowships from the National Endowment for the Humanities. He is the author of dozens of journal articles and book reviews.

STAFF

Theodore Knight   Managing Editor
David Brackley   Senior Developmental Editor
Juliana Gribbins   Developmental Editor
Rose Gleich   Administrative Assistant
Brenda S. Filley   Director of Production/Design
Juliana Arbo   Typesetting Supervisor
Diane Barker   Proofreader
Richard Tietjen   Publishing Systems Manager
Larry Killian   Copier Coordinator

AUTHORS

PATRICK J. BUCHANAN is a syndicated columnist and a founding member of three public affairs shows, *The McLaughlin Group, The Capital Gang,* and *Crossfire.* He has served as senior adviser to three American presidents, ran twice for the Republican nomination for president (1992 and 1996), and was the Reform Party's presidential candidate in 2000. He is the author of *A Republic, Not an Empire: Reclaiming America's Destiny* (Regnery, 1999).

JAMES MacGREGOR BURNS is the author of noted studies of presidents and other political leaders. As senior scholar, he teaches and researches leadership at the James MacGregor Burns Academy of Leadership at the University of Maryland in College Park, and he is an emeritus professor of political science at Williams College. He is coauthor of *State and Local Politics: Government by the People,* 10th ed. (Prentice Hall, 2001).

JOSEPH A. CALIFANO, JR., President Lyndon Johnson's special assistant for domestic affairs, currently runs the Center on Addiction and Substance Abuse at Columbia University. He is the author of *The Triumph and Tragedy of Lyndon Johnson: The White House Years* (Simon & Schuster, 1991).

CLAYBORNE CARSON is a professor of history at Stanford University in Stanford, California. He is also editor and director of the Martin Luther King, Jr., Papers Project at the university's Martin Luther King, Jr., Center for Nonviolent Social Change, which published in 2000 the fourth volume of a 14-volume edition of King's speeches, sermons, and writings. His publications include *A Knock at Midnight: Inspiration From the Great Sermons of Reverend Martin Luther King, Jr.,* coedited with Peter Holloran (Warner Books, 2000) and *Guide to American History* (Viking Penguin, 1999).

DANIEL DEUDNEY is an assistant professor in the Department of Political Science at the Johns Hopkins University in Baltimore, Maryland. He is the author of *Pax Atomica: Planetary Geopolitics and Republicanism* (Princeton University Press, 1993).

MELVYN DUBOFSKY is the Distinguished Professor of History and Sociology at the State University of New York at Binghamton. Since 1978 he has been a State University of New York Faculty Exchange Scholar, and he is a member of the Organization of Americans and the American Historical Association. He earned his Ph.D. from the University of Rochester in 1960, and he is the author of *The State and Labor in Modern America* (University of North Carolina Press, 1994).

ADAM FAIRCLOUGH is a professor at the University of Leeds, where he holds the chair of modern American history. He has written extensively on the civil rights movement, and he is the author of *Teaching Equality: Black Schools in the Age of Jim Crow* (University of Georgia Press, 2001) and *Race and Democracy: The Civil Rights Struggle in Louisiana, 1915-1972* (University of Georgia Press, 1999).

JO FREEMAN is a guerrilla and unaffiliated agitator. She is the author of *The Politics of Women's Liberation* (Longman, 1975), which won the American

Political Science Association prize for the best scholarly work on women and politics, and the editor of five editions of *Women: A Feminist Perspective* (Mayfield). She has a Ph.D. in political science from the University of Chicago (1973) and a J.D. from the New York University School of Law (1982). She currently practices law, politics, editing, and writing in Brooklyn, New York.

RICHARD M. FRIED is a professor of history at the University of Illinois at Chicago and the author of *The Russians Are Coming! The Russians Are Coming! Pageantry and Patriotism in Cold-War America* (Oxford University Press, 1998).

JOHN LEWIS GADDIS is the Robert A. Lovett Professor of History at Yale University in New Haven, Connecticut. He has also been Distinguished Professor of History at Ohio University, where he founded the Contemporary History Institute, and he has held visiting appointments at the United States Naval War College, the University of Helsinki, Princeton University, and Oxford University. He is the author of many books, including *We Now Know: Rethinking Cold War History* (Oxford University Press, 1997).

MICHAEL R. GORDON is chief defense correspondent for the *New York Times*. He has covered the Gulf conflict and the upheaval in Iraq, and he received the George Polk Award for International Reporting for his 1989 disclosures on Libya's chemical weapons program.

F. CAROLYN GRAGLIA is a writer and a lecturer. Her writings have appeared in such publications as *Harvard Journal of Law, Public Policy, The Weekly Standard*, the *Wall Street Journal*, and *The Women's Quarterly*. An attorney with the U.S. Department of Justice from 1954 through 1959, she later clerked on the Court of Appeals for the D.C. Circuit. Graglia consulted for several years on constitutional law and antitrust litigation and then began lecturing and writing on family issues. She received her law degree from Columbia University.

OTIS L. GRAHAM, JR., is a professor emeritus of history at the University of California, Santa Barbara. He is the editor of *The Public Historian* and the author or editor of many books on the environment, public policy, and modern America, including *Debating American Immigration, 1882–Present*, coauthored with Roger Daniels (Rowman & Littlefield, 2001) and *A Limited Bounty: The United States Since World War II* (McGraw-Hill, 1996).

JOHN EARL HAYNES is a twentieth-century political historian with the Library of Congress. He is coauthor, with Harvey Klehr and K. M. Anderson, of *The Soviet World of American Communism* (Yale University Press, 1998) and, with Harvey Klehr and Fridrikh I. Firsov, of *The Secret World of American Communism* (Yale University Press, 1996).

JOAN HOFF-WILSON is a professor of history at Indiana University in Bloomington, Indiana, and coeditor of the *Journal of Women's History*. She is a specialist in twentieth-century American foreign policy and politics and in the legal status of American women. She has received numerous awards, including the Stuart L. Bernath Prize for the best book on American diplomacy. She has published several books, including *Herbert Hoover: The Forgotten Progressive* (Little, Brown, 1975) and *Without Precedent: The Life and Career of Eleanor Roosevelt* (Indiana University Press, 1984), coedited with Marjorie Lightman.

STEPHEN HOLMES is a professor of law at New York University Law School. He has also been a professor of politics and law at the University of Chicago and a professor of politics at Princeton University. He specializes in democratic theory, the history of liberalism, the Russian legal system, and comparative constitutional law. He is editor-in-chief of the *East European Constitutional Review* and coauthor, with Cass R. Sunstein, of *The Cost of Rights: Why Liberty Depends on Taxes* (W. W. Norton, 1999).

G. JOHN IKENBERRY, currently a Wilson Center Fellow, is a professor of political science at the University of Pennsylvania and a nonresident senior fellow at the Brookings Institution. He is the author of *After Victory: Institutions, Strategic Restraint and the Rebuilding of Order After Major Wars* (Princeton University Press, 2000) and *American Foreign Policy: Theoretical Essays,* 3rd ed. (Addison-Wesley Longman, 1998).

TAMAR JACOBY, a senior fellow at the Manhattan Institute, writes extensively on race, ethnicity, and other subjects. Her articles and book reviews have appeared in a variety of periodicals, including the *New York Times,* the *Wall Street Journal, The New Republic, Commentary,* and *Foreign Affairs.* Before joining the institute, she was a senior writer and justice editor for *Newsweek.* Her publications include *Someone Else's House: America's Unfinished Struggle for Integration* (Basic Books, 1998).

D. CLAYTON JAMES holds the John Biggs Chair of Military History at Virginia Military Institute in Lexington, Virginia. He is the author of the best-selling and prize-winning three-volume work *The Years of MacArthur* (Houghton Mifflin, 1970–1985) as well as numerous other works of military history.

HARVEY KLEHR is the Andrew W. Mellon Professor of Politics and History at Emory University. He is coauthor, with Kyrill M. Anderson and John Earl Haynes, of *The Soviet World of American Communism* (Yale University Press, 1998) and, with John Earl Haynes and Fridrikh I. Firsov, of *The Secret World of American Communism* (Yale University Press, 1996).

MICHAEL L. KURTZ is dean of the Graduate School at Southeastern Louisiana University in Hammond, Louisiana, where he has also served as professor of history. He is editor of *Louisiana Since the Longs: Nineteen-Sixty to Century's End* (Center for Louisiana Studies, 1998).

STANLEY I. KUTLER is the E. Gordon Fox Professor of American Institutions at the University of Wisconsin–Madison and editor of *Reviews in American History.* He is the author of *Wars of Watergate: The Last Crisis of Richard Nixon* (Alfred A. Knopf, 1990) and the editor of *American Retrospectives: Historians on Historians* (Johns Hopkins University Press, 1995).

BJORN LOMBORG is an associate professor of statistics in the Department of Political Science at the University of Aarhus in Denmark and a frequent participant in topical coverage in the European media. His areas of professional interest include the simulation of strategies in collective action dilemmas, the use of surveys in public administration, and the use of statistics in the environmental arena. In February 2002 Lomborg was named director of Denmark's national Environmental Assessment Institute. He earned his Ph.D. from the University of Copenhagen in 1994.

H. R. McMASTER graduated from the U.S. Military Academy at West Point in 1984. Since then, he has held numerous command and staff positions in the military, and during the Persian Gulf War he commanded Eagle Troop, 2d Armored Cavalry Regiment in combat. He is the author of *A Distant Thunder* (HarperCollins, 1997).

DOUGLAS T. MILLER is the Distinguished Professor of History at Michigan State University in East Lansing, Michigan. He is the author of 10 books, including *On Our Own: Americans in the Sixties* (D. C. Heath, 1996).

CHARLES MURRAY is a Bradley Fellow at the American Enterprise Institute in Washington, D.C., a privately funded public policy research organization. His publications include *The Underclass Revisited* (American Enterprise Institute for Public Policy Research, 1999) and *Does Prison Work?* (Institute of Economic Affairs, 1997).

MARION NOWAK is a painter and writer who lives in Chicago, Illinois. During her career, she has studied weaving, lectured on history and art, and worked on newspapers.

THOMAS G. PATERSON is a professor of history at the University of Connecticut in Storrs, Connecticut. His articles have appeared in such journals as *Journal of American History* and *Diplomatic History,* the editorial boards of which he has served on, and *American Historical Review.* A former president of the Society for Historians of American Foreign Relations, he has authored, coauthored, or edited many books, including *Contesting Castro* (Oxford University Press, 1994).

COLIN L. POWELL became the 65th secretary of state of the United States on January 20, 2001. Prior to his appointment, he was the chairman of America's Promise—The Alliance for Youth, a national, nonprofit organization dedicated to mobilizing people from every sector of American life to build the character and competence of young people. Powell was a professional soldier for 35 years, during which time he held myriad command and staff positions and rose to the rank of four-star general. Following his retirement, he wrote his best-selling autobiography, *My American Journey* (Random House, 1995), and pursued a career as a public speaker.

PRESIDENT'S COMMISSION ON THE ASSASSINATION OF PRESIDENT JOHN F. KENNEDY was appointed by President Lyndon Johnson on November 29, 1963, to investigate the assassination of President Kennedy. Johnson directed the commission to evaluate matters relating to the assassination and the subsequent killing of the alleged assassin and to report its findings and conclusions to him. Commonly known as the Warren commission, after the commission's chair, Chief Justice Earl Warren, the commission's members included Representative Gerald R. Ford (R-Michigan) and Allen W. Dulles, former director of the CIA.

GEORGIA J. SORENSON is a senior scholar and founding director of the James MacGregor Burns Academy of Leadership at the University of Maryland. Formerly a senior policy analyst with the Carter administration, she has served as a consultant to four presidential campaigns.

JOHN S. SPANIER is a professor of political science at the University of Florida. In addition, he has lectured extensively at other universities, including the United States Military Academy at West Point and the Naval War College, where he was a visiting professor of strategy in 1983–1984. He is the author or coauthor of a number of publications, including *Games Nations Play,* 4th ed. (CQ Press, 1993) and *American Foreign Policy Since WWII,* coauthored with Steven W. Hook (CQ Press, 2000).

ATHAN THEOHARIS is a professor of history at Marquette University in Milwaukee, Wisconsin. A noted historian of the FBI files and records, he is a member of the Academy of Political Science and the Organization of American Historians. He has written several books, including *J. Edgar Hoover, Sex, and Crime: An Historical Antidote* (Ivan R. Dee, 1995). He earned his Ph.D. from the University of Chicago.

NICHOLAS THOMPSON is a Markle Fellow at the New America Foundation and a contributing editor of *The Washington Monthly.*

BERNARD E. TRAINOR, a retired lieutenant general of the U.S. Marine Corps, was the military correspondent for the *New York Times* from 1986 to 1990. He was also a military analyst for ABC News during the Gulf War. He now serves as director of National Security Programs in the John F. Kennedy School of Government at Harvard University.

BRIAN VANDEMARK teaches history at the United States Naval Academy at Annapolis. He served as research assistant on Clark Clifford's autobiography, *Counsel to the President: A Memoir* (Random House, 1991), and as collaborator on former secretary of defense Robert S. McNamara's Vietnam memoir *In Retrospect: The Tragedy and Lessons of Vietnam* (Times Books, 1995).

ANNE SHARP WELLS is an assistant editor with *The Journal of Military History.* She is the author of *Historical Dictionary of World War II: The War Against Japan* (Scarecrow Press, 1999) and coauthor, with D. Clayton James, of *America and the Great War, 1914–1920* (Harlan Davidson, 1998).

JOHN C. YOO is a professor of law at the University of California, Berkeley. He has also served as general counsel of the U.S. Senate Judiciary Committee and taught as a visiting professor at the Free University of Amsterdam. Yoo received the Paul M. Bator Award for excellence in legal scholarship and teaching from the Federalist Society for Law and Public Policy in 2001. He holds a J.D. from Yale Law School.

Index